Mixed-Use Development Handbook

Second Edition

ULI Development Handbook Series

 Urban Land Institute

About ULI–the Urban Land Institute

ULI–the Urban Land Institute is a nonprofit education and research institute that is supported by its members. Its mission is to provide responsible leadership in the use of land to enhance the total environment.

ULI sponsors education programs and forums to encourage an open international exchange of ideas and sharing of experiences; initiates research that anticipates emerging land use trends and issues and proposes creative solutions based on that research; provides advisory services; and publishes a wide variety of materials to disseminate information on land use and development. Established in 1936, the Institute today has more than 18,000 members and associates from some 70 countries representing the entire spectrum of the land use and development disciplines.

Richard M. Rosan
President

For more information about ULI and the resources that it offers related to mixed-use development and a variety of other real estate and urban development issues, visit ULI's Web site at www.uli.org.

For the *Mixed-Use Development Handbook*, visit www.mixeduse.uli.org.

Cover Photo: Southlake Town Square, Southlake, Texas.
Photographer: Mike Lewis; courtesy of Cooper & Stebbins

Project Staff

Rachelle L. Levitt
Senior Vice President, Policy and Practice
Publisher

Dean Schwanke
Vice President, Development Trends and Analysis
Project Director

Gayle Berens
Vice President, Real Estate Development Practice

Nancy H. Stewart
Director, Book Program

James A. Mulligan
Managing Editor

Barbara M. Fishel/Editech
Manuscript Editor

Betsy VanBuskirk
Art Director

Anne Morgan
Cover Design

Helene Y. Redmond/HYR Graphics
Book Design/Layout

Diann Stanley-Austin
Director, Publishing Operations

Recommended bibliographic listing:

Schwanke, Dean, et al. *Mixed-Use Development Handbook*. Second Edition. Washington, D.C.: ULI–the Urban Land Institute, 2003.

ULI Catalog Number: M39
International Standard Book Number: 0-87420-888-2
Library of Congress Control Number: 2003106616

Books in the ULI Development Handbook Series
Business and Industrial Park Development Handbook, Second Edition, 2001
Multifamily Housing Development Handbook, 2000
Shopping Center Development Handbook, Third Edition, 1999
Office Development Handbook, Second Edition, 1998
Resort Development Handbook, 1997
Residential Development Handbook, Second Edition, 1990

Authors

Principal Author and Project Director

Dean Schwanke
ULI–the Urban Land Institute
Washington, D.C.

Primary Contributing Authors

Patrick L. Phillips
Economics Research Associates
Washington, D.C.

Frank Spink
Spink Consultancy
Annandale, Virginia

Contributing Authors

Charles Lockwood
Topanga Canyon, California

David Versel
Economics Research Associates
Washington, D.C.

Case Study Authors

Steven Fader
Los Angeles, California

Leslie Holst
ULI–the Urban Land Institute
Washington, D.C.

Oliver Jerschow
Toronto, Ontario, Canada

Deborah Myerson
ULI–the Urban Land Institute
Washington, D.C.

Acknowledgments

The Urban Land Foundation, as part of its commitment to support ULI's core research program, provides major funding for the new and revised editions of the ULI Development Handbook Series. The *Mixed-Use Development Handbook* was funded in part by grants from the Foundation. The Urban Land Institute gratefully acknowledges these contributions.

This handbook would not have been possible without the contributions of many individuals. Although it is impossible to mention everyone who participated in the project, a number of individuals deserve special acknowledgment and thanks.

Acknowledgments are due first to the contributing authors. Frank Spink wrote the bulk of Chapters 6 and 7 on marketing and operations as well as the case study about University Park at MIT. Patrick Phillips and David Versel developed the financial spreadsheets that appear in Chapter 3 and wrote the text that explains these spreadsheets and the financial analysis process. Phillips also served as a reviewer for Chapters 2 and 3.

Charles Lockwood wrote the case study on Valencia Town Center Drive and contributed case study information used in Chapter 7. Oliver Jerschow wrote the case studies on Jin Mao Tower, Sony Center am Potsdamer Platz, and WestEnd City Center; Steven Fader the case studies of Addison Circle and Yerba Buena Center; and Deborah Myerson the case study of Peabody Place. Charles C. Bohl contributed text for the case study of CityPlace.

The book also incorporates articles that were previously published in *Urban Land* magazine or other sources; these authors and sources are cited with the articles in the text; their expertise and insights were invaluable additions to the book.

This book also draws on ideas, concepts, and text that were first developed by Robert Witherspoon, Jon P. Abbett, and Robert M. Gladstone in ULI's 1975 book on the subject, *Mixed-Use Developments: New Ways of Land Use.*

Many other individuals contributed to the book in a variety of ways. Special thanks are due to the ULI Advisory Committee and Reviewers, who provided valuable comments and astute insights that both shaped and enhanced the final product.

Thanks are also due to the many development firms that provided data, information, and insights for the case studies in Chapter 8, which are listed at the end of each case study. Many others provided information on other projects highlighted throughout the text.

Numerous firms and photographers were very helpful in providing photographs, renderings, site plans, and other graphics for the book; these images convey ideas that words cannot, and they have contributed greatly to the content of the book. The source for each image is generally noted with the image as it appears in the book.

In addition, several ULI staff and staff consultants were instrumental. Richard Rosan, Cheryl Cummins, and Rachelle Levitt provided the management direction and support necessary to undertake and complete the study. Gayle Berens reviewed the entire text and layout. Nancy Stewart, James Mulligan, Betsy Van-Buskirk, and Diann Stanley-Austin coordinated the editing and production of the book. Barbara Fishel thoroughly and expeditiously edited the manuscript. Helene Redmond molded the text and graphics into a handsome layout, and Anne Morgan prepared the cover design. Design guidelines for the ULI Development Handbook series were prepared by Michael Dennis and colleagues at Dennis Konetzka of Washington, D.C.

Numerous research interns provided assistance with photos. Jennifer Good spent many hours tracking down photos and graphics for the book, and Russell Gould assisted with photo placement and captions. Karrie Underwood provided assistance in managing the digital images and in finding additional photos. Clara Meesarapu provided administrative assistance for the review process and for file management.

To these individuals and firms, and to all the others who had a hand in this work, thank you.

Dean Schwanke
Principal Author and Project Director

Contents

Foreword

This handbook is part of the ULI Development Handbook Series, a set of volumes on real estate development that traces its roots to 1947, when ULI published the first edition of the *Community Builders Handbook.* That edition was revised and updated several times over the following 25 years, and a replica copy of the original edition was reissued in 2000. In 1975, ULI initiated the Community Builders Handbook Series with the publication of *Industrial Development Handbook.* A number of titles were published in that series over a period of years, covering industrial, residential, shopping center, office, mixed-use, downtown, and recreational development. The publication of *Resort Development Handbook* in 1997 marked the complete redesign of the handbook series, which was renamed the ULI Development Handbook Series.

ULI has had a longstanding and growing interest in mixed-use development that goes back to the early 1970s. ULI published its first book on the subject, *Mixed-Use Developments: New Ways of Land Use,* in 1975. In the 1980s, ULI held numerous conferences and published several other books—including *The Affordable Community: Adapting Today's Communities to Tomorrow's Needs* in 1982 and the first edition of the *Mixed-Use Development Handbook* in 1987—that sought to foster and encourage mixed-use development.

In the 1990s, ULI began publishing and promoting related concepts such as smart growth, place making, and town center development, all of which in part draw on the concept of mixed-use development. ULI held its first conference on smart growth in 1997 and its first conference on place making in 1999 and published *The Smart Growth Tool Kit* in 2002 and *Place Making: Developing Town Centers, Main Streets, and Urban Villages* in 2002.

This second edition of *Mixed-Use Development Handbook,* which draws on much of this earlier work, is a complete revision of the first edition. The nature of mixed-use development has changed enormously since 1975, and the quality of development and design has advanced substantially. This second edition looks at the development of mixed-use projects of all types, ranging from mixed-use towers to town centers, and includes ten new case studies as well as discussion of nearly a hundred other recent examples.

Like other ULI handbooks, this book covers all areas of the development process, including market and feasibility analysis, working with the public sector, planning and design, marketing and promotion, and operations and management. The book includes an international perspective and covers projects and practices in the United States, Europe, and Asia.

This book emphasizes the important role that mixed-use development can play in developing better urban environments while at the same time highlighting the many talents and skills required to succeed. The complexity and demanding nature of these projects remain barriers to widespread development of mixed-use properties; this book seeks to help development industry participants to address and overcome these challenges.

Dean Schwanke
Project Director

Mixed-Use Development Handbook

1. Introduction and History

In the history of urban development, the mixing of different land uses—residential, shopping, employment, entertainment, lodging, civic, cultural—in one relatively discrete area has been prevalent in human settlements ranging from small villages to large cities. The concept of mixed-use urban areas runs far back in history throughout the world, from the ancient towns and cities of Greece and China, to the tightly compacted and walled cities of medieval Europe, to the delightful mix of uses and buildings created over centuries that endure today in such vibrant cities as London, Paris, Cairo, Tokyo, and Beijing. Even the cores of many newer cities in North and South America and Australia, developed before the advent of the automobile, exhibit a high degree of integration among different land uses; prime examples are New York City, Toronto, Buenos Aires, and Sydney.

During the mid-20th century, however, several trends and developments converged to undermine this pattern of mixing uses closely in urban areas:

- The rise of the automobile as the dominant mode of transportation, which led to much more horizontal, low-density, and dispersed patterns of land use and development.
- Growing affluence, especially in North America and Europe, which has allowed a growing number of households to live in large homes—often detached single-family homes—on large lots, further encouraging horizontal land use patterns, reducing easy pedestrian connections, and encouraging physical separation of uses into discrete districts.
- The implementation of land use regulations and zoning laws, especially in the United States, that although intended to create order through the control and separation of land uses, essentially made it illegal to mix uses in newly developing areas.

The results of these trends and forces are still with us today. In much of the newly developing areas of many cities around the world, the dominant image and reality of housing is the low-rise, single-family residential subdivision. The image and reality of retail space is found in large regional shopping centers or strip retail space along major thoroughfares. And although a dominant image of office space is still the downtown high rise, the reality is that most office space in the United States—and much of the new space in other cities of the world—is now found in sprawling, low-density suburban office parks, districts, and corridors.

Although this pattern prevailed through much of the 20th century, new mixed-use development models emerged during the century that offered new approaches to both modern development and the mixing of uses. Although these new mixed-use developments have not been dominant, they have become increasingly influential.

This book documents the move toward modern mixed-use development and sets forth a broad guide, using many examples, for practitioners to use for developing quality mixed-use environments. It brings together ideas from

Renaissance Place in Highland Park, Illinois, mixes residential, retail, and office uses on an infill location.

leading developments and leading land use practitioners to address the issue of how best to create stimulating, compelling, and functional urban environments in which to live, work, shop, visit, and play.

The principal objectives of the book are to describe what has been learned through experience about developing mixed-use projects—from completing market analyses, feasibility studies, and development strategies to financing, planning and design, and marketing and management. Ten case studies delineate actual situations, strategies, and experiences, and the text draws on numerous examples throughout. The final chapter focuses on the most recent trends in mixed-use development and the outlook for this type of development.

Creating Mixed-Use Environments Today

Despite the trends leading away from mixed-use development throughout much of the 20th century, countervailing influences have now brought mixed-use development and urban place-making concepts back to the forefront of development trends around the world. The art of creating or enhancing viable and attractive mixed-use environments in cities and suburbs is flourishing and is being energized from many directions. Today, for example, mixed-use development examples and ideas pop up everywhere:

• Developers of master-planned communities incorporate mixed-use town centers into their developments to enhance a sense of place for their communities.
• Developers and redevelopment officials work together to stimulate revitalization and new mixed-use development in downtowns, urban infill locations, suburban downtowns, and suburban office districts.
• Many retailers, restaurant operators, and entertainment developers seek out new streetfront and open-air settings for their operations, notably town center, main street, and mixed-use environments.
• As a result of the growing number of childless households that prefer more urban lifestyles, higher-density housing increasingly is being developed in and around commercial areas—downtowns, town centers, transit stations, and suburban office districts—leading to more mixed-use development in those areas.
• Smart growth and new urbanism activists bring new ideas and policy initiatives to the table regarding mixed-use environments as a means for addressing numerous problems, from environmental degradation to urban decay to sprawl.
• Transit and local government officials promote transit-oriented development and transit villages that can increase transit use while also creating stimulating urban living environments.
• Suburban planners and officials encourage mixed-use town center development as a way to create identity and attractive pedestrian environments and gathering places for their communities.

• Asian cities such as Kuala Lumpur and Shanghai are building major high-rise mixed-use projects as an effective and attractive method for managing their rapid growth and urbanization.

Today the concept of urban place making—the creation of active, distinctive, pedestrian-friendly urban environments through effective programming and design of a mix of uses—is not simply a dream of urban planners; it is a marketable development concept that both the public and private sectors increasingly embrace.

The modern concept of mixed-use development that is being implemented today, however, is quite different from the historical models, largely because it incorporates many modern building forms—high-rise office buildings, large hotels, large apartment buildings, shopping and entertainment centers, convention facilities, health clubs, transit stations, and parking structures. Modern mixed-use developments are often characterized by the dramatic design, size, impact, and sense of place that is created—including significant public spaces and amenities—making them the subject of broad attention even when they are developed as small-scale projects.

Perhaps most distinctively, unlike most mixed-use environments of the past that evolved over time and involved many builders, modern mixed-use projects are usually developed over a relatively short period of time by one master developer under one master plan. For better or worse, they are very much designed and planned environments, presenting a fundamental challenge for developers and planners: how to plan urban buildings and environments that are not contrived, that feel authentic and "real."

Achieving success in developing mixed-use properties is not easy. Mixed-use development is complex and does not lend itself to the formulaic approach of many single-use projects. Each project and situation is different, and the development concept and outcome vary dramatically, depending on the particular site, market, developer, urban designer, and financing. Uses must be marketable in their own right, phased at the right time, and work together synergistically to create a whole that is greater than the sum of its parts.

What Is a Mixed-Use Development?

Since the publication in 1976 of ULI's first book on mixed-use development—*Mixed-Use Developments: New Ways of Land Use*—both the concept of mixed-use development and the actual product have evolved tremendously. The original definition developed in 1976, however, still holds today. Mixed-use developments are characterized by:

• three or more significant revenue-producing uses (such as retail/entertainment, office, residential, hotel, and/or civic/cultural/recreation) that in well-planned projects are mutually supporting;

CityPlace in West Palm Beach, Florida, exemplifies several trends currently driving mixed-use development: urban revitalization, smart growth, main street retailing, higher-density urban housing, and town centers.

- significant physical and functional integration of project components (and thus a relatively close-knit and intensive use of land), including uninterrupted pedestrian connections; and
- development in conformance with a coherent plan (that frequently stipulates the type and scale of uses, permitted densities, and related items).

Three or More Significant Revenue-Producing Uses

Although many real estate projects have more than one use, mixed-use developments as defined and discussed in this book generally include three or more major uses. The three or more uses should be significant (for example, retail space should offer more than site-serving convenience facilities) and should attract a significant market in their own right. In most mixed-use projects, the primary uses are usually income producing, such as retail, office, residential, and/or hotel facilities. Other significant uses might include arenas, convention centers, performing arts facilities, museums, and major civic buildings. In the case of cultural and civic facilities, some funding may be needed from philanthropic or public sources to make the use financially viable. The important factor is that they be significant uses that draw their own clientele to the project.

Physical and Functional Integration

The second characteristic of mixed-use developments is a significant physical and functional integration of

project components and thus an intensive use of land. All project components should be interconnected by pedestrian links, although this integration can take many physical forms:

- a vertical mixing of project components into a single mixed-use building or tower, often occupying only one city block;
- careful positioning of key project components around central public spaces (for example, a street, park, plaza, atrium, galleria, or shopping center);
- interconnection of project components through pedestrian-friendly pathways (including sidewalks along streets, interior walkways, enclosed corridors and concourses, retail plazas and mall areas, escalators, and aerial bridges between buildings).

Pedestrian circulation and orientation are critical elements in planning, because without them the project will not achieve the desired synergies and sense of place that are the hallmarks of good mixed-use developments.

This second characteristic distinguishes mixed-use developments from multiuse developments that may include three or more significant revenue-producing uses but do not integrate them. For example, such lower-intensity, more-spread-out developments might include low-density master-planned communities and business parks, both of which may include a variety of uses but whose densities and physical integration tend to be significantly less

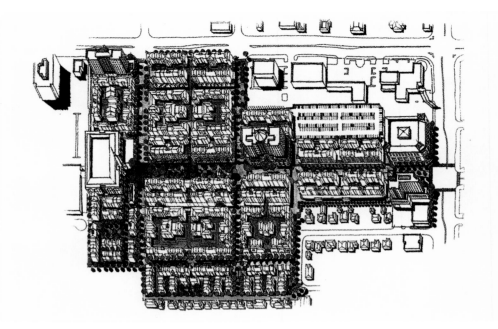

than mixed-use developments, resulting in less regular interaction between uses and more use of automobiles for movement within the project.

Development in Conformance with a Coherent Plan

Finally, mixed-use developments are conceived and executed following a coherent development strategy and plan. Master planning for a mixed-use development, compared with a single-purpose project, demands much more diverse and specialized participation from developers, market analysts, architects and land planners, property managers, and capital/financing sources. The planning process is therefore far more complex than for most other real estate projects. Such plans may comprise a collection of materials, including market studies, a development program (possibly with several options), land use and building configuration plans and models, working drawings, cost estimates, feasibility analyses, financing plans, marketing plans, and management plans.

Conceptual plans for mixed-use developments typically set forth at a minimum the types and scale of land uses, permitted densities, and general areas on the site where different kinds of development are to occur. Plans for projects entailing substantial public investment and/or control may also specify procedures for architectural review as well as the respective responsibilities and financial obligations of public and private sectors (for the provision of infrastructure, for example). These documents guide—in the case of some projects, govern—development as to the scale, timing, type, and density of buildings and relationships among project components, open space, and infrastructure at the site. This approach distinguishes such projects from the unplanned mixing of uses often resulting from the separate, unrelated actions of several different developers.

Physical and Structural Configurations

Although mixed-use developments include diverse types, sizes, and configurations, some basic physical and structural models can help to define these developments. The physical configuration of mixed-use developments generally can be grouped into three broad categories: mixed-use towers, integrated multitower structures, and mixed-use town centers/urban villages/districts. These types also represent three concepts on a continuum, with

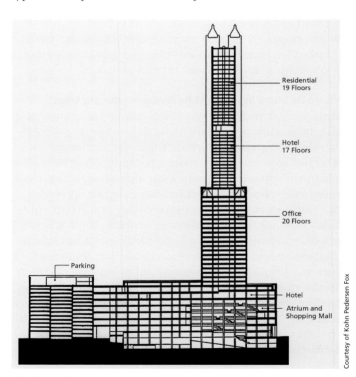

900 North Michigan Avenue in Chicago is a mixed-use tower that includes a large base structure with retail and parking, and a tower that includes office, hotel, and residential uses.

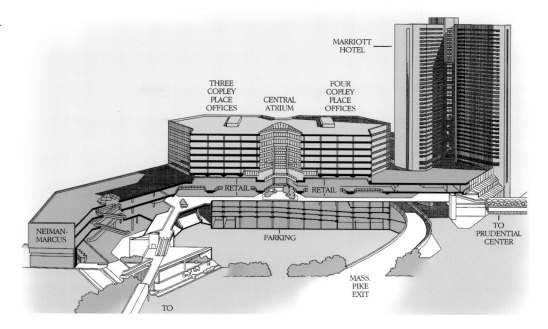

Copley Place in Boston, an integrated multitower mixed-use structure, includes two hotels, office space, and a retail mall.

mixed-use towers generally the highest density and town centers/urban villages the lowest.

Mixed-Use Towers

A mixed-use tower is a single structure, typically of considerable mass and height, whose uses principally are layered vertically. Several varieties are possible. One is a simple high-rise tower with three or more layered uses. The John Hancock Center in Chicago, one of the older and best-known examples of a mixed-use tower, includes residential units over office with retail at the base. Another example mixes residential and hotel uses over retail in one tower, such as was done at Park Tower in Chicago.

Another variation is a tower rising from an enlarged base structure, such as 900 North Michigan Avenue, which includes—top to bottom—condominiums, a hotel, office space, and a retail mall in the enlarged base, together with parking. Similarly, Water Tower Place in Chicago comprises a large ten-story base structure with a combination of retail, entertainment, and office uses out of which rises a 74-story tower that includes a hotel and residences.

A third variation is to attach a low-rise structure to a large tower. Jin Mao Tower in Shanghai (see Chapter 8), for example, includes hotel space stacked on top of office space, with a separate multilevel retail mall set to one side of the tower. Similarly, the 35-story Espirito Santo Plaza in Miami combines office, hotel, and residential uses in a single structure, with a large banking hall at its base. The office areas for the bank occupy the lower floors of the tower close to the banking hall, which is a large separate multistory structure at the base of the project. Residential and hotel uses are located atop the office space. A separate 11-story parking structure at the east end of the site includes a landscaped roof garden and health club with swimming pool and tennis court.

Among the most distinctive qualities of the mixed-use tower configuration is the consolidation of project mass into a single and therefore striking physical profile, establishing a dramatic project identity that is helpful in marketing the development. For example, both the Jin Mao Tower and the John Hancock Center can claim to be one of the tallest buildings in the world. Among the disadvantages is that little opportunity exists to create a compelling outdoor public space or civic realm.

Integrated Multitower Structures

Integrated multitower or multicomponent structures include individual buildings and towers architecturally connected by a common atrium, concourse, shopping complex, and/or underground parking structure that integrates all or most of the project components at the lower levels in a common base. They are typically found in downtown central business districts (CBDs) and higher-density suburban locations such as suburban downtowns. The Houston Galleria in Houston and Copley Place in Boston are classic examples.

Numerous variations are possible. The Fashion Centre at Pentagon City in Arlington, Virginia, includes a multilevel shopping center anchored by two department stores that offers direct structural connections to an office building, a hotel, and a multilevel parking structure, with a separate apartment building. Similarly, at WestEnd City Center in Budapest (see Chapter 8), office and hotel structures are connected at the base by a large retail mall, with parking in a structure to one side.

In some cases, buildings rise from a common platform or podium that may include several levels containing parking, service areas, and retail facilities. For example, Sony Center am Potsdamer Platz (see Chapter 8) includes eight buildings above a parking structure and lower-level service area that serves as the base for the entire site.

AOL Time Warner Center in New York is another variation, in this case involving two mixed-use towers that rise from a multistory base structure. The base structure includes two underground levels and ten levels above ground containing retail, office, and cultural facilities. Both towers include condominiums and office space, and one also includes a hotel.

Mixed-Use Town Centers, Urban Villages, and Districts

Mixed-use town centers, urban villages, and districts are organized around streets, parks, plazas, and/or squares and function more like an urban district than a single project. They frequently involve stacking uses—residential or office over retail, for example—in low- or mid-rise buildings, but they are predominantly made up of a variety of individual buildings arranged along streets and around public squares or other open spaces. Seven of the ten case studies in this book fall into this category: Addison Circle, CityPlace, Peabody Place, Phillips Place, University Park at MIT, Valencia Town Center Drive, and Yerba Buena Center. This configuration has become increasingly popular as more mixed-use projects are developed outside downtowns.

Mizner Park in Boca Raton, Florida, opened in 1990, is one of the earliest examples of this type of development. It is a town center organized around a two-block-long main street lined with retail space and a linear park with fountains and benches running down the middle of the street. Residential over retail uses line one side, office over retail space the other. The project has become an instant downtown for the city, which never before had

a real one. CityPlace in West Palm Beach, Florida, and Valencia Town Center Drive in Valencia, California, also use a main street configuration that includes retail, office, hotel, entertainment, and residential uses. A more urban example is Peabody Place, a major high-density mixed-use district and urban village in downtown Memphis. This redevelopment project includes office, retail, residential, hotel, and entertainment uses, and numerous historic buildings on seven blocks in downtown Memphis (see Chapter 8).

Mixed-use town centers and urban villages are clearly the direction that most mixed-use designs are moving today, and they are likely to become increasingly common as suburban mixed-use developments grow in popularity and urban redevelopment continues to focus on designing around existing streets in and around major downtowns. Such projects are often developed on large sites where buildings can be arranged and mixed horizontally as well as vertically and easily linked by open-air streets, pedestrian connections, parks, and squares. They also offer greater flexibility for timing and phasing projects, important factors in improving feasibility and reducing risk.

A Short History of Mixed-Use Development

Cities throughout history have provided many good models for intense mixed-use configurations that today's urban designers study carefully. Ancient cities of Greece

Phillips Place in Charlotte is a town center and urban village organized around a retail main street; it includes apartments, a hotel, and a cinema in addition to retail stores.

and Rome and historic villages and towns in Italy, France, and England are often cited, but perhaps the most illustrative example is the medieval town, relatively small and surrounded by high walls. To defend the city properly, it was necessary to keep the circumference of the protective exterior walls to a minimum, resulting in a compact city and necessitating relatively high densities and significant integration of governmental, commercial, and residential uses. An orientation toward pedestrian movement was inherent in these towns, not merely because of their small size and compact mass but also because of the relatively high cost of water-borne or animal-drawn transportation.

In the European cities that grew up as major centers during the Renaissance, a different, more open city form was developed in conjunction with the increased scale of economic activity. According to Howard Elkus of Elkus/Manfredi Architects, "The increase in wealth supported an increase in animal-drawn and water-borne transportation. . . . Streets became wider to support vehicular traffic. The increase in scale of economic, political, and religious activities created the need for more open areas within the urban fabric for markets and ceremonial functions. The need for walled enclosures as defensive boundaries continued nevertheless. . . . As many of these major centers grew, new ramparts were constructed beyond the limits of the old. These security requirements still provided an incentive for compact urban form. Such compact forms and limited transportation systems meant that mixing uses together in close proximity was the most sensible approach." Compactness, density, and mixed uses were the hallmarks of those cities.

Many older American cities to this day exhibit some of the same mixed-use traits. In Manhattan, residential, retail, hotel, office, and entertainment uses exist together on the same or adjacent blocks in many areas. In Washington, D.C., the Georgetown area includes a diverse collection of densely configured buildings containing individual shops, retail galleries, townhouses, apartment buildings, hotels, office buildings, and mixed-use projects. Even in many small American towns, main street blocks include retail uses at the ground level, office and residential units on the second level, and apartments or single-family houses on the back half of the block. Without belaboring the historical precedents, suffice it to say that mixing uses has been not only common throughout history but often the most logical land use configuration.

As outlined earlier, development trends and patterns in the 20th century changed radically. These changes have resulted in a whole new context and approach to planning and development and created new kinds of mixed-use developments and environments not seen before.

Early Twentieth-Century Mixed-Use Developments

Numerous developments established important models and precedents for modern mixed-use projects during the first half of the 20th century. They included town center and urban village models as well as high-rise downtown models.

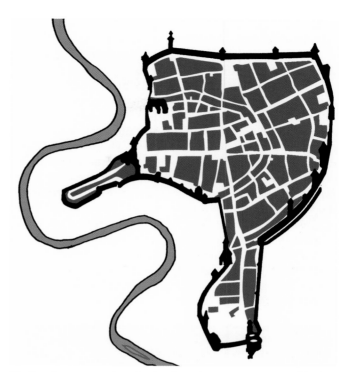

Medieval towns, such as Rothenburg in Germany, exemplify the compact mixed-use urban pattern that has been typical in cities and towns throughout history.

Early Urban Village Models. Many of the earliest 20th-century mixed-use models were related to the garden city movement. The team of Unwin and Parker, for example, planned numerous garden cities and suburbs in England that included town centers with a mix of uses.[1] The village center they planned for the model industrial village of New Earswick (1902), just northeast of York, included a modest folk hall, a village green, and a row of shops with residences above, all of which provided the village with a central gathering place and an identity true to its medieval motif. In the much larger town center that the team designed for Letchworth (1904), 12 streets and boulevards converge on a large town square dominated by major municipal and religious structures.[2]

The town center of Hampstead Garden Suburb (1906) near London is another example; it includes two imposing churches that face each other across a vast green, a smaller village green surrounded by a school, stores, various public buildings, tennis courts, and bowling greens, and an adjacent major shopping area that includes two blocks of Germanic medieval buildings positioned along the main highway, which serve as a monumental gateway to the town.

Among the more noteworthy early mixed-use developments in the United States are several town center–/urban village–style projects, including Market Square in Lake Forest, Illinois, and the Country Club Plaza District in Kansas City, Missouri.

The community of Lake Forest, Illinois, first started in 1856, resisted the notion of a town center for 60 years—until the addition of Market Square in 1916.[3] Market Square illustrates the shift away from traditional town centers anchored by religious and civic institutions toward centers devoted primarily to shopping.

Market Square's reputation is derived from the simple elegance of its traditional urban design, which features an arrangement of small-scale buildings along the street and surrounding a square. The formal common, complete with a memorial fountain honoring its architect, the open-air pedestrian arcades, and the prominent clock tower all contribute to a strong sense of place. The streetfront and the square are lined with two-story buildings containing ground-floor shops with offices and residences above. Angled, on-street parking spaces are provided in front of the shops; "shipping courts" located behind each block are reserved for deliveries, utilities, and trash collection.

Market Square continues to be widely hailed as a classic plan for an American town center conceived during the early automobile era. In 1979, it was added to the National Register of Historic Places as the first planned suburban shopping center.

Country Club Plaza, developed by J.C. Nichols, opened in 1922 as an outdoor shopping district in the heart of the Country Club residential district. Subsequent development added hotel and residential towers adjacent to the shopping district. It continues to prosper today and serves as a national model for retail and mixed-use development.

Country Club Plaza in Kansas City, like Market Square, is an early shopping center organized around streets, but its other uses are located on adjacent sites rather than above retail stores. One of the oldest suburban shopping centers in the United States, Country Club Plaza was initially developed in 1922 as a Spanish-inspired outdoor shopping district designed to appeal to people arriving by car. The Plaza was developed by J.C. Nichols, one of the founders of ULI, and was part of a larger planned district—the Country Club District—that included a variety of residential neighborhoods. During the 1950s, Miller Nichols, son of J.C. Nichols, expanded the retail uses and developed adjacent areas with high-rise apartments and hotels to create a mixed-use district.

Each decade since it was built, the Plaza has become larger, more productive, and more attractive to shop owners and the public alike. It attracts prominent national stores, receives top rents, and produces some of the highest sales volumes in the metropolitan area. Surrounding apartments, offices, and hotels all command the best rates in the market, and a new office building recently added to the heart of the plaza commands the highest rents in Kansas City. Through a combination of innovative site planning, rich architecture, careful maintenance, a mix of uses, self-imposed zoning restrictions, and continuous development and redevelopment, Country Club Plaza and District has thrived for more than 80 years. Today, the Plaza and District is a major tourist attraction; it has become a mid-town anchor for Kansas City and an important model and precedent for modern mixed-use town centers and urban villages.

Early Downtown Complexes. Several important downtown mixed-use projects from this period are also noteworthy, as they established a new scale for height and density in mixed-use development. They include the Cleveland Union Terminal complex in Cleveland, the Carew Tower complex in Cincinnati, and Rockefeller Center in New York City. Each remains a landmark today in its city.

One of the earliest high-density downtown mixed-use projects in the United States was the Cleveland Union Terminal complex, opened in 1930 and centered around a train station in downtown Cleveland. In addition to the train station, the development included the Harvey shops and restaurants and other terminal conveniences, Public Square as the heart of the city and hub of urban transportation, the Hotel Cleveland, the 18-story Medical Arts Building, the 18-story Builders' Exchange Building, the 18-story Midland Bank Building, a post office building, the 52-story Terminal Tower, and a modern 12-story department store.

The development also included an extensive railroad infrastructure of tracks, bridges, signals, electrical catenary structures, and yard buildings necessary to switch passenger coaches from steam to electricity and bring them into the downtown area. The original marketing materials for the project noted that "other companion units will be designed and built from time to time, em-

The Cleveland Union Terminal complex, which opened in downtown Cleveland in 1930, was one of the earliest large-scale high-rise mixed-use projects in the United States. Much of this complex was redeveloped in the late 1980s and is now known as Tower City Center.

bodying beauty of mass and proportion, balance, rhythm, and variety in unity."

The project, undertaken by the Cleveland Union Terminals Co. and the Cleveland Terminals Building Co. "was a massive urban redevelopment project that foreshadowed the Rockefeller Center in New York, gave Cleveland the second-tallest building in the world in 1930, and forever changed the face of Public Square and wide swaths of adjoining neighborhoods."[4]

Another early high-rise mixed-use development was also in Ohio: the Carew Tower complex in downtown Cincinnati. Begun in September 1929, one month before the stock market crashed, the original development included a 49-story office building, a 28-story hotel with 800 rooms, and a through-block retail arcade with 20 shops and two department stores that joined the office and hotel and connected to the surrounding streets. A 25-story, fully automated parking garage held 750 cars in a separate structure. The project was located on a prime downtown site measuring 216 by 142 feet (65 by 43 meters). The project was undertaken by John J. Emery, Jr., a Cincinnati industrialist and real estate developer.

The Carew Tower complex, despite its large size and internal arcade, was a good fit for its site; it has been a landmark for the city to this day. "The Carew complex did not essentially change or disrupt certain patterns of social and commercial life in downtown Cincinnati. On the contrary, the complex enhanced them, for all its major functions were modernized versions of well-known businesses already on or adjacent to its site."[5]

Rockefeller Center in New York was started two years later, in 1931. A landmark mixed-use project driven largely by office demand but including retail, hotel (in a later phase), and performing arts space, Rockefeller Center in New York City was one of the most innovative and successful commercial real estate developments of the 20th century. The integration of numerous office buildings with retail, recreational, and cultural facilities—all surrounding landmark public spaces—in one development

is exemplary, and the project is one of the earliest and most important models for the mixed-use developments that sprang up in the latter half of the century.

A pioneering development in concept, scale, physical design, and services, Rockefeller Center today is a massive business, retail, and entertainment center. Built in roughly two stages (1931 to 1940 and 1946 to 1975), the center has continued to expand and change over the years, including an ongoing modernization program. Its total rentable area is 17 million square feet (1.6 million square meters), comprising 21 buildings on nearly 24 acres (10 hectares) in the heart of New York City. Each building in the first phase of this city within a city has an established relationship with the others and with the surrounding urban fabric, with a 70-story tower at the center. Nearly one-fourth of the land area has been left open to permit the proper play of light and air, to facilitate the flow of traffic, and to provide for beautifully landscaped pedestrian areas.

A project of continuing contemporary relevance, Rockefeller Center has manifestly influenced many developers of other downtown mixed-use projects. This colossal development has much significance for contemporary mixed-use projects:

- accommodation of pedestrian and vehicular traffic through such farsighted concepts as an "extra" street (Rockefeller Plaza, which breaks the monotony of long city blocks) and underground passageways (the Concourse);
- the concept of total services for commercial developments whereby convenience retail space and a wide variety of tenant services are available;
- dynamic evolution of the center over time, through an active program of expansion and modernization that has included construction of new buildings and the updating of existing space to keep all center buildings fully competitive with new structures;

Rockefeller Center is a landmark development that today includes 21 buildings with office, retail, and performing arts space, and a hotel. Among its most distinctive and memorable features is the world-famous plaza, pictured here at Christmas.

- the attendant changes in physical relationships among project components, building use, and occupancy patterns over time; and
- management's continuing attention to tenants' needs, a key to the center's commercial success.

The result was a business and entertainment complex far ahead of its time. The three-dimensional approach to urban design—with skyscrapers planned in relation to one another, to the open space, and to the concourse—has served as the prototype for similar developments around the world.

The Emergence of Modern Mixed-Use Projects in the 1960s

Mixed-use development was largely dormant during the 1940s and early 1950s, but the late 1950s and especially the 1960s witnessed a new era when modern mixed-use projects came to the fore. These projects arose initially in downtowns with commercial uses as drivers but eventually incorporated residential uses and moved beyond the downtown. Sizable mixed-use towers also first emerged during this period. Many of the projects reflect the international school of architecture—often featuring glass-box buildings or dramatic architecture with hardscape plazas—that in many cases has not aged well in most eyes. Nevertheless, they were ambitious projects and important experiments in city building and large-scale development, and most are still evolving today.

This new era of modern mixed-use projects first appeared on the North American scene as primarily public/private efforts to revitalize downtown commercial cores. These areas had served for many years as diverse urban centers, but over the years, many had declined as affluent residents moved to the suburbs, where new shopping centers and employment centers began to spring up. Revitalization programs were frequently geared toward large-scale efforts to reestablish downtown vitality by incorporating multiple uses that could extend the activity cycle of the area.

Among these early downtown mixed-use projects:

- Penn Center in Philadelphia, an office/hotel/retail project that was originally developed according to a master plan prepared by the city planning commission, with actual development (begun in 1954) undertaken by several developers.
- Midtown Plaza in Rochester, New York, a project initiated by downtown businesspeople concerned about deterioration in the central city; the project opened in 1962.
- Constitution Plaza in Hartford, Connecticut, an 11-acre (4.4-hectare) office/hotel/retail mixed-use project conceived by the Hartford Redevelopment Agency and subsequently developed by Travelers Insurance Company. Construction began in 1960 and was completed in 1964.
- Prudential Center in Boston, a privately financed mixed-use project in a downtown area. This very large

project included 52-story and 25-story office towers, a 29-story hotel, four low-rise commercial/retail buildings, the John B. Hynes Civic Auditorium, and three 28-story apartment buildings. Construction began in 1959; it has recently been updated with the addition of an office tower, an expanded retail area at the base, and condominiums.

- Charles Center in Baltimore, first conceived in 1957. The project was implemented for the city by Charles Center–Inner Harbor Management, Inc., a special, private, nonprofit corporation formed to manage downtown redevelopment under contract to the Baltimore Department of Housing and Community Development. The project includes office space, retail space, residential and hotel facilities, a live theater, underground parking, and extensive first- and second-level pedestrian plazas and walkways.

These early public/private mixed-use projects were early signals of the public sector's growing interest in creating diverse integrated uses within a downtown redevelopment area; most previous public planning efforts had emphasized the separation of uses, and this new approach was the beginning of an important shift in public planning theory that has significantly fueled mixed-use development.

While the revitalization of commercial cores proceeded, several pioneering efforts created residentially oriented mixed-use projects in central cities as well. Two early examples include Marina City in Chicago and the Watergate in Washington, D.C. Both involved central city revitalization, but they were initiated primarily by the private sector and were different from the previously discussed projects in that they both began as primarily residential projects. A third early example was Golden Gateway Center in San Francisco, part of a larger redevelopment effort in downtown San Francisco.

Marina City was completed in 1963 and continues to be internationally recognized for its distinctive architectural design. Marina City is located on a 3.2-acre (1.3-hectare) site in the heart of downtown Chicago. Although residential uses dominate, other components include office space, retail areas, a marina, movie theaters, an ice rink, a health club, and parking. Marina City was a pioneer because of its emphasis on residential uses in a largely downtown commercial area and because it was one of the first privately initiated ventures to employ the mixed-use concept.

Although downtown locations were frequently preferred, mixed-use projects in the latter part of the 1960s also found strong market potential in more outlying areas. As affluent residential areas continued to be developed in the suburbs and new transit systems were developed, many areas on the edge of downtown and beyond became very attractive locations for a mixed-use development. Four projects that helped to pioneer mixed-use projects in more outlying areas were Westmount Square in Montreal, la Défense in Paris, Century City in Los Angeles, and Crystal City in Arlington, Virginia, near Washington, D.C.

Westmount Square is one of the earliest projects to demonstrate the viability of a commercially oriented mixed-use project outside the commercial core and the potential for mixed uses around a transit station. It is a tightly configured mixed-use development covering 5.5 acres (2.2 hectares). Land uses in the first phase included a 24-story office tower, two luxury high-rise apartment buildings, 45 exclusive retail shops situated under a plaza covering almost the entire site, a 700-seat movie

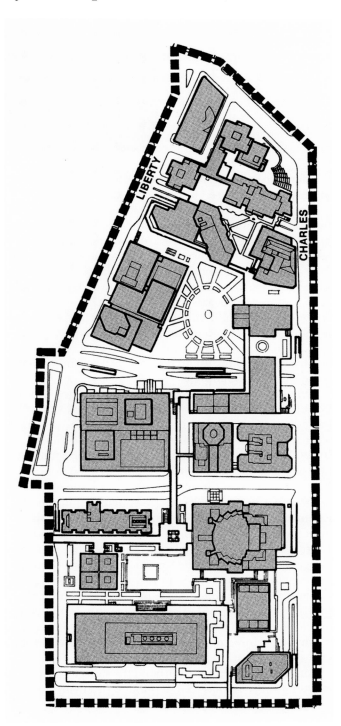

The site plan for Charles Center in downtown Baltimore highlights the large-scale multiblock configuration of this mixed-used project, conceived in the late 1950s and built largely in the 1960s.

La Défense is a world-famous mixed-use project in Paris that was begun in 1958. The office building in the foreground, la Grande Arche, was designed to be a postmodern reflection of l'Arc de Triomphe. Located on the edge of central Paris, la Défense is free from the height restrictions of the city center, allowing it to explore the world of modern high-rise architecture.

Gérald D. Morand

theater, and parking. All components in the first phase of development were built between 1965 and 1968.

Another early example of a project on the edge of the historic city center is la Défense in Paris, a monumental project that began in earnest around 1958. This mixed-use project includes offices, a shopping center and restaurants, housing, an exhibition hall, and large public open spaces and gardens. The project was intended to extend the Champs-Élysées axis. It is served by two subway stops and includes the monumental Grande Arche, completed in 1983, a world-famous building in the shape of a cube with a square arch through the middle of it. The project draws on modernist architectural styles and includes some stunning buildings.

One of the earliest mixed-use projects to go entirely beyond the downtown to establish a truly new suburban location was Century City in Los Angeles, developed from scratch on a 180-acre (73-hectare) abandoned movie studio lot; the development includes a massive amount of space that was started in 1961 and has been developed over 40 years. In addition to its scale, extended development period, and colossal investment requirements, Century City ranks as one of the first large-scale, office-oriented suburban mixed-use centers to appear in the United States. The original scale and objectives for this project, however, like those for many suburban commercial developments, provided for somewhat limited physical and functional integration of uses throughout the project or easy pedestrian circulation, although recent development and urban design efforts have sought to create better integration and a more pedestrian-friendly environment.

Another pioneering suburban effort was Crystal City in Arlington, Virginia. Also developed strictly by the private sector, today it is large enough to be described as a mixed-use district; it contains as much space as many small cities have in their entire downtowns. The project is similar in some ways to Century City, but it has a more linear orientation and a much greater emphasis on physical and functional integration and pedestrian connections between uses. Started in 1964, it includes apartments, office space, retail facilities, hotels, movie theaters, a subway transit station, and recreational facilities.

These projects were instrumental in pioneering mixed-use concepts outside CBDs. Their developers recognized the potential of these locations where others did not, and the mixed-use concept was particularly useful in both instances in establishing a sense of place where none had existed before. In effect, these projects helped to shape and focus growth patterns in their respective cities and thus highlighted the growing potential of building mixed-use projects in a variety of locations.

The 1960s also saw the first major mixed-use tower. Among the earliest examples of a mixed-use project within a single vertical structure is the John Hancock Center in Chicago. Most mixed-use projects discussed up to this point emphasized horizontal integration of uses, but vertical stacking and integration have come to play important roles in modern mixed-use development as well; the John Hancock Center, one of the tallest buildings in the world, was a major landmark in the development of mixed-use towers. This 100-story tower with 2.8 million square feet (260,000 square meters) of gross building area includes residential uses on floors 44 to 92 and office space on floors 13 to 41. The first five floors were programmed for retail and commercial uses, and parking for 650 cars is provided on floors 6 through 12, served by an external spiral ramp. The project was conceived in 1964, construction began in 1965, and the first occupants moved in 1969.

Mixed-use projects of the 1960s pioneered the concept of dramatic interior spaces—large atriums and gallerias, for example—in modern buildings; Peachtree Center in Atlanta was a leader in this effort. The atrium and other design concepts incorporated into the Atlanta Hyatt Regency Hotel were striking departures in hotel and mixed-use design, elements that have been emulated in numerous projects throughout the country and around the world. Jin Mao Tower in Shanghai, which incorporates a major soaring atrium within its hotel, is a recent example. The additions of the Westin and Marriott Hotels to Peachtree Center, each with its distinctive atrium, furthered the concept at Peachtree Center. Peachtree Center combines office, retail, hotel, and wholesale showroom facilities on 12 acres (4.8 hectares) in the heart of downtown Atlanta.

Finally, one very different kind of mixed-use project was started in the 1960s—a resort village—that was remarkably ahead of its time. Vail Village, the village center at the heart of the large Vail Resort in Colorado, first opened in 1961. The design concept integrated a variety of European town-planning principles, including narrow streets, an irregular street pattern, automobile-free pedestrian zones, a mix of retail, lodging, and residential uses, a Tyrolean architectural style, and prominently located public spaces. It was and is an important precedent for the town center and urban village projects that have become so popular today.

Among the most distinctive qualities characterizing the early projects, in contrast to the mixed-use projects of the 1970s, was their residential orientation. Most of the projects of the 1960s included substantial residential space, and many actually began as primarily residential projects.

A second distinctive quality was their relative openness to surrounding areas. For the most part, although they did not necessarily fit in well with the surrounding fabric, they were at least somewhat porous and did not try to become fortresses like many of the projects that would follow in the 1970s. Third, most projects were built using International-style architectural principles, a style not particularly strong in creating attractive pedestrian areas or people places. Many of the projects incorporated platforms and underground space, just as Rockefeller Center did, but none came close to capturing the kind of vitality and design quality of Rockefeller Center's

John Hancock Center in Chicago is the first major mixed-use tower built in the United States. Its vertical layering integrates and stacks (from bottom to top) parking, retail and restaurants, offices, and residences in a single structure. With its height and distinctive tapered shape, this building is one of the most recognizable in the world.

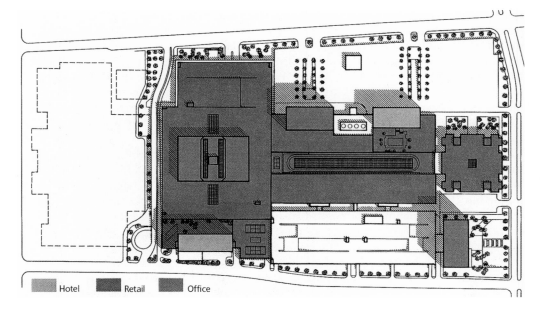

The Houston Galleria is one of the earliest mixed-use projects to include a major suburban retail mall. The initial plan arranged three office buildings and two hotels around the mall. The development has been expanded considerably since this initial plan was developed.

Hotel　Retail　Office

public spaces. Many of them were examples of podium developments, which often placed pedestrian plazas on second levels, separating pedestrians from the surrounding streets. Most of these projects suffered from some of the undesirable characteristics of the International style of architecture—with its emphasis on hard-surfaced plazas and glass boxes—that was still dominant in the 1960s, which contributed to the poor quality of many of the public areas.

In general, not many projects were completed during this decade. A ULI survey conducted in the 1980s identified only 23 projects that were started in the 1950s or 1960s, compared with 65 started in the 1970s and many more than 100 in the 1980s.

Internal Orientation in the 1970s

The 1970s brought a trend of increasing internal orientation. Although many of the projects of the 1960s maintained a certain open quality and paid some homage to the surrounding environment, many of the projects of the 1970s were enclosed and internally focused, the result of the increasing popularity of enclosed malls and large atriums in mixed-use developments. It was the full development of these concepts, together with the turmoil of central cities in the later 1960s, that pushed many of the mixed-use projects of the 1970s toward greater internal orientation and more defensive architecture.

The evolution of the shopping mall affected mixed-use projects in two important ways. First, the internally oriented shopping center under one central management emerged as a key component in the development of many downtown mixed-use projects that sought to compete with suburban malls, and the mall concept in general permeated a high percentage of mixed-use projects that were developed in the 1970s and 1980s.

Second, the suburban shopping center itself became a hub around which numerous uses were developed, and some developers saw the chance to create much more than scattered, peripheral structures and a sea of park-

ing in a shopping center setting. Some saw the possibility of creating fully integrated mixed-use projects.

Such was the case with the Houston Galleria. Perhaps the most influential suburban mixed-use project of the 1970s, the Houston Galleria is among the earliest examples of a mixed-use project that is focused and planned around a suburban shopping center; it has subsequently become the focus of a major suburban business center in the Houston area. The Galleria is a large-scale mixed-use project located about 6.5 miles (10.5 kilometers) west of downtown Houston in an upper-income, multiuse area known as City Post Oak.

Started in 1967, the project's initial centerpiece was a 450,000-square-foot (41,800-square-meter), three-level shopping mall that serves as a focus for office, hotel, and recreational components. It is a 20th-century interpretation of the famed 19th-century Galleria Vittoria Emmanuelle in Milan (c. 1865 to 1867). A barrel-vault skylight, 550 feet long and 50 feet wide (168 meters by 15 meters), covers the mall. Office, hotel, recreation, and parking components feed into this dramatic central space through a carefully planned system of pedestrian circulation. This mall subsequently has been expanded substantially. The project helped to set the precedent of mixed-use projects focused primarily on three commercial elements—office, retail, and hotel. This mix of uses became the most popular and feasible mix in projects developed in the 1970s and 1980s.

A similar mix of office, retail, and hotel uses is configured in a much different way in another landmark project of the early 1970s, the IDS Center in Minneapolis. The office tower is the dominant feature in this case, with the other elements of the project spread out at the base to create a lively urban experience. The IDS Center is one of the earliest mixed-use projects to use an atrium—Crystal Court—as the central focus and organizing space for the project; this central atrium serves as an excellent example of how a well-designed public space can contribute to the success of a mixed-use development.

Crystal Court, which joins the IDS Tower with the hotel tower and other structures, is a skylighted atrium with shops, restaurants, service facilities, and exhibit areas. Designed by John Burgee and Philip Johnson of New York, the IDS Center was initially conceived as a half-block project in 1962. Construction began in 1969 and was completed in 1973.

The IDS Center is a landmark among mixed-use projects because of its outstanding architecture, its careful balance of uses, its contribution to the downtown environment exemplified by the people-oriented Crystal Court, and its integration with other elements of downtown Minneapolis. Moreover, it is one of the earliest major downtown office buildings to move away from the "windswept plaza" approach to urban design, providing an exciting enclosed, skylighted atrium at its base.

The 1970s also witnessed the opening of three of the largest mixed-use projects to date—the World Trade Center (WTC) in New York City, Illinois Center in Chicago, and Embarcadero Center in San Francisco. The World Trade Center opened in 1970 and became an instant international landmark and icon for New York City. Much of the world thought of the WTC as two skyscrapers, but it was in fact a mixed-use project that included six office buildings and a hotel surrounding a plaza, with a retail concourse and transit connections beneath. Although this development did include significant open space, the plan did not bring any of the surrounding streets into the site plan, and the plan essentially created an island apart from the rest of the city, breaking up the fabric of surrounding streets, placing retail shops in lower-level concourses, and creating an isolated, stand-alone project. Although design of the WTC sought to create a pedestrian-friendly enclave by restricting auto access, the pedestrian areas and plazas were in reality not pedestrian friendly at all and were essentially the epitome of windswept plazas. Following its destruction on September 11, 2001, redevelopment planning for the site is addressing these shortcomings, and the final plan will likely result in much improved and far more compelling urban spaces.

Illinois Center used a similar approach, incorporating a series of high-rise buildings connected by plazas and retail concourses. The project is a colossus among mixed-use projects in investment, acreage, buildable floor area, and time frame of development. Located adjacent to Chicago's Loop and immediately south of the fashionable North Michigan Avenue area, the 83-acre (33.6-hectare) site was formerly a rail yard. Begun in 1969, the project's master plan calls for a multilevel circulation network that will eventually cover the entire site and serve as a base for all development. Designed by the office of Mies van der Rohe with Solomon, Cordwell, Buenz & Associates, the infrastructure provides for three distinct vehicular street levels and a separate, uninterrupted, enclosed pedestrian walkway throughout the project.

The project includes several hotels and numerous high-rise office buildings, including an 82-story skyscraper, residential towers, and retail space. Such a massive project expanded the meaning of mixed use, highlighting the

The IDS Center is one of the finest examples of a mixed-use development organized around a central enclosed atrium and courtyard. The Crystal Court serves to internally connect the various uses of the project, which include a 57-story office tower, a 19-story hotel, parking, restaurants, and retail space, occupying a total of 2.25 million square feet (209,000 square meters).

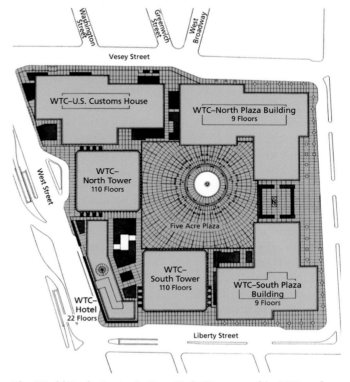

The World Trade Center in New York City opened in 1970 and stood as one of the most recognizable landmarks in the world before it was destroyed in 2001. It included six office buildings and a hotel surrounding a plaza, with a retail concourse, parking, and transit connections beneath.

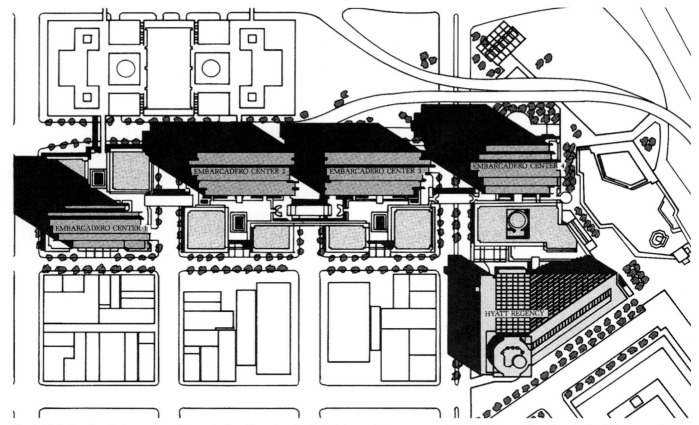

The initial plan for Embarcadero Center in San Francisco included four office towers with an 804-room hotel and 325,000 square feet (30,200 square meters) of ground-level retail space.

issue of phasing as a critical part of the mixed-use concept and illustrating clearly the advantages and challenges of building on a large scale.

Embarcadero Center in San Francisco, also among the largest of mixed-use projects of the time, pursued a more open approach. It initially involved four large office towers with 2.7 million square feet (251,000 square meters) of space, an 804-room Hyatt Regency Hotel (including a large atrium), and 325,000 square feet (30,200 square meters) of ground-level retail space, all set amid open plazas and walkways in a signature location in downtown San Francisco near the waterfront. Unlike many of the projects of the 1970s, it was relatively well integrated with surrounding uses, although it did separate pedestrians from surrounding streets through the use of plazas and elevated walkways over the several streets that bisected the project. But it was not a fortress, and it did not place retail in enclosed concourses underground or above grade but at the ground level and largely within the base of the office buildings, making them easily accessible from surrounding streets.

The 1970s also brought a second major vertical mixed-use project to Chicago (sited near the existing John Hancock Center), a ground-breaking venture in its successful implementation of a vertical downtown retail mall, its incorporation of four major uses in one primarily vertical structure, and its reliance on nonoffice uses as the primary components. Water Tower Place comprises a dramatic L-shaped megastructure that includes a 12-story base building and a tower rising to 74 stories. The project was developed by Urban Investment and Development Company on a full city block on North Michigan Avenue.

Included in the complex is a 450-room hotel, 199,000 square feet (18,500 square meters) of office space located on floors 8 and 9, 260 luxury condominium units on the upper floors of the tower, and 613,700 square feet (57,000 square meters) of retail space on eight levels, arranged around a grand atrium. The retail component features two department stores as well as more than 100 specialty shops. Construction began in 1972 on this privately financed development and was completed in summer 1976. Although retail malls had appeared in downtown mixed-use projects well before Water Tower Place, few included so much retail space, and none configured it in such a vertical fashion.

Several mixed-use projects of this era went to extremes to internalize space and have been criticized for turning their backs on the surrounding city. One often cited example is the Renaissance Center in Detroit. The first phase of Renaissance Center, which is located on 32 acres (13 hectares) along Detroit's riverfront, consists of four office towers containing 2.2 million square feet (204,500 square meters) of space surrounding a hotel tower containing 1,464 rooms. These five towers are constructed on a base structure and connected by a circular atrium that originally contained restaurants, an 800-seat theater, retail shops, and parking for 1,200 cars.

The entire first phase is organized around a central circular atrium, out of which rises the hotel. The office towers are located on four sides, and the retail space is distributed around several levels of the central atrium. The architecture, especially of the interior space, is dramatic and very futuristic but also very confusing and not very amenable to retailing. Architectural critic Colden Florance writes:

> The character of the interior is unsettling. Thrilling on the one hand, it seems bombastic and stagy on the other. Very well thought out and remarkably consistent in design, its plan nevertheless disorients the visitor, who must depend on ubiquitous attendants to find the way around. One thing is very certain, however. People get a tremendous kick out of being there.[6]

Moreover, the original exterior street frontages visually set the project apart from the surrounding city. Large structures at the base housed mechanical equipment, lacking appeal to draw visitors inside the project from the surrounding areas. The project has experienced numerous difficulties, and it has been modified several times in an effort to overcome the design problems and change both the exterior and interior to soften the project's fortress-like quality.

Mixed-use projects from the 1970s are distinctly different from their predecessors of the 1960s on several counts. First, residential uses are not nearly as prominent in the latter projects: only two of the seven projects mentioned include residential uses. In fact, the projects of the 1970s emphasize a standard mix of uses that relies heavily on the office/retail/hotel configuration; five of the seven projects use it. Second, nearly all the projects of the 1970s discussed here include large interior atriums, galleria, or retail concourse spaces, and in general they have a much more enclosed environment than the projects of the 1960s.

Perhaps most important, however, the 1970s saw the mixed-use concept catch hold on a broad scale. Developers, architects, and urban planners alike in great numbers began to see the importance of the concept, the promising possibilities it represented, and the pitfalls. Mixed-use projects achieved significant recognition and praise— as well as strong criticism—through the course of the decade, which led to some new approaches later.

Key to pioneering some of the new approaches that would follow was one important retail project of the 1970s—Faneuil Hall Marketplace—that led the resurgence of open-air retail districts. The success of this project, which would later add office space, helped to resurrect the idea of urban and main street retailing in mixed-use projects, an important concept for mixed-use projects in the following decades, especially the 1990s and 2000s.

Postmodernism and More Openness in the 1980s
The 1980s witnessed the increasing application of postmodern design themes and approaches and a new emphasis on quality urban design that focused attention not simply on the buildings but on the space between the buildings. These approaches represented a significant shift that drew on old models and forms that predated modernism in architecture, including historic buildings, districts, public spaces, and town centers. The trend began to lead mixed-use projects toward the creation of mixed-use districts rather than megastructures.

One of the leading early examples of this trend was the Crescent in Dallas. The Crescent is a mixed-use development near downtown Dallas that contains 1.25 million square feet (116,000 square meters) of office space in three towers, a 218-room hotel, and 175,000 square feet (16,300 square meters) of specialty retail space in a three-level open mall. Designed as an upscale alternative to downtown developments, the Crescent is located between downtown Dallas and some of Dallas's most prestigious neighborhoods. The project was developed by Rosewood Properties, Inc., and designed by John Burgee Architects with Philip Johnson.

Water Tower Place in downtown Chicago (in the foreground) stands adjacent to the John Hancock Center and includes retail, office, hotel, and residential uses, layered vertically. Retail and restaurants are arranged around a grand central atrium that comprises the bottom eight floors, with two floors of office space above that. The tower comprises hotel and residential uses.

For this in-town location, the developers believed that a dramatic, instantly recognizable project with high-quality construction would succeed. Accordingly, they employed a well-known architectural firm to design a project of distinctive appearance. Oriented toward a high-income market, each use is large enough to stand alone yet is planned to function interdependently.

The Crescent brought together a large office building in three 18- and 19-story linked towers, the Hotel Crescent Court in a separate five- and eight-story building, and a three-story retail center called the Shops and Galleries. All these uses are constructed above three to five parking levels that contain 4,200 parking spaces. The entire complex opened in April 1986.

The plan called for building heights to be scaled down from high buildings on the site's downtown end to lower buildings at the neighborhood end. The office structure therefore was placed on the site's wide end nearest downtown. The five- and eight-story hotel is separated from the office building by entrance drives that provide a front door to the site. At the apex of the triangular site, the lower retail center compares in height with nearby buildings.

Although each building functions independently, access between them is convenient. At ground level, pedestrians can walk from the office towers across a small parking plaza, through the hotel lobby across a smaller courtyard, to the open-air retail courtyard. Within the retail center, shoppers ascend and descend by escalators and

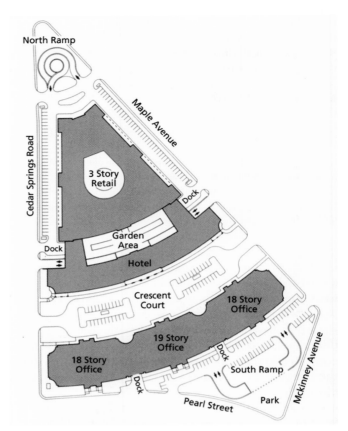

Site plan for the Crescent in Dallas, which arranges office, hotel, and retail uses around open-air courtyards.

The hotel at the Crescent. The Crescent was designed by Philip Johnson and John Burgee and is one of the first mixed-use developments to be designed in a postmodern style using strong historical allusions.

elevators. The Crescent is one of the first mixed-use projects to be designed in a distinctly postmodern style with strong historical allusions, and its attention to context and the use of outdoor public spaces and streetscapes, while not altogether successful in enlivening the area, was a push in the right direction for mixed-use design.

Another important example of this era is Miami Lakes Town Center, an early town center noted as one of the earliest prototypes for the new wave of mixed-use suburban town centers now found throughout the United States. Although the entire project comprises 90 acres (36 hectares), it is the Main Street core area of about 50 acres (20 hectares) that has helped to inspire a new interest in the development of traditional small-town commercial centers. The narrow, slightly curved street is lined with street-level storefronts with offices and apartments built above. The street is open to automobiles, with limited on-street parking provided. Although the specialty shopping street is unanchored in traditional terms, a hotel and movie theater are located at opposite ends of the street and serve as substitute anchors. Miami Lakes is a 3,000-acre (1,215-hectare) master-planned community started in 1962 about 15 miles (24 kilometers) northwest of downtown Miami. Like the larger community where it is located, Miami Lakes Town Center was developed by the Graham Companies, a closely held family-owned and -operated business.

Master planning for the town center was driven by William A. Graham's belief that every town needs a hub where people can gather to eat, shop, and socialize. The 1962 Miami Lakes master plan designated a 90-acre (36-hectare) "town center" for such purposes, but the area was not planned in detail until the 1970s, after much of the surrounding development was well underway. The Graham family worked closely with New York– and Florida-based planner Lester Collins to devise the final plan.

The town center street system features a spiral design often likened to the chambers of a nautilus shell. Bisecting this spiral in a north/south direction is Ludlam Road, a four-lane arterial roadway. Bisecting the spiral in an east/west direction is Main Street, the core of the town center.

Main Street is designed with a curb-to-curb distance of 29 feet (8.8 meters). Buildings facing the street are typically 71 feet (21.5 meters) apart, but this distance narrows to as little as 47 feet (14.3 meters) to provide a sense of enclosure at certain points. Parking for retail, residential, and office uses along Main Street is provided primarily in surface parking lots at the rear of buildings. Covered arcades at mid-block allow people to pass between the street and the parking lots; storefronts line the arcades to add vitality to these spaces. Phases I and II of Main Street constitute 27.43 acres (11.1 hectares). The extension of Main Street across Ludlam Road to the east remains to be built and will make up the third and final phase of the core area.

Among the key lessons learned from this early town center are that apartments located near a movie theater

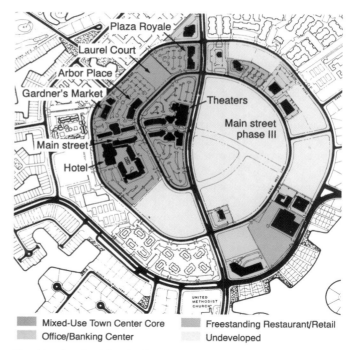

Mixed-Use Town Center Core   Freestanding Restaurant/Retail
Office/Banking Center   Undeveloped

The site plan for Miami Lakes Town Center, a mixed-use town center in the master-planned community of Miami Lakes near Miami. Main Street's design features brick sidewalks, small gardens and courtyards, fountains, and Mediterranean-style buildings with red barrel-tile roofs. One- and two-story apartments above storefronts line the street, giving the neighborhood a traditional feel.

can be more difficult to lease because of concerns about noise, that offices are more marketable and successful when they have private access that is easily identified from the street and does not share elevators or access stairs with apartments, and that hotel restaurants should have direct access to the main street.

Other important projects from the 1980s exhibited postmodern approaches and/or much more open designs:

- the Atlanta Galleria, which arranged numerous high-rise office buildings and a hotel/retail complex around a park;
- 900 North Michigan Avenue, a mixed-use tower that employed a postmodern design to considerably enhance and soften the size and complexity of this retail, office, hotel, and residential skyscraper in Chicago;
- Rowes Wharf, which used a dramatic arch, a waterfront promenade, and a series of buildings on wharves to create an attractive mixed-use setting along the Boston harbor;
- Janss Court, a mixed-use building with a cinema and retail, office, and residential uses that contributed greatly to the revitalization of the Third Street Promenade area in Santa Monica;
- the Willard in downtown Washington, D.C., which demonstrated how a historic hotel can be sensitively renovated and combined with new office and retail

development to restore and enhance an existing landmark and its surroundings; and

- Princeton Forrestal Village near Princeton, New Jersey, which arranged office, retail, and hotel uses around a main street to create a town center within a suburban business park.

Although postmodern design ideas drove mixed-use development in the United States, modernist design trends remained strong in mixed-use projects in other parts of the world, especially Asia. The decade witnessed the emergence of major new mixed-use projects in Asia, including Raffles City in Singapore and Pacific Place in Hong Kong. Both of these projects used design models emphasizing high-rise towers connected at ground level by enclosed shopping malls. Raffles City, opened in 1986, included two high-rise hotels, one 73 stories and the other 26, a 42-story office tower, a four-level shopping center within a base building, and a convention center. The project, designed by I.M. Pei & Partners, became an instant landmark for the city. Pacific Place in Hong Kong, which opened in 1988, used a similar format and mix, including three high-rise hotels and one high-rise office building connected at the base by a multilevel shopping mall.

Perhaps the most significant trend of the 1980s was the growth in the number of mixed-use projects developed in the suburbs, especially in the United States. A second was the decreased average total floor area of proj-

ects started in the 1980s. Projects were developed on much smaller scales in the 1980s, especially in the United States, evidence of the concept's continuing evolution and a growth in the acceptance of mixed-use projects in smaller-scale environments and locations.

A third trend was the changing mix of uses, with an increase in the popularity of residential uses in the 1980s. Research conducted by ULI found that residential uses were included in 46.2 percent of projects in the 1960s, 19.4 percent of projects in the 1970s, and 49.4 percent of projects in the first half of the 1980s. Generally, the mixed-use projects of the 1970s were an aberration in their lack of residential uses, compared with earlier and later projects.

Numerous other trends were apparent as well in the 1980s, including a striking shift to new postmodern and historicist architectural themes and approaches, more openness and sensitivity to the total urban environment, greater use of renovation and historic rehabilitation of existing buildings, and more infusion of entertainment and cultural uses into mixed-use projects.

Town Centers and Urban Villages in the 1990s and Early 2000s

The 1990s saw the continued refinement and evolution of previously discussed models as well as the emergence and rapid growth of the mixed-use town center and urban village concept, which really took hold in the 1990s. This evolution was exemplified by two very significant new

Janss Court is a small mixed-use building that includes ground-level retail and cinema uses, office space above, and wood-frame residential uses that rest on top of the office building.

Raffles City (right), designed by I.M. Pei, features two hotel towers, an office tower, and a retail mall, and has become a distinctive landmark for the city of Singapore. The surrounding area, which includes a central transit station, has expanded considerably since Raffles City was completed in 1986; it now includes the Suntec City mixed-use project (including the convention center at bottom left) and One Raffles Link (near the corner of the convention center), an office/retail project designed by Kohn Pedersen Fox.

projects that opened in 1990 to set a new tone for mixed-use development in the decade: Reston Town Center in Reston, Virginia, and Mizner Park in Boca Raton, Florida. They essentially established a new vision for creating mixed-use projects organized around main streets in a town center. The decade also saw the mixed-use development trend take hold internationally, especially in Asia. Numerous very large projects—such as Jin Mao Tower in Shanghai, Kuala Lumpur City Centre (including the two Petronas Towers), Canal City Hakata in Japan, and Canary Wharf in London—were proposed and built in major cities around the world.

But the emergence of a new approach to urban design for mixed-use developments was the most interesting development of the decade. Reston Town Center opened in October 1990, establishing a new precedent for mixed-use development by arranging a variety of major commercial uses, including two office towers, a Hyatt Regency Hotel, a cinema, and retail space, in the configuration of a a main street town center. The project expanded on the precedent of Miami Lakes but with a more ambitious plan. Later phases added more office space, a substantial amount and variety of residential uses, additional retail space, and more open space to solidify its position as perhaps the largest town center project to be built to date.

The Reston Town Center urban core is an 85-acre (34-hectare) mixed-use urban center located in a 460-acre (186-hectare) town center district that was identified in Reston's original 1962 master plan. The first phase of the urban core, completed in 1990, includes 530,000 square feet (49,300 square meters) of office space; 240,000 square feet (22,300 square meters) of retail, restaurant, and entertainment space; and a 514-room hotel. Recognizing that the community would soon be able to support its own downtown, Reston Land Company (RLC), a subsidiary of Mobil Land Development Corporation and Reston's master developer since 1978, initiated detailed planning for the urban core in 1981.

The first phase of Reston Town Center opened in 1990, occupying 20 acres (8 hectares) on the eastern end of the urban core. The mixed-use project includes twin 11-story office buildings; a Hyatt Regency Hotel with extensive conference facilities and an executive fitness center; street-level retail, restaurants, and entertainment uses with professional offices above; and surface and structured parking for more than 3,000 cars. Its centerpiece is Fountain Square, an open-air civic plaza and pavilion that contains a major fountain, outdoor seating, artwork, and, in winter, an ice-skating rink.

Much of the retail space in Phase I is located along Market Street, which extends east/west through Fountain Square. Market Street is the the town center's pedestrian spine; a private street, it is usually open to one lane of traffic in each direction but can be closed for community events and concerts.

Master planning for the Town Center District started in February 1982. RTKL Associates, Inc., a national archi-

Canal City Hakata in Fukuoka, Japan, is a dramatic and colorful mixed-use design that features office, hotel, retail, and performing arts space surrounding a central canal and public open spaces.

Reston Town Center is one of the most influential mixed-use town centers developed to date. Its first phase opened in 1990 with office, hotel, retail, restaurant, and cinema uses. Stately facades, domed towers, and a fountain plaza give the first phase of development a sense of civic scale and importance.

tectural firm with planning capabilities that had provided planning assistance for Reston's neighborhoods and villages during the 1970s and early 1980s, devised a master plan and development concept. The plan intentionally incorporated positive characteristics of both urban and suburban development: pedestrian-scale streets, a variety of uses and services, green open spaces, easy vehicular access, and ample parking. Before deciding on a traditional street grid, RTKL evaluated the evolution of town centers in search of organizational schemes to make the core distinct from the rest of Reston. RTKL also looked at ways other communities created public spaces and integrated automobile use.

The plan was presented to a panel of ULI members in 1983. The panel challenged RLC to decide whether the project should be urban or suburban and then to stretch the boundaries of the chosen direction. To create an urban center, the panel recommended higher densities, the addition of a hotel to the downtown mix, and the inclusion of a cultural and civic component. During 1984 and 1985, Reston Land completed a national search for a master developer and formed a partnership with Himmel/MKDG, whose principals had led the development of numerous other large-scale projects, including Water Tower Place in Chicago and Copley Place in Boston. Working with the new development partnership, RTKL refined the concept plan for the core area and responded to the increased development program and density.

In 1986, in an invited national competition, RTKL produced the winning design for the first phase and became the project architect. The firm designed Phase I's five structures simultaneously, establishing a visual and stylistic vocabulary that provided a strong identity for the new town center. Ken Wong, the partnership's development executive, explained that they were looking for "a pedestrian-friendly, retail-driven plan that created a *there* there. RTKL's diagram of a main street with the U-shaped fountain plaza at the heart was instantly well received and has been emulated in many projects since."

Sasaki Associates's plan for the streetscape recalls European shopping streets and public squares as well as such American prototypes as Country Club Plaza in Kansas City. Custom-designed paving and benches complement the architecture and reinforce human-scale comfort and accessibility. Large trees and seasonal planting beds give the streets and plazas a sense of liveliness and maturity. The streets and sidewalks are proportioned to balance spaciousness and ease of movement with an intimate, human scale. The sidewalks are wider on the sunny side of the street, and the cartway is narrow so that pedestrians are encouraged to cross from one side of the street to the other.

The developers realized that a variety of customized retail storefronts would help to create a vibrant pedestrian experience. They engaged Philip George, a New York–based retail designer, to test the layout of food, entertainment, and specialty retail uses and to identify the visual characteristics critical to its success. RTKL then designed the buildings to accommodate storefronts at the ground level of every building, with variations in setbacks, entrances, awnings, bay windows, and signage to produce a recurring sense of surprise and the impression that the town has evolved over time. Every ground-level wall was designed with a pedestrian retail experience in mind.

Mizner Park in Boca Raton, Florida, used a very different mix, relying more heavily on residential uses from the start; it also very much redefined the nature and importance of well-designed public open space as a central organizing element for a mixed-use project. Developed by Crocker and Company and designed by Cooper Carry Inc., the initial phase of Mizner Park involved the development of a 398,000-square-foot (37,000-square-meter) mixed-use development configured as a traditional downtown center for Boca Raton. The project's first phase included four principal mixed-use buildings surrounding a two-block-long public park and containing 156,000 square feet (15,000 square meters) of specialty retail space, with six restaurants and an eightplex cinema, 106,000 square feet (9,850 square meters) of rentable office space, 136 over-the-shop rental apartments, a performing arts amphitheater, and the International Museum of Cartoon Art (since closed). Later phases included a Jacobson department store, an additional apartment building, townhouses, and two museums; a performing arts center is also planned for a future phase.

The project is especially noteworthy because of its careful attention to urban design and the creation of a sense of place; its mix of uses and town center configuration, and especially its restaurants and streetfront retail bordering a central public park, have stimulated a vibrant, round-the-clock mosaic of activity that brings new life to the city's downtown core.

City planners, the developers, and their architects looked to many other models, old and new, in developing the concept, including East Hampton on Long Island, Old Town Alexandria, Virginia, Worth Avenue in Palm Beach, South Street Seaport in New York, and Cross Keys in Baltimore. Mizner Park, configured as a village within the city, encompasses two city blocks on either side of a grand central public park/open space. Conceived as a traditional downtown, the project involves four main mixed-use buildings facing each other across the park and public space and creates a visually uninterrupted ambience that visitors often compare with a charming European city.

The central space for the project contains two public streets designed with pavers and plaza details to provide vehicular access, over-the-curb parking, and pedestrian access. Thus, the needed circulation elements are combined with open-space amenities, furthering the traditional main street atmosphere. One of the key advantages of the park's being surrounded by two streets is that this configuration affords ample on-street parking in front of the stores and restaurants, as cars can be parked on both sides of both streets.

Outdoor dining plazas and apartment balconies overlooking the activities below contribute to a buzz of activity. The grand central public space is well on its way to becoming the community center of Boca Raton. The architecture reflects a strong, highly appropriate style and sense of place, building as it does on Boca Raton's well-known design traditions and adapting the fanciful, highly articulated style of 1920s architect Addison Mizner to the demands of the 1990s.

Numerous other projects were developed in the 1990s using a mixture of enclosed and open spaces to create interesting mixed-use configurations. For example, CambridgeSide Galleria in Cambridge, Massachusetts, combines an innovative shopping center with an office building, parking garage, hotel space, and housing, bringing round-the-clock uses to a former industrial area by the Charles River just across from downtown Boston. The master plan integrates public open space into the new private development, enriching city street life, improving traffic circulation, creating a new park, and providing access to the recreational amenities of the Charles River. It centers around a three-level retail mall that opens onto public parks at both ends.

The regional shopping center, which opened in 1990 in East Cambridge, breaks many of the cardinal rules of mall development. Departing from the conventional formula of department stores located at the ends of a retail arcade lined with specialty shops, CambridgeSide Galleria anchors its arcade with two municipal open spaces and places the department stores on side aisles. Many shopping centers locate their food courts on second floors to lure shoppers to the center's out-of-the-way places. At CambridgeSide, a first-floor food court connects directly to an outdoor esplanade that skirts Lechmere Canal. Access to enclosed shopping centers often is limited and carefully controlled, but here, two of the three anchor stores and the three streetfront restaurants open directly onto city sidewalks. Most malls are inward-gazing fortresses, but CambridgeSide features large display windows on all levels and a vaulted skylighted arcade parallel to Cambridge's

Mizner Park in Boca Raton, Florida, includes apartments, and office, retail, and restaurant space around a main street and a village green with a central fountain, gazebos, walkways, extensive landscaping, and flower arrangements. Mizner Park was opened in 1990 and became an "instant downtown" for Boca Raton and a popular gathering place throughout the day and night.

Courtesy of Cooper Carry Inc.

CambridgeSide Galleria in Cambridge, Massachusetts, includes a retail mall, offices, housing, hotel space, and public open space. This public/private development satisfies the city's need for a dynamic and open pedestrian area—a true focal point of activity near the waterfront—while working as a profitable mixed-use development.

north/south streets that acts as an extension of the city's street grid.

A major new mixed-use project also emerged in London during the 1990s that has become an important model for office-oriented mixed-use projects. Canary Wharf, so called because when it was used as a dock many of the imports were from the Canary Islands, is planned on a grand scale yet with meticulous attention to detail. The estate extends to more than 86 acres (35 hectares). Approximately 6 million net square feet (558,000 square meters) of office and retail space has been constructed to date, with another 8.1 million square feet (753,000 square meters) under construction.

The first tenants moved to Canary Wharf in August 1991. Today, more than 35,000 people work at the site. The first phase of development comprises ten office buildings, a retail center, a conference and banquet center, a Docklands light-rail station, landscaped grounds, and five car parks (in addition to car parking below the office buildings).

In Asia, the new Kuala Lumpur City Centre set a new height standard for both skyscrapers and mixed-use projects. This huge development includes the twin Petronas Towers, each 1,483 feet (452 meters) tall (88 floors), the tallest buildings in the world. The development also includes several other office buildings with a total of 8 million square feet (743,500 square meters) of office space as well as 1.5 million square feet (140,000 square meters) of retail and entertainment facilities, a 643-room hotel, a conference center, a museum, and a concert hall.

The 1990s witnessed a transformation of mixed-use development from project building to place making, from megastructures to urban districts—fundamental shifts that have greatly improved the quality and potential of mixed-use development and greatly enhanced the contribution they have made to the urban environment. Numerous other examples of projects developed later in the 1990s are discussed in Chapter 8 and throughout this book.

Factors Favoring Mixed-Use Development

The factors that have led to the emergence and blossoming of these new mixed-use developments over the past several decades encompass numerous trends—economic and financial; political, social, and regulatory; property and design. Not all the factors appeared at once, and new ones are arising and growing even as others have run their course or been replaced by more contemporary concerns.

Economic and Financial Trends

The concentration of talent in a number of large, experienced, and sophisticated development entities capable of undertaking large, complex, financially demanding mixed-use projects has increased. The real estate development community has grown more sophisticated, and more firms are willing to and capable of tackling larger and more complicated projects. Many U.S. firms—among them the Related Companies, Hines, Tishman Speyer Properties, and Forest City Enterprises—now are national or international in scope, are well capitalized, and have developed substantial track records in mixed-use development. Several large firms in Asia and Europe are also now capable of undertaking these projects, and many smaller firms have become more sophisticated and are pursuing mixed-use development as an underserved niche.

Although ups and downs in liquidity have occurred, generally the increasingly sophisticated and liquid real estate capital markets have become very efficient, providing a new source of capital for well-planned mixed-use development projects.

Land costs throughout major metropolitan areas have risen, particularly in commercial areas where more intensive development has occurred. As land costs have climbed, developers have sought ways to build greater "supportable values" through higher-density and mixed-use development. They have also sought to build out their projects more quickly by diversifying uses, which hastens absorption and reduces carrying costs on the undeveloped land. As suburban land prices rise and those areas become more densely developed, mixed-use projects will become increasingly more feasible and provide optimal solutions there as well.

Political, Social, and Regulatory Trends

The thinking of influential urban planners and writers who have questioned and challenged single-use zoning increasingly has affected the policy and practice of planning and development. Jane Jacobs, author of the landmark *Life and Death of Great American Cities* published in 1961, was among the early leaders in this effort and has been instrumental in championing urbanity, pedestrian streets, a mix of old and new, and a mix of uses as the means for creating vibrant, interesting, and safe urban environments. The book is one of the most influential books ever written on the subject of urban planning and development and has helped mixed-use concepts to reemerge in urban planning and development. Other influential authors, such as Lewis Mumford *(The City in History)* and Victor Gruen *(Centers for the Urban Environment),* also wrote persuasively during the 1960s about mixed-use environments and the diversity of true urban environments. Numerous authors and designers continue to propound these ideas; Andrés Duany and Peter Calthorpe, among others, have written persuasively on new urbanism and mixed-use development.

Planned unit development (PUD) ordinances, mixed-use zoning, and other flexible zoning ideas that emerged in the 1960s and 1970s allowed local communities to relax single-purpose zoning and permit a mix of uses. These new approaches, reflected in both mixed-use redevelopment plans and large-scale planned communities, resulted in large-scale planning and development of multiuse environments.

The increasing importance of redevelopment planning over the past several decades has become a necessity in many older urban and suburban locations needing revitalization. The need to revitalize and diversify central urban cores—areas that are often blighted or simply dull —has been the setting from which mixed-use projects first began to spring in the late 1950s and early 1960s. Redevelopment has led to many comprehensively planned mixed-use projects in downtowns, along waterfronts, and in other central city areas and older suburbs.

The smart growth movement, which seeks a balance of economy, community, and environment to create more livable communities while reducing sprawl, has grown tremendously since it first appeared in 1997. The development of higher-density mixed-use neighborhoods and commercial centers is one of the favored strategies for implementing smart growth. Proponents of mixed-use development view smart growth as a means of creating more attractive and functional urban environments. Smart growth has become increasingly popular among public officials, designers, and developers alike, affording new opportunities for mixed-use development in a variety of locations.

Bethesda Row in Bethesda, Maryland, is an urban village of retail, office, and residential uses that was built through a public/private partnership. Located on a suburban downtown infill site, it uses existing streets as central arteries and pedestrian spaces.

The growing social and political demand for real places in the placeless suburbs has also spurred mixed-use developments. Many suburbs have little or no sense of community or sense of place, in part because they have no town centers or central civic place for people to gather in or identify with. Local jurisdictions increasingly favor mixed-use town centers and urban villages as a means to counter this problem. Mixed-use projects have often come to be necessary focal points, areas of urbanity in the midst of a sprawling undefined suburbia.

Growing traffic congestion and air pollution have led to increased support for new transit development and transit-oriented development. Transit villages and other developments around transit stations frequently take on the characteristics of mixed-use development. Increasing congestion in general has forced developers and planners to consider land use patterns that can reduce the need for auto trips and increase pedestrian movement.

Property and Design Trends

New urbanist and smart growth design and development concepts have championed mixed-use town centers, transit villages, and urban villages that are pedestrian oriented and include a wide mix of uses. The ideas of Andrés Duany, Elizabeth Plater-Zyberk, and Peter Calthorpe, leading thinkers and practitioners of the new urbanism, increasingly have affected development, zoning, and regulations in local jurisdictions across the United States and internationally.

The tremendous growth in office employment and the resulting demand for office space (and increasingly larger office buildings) over the past two decades have supported demand for mixed-use projects. Office space is frequently a cornerstone of a mixed-use project, and many of the largest office projects can generate substantial demand for surrounding amenities and uses. Although this demand alone may not justify the development of a full mixed-use project, it can provide the added market necessary to tip the scales in an area already poised for such growth and diversification. The larger the office project, the greater the need for amenities like restaurants and retail shops to serve office workers, hotels to provide lodging for business clients, and nearby residential units to house office employees.

Main street retailing and urban entertainment centers thrive on dense surrounding locations, strong pedestrian environments, and a mix of uses. Urban entertainment centers in particular have become major forces on the development scene, and they can become important cornerstones for a mixed-use project.

Full-service hotels are now more sophisticated and include a variety of ancillary uses such as convention facilities, restaurants, retail shops, and recreational amenities that make them well suited for mixed-use environments. Office tenants view these large facilities as amenities, and they must be close to major office users to thrive. They also benefit from strong surrounding amenities that mixed-use environments offer. Moreover, they are increasingly being viewed as important amenities for upscale residential properties.

Interest is growing in pedestrian-friendly communities, intown and urban housing, and urban lifestyles. Demographic changes have and will continue to see a growth in affluent childless households that frequently favor more urban lifestyles and urban housing—in both cities and suburbs—that fit well with mixed-use concepts.

Problems and Opportunities in Mixed-Use Development

Mixed-use development has and will benefit from these trends, and the field holds promising opportunities. But before mixed-use development can achieve its high potential for financial success and make a positive contribution to the urban environment, numerous problems and pitfalls must be recognized and overcome:

- From a business point of view, mixed-use development calls for extraordinary planning, management, political patience, and capital resources, and a high appetite for risk to cope with the more intricate planning, higher front-end costs, and heavier upfront negative cash flows typically associated with it, making the developer's job much tougher and requiring a broader, deeper range of expertise.
- From the viewpoint of the urban environment, the design of mixed-use projects, because of their typical size, diversity, and density, requires much more skillful urban design talent if these developments are to avoid becoming monolithic, dysfunctional, or unwelcome additions to the urban fabric. Some mixed-use projects of the past have been criticized for disorienting their visitors, destroying the existing fabric, creating islands and fortresses, and replicating suburban sprawl in downtown areas. Good mixed-use design requires

not just talented architects but also talented urban designers.

It should never be assumed that a mixed-use concept will automatically lead to greater financial returns or a better urban environment. Mixed-use projects, as easily as other projects, can be failures on both these counts.

These problems and pitfalls can be overcome, however, and mixed-use projects do offer opportunities for greater financial returns and better urban environments that are more satisfying and relevant to human needs. Mixed-use projects offer many advantages over single-use real estate projects in terms of place making, synergy, economies of scale, critical mass, operational efficiencies, and impact on the community.

- In some cases, mixed-use development is the only feasible approach. Under some circumstances, successful development requires creation of an essentially new physical environment on a large scale to overcome blighting influences of adjacent areas. Many of the projects surveyed for this publication were successful in overcoming adjacent blight, and some have also served as catalysts for further improvements and development beyond the project's boundaries.
- Mixed-use development can be used to achieve higher densities while also creating more amenities and more usable and pleasant public open space. Mixed-use zoning frequently provides density bonuses if certain conditions are met, which can result in a win-win situation for both the public and private sectors.
- Mixed-use development can be used as a means of more rapid development of the site's potential. By offering several uses and product lines simultaneously, mixed-use projects can enable a faster absorption schedule, thus increasing the present value of investment and reducing land carrying costs.
- Mixed-use development can be used as a means of differentiating products and encouraging superior design through aggregation of individual uses and/ or provision of superior amenities or public spaces. Even though markets for individual uses by themselves may be questionable, appropriately scaled mixed-use projects that combine these uses may be very competitive because they offer more than single-purpose projects. A superior design can often be achieved as a result of a larger development budget and the potential for integrating attractive public spaces, creating a place where users want to be.
- Mixed-use development can result in shared infrastructure, thereby making possible economies of scale in development. Developers' opinions are mixed on this subject, and although some point to economies of scale in key project components (parking, for example), a valid database is not available for drawing definitive generalizations. At any rate, such savings as the result of economies of scale in some project components are frequently eaten up elsewhere in the development (increased cost for landscaping,

When completed, Atlantic Station in Atlanta will include office, retail, hotel, and residential uses. The project is a major redevelopment on an infill brownfield site near downtown Atlanta.

Courtesy of Jacoby Development

artwork, or other amenities, for example). In larger mixed-use developments, scale can actually lead to diseconomies.

- Mixed-use development can result in superior project performance (for example, higher rents or prices, higher occupancy). Superior performance can be derived from creation of a special place or quality address, thereby permitting premium prices or rents or faster sales and leasing. Superior performance can also derive from synergies created within the project by uses that are mutually supportive of each other. Most developers see evidence of market synergy, and many have established premium prices or rents accordingly. Synergy does not occur naturally or through happenstance, however; it is the deliberate outcome of careful planning, design, and management.

- Mixed-use development can achieve economies of scale in operation, including savings on items such as parking operations, common area maintenance, central HVAC (heating, ventilation, and air-conditioning) systems, and marketing and promotion.

- Mixed-use development can achieve greater long-term appreciation in land and property values. By creating a special place through the innovative mixing of uses and a creative urban design, owners can benefit greatly in the long term from the appreciation in value of both the project itself and the surrounding undeveloped land.

Underlying these observations, of course, is the opportunity afforded by mixed-use projects to better satisfy consumers' needs and preferences by offering the right mix and scale of real estate products, services, and place identity within an overall physical configuration that is pleasing, functional, and even exciting. By virtue of their scale and functional diversity, mixed-use developments can have a far greater impact on community develop-

ment than single-purpose projects. Mixed-use projects, for example, are viewed as an important solution to improving and revitalizing urban areas that are dead during nonworking hours through the introduction of new residential, transient, and/or recreational activities. They are also viewed as a means for creating new urban places in the suburbs, areas that often lack town centers and other pleasant and enjoyable pedestrian environments for workers, shoppers, residents, and visitors alike.

Two key considerations should be kept in mind when undertaking a mixed-use project. First, when mixed-use projects succeed or fail, they do so on a much larger financial and environmental scale than single-use projects. Second, when the project works as a whole, it can become an entity greater than the sum of its parts, but when only one element fails, it can negatively affect the entire project. In short, the mixed-use concept can magnify both success and failure in a development venture, and it should be approached with the understanding that such magnification increases both the risks and potential rewards for both the private and public sectors.

Notes

1. Material on Unwin and Parker is adapted from Charles C. Bohl, *Place Making: Developing Town Centers, Main Streets, and Urban Villages* (Washington, D.C.: ULI–the Urban Land Institute, 2002).
2. Peter Hall, *Cities of Tomorrow* (Oxford, England: Blackwell, 1988).
3. Bohl, *Place Making.*
4. www.csuohio.edu/CUT/tower2.htm, accessed March 18, 2003.
5. Edward W. Wolner, "Design and Civic Identity in Cincinnati's Carew Tower Complex," *Journal of the Society of Architectural Historians,* March 1992, pp. 35–47.
6. Colden Florance, "MXD," *AIA Journal,* September 1977, p. 30.

2. Evaluating Markets and Development Potential

Success in mixed-use development begins with and requires a capable and diverse development team, sound and thorough market analysis, a creative development strategy and program to meet the market, and much creativity. An inexperienced development team can seldom carry out such a complex undertaking successfully, nor can such projects be undertaken hastily. The initial steps in the process involve identifying the objectives, the site, and the potential for developing various uses on that site.

Development typically begins with an idea and usually proceeds along one of two paths, either the search for a use (or uses) for a site or the search for a site for an already identified use (or uses). Mixed-use development, however, is not quite so simple, and both approaches can often play a role in the same project. Many mixed-use projects, for example, involve both a landowner (often a public entity) that is looking for new uses for a site and a private developer that is looking for a site for a mixed-use concept. In other cases, a development entity might be searching for a site for a mixed-use project but may not be certain about the exact mix of uses. Thus, the development process often follows a convoluted path, depending on the players and objectives involved.

Canal City Hakata in Fukuoka, Japan, is a large-scale urban project featuring office, hotel, retail, entertainment, and performing arts space, and a promenade along an interior canal.

Development Objectives and the Development Entity

Both financial and nonfinancial development objectives must be well defined and well understood from the outset. The nature and relative importance of these objectives will shape the project, and as planning and development continue, all decisions will be tied in one way or another to these initial objectives—either in their conformance to the spirit of the objectives or as feedback leading to a reassessment of the initial objectives.

Moreover, in a complex deal with numerous players from the public and private sectors—often the case with mixed-use projects—usually more than a few differing objectives lead to conflicts. Thus, it is important that all parties seek to understand the other parties' objectives. Whatever the development entity—landowner, public sector, or private developer—perhaps the most important task is to make explicit the nonfinancial objectives so that their effect on the project's financial performance can be estimated, understood, and justified.

Development objectives and programs for any mixed-use development are heavily influenced by the development entity that initiates the project. These entities can be broadly grouped as landowners, public sector organizations, and private developers. In some cases, all three entities are involved, usually entailing different objectives and compromises.

The development of University Park at MIT was initiated by the landowner, in this case the Massachusetts Institute of Technology. When fully complete in 2004, the 27-acre (11-hectare) formerly abandoned industrial site will be transformed by developer Forest City Enterprises into a complex comprising 2.3 million square feet (214,000 square meters), including ten research and office buildings; three residential complexes; 250,000 square feet (23,200 square meters) of hotel, restaurant, and retail space; and structured parking for 2,800 cars.

Landowners

Landowners who have owned their properties for some time have initiated many mixed-use projects; often the land has been used for other purposes or is adjacent to other properties being used or developed by the landowner. Landowners that fit this category include railroads, universities, large corporations, families, small businesses with little expertise in real estate, and developers of master-planned communities.

Development entities in this category can be motivated by numerous objectives that go beyond the project itself. For example, a university may wish to create a property to further its research capacity or add needed retail or hotel space. The developer of a master-planned community may wish to create an important focal point for a community that will enhance the value of surrounding properties and homes. In both these cases, owners may accept lower returns if their other objectives are met.

Long-term landowners also often own the land outright with little or no debt to carry, making project financing easier. They also often own a lot of land, creating the possibility of developing a fairly large project. As a result of these factors, mixed-use projects initiated by landowners often lead to unusual project economics, development strategies, and project designs.

One example is University Park at MIT, a project initiated by a university. The Massachusetts Institute of Technology had been acquiring land for 25 years for the development of a corporate office research and develop-

ment (R&D) park adjacent to its campus. It was to be the part of its strategy for the investment of its endowment fund that would help accelerate the transfer of technology into the commercial marketplace. In 1992, with a site assembled, MIT issued a Request for Proposals (RFP) for a mixed-use project that would include office, R&D, hotel, retail, and residential uses. The project is largely developed, with only a few phases yet to be completed.

A second example is Valencia Town Center Drive, a mixed-use town center launched by the Newhall Land and Farming Company, originally a ranching and farming company that has become a developer of master-planned communities and mixed-use town centers in the Los Angeles region. The company is currently developing two large master-planned communities north of Los Angeles—Valencia and Newhall Ranch—on 37,000 acres (15,000 hectares) of land. Town Center Drive is essentially a new downtown for these new communities.

A very early example is Chicago's Illinois Center, the impetus for which came from the Illinois Central Railroad, the owner of the once underused 83-acre (34-hectare) site in downtown Chicago where the project stands. In this case, the property owner entered into a joint venture—dubbed the Illinois Center Plaza Venture—with developer Metropolitan Structures to develop the property. ICPV served as the land developer, purchasing land from the railroad and selling prepared sites to other development groups. The railroad's objective was clearly financial, directed toward maximizing profits on a long held and long underused property. The situation was unusual in that the railroad owned outright such a large parcel in such a prime location, creating opportunities for major high-density, mixed-use development. This situation and the developer's objectives resulted in a large-scale high-rise project phased over more than 30 years.

Public Sector Entities

Projects initiated by the public sector are often highly complex, involving numerous players and objectives. The process usually involves the public sector's establishing objectives for redevelopment for a particular area, assembling land, and soliciting development proposals. Mixed-use projects often fit nicely with redevelopment objectives, because they both usually involve the creation of lively urban environments. Some recent examples of publicly initiated mixed-use developments include CityPlace in West Palm Beach, Florida; Downtown Silver Spring in Silver Spring, Maryland; Smyrna Town Center in Smyrna, Georgia; the Jin Mao Tower in Shanghai, China; Yerba Buena Center in San Francisco, California; and Sony Center am Potsdamer Platz in Berlin, Germany.

Many of these projects would not have proceeded without public intervention—land assembly, public improvements, public financial assistance, master planning, or coordination of development, for example. Seldom does the public sector actually act as the developer of most buildings in the project, but it often acts as the land developer. Because of the critical role the public sector can play in initiating the project, its objectives are often the primary shapers of the development.

Public objectives may often sway the project in unusual directions—toward social priorities and away from strictly profit-motivated goals. A market analysis, for example, might show strong support for office and hotel uses on a site, while public objectives might be oriented more toward residential and retail uses. As a result, the ultimate selection and sizing of the various uses in the project can result as much from public as private objectives, although the overall project must be structured so that it is financially feasible for the private developer before it will proceed.

If public objectives lead to financial infeasibility for part or all of the project, then the public sector will have to subsidize part of the development or provide development incentives or bonuses to increase the size of the more profitable uses. Basic options for providing subsidies include reducing the developer's capital costs, reducing the project's operating expenses, and reducing entitlement risk and other upfront costs.

Developers and Property Companies

Developers and property companies with no landholdings also initiate many mixed-use projects on their own. They are in the business of seeking out profitable development opportunities and continuously look for good sites in strong market areas that can support new development. They are motivated primarily by profit, but they often undertake projects for ego or personal reasons as well.

The private developer's specific financial objectives vary, which may affect the nature of the project. These objectives might include selling part or all of the project shortly after development and leasing are complete to cash in on gains immediately, or they might include holding the property for a longer term to take advantage of opportunities for substantial residual values or downstream development opportunities.

The size and nature of the private developer also affect the objectives and nature of the project. Only large, experienced, and diversified developers will likely undertake large projects, while smaller projects are more likely to be undertaken by small developers. In some cases, teams of smaller local developers engage in a larger mixed-use project.

Although financial gain is always a primary objective and concern for the private developer, in many cases part of the motivation for doing a mixed-use project is the perception that mixed-use development is the state of the art—the highest form of real estate development—and offers the best opportunity for shaping the urban environment in the most positive and lasting way. The personal and ego gratification that goes with developing a successful mixed-use project has been a driving force in many projects; mixed-use development allows the developer to have a greater impact on the urban environment and to make a greater contribution to the shape of the city. This element should not be underestimated in the development process; in fact, the developer's ego-driven "wants factor" may need to be restrained.

Development Management

Whatever entity initiates the project and however many participants are involved in the venture, ultimately the project must be undertaken and controlled by a master developer. Master developers of mixed-use projects should have at a minimum:

- Enough organizational depth, through a multitalented, resourceful real estate team, to respond to opportunities and problems. Entrepreneurial spirit is necessary, but it is no substitute for strong management and specialists on the staff.
- The ability to live with high risks and long lead times (typically at least five years) before profits are realized.
- Access to sizable financial resources (and "patient money"), especially at the early stages. During the project's most critical early stages, financing arrangements must allow the developer great flexibility in funding and in deferring amortization of debt capital.
- Substantial control over the subject property and all major aspects of the development process. When an unforeseen marketing, financial, engineering, or political problem arises, the master developer must be able to assess its impact on the entire development swiftly and, if necessary, rearrange financing or scheduling. Having to answer to numerous sources and levels of command is a definite liability for the developer of a mixed-use project.

Mixed-use projects throughout the world usually start with the vision of the developer. Although *developer* can mean many things to different people, development entities consistently fall into one of three categories: major property owners, public organizations, or private developers.

The most common form of mixed-use developer outside the United States is the major property owner. Given that the availability of well-located adjacent parcels of land drives the development process, the major property owner who already has assembled large contiguous pieces of land in prime locations is the only entity able to move on large-scale mixed-use projects.

Internationally, mixed-use sites typically are corporate holdings (former factory sites in urban settings, urban infill sites near or on transportation hubs, and so on) or family-owned parcels near existing commercial projects. Although these corporate entities or family enterprises may have developed a number of commercial projects, rarely have they had much experience in mixed-use development. Most of them are not prepared for the complex development process required of a mixed-use project or have a staff with such experience. Therefore, they turn to international consultants with the expertise to make an envisioned project viable.

Although public agencies and organizations are a common catalyst in the United States for mixed-use projects, they are nearly unheard of in most emerging nations or in those countries whose governments are very probusiness. The need to renew city centers through mixed-use developments is left to property owners or private developers, which creates a climate not always conducive to development.

Many formerly communist and socialist countries have in place a multilayer review and approval process, which mandates that local professional associations of architects and engineers approve all developments. As many U.S. developers can attest, trying to get 100 architects or engineers to agree on one issue can be a nightmare. This system can be incredibly cumbersome and requires having well-grounded relationships with local government officials to help move the development process forward. Obtaining input from the leaders of these professional associations during the design process also is imperative for creating a successful development.

Although private developers are the largest force in mixed-use development in the United States, singular-entity private developers are not nearly as prevalent on the international scene. Large corporate entities have internal groups that function as their development arm, but usually these groups are guided by the corporation's

Nowe Miasto is an office, retail, and hotel project in downtown Krakow, Poland, that is being developed by Tishman Speyer Properties, with RTKL providing architectural services.

Courtesy of Tishman Speyer Properties

own growth and internal goals. For example, some Asian conglomerates develop mixed-use projects as "centers of business" for their interests in a foreign country. The primary focus of such a project is to serve employees' needs (for office space, housing, hotels, et cetera). Only secondarily is the project used to provide commercial opportunities in its context. Certainly, as the world of trade continues to expand and impediments to business are overcome, the need for the private developer—both as a partner with local developers and as the sole creator of mixed-use projects—will increase internationally.

The one constant in all serious mixed-use developments is the feasibility study, which is conducted through the use of market analysis. As one might assume, when investors look at the amount of development dollars needed for a mixed-use project, they tend to be conservative in their investment. The proper mix of uses is always the key to a successful project, but knowing what uses work well in each country and culture requires local investigation and analysis.

International market analysis can be quite challenging, as good market data are often hard to come by and/or expensive to collect. Notes Paris Rutherford of RTKL Associates in Dallas, "Market analysis in international settings is often very difficult to undertake at the level of detail achieved in the United States."

Office Use

Although the speculative office market may be strong in many countries, governments restrict speculative development in some areas. In Korea, for instance, an office building must be at least 10 percent occupied by the developer or its subsidiaries. This requirement certainly restricts the overbuilding of office space, but it also makes offices much less desirable as a potential use.

Large international companies are the desired tenants in mixed-use projects, not only because they will lease large portions of the project but also because of the cachet of their name in marketing to smaller tenants. Thus, the strongest portion of the office market in international mixed-use projects appears to be the U.S. equivalent of Class A office space. In emerging nations where the desire is to attract global companies, amenities such as larger floor plates, proper elevator sizes and capacities, raised-access flooring, and modern computer and telecommunications systems are considered standard in developing a successful office component for the project.

Unfortunately, in many countries, the services provided are only as good as the infrastructure providing them. Trying to offer U.S. standards can fall dramatically short in many countries where the infrastructure simply cannot provide the electricity, water, or telecommunications necessary to create Class A space. On the other hand, a lack of existing infrastructure means that no equipment must be removed and updated; thus, it is easier to implement new fiber-optic and cell phone technologies in those countries.

Hotel Use
The mix of hotel and office space (usually with retail as a third use) always has been a most potent combination in mixed-use development. The ability to bring business travelers to a prime location can be a strong marketing tool. In the United States, a hotel functions primarily as a place for businesspeople to stay while conducting business elsewhere in the city. In Asia and the Middle East, business is conducted in the hotel lobby and its many restaurants. Thus, the international hotel market requires 200 to 300 percent more public space than comparable U.S. hotels.

In some parts of the Middle East, hotels may be the only socially sanctioned space in which to entertain in a business setting, because Muslim countries generally restrict access to alcohol in all places except hotels. Although hotels hold great development potential because of this factor, many Muslim clients or developers who follow strict Islamic teachings will not build or operate hotels because of their connection with alcohol consumption.

Residential Use
Like developers in the United States, international developers look for ways to extend the daily life of a mixed-use project. Residential components of a mixed-use project not only provide the critical mass needed to sustain round-the-clock activity in a development but also lend a greater feeling of permanence. Although residential tenants like the convenience of mixed-use projects, privacy and security are of even greater importance to them. Thus, the residential components must be clearly separated from the hotel and the coming and going of its guests.

Replacing the hotel component with furnished apartments rented by the day, week, or month that provide maid service and other amenities ("serviced apartments") may solve part of this problem. But the need then arises to provide separate amenities (such as a health club, pool, or common garden areas) for residents of permanent apartments and serviced apartments.

In countries with expanding tourist markets, serviced apartments can be a positive program addition if hotel uses are not feasible. Serviced apartments provide a greater return for the developer than a standard apartment; premium rates can be charged because the rental period is limited. Nevertheless, serviced apartments do require management staff to handle the hotel-like quality of service needed.

Retail and Entertainment Use
In the United States, retail uses associated with mixed-use projects usually are ancillary to the entire development. Typically, small amounts of specialty retail space with some food and beverage outlets are enough to round out the program. In most areas of the world, however, retail is viewed as the primary driver of a mixed-use development, and entire regional shopping centers with numerous entertainment venues are incorporated in mixed-use projects. This heavy mix of retail and entertainment space completes the synergy of uses necessary to make the project work: office, residential, and hotel all are perceived to be more ideally located when convenient, substantial retail is present.

It is this synergy of uses that fires international mixed-use projects. Most cultures have not yet reached America's readiness to "de-mall": they still regard shopping centers as a novelty. The inclination toward new, large centers allows designers and developers to fashion retail projects without the problems (such as the faceless boxes) to which many Americans now react negatively.

International retail centers typically offer an unusual mix of merchandising. Most successful regional centers contain a supermarket or hypermarket that offers more variety and value-oriented products than local markets and fits well with the convenience and diversity of mall shopping.

Entertainment venues also do not always conform to the typical American approach. For U.S. cinemas, bigger is better. International markets seem to max out at ten to 12 screens per location, partly because no copyright law enforcement exists, which makes it cheaper in many countries to buy a pirated video than go to the cinema. Internationally, cinema operators and distributors are the same entity, a practice prohibited by antitrust laws in the United States.

Internationally, the demand is strong for American brands in the entertainment market. Although European developers tend to take more risks in implementing new ideas, American entertainment development tends to rely on tested formats. In the United States, if the cinema experience can be tied to food and beverage, the viability of cinemas is greatly increased. Theme restaurants and game-oriented food and beverage outlets, considered very American, always are popular. Still, like hotels, if a culture does not accept alcohol, food and beverage venues may find it hard to stay afloat. Because most food and beverage revenues derive from beverages, the American theme restaurant would be harder to pencil out.

Cultural Use

Cultural uses pose difficult questions in the international market. Without strong government and public support, they have little ability to remain in a development pro forma. As uses generating low profits, they may draw people, but they will have difficulty paying their own way. If a strong tourist entertainment attraction can be integrated into a mixed-use program, the project stands a better chance of surviving.

Parking Use

Parking can make or break a mixed-use project. If a project cannot deal with the volume of cars moving in and out of the site, people will not return. Mixed-use projects offer convenience by bringing many uses together in one location, but multiple uses also bring a high concentration of vehicles in a confined space. Most municipalities play an increasingly active role in reviewing the traffic impact that a project will bring.

American standards for parking ratios based on gross areas are high compared with many international code requirements. Meeting the code requirement is usually easy; meeting the realistic needs can be difficult. Understanding cultural use patterns can help to identify patterns among all uses, enabling developers to limit to a workable number the car spaces that must be built. For example, in the United Arab Emirates, typical office work hours are between 8:00 a.m. and 7:00 p.m. Peak retailing begins at 8:00 p.m. This pattern allows the overflow from retail parking during peak hours to use parking spaces for the office use.

Source: Adapted from Raymond Peloquin, "Into the Fabric Woven," *Urban Land,* April 1999, pp. 77–79, 92–93.

■

Courtesy of Birkdale Village

Birkdale Village in Huntersville, North Carolina, which includes retail, residential, office, and entertainment uses, has been developed by a partnership between two development firms, Crosland and Pappas Properties.

- An acute awareness of and appreciation for the importance of urban design.

With such requirements, prospective entrants into the field should be justifiably wary, and small and inexperienced firms should be especially wary. Often developers of mixed-use projects have been very large, including major public companies such as Catellus in San Francisco, Trammell Crow in Dallas, and Forest City Enterprises in Cleveland. Several large real estate investment trusts (REITs), such as Federal Realty Investment Trust, Post Properties, and Trizec Properties, have initiated major mixed-use developments as well, but recently these three firms have moved away from this business. For the near future, most REITs likely will avoid the role of master developer in mixed-use development because they are focused primarily on one property type—for instance, apartments, retailing, or office. Some, however, are and will remain active in developing components of mixed-use projects.

Although small firms seldom undertake mixed-use developments, these projects are not strictly the purview of large firms either. Most mixed-use projects today are developed by large or medium private developers and property companies. Larger private firms that have developed a number of mixed-use projects in various parts of the United States and/or international markets include Tishman Speyer Properties in New York, Hines in Houston, Related Companies in New York (through its Related Urban Group, formerly known as the Palladium Company), Millennium Partners in New York, and Mori Building Co. Ltd. in Tokyo. Several leading small and medium firms that have focused on mixed-use development, frequently in a defined local area, include Jacoby Development, Inc., in Atlanta, Cooper & Stebbins in Dallas, de Guardiola Development Ventures in West Palm Beach, Pappas Properties in Charlotte, the Peterson Companies in Fairfax, Virginia, the CIM Group LLC in Hollywood, California, McCaffery Interests in Chicago, Granit Polus R.A. in Budapest, and Raffles International in Singapore.

Finally, and by definition, master developers of mixed-use projects are involved in multiple product lines, not a single type of real estate. This factor in itself can create significant problems in that these product lines vary significantly and require diverging approaches and skills. Many developers who are highly proficient in one type of product have run into major pitfalls when trying to develop another. Thus, many master developers have chosen to develop partnerships with developers who excel in certain specialties. For example, a master developer with expertise in office development might choose to bring in a retail developer, apartment developer, or hotel developer to develop, own, and/or operate a portion of the project.

In many cases, large and complex mixed-use projects involve several development partners. For example, Federal Realty Investment Trust and Post Properties have worked together on a number of projects that combine retail and apartment uses, allowing each to draw on the expertise of the other. Other partnerships can involve a large national or international developer partnering with a small local developer for its local knowledge and contacts. WestEnd City Center in Budapest (see Chapter 8), for example, was developed by TriGranit, a joint venture of Canada's TrizecHahn Corporation (now known as Trizec Properties) and Granit Polus R.A., a Hungarian company with extensive development experience in the Eastern European market.

Redevelopment of the Edinburgh Royal Infirmary is being undertaken by Taylor Woodrow Capital Developments and its partners, Bank of Scotland and Kilmartin Property Group. The 19-acre (7.7-hectare) city center site is one of the most prominent and best development opportunities in Europe. The development, with Foster and Partners as master plan architect, will involve a mix of uses, including residential accommodations, hotel/leisure uses, and offices.

Some projects may require highly specialized expertise and a range of development partners. For example, the development team for the Bryant Street Pier in San Francisco, which will include a major cruise terminal and a variety of other land-based uses, includes four equity partners: Lend Lease Group, a global property and financial services group of companies; PSA Corporation, Ltd., which owns and operates the port of Singapore and the Singapore Cruise Center; Chinese Maritime Transport Ltd., which has a long maritime history; and Whittney Cressman, LLC, a commercial real estate advisory and brokerage firm with significant experience in local retail and commercial leasing.

Evaluating Sites and Opportunities for Development

The initial identification of a potential site suitable for mixed-use development is as much an art as a science; it is based on the observations of an experienced individual with a thorough understanding of mixed-use development, of the specific property types being considered for the development, and of the local market.

To evaluate a site, it is desirable to begin with an examination of its positive and negative attributes relative to each potential use:

- proximity (adjacent land uses, nearby activity centers);
- access and visibility (highways, transit systems, pedestrians);

Courtesy of Lend Lease Development

Bryant Street Pier in San Francisco is a complex waterfront project that is being developed by an international partnership comprising firms from Australia, Singapore, China, and the United States.

A model of the Market Commons Clarendon in Arlington, Virginia. The project has been developed by McCaffery Interests, a development firm that targets opportunities in urban or suburban infill locations with high pedestrian traffic, proven residential or office markets, and access to public transportation.

Courtesy of Antunovich Associates

- the site itself (size, shape, topography, soils);
- services (utilities, roads, public facilities);
- land use controls (zoning, subdivision regulations, building codes, local government's attitudes);
- social and political issues and sensitivities;
- potential use (type and quality of use programmed, timing and size of markets);
- landownership (availability, assembly requirements);
- land cost in relation to these factors.

Although the characteristics of sites for mixed-use development vary widely, they generally have several features in common. First, they must be substantially sized and/or allow for relatively high-density development to accommodate multiple uses. Thus, the amount of space that can be built on the site, either by virtue of its significant acreage or its substantial allowable density, in most cases has to be quite large to accommodate all potential uses. Sites can be small but only if they allow for stacking uses to fairly high levels, like many mixed-use towers. High-density mixed-use towers in downtown locations often have 20 to 30 stories or more. It is generally not feasible to stack three uses in a building of ten or fewer stories.

Second, sites for mixed-use projects usually have excellent access and good exposure. Because such facilities are likely to generate considerable auto and pedestrian traffic, sites should be proximate to existing travel patterns and numerous access points.

Third, sites for mixed-use projects are usually located in an existing, larger multiuse environment. Sites are often the center of a confluence of activities or a transitional area between different uses and activities, providing the site with proximity to multiple land use markets. Good mixed-use sites can become focal points for their immediate areas.

Fourth, sites for mixed-use projects must be located in a jurisdiction that is predisposed to favor such development and/or allows flexible or mixed-use zoning. If

the parcel is not already zoned for mixed uses, the zoning must be achievable in a reasonable amount of time with a reasonable amount of effort. An experienced local land use attorney should be consulted to evaluate this issue (see Chapter 4).

Developers sometimes have their own specific criteria for sites. For example, McCaffery Interests in Chicago, which has developed mixed-use properties in various cities in the United States, pursues development sites and opportunities as follows:

> The purpose of the company is to add value through the opportunistic acquisition and subsequent development or redevelopment of land or buildings in high-quality urban locations. McCaffery Interests targets such opportunities in what are typically identified as 24-hour cities. Upon acquisition, the company will focus on identifying a creative solution for the reuse of the property that addresses the fundamental real estate attributes of the asset. Typical targeted properties [are located near] high pedestrian traffic; . . . vibrant shopping districts; proven residential and/or office [centers]; access to public transportation; and . . . cultural or sporting activities.[1]

The types of sites frequently used in mixed-use projects range from downtown sites to master-planned communities.

Downtown Sites

Downtown sites are frequently chosen for mixed-use development, especially underused or blighted sites in diverse downtown areas, often with transit nearby. The edges of downtowns—transition areas between districts of differing character and use—are often good locations for mixed-use projects. The major impediment of such locations, however, often is the difficulty of assembling a large enough site to support a mixed-use development. The major asset is the diverse nature of such downtown areas, which can usually support three or more uses in a mixed-use project if the timing and sizing of the project are appropriate.

A good example in the United States is Tower City Center, a redevelopment project that capitalizes on existing structures and design opportunities to help rejuvenate the lakefront sector of downtown Cleveland. The historic Cleveland Union Terminal complex (constructed in the late 1920s) was once a thriving regional business and transportation hub but had fallen on hard times. The developer of the revitalized center, Forest City Enterprises, sought to make Tower City Center a new focus for downtown shopping by linking an existing department store with a new retail mall. To generate sufficient marketable space to support development, Forest City Enterprises incorporated both new and renovated office buildings and a hotel into the project and retained and improved important physical connections to adjoining office and hotel buildings and transit facilities. Other examples in the United States include Peabody Place in Memphis, Yerba Buena Center and Embarcadero Center in San Francisco, and CityPlace in West Palm Beach.

Such projects are also common internationally. A new urban regeneration project on a site in Portsmouth, England, home of the Royal Navy, will involve mixed-use development. U.K. property developers Centros Miller and Taylor Woodrow have formed a partnership with Los Angeles–based Jerde Partnership International as master planner to undertake the project. It is expected that the mixed-use project, which will focus on the redevelopment of a city-center site that formerly housed the Tricorn shopping center, will be completed in 2005. Among the planned uses on the 20-acre (13.5-hectare) site will be more than 200 residential units, a hotel, and 750,000 square feet (70,000 square meters) of leisure and retail space. According to Jerde senior vice president and project designer David Moreno, "Our goal is to reconnect the important existing civic components of the urban core into a seamless pedestrian network of compelling shopping streets, plazas, and gardens." (See also the case studies on Sony Center am Potsdamer Platz, West End City Center, and Jin Mao Tower in Chapter 8.)

Convention centers and arenas, especially in or near downtown areas where office markets are strong, are sometimes attractive places for mixed-use projects because of the visitor traffic they generate, which in turn can support hotel and retail facilities. The recently updated Prudential Center in Boston, which is connected to the Hynes Convention Center, incorporates major hotel and retail facilities that benefit from proximity to the convention center. Plans for the area around the Staples Arena in downtown Los Angeles combine hotel, residential, retail, and public spaces. Convention centers generally are not, however, a good use with residential space unless the two uses are sufficiently separated.

Waterfront redevelopment sites in downtown areas are a natural location for mixed-use projects, as they frequently offer a prime location adjacent to a natural amenity that can enhance the marketability of a variety of uses. Mixed-use projects that have been proposed or developed on downtown waterfront sites include Rowes Wharf in Boston, the Ritz-Carlton and Residences Georgetown in Washington, D.C., Bryant Street Pier in San Francisco, Inner Harbor East in Baltimore, and the International Finance Centre in Hong Kong.

Transit Station Sites

Sites near or over subway or light-rail transit stations are often superb sites, offering excellent access, higher-density zoning, or zoning that encourages a variety of uses. Carlyle in Alexandria, Virginia; Arlington Town Square in Arlington Heights, Illinois; Orenco Station near Portland, Oregon; Mockingbird Station in Dallas; WestEnd City Center in Budapest, and the proposed Lindbergh City Center in Atlanta are examples.

In many cases, such sites are also former industrial or railroad sites. For example, EmeryStation Plaza in Emeryville, California, is a three-building, 550,000-square-foot (51,000-square-meter), mixed-use transit village complex on the north, east, and south sides of the Emeryville Amtrak station. The first phase of the project,

Developed by Forest City Enterprises, Tower City Center is located in downtown Cleveland and comprises 6.5 million square feet (604,000 square meters) of office, retail, and hotel space. The central downtown site incorporates numerous historic structures, including the historic Terminal Tower building and the former city railway station.

Courtesy of Forest City Enterprises

by Wareham Development, consists of a 247,000-square-foot (23,000-square-meter), five-story office building with 16,900 square feet (1,570 square meters) of ground-floor retail space and two levels of parking below. Succeeding phases will include additional commercial and residential space. The complex is a major component of the transit business village evolving around the Amtrak station. The 10.6-acre (4.3-hectare) site is the former location of a Westinghouse Corporation facility used for manufacturing transformers that had been vacant for more than 20 years.

A prominent international example is the JR Central Towers and Station in Nagoya, Japan. This mixed-use station complex contains 4.4 million square feet (409,000 square meters) of office, hotel, retail, transportation, and cultural facilities. Developed by Japan Central Railways and designed by Kohn Pedersen Fox Associates, this commercial development includes a 20-story base building that houses retail uses and the transit station, and two 50-story towers housing separate office and hotel uses. The project involved major improvements to the main regional transportation hub serving the high-speed bullet train, the national railway network, several commuter rails, and subway and bus lines.

Industrial, Railroad, and Military Sites

Underused railroad or other industrial holdings in or near central cities can also provide good opportunities for mixed-use projects because of their size and central locations. Illinois Center in Chicago is an early example; more recent examples include Mission Bay in San Francisco, Potomac Yard in Alexandria, Virginia, and the Salt Lake City Gateway project.

Salt Lake City Gateway is a 40-acre (16-hectare) mixed-use development on Union Pacific's abandoned railroad yards. Capping the northernmost area of downtown, the site is part of a brownfield redevelopment project supported by the U.S. Environmental Protection Agency (EPA) and is a catalyst for urban infill between the downtown area and the site. The historic Union Pacific depot serves as the project's gateway. Other major brownfield sites in the early stages of redevelopment include Atlantic Station in Atlanta and Victory in Dallas.

Numerous surplus military sites are being planned or developed as mixed-use properties, including the Orlando Naval Training Center, Lowry Town Center near Denver, and Truman Annex in Florida. These very large properties generally require long time frames for development.

The special issues involved in redeveloping such sites are numerous and well illustrated by the Truman Annex, once a strategic naval station in Key West, Florida. The project's principal developer faced formidable challenges throughout the project, including environmental contamination requiring significant remediation, the need to replace obsolete infrastructure that did not comply with local codes, extensive and unpredictable entitlements, a national economic recession, and intense community involvement.

JR Central Towers and Station in Nagoya, Japan, incorporates a rail station at its base and also includes retail, office, hotel, and cultural facilities in a base structure and two towers.

Courtesy of Kohn Pedersen Fox

Salt Lake City Gateway is a 40-acre (16-hectare) mixed-use development on Union Pacific's abandoned railroad yards at the edge of downtown Salt Lake City. The Union Pacific station has been restored as part of the development.

Used as a naval base since 1822, the annex comprised single-family residences, barracks, industrial buildings, administrative buildings, fuel and water tanks, dock areas, and supporting utilities.

Upon acquiring the site, the developer took possession of approximately 1.1 million square feet (102,200 square meters) of abandoned buildings, a majority of which were rotting and condemned. The property's infrastructure was functionally obsolete and required removal and replacement. Given the former industrial activities that took place on the site, the extent of contamination was fairly modest, but pollutants such as cadmium, lead, chromium, PCBs (polychlorinated biphenyls), and asbestos required remediation.

The redeveloped Truman Annex comprises 60,000 square feet (5,580 square meters) of commercial space, 425 residential units, 244 hotel rooms/timeshare units, and 22,000 square feet (2,045 square meters) of museum space.

Like most large-scale and long-term initiatives, the redevelopment of military bases and industrial sites involves substantial risk. Given the multiple entities involved, predevelopment can be incredibly complex, often requiring regulatory permits and approvals from local, state, and federal agencies. Developers and regulatory officials need a high level of flexibility and commitment for these projects to succeed and to survive changing economic conditions over long development periods.

Suburban and Satellite Downtowns

Suburban and satellite downtowns around many cities, like many CBDs, are undergoing redevelopment in areas where markets are strong and where underused but well-located sites can be developed to become the center piece of the suburban downtown. Because market pressure often favors offices and hotels in suburban downtowns while public pressure favors residential and retail uses, mixed-use projects are often a good solution and compromise. One early example is Janss Court in down-

town Santa Monica, which was a major catalyst for the revitalization of the downtown area (see the accompanying feature box). A more recent example is Renaissance Place in Highland Park, Illinois, which sensitively incorporates retail, office, and residential uses at the center of this affluent Chicago suburb in a main street configuration.

Numerous other examples are in various stages of completion. Downtown Pleasant Hill in the San Fran-

Renaissance Place is located on an infill site in Highland Park, Illinois, a suburban downtown north of downtown Chicago. The design sensitively incorporates retail, office, and residential uses into the downtown fabric.

Photographer: Alise O'Brien Photography; courtesy of Suttle Mindlin Architects

In the 1960s, the city of Santa Monica, hoping to breathe new life into its downtown retail district, decided to convert one of its main shopping streets into a pedestrian mall. Three blocks of Third Street between Broadway and Wilshire Boulevard were closed to traffic and landscaped for pedestrians. By almost every measure, the pedestrian mall failed.

In 1986, Santa Monica adopted a Specific Plan for the redevelopment of the mall and prepared regulations to guide private development along Third Street. Janss Court was the first major project built under the new plan. It embodies many of the city's redevelopment objectives for privately owned parcels fronting the mall: mixed uses, pedestrian access to city parking structures, ground-level commercial sites, night-oriented activities, and attention to design. Because Janss Court was considered an important private project consistent with public redevelopment, the city streamlined the approvals process. The project occupies an important site at the southern terminus of the Third Street Promenade in downtown Santa Monica, directly adjacent to an enclosed downtown regional shopping center. Notes David Marks of Marketplace Advisors, Inc., in Maitland, Florida, "Third Street Promenade has become one of the best examples of mixed-use main street development in the United States; its energy and vitality have turned it into a world-class destination."

Janss Court is a seven-story, 131,000-square-foot (12,200-square-meter) building located on a 30,000-square-foot (2,800-square-meter) parcel. The ground floor (and a small area below grade) houses a fourplex theater and two restaurants within 33,800 square feet (3,140 square meters). Located above are three floors of office space

Janss Court in Santa Monica is a seven-story mixed-use building with retail, cinema, office, and residential uses that was instrumental in revitalizing the Third Street Promenade, now one of the most vibrant sites in the Los Angeles area.

within about 59,000 square feet (5,500 square meters). The building is topped with 32 upscale rental apartments located on three floors. Although not required by the city, 203 parking spaces for office and residential tenants are provided below grade in a 3.5-level poured-in-place concrete garage.

■

cisco suburb of Pleasant Hill is a mixed-use development that aims to bring new life and identity to this Bay Area community. The new downtown plan includes a 355,000-square-foot (33,000-square-meter) shopping district integrated with townhouses, a 120-room hotel, an office building, and the Charles Moore–designed Civic Center that creates a focal point for the community. The new urban design is carefully oriented toward pedestrians. A curving street, Crescent Drive, links shops and middle-market anchor tenants with plazas, restaurants, parking, and a multiscreen theater complex.

Bethesda Row is located just off Wisconsin Avenue, a major artery in the Washington, D.C., metropolitan area and the heart of downtown Bethesda, Maryland. Bethesda, an inner-ring suburb immediately northwest of the city, has one of the highest median household incomes in the country. Adjacent uses include high-rise office buildings, the Metro (subway) station, and lower-density residential areas. As a whole, the site for Bethesda

Row covers seven contiguous city blocks. Previous uses on the site included warehouses, a cement plant, low-rise office buildings, and small-scale retailers. Almost all of the land was in the hands of a single owner, whose family had long held on to the site. Through negotiations with this individual, the developer, Federal Realty Investment Trust, was able to gain control of the site at an acceptable cost. Federal Realty negotiated long-term ground leases for Phases I, II, and III and bought the land for Phase IV.

Suburban Activity Centers and Business Parks

More fragmented suburban activity centers, edge cities, and business parks are also good locations for mixed-use projects; they usually already provide multiple uses but usually lack a central focal point or a pedestrian-friendly environment. Such areas often include fairly expensive land parcels that often require fairly high-density development to achieve reasonable returns. Mixed-use projects can easily be the most profitable use in this context;

they can offer a much needed pedestrian-friendly environment in these auto-dominated environments.

Numerous opportunities are available to invigorate an existing suburban business center with a broader mix of uses, and a significant demand is largely unmet for suburban office space that offers a mixed-use, pedestrian-friendly environment. Phillips Place in Charlotte, North Carolina, is a good example; the project is a mixed-use town center in the South Park area, a major suburban office and retail location (see Chapter 8).

Legacy Town Center in the Legacy development near Dallas is another example. The developers are building a town for its corporate citizens in the heart of a business park/edge city that is home to 36,000 employees and some of the country's largest corporations. The 155-acre (63-hectare) Legacy Town Center came about after extensive discussions among representatives of the Dallas suburb of Plano, Legacy, the community, local businesses, and Atlanta-based Post Properties. Notes Marilyn Kasko, director of Legacy business park for developer Electronic Data Systems, "This town center is the ultimate amenity for the employees in Legacy, as well as for those in the surrounding communities."

Shopping Center Sites

Many regional shopping malls and retail commercial strips have failed in recent years, and many others are performing poorly,[2] creating opportunities for redevelopment of these sites, frequently referred to as *greyfields*. A 2001 study found that "approximately 7 percent of existing regional malls are greyfield malls, with an additional 12 percent of regional malls vulnerable to future greyfield mall status. . . . The majority of greyfield malls are in moderate-income neighborhoods with older, affordable housing."[3] The estimated total number of greyfield malls (defined in the study as those with sales of $150 per square foot [$1,600 per square meter] or less) in the United States in 1999 was somewhere between 114 and 140.

Unlike many other redevelopment sites, greyfield redevelopment sites can be very attractive because they are usually well served by existing roads, they are quite large (averaging 45 acres [18 hectares], according to PricewaterhouseCoopers), they are owned by a single entity and thus land assembly is not an issue, and they seldom involve environmental cleanup. They also often include large areas that are occupied only by parking lots and by buildings that can easily be reconfigured or demolished, keeping demolition and redevelopment costs relatively low while also providing a clean slate for a new design. Greyfield redevelopment sites were typically developed more than 30 years ago and have become urban infill sites, usually increasing their potential for commercial development.

ULI has identified 12 mixed-use projects on former shopping center sites that have been completed or where planning is underway: Brainerd Town Center, Chattanooga, Tennessee; Belmar, Lakewood, Colorado; CityCenter Englewood, Englewood, Colorado; DownTown Park Forest, Park Forest, Illinois; Downtown Kendall, Miami, Florida; Mashpee Commons, Mashpee, Massachusetts; Mizner Park, Boca Raton, Florida; North Hills, Raleigh, North Carolina; Paseo Colorado, Pasadena, California; Santana Row, San Jose, California; Village at Shirlington, Arlington, Virginia; and Winter Park Village, Orlando, Florida. Many of these redevelopments involve scraping the site completely (Mizner Park, Belmar, and Santana Row, for example), but others retain some of the buildings. Smaller shopping centers, such as those that existed on the sites for Mashpee Commons and the Village at Shirlington, frequently can be redeveloped by retaining and redesigning many of the existing buildings and carefully placing new buildings to shape a more urban town center. Redevelopment sometimes retains a department store, as at Winter Park Village, a new mixed-use town center that has been developed on the site of the defunct 500,000-square-foot (46,500-square-meter) Winter Park Mall near Orlando. The former Dillard's depart-

Winter Park Village in Winter Park, Florida, is a town center built on the site of the defunct 500,000-square-foot (46,450-square meter) Winter Park Mall. Although the redevelopment involved significant demolition, the plan also transformed a department store into residential and retail space.

Fairview Village near Portland, Oregon, is a planned community that includes a mixed-use town center with retail, residential, and civic uses. Pictured is the village post office.

ment store has been redeveloped into loft apartments, a Cheese Cake Factory restaurant, and retail space.

Several proposed or implemented mall redevelopment projects, among them Brainerd Town Center and Downtown Kendall, use an incremental and phased transition from mall to mixed uses. And some malls retain portions of the existing center for retail uses and are redeveloped largely in one phase, such as at Paseo Colorado. The 600,000-square-foot (55,760-square-meter) Plaza Pasadena, which opened in 1980, was in all respects, except its location, a suburban mall. An enclosed mall with three department store anchors, the mall was almost completely inward looking, left a two-block-long retail dead zone along Colorado Boulevard, and was perhaps the worst possible use from an urbanist point of view. In addition to severing the pedestrian and retail continuity of Colorado Boulevard, the mall closed off Garfield Avenue, a key north/south street that was part of the historic 1925 Bennett Plan for Pasadena. Previously, the vista down Garfield Avenue had been terminated by the historic Central Library at one end of the street and by the Pasadena Civic Auditorium at the other. In the Plaza Pasadena plan, the grand axis was replaced with a glass entry wall, signifying the axial view that was lost. And in place of the beaux arts and Mediterranean-style structures that preceded it, the new mall presented a mostly blank brick facade to the street.

The concept for Paseo Colorado entailed the demolition of everything above the subterranean parking structure except the Macy's department store. The new center, built on top of the previous mall's two-level underground parking structure, mixes retail space, restaurants, entertainment uses, and housing around a new series of pedestrian promenades and paseos that reestablishes the vistas along Garfield Avenue. The project includes 56 retail shops, a full-line Macy's department store, seven destination restaurants, six quick-service cafés, a health club, a day spa, a supermarket, a 14-screen cinema, and 387 units of rental housing.

Planned Communities

Master-planned communities and traditional neighborhood developments are excellent locations for mixed-use projects, especially mixed-use town centers. Many master-planned communities seek to establish a sense of place and a distinct identity, and town centers are viewed as a primary tool for achieving these objectives. New mixed-use town center developments in fact began in planned communities, including developments such as Miami

figure 2-1

Town Centers in Master-Planned Communities in the United States and Canada

Town Center	Location
McKenzie Towne Town Center	Calgary, Alberta
Cornell Town Center	Markham, Ontario
Playa Vista	Los Angeles, California
San Elijo Town Center	San Marcos, California
Valencia Town Center Drive	Valencia, California
Abacoa Town Center	Jupiter, Florida
Market Street at Celebration	Celebration, Florida
Haile Village Center	Gainesville, Florida
Miami Lakes Town Center	Miami Lakes, Florida
Coffee Creek Center	Chesterton, Indiana
Kentlands Market Square	Gaithersburg, Maryland
Southern Village	Chapel Hill, North Carolina
Vermillion Town Center	Huntersville, North Carolina
Easton Town Center	Easton, Ohio
Fairview Village	Fairview, Oregon
Orenco Station	Hillsboro, Oregon
I'On Square	Mount Pleasant, South Carolina
Woodlands Town Center	The Woodlands, Texas
Reston Town Center	Reston, Virginia

Courtesy of Intrawest Corporation

Station Mont Tremblant in Tremblant, Quebec, is a mountain resort that features a resort village with condo units, a hotel, townhouses, 80 commercial spaces for dining and shopping, and resort amenities.

Lakes Town Center in Miami Lakes, Florida, and Reston Town Center in Reston, Virginia (see also Figure 2-1).

A strategic location in the master-planned community that provides good access to major amenities and markets outside the community is important as well. Abacoa Town Center, for example, is located within the 2,055-acre (832-hectare) master-planned community of Abacoa, but the site is also strategically located adjacent to the John D. MacArthur campus of Florida Atlantic University in Jupiter on one side and Roger Dean Stadium, site of spring training for the St. Louis Cardinals and the Montreal Expos, on the other. Reston Town Center is at the heart of Reston but also directly accessible from the Dulles Toll Road, a major highway and development corridor in northern Virginia.

Resort Areas

Resort areas provide excellent opportunities for creating mixed-use villages that include non-office-oriented combinations, such as residential, hotel, retail, entertainment, and recreation uses. Many resort areas in the United States have traditionally lacked town- and village-style amenities such as those found in many European resort towns and areas. The leading exception is Aspen, a phenomenally successful and exclusive resort area in Colorado whose success in large part stems from its historic village center. A pioneering early example of the creation of a new village center is Vail Village in Vail, Colorado, developed in 1961. And Seaside, a resort community in the panhandle of Florida, has grown into a town center as the community has matured. The village atmosphere now rivals the oceanfront setting as a primary amenity for the project.

All three of these projects have strongly demonstrated the value of a mixed-use village in enhancing the success of resort destinations, and several developers are now employing this strategy in their developments. Intrawest Corporation—one of the largest resort developers and operators in North America—now describes itself as "the leading developer and operator of village-centered desti-

nation resorts across North America." It creates mixed-use villages with hotels, condominiums, retail space, restaurants, and recreation uses in an attractive village setting.

For example, the proposed commercial master plan for the Village at Squaw Valley USA consists of approximately 80 shops and restaurants in 11 distinct commercial neighborhoods intermixed with lodging and residential uses. Creating many varied and interactive guest experiences in the pedestrian village and populating each space with distinctive operators ensure long-lasting positive memories for guests, notes Max Reim, vice president, Intrawest–The Village People.

The recently completed Bay Harbor Marina District, just north of Traverse City, Michigan, is based on a similar concept. A major resort destination, the district includes 190,000 square feet (17,660 square meters) of condominium, retail, restaurant, vacation retreat, and office space as well as a marina in a new urban resort village setting on Lake Michigan. Numerous other such resorts are being planned, including the 28-acre (11-hectare) Village of Baytowne Wharf at the Sandestin golf and beach resort in Florida and the 21-acre (8.5-hectare) MonteLago Village planned for Lake Las Vegas, which will include restaurants, shops, offices, condominiums, a Ritz-Carlton hotel, and a casino.

Hines Resorts has also pursued mixed uses at Aspen Highlands Village in Colorado, a pedestrian-friendly, ski-in/ski-out village comprising retail shops, restaurants, condominiums, townhouses, the Ritz-Carlton Club, skier and visitor services, public gathering places, and transportation facilities oriented around a central plaza at the base of the mountain. The master plan calls for 27,000 square feet (2,500 square meters) of retail space and 21,730 square feet (2,000 square meters) of restaurant space located around a spacious pedestrian plaza at the base of Aspen Highlands ski area. In addition, 31 single-family homesites, 31 direct–ski access townhouse residences, 73 village condominiums, and 111 affordable housing units are included.

Spanning 138 acres (56 hectares) at the nexus of I-75 and I-85 in the northwest corner of Atlanta's resurgent Midtown district, the site of Atlantic Steel Industries first came to life almost 100 years ago, when the company produced steel for wagon wheels and cotton bales. In recent decades, however, foreign competition and industry consolidation have taken their toll. But as the property's utility as a steel rolling mill diminished, its redevelopment potential increased.

In 1997, James Jacoby, chair of Atlanta-based Jacoby Development, Inc., employed LAW Environmental Engineering to conduct a feasibility study to determine whether the property could be remediated and redeveloped. LAW, in conjunction with the state Department of Natural Resources's Environmental Protection Division, developed a risk-based remediation plan that not only served the bottom line but also guaranteed a more important goal—restoring the property to an acceptable environmental condition and beneficial use.

Jacoby recognized that the Atlantic Steel property could serve as the site of a major gateway to the CBD and eventually teamed up with Charles Brown's CRB Realty Associates to serve as master developers of the site. The concept of multiple uses was adopted early in the redevelopment process for Atlantic Steel—renamed Atlantic Station—and is inherent in the current site plan.

The property is blessed with an ideal location but is inadequately served by the local transportation infrastructure, a situation that plan rectifies through the construction of a new multimodal bridge and modified ramp system. The bridge will tie directly into Midtown's street network and provide for an uninterrupted interface with the MARTA (Metropolitan Atlanta Rapid Transit Authority) Arts Center subway station. Although it will provide four lanes of general vehicular traffic, the bridge's primary purpose will be to serve as a linear park accommodating pedestrian, bicycle, and transit movement between Midtown and Atlantic Station. The multimodal connection will allow development of a mixed-use community of residential, retail, entertainment, office, and hotel uses offering a variety of transportation options. Existing interstate exit ramps will be modified to permit vehicle access to the interstate highway, the northern area of Midtown, and Atlantic Station.

The site has few constraints other than conditions resulting from operation of the steel mill. The eastern portion will be the center of activity, a truly urban environment focused on creating a 24-hour city where people can live, work, and play. The residential village will center around a manmade lake and will be interlaced with a series of parks and green spaces that connect to neighboring areas. The plan also calls for 4 million to 5 mil-

Atlantic Station is being built on the former Atlantic Steel industrial site, a brownfield site that has been cleaned up; the site is well situated to serve as a gateway development for the central business district.

Courtesy of Headline Group

lion square feet (372,000 to 465,000 square meters) of office space and roughly 1,200 hotel rooms.

Assistance has come from an innovative EPA program called Project XL (eXcellence & Leadership). Although federal restrictions now exist on area transportation projects—a result of Atlanta's failing to meet federal air quality standards—Project XL provides a means of moving the project forward. Project XL provides flexibility in its regulations, policies, and procedures when superior environmental performance can be attained through a particular alternative. Jacoby Development and CRB Realty have applied for and obtained regulatory flexibility for this development because of the environmental benefits of the brownfield remediation and of particulars related to site design and construction, including commitments to long-term air quality.

The citizens and leaders of Atlanta have vowed to cooperate to address future land use and transportation issues through a regional plan and smart growth. Atlantic Station is an exemplary project in this regard: it involves infill development near the city center, a mix of uses, environmental remediation of a brownfield, and a pedestrian- and transit-friendly design.

Source: Adapted in part from Brian Leary, "Steel Away," *Urban Land,* April 1999, pp. 48–51.

Site Control and Analysis

Once a site is identified as suitable for a mixed-use development, more in-depth analyses are required to confirm or refute the initial judgments. At this stage, developers generally prefer to control a site rather than to obtain outright fee simple ownership of it. If the site is owned by the public sector, a phased takedown of the land on a mutually agreeable schedule in often employed. If the land is privately owned, several options are available, including a joint venture with the landowner, or an option contract that allows the developer to establish terms of purchase and the exclusive availability of a desirable site but preserves the right to escape from the contract at a small cost. This choice allows time to complete due diligence (market research and feasibility analysis, soil tests, development approvals, and so on).

Site acquisition should be preceded by some level of due diligence and market analysis. Determining the market potential must focus on assessing multiple market potentials. The process involves data collection, field research, and statistical analysis to determine supply and demand for each potential use in specified market areas (which frequently differ for each use under consideration), quantitative identification of market potentials by time period and product line, and determination of development potential for the specific mixed-use project being analyzed. Market studies should consider typical market potential associated with each individual use as well as the market synergy resulting from a combination of uses in a single complex. As a rule, however, each element of the project should be able to stand on its own as a marketable and financially feasible component, and the analysis should not overstate possible synergies or competitive advantages.

The development potential for public, non-revenue-generating, and/or ancillary uses should also be considered at this time to determine the market support for them and/or their potential contribution to the other uses in a project. The addition of a cultural facility to the project, for example, needs to be assessed to determine whether the facility would attract patrons, how the facility could benefit other uses, and whether sufficient public, institutional, or other support is available to make such a use financially feasible. The following sections discuss assessment of the development potential for specific property types.

Office Uses

Office uses have historically been the driving force behind many mixed-use projects. A sound analysis of market potential will determine not only market support for the project but also what office building and office environment features are in demand and/or underserved in the market. Frequently, the words used to describe some of the important factors in selling office space are *amenity packages* and *on-site services*. A potential office tenant's interest in such extras must be carefully gauged in the market analysis to determine the value that a mixed-use environment might add to the office component. Some tenants look for these extras and are willing to pay a premium to obtain them; others are much more focused on space and price. In addition, a premium can usually be obtained from an office product that is new and fresh and offers new ideas.

Analyzing Office Markets

In general, any analysis of the market for and feasibility of new office space in a given area, whether freestanding or part of a mixed-use project, begins with an estimate of the supply of and demand for office space in the metropolitan area and then proceeds to an assessment for a particular submarket, node, and site.

Estimates of office space absorbed should be analyzed by category—e.g., finance, insurance, real estate, legal, business services, corporate—and trends in the growth

The office building at Riverside in Atlanta, a project built by Post Properties and designed by Duany Plater-Zyberk & Company. Riverside is reminiscent of an Italian village featuring a central "piazza," an urban square surrounded by a pedestrian environment of cafés, shops, and recreational facilities.

or decline in each sector identified. Special attention should also be given to characterizing each tenant type's space needs and preferences and the trends in those preferences. Not only do different users prefer different locations; their preferences also differ in terms of the quality, nature, and price of the space they occupy. The size of floor plates is an especially important driver and varies substantially by sector.

Understanding demand for office space is only half the equation; perhaps the most important analysis, especially for mixed-use development, is to assess the existing and projected supply of office space and existing vacancy levels. Most important for mixed-use projects, the overall analysis of the office supply should stratify the competition by product type, primarily comparing freestanding suburban office space with offices in mixed-use environments.

Special attention should be given to evaluating how recently developed office space in mixed-use environments has leased compared with freestanding office space, whether rents differ between office space in mixed-use environments and comparable freestanding projects, and how the tenant profile for offices in mixed-use environments differs significantly from that for freestanding projects. In some markets, office space in mixed-use environments performs better than that in freestanding buildings; other markets may see little difference.

Although the strength and direction of the overall metropolitan market paint a broad picture, it is also necessary to focus on the particular node or area where the development site is located and whether it is downtown or suburban. Such an analysis should look at old, new, and planned office buildings, noting the age, condition, and occupancy rate of existing facilities and correlating this information with existing rental rates. It is especially important to focus on buildings planned or under construction, particularly those in competing mixed-use environments, to get a current picture of the latest competition.

These office buildings are signature elements at Reston Town Center in Reston, Virginia. Office rents in Reston Town Center are among the highest in all of northern Virginia.

The most difficult judgment in the market analysis is to assess what percentage of the nodal demand can be captured by the particular development site and the project proposed—and at what price. At this stage, the art of real estate development comes into play. Although the oldest cliché in real estate—location, location, location—is critical, the nature of the project itself has a major impact on market capture rates and rents. This concept is particularly critical for a mixed-use development, because mixed-use projects offer an environment and amenities not found in other office buildings; well-conceived projects should lease more quickly at higher rental rates. The previously gathered information comparing the performance of office space in mixed-use environments with that in freestanding buildings is helpful in making this final judgment.

Ultimately, analyzing the potential for office development must focus on what kinds of tenants will be targeted for the project and what their space requirements are likely to be. Tenants' characteristics most pertinent to this analysis include size of the tenant's operation and the nature of office functions that will take place. Size is important in terms of determining the most desirable size of floor plates and the size and height of the office building or buildings, but more important, it affects the kinds of amenities desirable for the project.

The Role of Office Space
The amount of office space the site can support must be determined in relation to the programming for other uses to estimate overall project size and the amount of space allocated for each use. This process involves both feasibility and sensitivity analyses for each use (see Chapter 3). Once the initial analysis and allocation are complete, the relative importance of the office component compared with other uses becomes evident: the office component can be a primary, secondary, or balanced use. The importance of the office space to the project's overall success clearly affects how the office space is configured, and in turn the configuration clearly affects the leasability of the space and the kinds of tenants it will attract.

Office space is frequently configured as the dominant use in a mixed-use project—especially for projects developed in the 1980s—usually leading to secondary and supporting uses like hotel and retail facilities. In such projects, office space is usually prominently positioned and drives the overall conceptual design like, for example, the IDS Center in Minneapolis, California Plaza in Los Angeles, Reston Town Center near Washington, D.C., and Redmond Town Center in Redmond, Washington (see also the Sony Center am Potsdamer Platz, Jin Mao Tower, and University Park at MIT case studies in Chapter 8). The key issues in such projects are related to the identity of the office space within the overall scheme, the compatibility and supporting nature of the other uses, the maintenance of a strong office/corporate environment, and the amenities that will be most suitable for targeted office tenants.

Many mixed-use projects—especially those developed in the 1990s and 2000s—include moderate amounts of office space, often balancing such space with other components. Valencia Town Center Drive in Valencia, California, Addison Circle near Dallas, WestEnd City Center in Budapest, and Peabody Place in Memphis all balance office space with retail, hotel, and residential uses. In such cases, each use is more likely to stand on its own, and the design and planning of the office space must compete with other uses for its place within the project.

Office space in a balanced project often does not achieve the same identity that a freestanding office building does, which can mean the project will not appeal to tenants who want to achieve a strong corporate profile in a distinct building. But although the building itself may not have as strong an identity, its association with the larger mixed-use project can give it a brand and place identity that may benefit the space. Every local market is different, and such issues should be carefully analyzed; in many suburban markets, for example, developers of freestanding office buildings have emphasized the distinct identity they can provide a tenant, including visibility along major roadways and naming rights to the building.

Projects in which office space is a secondary use often have a completely different feel and look, and the office space is usually positioned and marketed much differently. In such projects, the surrounding office market is usually small and often made up of small tenants, and the demand for new office space is usually modest; in fact, the developer may hope to capture tenants currently in less attractive or substandard space by marketing the sense of place created by the mixed-use environment. The profile, identity, and forward-thinking image that can come with location in a mixed-use project can be valuable to community-based businesses and other small firms.

Problems can occur in projects where office space is secondary: the space lacks identity, entrances are sometimes difficult to find, and a proper corporate environment is difficult to achieve. Including small amounts of office space can be an effective option, however, especially where 1) the demand for new office space is modest and will support only a small amount of space on site, 2) it is necessary to make the best use of development potential or space that is not suitable for other uses, or 3) public policy or zoning restricts the amount of office space allowed.

Entitlements for office space are sometimes difficult to obtain in many locations, and mixed-use environments can be helpful in obtaining them. Paris Rutherford of RTKL Associates in Dallas says, "Residential and retail have frequently been the driving force behind a mixed-use project over the past decade; in many instances, these uses allowed office entitlements to be approved."

However the office space is positioned, it should be carefully developed and managed, as it offers significant upside potential to the developer. Office space traditionally achieves among the highest rents per square foot of any type of real estate and thus can be a primary source of income, profit, and capital appreciation in a mixed-use project. It can also generate demand for other uses, especially hotel and retail facilities.

Premiums for Offices in Mixed-Use Projects

Evidence suggests that quality mixed-use environments can achieve superior office rents and performance. According to Eric Smart of Bolan Smart Associates in Washington, D.C., "In general, it is reasonable to expect a rent premium of 5 to 25 percent for an office product in a well-conceived and -executed mixed-use development."

Office space in Reston Town Center in Reston, Virginia, for example, as of 2002 had achieved the highest rents in northern Virginia, above the levels of buildings in other high-profile locations even closer to the city, such as Tysons Corner. At Winter Park Village in Winter Park, Florida, the town center and retail main street design was so compelling that the developer discovered a strong demand for office space on the property, significantly exceeding the developer's expectations. And at Legacy Town Center in Plano, Texas, the developers were able to lease space in a soft office market to several major users, including Compaq Computers and Marriott, because they preferred the mixed-use environment over many more conventional competing sites.

Offices in mixed-use environments have both pros and cons. Ken Hughes of Kenneth H. Hughes Interests in Dallas says, "Office buildings close to restaurants and other shopping are more popular with many tenants, and I suspect that on average individual tenants stay in the same building longer. This is particularly true of small and medium-sized tenants." But the flip side, according to Patrick Phillips of Economics Research Associates in Washington, is that "large tenants may perceive a conflict —any use other than office may be seen as compromising their identity."[4]

Residential Uses

Residential uses often were not included in mixed-use projects of the 1970s and 1980s, but in recent years they have come to play a prominent role, accounting for a high percentage of mixed-use projects developed over the past decade. Most of the growth in residentially oriented mixed-use projects has been in the suburbs, often in the form of town centers or urban villages. Upscale and luxury condominiums in upscale downtown markets have also shown strength, as exemplified by projects such as Park Tower and River East in Chicago and numerous projects by Millennium Partners in New York, Washington, Boston, and San Francisco.

The market for residential space in mixed-use and urban environments is particularly favorable among households without children, which is expected to be a very strong segment of the housing market over the next ten years. Within this group are various segments that should be carefully studied, as each has its own pref-

Office space in a mixed-use project need not always be located in major office buildings. Much more modest facilities are suitable and marketable in some locations. For example, Celebration's downtown area, Market Street, is a traditional retail and business district modeled after those found in small American towns. The downtown area features a variety of professional and health care offices, a town hall, a post office, the Sun-Trust Bank, and Town Hall. The 18-acre (7.3-hectare) site surrounds a lakeside promenade.

Commercial space totaling 84,467 square feet (7,850 square meters) is designed to meet the needs of the community and nearby residents.

		Square Feet (Square Meters)	
Preview Center	700 Celebration Avenue	12,240	(1,140)
Town Hall	690 Celebration Avenue	2,991	(280)
Bank	650 Celebration Avenue	5,064	(470)
Seminole Building	610 Sycamore Street	32,250	(3,000)
C-1	741 Front Street	18,181	(1,690)
M-11	671 Front Street	2,678	(250)
M-1	715 Bloom Street	4,663	(435)
H-5	660 Celebration Avenue	6,400	(595)

All the commercial office space in the downtown area is equipped with security systems. The two primary office buildings are 741 Front Street and 610 Sycamore Street. The 741 Front Street building, designed by Robert A.M. Stern, is three stories high and is designed as a "typical small town office block," a building of stucco with minimal ornamentation other than a bracketed cornice over the third-story windows. It draws on its antecedents, buildings designed to mean business.

The 610 Sycamore Street building, three stories high, is the largest building in the downtown area. It is a taupe-colored stucco building, which is, in the words of master-plan architect Jaquelin Robertson, "symmetrical, vertical, formal, and repetitive, mixing classical and vernacular Gothic motifs [on] a no-nonsense traditional office block."

The Celebration Bank building, designed by Venturi, Scott Brown & Associates, is two stories high. The bank's design is an abstraction of a pure neoclassical style, typical of many turn-of-the-century banks, stripped down and flattened out—as much a building of today as yesterday.

Market Street was developed and is owned by the Celebration Company and is managed by Celebration Realty, Inc. Several prominent, internationally known architects have given each building a distinctive character, providing the variety of style found in other American towns that have evolved over the years.

In addition to the commercial office space, the downtown area offers more than 20 retail shops and restaurants and the Celebration Golf facilities. The AMC Celebration 2 theater, which can be leased for business meetings or seminars, is the first in central Florida to feature plush high-back Eurochairs and stadium-style seating.

Source: Adapted from www.CelebrationFL.com, accessed March 20, 2002.

Office space at the town center in Celebration near Orlando, Florida, is modestly scaled and oriented toward small tenants.

Courtesy of Celebration

erences. At Paseo Colorado in Pasadena, for example, residents were attracted to the urban lifestyle of the project, especially the convenient shopping and entertainment. Residents are mainly singles and couples ranging from young professionals to empty nesters. Not surprisingly, tenants of the loft-style apartments in the project are younger than the tenants of conventional units.

Analyzing Housing Markets

An analysis of any residential housing market—generally a local market—involves several operations:

- delineation of the local market area;
- analysis of that area's economic trends; and
- determination of the demand factors, such as employment and population growth trends, the political climate, disposable income, household characteristics, and the current and projected absorption rate.

In some cases, successful projects have been able to attract buyers and renters from a much larger area than competing projects.

Various supply factors must also be examined—level of current residential construction, housing inventory by product type, and current market conditions, such as vacancies, unsold inventory, prices, rents, building costs, marketability of for-sale and rental units, and mortgage defaults and foreclosures. The analysis should focus on voids in the market or underserved segments of the mar-

ket. Specifically, the analysis should assess to what degree the housing market is underserved in terms of attractive urban or village living environments, both downtown and in more suburban areas—essentially what most mixed-use projects with residential uses offer. Although mid- and high-rise apartment buildings are common in suburban areas today, few are set in pedestrian-friendly environments. The suburbs of many large metropolitan areas often are underserved in this area and should be carefully explored.

The analysis should evaluate the potential for a whole range of higher-density urban and intown housing products, including townhouses, stacked flats, live/work units, loft apartments, condominiums, walkup apartments, mid- and high-rise apartments, and, especially, residential over retail uses. The analysis should also evaluate what amenities are in most demand for these various segments. Paris Rutherford of RTKL Associates in Dallas observes, "We have found that in urban mixed-use settings, rental multifamily pioneered the market, paving the way for luxury condominiums and townhouses."

Development Issues and Options

Residential use has come to the forefront in mixed-use projects, especially in town center formats. Among the earliest and best examples of housing as a primary use in a mixed-use town center is Mizner Park in Boca Raton, which also includes retail and office uses. Residential today is usually part of a balanced program that may include hotel, retail, and/or office uses as well.

Residential uses at CityPlace in West Palm Beach are located above retail stores along main streets.

At Mockingbird Station in Dallas, located adjacent to a transit station, loft apartments rent for 20 percent more than comparable neighboring apartments.

Many apartment developers now actively seek out mixed-use environments for their projects. For example, Trammell Crow Residential's new Alexan CityCenter development involves a combination of residential and retail in the larger CityCenter Englewood mixed-use project in Englewood, Colorado. Alexan CityCenter includes 438 residential rental units in two buildings, approximately 28,000 square feet (2,600 square meters) of ground-floor, streetfront retail space, and an adjacent four-story parking structure.

The case studies in this book exemplify a wide range of housing options used successfully in mixed-use projects (see Chapter 8). CityPlace and Phillips Place offer rental apartments over retail as well as other apartments in a town center. Valencia Town Center Drive uses a main street as well but places the apartment buildings at one end of it, not over retail space, while Addison Circle uses the concept of an urban village that organizes apartments around streets and above a modest retail component. The adaptive use of historic buildings at Peabody Place and University Park at MIT creates attractive mid-rise housing products; the latter also includes new wood-frame affordable housing around a courtyard. Sony Center and Yerba Buena Center include both rental and condominium buildings; Yerba Buena Center also includes senior housing, a wide range of freestanding residential buildings, and mixed-use buildings that include residential. Only Jin Mao Tower and WestEnd City Center do not include housing at all.

A key issue to consider is whether to place residential over retail in a layered configuration. For much of the 1970s and 1980s, people generally believed that residential over retail was difficult to market, but more recent trends and evidence now suggest that it is not necessarily true. In fact, apartment units overlooking attractive main street environments, for example, can actually be rented for a premium, as they have been at Phillips Place in Charlotte, North Carolina. At Mockingbird Station in Dallas, which includes loft apartments over retail next

to a transit station, residential rents are $1.52 per square foot ($16.35 per square meter), more than 20 percent above comparable neighboring apartment rents of $1.25 per square foot ($13.45 per square meter). These premiums are the result of both the transit station and the distinctive mixed-use environment that was created.

In general, premiums for residential uses in mixed-use environments should be estimated and quantified, and extra delivery and operating costs should be assessed and carefully managed. The tradeoffs between stick-built construction versus concrete or steel should also be assessed in light of market realities. The fire code's impact on residential over retail and the associated costs should also be carefully assessed.

Several other key issues should be considered upfront: planning for privacy, noise control, and security; marketing and management, which often differ greatly from that for other components, especially for for-sale units; and financing, which also may differ greatly from that for other components.[5]

Hotel Uses

The hotel industry includes many types of hotels: budget, economy, mid-price, upscale, and luxury. For many mixed-use projects developed before the 1990s, hotels were usually of the upscale and luxury categories and often quite large, with 300 or more rooms the norm; many of them were associated with larger convention facilities. With the advent of mixed-use town centers and other smaller projects, many hotels in mixed-use projects are now smaller—sometimes of the boutique variety—and some have been developed in the mid-price segment. Seldom are budget or economy hotels developed in mixed-use projects.

Hotels are strong contributors to mixed-use projects:

- Hotels with strong brands can enhance a project's image, create a special address, or provide name recognition for the project through an established name and proven effective marketing program.
- Hotels bring 24-hour vitality to the project, attracting people and groups throughout the day and evening.
- Hotels can provide dining, entertainment, recreation, and other amenities that serve not only hotel guests but also office and residential tenants.

Hotels also can benefit greatly from a mixed-use environment, especially if pedestrian, retail, and/or entertainment facilities enhance the hotel's image and guests' experiences during their stay. Hotels also benefit directly from the demand generated by office and/or residential components of the project. Depending on the type of office tenants in adjacent buildings, the demand for hotel rooms may be quite significant from on-site office users. Similarly, high-end residential condominium residents also frequently use the hotel's services, and at least one developer working today—Millennium Partners—

The Hampton Inn at Phillips Place in Charlotte anchors one end of this main street, which also includes retail, apartment, and cinema uses.

combines luxury condominiums with luxury hotels, taking advantage of this synergy.

Analyzing Hotel Markets

The decision to build a hotel must be based on an accurate assessment of current and future economic and market conditions. First, the developer or his consultant must collect the data that will form the basis for that assessment, which entails delineating the market support area, determining the sources of lodging demand, evaluating the existing and proposed supply of lodging, evaluating the suitability of the site for development, analyzing the market demand, recommending size and amenities for the facility, and preparing projections of occupancy levels and room rates.

Both demand and supply should be carefully evaluated for a defined market area surrounding the site. First, the developer should analyze the sources of lodging demand, which may be segmented into three general categories—commercial, convention, and leisure travelers. Other elements of the mixed-use project may generate varying degrees of room-night demand, depending on their type and market orientation. For example, corporate offices in a mixed-use project, like national financial or business services firms and similar operations that bring frequent out-of-town visitors and/or require training seminars, are compatible with hotel development. Such business operations generate significant hotel demand. By comparison, local government, back-office operations, and small local businesses generate far less hotel demand. The distance from the proposed hotel to sources of travel demand (convention centers, office space, visitor attractions) as well as expenditure patterns of commercial, convention, and vacation travelers to the area should also be assessed.

The developer should then inventory existing and proposed competing facilities in the market support area, noting the size, location, brand, segment (budget, economy, mid-price, upscale, or luxury), amenities offered,

room and occupancy rates (including weekly and seasonal variations), ownership status, and strengths and weaknesses of competitors.

The proposed site itself should be analyzed for its adequacy as a hotel location. Is the site accessible from major highways or near public transportation, and is it easily accessible from potential generators of room-night demand? What are its physical characteristics, and can it functionally accommodate a hotel? What is the status of the existing infrastructure? Are the surrounding land uses now compatible with a hotel, and will they stay that way? Underserved market segments should be evaluated to determine what the potential is for a hotel on the site. What are the voids in the market, and what likely market segments can be attracted to this new facility?

At this point, if the team decides to proceed, the initial hotel size, range of amenities, room rates, and occupancy levels should be proposed for further testing. The developer must not lose sight of the overall market position of the mixed-use project as a whole. A mismatch between the market positioning of the hotel and other elements of the project can doom the hotel or even the entire project.

In general, hotels in well-conceived mixed-use projects should generate some premiums, especially as related to occupancies. It can be especially evident in weekend occupancies, which are typically quite low in full-service hotels in auto-dominated environments. Once the market potential has been established, two very important issues still need to be considered: selecting a hotel operator and evaluating the hotel's role in the mixed-use project.

Determining the Hotel's Role

Hotels are seldom the dominant use in a mixed-use project unless the project is in a resort location or near a convention center. Neither are they usually a minor use, because certain economies of scale involved in marketing and operating a typical commercial, luxury, or convention hotel—the kinds most often found in mixed-use projects—mean that these facilities usually must be at least several hundred rooms to operate effectively. A key question that should be addressed at the outset is whether the hotel is to be the crown jewel of the mixed-use project or merely a service element to attract office tenants and serve surrounding transient demand.

Hotel uses are a major part of several contemporary mixed-use developments. Copley Place in Boston, near the Hynes Convention Center, includes two high-rise hotels—a Westin and a Marriott—totaling 1,951 rooms as well as substantial office and retail space. Peachtree Center in Atlanta includes three major hotels—Hyatt, Westin, and Marriott—with more than 4,000 total rooms that serve surrounding office markets as well as conventions and the merchandise marts in the project. Northbridge in Chicago includes 2,500 hotel rooms operated by Marriott, Hilton Garden Inn, Le Méridien Hotels, Marriott Courtyard, and Homewood Suites. Pacific Place in Hong Kong has three major high-rise hotels.

Some developers have recognized the marketing strength of hotels and have used them as anchors for their overall development strategies. Millennium Partners has established a mixed-use format for hotels that combines luxury hotels such as Ritz-Carlton and Four Seasons with luxury condominiums and apartments in prime center city locations around the country. One of the company's two projects in Washington, D.C., the Ritz-Carlton Hotel and Residences Georgetown, includes a 91-room Ritz-Carlton hotel, 28 luxury residential condominiums, a 3,000-seat multiplex cinema, and 13,000 square feet (1,200 square meters) of retail space.

Seven of the ten case studies featured in this book include a hotel, and two others have plans for one. At Peabody Place, the restoration of the historic Peabody Hotel was a major catalyst for the overall project; the hotel serves as a major signature building in the development. At Yerba Buena Center, the Marriott Hotel was one of the first major elements completed following the completion of the Moscone Convention Center. At CityPlace, the hotel is planned for a site adjacent to the new convention center across a major arterial from the main part of the development. At Jin Mao Tower, the hotel sits atop the office building, providing dramatic views of Shanghai. At Valencia Town Center Drive, a hotel that includes modest conference facilities was placed near the center of the main street, while at Phillips Place an all-suite hotel with limited services anchors one end of main street. University Park includes a modest hotel at the heart of the project off the commons, and WestEnd City Center places a hotel above an internal mall. Sony Center is the only case study in this book with no plans for a hotel.

Determining the right approach, brand, and hotel operating company for a hotel in a mixed-use project must be addressed upfront. The market analysis should involve discussions with various hotel brands and/or operators to determine their level of interest in the site and the proposed project. Without a reputable brand and/or operator, a hotel is difficult to develop and

The entrance to the hotel at the Ritz-Carlton Hotel and Residences Georgetown in Washington, D.C. The project was developed by Millennium Partners and combines the Ritz-Carlton Hotel with luxury condominiums, a multiplex cinema, and retail; the project includes both historic and new buildings.

finance. A national operator of an upscale or luxury hotel, such as Hyatt, Marriott, Ritz-Carlton, Four Seasons, Westin, or Hilton, with its strong international reservations system, can provide a definite marketing advantage for a mixed-use project. Other hotel chains may be used merely to provide hotel services at a lower price and may not add a strong brand name to the project.

Whatever the role of the hotel, it is clear that if a hotel is to be included, it will necessarily become a substantial factor in the planning process; it cannot be approached as simply a minor or supporting use. The hotel must be able to tap a substantial market beyond the other uses in the project and must be properly positioned in the project for effective market appeal.

Retail Uses

Retail uses—especially when they are configured as major place-making elements such as an urban entertainment center, a retail main street, or a major retail mall—are usually critical to the success of a mixed-use project. They are often the defining element and the signature for the development—the straw that stirs the drink—and occupy the primary public place in the project, defining the character of much of the space. Retail is also the most difficult program to develop successfully.

Nearly every mixed-use project contains retail space, whether a small amount of convenience and/or service retail space ancillary to the project's major components or a regional or super regional shopping center offering a full array of shopping goods and services. A decision about the size, type, and timing of retail space to be included in the project should be based on a thorough market study conducted by an experienced retail market analyst.

Developers should be aware that retail uses are often oversized in mixed-use projects. Thus, in general it is better to err on the side of too little rather than too much retail space, as the retail space often can be expanded later. Decreasing the amount of retail space, on the other hand, is difficult to do and presents an image of failure.

Support for the retail component of a mixed-use project can come from four markets:

- the on-site market—the project's office employees, hotel guests, residents, and visitors drawn by the project's other components;
- the nearby/local market—residents and employees of the immediate area (generally within five to seven minutes of travel time) as well as visitors to the general area;
- the regional market—residents, employees, and visitors within roughly 30 minutes of travel time;
- the transient drive-by market—auto travelers passing by the development on their way to other destinations.

The Shops at North Bridge in Chicago is located in a prime location on vibrant North Michigan Avenue, one of the leading retail streets in the world. The project also includes entertainment, hotel, and office uses, and serves an affluent downtown residential, office, and transient market.

The retail stores in Redmond (Washington) Town Center draw on a substantial on-site office population as well as local residents and destination shoppers who are attracted to the activity generated by the concentration of amenities and the pedestrian-oriented environment.

Courtesy of LMN Architects

The market analysis depends on the nature of the retail component being considered. For example, if a major regional shopping mall, urban entertainment center, or main street retail project is contemplated for a suburban mixed-use project, identifying the regional market at the outset is important. This regional analysis is then followed by analyses of the local and on-site markets to determine overall development potential and options.

On the other hand, if the retail component is expected to be oriented toward service and convenience retail shops, the market analysis must focus on the local and on-site markets. In this case, retail use depends to a great degree on the project's other components; thus, the ultimate potential cannot be determined until these components are clearly defined. In general, on-site and local markets are basic generators of shoppers for commercial space in mixed-use projects, but most mixed-use projects with a significant retail component must draw from a much larger area to be viable.

Identifying On-Site and Local Markets

An estimate of potential support from the local market (within five to ten minutes of travel time) requires an evaluation of several items:

- existing and future population of office workers in the area;
- local residential population, including a careful review of the demographics of the residential market (including income levels, spending patterns, unique demographic groups such as university students, and lifestyles);
- size and spending patterns of visitors;
- extent, nature, and proximity of retail competitors in the area.

In general, an estimate of the project's on-site market support for retail uses requires a thorough analysis of each nonretail component. Although it is tempting to

apply rules of thumb or quick-and-dirty analyses to quickly determine potential on-site market support, such a process is unrealistic. Each mixed-use project is distinct, and on-site market support for retail uses can vary significantly, depending on the nature of the project and its mix of uses, the location of the project, the project's design and configuration, and the nature of the proposed retail component.

Office Workers' Spending. The extent of the on-site market depends on the type, size, character, and location of the other land uses in the mixed-use project. Support from on-site office workers can be estimated by first calculating the total number of office workers, which can be derived by the total occupied space, and then projecting the average retail expenditure per employee, broken down by expenditures for food services, apparel, and other items. Information required to project expenditures can be obtained by surveying office workers in the area to ascertain their shopping and spending patterns.

A 1995 study by the International Council of Shopping Centers found, for example, that in downtown Indianapolis, following the completion of the new 800,000-square-foot (74,350-square-meter) Circle Centre mall, office workers ate lunch during the workday an average of 4.4 times per week and that 29 percent brought lunch from home, 25 percent ate at fast-food restaurants, 17 percent bought lunch at carryouts, 13 percent ate in sit-down restaurants, 7 percent used the company cafeteria, 5 percent ate in shopping center food courts, and 3 percent used another facility. The average expenditure for purchased lunches was $5.20 per lunch.[6] Using this data, the average daily lunch expenditure per downtown office worker can be estimated as follows:

$5.20 average lunch purchase x 70% of workers who purchase lunch during workday x 88% likelihood of eating lunch at work on any given day = $3.20 average daily lunch expenditure per downtown office worker (1995 dollars).

The study also found that 12 percent of the office workers bought apparel or accessories during the previous week, for a median expenditure of $27.17. The average daily expenditure per downtown office worker was approximately $0.65 for apparel. The study also found that 49 percent of the office workers bought other nonfood items during the previous week—a median expenditure of $9.50—amounting to an average expenditure per downtown office worker of approximately $0.93 per day on other nonfood items.

Totaling these expenditures yields an average expenditure per downtown office worker of $4.78 per day in 1995 dollars or roughly $5.60 in 2003 dollars. This figure varies considerably, of course, depending on the median income of employees in the immediate area and other factors. The percentage of these sales that can be captured in the project depends on the nature and extent of the retail services offered in the project and in the surrounding area.

These figures can, however, yield a rough idea of the possibilities for retail sales that can result from on-site office space. To illustrate, if a mixed-use project includes 400,000 square feet (37,200 square meters) of leasable office space with an average of one worker per 225 square feet (20 square meters)—a figure that also varies—it would amount to approximately 1,777 office workers in the building. If the project is in the suburbs where little immediately accessible competition exists and the project includes a substantial 150,000-square-foot (14,000-square-meter) retail component, then each worker would reasonably be expected to make 50 percent or more of his workday purchases in the retail component of the project, yielding the following potential annual retail sales:

> 1,777 office workers x $5.60 average per worker per day in expenditures x 260 work days per year x 0.5 capture rate = $1,293,656 annual retail/restaurant sales for the retail component, or $8.62 per square foot ($92.75 per square meter) for a 150,000-square-foot (14,000-square-meter) retail center.

New retail centers of this size and type in the United States would generally need to generate sales of $300 per square foot ($3,230 per square meter) or more annually; thus, a 400,000-square-foot (37,200-square-meter) office building would provide a very small percentage (roughly 3 percent) of the sales needed to make a 150,000-square-foot (14,000-square-meter) shopping center viable if all these variables were to hold true. Put another way, if sales are $300 per square foot ($3,230 per square meter), the office workers can support only about 4,500 square feet (420 square meters) of space in this example. A single 400,000-square-foot (37,200-square-meter) office building is not a major source of retail sales in and of itself, but if the development includes other buildings, the office worker market can start to make a difference.

Retail/office ratios in many downtown areas are about one square foot of retail space for every 35 to 60 square feet of office space (10.8 square meters of retail space to 375 to 645 square meters of office space), according to Eric Smart of Bolan Smart Associates in Washington. Although this retail space attracts more than just office workers, the ratio still provides an informative benchmark.

Residents' Spending. Residents of a mixed-use development have very different spending patterns from office workers. Their overall retail expenditures not associated with working are much higher than those of office workers, but the share of this spending on site is likely to be much lower. Their spending also represents a much broader range of goods and services, including food service and entertainment (at night and on weekends), groceries, apparel, personal services, and all the other retail categories found in shopping centers.

The number of residential units proposed for the project as well as their sale prices or rents are key determinants in identifying support for the retail segment from the project's residents. Proposed unit sales or rental prices can be used to estimate incomes and buying power. Estimating annual household retail expenditures and applying a capture rate yields an estimate of sales per square foot that can be derived from on-site residential spending. For example, a development of 400 occupied residential units with annual retail/entertainment expenditures of roughly $15,000 per unit and a retail component that captures 20 percent of the sales yields the following result:

> 400 residential units x $15,000 per year retail spending x 0.20 = $1,200,000 annual retail sales for the retail component, or $8.00 per square foot ($86 per square meter) for a 150,000-square-foot (14,000-square-meter) retail center.

This amount represents 2.7 percent of sales in a shopping center with sales of $300 per square foot ($3,230 per square meter) annually, a very small part of the market necessary to support the retail component. If, however, the project contains substantially more residential space, household income and expenditures are higher, or a significant number of other housing units are close by, especially within easy walking distance, this on-site/local market can start to add up. Capture rates, however, go down as the distance from the project increases.

Hotel Guests' Spending. The type of hotel and guest mix and proposed room rates are key factors in determining on-site support for a retail component from hotel guests. The type of hotel—whether it is a convention hotel serving primarily conventioneers, a commercial hotel serving primarily business travelers, or a resort hotel serving primarily leisure travelers—affects consumers' spending patterns. For example, according to D.K. Shifflet and Associates in Falls Church, Virginia, expenditures for business travelers in the United States during 2001 broke down as follows: 48.1 percent for lodging, 26.5 percent for food, 10.8 percent for shopping, 8.3 percent for entertainment, and 6.2 percent for miscellaneous purchases. Expenditures for leisure travelers broke down quite differently: 24.6 percent for lodging, 29.6 percent for food, 19.6 percent for shopping, 19.8 percent for en-

Birkdale Village in Huntersville, North Carolina, near Charlotte, features main street–style retail with tenants such as Chico's, the Gap, the Yard Shop, and Planet Grill as well as a 16-screen cinema, offices, and apartments.

Courtesy of Birkdale Village

tertainment, and 6.2 percent for miscellaneous purchases.[7] Leisure travelers clearly have a higher propensity to spend money on shopping and entertainment.

Convention travelers have their own special spending patterns, likely somewhere between those for business and those for leisure travelers. The International Association of Convention and Visitor Bureaus has collected data on convention delegates' spending per day and found that in 2001, delegates' average daily spending included $34.00 on hotel food and beverage, $31.00 on other food and beverage, and $25.00 in retail stores.[8] Thus, a mixed-use project that includes a 300-room hotel with an average occupancy rate of 65 percent and average expenditures outside the hotel per occupied room per day of $56.00 (with the retail component capturing 30 percent of these sales) would yield:

300 hotel rooms x 365 days per year x 0.65 occupancy rate x $56 average spending per day x 0.30 capture rate = $1,195,740 annual retail/restaurant sales for the retail component, or $7.97 per square foot ($85.75 per square meter) for a 150,000-square-foot (14,000-square-meter) retail center.

These figures represent about 2.7 percent of sales in a 150,000-square-foot (14,000-square-meter) shopping center with sales of $300 per square foot ($3,230 per square meter), again a very small part of the market necessary to support this amount of retail space.

One factor to consider is the level of restaurants, entertainment, and retail services offered in the hotel itself, which will affect the potential for such services in the restaurant/retail/entertainment component of the project. Most first-class hotels have their own restaurants and bars, but some mixed-use projects have successfully incorporated limited-service hotels and then provided restaurants nearby to create a package closer to full service for the hotel. For example, at Phillips Place, the Hampton Inn does not include a restaurant; thus, a first-class restaurant was located adjacent to the hotel entrance

in a main street setting, with several other restaurants farther down the street as added amenities.

In some cases, hotels can serve as major markets for retail uses in mixed-use projects. For example, Copley Place in Boston includes two upscale hotels, major multilevel malls, and office space. It offers 1,951 hotel rooms in a Westin and a Marriott that cater to generally upscale travelers. The hotels generate substantial retail sales for the center and were major market factors in the retail leasing program for the project.

Identifying the Regional Market

The regional market for a mixed-use project's retail component, if it is to be a regional competitor, comprises residents, workers, and visitors within approximately 20 to 30 minutes of travel time. Determining the potential regional market requires an analysis of the competition, population data, and buying power and sales potential in the defined trade area. The ability of a mixed-use project's retail component to tap the larger regional market and compete with other shopping centers requires that the retail component be sufficiently sized and tenanted to function as a destination, drawing shoppers from a large geographic area.

The ability of the project and its retail component to function as a destination depends on its location and the proximity of major competitors, the design and character of the retail component, and the overall sense of place that can be created. In general, modestly sized retail components in mixed-use projects can attract regional markets if they offer something unusual. In the early 2000s, for example, many mixed-use projects configured as suburban town centers are in a favorable position to draw a regional market with 200,000 or fewer square feet (18,600 square meters), as these kinds of retail environments are in demand and are still relatively rare. (In contrast, an average regional mall is around 550,000 square feet [51,000 square meters], a super regional mall just over 1 million square feet [93,000 square meters].) People will go out of their way to visit an attractive main street retail environment that includes a cinema, a variety of restaurants, attractive shops, and a strong sense of place.

To identify regional market support requires a detailed demographic and market analysis, including an analysis of the size of the existing population within one, three, and five miles (1.6, 4.8, and 8 kilometers), projections of future population and employment growth, and the composition of the population according to age, income, and size of household units. The size of the population in the immediate market area influences the amount of retail space that can be supported, while the composition of the population indicates the type of retail tenants needed or wanted in the market area.

Although the development of new retail space in a trade area does not create new buying power or new consumers, it can result in changes in consumers' purchasing behavior and a redistribution of their retail expenditures. Notes Ken Hughes of Kenneth H. Hughes Interests in Dallas, "Mixed-use retail can stimulate new sales from the existing customer base if the environment is unique." Thus, mixed-use retail can and often does tap unserved demand, even in relatively mature retail markets.

The Retail Concept and Tenant Mix

Beyond assessing the size and character of the market, it is also important to assess the competition and to identify voids in the market. Retail concepts for mixed-use projects vary widely. CityPlace in West Palm Beach, for example, includes a major main street–style regional shopping center, while WestEnd City Center in Budapest includes an enclosed regional mall. Jin Mao Tower includes a multilevel mall that is only partially occupied; Phillips Place and Valencia Town Center Drive include modestly sized main street retail and entertainment uses in a suburban setting that could be characterized as lifestyle centers. Peabody Place and Yerba Buena Center feature streetfront retail shops as well as major urban entertainment centers in their own buildings in downtown settings, and Sony Center includes a major entertainment component in a downtown setting.

Retailers increasingly are considering mixed-use and main street environments as alternatives to more conventional shopping centers. Such well-known retailers as Pottery Barn, Restoration Hardware, and the Gap have been actively seeking out such locations, and even some department stores have pursued this strategy. Macy's has a store at CityPlace in West Palm Beach, and Bon Marché recently opened a store in the Redmond Town Center in Redmond, Washington. Dan Edelman, chair and CEO of the Seattle-based division of Federated Department Stores, says that "Redmond Town Center's attractive open design and location will enhance Bon Marché's offerings."

Retail stores in mixed-use projects seldom fit neatly into one of the categories of shopping centers: neighborhood, community, power, regional, and super regional. It is perhaps more useful to describe the types of retail goods and services most often found in these develop-

A corner bakery and café at Southlake Town Square in Southlake, Texas. Retail concepts in mixed-use projects frequently rely heavily on food and impulse purchases.

ments. Retail categories overlap, and mixed-use projects frequently contain more than one type of retailing.

Service and Convenience Retail. Service retail is generally oriented to consumers on site or nearby; it features personal and business services (such as dry cleaners, travel agencies, banks) and certain modest eating and dining establishments. It should be located so as to require little time or effort to visit or shop. Service retail elements can be small, totaling 10,000 to 25,000 square feet (930 to 2,325 square meters) of gross building area. The target market for service retail comprises mainly captive shoppers, primarily those within five minutes of the project. Service retail in a mixed-use setting is generally developed at grade (the ground floor of office buildings) or along a main street or concourse, frequently in a nonprime location.

Convenience retail goods (food, drugs, liquor, sundries) are generally bought at the location the purchaser can most easily reach. Oriented toward captive and nearby market segments, convenience retail, like service retail, is highly sensitive to location, as few patrons go out of their way to find such goods. Typically, convenience retail is anchored by a grocery store or drugstore, and it includes smaller shops selling comparison goods (such as books, records, accessories) and eating and drinking establishments.

The target market for convenience retail goods comprises mainly captive and drive-by shoppers, primarily those within ten minutes of the project. Location plays an important role, along with strong anchors (such as a good independent or chain grocery) to draw destination shoppers, particularly if the store's merchandise lines are not well represented in the market.

Comparison Retail. Comparison retail goods (clothing, appliances, jewelry) are generally purchased after some shopping around. Comparison retail space is typically anchored by one or more major department stores and complemented by specialty and lifestyle retailers with comparable merchandise and price-point orientation. It features goods such as general merchandise, apparel, furniture, and other specialty items.

Comparison retail facilities are typically much larger than service and convenience retail formats and can reach 300,000 square feet (28,000 square meters) and up. The target market for comparison retail goods comprises mainly destination shoppers, primarily those within 20 minutes of the project.

Increasingly, comparison retail is found in big-box stores. A key issue facing mixed-use projects today is how to incorporate such big-box retailers as stores become ever larger and require dedicated parking. But Wal-Mart has built a 134,000-square-foot (12,500-square meter) store at CityCenter Englewood in Englewood, Colorado, a mixed-use town center that includes residential space as well. Wal-Mart anchors the retail portion of the mixed-use development.

The design of the attractive new store includes red brick, landscaping, and a public art wall. "As a result of our alliance with the city of Englewood, we have designed a store that fits the architectural theme of City-Center and the community," says Daphne Davis, community affairs director of Wal-Mart Stores, Inc. "Wal-Mart has integrated itself positively into our transit-oriented development," adds Bob Simpson, Englewood community development director. "The scale of the building, the color scheme, the use of landscaping, and the integration into the street pattern all blend positively with the rest of the project site. We believe this relationship has produced a very important partner for our community." CityCenter, site of the former Cinderella City shopping mall, is being redeveloped as a transit-oriented development to include retail, residential, civic, and cultural elements with an emphasis on light rail as a major transportation force.

In mixed-use projects, comparison retail space is often the cornerstone land use, thus requiring ample frontage, access, and parking. It anchors mixed-use projects in strong retail markets, providing support for other higher-density development such as apartments, office buildings, and hotels in response to market demand.

Specialty, Lifestyle, and Entertainment Retail. Specialty and lifestyle retail refers to distinctive merchandise presented in a unique way; it increasingly is the driving retail concept behind many main street and town center projects. Such shops offer one-of-a-kind merchandise (such as a fine luggage shop) or traditional goods and services presented in an interesting format (such as a

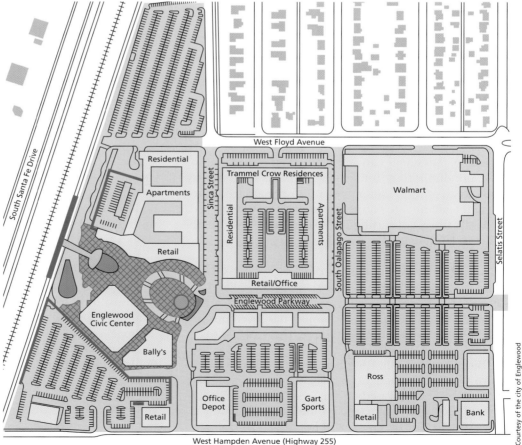

CityCenter Englewood in Englewood, Colorado, is a town center with a main street and civic buildings, but it also incorporates several big-box retail stores, among them Wal-Mart, Ross, and Office Depot.

Courtesy of the city of Englewood

Mixed-use projects frequently include an unusual tenant mix that involves restaurants, entertainment, recreation, and service, both traditional and specialty retail, and even supermarkets. Paseo Colorado in Pasadena, for example, features 565,000 square feet (52,500 square meters) of retail stores, dining, and entertainment plus 387 upscale residential units and office components. Anchored by Pacific Theatres's Paseo 14, Gelson's Super Market, Amadeus Spa & Salon, a newly renovated Macy's, and the first West Coast location of Equinox Fitness Club, Paseo Colorado features 60 distinct specialty retail shops. Nearly three-quarters of the village's retailers are new to Pasadena. The complex is located along three city blocks in the heart of historic Pasadena.

The retail strategy for Paseo Colorado was complicated by the city of Pasadena's political and financial interests in the adjacent retail areas of Old Pasadena, the Playhouse District, and Lake Street. The city's mandate to TrizecHahn was, in effect, provide an active and successful mix of retailers, but do not steal from other Pasadena venues. In addition, the competition facing Paseo Colorado included two successful regional malls in nearby communities. And although Old Pasadena was a proven success for retailers, the Paseo Colorado location had not been successful, and the concept of an urban village was somewhat new to the retail community.

The developers of Paseo Colorado, however, could look to four complementary market strengths to offset these constraints: a large primary trade area (941,000 persons within a radius of 7.5 miles [12 kilometers]); a daytime office market within walking distance; a visitor/tourist market (including the adjacent Pasadena Conference Center); and the planned on-site residential market and a growing nearby residential base. Playing to these multiple markets, Paseo Colorado has pieced together a roster of tenants that creates an active, mixed-use destination while not duplicating (or stealing) tenants from nearby retail areas. Macy's, the one tenant to remain from the original mall, invested approximately $1 million to remodel its store, converting the space from a discount outlet to a full-line store.

One of the strengths of Paseo Colorado is food. Given the market's demand (workers, visitors, and local and on-site residents), food service has been elevated to anchor status at Paseo Colorado. The project has seven upscale destination-type restaurants, ranging from 10,000 to 12,000 square feet (930 to 1,115 square meters), including Bice, Border Grill, P.F. Chang's China Bistro, and Tokyo Wako, a Japanese steakhouse. The restaurants have been strategically located on the second level, offering views of the Civic Center, the mountains, and, closer to home, Garfield Promenade and Fountain Court. Similarly, the food court is located on the second level, near

Courtesy of Trizec Properties

Paseo Colorado draws on four primary markets: a large and affluent primary trade area, a substantial daytime office market, a growing nearby residential base and an on-site residential population, and a busy visitor/tourist market.

the movie theaters. The food court eateries have indoor seating in each shop and a common outdoor seating area overlooking the Paseo. Visibility and access are critical to the success of second-floor restaurants. At Paseo Colorado, access is gained by several grand stairways and visible second-level plazas as well as by multiple elevators and escalators throughout the project. The design in this case creates curiosity, luring pedestrians up, and several of the spaces offer attractive vistas as well.

Complementing the food service is the cinema, the largest in the Pasadena area, with state-of-the-art features such as stadium seating, high-back "loveseat" chairs with retractable armrests, curved screens, and digitally enhanced sound. The theater also goes a step beyond the norm in food service, offering pizza made on site and "Pink's famous hot dogs, a Hollywood legend."

Retail shops at Paseo Colorado include many national and regional tenants, among them Ann Taylor Loft, Sam Goody, and Brookstone. But TrizecHahn has also brought in a variety of lesser-known and distinctive retailers such as Japanese Weekend Maternity, A Snail's Pace running shop, and Elements Furniture and Gifts. There is no bookstore at Paseo Colorado, as the major booksellers are already located in nearby Old Pasadena. In the end, only three of Paseo Colorado's tenants came from adjacent Pasadena retail areas: two relocated because they were in undersized spaces where they could not expand, and one opened a second location at Paseo Colorado. ■

boutique or theme restaurant). Specialty centers share certain common elements:

- an unusual setting or striking architecture;
- a strong food statement, with restaurants replacing traditional retail anchors;
- an emphasis on gifts and crafts, often with a distinctive local or regional orientation;
- a visual openness designed to create clear, interesting vistas and strong store-to-store sight lines; and
- a large number of relatively small shops (400 to 2,000 square feet [37 to 185 square meters]).

Typically, such centers have no traditional retail anchors. Rather, the emphasis is on merchandising depth—several tenants in the same category. The specialty image can be carried out through merchandising (primarily in apparel, household, and specialty goods, food, and entertainment), architectural design, and overall shopping ambience. Centers can range from 40,000 to more than 300,000 square feet (3,700 to 28,000 square meters). The target market for specialty retail goods ranges from captive and drive-by patrons to destination shoppers drawn to the center's special character from a wide regional area.

Specialty retail shopping provides the focal point for certain mixed-use projects through evocative architecture and a careful positioning of key project components around central places (such as a main street or shopping gallery). For many mixed-use projects, this retail element creates a distinct identity in a crowded market. Some mixed-use projects use relatively unusual retail elements, such as temporary farmers' markets, to create lifestyle features and draws. Santana Row in San Jose, for example, incorporates a farmers' market two days per week.

Finally, entertainment tenants, discussed in greater detail in the following section, increasingly can define a center. Mixed-use retail is increasingly about restaurants, cinemas, and/or media retailers, including bookstores such as Barnes & Noble and Borders, media outlets such as Virgin Megastore, and entertainment corporation stores such as the Disney Store and Warner Bros.

Development Issues and Options

The market analysis for the retail component of a mixed-use project must carefully address the location, accessibility, and configuration of the retail element. It is critical that the location, design, and size of the retail component be compatible with projected market support. For example, a major retail component that is expected to draw heavily from the regional market and to a lesser extent from the on-site and local markets must be located and designed so that it is highly visible, readily identifiable, and easily accessible, especially by auto, with adequate parking. It often will serve as the project's focal point and should meet or exceed the visibility and accessibility of competing regional shopping centers. But a mixed-use retail center must also offer something different, or it is just another mall. Thus, most mixed-use developers include retail components that offer something relatively unusual for the market, either tenants or the shopping environment, and frequently a more urban environment.

If substantial residential uses are included in the project, the retail strategy should seek to include retail services to support that residential population, as the presence of such services can be an important marketing tool for the residential component. Grocery stores, drugstores, dry cleaners, and hair salons are particularly important. Both Paseo Colorado in Pasadena and Pentagon Row in Arlington, Virginia, for example, include supermarkets that serve as major amenities for the large number of apartments in these two projects.

A major retail component should be included in a mixed-use project only if a separate and definite market exists for the retail portion apart from the project's other uses. The retail use must have its own demand and make

Santana Row in San Jose includes a main street retail/entertainment component of 445,000 square feet (41,342 square meters), with a variety of retail streetfront designs. The project, built on the former site of the defunct Town and Country Mall, also includes 255 rental apartments and a 213-room hotel in its first phase.

Courtesy of Federal Realty Investment Trust

sense in and of itself. It must be able to stand on its own and should not be included merely to obtain higher office, apartment, or hotel rents or occupancy rates. The opportunity to create a ready-made market for major retail space from other project components in a mixed-use project is often overstated. Jin Mao Tower in Shanghai, for example, is the world's tallest building and includes both office and hotel uses above a retail mall that is largely vacant.

If done correctly and creatively, successful mixed-use retail projects can create very attractive real estate values and investment returns. The mixed-use retail facility can benefit from a longer selling day for more peak period sales, and from sustained demand from captive shoppers on site. If done incorrectly, the retail element may severely underperform compared with its competitors. In the end, the retail market analysis and programming is critical for the overall project; the success of the retail

Main Street Retailing and Entertainment at Easton Town Center

A major example of the main street retail trend is Easton Town Center in Columbus, Ohio. This roughly 1.5 million-square-foot (140,000-square-meter) retail/entertainment complex is located about eight miles (13 kilometers) from the CBD but within city limits and within the I-270 beltway. Easton Town Center is a destination project with a main street that includes restaurants, a brew pub, a comedy club, a book superstore, a fitness center, a home furnishings store, a cybercafé, more than 50 upscale boutiques and shops, and a 30-screen cineplex. A centrally located town square completes the village theme, providing an identity for the project and a gathering spot for social activities; a new fashion district was recently added that doubled the original retail square footage of the development. The project also includes two hotels, office space in the second phase, and a luxury apartment and townhouse community called Easton Commons.

Easton Town Center offers customers a variety of ways to spend their leisure time. As a lifestyle center, it has no true anchors. Shops are laid out around a town square and along urban streets. The development team wanted not just a main street, but a *Columbus* main street. They sought out local restaurateurs to develop new concepts based on local preferences; two that have succeeded are the Ocean Club and Brio Tuscan Grille, serving seafood and Italian fare, respectively. Life Time Fitness, a Minneapolis-based health club, leased its own 95,000-square-foot (8,800-square-meter), two-story building to house its facilities: aerobic studios, a sauna, fitness equipment, two swimming pools, two basketball courts, squash courts, climbing walls, and a child-care facility.

Source: ULI Development Case Studies, www.uli.org, accessed March 20, 2003. ∎

Easton Town Center in Columbus, Ohio, is one of the largest town center/main street developments in the country, with more than 1.5 million square feet (140,000 square meters) of retail and entertainment space. Office space is located on the second level of several buildings, and residential and hotel uses are located at the edges of the development.

At CityPlace in West Palm Beach, the 20-screen Muvico Theater is located on the second level of this town center. The theater can be accessed from a grand staircase at ground level or directly from the second level of the adjacent parking structure.

space, because it is usually the most prominent part of the mixed-use project, is essential if the project as a whole is to succeed.

Entertainment Uses

Often the key factors affecting the success of a mixed-use project are related to the sense of place and identity that the project can create. Entertainment facilities—cinemas, restaurants, clubs, and bars—serve this objective well, and they have become key ingredients in many mixed-use projects. Less often, more elaborate and unusual entertainment may be included, such as amusement rides, commercial entertainment venues, and even arenas and stadiums.

The process of analyzing the potential for entertainment uses is very similar to that for retail, but several major issues need to be carefully considered. Patrick Phillips of Economic Research Associates in Washington, D.C., says, "The expenditures for entertainment are highly discretionary, and consumers can be very fickle. Moreover, the fit-out costs are high relative to potential rents, and operating characteristics can be complex. One strong benefit for entertainment uses is that they offer great opportunities for shared parking."

Entertainment uses can be integrated with general retail or can be included in a designated entertainment facility. For example, Yerba Buena Center (see Chapter 8) includes Metreon, an urban entertainment center jointly developed by Sony and Millennium Partners/WDG. Located at the heart of the project, Metreon has surpassed attendance expectations, with estimates of 8 million to 10 million visitors for its first year of operation. The 350,000-square-foot (32,500-square-meter) complex includes themed amusements based on the work of well-known authors, games, one-of-a-kind retail tenants such as Sony Style and a Discovery Channel store, several

restaurants, and a 16-theater cineplex offering a Sony IMAX theater.

Phillips Place in Charlotte (see Chapter 8), on the other hand, uses a more modest approach, placing a multiplex theater at one end of a main street and a variety of restaurants along the street.[9]

Restaurants, Bars, and Live Entertainment Clubs

The most common entertainment uses found in mixed-use projects are restaurants, bars, and clubs. Restaurants, bars, and live entertainment clubs can be primary anchors in the retail/entertainment component of a mixed-use project; they frequently make up a larger percentage of the tenants. At Phillips Place in Charlotte, for example, restaurants occupy 25 percent of the 126,739 square feet (11,800 square meters) of retail/entertainment space, and the cinema occupies an additional 24 percent. With nearly 50 percent of the space, these uses are clearly the anchors for this development; they serve the important purpose of drawing people on evenings and weekends.

A broad range of restaurants can position the development as a dining destination that customers will return to over and over. Reston Town Center in Reston, Virginia, for example, has 18 restaurants and food outlets ranging from cafés to fine dining. Highly regarded restaurants can become major signatures for a mixed-use development. Reston Town Center became a restaurant destination when Clyde's of Georgetown, a leading Washington, D.C., restaurant, located in Reston Town Center. Atago Green Hills incorporates one of the finest Japanese vegetarian restaurants in Tokyo.

Live entertainment venues in commercial establishments are also popular draws, but they must be carefully controlled. The major concern when live entertainment is included is to ensure that the sounds and festive nature do not detract from residential, hotel, and office uses. These uses must be carefully placed and soundproofed to avoid such conflicts.

Regal's theater complex serves as a main anchor for New Roc City, ensuring crowds on weekends and in the evenings, but the project also includes the Huguenot Tower Space Shot Ride.

Cinemas

Cinemas also draw people to the mixed-use project on evenings and weekends; increasingly, they are viewed as anchors for the retail component of a mixed-use project. According to Patrick Phillips of Economics Research Associates in Washington, D.C., "Despite their challenges, cinemas are the single best generator of repeat visitation by regional residents because of Hollywood's marketing muscle."

The trend for such complexes has been toward multiplex cinemas, frequently including eight to 24 screens or more. This arrangement creates a continuous flow of people into and out of the cinema, with movies starting as frequently as every five or ten minutes, depending on the size of the complex. Abacoa Town Center in Jupiter, Florida, for example, includes a 16-screen Crown Theatre complex as well as a one-acre (0.4-hectare) theater green with an open-air stage. Of the ten case studies in this book, seven include cinemas. At Phillips Place, the cinema anchors one end of the main street, and at City-Place, the cinema, located on a second level, is a key anchor and a major attraction for the project. Peabody Place, Valencia Town Center Drive, and Yerba Buena Center use cinemas to anchor major entertainment facilities or zones that include restaurants.

IMAX theaters are also being used in mixed-use projects, usually together with conventional cinema complexes, but their installation should be considered carefully. Notes Patrick Phillips, "Developers and owners are

fairly skeptical these days about commercial IMAX. The track record has not been strong, mainly because of the lack of sufficient movies in the format." IMAX theaters are quite large and tall and thus can be difficult to position in a mixed-use project. A recent example is the Regal IMAX Theater at New Roc City, a 1.2 million-square-foot (111,500-square-meter) mixed-use project in downtown New Rochelle, New York. The IMAX features 380 seats with a six-story screen and a 12,000-watt, six-channel high-fidelity motion picture sound system. The IMAX offers technology in which realistic three-dimensional images are projected onto the giant IMAX screen. The project also features 18 state-of-the-art theaters, all with stadium-style seating. The theater lobby also offers a café for dining.

Amusements and Rides

In some cases, the entertainment component is quite elaborate—even including amusement rides—and may become a defining element for the project. For example, in addition to cinemas, New Roc City offers several amusement attractions. The Sports Plus entertainment center features the Huguenot Tower Space Shot Ride, other thrill rides, simulators, laser tag, bumper cars, climbing walls, a Kidz Zone, and two ice skating rinks. Birthday party packs and special group packages are available.

In other situations, the entertainment may have a more educational focus with the use of interactive learning technology. At Sony Center am Potsdamer Platz in Berlin, for example, Sony has contributed to the entertainment facilities in the form of the Music Box, whose theme is music in all its variations. Using cutting-edge technology, the Music Box offers patrons a variety of interactive and informative activities, including the Beatles Yellow Submarine Adventure, in which participants ride in a simulated-motion submarine. Standing in front of a series of screens, riders can try conducting the Berlin Philharmonic Orchestra. A harp makes music with jets of running water instead of strings, and a recording studio brings a virtual Beethoven back to life. The focus is on having fun in an environment that is both stimulating and educational, using the latest in computer technologies.

Numerous firms now offer family entertainment that includes interactive games. North Bridge—a 2.1 million-square-foot (195,000-square-meter), nine-block mixed-use development in Chicago, includes DisneyQuest, an indoor interactive theme park that combines Disney themes with technologies such as virtual reality. Similarly, Centro Ybor in Tampa includes GameWorks, which combines a restaurant/bar with interactive games. And at the Stacks at the Waterfront, a $300 million industrial reuse project now rising on the Monongahela River directly across from Pittsburgh, a Dave and Busters is planned, combining a restaurant/bar with interactive games.

Arenas and Stadiums

In a few cases, arenas and stadiums are major parts of mixed-use developments or districts. Sports arenas and stadiums are frequently used to create or stimulate a lively mixed-use, round-the-clock atmosphere for downtowns, but this effect does not always happen naturally and planners have become more proactive in the use of mixed-use districts around these facilities. In many cases, these stadiums and arenas take on mixed-use characteristics of their own.

For example, the San Diego Padres's new ballpark, scheduled to open in 2004, will become part of a ballpark district featuring offices, hotels, and residences in downtown San Diego. MCI Arena in Washington, D.C., is located downtown and includes both stores and restaurants open to the street. Oriole Park at Camden Yards, adjacent to downtown Baltimore, includes several historic buildings that now house office space overlooking the field. The Victory, a project adjacent to downtown Dallas, includes an arena, American Airlines Center. AutoZone Park, a minor league baseball park in Memphis, includes plans for a surrounding mixed-use district.

Although stadiums and arenas are large and often freestanding to some degree—and can dominate surrounding uses—they can significantly and positively affect surrounding areas if they are carefully sited and sensitively designed. Sports arenas and stadiums today typically have a large seating capacity and the flexibility to accommodate a variety of events apart from sports, from circuses to rock concerts. At a minimum, arenas and stadiums can serve to acquaint a larger public with a given mixed-use project or district, but they can also generate

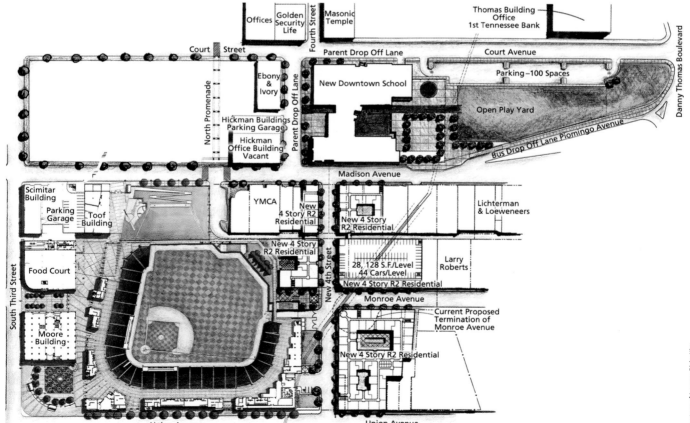

Plans for AutoZone Park in Memphis, a minor league baseball field, include a surrounding mixed-use ballpark district.

The International Spy Museum is a featured use at the 800 F Street Historic Row development in Washington, D.C. The project, combining old and new buildings, includes 20,000 square feet (1,860 square meters) of residential space, 54,468 square feet (5,060 square meters) of office space, and 55,956 square feet (5,200 square meters) of ground-level museum and retail space.

revenue for hotels, retail stores, and restaurants in a mixed-use district.

Several older mixed-use projects also incorporate arenas, such as CNN Center in Atlanta, which contains a 16,000-seat arena connected to office, hotel, retail, and entertainment space. Lexington Center in Lexington, Kentucky, includes an arena, a convention center, and hotel and retail uses. The Rupp Arena there plays a particularly important role, because it is the home of the University of Kentucky Wildcats basketball team and has been the site for many nationally televised basketball games and tournaments. The arena draws thousands of visitors annually, adding a great deal to the project's identity.

The facility should be in use throughout the week and most of the year. Thus, stadiums that are used principally for football on weekends in the fall are not a good fit for a mixed-use project or district.[10]

Cultural Uses

Increasingly, cultural uses such as performing arts centers, museums, religious facilities, or art in the built environment are developed in mixed-use projects, usually requiring an innovative approach that may involve subsidies for the uses. Cultural facilities can give the development a strong identity and prestigious image that money often cannot buy. Cultural uses often do not generate enough revenue to cover operating expenses and debt service, however, and thus often require substantial support from the public, institutional, and philanthropic sectors if they are to be financially feasible.

To manage and finance the development of cultural elements, innovative partnerships are frequently forged among private developers, public agencies, and arts organizations. The inclusion of an arts component in a mixed-use project usually depends on the kind of deal that can be worked out. Generally, it is almost universally

agreed that cultural facilities can provide substantial amenities, identity, and drawing power for a mixed-use project. The tough part to agree on is how much money can be devoted to cultural uses from the project's budget, if any, and how much must come from outside sources. Moreover, raising money from outside sources is generally difficult and time-consuming.

To incorporate an arts component into a mixed-use project often involves strong leadership by a single individual dedicated to the goal, and it usually involves a longer period for predevelopment and intensive negotiations among the developer, the public agency, and the arts sector. In some cases, the public sector actually initiates a mixed-use project with cultural facilities because it can use a well-located property that it controls and can require that certain cultural elements be incorporated in the overall plan (Yerba Buena Center in San Francisco and California Plaza in Los Angeles, for example). In some larger projects, the arts component includes both performing arts facilities and major museums.

Yerba Buena Center (see Chapter 8) is perhaps the leading example of major cultural facilities used as strong anchors for mixed-use development. Yerba Buena Center includes the San Francisco Museum of Modern Art, the nonprofit Yerba Buena Center for the Arts, which hosts the productions of local arts groups as well as national and international artists and performers, Jewish and Mexican museums, and the African American Cultural Institute.

When major facilities are involved, the developer must take a long, hard look at the situation before proceeding.

Many developers who might be interested in initiating such projects simply do not have the resources; this type of development requires substantial front-end investment, complex phasing, and intricate management systems once the project is open. A developer must be prepared to defer immediate returns for longer-term rewards, some of which may be difficult to quantify. Real estate organizations therefore often prefer to concentrate on more traditional opportunities. The developers who do get involved with arts-inclusive projects tend to be large, multitalented organizations that have gained the requisite expertise through their work on smaller mixed-use projects or elaborate adaptive use projects.

Any developer who initiates such a project is likely to exhibit strong entrepreneurial leadership. Developers may be most open to the challenge of doing something grand and magnificent when it can be considered a capstone to their careers. In such situations, [when] the demands of return on investment still must pencil out, developers tend to be more willing to include a range of amenities that may not be immediately profitable.[11]

Performing Arts Facilities

Performing arts facilities are especially good at creating a strong positive image for a mixed-use project and for drawing patrons on evenings and weekends. They add activity and excitement to mixed-use projects during these key time periods, and they are major place makers that can add an aura to a project that is hard to match. They can be costly to construct, however, and private developers should carefully assess the costs and benefits if they are expected to cover a portion of development costs.

CityPlace in West Palm Beach, for example, holds events in the Harriet Himmel Gilman Theater for Cultural and Performing Arts in a restored church. The Centre for the Arts at Mizner Park features a new state-of-the-art amphitheater and concert green accommodating 5,000 people and an 1,800-seat acoustically superior concert hall. AOL Time Warner Center in New York includes Jazz at Lincoln Center, with space that will house "the first and only performance spaces in the world created specifically for jazz." The new spaces include a concert theater of 1,100 seats, a 600-seat performance atrium, a 140-seat jazz café, recording studios, and classroom space. The development's proximity to Lincoln Center made this cultural use a natural fit.

Hollywood & Highland in Hollywood, California, includes the Kodak Theatre, permanent home of the Academy Awards® ceremonies and host of numerous

other events, including American Ballet Theater productions, Sesame Street Live, the Moscow Ballet, Blues Clues, performances by popular entertainers, and numerous nationally televised specials. Kodak Theatre has featured artistic performances for the Chinese, Korean, Persian, Armenian, and Russian communities. Despite the prestige and the events the theater has brought and its retail and hotel uses, however, Hollywood & Highland has not been financially successful.

Outdoor performing arts facilities such as Abacoa Town Center in Jupiter, Florida, and Reston Town Center in Reston, Virginia, are also increasingly popular. Although generally much more modest in scope and cost, such centers can add considerable life and value to a project, drawing large numbers of visitors to the site.[12]

Museums

Although performing arts venues are usually better for drawing people during evenings and weekends, museums are stronger during daytime hours, especially on weekends. Museums in mixed-use projects are usually not major institutions, although there are exceptions. California Plaza at Bunker Hill in Los Angeles, for example, incorporates the Museum of Contemporary Art and the Bella Lewitzky Dance Gallery, Mizner Park includes the 44,000-square-foot (4,100-square-meter) Boca Raton Museum of Art, and Yerba Buena Center incorporates more than 20 museums and galleries, including the San Francisco Museum of Modern Art, a major institution.

In general, smaller and/or specialized museums are the most likely candidates for mixed-use projects. An example is South Street Seaport in New York, which incorporates a seaport museum and also stands as an important historical artifact through preservation of the last vestiges of a 19th-century port that helped make New York a world center of commerce. The South Street Seaport Museum, chartered by the state of New York, is acquiring and restoring landmark buildings and sailing ships to create a major maritime museum.

Hollywood & Highland includes the new Kodak Theatre, seen here during construction, that is now the home of the annual Academy Awards® ceremony.

Peabody Place Museum and Gallery in Memphis offers Chinese art and sculpture—from the developer's personal collection—extending back as far as 2,000 years. The collection also includes Judaica, European contemporary art glass, a mineral collection including a 75 million-year-old bird fossil and a petrified dinosaur egg, and Italian mosaics, boxes, and obelisks. Roppongi Hills in Tokyo (see the accompanying feature box) is another example of a small museum.

Religious Facilities

Religious facilities are also occasionally incorporated into mixed-use projects. The site of Atago Green Hills in Tokyo was originally owned by a temple that included a complex of historic buildings needing repair. The temple negotiated a deal with Mori Building Company, allowing it to develop two high-rise towers—one office and one residential—while preserving and incorporating the temples into the overall site design. Although the towers dominate the skyline, the temple buildings are defining elements at street level, and they have actually become more visible and more prominent in the neighborhood as a result of the development and restoration. They draw people to the project from the surrounding areas. Kuala Lumpur City Centre includes the new 6,000-person-capacity Asy-Syakirin Mosque. Skilled Uzbekistan craftsmen were employed to render intricate carvings and calligraphy on the interior of the building and the internal facade of the dome. At Riverplace in Minneapolis, a historic church near the center of the site was restored and still operates as a church.

Sculpture and Paintings

It should not be forgotten that cultural uses can be incorporated into a project or district on a more modest scale as well. For example, sculpture and paintings can be used to enhance public areas and lobbies. Small stages can be used to provide entertainment in retail areas or

A Penthouse Arts Center at Roppongi Hills

Courtesy of Mori Building

Roppongi Hills in Tokyo features the Mori Art Center, a 65,000-square-foot (6,039-square-meter) contemporary art gallery, at the top of the tallest skyscraper pictured here.

When Minoru Mori was approached with the idea of creating an arts center on the top of a skyscraper in the new Roppongi Hills mixed-use project in Tokyo, he thought it was one of the craziest ideas he had ever heard. "But then I thought it over. I thought because it was crazy, it just might work. We could combine this tremendous attraction—a museum—with an observation deck. It would be like a lighthouse, a symbol of the city, a sort of jewel in the crown," says Mori.

With its distinctive gallery spaces totaling 65,000 square feet (6,039 square meters), its strong commitment to the arts, and its ambitious educational programs, the Mori Art Center aspires to be one of Asia's preeminent modern contemporary art institutions. "A museum can be a focal point, a way of enriching the lives of individuals," comments Glenn D. Lowry, director of the Museum of Modern Art (MoMA) in New York. "The Mori Art Center is one of the most innovative programs anywhere in Asia."

Mori is excited about the art center because it will serve as a cultural beacon for the Roppongi Hills project and for the city of Tokyo. When he first created his Ark Hills redevelopment project, the largest urban redevelopment in Tokyo in the 1980s, he wanted the complex to have a symbol; thus was born a concert hall that has contributed to the quality of concerts in Tokyo. With Roppongi Hills, Mori wants to contribute a new arts center.

The museum focuses on architecture and design as well as modern and contemporary art. It aims to bring the best western art to Japan while also focusing on Asian artists. MoMA serves as principal cultural partner and artistic adviser to the Mori Art Center, and an advisory committee has been formed that includes arts officials from London, Paris, and Bonn.

Mori anticipates that the new museum will become a cultural centerpiece for Tokyo. "The new Mori Art Center is destined to become a major attraction for the local community and international visitors," he says.

Source: Adapted from Bradley C. Grogan, "Cultural Heart," *Urban Land*, November/December 2000, pp. 58–61.

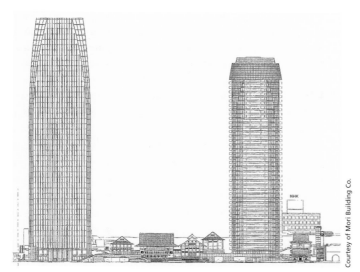

Atago Green Hills in Tokyo is built on the site of a temple whose buildings have been renovated and restored.

other public open spaces. Such uses can often be supported by the project's budget as worthwhile amenities. For example, University Park at MIT includes numerous sculptures on the green that depict industrial uses that once operated on the site.

Addison Circle in Dallas includes *Blueprints at Addison Circle,* a piece of public art located in the central circle that celebrates Addison's history and its future. The piece, consisting of 25 metal poles topped with five floating art panels depicting blueprints of some phase of Addison's past and future, is intended to symbolize the town and its development concept. Total cost for the sculpture—shared between the city of Addison and the developer—was $2.1 million.

Public and Civic Facilities

Public, civic, educational, and transit uses are frequently found in mixed-use projects, especially town center and transit village projects in the suburbs. Such facilities may include city halls and government offices, courthouses, libraries, post offices, educational facilities, community/civic centers, and various types of transit stations.

Civic and Educational Uses
Many mixed-use town centers are initiated by the public sector and often include civic uses as primary elements. Projects that incorporate city halls or government buildings include Southlake Town Square in Southlake, Texas, Smyrna Town Center in Smyrna, Georgia, Cathedral City Downtown in California, Fairview Village in Portland, Oregon, Cornelius Town Center in North Carolina, and CityCenter Englewood in Colorado.

Cornelius, North Carolina, for example, recently undertook to build a town center that features at its center a 25,000-square-foot (2,300-square-meter) town hall. The new facility houses town administrative functions as well as several public meeting spaces, including

a large council chamber and town meeting hall. The town hall was designed to serve as an identifiable landmark for the town. Reminiscent of many of North Carolina's older courthouses and municipal buildings, it has a dominant location in the plan. The town hall also contains approximately 3,000 square feet (280 square meters) of office space designed for the relocation of professional offices to the town center. A later phase will add a recreation center with a police station below it directly across the street from the town hall. These two civic buildings are set in a green space at the heart of the ten-acre (4-hectare) town center, which is planned to include main street retail and office space and residential uses.

In Englewood, Colorado, the city's administrative offices, municipal court, and public library are located in the Englewood Civic Center, part of CityCenter Englewood. The civic center is the former Foley's Department Store building, which was gutted and remodeled. CityCenter Englewood is being developed as a transit-oriented mixed-use development that will also include a light-rail station, retail, restaurants, apartments, office space, cultural arts, and open space. The Englewood Civic Center is centrally located to play a major role in the lives of Englewood citizens.

One caveat regarding civic uses relates specifically to courthouses; although they can be an important civic symbol for a project, they can also bring a steady stream of unhappy people through the development—from suspected criminals to couples seeking divorces. The potential for a poor image and tone for the area should be considered in the development strategy.

Educational facilities can frequently be operated in the evening, helping to animate the development during these hours. For example, at Eastwood City CyberPark, a large and dense mixed-use project being developed in downtown Manila, the University of Asia and the Pacific has collaborated with developers to establish a world-class graduate school for information technology professionals. The International Centre for Information Technology

City Hall is a principal anchor for Smyrna Town Center in Smyrna, Georgia.

Education will offer degree programs and certification and distance learning courses in an environment where students can interact with established professionals in the field. The graduate school will also provide a ready pool of experts for CyberPark tenants and serve as an incubation ground for new ideas.

Transit Uses

Transit-oriented development and transit villages are old ideas that have come back in vogue in recent years. Transit stations are often part of mixed-use projects because of the obvious advantages of location and access such sites and transit facilities can offer. Although many downtown mixed-use projects have been sited adjacent to transit stations, more recently many mixed-use projects have been developed around transit stations in the suburbs to create what are sometimes called *transit-oriented developments* or *transit villages.*

Transit-oriented developments can offer both opportunities and challenges. In the suburbs, although transit stations create higher property values and potentially strong demand for a variety of uses, the facilities are often above ground, dividing an area in half and creating circulation problems. With good design, however, most problems can be overcome, and the transit station can be planned as a featured element that will draw attention to the project.

A well-known example of a transit village is Orenco Station in Hillsboro, Oregon, a development that became possible when the Orenco light-rail station, originally located near an existing low-density development, was relocated by the regional transportation agency to a site adjacent to developable land. The development on the adjacent land, named Orenco Station, is a mixed-use pedestrian-oriented community that includes residential (rowhouses, cottages, townhouses, condominiums, and lofts), retail, and office space.

Another planned project is CascadeStation, on 120 acres (49 hectares) along the south side of the gateway to Portland International Airport. To contain a mix of office buildings, hotels and conference facilities, and retail and entertainment uses, the project will feature proximity to a freeway and the airport and access to on-site light-rail transit service in two stations. Cascade-Station, designed around a linear park, will be centered along the new Airport MAX light-rail line, providing direct service between downtown Portland and the airport. It is expected to carry 7,500 passengers a day by 2015. CascadeStation is approved for a maximum of 1,325,000 square feet (123,000 square meters) of office space, 1,200 hotel rooms, 400,000 square feet (37,000 square meters) of retail space, and a 24-screen cinema.

Of the case studies in this book, Addison Circle, Sony Center, West End City Center, and Yerba Buena Center are located adjacent to or incorporate rail transit stations. Other mixed-use projects incorporating rail transit include Arlington Town Square in Arlington Heights, Illinois, the proposed Lindbergh City Center in Atlanta,

The civic center is a featured element in the new Downtown Cathedral City, California, a development initiated by the city.

JR Central Towers in Nagoya, Japan, and Mockingbird Station in Dallas.

Convention Facilities

Convention facilities in mixed-use projects usually take two forms: a major convention center, often developed by the public sector, or a more modest facility in a convention hotel. In either case, convention facilities can be attractive components of mixed-use projects because of their compatibility with hotels, the support they can lend to the retail and restaurant components of a project, and the after-five activity and business generated by convention goers. They can also, however, be giant behemoths that consume a great deal of land and can detract from a pedestrian-friendly atmosphere.

In some mixed-use projects, major convention centers have become a primary use for the project and a major impetus for development of the mixed-use project. The development of a major convention center invariably involves a public sector initiative, and thus the public sector usually assesses the facility's potential and feasibility. The analysis takes into consideration the marketability of the city as a convention destination, the nature of existing facilities, and the untapped potential that a new facility could capture.

Many cities have developed substantial convention facilities in recent years where none existed before, hoping to attract visitors to the city and generate new business activity and revenue. Many of those facilities have been successful and have attracted much new business to the city; in other cases, the market has been very shallow and the decision to proceed highly speculative, based more on public goals than on market demand. The newest convention centers, especially those in major cities, are now so large that they are often freestanding facilities on the edge of town.

When convention space is included in a mixed-use development and the market for attracting conventions to the facility is highly speculative, the mixed-use project may be on shaky ground as well, even if the costs for the convention center itself are covered by public monies. A hotel in a mixed-use project will not succeed if one of its major markets is to be a convention center that does not draw conventions.

In short, a private developer must independently assess the potential drawing power of a major convention facility, even when it is being developed with public monies. This assessment in turn plays a major role in determining the on-site support for the hotel and retail components of the project, and the overall analysis may involve market specialists from all three of these areas. Hotel operators also make such analyses before committing themselves to the operation of the hotel.

An example of a major convention center in a recently developed mixed-use project is Suntec City, a 28.9-acre (11.7-hectare) mixed-use project in the new, master-planned Marina Centre CBD of Singapore. The project

Mockingbird Station in Dallas includes a Dallas Area Rapid Transit station, located adjacent to the project on the right.

comprises the Singapore International Convention and Exhibition Centre, one of the largest in southeast Asia; five blocks of office space, including one 18-story and four 45-story office towers totaling 2.3 million square feet (214,000 square meters); Suntec City Mall, a shopping and entertainment center offering 880,000 square feet (82,000 square meters) of prime retail space; and amenities such as the Fountain Terrace, a swimming pool, two tennis courts, a garden pavilion, and two basement levels of parking for 3,200 cars.

The 1.08 million-square-foot (100,000-square-meter) convention and exhibition center is eight stories with a column-free convention hall on Level 6 that can seat up to 12,000 delegates; it also has a custom-engineered telescopic seating system with 7,560 seats. The exhibition hall has an acoustic floating floor system to dampen sound and vibration and can be subdivided into three smaller halls by moving the walls. The exhibition hall also houses a 600-seat auditorium, 26 meeting rooms catering to groups of 20 to 400 people, a 35,500-square-foot (3,300-square-meter) art gallery, a ballroom accommodating up to 2,000 people, an 18,300-square-foot (1,700-square-meter) central kitchen designed for on-site catering, direct two-way access to the convention floor for container trucks for easy installation and removal of exhibits, state-of-the-art audio, visual, and lighting equipment, with teleconferencing and videoconferencing available via satellite, and a simultaneous interpretation system for up to 12 languages.

The Diagonal Mar development in Barcelona will include a 540,000-square-foot (50,000-square-meter) convention facility developed by the city. Diagonal Mar is a large-scale mixed-use project on 84 acres (34 hectares), covering 4 million square feet (372,000 square meters) of construction on Barcelona's seafront. The project consists of a super regional retail and leisure center, 1,400 apartments in five independent phases, three hotels with a total of 950 rooms, two Class A office buildings, and the convention facility. Of the case studies in this book,

CambridgeSide Galleria in Cambridge includes residential uses and a large enclosed mall but also features parks and pedestrian-friendly outdoor areas. It was developed through a public/private partnership.

Yerba Buena Center began with the development of the Moscone Convention Center, and CityPlace includes a publicly funded convention center.

Convention and meeting facilities developed on a much smaller scale in a hotel in a mixed-use project are often not separated into distinct facilities; they act simply as part of the hotel. The market for such facilities should be determined in conjunction with the proposed hotel operator, which will likely be solely responsible for marketing and managing the meeting spaces.

The impact of a large or small convention facility can be significant for a mixed-use project in terms of supporting other uses, creating an identity, and generating 24-hour activity. The developer should remember, however, that such facilities may not be profitable in themselves and that their usefulness must thus be evaluated in terms of benefits for the overall project and in light of available public support.[13]

Recreational Uses

Recreational uses in mixed-use projects can serve several of the same purposes as entertainment or cultural facilities: they extend the activity cycle for the project, they draw people who might not otherwise visit, and they provide an amenity for tenants, residents, and guests. Recreational uses found most often in mixed-use projects are parks, marinas, athletic/health clubs, and ice rinks.

Public Parks and Recreation Facilities

Public parks and recreation facilities may range from parks and paths to swimming pools and gymnasiums, and they can become major destinations in themselves. In fact, some developments, such as Mizner Park in Boca Raton, have found that the park is so attractive that residents come to it just to visit, increasing parking demand beyond projections.

Often parks and recreation facilities are included as a result of public participation in the project. The City Heights Urban Village development in San Diego includes a recreation center, playing fields, a public swimming pool, a municipal gymnasium, a performance area, a police substation, a library, an elementary school, a retail center, and an adult learning center. Still under construction are offices and 116 townhouses. The urban village covers ten city blocks; it has re-created the core of the City Heights community and established a pedestrian-friendly town square with important city facilities and centers of learning. The project is a partnership of the city of San Diego, the city's Redevelopment Agency, San Diego Foundation, CityLink Investment Corp., and Price Charities.

For very large projects, parks can take on large proportions. At Kuala Lumpur City Centre, a large project that includes the two largest towers in the world, a 50-acre (20-hectare) tropical landscape in the heart of the development, intended to provide an urban sanctuary for all Malaysians, is open to the public throughout the year. The public park and garden reflect the tropical greenery, vibrant colors, and patterns of the country's cultural heritage. The greenery and water features are old-fashioned contrasts to the modernity of the new-age materials and structures around it. The park features amenities such as a two-acre (0.8-hectare) children's playground, fountains, a wading pool, a jogging track, shelters and benches, patterned footpaths, sculptures, and murals. As the park approaches the commercial buildings in the development, it merges with the private gardens of each building to make them an integral part of the park.

Approximately 1,900 indigenous trees and palms representing 74 species are planted to encourage biodiversity in the park areas. The park also includes the Lake Symphony, two water fountains that are programmed to provide 150 colorful and dramatic animations. Part of the park is also a haven for birds and other local fauna. Much research preceded the selection of the trees that would attract local and migratory birds.[14]

Similarly, Diagonal Mar has built and dedicated a major park to the city. Surrounding the 85-acre (34-hectare) Diagonal Mar project, the 35-acre (14-hectare) public park features three lakes, pedestrian walkways shaded by 12-foot-high (3.6-meter-high) pergolas, bicycle and skating paths, three children's play areas, an area for walking dogs, and multiple water features. Dedicated to the city by the developer, the park will be the third largest park in Barcelona. The Diagonal Mar project is scheduled to be completed by mid-2004.

Parks should be carefully sized and placed to ensure they enhance other uses in the development. Paris Rutherford of RTKL Associates observes, "Parks are often planned to be the core of an intended activity center. This use should be carefully thought through, as large parks can create difficult single-loaded conditions not conducive to retail activity."[15]

Marine Facilities

A great many mixed-use projects have been developed on waterfronts, leading to marinas as a natural and attractive element in these projects. Marinas in mixed-use projects take on different characteristics from facilities used only as marinas. For example, in mixed-use projects with a significant retail component, the marina might include significant short-term "parking" for boaters who wish to shop or to eat at a restaurant. In mixed-use projects with a heavy office orientation, slips might be set aside for commuters and for water taxis that carry workers from other locations. In projects designed to attract tourists, facilities for tour boats and/or for boat rentals are desirable and potentially profitable amenities. In residentially oriented projects, the marina might be strictly private, with slips sold as condominiums.

The obstacles to marina development, however, are significant. Environmental regulations have lengthened the approval process by requiring costly environmental impact mitigation measures and have greatly reduced the number of potential marina sites. Developers con-

The developers of Diagonal Mar in Barcelona built a 35-acre (14-hectare) park as an integral element of the project. The park, with lakes, paths, and play areas, has been dedicated to the city.

Officially known as the Bryant Street Pier project and the James R. Herman International Cruise Terminal, Bryant Street Pier is situated next to the San Francisco Bay Bridge in the heart of the dynamic South Beach neighborhood. When completed in 2003, the development will house the James R. Herman Cruise Terminal, offices, retail and entertainment space, a hotel and timeshare accommodations, apartments, and a marina. Initial estimates call for 80 to 85 visits from cruise ships per year, carrying a total of 400,000 people into the city. The terminal will also function as a variety of year-round uses, from conventions to community and civic events.

The Bryant Street Pier project, located on the waterfront along San Francisco's famed Embarcadero, is the equivalent of four downtown city blocks. The focal point of the project is the James R. Herman International Cruise Terminal, a state-of-the-art complex that will position San Francisco as a leader in the cruise industry.

Key to the plan is the Town Center and Lagoon, which serves as a centerpiece for the project and for the adjacent South Beach neighborhood. This vibrant residential community also is home to many of San Francisco's multimedia firms and the San Francisco Giants's new ballpark. The plan features 156,000 square feet (14,500 square meters) of retail space, including neighborhood shops; 300,000 square feet (28,000 square meters) of commercial space, which will be managed under the World Trade Center banner; a fashionable hotel with extended-stay residences; an independent cinema; a public day-use marina; and a jazz club.

More than 50 percent of the ground space in the plan is earmarked for public open spaces, pedestrian walkways, and promenades. The project includes parking and is configured to encourage the use of public transit and other alternatives to automobile use.

The Bryant Street Pier in San Francisco will include a major cruise terminal.

Courtesy of Lend Lease Development

templating a marina in most states must now convincingly prove that their proposal is compatible with the public's environmental goals. Because marinas developed in conjunction with mixed-use projects are often part of waterfront redevelopment plans, however, the public sector's support of the marina is usually much easier to obtain, especially when the plan calls for a lively tourist-oriented facility that can be a major attraction for the city.

In analyzing the potential for marina development, the developer must consider numerous factors that are highly specialized and often beyond the realm of his normal range of expertise; environmental, regulatory, and market analyses for marinas involve issues that usually require the services of specialized consultants.

Numerous models exist for incorporating marinas into mixed-use projects; one of the earliest is Marina City in Chicago. The marina was instrumental in positioning

Rowes Wharf in Boston includes 38 marina slips, a dock for the Airport Water Shuttle, and docking facilities for commuter and excursion boats. Rowes Wharf also includes retail, offices, restaurants, and a hotel on a 5.4-acre (2.2-hectare) land and water site.

the project in the marketplace. This largely residential mixed-use project is unusual in that it does not incorporate waterfront slips. Located along the Chicago River, it is oriented around dry dock and boat-launching facilities. The marina, which originally included berths for 500 boats, is located on the lower levels of the platforms that support high-rise towers. Boats are moved by forklift.

Rowes Wharf in Boston includes two residential buildings that project into the harbor on wharf structures; the project also included at the outset 38 marina slips for residents and transients, a dock for the Airport Water Shuttle, and docking and terminal facilities for commuter and excursion boats. Washington Harbour in Washington, D.C., includes a boardwalk along the Potomac River that is used for short-term parking for boats visiting the restaurants; it is popular on evenings and weekends during the summer when the restaurants are especially busy. Bryant Street Pier in San Francisco (see the accompanying feature box) and RiverPlace in Portland, Oregon, are other examples.

Marinas often play major roles in mixed-use projects, providing amenities, projecting an image, and creating a sense of place. They may or may not be profitable ventures, and they often require public investment to be successful, especially where land values are high. They can provide a significant amenity for residents, hotel guests, and office workers, however, increasing the marketability of each component while also drawing off-site markets to the project that in turn can benefit retail and restau-

rant uses. In the right situation, they can play a key role in transforming an underused redevelopment area into a dynamic and lively mixed-use development or district.

Athletic/Health Clubs

Athletic/health clubs are probably the most popular recreational uses found in mixed-use projects, having grown in popularity with the fitness and weight-loss boom of the past several decades. They are frequently placed in nonprime lower-level or second-level spaces.

The inclusion of a single athletic/health facility accessible by all the project's tenants, guests, and residents can create significant economies of scale, taking advantage of the substantial on-site market. In many single-use residential or office projects, for example, certain recreational facilities such as racquetball courts may be included to help market the project, even though tenants might not use them often. In a mixed-use project, the cost of this marketing amenity can be spread across numerous uses; moreover, actual use will likely justify inclusion of the facility.

Each on-site market must be assessed to determine the support available for an athletic/health club and what mix of recreational activities each market segment demands. Some care must be taken to ensure that all on-site markets will want to use a facility that is shared among office, hotel, and residential users. In luxury residential projects, for example, it may be necessary to provide some separate and exclusive facilities for residents only.

Another important issue is how to support the capital and operating costs for such a facility when it draws on multiple markets. For example, on-site residents and hotel guests might be offered reduced rates for use of the facilities, while office tenants and/or the general public must pay a membership fee. Somehow revenues generated from the residential and hotel components must be allocated equitably to help defray the operating expenses of the athletic club.

An initial difficulty in developing such facilities in a mixed-use project is the availability of suitable land or building space. Second-floor areas of retail facilities increasingly are chosen. For example, the new Pentagon Row project in Arlington, Virginia, includes an athletic club on the second level overlooking a central retail courtyard. Another possibility is the approach used at Waterfront Place in Seattle, where an outdoor racquet club was developed on top of a parking facility connected by skyway to a mixed-use building containing offices, residential condominiums, and ground-level retail space. The facility includes two tennis courts and three racquetball courts.

The quality and price of membership facilities, operated by a variety of firms, vary substantially by facility and brand. Sports Club/LA, for example, is a high-end club, as exemplified by one of its newest incarnations in the new Ritz-Carlton Hotel and Residences in Washington, D.C. The 100,000-square-foot (9,300-square-meter) club offers its members an array of fitness and recreational options in an urban country club and resort-like atmosphere: weight training, group exercise studios, a junior Olympic swimming pool, basketball/volleyball and squash courts, yoga, martial arts, boxing, steam rooms and a sauna, private trainers, a pro shop, child care, and nutritional services.

Although health and fitness facilities increasingly are offered as membership-only facilities and for-profit operations, one distinguishing feature of them in mixed-use projects is that they can be viewed as an amenity and thus the operation's profitability can be subsidized if needed or desired. Although developers of mixed-use projects are inclined to develop and operate a profitable facility, often the more important consideration is the marketing value of such a facility for the overall project. In some situations, a developer may provide tenants with free or subsidized access to a modest facility as part of the lease agreement or may rent space to an operator at a favorable rate. The value of the facility to the overall development in hard dollars is often difficult or impossible to calculate, however, making the decision to include such amenities more one of informed judgment and experience than cold financial analysis.

Ice Rinks

Ice rinks have become popular in mixed-use projects for several reasons:

- Like other recreational uses, they can extend the project's activity cycle and draw visitors who might not otherwise come to the project.
- They are place makers, and their entertainment value for spectators is as important as their utility for skaters.
- They can provide an important visual amenity, creating a sense of movement and activity in public spaces.

Most ice rinks in mixed-use projects have been developed in conjunction with the retail portion of the project, and they are usually viewed as an amenity rather than a significant revenue generator. In mixed-use projects of the 1960s, 1970s, and 1980s, most ice rinks were located indoors, and they were particularly popular in warm climates. Among the earliest ice rinks to appear in a mixed-use project was the one in the Houston Galleria, where the ice rink is the central feature of a retail mall. Williams Center in Tulsa and Plaza of the Americas in Dallas are other early examples.

More recently, ice rinks have been included as outdoor seasonal amenities. For example, Reston Town Center includes a pavilion that is used for various events during warm months and for ice skating in the winter. It has become a very important amenity for the project throughout the year, drawing visitors and creating a sense of place, greatly benefiting the retail and restaurant uses in the project.

Another example is New Roc City in New Rochelle, New York, which features a Sports Plus entertainment complex with two ice skating rinks. Its Central Park skating pond features a sculptured ice surface, iron rails, park benches, lampposts, and a floating island. The skating arena offers hockey games, figure skating, and special events and shows. At Pentagon Row in Arlington, Virginia, the ice rink is at the center of a retail plaza.

Parking Demand and Shared Parking

Many factors affect the demand for parking in a real estate development: type and size of land use, location of the project, character and income level of the population using the real estate, availability and cost of mass transit, amount of walk-in traffic, design of parking structures, parking fees, and use of shared parking. For example, Sony Center am Potsdamer Platz in Berlin (see Chapter 8) includes 1.4 million square feet (130,000 square meters) of office, retail, residential, and entertainment space in a downtown location but has only 980 parking spaces. Using conservative parking generation ratios, a project of this size and mix could generate demand for more than 4,000 parking spaces in a suburban U.S. location. The lower number at Sony Center is largely because of the project's location adjacent to a transit station in the downtown of a major European city where demand for auto use is considerably lower than a suburban U.S. location; shared parking likely played a role as well.

Various participants have many different perspectives on parking in mixed-use developments:

- Voters and their elected officials want no parking problems spilling over from office, retail, entertainment, apartment, or transit station developments into single-family residential areas, but they also want more smart growth, fewer paved areas, and less environmental degradation in their communities.
- Retail and entertainment tenants want lots of parking close to their operations and want to ensure that the parking is readily available at peak evening, weekend, and holiday shopping periods. For major shopping centers, holiday peak periods require substantially more parking than would be required for any other month or time of the year; thus, much of it goes unused for most of the time.
- Residents of new apartments and condominiums often want their own specific parking spot in a secure environment and resist shared parking, except possibly for visitors.
- Office tenants want priority use of office parking areas during daytime office hours.

- Hotels want adequate parking for guests at night and, to varying degrees, for conference attendees during the day.
- Lenders want to ensure that parking is adequate and do not want to take chances on this issue; they tend to err on the side of more rather than less parking, and they are not particularly concerned about how much it will cost the developer so long as their debt is adequately secured.
- Developers want to build neither too much nor too little parking, seeking to meet tenant demands while minimizing parking construction and land costs.

With this many stakeholders involved and a shortage of up-to-date and reliable real-world data on shared parking, determining the optimal parking program for a new mixed-use development can be challenging and frustrating. One developer undertaking a mixed-use project observed:

> In our recent rezoning for a suburban mixed-use project, we produced anecdotal evidence to show that much more sharing is possible than the ULI *Shared Parking* study permits. The local jurisdiction, however, insisted on the standards in the ULI *Shared Parking* study, and as a result we are building much more parking than we know from our experience is needed. For example, a multiplex theater in a community produces abundant parking that is used only on nights and weekends. It makes office and hotel parking highly complementary; few public bodies really understand that. Their philosophy is to build so much excess parking that no one will ever complain, and the lenders are with the public officials on it.

At Addison Circle in Addison, Texas, although the city, the developer, and the lead tenants in a portion of the project were satisfied with the shared parking that was planned, the lender was not and the strategy thus was not implemented. Once the development was complete, it became apparent that too much parking had been provided.[16]

Estimating Parking Demand

The demand for parking in a mixed-use project can be highly variable, and estimation of parking demand for such a project is more complex than for a single-use development. An accurate estimate of the parking demand at a mixed-use project must not only reflect the variables that affect parking demand for each use but also recognize the fact that total peak parking demand for the entire project will likely be less than the sum of the peak demand values for the project's individual land uses.

Because of the different activity cycles of different land uses, the peak parking accumulations for individual land uses in a mixed-use project often occur at different hours of the day, days of the week, and seasons of the year (Figure 2-2). Thus, simply adding together the estimated peak parking demand for individual land uses to arrive at the estimated total peak demand for the project produces an estimate that is too high, unless parking is

figure 2-2
Parking Accumulation

Office Parking Accumulation

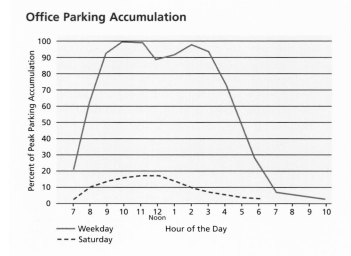

Regional Retail Parking Accumulation

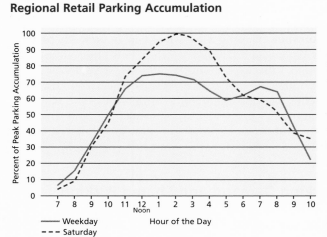

Restaurant/Lounge Parking Accumulation

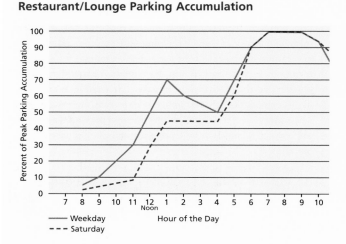

Cinema Parking Accumulation

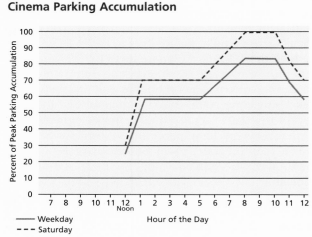

Hotel Parking Accumulation—Guest Rooms and Employees

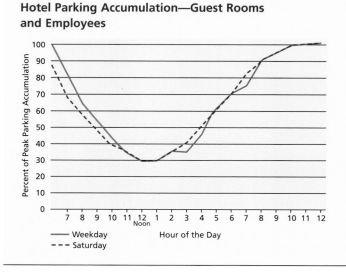

Residential Parking Accumulation

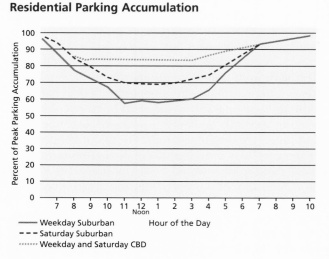

Source: ULI–the Urban Land Institute, *Shared Parking* (Washington, D.C.: Author, 1983).

segregated for each use. Calculations of demand must reflect the different demand patterns of the various land uses.

The synergistic relationship among different land uses in a mixed-use project also often encourages multi-purpose trips in which people attracted to the mixed-use project often visit more than one land use on a single trip. Thus, a single parking space can in effect serve several land uses. This phenomenon, which has been referred to as the *captive market effect,* also must be considered when estimating parking demand for a mixed-use project. The effect of this phenomenon on parking demand is not clearly understood, however. Notes Gerald Salzman of Kimley-Horn and Associates, "I don't think that anyone has been able to document it very well, and I have always believed that the captive market ends up being simply additional customer base."

Because different uses generate different levels of parking demand at different times, it is possible for these uses in a mixed-use project to share parking without conflict or encroachment. The significance of shared parking in mixed-use projects lies in the opportunity to plan and design efficient parking facilities that contain an adequate number of parking spaces to accommodate demand rather than creating a large surplus of spaces. The reduction in the amount of parking required for a mixed-use project as the result of shared parking presents significant opportunities for cost savings but brings with it critical conditions for design and operation.

A comprehensive ULI study undertaken in 1982 and 1983 includes a four-step methodology that can be used to estimate parking demand for a mixed-use project. The methodology recognizes the variation in peak parking demand among different land uses as well as the captive market effect of mixed-use projects, making it possible to estimate parking demand more accurately.

The methodology first requires that peak parking demand factors be determined for the various land uses; peak demand factors for individual land uses were identified by surveys in the United States undertaken for the study, but these data are now quite old—and were drawn from projects that are very different from those being built today. Therefore, they should not be relied on as a standard, merely as a rough starting point and rule of thumb. Moreover, as these data were derived from experience in the United States, they have little relevance for international projects where auto use is different.

The peak parking demand factor selected for each land use must be multiplied by the quantity of the land use to produce an estimate of the peak parking demand for each use. This value must then be adjusted to reflect hourly and seasonal variations and for mass transit use. For example, at Pentagon City in Arlington, Virginia, which includes a major mall with two department stores and high-rise office and hotel buildings near a transit station, the required parking ratios were as follows:

- Office—Two spaces per 1,000 gross square feet (93 square meters);

At Mockingbird Station in Dallas, the local jurisdiction allowed the developer to reduce parking from the required 2,200 spaces to 1,600 because of the mix of uses and shared parking.

- Hotel—0.75 space per room;
- Residential—1.125 spaces per unit for the first 200 units, one space per unit thereafter;
- Retail—5.2 spaces per 1,000 square feet (93 square meters) of gross leasable area (GLA).

The ratios were substantially below the standards of the original ULI shared parking study for office, hotel, and residential uses, partly because of the proximity to transit.

In 2002, ULI began to revise and update the original shared parking study to better reflect current conditions. An advisory group was formed to guide the new study; its initial assessment was that the basic methodology was still sound. What has changed are some of the demand factors. Anecdotal evidence from the advisory group suggests that several demand factors have changed since the original study:

- A study for expansion of a mixed-use project in Boca Raton, Florida, measured existing parking demand at about 10 percent higher for the retail segment than rates in the ULI shared parking study but substantially below local codes. Office ratios were slightly below ULI's study rates and well below the county rates, and hotel ratios were about 20 percent below ULI study rates.
- A project in Burbank, California, used office ratios that matched ULI's and retail ratios higher than ULI's but matching ratios in a new ULI shopping center parking study.
- Developers of a project near Phoenix found that the ULI study rates for cinemas needed to be substantially increased and for restaurants slightly increased. Their initial conclusions suggest that cinema, retail, and restaurant parking demand are the areas that most need revision.[17]

Mary Smith, senior vice president with Walker Parking Consultants in Indianapolis, who is the lead researcher

Parking requirements were key determinants in the overall sizing of Mizner Park in Boca Raton; a shared parking scheme reduced parking requirements by more than 25 percent.

on the new ULI shared parking study, has updated some of the ULI standards in her recent chapter on parking in *Transportation Planning Handbook:*

> The parking demand at retail uses in the evening hours has been increased to reflect changes in shopping patterns that have occurred since the publication of both *Parking Requirements for Shopping Centers* and *Shared Parking.*
>
> The factors for cinemas have also been adjusted, based on studies of parking needs at today's multiscreen megaplexes: the time of day and seasonal adjustment factors in *Shared Parking* are too low in places and can result in an underestimation of the parking needs of today's cinemas.

In developing a shared parking plan, it should be kept in mind that although it is important to provide adequate parking, it is in everyone's best interest not to provide too much parking for a new development, as it is both costly and environmentally undesirable. The less land paved over unnecessarily, the better.[18]

Implementing Shared Parking

Although shared parking is cost-effective and environmentally friendly, it is not easy to implement for a number of reasons. First, public officials often view shared parking skeptically during the approval process. Second, the data to support shared parking are not easy to obtain. Third, some project users, primarily residents, may want dedicated parking areas or spaces for their exclusive use. High-end residential components of mixed-use properties, for example, increasingly require dedicated or reserved parking for tenants, eliminating the opportunity to share parking with a complementary use such as office space (although guest parking spaces may still be shared with other uses).

Local jurisdictions' views on shared parking vary, from very proactive to general opposition. Even when they are favorably disposed to the concept, there is a limit to how much they will reduce parking as a result of sharing.

At Janss Court in Santa Monica, California, for example, the Specific Plan included no requirement for on-site parking, because the Third Street Promenade area where the project was located was already served by more than 3,000 parking spaces in city-owned structures. In response to market demand, however, the developer built 203 spaces below grade; residential units are given one space for each bedroom, and parking for offices is allocated at three spaces per 1,000 square feet (93 square meters) of floor area. No on-site parking is provided for restaurant and theater users, but plenty of parking is available in the adjacent structure.

At Reston Town Center in Reston, Virginia, a shared parking agreement was negotiated as part of the approval process with the county, thereby reducing the parking requirement for Phase I from 4,100 to 3,100 spaces. The developer also agreed to establish a transportation management association to educate the public on transportation alternatives, refine regional transit routing to the development, and advocate various strategies to reduce demand.

At Mockingbird Station in Dallas, the local jurisdiction allowed for shared parking within strict limits. The development, which is adjacent to a Dallas Area Rapid Transit (DART) station, includes 211 upscale loft residences; 180,000 square feet (16,700 square meters) of retail, theater, and restaurants; 140,000 square feet (13,000 square meters) of offices; and a proposed hotel. Although the city allowed the developers to build only 1,600 spaces (when 2,200 were required) by granting a parking reduction credit, it refused to reduce parking further to reflect the proximity of the transit station. The developer estimates that he had to build $6 million worth of excess (structured) parking for the project and that the project may have needed only 1,300 spaces, acknowledging that some tenants may have resisted the lower figure.

At Mizner Park, a public/private development, the parking requirements were key determinants in the overall size of the project, with the mix (residential, office, retail, and cultural) affording the advantages of a shared parking scheme. The parking structures are located to maximize the use of shared parking for the cultural facilities, in a move that is estimated will reduce the number of parking spaces by more than 25 percent.

In some cases, even small portions of a project can share parking. At RiverPlace in Portland, for example, the athletic club and restaurants share parking facilities, because they have different peak hours.

Among the case studies in this book, some use shared parking extensively, others only minimally or not at all. At Valencia Town Center Drive, developers took advantage of the mix of office, hotel, and retail/entertainment uses to share parking in two separate parking structures on separate portions of the town center site. The main structure generally makes sharing possible for office, retail, restaurant, and cinema uses. A second structure provides shared parking for hotel and office uses. The developer estimates that sharing has resulted in a 30 to 40 percent reduction in structured parking.

At Peabody Place, office tenants can rent spaces in the 700-car parking garage attached to the Tower at Peabody Place for $90.00 per month, while apartment residents of Gayoso House and Pembroke Square may lease parking spaces there for $35.00 per month.

WestEnd City Center in Budapest, which includes roughly 900,000 square feet (84,000 square meters) of leasable area in a downtown location adjacent to a transit station, currently provides 1,500 parking spaces in both underground garages and a multilevel parking structure. Such a project in a suburban U.S. location with no transit connection and no shared parking would likely require nearly 3,000 spaces. But WestEnd City Center has more than enough parking. Part of the issue is the cost of parking, because patrons of the shopping center have to pay to use the parking structure.

Several projects in other case studies—Phillips Place in Charlotte, for example, which combines residential, retail, and hotel uses—do not offer shared parking, and the retail and residential parking areas are strictly separated. At Addison Circle, residential and nonresidential uses share the same parking garages but do not share space in the garages; the number of parking spaces required by code is met or exceeded for each land use.

Providing less parking than codes require usually involves a special exception in most communities. A parking management program is often required to support shared parking, such as around transit stations in Denver. Public participation can help, as in Silver Spring, Maryland, where a parking authority can subsidize spaces needed for infill development until they become profitable.

Zoning ordinances increasingly allow for some shared parking, including flexibility in approving it, although they frequently require evidence to support the parking reduction. For example, a Springfield, Oregon, mixed-use zoning ordinance states:

> Surface parking shall meet the minimum parking requirement for the various use categories. . . . The Director may reduce the mini-

mum number of parking spaces required, based on a parking generation study, without need for a variance. The study shall demonstrate how a proposal to reduce parking is justified by estimated peak use, easy pedestrian access, availability of transit service, and adjacent on-street parking. This reduction shall be limited to 20 percent of the established standard.

The Portland region and its regional planning organization have been leaders in developing and adopting shared parking; they have developed numerous resources for implementing shared parking, including *Shared Parking Handbook,* which includes survey results from developers, business owners, and government officials on the pros and cons of shared parking, an overview of shared parking principles, a model shared parking ordinance, and a model shared use agreement for parking facilities.[19]

Although obstacles must be overcome, both developers and local governments increasingly agree that shared parking is desirable. Although parking demand varies from situation to situation and makes implementation difficult, the high economic and environmental costs of building parking spaces require that parking be used efficiently. All these parties must continue to work together to implement shared parking wherever possible.

Assessing Market Synergy

In assessing market potential, the developer should seriously evaluate on-site market support for each use and overall market synergy only after determining that a sufficient market exists for each major use. Three kinds of market synergy can be achieved in a mixed-use project: direct support (on-site market support), indirect support, and place-making synergy.

Direct Support

One type of market synergy is derived from direct on-site market support. For example, office workers, hotel guests, and residents will support a certain volume of nearby retail and restaurant business, and office tenants will generate a certain level of business for a nearby hotel and a certain number of occupants for nearby residences. The proximity of uses and the project's pedestrian access are critical for the success of this kind of synergy.

Such synergy can usually be calculated based on sound market data and techniques for market analysis similar to those described in this chapter. Market estimates for on-site retail space are particularly critical, because retail space often draws a significant market from on-site users.

Indirect Support

The second kind of synergy involves the indirect benefits of other uses as amenities. For example, retail and hotel uses do not directly generate revenues for office tenants or residents, but they can serve as important amenities for those uses—which can lead to faster lease-up at higher rents for the office and residential space. Retail and restaurant uses can provide an attractive and convenient shopping environment and sense of place for hotel guests, office tenants, and residents, improving the marketability of each component.

Hotels can also serve this purpose. For example, Millennium Partners in New York has undertaken numerous downtown mixed-use projects around the country that combine luxury condominiums with luxury hotels; many of the condominiums are marketed for more than $1 million; the residential portions of these projects clearly benefit from the luxury services and image that the hotel offers to the residences. One of its projects —the Ritz-Carlton Hotel and Residences—emphasizes the marketing strength of the hotel name for both the hotel and the residences. Hotels can also contribute to synergy by enhancing the marketability of the office component.

Other uses, such as recreational, cultural, or entertainment facilities, can also contribute to this kind of synergy by enhancing the project's image and making each component and the project as a whole more marketable. Although in the first example the main beneficiary is the retail and hotel component, in the second type the main beneficiaries are the office, residential, and hotel components, which gain marketability from the other uses as amenities.

Place Making
The third kind of synergy is derived from the opportunity that mixed-use development offers for place making, for creating a compelling new address and location in the urban landscape. For example, the strong mixed-use setting of Winter Park Village in Winter Park, Florida, attracted office uses not originally envisioned for the site. Good design and place making can unearth markets in some cases—although it is unwise to bank on its happening to any large degree.

Mixed-use developments have frequently been used to help transform blighted central city areas that could not attract or nurture single-use projects. For example, a location surrounded by blight that could not support the development of any single-use project might overcome these shortcomings—often with the help of the public sector—if several uses are combined on a relatively large scale to create a place that is amenable to and marketable for numerous purposes. Major downtown redevelopment almost always involves mixed-use development.

Mixed-use developments are also used for place making in the suburbs, taking the form of town centers or urban villages and creating new pedestrian-friendly environments that are fast becoming the signature places and the civic identity for many suburban communities. These places often include city halls and libraries to enhance the identity and civic nature of the developments.

Unlike most single-use developments, mixed-use developments can create a whole new sense of place for an area or district. Mixed-use developments, by virtue of

An early rendering of Legacy Town Center. Unlike most single-use developments, mixed-use developments can create a whole new sense of place for an area or district. Legacy Town Center is intended to provide such a place for the surrounding Legacy business community in Plano, Texas.

their larger scale, variety of uses, multiple buildings, and large construction budgets, allow for the shaping of new urban spaces and places. In fact, the quality of the public urban spaces created in these projects can be the defining element and the most important amenity in the project if they are well designed. In general, a mix of uses is fundamental in achieving success in place making and city building.

Compared with direct and indirect synergy, where some uses generate markets or value while others take advantage of them, all uses tend to benefit more evenly in the sense of place created. The point is to create a project of sufficient size, diversity, impact, and quality that becomes greater than the sum of its parts, a place or district rather than simply a building or project.

Achieving this kind of synergy is the ultimate reward derived from good planning and urban design. Some projects, for example, have been developed in areas where market analyses did not show strong support for any of the proposed uses as freestanding entities, because none could establish a sufficient sense of place to overcome the site's shortcomings. When the uses were developed together, however, in sufficient scale and with the right design, they succeeded.

In general, assessment of the synergy that can be created must rely on seasoned judgment and experience and on the study of other mixed-use projects and how the uses in them have performed in comparison with competitive single-use projects. Developers should remember that overly optimistic assumptions about synergy have been the weak points in many mixed-use projects that tried to include or oversize questionable uses for the location.

A Framework for Assessing Synergy
To provide an overview of the effects of market synergy, Figure 2-3 outlines a general framework showing each use's potential positive effect on the others. Overall, this chart suggests that the use that can potentially derive the

figure 2-3

Framework for Estimating On-Site Support and Synergy in a Mixed-Use Project

Use	Degree of Support for and Synergy with Other Uses
Office	
Residential	• •
Hotel	• • • • •
Retail/Entertainment[a]	• • • •
Cultural/Civic/Recreation	• • •
Residential	
Office	• • •
Hotel[b]	• • •
Retail/Entertainment	• • • •
Cultural/Civic/Recreation	• • • • •
Hotel	
Office	• • • • •
Residential	• • •
Retail/Entertainment	• • • •
Cultural/Civic/Recreation	• • • •
Retail/Entertainment	
Office	• • • • •
Residential	• • • • •
Hotel	• • • • •
Cultural/Civic/Recreation	• • • •
Cultural/Civic/Recreation	
Office	• • • •
Residential	• • • • •
Hotel	• • • • •
Retail/Entertainment	• • •

1 = Very weak or no synergy.
2 = Weak synergy.
3 = Moderate synergy.
4 = Strong synergy.
5 = Very strong synergy.

[a]Restaurants and food services are the main source of benefit for offices.
[b]Synergy is strongest between high-end hotels and condominiums, less for mid-priced hotels and residences.

most support from on-site uses is retail space, followed in order by cultural/civic/recreation facilities, hotels, residential, and offices. This framework is intended only as a general guide; the actual on-site support and synergy vary from project to project and place to place.

Notes

1. www.mccafferyinterests.com, accessed January 13, 2003.
2. Many other nonmall shopping centers and strip commercial areas are also prime candidates for conversion to mixed-use projects. In Chicago, for example, of 700 linear miles (1,130 kilometers) of commercial strip space in the city, officials of the Planning Department deem only 200 to 300 miles (322 to 484 kilometers) viable.
3. PricewaterhouseCoopers, *Greyfield Regional Mall Study* (San Francisco: Congress for the New Urbanism, 2001), p. 16.
4. For more in-depth coverage of assessing the potential for office development, see Jo Allen Gause et al., *Office Development Handbook*, 2nd ed. (Washington, D.C.: ULI–the Urban Land Institute, 1998).
5. For more in-depth coverage of assessing the potential for residential development, see Adrienne Schmitz et al., *Multifamily Housing Development Handbook* (Washington, D.C.: ULI–the Urban Land Institute, 2000).
6. "Office Workers Revisited," *ICSC Research Quarterly,* Winter 1995, pp. 1–4.
7. www.ahma.com, accessed January 7, 2003.
8. Personal communication, Mary Tack, director of research, International Association of Convention and Visitor Bureaus, January 2003.
9. For more information on this topic, see Michael D. Beyard et al., *Developing Retail Entertainment Destinations* (Washington, D.C.: ULI–the Urban Land Institute, 2001).
10. For more information on this topic, see David C. Petersen, *Developing Sports, Convention, and Performing Arts Centers* (Washington, D.C.: ULI–the Urban Land Institute, 2001).
11. Harold Snedcof, *Cultural Facilities in Mixed-Use Development* (Washington, D.C.: ULI–the Urban Land Institute, 1985), p. 10.
12. For more information, see Peterson, *Developing Sports, Convention, and Performing Arts Centers.*
13. Ibid.
14. Adapted from a press release from the Public Affairs Department of KLCC, May 7, 1998 (www.klcc.com.my).
15. For more information on this topic, see Alexander Garvin et al., *Urban Parks and Open Space* (Washington, D.C.: ULI–the Urban Land Institute, 1997); and Peter Harnik, *Inside City Parks* (Washington, D.C.: ULI–the Urban Land Institute, 2000).
16. Personal communication, Paris Rutherford, RTKL Associates, Dallas, Texas, February 2003.
17. Cinema operations and theater design have changed dramatically since the original study was completed; some new data are available from the Institute of Transportation Engineers (ITE) on cinema parking. Retail parking demand has also changed, and a new ULI/ICSC study, *Parking Requirements for Shopping Centers,* contains more current information. Restaurant demand may have been understated for the restaurants typically found at main street centers that attract singles and couples rather than families.
18. For further information, see Barton-Aschmann Associates and ULI–the Urban Land Institute, *Shared Parking* (Washington, D.C.: ULI–the Urban Land Institute, 1983).
19. See www.metro-region.org.

3. Feasibility Analysis and Financing

The previous chapter highlights the multiplicity of market and development issues that must be addressed at the outset when undertaking a mixed-use project. The developer and his team must be intimately familiar with a wide variety of uses, data, and concepts before they can begin to think about alternative development programs, and each potential use must be carefully and independently assessed before a program can be developed.

Once these initial investigations are complete, the development team needs to outline one or more project concepts, analyze the feasibility of each, and develop a financing strategy. Specifically, the developer needs to:

- Define alternative development programs and strategies for the mix and scale of uses, the necessary critical mass, the initial configuration, timing and phasing, and land assembly;
- Determine the financial feasibility of each alternative program by estimating development costs, operating costs and revenues, and long-term cash flow—and ultimately the financially optimal program;
- Structure the financing, including equity structures and ownership, ownership and financing of separate

Detail from the residential entrance to Park Tower in Chicago, a mixed-use tower on North Michigan Avenue that includes residential, hotel, and ground-level retail uses.

components, public financing, and the number and type of debt financing sources to be involved.

These efforts determine the fundamental development concepts and approaches for the project. They require input from the entire development team—market analysts, planners, architects, engineers, contractors, financial analysts, financial institutions, and property managers—all working closely with the developer.

For each alternative program, the parties test the project's mix, feasibility, investment returns, and financing structure. (Although the process is iterative, it is described here as essentially a three-step process.) With each step, this testing becomes more demanding and leads to more irrevocable commitments of resources at risk. Mixed-use projects in particular may require several iterations until the best fit is found; the program must be marketable, feasible, and financeable, and must also be able to receive public approval. This latter fact should not be underestimated, as the approval process can substantially affect the final program.

Feasibility analysis requires the consideration of all relevant profit centers, individually and combined, and complex issues of cost allocation. Comprehensive economic models are generally used, for they can deal with the special development issues arising from such projects, such as evaluating timing and phasing issues and the mix of uses throughout the development program. These economic models seek to incorporate techniques of optimization and sensitivity testing to establish the highest and best use for mixed-use projects; the models are used repeatedly throughout the process as conditions change.

Likewise, the financing of mixed-use projects can be more difficult than for single-purpose projects as a result of substantial capital requirements, the multiple uses that must be underwritten, and the numerous owners and financing sources involved. Because of these and other complicating factors discussed throughout this book, investors frequently seek and expect a risk premium when undertaking mixed-use projects.

The Development Program

The development program must specify the mix and scale of uses, the configuration and massing of the project, and the timing of the development and phasing of elements. The development program is essentially the grand plan laid out in some detail.

Mix and Scale of Uses

As the first step, principal components of the project's development program must be specified (housing units, office or retail square footage, hotel rooms, for example), taking into consideration timing, phasing, and allocated acreage; several alternative programs should also be developed. The mix and scale of uses are derived from several sources, including the creative ideas of the developer and his team, the market analysis, characteristics of the site, physical constraints and opportunities, the financing environment and financing constraints, public objectives and requirements, zoning regulations, and the developer's specific objectives and capabilities. The process begins with determining a cornerstone use and complementary uses, then developing several alternatives for configuring and phasing the project.

Determining the Cornerstone Use. The market analysis yields information on the relative market support for each use on the site, and from that analysis the developer often proceeds with the idea that one of the uses will be the cornerstone use—the most viable and profitable use in the project. In some cases when market support is relatively balanced among uses, numerous cornerstones may be possible, but usually one is the cornerstone.

Moreover, in some cases the dominant use may not be the cornerstone use in terms of profitability. This situation often occurs for publicly initiated projects that mandate a large amount of residential space; the residential space might be the dominant use, but the office or retail space might be the most profitable, making it the cornerstone use that generates the most revenue for the project. Because public policy can play an important role in shaping some projects, profitability is not always the primary determinant in establishing the mix of uses.

In most privately sponsored projects, however, the dominant and cornerstone uses are the same, and the cornerstone uses become obvious at an early stage; in

Worldwide Plaza in New York is a high-rise mixed-use project where office space is the cornerstone use. The project features a landmark office tower, a smaller residential tower, and ground-level retail.

fact, one use might already have surfaced as the assumed cornerstone even before the formal market analysis begins. The cornerstone use often drives the development concept as well as the decisions regarding the suitability and compatibility of other uses, which generally become either primary or auxiliary uses.

Office Space as the Cornerstone. In many mixed-use projects begun in the 1970s and 1980s—Embarcadero Center in San Francisco, the IDS Center in Minneapolis, Illinois Center in Chicago, for example—the office space is the cornerstone and dominant use. In these situations, the office component clearly establishes much of the project's character; in some cases, a large amount of office space can serve as a significant part of the market for other uses, such as hotel and retail space.

Numerous factors determine mix and scale in an office-oriented mixed-use project. For example, if the developer begins with a prelease commitment from a very large tenant, then the project will likely be configured to meet the needs of that user first, and the other uses may come second. At the IDS Center in Minneapolis, for example, the identity of the office building was of paramount importance because of the prime downtown location and the large corporate tenant, and the final product took the form of a dramatic skyscraper that dominates not only the project but also the entire skyline. Other uses of less importance include retail space and a hotel.

Numerous mixed-use projects recently developed or under construction in the Pacific Rim, including Japan, China, Thailand, and Malaysia, also use office space as the cornerstone and dominant use. Kuala Lumpur City Centre and International Finance Centre in Hong Kong, for example, both include major landmark office towers. Among the case studies in this book, Jin Mao Tower, Sony Center, and University Park all use office space as the cornerstone. Other recent examples where office space is the cornerstone include Worldwide Plaza and AOL Time Warner Center in New York, and Espirito Santo Plaza in Miami. In these and similar cases, where very large office buildings are defining elements, the demand for a large amount of office space must be clearly demonstrated. The developer will likely need to prelease much of the space early to make the project work and to avoid the costs associated with excessive vacancies.

Rather than one large building, however, most mixed-use projects use several smaller office buildings, especially in suburban areas, where many of these projects are being built today. The use of several smaller buildings benefits the program in several ways: it allows for greater flexibility in floor layouts and sizing; it allows the developer to phase the buildings and lowers the risk of excessive vacancies; and it allows for separate buildings with separate identities, opening up the possibility of attracting smaller lead tenants who could not occupy an entire large building but could take the lead in a smaller building. Reston Town Center in Reston, Virginia, and Redmond Town Center in Redmond, Washington, are two examples of this approach.

Residential or Retail Use as the Cornerstone. Although many of the projects of the 1960s, 1970s, and 1980s involved office space as the cornerstone, mixed-use projects in the 1990s and early 2000s have been much more varied, and many included residential or retail/entertainment uses as the cornerstone. In general, projects in which residential or retail/entertainment uses are cornerstones often have a completely different feel and look from office-oriented projects. Residential and retail/entertainment uses were increasingly prominent cornerstones in the 1990s, especially in suburban areas.

Such projects frequently take the form of town centers or transit villages. Mizner Park in Boca Raton, Florida, for example, includes 248 apartment units and 24 townhouses, main street retail/restaurants, and a modest amount of office space. The retail and entertainment uses—configured as a main street—provide the defining character for the project, while residential is the cornerstone and dominant use, helping support the retail by providing many housing units within walking distance. The office space plays a minor role.

Similarly, Phillips Place in Charlotte, North Carolina (see Chapter 8), includes main street retail establishments, 402 apartment units, and a hotel—but no office space. The development program at Addison Circle is driven largely by apartment uses with some retail and office space, while CityPlace is driven largely by retail space, although it also has residential and office uses.

A Balance of Uses. Some projects have no clearly dominant use but a careful balance of uses. For example, the mixed-use complex developed in the 1980s at Pentagon City in Arlington, Virginia, features the Fashion Centre at Pentagon City, the Ritz-Carlton Pentagon City, an office building, and an apartment building. Each use is carefully balanced in the program and the plan; in fact, all the uses are named individually, with no single name for the entire project. Each use has prominent frontage along the major street adjacent to the project. Office, hotel, and residential uses are configured in high-rise

Phillips Place in Charlotte, North Carolina, is a suburban town center with residential and retail/entertainment as the cornerstone uses; the project also includes a hotel.

buildings, and retail space is configured as a four-level mall that spreads out around them. Each use has its own distinct identity and entrances.

Uses at Rowes Wharf in Boston are balanced; the space includes 330,000 square feet (30,700 square meters) of offices, a 230-room hotel, and 100 luxury condominiums in a distinctive design in an attractive waterfront location along the Boston harbor. The condominiums are placed on wharfs that protrude into the harbor, and the office and hotel space is located on the city side of the project in a large building featuring two towers divided by a grand archway.

Compatibility. Whatever the mix and scale of uses chosen, the uses must be compatible and appealing to similar markets. Some of this compatibility occurs naturally; for example, a first-class hotel operator is not likely to be attracted to a mixed-use project unless the office, residential, and retail portions of the project are planned to be equally upscale.

The area where incompatibility most often becomes a problem is retail, because the retail portion usually must appeal to multiple markets to be successful, and most of the market will be off site. If the retail market is more downscale than other uses, conflicts and problems of image may occur. This problem is a particularly critical one to be resolved, as the retail portion usually plays a major role in creating the image and identity for the project.

Moreover, some office tenants might view some potential uses in a project—significant amounts of retail space or a convention center, for example—as detracting from a desirable corporate environment. Such conflicts can often be handled through effective design, but the issue should be addressed early in the planning process.

Project Configuration and Critical Mass

Once the mix and scale of uses are determined, an initial plan and configuration must be developed that masses each use on the site. This process need not pro-

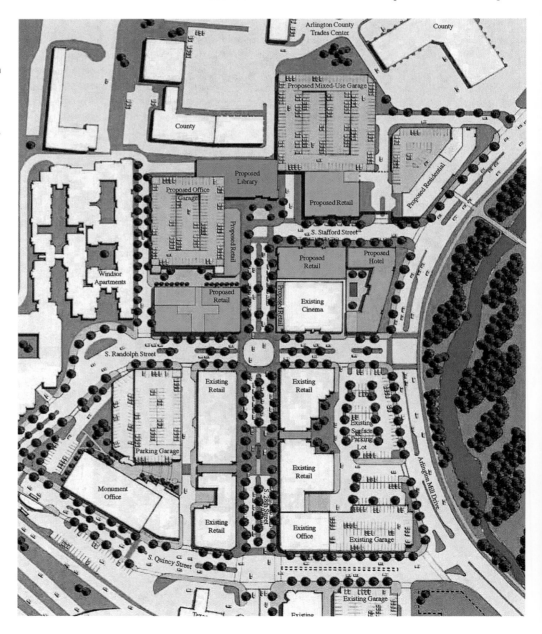

The first phases of the Village at Shirlington, completed in 1987, consisted of office and retail space, restaurants, and a cinema. The development has been a popular entertainment destination but has not established a strong retail presence. A proposed expansion (highlighted areas)—designed by Cooper Carry Inc.—will add more retail and office space, a hotel, and a library, which should greatly increase the project's critical mass.

CityPlace included 1.3 million square feet (121,000 square meters) in its first phase; an additional 1.1 million square feet (102,000 square meters) of office, hotel, and convention space is under construction or planned.

vide precise designs or sizes, but it should place each use on the site in a suitable location. Doing so will essentially test the program for a physical fit. Also critical to this effort is the massing of open space, because this element is important in establishing a sense of place for any successful mixed-use project. The developer should have an overall urban design concept in mind when undertaking initial massing and configuration (Chapter 5 provides more detail on this process).

A key concept in this initial configuration is to ensure the achievement of a critical mass within the confines of the site and the market. Although each use will have a certain minimum size simply to achieve operational efficiency, these minimums are usually exceeded in mixed-use environments. Hotels, for example, can include as few as 60 or 70 rooms, but hotels in mixed-use projects are likely to be at least 125 rooms and more likely around 300 rooms. Apartment buildings in mixed-use projects usually have at least 150 units and usually 300 or more. Retail and entertainment space, if it is intended to be a significant use, usually involves at least 125,000 square feet (11,600 square meters). And office space in a mixed-use project is seldom smaller than 100,000 square feet (9,300 square meters) and frequently involves 400,000 square feet (37,200 square meters) or more. Thus, a typical mixed-use project that includes three of these four uses would likely have at least 300,000 square feet (28,000 square meters) and typically more than 1 million square feet (93,000 square meters).

If the site and market suggest that a project with greater impact is desirable and marketable, the size of each component may increase significantly. For example, the smallest of the ten case studies in Chapter 8 is Phillips Place in Charlotte, North Carolina, which is around 600,000 square feet (56,000 square meters) and includes 402 apartments, 125,000 square feet (11,600 square meters) of retail and entertainment space, and 124 hotel rooms. This sizing, together with an attractive main street configuration, was sufficient to allow the development to achieve a strong sense of place in a competitive market.

Other case studies present much larger projects. CityPlace currently includes more than 1.3 million square feet (121,000 square meters) of retail and residential space, with an additional 1.1 million square feet (102,200 square meters) of office, hotel, and convention space planned. Sony Center includes 1.4 million square feet (130,000 square meters), WestEnd City Center 2.1 million square feet (195,000 square meters), and University Park at MIT 2.3 million square feet (213,700 square meters). Addison Circle includes 2.5 million square feet (232,300 square meters) and, when built out, is planned to be 5 million square feet (465,000 square meters). Yerba Buena Center, which includes a diverse set of projects undertaken by many developers, includes more than 10 million square feet (930,000 square meters).

Scale and density alone do not necessarily provide sufficient critical mass for a project, however. Physical and functional integration is the final ingredient that

After the parking structure at Lincoln Square in Bellevue, Washington, was completed, construction was temporarily halted in mid-2002 as a result of significant market shifts. Developers used the pause to reevaluate the program, phasing, and timing, especially for the office component. The original program and concept, depicted here, consisted of an office tower and a residential/hotel tower atop a 330,000-square-foot (30,700-square-meter) podium containing retail and restaurants.

will ensure critical mass and the resulting synergy. The role of planning and design is extremely important at this early stage in determining basic physical and functional relationships. Moreover, this initial configuration must consider the open and public areas that will be important elements in the project's success. According to Peter Pappas of Pappas Properties in Charlotte, "Functionality is key; location of parking and service areas, ingress and egress for vehicles to parking and service areas, and locations of elevators and escalators should be part of the early design process."

Initial massing and configuration generally include numerous alternative plans, often drawing on several alternative programs for mix and scale of uses. The initial massing and design are only preliminary, but the preliminary conceptual design is the most important stage in the design process, providing the fundamental concepts that will determine the completed project's physical relationships. In developing the concept, notes Ken Wong of Related Urban Group in Los Angeles, "Key elements are an integrated consumer proposition, an overall physical vision or image, and a master strategy that can accommodate change but still deliver the concept."

Once the alternative configurations are outlined, preliminary financial analyses are necessary to determine whether the program and configuration are financially feasible and which alternative is financially optimal. This process involves determining costs, revenues, and anticipated return on investment for each alternative (all of

which are discussed in more depth in "Financial Analysis" and "Financing").

Timing and Phasing

Because mixed-use projects usually involve a long period of time for predevelopment planning and construction, the likelihood that the overall development climate will change during planning is greatly increased. In very large projects where preliminary planning costs millions of dollars even before one shovel of dirt is turned, the risks are substantial.

Timing. Time is money. Timing is everything. Mixed-use projects are perfect for illustrating the truth in these well-worn phrases. If the timing is poor or unlucky or if time is not well managed in mixed-use development, profits disappear. For example, at the Heritage on the Garden in Boston, the Druker Company managed to sell all the condominiums and lease nearly half the office space before the real estate market crashed in the late 1980s. If sales and leasing at the Heritage had started just six months later, prices would have been substantially lower.

Mixed-use projects by definition involve different land use markets, with their own cycles apart from the overall economy. If the market for one use should sour during the planning process, it could wreak havoc on carefully laid plans, especially when a carefully crafted balance of uses is important to a project's success and market shifts necessitate a change in the balance. At Lincoln Square in Bellevue, Washington, development proceeded through completion of the parking structure at the base before construction was temporarily halted in mid-2002 because of significant market shifts. The original project plans called for a 27-story office building in one tower, a 200,000-square-foot (18,600-square-meter) retail building, a 65,000-square-foot (6,040-square-meter) health club, and a 41-story mixed-use tower housing a Westin Hotel and 148 condominium units. The developers halted the project for more than six months to reevaluate the program, phasing, and timing, especially the office component, as office vacancy rates in the area soared to 25 percent.

Such problems make it important to allow for as much flexibility as possible so that the various components can change during the planning process without compromising the viability of other components. For example, the Santana Row development in San Jose—scheduled for opening in 2002—experienced a major fire toward the end of construction that destroyed much of the residential portion of the project. As a result of softening in the housing market after construction began, the developers are seriously considering scaling back the residential portion before they begin rebuilding it.

Phasing. Phasing is the means by which many developers address problems of timing; phasing allows developers to build only as much as the market can absorb in a reasonable period of time, allowing them to minimize their risks and hedge their bets. Although phasing is the only logical approach in very large mixed-use projects covering large areas, smaller projects can also benefit from the concept. Tradeoffs are always necessary, however, between developing the project in increments or all at once. Each situation offers a range of different phasing strategies.

No one approach is best for phasing mixed-use projects, but phasing for mixed-use projects should take into account several issues:

- Inherent uncertainties in the development process should be recognized upfront, and flexibility must be built into the phasing plan from the start. The list of risks is long in mixed-use development, particularly

for large-scale projects. One important way to reduce such risks is to insulate one phase from the next so that each could substantially survive without the other. Although this approach is sometimes impossible or ill advised, the strategy should be considered where the situation warrants it.

- The first phases of the project set its tone and create its image. They must succeed on their own to get the project off on the right foot.
- The development team's capabilities and capacity to undertake the various elements of the project should be carefully managed to ensure the project can proceed in a timely fashion without overtaxing the developer's staff. Competing demands from the simultaneous development of several project components can overload the staff.
- Although the current phase is important, the developer must always think ahead. Each building phase must be functionally and financially viable while allowing flexibility for further development should the market or program change.

Some mixed-use projects developed in stages have suffered from the image of the first component constructed. Unless the promise of complementary project components is kept clearly in public view, this image can be a liability in marketing. The advantages of carefully staged development are many, however, and a phasing program is a necessity for most mixed-use projects.

Generally, when retail is a cornerstone use, opening as much retail space as possible at the same time is important, but not always possible. This concept can create phasing issues, especially for main street–oriented mixed-use projects where retail space is configured as street-level stores on the lower level of office, hotel, or residential buildings, many of which may be planned for future phases.

Phasing by Parcel. The possibilities for phasing are as varied as the projects themselves. At Cornelius Town Center, a small mixed-use development in Cornelius,

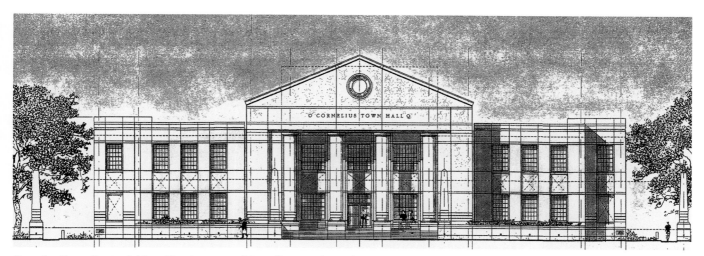

Cornelius Town Center, initiated by the town of Cornelius, North Carolina, includes a new 25,000-square-foot (2,300-square-meter) town hall in the second phase.

Courtesy of Cooper Carry Inc.

Incremental phasing at Bethesda Row in Bethesda, Maryland, helped to mitigate development risk. The project proceeded in four initial phases that were completed in 1997, 1998, 1999, and 2001.

North Carolina, initiated by the town of Cornelius, the plan calls for three initial phases, although the master plan depicts development potential and a suggested way in which the new town infrastructure should continue to evolve beyond the initial phases. The first phase consisted of demolition of old warehouse and mill structures on site, installation of new public roads and utilities, and construction of a new 40,000-square-foot (3,700-square-meter) grocery store and seven small retail shops. The second phase provided for the construction of additional infrastructure such as site lighting and the construction of a new 25,000-square-foot (2,300-square-meter) town hall.

The third phase will see the development of two- and three-story "main street" buildings fronting along the main thoroughfares and approximately 40 new townhouses. The development of the second and third phases has been slowed by slower real estate markets in 2002 and 2003. Future phases include a light-rail station, structured parking, a police station or other civic use, renovation of a mill building, and multifamily residential units. The master developer is the town of Cornelius; the city provides infrastructure and delineates land uses, and then sells parcels to developers.

At Bethesda Row in Bethesda, Maryland, a main street–oriented mixed-use project in an existing urban district, phasing the development on multiple blocks was a key element of the strategic plan. By phasing development over a number of years, Federal Realty was able to mitigate some development risk and create sufficient cash flow to cover subsequent development costs. Like its other retail properties, Federal Realty found that the benefits of its improvements and renovations accrued to nearby property owners; by building a bigger project, Federal hoped to be able to capture for itself more of the benefits of its work. The project proceeded in four initial phases that were completed in summer 1997, fall 1998, fall 1999, and spring 2001. Phasing allowed the project to achieve a sizable critical mass without having too much under development at one time.

Even larger projects may be phased over even longer periods. The Illinois Center in Chicago, for example, was begun in 1969 and is still not complete today. The initial phasing plan for Atlantic Station in Atlanta phased development over ten years (see the accompanying feature box). Adverse market conditions and other factors can easily lengthen such phasing plans; thus, contingency plans should be in place to make certain the project can withstand a phasing and buildout plan that is longer than initially expected.

Phasing may involve new owners. At Reston Town Center, for example, ownership of the project has evolved over time. The original developer, Reston Land Corporation and Himmell & Co., sold the project; the first completed phase is now owned by Equity Office Properties, while the land for the second phase was sold to Terrabrook, which is developing it. Phase I focused predominantly on office buildings and Market Street's shops and restaurants. Phase II seeks to expand on these uses while adding residential uses to the mix. Several phases were developed simultaneously during 2001 and 2002 on separate portions of the site, including residential uses at the far end of the main street and center and office uses near the center. The phasing plan includes the use of flexible blocks and a strong sense of districts in the town center.

Phasing in Integrated Structures. Even integrated complexes and vertical mixed-use structures can be phased, although doing so can create complications. At the Grand Pier Center in Chicago, an integrated mixed-use structure with two towers rising from a multilevel base, construction began on the base structure, which includes retail, cinema, and parking, before financing was in place for the high-rise residential and hotel towers above it. Metro Center, a multiblock mixed-use project in Washington, D.C., first started in the 1980s, included a large Hecht's department store that was designed so that office space could be built above in a later phase. That office space was not actually added for more than ten years, with completion scheduled for 2003 by a different developer. Parking for the new office space had to be provided on adjacent parcels.

In some cases, the project may be built roughly all at once but still opened in phases by component or use. For example, at WestEnd City Center (see Chapter 8) all components of the project were built simultaneously but completed at slightly different times to accommodate the needs of different users. To open the retail component in time for the Christmas rush in 1999 required a push from the project management team and construction crews. This rush to completion was not considered as essential for the other components of the project, so they opened later. Offices were opened in July 2000, the hotel in September 2000.

Financial Analysis

Once alternative programs and concepts are proposed, they must be tested to determine their feasibility and which program is financially optimal. The financial analysis seeks to model capital costs, operating revenues and expenses, and return on investment, entailing a complex analysis of cash flows over a ten- or 15-year period. A financial analysis involves a model that can respond to change. For most mixed-use projects, the purpose of this financial analysis is to define and optimize the development program, to assess the prospects of financial success or failure with reasonable accuracy, and to determine whether or not to proceed.

In undertaking the financial analysis, the developer is well advised to model a single-use project as one alternative, because it likely will be the lowest-risk alternative and can provide an important baseline for evaluating risk and return. For example, McCaffery Interests of Chicago, which has developed numerous retail-oriented mixed-use projects around the country, uses the following approach to analyze and manage risk in its projects:

A focus on minimizing risk and a determination to develop "the right thing" has led McCaffery Interests to consider property development and redevelopment opportunities from a unique perspective—the perspective of risk management. This approach has led the company to identify the *lowest and best use* for a property that produces an acceptable market financial return. Seeking to identify a lowest and best use ensures that "risk" receives equal or greater consideration than "return" in McCaffery Interests's business plan. Mitigation of risk, identification of the best use, and creation of relative surety in returns are prime motivators in the company's philosophy.[1]

Issues in Financial Modeling

Mixed-use projects frequently involve very different costs and revenues from single-use projects; those differences might involve a number of factors:

- Because sites for mixed-use projects must appeal to multiple markets, they are usually well located and often very expensive.

Atlantic Station: Initial Timetable and Phasing Plan

Atlantic Station, the $2 billion redevelopment of the former Atlantic steel mill in Atlanta, was planned as of 2001 to be phased over ten years. This plan for the transformation of 138 acres (56 hectares) involved three major phases:

- Phase I, started in late 2001, features 1.2 million square feet (111,500 square meters) of retail and entertainment space, 1 million square feet (93,000 square meters) of commercial office space, 500,000 square feet (46,500 square meters) of high-tech office space, 1,250 residential units, and 500 hotel rooms.

- Phase II, scheduled for completion in fall 2006, will feature 300,000 square feet (28,000 square meters) of retail space, 500,000 square feet (46,500 square meters) of commercial office space, 500,000 square feet (46,500 square meters) of high-tech office space, 750 residential units, and 250 hotel rooms.
- Phase III, scheduled for completion in fall 2012, will feature 100,000 square feet (9,300 square meters) of retail space, 2.5 million square feet (232,300 square meters) of commercial office space, 500,000 square feet (46,500 square meters) of high-tech office space, 1,600 residential units, and 750 hotel rooms.

Source: Long Aldridge & Norman, CRB Realty Associates. ■

Atlantic Station in Atlanta, located on a 138-acre (56-hectare) site, will be phased over at least ten years.

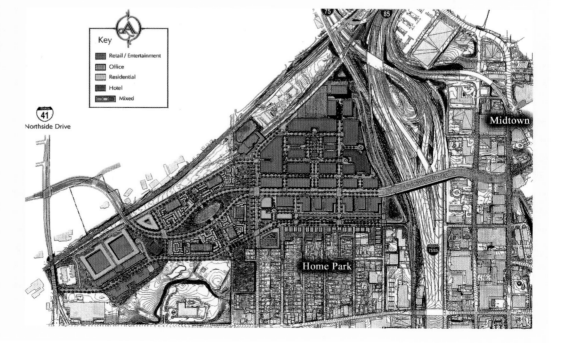

- Because of the complicated nature of mixed-use projects, initial planning costs may be greater than for single-use projects. For a large and complicated project, it is not unusual for the developer to have $10 million to $20 million tied up before making the first draw on the construction loan. In fact, it is easy to have $5 million invested before the developer knows for sure that he has a project to develop at all. This factor often results in a higher-than-normal proportion of development costs allotted to soft costs.

- Land carrying costs are often quite different from those associated with single-use projects. On the one hand, because of the large size of mixed-use projects, land parcels are often larger and land carrying costs greater than for competitive single-use projects on a small parcel. On the other hand, land carrying costs can be less than those associated with a large single-use project requiring vast acreage, such as an office park, because a mixed-use project with numerous uses can be absorbed more quickly and thus built out faster than a single-use office project. Moreover, mixed-use projects frequently involve public participation, often involving land leases, land writedowns, or other incentives that can reduce the cost of the land.

- Because public review bodies often look favorably on mixed-use projects, achievable densities may be higher than for a single-use project, effectively lowering the cost of land per square foot or square meter of devel-

oped space when the land is owned or controlled before a rezoning.

- Construction costs per square foot or square meter for individual uses may differ significantly from construction costs for single-use projects. In a mixed-use building, for example, structural costs will likely be higher than for a single-use building of similar size.

- The amount and cost of common areas and amenities, which must be reflected in the pro forma analyses for individual uses, might be greater or less than those normally associated with single-use projects.

- Because of the potential for shared parking, the amount of parking required and the associated construction costs will likely be less than if the uses in the project were developed separately (although shared parking is not always feasible).

- Operating costs may be higher or lower than for single-use projects, depending on the nature of the project.

- The project's performance might be superior to that of competing single-use projects, resulting in potentially faster leasing and higher rents for offices, faster leasing and greater rents and overages for retail space, higher occupancy and room rates and greater revenues from restaurants and meeting spaces for hotels, and faster renting or sales at higher prices for residential uses.

It is impossible to say categorically to what degree costs or revenues will vary for most of these issues, because the

Vancouvercenter in Vancouver, Washington, includes 194 apartments, 68 condominiums, and 165,000 square feet (15,000 square meters) of office and ground-floor retail space. The complex includes four buildings; two buildings of six and seven stories contain apartments, and nine- and 11-story buildings each contain offices, condominiums, and retail space.

Courtesy of Otak, Inc.

Hollywood & Highland includes retail/entertainment uses, a hotel, and the Kodak Theatre.

configuration and success rate of projects differ greatly. Although separate financial analyses must be performed for each use to ensure that each is feasible in its own right, the analyses must also take into consideration the peculiarities of mixed-use projects that will affect costs and revenues. Perhaps more important, these issues mean that the process of estimating costs and revenues is more complicated than for single-use developments and subject to greater miscalculations, requiring larger contingency funds than for single-use projects.

Targeting Returns and Projecting Performance

In general, targets for financial performance and returns for mixed-use projects should be above those of most other real estate property types to provide an adequate return for the additional complexity involved. Notes Peter Pappas of Pappas Properties in Charlotte, "The targeted return should be higher than the expected return on a less complicated project." The additional risk that goes with complexity should be financially rewarded, or it will not be worth the effort.

Some recent high-profile projects highlight the financial pitfalls that ambitious mixed-use projects may encounter. For example, the publicly traded Trizec Properties (formerly TrizecHahn Corporation) recently undertook two *major* mixed-use projects in California, Hollywood & Highland in Hollywood and Paseo Colorado in Pasadena. Anticipated financial returns for the two properties were initially 11 percent for projected stabilized return on cost, 19 percent for projected stabilized return on Trizec equity, and approximately 25 percent for a leveraged internal rate of return to Trizec.

Hollywood & Highland opened in fall 2001 with 425,000 square feet (39,500 square meters) of retail space, 180,000 square feet (16,730 square meters) of theater space, a 40,000-square-foot (3,700-square-meter) ballroom, and a separately developed hotel. The project offered significant opportunities for additional revenue from sponsorship, naming rights, advertising and special

events; it is the new home of the Academy Awards®. Trizec owns 100 percent of the project. Ownership of the 640-room Renaissance Hollywood Hotel was initially structured as an 84 percent/16 percent joint venture between Trizec and Marriott, anticipating a 91 percent/9 percent (Trizec/Marriott) joint venture at opening. Paseo Colorado also opened in fall 2001, with 565,000 square feet (52,500 square meters) of retail space owned by Trizec and separate apartments owned and developed by Post Properties.

Initial financial results for Hollywood & Highland, however, were not as anticipated, highlighting the issue of market risk, the pitfalls of estimating and managing costs, and the real possibility of development cost overruns that can result from complex construction and development programs. In 2003, Trizec Properties wrote down its investments in Hollywood & Highland by a total of $181.4 million, a loss that resulted from development cost overruns, conceptual mistakes in project programming and design, and a slowing economy and tourism market that followed the events of September 11, 2001.

As with all financial analyses, the analyst's assumptions about the mixed-use project's performance over time are critical factors that must be carefully scrutinized. First, the lease rates used to estimate gross income must be realistic for the market. In slowing or overbuilt markets, for example, lower rents or rent concessions may result, preventing the pro forma rents from being achieved. Second, expected vacancy projections must be realistic. If a project fails to lease in the time projected or vacancy rates persist at levels above those projected, the project underperforms.

The key to performance projections, then, is the reliability of assumptions being used to produce them. Computer software is available to help determine the numbers and projections, but often too much importance is placed on the model and underlying assumptions are insufficiently analyzed. For this reason, it is also important to undertake sensitivity testing of the performance to determine how higher vacancies or lower rents will affect the project's performance.

The financial analysis model described in the following pages reviews only one alternative program and scenario to highlight the methodology and the issues involved. The assumptions in this model can easily be changed to test other programs or different scenarios; a financial analysis for a mixed-use project must involve a variety of scenarios to get a clear picture of a range of possible outcomes.

Financial Modeling: The Process

The primary thrust of the financial model is to measure the expected profitability and rates of return of alternative development scenarios for a particular project. The results of the model will help determine whether or not a proposed alternative meets the developer's objectives and which variables of the program should be altered to improve the project's financial performance.

An effective financial model not only yields measures of expected returns but also allows for sensitivity analyses of the variables in the model to determine ways to make the project more profitable. Making good use of the financial model eases the process of selecting a preferred program alternative and helps to shape the decision-making process throughout the project's implementation phase.

The financial model consists of four basic steps: 1) create alternative development programs, 2) estimate development costs, 3) calculate the expected revenue stream, and 4) compare costs and revenues. For each step, the developer must consider a number of different variables and parameters. Each decision, no matter how small, will in some way affect the project's profitability; therefore, it is vital to understand how sensitive the model will be to different variables. For example, the diminishing value of money over time affects the results of a model significantly, as an annual income stream of $500,000 today is worth considerably more than an income stream of $500,000 ten years from now. When making decisions about a development program, the timing of its construction can have serious implications on the rate of return.

The following points briefly describe each of the four steps and the various considerations within each step.

- Create Alternative Development Programs—Creating a development program for a mixed-use project involves three major considerations: project concept (types of uses), volume of each use type, and timing of development. A large number of these decisions will likely be shaped by previous decisions resulting from site analysis and market research. To effectively compare which project elements are more productive than others, however, it is useful to create multiple development scenarios, each of which may emphasize one element over another. It is also useful to look at the effects of a more rapid buildout on the bottom line and to evaluate the costs and benefits of higher densities and/or vertical integration of uses.
- Estimate Development Costs—Development costs involve three different aspects: hard and soft construc-

Courtesy of Torti Gallas and Partners–CHK Inc.

The proposed Twinbrook Commons in Rockville, Maryland, is a transit-oriented development on a 26-acre (10.5-hectare) site that is planned to include 620,000 square feet (56,000 square meters) of office space, 805 high-rise residential units, 490 low-rise residential units, and 160,000 square feet (15,000 square meters) of retail.

tion, contingencies, and infrastructure. Hard and soft construction costs of a mixed-use project depend on variables like construction materials, the size of residential units, the cost of professional services (architecture, site planning, engineering, and so on), and the quality of construction. Projects with higher construction costs mandate higher pricing on the revenue side; therefore, construction costs must be carefully considered. Contingencies typically are calculated as a function of hard and soft construction costs, so they are not an independent variable. Infrastructure costs are a function of two factors: density and quality. A higher-density project requires fewer linear feet of infrastructure per unit of revenue-producing space and therefore reduces costs. Many such projects use high-quality paving materials, more street trees, expensive street lighting, and other elements, however, that add to the cost per linear foot of infrastructure. Infrastructure costs must be rationally allocated to each use.

- Calculate Expected Revenue Stream—As mentioned, the required revenue stream from a mixed-use project often depends on the amount of cost put into the project. Revenues can be expected to rise only as high as the market will support, however. For each project element, an understanding of the market must inform revenue assumptions to avoid overestimating the project's potential. Beyond market considerations, however, many mixed-use projects create premium values for themselves through the relationships of compatible uses, the creation of attractive public spaces, and other amenities. For each use, expected unit values should therefore be set through comparisons of market support, development costs, and expected premium values. It is also important to determine what the net revenue after operating costs will be for each use. A final consideration in this step is to determine value appreciation, as many mixed-use projects experience real appreciation in value over inflation over time.

- Compare Costs and Revenues—In this final step, the net cash flow is calculated by subtracting costs from revenues for each year of the development program. The annual cash flow is then evaluated to calculate the project's rate of return and net present value. Although the results of tinkering with other elements of the model are displayed during this step, the actual assumptions that change come from one of the three preceding steps. The only variable in this step is the discount rate used to calculate the project's net present value.

The remainder of this section outlines the financial analysis of a sample mixed-use development that was developed in accordance with the four steps listed above.[2]

A Sample Mixed-Use Financial Model
The following analysis presents the assumptions and results of the analysis of a hypothetical urban mixed-use development in an urban infill area. The hypothetical high-density project is built into a city grid and features streetfront structures with parking located on the interior of blocks. Infrastructure costs have been set at a fairly high level to reflect a high-quality urban environment with attractive landscaping and substantial public open space.

The project includes 450 units of rental housing, 100 units of for-sale housing, 750,000 square feet (70,000 square meters) of office/commercial space, 250,000 square feet (23,000 square meters) of retail space, a 300-room hotel, and 3,000 spaces of structured parking. The full set of tables for the analysis can be found on pages 102 to 119. The development pro forma summary (Figure 3-1) and the proposed development program (Figure 3-2) outline a multiyear schedule of development for the previously mentioned uses covering 15 years, including two five-year development phases. Unit development costs for the different use types are displayed in Figure 3-3. The following paragraphs describe the model's structure and assumptions.

California Plaza in downtown Los Angeles includes two major office towers as well as residential, hotel, retail, and museum space.

Land Acquisition Costs. The model ignores the cost of land acquisition, as it assumes that the property will be part of a major redevelopment. As a result, the land will be leased to the developer or will be subject to incentives (such as property tax abatements) that will defray the costs of property acquisition. Thus, the residual value, or the present value of the net cash flow, also represents the supportable land cost.

Infrastructure Costs. Figures 3-3 through 3-5 show the calculation of the project's infrastructure costs. Infrastructure costs are allocated to each type of use based on each use's percentage of the project's total square footage. For example, if the office/commercial component accounts for 250,000 square feet (23,200 square meters) of a 1 million-square-foot (93,000-square-meter) project, 25 percent of the infrastructure costs are attributed to the office/commercial component. (This allocation method can penalize space-intensive uses; another approach allocates infrastructure costs based on the proportion of total project cost represented by each use.) The cost of infrastructure in the model has been set at $70.00 per square foot ($750 per square meter) of paved area, including all utility lines, paving, sidewalks, and streetscape. For timing, all infrastructure costs for each project phase are assumed to be paid in the first year of each phase (Years 1 and 6).

Rental Housing. The program proposes 450 rental housing units, with a four-year absorption period, beginning in Year 2 (Figure 3-6). The following assumptions were made for this use:

- Average Unit Size—1,000 square feet (93 square meters), with 840 square feet (78 square meters) of net rentable area
- Development Costs, including Contingencies—$143,000 per unit ($143.00 per square foot [$1,600 per square meter])
- Rent—$1,638 per unit ($1.95 per square foot [$21.00 per square meter])
- Annual Operating Expenses—$6.50 per square foot ($70.00 per square meter).

For-Sale Housing. The program calls for 100 for-sale housing units to be sold over a four-year period, beginning in Year 2 (Figure 3-7). Thus, average annual absorption is 25 units. The following assumptions were made for this use:

- Buildings—Low-rise structures of wood-frame construction
- Average Size—1,600 square feet (150 square meters)
- Development Costs, including Contingencies—$247,500 per unit ($154.68 per square foot [$1,665 per square meter])
- Sale Price—$352,000 per unit ($220 per square foot [$2,370 per square meter])
- Cost of Sale: 5 percent of gross unit price ($17,600 per unit).

Office/Commercial. The office/commercial component includes 750,000 square feet (70,000 square meters) of gross leasable area (Figure 3-8). Leasing is suggested to begin in Year 2 and to continue through Year 9, an eight-year absorption period. The following assumptions were made for this use:

- Development Costs, including Contingencies—$165 per square foot ($1,775 per square meter)
- Lease Rate—$26.00 per square foot ($280 per square meter)
- Operations and Maintenance, excluding Insurance and Common Area Maintenance (CAM)—$6.00 per square foot ($65.00 per square meter)
- Vacancy Factor: 5 percent.

Retail. The retail component consists of 250,000 square feet (23,200 square meters) of gross leasable area (Figure 3-9). Leasing begins in Year 4 and does not conclude until Year 9, representing a six-year absorption period. The following assumptions were made for this use:

- Development Costs, including Contingencies—$203.50 per square foot ($2,200 per square meter)
- Lease Rate—$33.00 per square foot ($355 per square meter)
- Operations and Maintenance, excluding Insurance and CAM—$5.50 per square foot ($60.00 per square meter)
- Vacancy Factor: 5 percent.

Hotel. The program includes a 300-room hotel to be built in Year 7 of the development period (Figure 3-10). The following assumptions were made for this use:

- Development Costs, including Contingencies—$192,500 per room
- Average Daily Room Rate: $175
- Operating and Maintenance Expenses—72 percent of gross revenue
- Occupancy Factor—72 percent.

Structured Parking. In addition to dedicated parking for the project's residential and hotel components, the project will also contain 3,000 spaces of structured parking to serve its office/commercial, retail, and public components (Figure 3-11). The following operating assumptions were made concerning parking operations:

- Development Costs, including Contingencies—$17,600 per space
- Monthly Parking Operations—35 percent of spaces
  - Monthly Parking Charges—$150 per space
  - Occupancy Factor—95 percent
- Hourly Parking Operations—65 percent of spaces
  - Hourly Parking Rate—$2.75
  - Number of Nonwork Days—115
  - Nonwork Day Parking Hours—14
  - Nonwork Day Occupancy Factor—25 percent
  - Number of Work Days—250

- Work Day Parking Hours—10
- Work Day Occupancy Factor—25 percent
- Operating Expenses—25 percent of gross revenues.

Public Elements. In addition to all these real estate components, the hypothetical project would also contain a substantial amount of public space—parks, walking/ bicycle paths, and gathering spaces, for example. For purposes of the financial model, the total value of these elements has been estimated at $4 million, and the entire amount will be paid in Year 1 of the program.

Results of Model. Figure 3-1 displays the results of the financial model, given all these assumptions. The model solves for annual cash flow on an unleveraged (prefinancing) basis, which is an effective initial test of feasibility. The model assumes that the developer will continue to operate all ongoing uses (that is, all uses except for-sale housing) until Year 15. At that time, the operating assets will be sold, and the proceeds will be added to the project's revenue stream. The value of the sale has been estimated by capitalizing the Year 15 revenue stream at 10 percent and deducting 5 percent to account for the costs of sale.

In addition to the overall results shown in Figure 3-1, each cash flow analysis for individual uses (Figures 3-6 through 3-11) shows the results for that use. The following table summarizes the results of this hypothetical model.

Use	Net Present Value of Cash Flow (10 Percent Discount Rate)	Unleveraged Internal Rate of Return
Rental Housing	$1,723,500	10.4 percent
For-Sale Housing	$544,300	12.6 percent
Office/Commercial	$4,042,900	10.6 percent
Retail	$19,049,100	16.5 percent
Hotel	$11,042,100	14.3 percent
Structured Parking	$5,238,200	11.8 percent
Total[1]	$38,003,700	11.9 percent

[1]Other infrastructure costs are not allocated among each of the uses. Therefore, the project net present value is less than the sum of the net present values for the individual uses.

Financing

Ultimately, the feasibility of a development depends on whether it can be financed. Thus, even if market and financial studies support the feasibility of the development, it will not proceed until a suitable financing strategy is devised and effectively implemented at the right time to successfully develop the project. Issues such as conditions in the financial marketplace and the proper structuring of financing are just as important as market demand and a sound development program.

Key Financing Considerations
Several issues are key when seeking financing for a mixed-use project:

Construction at Grand Pier Center in Chicago, an integrated mixed-use structure, began on the base before financing was in place for the high-rise residential and hotel towers above it.

- Financial Market Conditions—Interest rates and the cost and availability of equity and construction and permanent financing significantly affect the project's financial feasibility and the ultimate financing decision.
- Developer Equity and Upfront Costs—Financing begins with the developer's equity. Developers of mixed-use projects need considerable equity upfront to finance land options, market and feasibility studies, land acquisition, and other predevelopment costs. This equity is at considerable risk, and thus much of it will likely be supplied by the development firm itself.
- Equity Partners—Many private developers seek equity partners and create limited partnerships, joint ventures, new corporations, and other ownership structures. Pulling together a viable ownership structure is fundamental and perhaps the most difficult part of real estate development. Few guidebooks have been written on how to attract equity capital to a development project, and few substitutes are available for having in place an experienced development entity that already has developed strong contacts and relationships with equity investors. The amount of equity the developer can put into the deal affects not only whether the project can be financed but also the cost of financing.
- Relationships with Lending Institutions—Some developers, especially larger ones involved in mixed-use projects, have established relationships with debt sources that can make financing easier. Without a good relationship between developer and lenders,

figure 3-1
Summary of Results: Sample Mixed-Use Development Pro Forma
Thousands of Dollars

	Year 1	Year 2	Year 3	Year 4	Year 5	Year 6	Year 7
Net Operating Income							
Rental Housing	$0.0	$1,312.3	$2,703.4	$4,524.7	$6,453.0	$6,646.6	$6,846.0
For-Sale Housing	0.0	8,940.1	9,208.3	12,646.0	0.0	0.0	0.0
Office/Commercial	0.0	861.6	1,772.6	3,659.7	5,634.0	7,736.3	9,990.4
Retail	0.0	0.0	0.0	2,905.5	4,351.3	5,092.3	6,361.1
Hotel	0.0	0.0	0.0	0.0	0.0	0.0	7,792.0
Structured Parking	0.0	290.6	598.7	1,850.0	2,826.5	3,696.4	4,717.0
Total Net Operating Income	$0.0	$11,404.7	$14,282.9	$25,586.0	$19,264.8	$23,171.6	$35,706.5
Development Costs							
Rental Housing	$17,233.8	$15,170.9	$19,532.5	$20,118.5	$0.0	$0.0	$0.0
For-Sale Housing	8,538.3	7,877.2	10,818.0	0.0	0.0	0.0	0.0
Office/Commercial	11,573.7	9,627.7	19,833.0	20,428.0	21,040.8	23,930.5	27,902.8
Retail	918.4	0.0	22,237.0	10,306.8	4,718.2	9,053.1	6,257.0
Hotel	0.0	0.0	0.0	0.0	0.0	69,924.4	0.0
Structured Parking	5,785.4	2,800.8	11,539.2	8,616.9	7,345.2	11,247.9	9,740.6
Other Infrastructure[1]	4,000.0	0.0	0.0	0.0	0.0	0.0	0.0
Total Development Costs	$48,049.7	$35,476.5	$83,959.7	$59,470.2	$33,104.2	$114,156.0	$43,900.3
Annual Cash Flow							
Net Operating Income	$0.0	$11,404.7	$14,282.9	$25,586.0	$19,264.8	$23,171.6	$35,706.5
Total Asset Value @ 10%							
Total Costs of Sale @ 5%[2]							
Total Development Costs	(48,049.7)	(35,476.5)	(83,959.7)	(59,470.2)	(33,104.2)	(114,156.0)	(43,900.3)
Net Cash Flow	$(48,049.7)	$(24,071.8)	$(69,676.8)	$(33,884.2)	$(13,839.5)	$(90,984.4)	$(8,193.9)

Net Present Value @ 10%: $38,003.7 **Unleveraged IRR: 11.9%**

[1]Other infrastructure costs are not allocated among each of the uses. Therefore, the project net present value is less than the sum of the net present values for the individual uses.

[2]Assumes asset sale in Year 15.

Source: Economics Research Associates, Washington, D.C.

	Year 8	Year 9	Year 10	Year 11	Year 12	Year 13	Year 14	Year 15
	$7,051.3	$7,262.9	$7,480.8	$7,705.2	$7,936.3	$8,174.4	$8,419.7	$8,672.3
	0.0	0.0	0.0	0.0	0.0	0.0	0.0	0.0
	12,830.5	15,866.9	16,332.0	16,855.9	17,374.5	17,887.3	18,394.5	18,959.8
	7,367.1	8,442.2	8,673.4	8,950.4	9,225.8	9,499.5	9,771.4	10,065.3
	8,025.7	8,266.5	8,514.5	8,769.9	9,033.0	9,304.0	9,583.1	9,870.6
	5,899.6	7,149.0	7,363.5	7,584.4	7,811.9	8,046.2	8,287.6	8,536.3
	$41,174.4	$46,987.4	$48,364.1	$49,865.9	$51,381.5	$52,911.6	$54,456.3	$56,104.2
	$0.0	$0.0	$0.0	$0.0	$0.0	$0.0	$0.0	$0.0
	0.0	0.0	0.0	0.0	0.0	0.0	0.0	0.0
	28,739.8	0.0	0.0	0.0	0.0	0.0	0.0	0.0
	6,444.7	0.0	0.0	0.0	0.0	0.0	0.0	0.0
	0.0	0.0	0.0	0.0	0.0	0.0	0.0	0.0
	10,032.8	0.0	0.0	0.0	0.0	0.0	0.0	0.0
	0.0	0.0	0.0	0.0	0.0	0.0	0.0	0.0
	$45,217.4	$0.0	$0.0	$0.0	$0.0	$0.0	$0.0	$0.0
	$41,174.4	$46,987.4	$48,364.1	$49,865.9	$51,381.5	$52,911.6	$54,456.3	$56,104.2
								561,042.2
								(28,052.1)
	(45,217.4)	0.0	0.0	0.0	0.0	0.0	0.0	0.0
	$(4,043.0)	$46,987.4	$48,364.1	$49,865.9	$51,381.5	$52,911.6	$54,456.3	$589,094.3

figure 3-2

Multiyear Development Program: Sample Mixed-Use Development Pro Forma

	Total Buildout	Year-by-Year Cumulative Absorption					
		Year 1	Year 2	Year 3	Year 4	Year 5	Year 6
Project Buildout by Development Units							
Rental Housing	450 units	0	100	200	325	450	450
For-Sale Housing	100 units	0	30	60	100	100	100
Office/Commercial	750,000 square feet	0	50,000	100,000	200,000	300,000	400,000
Retail	250,000 square feet	0	0	0	100,000	145,000	165,000
Hotel	300 rooms	0	0	0	0	0	0
Structured Parking	3,000 spaces	0	150	300	900	1,335	1,695
Project Buildout by Square Feet							
Rental Housing	450,000	0	100,000	200,000	325,000	450,000	450,000
For-Sale Housing	160,000	0	48,000	96,000	160,000	160,000	160,000
Office/Commercial	750,000	0	50,000	100,000	200,000	300,000	400,000
Retail	250,000	0	0	0	100,000	145,000	165,000
Hotel	150,000	0	0	0	0	0	0
Structured Parking	975,000	0	48,750	97,500	292,500	433,875	550,875
Total	2,735,000	0	246,750	493,500	1,077,500	1,488,875	1,725,875

Source: Economics Research Associates, Washington, D.C.

figure 3-3

Unit Development Costs and Infrastructure Costs: Sample Mixed-Use Development Pro Forma

Commercial Development Unit Costs

Contingency Costs: 10% of Development Costs

	Unit Cost before Contingency	Contingency Cost	Total Unit Cost, including Contingency
Rental Housing	$130,000 per unit	$13,000 per unit	$143,000 per unit
For-Sale Housing	225,000 per unit	22,500 per unit	247,500 per unit
Office/Commercial	165.00 per square foot	16.50 per square foot	181.50 per square foot
Retail	185.00 per square foot	18.50 per square foot	203.50 per square foot
Hotel	175,000 per room	17,500 per room	192,500 per room
Structured Parking	16,000 per space	1,600 per space	17,600 per space

Infrastructure Development Costs

Commercial Infrastructure

Linear Feet of Infrastructure (Feet)	2,800
Average Street Width (Feet)	55
Total Square Footage (Square Feet)	154,000
Infrastructure Cost per Square Foot	$70.00
Subtotal	$10,780,000

Other Infrastructure Improvements

Park/Landscaping	$4,000,000
Total Infrastructure Costs	$14,780,000

Source: Economics Research Associates, Washington, D.C.

Year 7	Year 8	Year 9	Year 10	Year 11	Year 12	Year 13	Year 14	Year 15
450	450	450	450	450	450	450	450	450
100	100	100	100	100	100	100	100	100
500,000	625,000	750,000	750,000	750,000	750,000	750,000	750,000	750,000
200,000	225,000	250,000	250,000	250,000	250,000	250,000	250,000	250,000
300	300	300	300	300	300	300	300	300
2,100	2,550	3,000	3,000	3,000	3,000	3,000	3,000	3,000
450,000	450,000	450,000	450,000	450,000	450,000	450,000	450,000	450,000
160,000	160,000	160,000	160,000	160,000	160,000	160,000	160,000	160,000
500,000	625,000	750,000	750,000	750,000	750,000	750,000	750,000	750,000
200,000	225,000	250,000	250,000	250,000	250,000	250,000	250,000	250,000
150,000	150,000	150,000	150,000	150,000	150,000	150,000	150,000	150,000
682,500	828,750	975,000	975,000	975,000	975,000	975,000	975,000	975,000
2,142,500	2,438,750	2,735,000	2,735,000	2,735,000	2,735,000	2,735,000	2,735,000	2,735,000

figure 3-4

Infrastructure Allocation by Distribution of Space: Sample Mixed-Use Development Pro Forma

	Square Feet	Percent of Total
Rental Housing	450,000	16.5%
For-Sale Housing	160,000	5.9%
Office/Commercial	750,000	27.4%
Retail	250,000	9.1%
Hotel	150,000	5.5%
Structured Parking	975,000	35.6%
Project Total	2,735,000	100.0%

Source: Economics Research Associates, Washington, D.C.

figure 3-5

Infrastructure Costs by Year, Allocated by Use Types: Sample Mixed-Use Development Pro Forma Based on Distribution of Space

Thousands of Dollars/Inflation: 3%

		Phase I					Phase II
		Year 1	Year 2	Year 3	Year 4	Year 5	Year 6
Inflation Factor		1.03	1.06	1.09	1.13	1.16	1.19
Commercial Infrastructure							
Rental Housing	16.5%	$2,504.8	$0.0	$0.0	$0.0	$0.0	$0.0
For-Sale Housing	5.9%	890.6	0.0	0.0	0.0	0.0	0.0
Office/Commercial	27.4%	2,226.5	0.0	0.0	0.0	0.0	2,258.4
Retail	9.1%	918.4	0.0	0.0	0.0	0.0	548.5
Hotel	5.5%	0.0	0.0	0.0	0.0	0.0	967.9
Structured Parking	35.6%	3,066.2	0.0	0.0	0.0	0.0	2,736.7
Subtotal	100.0%	$9,606.5	$0.0	$0.0	$0.0	$0.0	$6,511.6
Other Infrastructure							
Park/Landscaping		$4,120.0	$0.0	$0.0	$0.0	$0.0	$0.0
Subtotal		$4,120.0	$0.0	$0.0	$0.0	$0.0	$0.0
Total Infrastructure Costs							
Total Costs		$13,726.5	$0.0	$0.0	$0.0	$0.0	$6,511.6

Net Present Value of Costs @ 10%: $16,154.2

Source: Economics Research Associates, Washington, D.C.

	Year 7	Year 8	Year 9	Year 10	Phase III Year 11	Year 12	Year 13	Year 14	Year 15
	1.23	1.27	1.30	1.34	1.38	1.43	1.47	1.51	1.56
	$0.0	$0.0	$0.0	$0.0	$0.0	$0.0	$0.0	$0.0	$0.0
	0.0	0.0	0.0	0.0	0.0	0.0	0.0	0.0	0.0
	0.0	0.0	0.0	0.0	0.0	0.0	0.0	0.0	0.0
	0.0	0.0	0.0	0.0	0.0	0.0	0.0	0.0	0.0
	0.0	0.0	0.0	0.0	0.0	0.0	0.0	0.0	0.0
	0.0	0.0	0.0	0.0	0.0	0.0	0.0	0.0	0.0
	$0.0	$0.0	$0.0	$0.0	$0.0	$0.0	$0.0	$0.0	$0.0
	$0.0	$0.0	$0.0	$0.0	$0.0	$0.0	$0.0	$0.0	$0.0
	$0.0	$0.0	$0.0	$0.0	$0.0	$0.0	$0.0	$0.0	$0.0
	$0.0	$0.0	$0.0	$0.0	$0.0	$0.0	$0.0	$0.0	$0.0

figure 3-6
Income Statement—Rental Housing: Sample Mixed-Use Development Pro Forma
Thousands of Dollars/Inflation: 3%

		Year 1	Year 2	Year 3	Year 4	Year 5	Year 6
Revenue Assumptions							
Inflation Factor	3.0%	1.03	1.06	1.09	1.13	1.16	1.19
Projected Unit Absorption	450	0	100	200	325	450	450
Average Unit Size	1,000	0	100,000	200,000	325,000	450,000	450,000
Net Rentable Area	840	0	84,000	168,000	273,000	378,000	378,000
Monthly Rent per Square Foot	$1.95	$2.01	$2.07	$2.13	$2.19	$2.26	$2.33
Occupancy Factor	96.0%						
Net Operating Income							
Gross Lease Revenues		$0	$2,001.9	$4,123.9	$6,902.4	$9,843.9	$10,139.2
Annual Operating Expenses per Square Foot	$6.50	$0	$689.6	$1,420.5	$2,377.6	$3,390.9	$3,492.6
Net Operating Income		$0	$1,312.3	$2,703.4	$4,524.7	$6,453.0	$6,646.6
Development Costs							
Percent Built by Year		22.2%	22.2%	27.8%	27.8%	0.0%	0.0%
Development Costs	$64,350.0	$14,729.0	$15,170.9	$19,532.5	$20,118.5	$0	$0
Infrastructure Costs		$2,504.8	$0	$0	$0	$0	$0
Total Development Costs		$17,233.8	$15,170.9	$19,532.5	$20,118.5	$0	$0
Annual Cash Flow							
Net Operating Income		$0	$1,312.3	$2,703.4	$4,524.7	$6,453.0	$6,646.6
Asset Value[1] @ 10%							
Costs of Sale @ 5%							
Total Development Costs		$(17,233.8)	$(15,170.9)	$(19,532.5)	$(20,118.5)	$0	$0
Net Cash Flow		$(17,233.8)	$(13,858.6)	$(16,829.1)	$(15,593.7)	$6,453.0	$6,646.6

Net Present Value @ 10%: $1,723.5   **Internal Rate of Return: 10.4%**

[1]Assumes asset sale in Year 15.

Source: Economics Research Associates, Washington, D.C.

Year 7	Year 8	Year 9	Year 10	Year 11	Year 12	Year 13	Year 14	Year 15
1.23	1.27	1.30	1.34	1.38	1.43	1.47	1.51	1.56
450	450	450	450	450	450	450	450	450
450,000	450,000	450,000	450,000	450,000	450,000	450,000	450,000	450,000
378,000	378,000	378,000	378,000	378,000	378,000	378,000	378,000	378,000
$2.40	$2.47	$2.54	$2.62	$2.70	$2.78	$2.86	$2.95	$3.04
$10,443.3	$10,756.6	$11,079.3	$11,411.7	$11,754.1	$12,106.7	$12,469.9	$12,844.0	$13,229.3
$3,597.4	$3,705.3	$3,816.5	$3,931.0	$4,048.9	$4,170.4	$4,295.5	$4,424.3	$4,557.1
$6,846.0	$7,051.3	$7,262.9	$7,480.8	$7,705.2	$7,936.3	$8,174.4	$8,419.7	$8,672.3
0.0%	0.0%	0.0%	0.0%	0.0%	0.0%	0.0%	0.0%	0.0%
$0	$0	$0	$0	$0	$0	$0	$0	$0
$0	$0	$0	$0	$0	$0	$0	$0	$0
$0	$0	$0	$0	$0	$0	$0	$0	$0
$6,846.0	$7,051.3	$7,262.9	$7,480.8	$7,705.2	$7,936.3	$8,174.4	$8,419.7	$8,672.3
								$86,722.6
								$(4,336.1)
$0	$0	$0	$0	$0	$0	$0	$0	$0
$6,846.0	$7,051.3	$7,262.9	$7,480.8	$7,705.2	$7,936.3	$8,174.4	$8,419.7	$91,058.7

figure 3-7

Income Statement—For-Sale Housing: Sample Mixed-Use Development Pro Forma

Thousands of Dollars/Inflation: 3%

		Year 1	Year 2	Year 3	Year 4	Year 5	Year 6
Assumptions							
Inflation Factor	3.0%	1.03	1.06	1.09	1.13	1.16	1.19
Number of Units	100						
Average Unit Size[1]	1,600	0	48,000	48,000	64,000	0	0
Net Usable Area	84%	0	40,320	40,320	53,760	0	0
Sale Price per Square Foot[1]	$220.00						
Net Operating Income							
Sale Revenues		$0.0	$9,410.6	$9,692.9	$13,311.6	$0.0	$0.0
Builder Profit (Percent of Revenue)	15.0%	$0.0	$1,411.6	$1,453.9	$1,996.7	$0.0	$0.0
Cost of Sales (Percent of Revenue)	5.0%	$0.0	$470.5	$484.6	$665.6	$0.0	$0.0
Net Operating Income		$0.0	$8,940.1	$9,208.3	$12,646.0	$0.0	$0.0
Development Costs							
Percent Built by Year		30.0%	30.0%	40.0%	0.0%	0.0%	0.0%
Development Costs	$24,750.0	$7,647.8	$7,877.2	$10,818.0	$0.0	$0.0	$0.0
Infrastructure Costs		$890.6	$0.0	$0.0	$0.0	$0.0	$0.0
Total Development Costs		$8,538.3	$7,877.2	$10,818.0	$0.0	$0.0	$0.0
Annual Cash Flow							
Net Operating Income		$0.0	$8,940.1	$9,208.3	$12,646.0	$0.0	$0.0
Total Development Costs		$8,538.3	$7,877.2	$10,818.0	$0.0	$0.0	$0.0
Net Cash Flow		$(8,538.3)	$1,062.9	$(1,609.7)	$12,646.0	$0.0	$0.0

Net Present Value @ 10%: $544.3   **Internal Rate of Return: 12.6%**

[1]Unit Size Includes garage in each unit, and Sale Price per Square Foot considers presence of unfinished garage space.

Source: Economics Research Associates, Washington, D.C.

Year 7	Year 8	Year 9	Year 10	Year 11	Year 12	Year 13	Year 14	Year 15
1.23	1.27	1.30	1.34	1.38	1.43	1.47	1.51	1.56
0	0	0	0	0	0	0	0	0
0	0	0	0	0	0	0	0	0
$0.0	$0.0	$0.0	$0.0	$0.0	$0.0	$0.0	$0.0	$0.0
$0.0	$0.0	$0.0	$0.0	$0.0	$0.0	$0.0	$0.0	$0.0
$0.0	$0.0	$0.0	$0.0	$0.0	$0.0	$0.0	$0.0	$0.0
$0.0	$0.0	$0.0	$0.0	$0.0	$0.0	$0.0	$0.0	$0.0
0.0%	0.0%	0.0%	0.0%	0.0%	0.0%	0.0%	0.0%	0.0%
$0.0	$0.0	$0.0	$0.0	$0.0	$0.0	$0.0	$0.0	$0.0
$0.0	$0.0	$0.0	$0.0	$0.0	$0.0	$0.0	$0.0	$0.0
$0.0	$0.0	$0.0	$0.0	$0.0	$0.0	$0.0	$0.0	$0.0
$0.0	$0.0	$0.0	$0.0	$0.0	$0.0	$0.0	$0.0	$0.0
$0.0	$0.0	$0.0	$0.0	$0.0	$0.0	$0.0	$0.0	$0.0
$0.0	$0.0	$0.0	$0.0	$0.0	$0.0	$0.0	$0.0	$0.0

figure 3-8

Income Statement—Office/Commercial: Sample Mixed-Use Development Pro Forma

Thousands of Dollars/Inflation: 3%

		Year 1	Year 2	Year 3	Year 4	Year 5	Year 6
Assumptions							
Inflation Factor	3.0%	1.03	1.06	1.09	1.13	1.16	1.19
GLA Absorbed	750,000	0	50,000	100,000	200,000	300,000	400,000
Net Rentable Area	90%	0	45,000	90,000	180,000	270,000	360,000
Vacancy Factor	5%						
Net Lease Revenue per Square Foot	$26.00	$26.80	$27.60	$28.40	$29.30	$30.10	$31.00
Net Operating Income							
Leasing Revenues		$0.0	$1,179.9	$2,428.2	$5,010.3	$7,720.7	$10,602.0
Operations and Maintenance Expenses per Square Foot	$6.00	$0.00	$318.3	$655.6	$1,350.6	$2,086.7	$2,865.7
Net Operating Income		$0.0	$861.6	$1,772.6	$3,659.7	$5,634.0	$7,736.3
Development Costs							
Percent Built by Year		6.7%	6.7%	13.3%	13.3%	13.3%	13.3%
Development Costs	$136,125.0	$9,347.3	$9,627.7	$19,833.0	$20,428.0	$21,040.8	$21,672.0
Infrastructure Costs		$2,226.5	$0.0	$0.0	$0.0	$0.0	$2,258.4
Total Development Costs		$11,573.7	$9,627.7	$19,833.0	$20,428.0	$21,040.8	$23,930.5
Annual Cash Flow							
Net Operating Income		$0.0	$861.6	$1,772.6	$3,659.7	$5,634.0	$7,736.3
Asset Value[1] @ 10%							
Costs of Sale @ 5%							
Total Development Costs		$(11,573.7)	$(9,627.7)	$(19,833.0)	$(20,428.0)	$(21,040.8)	$(23,930.5)
Net Cash Flow		$(11,573.7)	$(8,766.0)	$(18,060.4)	$(16,768.3)	$(15,406.9)	$(16,194.2)

Net Present Value @ 10%: $4,042.9   **Internal Rate of Return: 10.6%**

[1]Assumes asset sale in Year 15.

Source: Economics Research Associates, Washington, D.C.

	Year 7	Year 8	Year 9	Year 10	Year 11	Year 12	Year 13	Year 14	Year 15
	1.23	1.27	1.30	1.34	1.38	1.43	1.47	1.51	1.56
	500,000	625,000	750,000	750,000	750,000	750,000	750,000	750,000	750,000
	450,000	562,500	675,000	675,000	675,000	675,000	675,000	675,000	675,000
	$32.00	$32.90	$33.90	$34.90	$36.00	$37.10	$38.20	$39.30	$40.50
	$13,680.0	$17,580.9	$21,738.4	$22,379.6	$23,085.0	$23,790.4	$24,495.8	$25,201.1	$25,970.6
	$3,689.6	$4,750.4	$5,871.5	$6,047.6	$6,229.1	$6,415.9	$6,608.4	$6,806.7	$7,010.9
	$9,990.4	$12,830.5	$15,866.9	$16,332.0	$16,855.9	$17,374.5	$17,887.3	$18,394.5	$18,959.8
	16.7%	16.7%	0.0%	0.0%	0.0%	0.0%	0.0%	0.0%	0.0%
	$27,902.8	$28,739.8	$0.0	$0.0	$0.0	$0.0	$0.0	$0.0	$0.0
	$0.0	$0.0	$0.0	$0.0	$0.0	$0.0	$0.0	$0.0	$0.0
	$27,902.8	$28,739.8	$0.0	$0.0	$0.0	$0.0	$0.0	$0.0	$0.0
	$9,990.4	$12,830.5	$15,866.9	$16,332.0	$16,855.9	$17,374.5	$17,887.3	$18,394.5	$18,959.8
									$189,597.7
									$(9,479.9)
	$(27,902.8)	$(28,739.8)	$0.0	$0.0	$0.0	$0.0	$0.0	$0.0	$0.0
	$(17,912.4)	$(15,909.3)	$15,866.9	$16,332.0	$16,855.9	$17,374.5	$17,887.3	$18,394.5	$199,077.6

figure 3-9

Income Statement—Retail: Sample Mixed-Use Development Pro Forma

Thousands of Dollars/Inflation: 3%

		Year 1	Year 2	Year 3	Year 4	Year 5	Year 6
Assumptions							
Inflation Factor	3.0%	1.03	1.06	1.09	1.13	1.16	1.19
GLA Absorbed	250,000	0	0	0	100,000	145,000	165,000
Net Rentable Area	85%	0	0	0	85,000	123,250	140,250
Vacancy Factor	5%						
Net Lease Revenue per Square Foot	$33.00	$34.00	$35.00	$36.10	$37.10	$38.30	$39.40
Net Operating Income							
Leasing Revenues		$0.0	$0.0	$0.0	$3,524.5	$5,275.8	$6,176.0
Operations and Maintenance Expenses per Square Foot	$5.50	$0.0	$0.0	$0.0	$619.0	$924.5	$1,083.6
Net Operating Income		$0.0	$0.0	$0.0	$2,905.5	$4,351.3	$5,092.3
Development Costs							
Percent Built by Year		0.0%	0.0%	40.0%	18.0%	8.0%	14.0%
Development Costs	$50,875,000	$0.0	$0.0	$22,237.0	$10,306.8	$4,718.2	$8,504.6
Infrastructure Costs		$918.4	$0.0	$0.0	$0.0	$0.0	$548.5
Total Development Costs		$918.4	$0.0	$22,237.0	$10,306.8	$4,718.2	$9,053.1
Annual Cash Flow							
Net Operating Income		$0.0	$0.0	$0.0	$2,905.5	$4,351.3	$5,092.3
Asset Value[1] @ 10%							
Costs of Sale @ 5%							
Total Development Costs		$(918.4)	$0.0	$(22,237.0)	$(10,306.8)	$(4,718.2)	$(9,053.1)
Net Cash Flow		$(918.4)	$0.0	$(22,237.0)	$(7,401.4)	$(366.9)	$(3,960.8)

Net Present Value @ 10%: $19,049.1   **Internal Rate of Return: 16.5%**

[1]Assumes asset sale in Year 15.

Source: Economics Research Associates, Washington, D.C.

Year 7	Year 8	Year 9	Year 10	Year 11	Year 12	Year 13	Year 14	Year 15
1.23	1.27	1.30	1.34	1.38	1.43	1.47	1.51	1.56
200,000	225,000	250,000	250,000	250,000	250,000	250,000	250,000	250,000
170,000	191,250	212,500	212,500	212,500	212,500	212,500	212,500	212,500
$40.60	$41.80	$43.10	$44.30	$45.70	$47.10	$48.50	$49.90	$51.40
$7,714.0	$8,934.8	$10,236.3	$10,521.3	$10,853.8	$11,186.3	$11,518.8	$11,851.3	$12,207.5
$1,352.9	$1,567.6	$1,794.1	$1,847.9	$1,903.3	$1,960.4	$2,019.2	$2,079.8	$2,142.2
$6,361.1	$7,367.1	$8,442.2	$8,673.4	$8,950.4	$9,225.8	$9,499.5	$9,771.4	$10,065.3
10.0%	10.0%	0.0%	0.0%	0.0%	0.0%	0.0%	0.0%	0.0%
$6,257.0	$6,444.7	$0.0	$0.0	$0.0	$0.0	$0.0	$0.0	$0.0
$0.0	$0.0	$0.0	$0.0	$0.0	$0.0	$0.0	$0.0	$0.0
$6,257.0	$6,444.7	$0.0	$0.0	$0.0	$0.0	$0.0	$0.0	$0.0
$6,361.1	$7,367.1	$8,442.2	$8,673.4	$8,950.4	$9,225.8	$9,499.5	$9,771.4	$10,065.3
								$100,652.9
								$(5,032.6)
$(6,257.0)	$(6,444.7)	$0.0	$0.0	$0.0	$0.0	$0.0	$0.0	$0.0
$104.2	$922.4	$8,442.2	$8,673.4	$8,950.4	$9,225.8	$9,499.5	$9,771.4	$105,685.6

figure 3-10

Income Statement—Hotel: Sample Mixed-Use Development Pro Forma

Thousands of Dollars/Inflation: 3%

		Year 1	Year 2	Year 3	Year 4	Year 5	Year 6
Assumptions							
Inflation Factor	3.0%	1.03	1.06	1.09	1.13	1.16	1.19
Rooms Completed	300	0	0	0	0	0	0
Vacancy Factor	28%						
Occupancy Factor	72%						
Average Daily Room Rate	$175.00	$180.25	$185.66	$191.23	$196.96	$202.87	$208.96
Net Operating Income							
Room Revenues		$0.0	$0.0	$0.0	$0.0	$0.0	$0.0
Other Revenues		$0.0	$0.0	$0.0	$0.0	$0.0	$0.0
Total Revenues		$0.0	$0.0	$0.0	$0.0	$0.0	$0.0
Total Expenses as Percentage of Gross Revenue	72%	$0.0	$0.0	$0.0	$0.0	$0.0	$0.0
Net Operating Income		$0.0	$0.0	$0.0	$0.0	$0.0	$0.0
Development Costs							
Percent Built by Year		0.0%	0.0%	0.0%	0.0%	0.0%	100.0%
Development Costs	$57,750.0	$0.0	$0.0	$0.0	$0.0	$0.0	$68,956.5
Infrastructure Costs		$0.0	$0.0	$0.0	$0.0	$0.0	$967.9
Total Development Costs		$0.0	$0.0	$0.0	$0.0	$0.0	$69,924.4
Annual Cash Flow							
Net Operating Income		$0.0	$0.0	$0.0	$0.0	$0.0	$0.0
Asset Value[1] @ 10%							
Costs of Sale @ 5%							
Total Development Costs		$0.0	$0.0	$0.0	$0.0	$0.0	$(69,924.4)
Net Cash Flow		$0.0	$0.0	$0.0	$0.0	$0.0	$(69,924.4)

Net Present Value @ 10%: $11,042.1   **Internal Rate of Return: 14.3%**

[1]Assumes asset sale in Year 15.

Source: Economics Research Associates, Washington, D.C.

Year 7	Year 8	Year 9	Year 10	Year 11	Year 12	Year 13	Year 14	Year 15
1.23	1.27	1.30	1.34	1.38	1.43	1.47	1.51	1.56
300	300	300	300	300	300	300	300	300
$215.23	$221.68	$228.34	$235.19	$242.24	$249.51	$256.99	$264.70	$272.64
$16,968.6	$17,477.6	$18,002.0	$18,542.0	$19,098.3	$19,671.2	$20,261.4	$20,869.2	$21,495.3
$10,859.9	$11,185.7	$11,521.3	$11,866.9	$12,222.9	$12,589.6	$12,967.3	$13,356.3	$13,757.0
$27,828.5	$28,663.3	$29,523.2	$30,408.9	$31,321.2	$32,260.8	$33,228.6	$34,225.5	$35,252.3
$20,036.5	$20,637.6	$21,256.7	$21,894.4	$22,551.2	$23,227.8	$23,924.6	$24,642.4	$25,381.6
$7,792.0	$8,025.7	$8,266.5	$8,514.5	$8,769.9	$9,033.0	$9,304.0	$9,583.1	$9,870.6
0.0%	0.0%	0.0%	0.0%	0.0%	0.0%	0.0%	0.0%	0.0%
$0.0	$0.0	$0.0	$0.0	$0.0	$0.0	$0.0	$0.0	$0.0
$0.0	$0.0	$0.0	$0.0	$0.0	$0.0	$0.0	$0.0	$0.0
$0.0	$0.0	$0.0	$0.0	$0.0	$0.0	$0.0	$0.0	$0.0
$7,792.0	$8,025.7	$8,266.5	$8,514.5	$8,769.9	$9,033.0	$9,304.0	$9,583.1	$9,870.6
								$98,706.3
								$(4,935.3)
$0.0	$0.0	$0.0	$0.0	$0.0	$0.0	$0.0	$0.0	$0.0
$7,792.0	$8,025.7	$8,266.5	$8,514.5	$8,769.9	$9,033.0	$9,304.0	$9,583.1	$103,641.6

figure 3-11

Income Statement—Structured Parking: Sample Mixed-Use Development Pro Forma

Thousands of Dollars/Inflation: 3%

		Year 1	Year 2	Year 3	Year 4	Year 5	Year 6
Assumptions							
Inflation Factor	3.0%	1.03	1.06	1.09	1.13	1.16	1.19
Parking Spaces	3,000	0	150	300	900	1,335	1,695
Monthly Fees							
Monthly Parking Fee	$150						
Allocation to Monthly Use	35%	0	53	105	315	467	593
Percent Occupancy by Monthly Contracts	95%						
Hourly Fees							
Number of Spaces	1,950	0	98	195	585	868	1,102
Nonwork Days	115						
Daily Parking Hours	14						
Percent Utilization	25%						
Work Days	250						
Daily Parking Hours	10						
Percent Utilization	25%						
Hourly Parking Rate	$2.75						
Expenses							
Operating Expenses (Percent of Gross Revenue)	25%						
Net Operating Income							
Parking Revenue							
Monthly Parking		$0.0	$95.2	$196.2	$606.3	$926.3	$1,211.3
Hourly Parking		$0.0	$292.3	$602.1	$1,860.5	$2,842.5	$3,717.2
Total Parking Revenue		$0.0	$387.5	$798.3	$2,466.7	$3,768.7	$4,928.6
Expenses		$0.0	$96.9	$199.6	$616.7	$942.2	$1,232.1
Net Operating Income		$0.0	$290.6	$598.7	$1,850.0	$2,826.5	$3,696.4
Development Costs							
Percent Built by Year		5.0%	5.0%	20.0%	14.5%	12.0%	13.5%
Development Costs	$52,800	$2,719.2	$2,800.8	$11,539.2	$8,616.9	$7,345.2	$8,511.2
Infrastructure Costs		$3,066.2	$0.0	$0.0	$0.0	$0.0	$2,736.7
Total Development Costs		$5,785.4	$2,800.8	$11,539.2	$8,616.9	$7,345.2	$11,247.9
Annual Cash Flow							
Net Operating Income		$0.0	$290.6	$598.7	$1,850.0	$2,826.5	$3,696.4
Asset Value[1] @ 10%							
Costs of Sale @ 5%							
Total Development Costs		$(5,785.4)	$(2,800.8)	$(11,539.2)	$(8,616.9)	$(7,345.2)	$(11,247.9)
Net Cash Flow		$(5,785.4)	$(2,510.1)	$(10,940.5)	$(6,766.9)	$(4,518.6)	$(7,551.5)

Net Present Value @ 10%: $5,238.2   **Internal Rate of Return: 11.8%**

[1]Assumes asset sale in Year 15.

Source: Economics Research Associates, Washington, D.C.

Year 7	Year 8	Year 9	Year 10	Year 11	Year 12	Year 13	Year 14	Year 15
1.23	1.27	1.30	1.34	1.38	1.43	1.47	1.51	1.56
2,100	2,550	3,000	3,000	3,000	3,000	3,000	3,000	3,000
735	893	1,050	1,050	1,050	1,050	1,050	1,050	1,050
1,365	1,658	1,950	1,950	1,950	1,950	1,950	1,950	1,950
$1,545.8	$1,933.3	$2,342.7	$2,413.0	$2,485.4	$2,560.0	$2,636.8	$2,715.9	$2,797.3
$4,743.6	$5,932.9	$7,189.3	$7,404.9	$7,627.1	$7,855.9	$8,091.6	$8,334.3	$8,584.4
$6,289.4	$7,866.2	$9,532.0	$9,817.9	$10,112.5	$10,415.9	$10,728.3	$11,050.2	$11,381.7
$1,572.3	$1,966.5	$2,383.0	$2,454.5	$2,528.1	$2,604.0	$2,682.1	$2,762.5	$2,845.4
$4,717.0	$5,899.6	$7,149.0	$7,363.5	$7,584.4	$7,811.9	$8,046.2	$8,287.6	$8,536.3
15.0%	15.0%	0.0%	0.0%	0.0%	0.0%	0.0%	0.0%	0.0%
$9,740.6	$10,032.8	$0.0	$0.0	$0.0	$0.0	$0.0	$0.0	$0.0
$0.0	$0.0	$0.0	$0.0	$0.0	$0.0	$0.0	$0.0	$0.0
$9,740.6	$10,032.8	$0.0	$0.0	$0.0	$0.0	$0.0	$0.0	$0.0
$4,717.0	$5,899.6	$7,149.0	$7,363.5	$7,584.4	$7,811.9	$8,046.2	$8,287.6	$8,536.3
								$85,362.6
								$(4,268.1)
$(9,740.6)	$(10,032.8)	$0.0	$0.0	$0.0	$0.0	$0.0	$0.0	$0.0
$(5,023.6)	$(4,133.2)	$7,149.0	$7,363.5	$7,584.4	$7,811.9	$8,046.2	$8,287.6	$89,630.7

Financing mixed-use projects can be challenging because of their large size, diverse mix of uses, and long development time frames. Fairfax Corner in Fairfax, Virginia, is planned to include 900,000 square feet (84,000 square meters) on 45 acres (18 hectares), with apartment, office, retail, and cinema uses.

Building H South Elevation

Building H West Elevation

Building O South Elevation

Building O East Elevation

financing for an expensive and risky project like a mixed-use project is more difficult.

- Availability of Public Financing—The community's commitment to the project can play an important role in attracting other sources of financing; public financing often makes the difference between a project's being viable or nonviable.
- Uses Involved—With property cycles varying for different uses, the ability to finance specific uses should be considered. For example, in early 2003, hotels and cinemas were particularly difficult to finance.
- Financing by Component—Financing can be arranged by component if separate components have separate owners or if the developer desires the flexibility of separately financing or selling components in the future. Structuring the financing so that it is acceptable to the financing community is critical. Legal documents that clearly delineate the separate components and their legal relationship to the other components are also critical.

- Project's Complexity, Size, and Phasing—These factors affect the kind of financing sources that could be attracted to the project, the amount of capital that is needed, the number of financial institutions that will be involved, and the possible phasing of the financing.

It is beyond the scope of this text to provide a comprehensive technical guide to real estate and/or development finance, as entire textbooks are devoted to the many issues and techniques involved in real estate finance.[3]

The Financing Challenge

Mixed-use projects are difficult to finance because of a variety of complicating issues. Compared with most single-use projects, mixed-use projects are more likely to involve larger capital requirements, more numerous financing sources, higher equity requirements, a longer development period, more complicated underwriting as a result of the numerous uses that require separate underwriting, skeptical public capital markets, investors' preferences for risk premiums, and/or complications resulting from the inclusion of public financing or financial participation.

Large Capital Requirements and Numerous Financing Sources. The substantial development costs often associated with mixed-use projects usually mean that only a limited number of developers and financial institutions have the resources and/or interest in financing such demanding projects. Because mixed-use developments combine several types of products into one project, they generally are among the largest type of project being built today and require a correspondingly large financial commitment. Many mixed-use projects cost upward of $400 million to build. The very substantial amount of capital required for a single development eliminates many of the smaller financial players that would be interested in a project. It is especially difficult to find financial institutions that are willing to be the single source of debt financing for loans of this size and complexity. As a result, several sources of both debt and equity financing are often involved.

Many mixed-use projects involve such high costs that they can strain the financial resources of even the largest and most experienced developers. In other situations, the mixed-use project under development may be the largest and most complex the developer has ever undertaken, suggesting that the developer may be faced with the prospect of risking substantial portions of his equity asset base. For this reason, joint ventures, strong equity partners, and/or multiple financing sources are inevitably required to make a mixed-use project work.

Higher Equity Requirements. The developer may also need more equity than for standard single-use projects. Because they are frequently not well understood by lenders and are considered riskier than other developments, mixed-use projects often require higher levels of equity than single-use projects. For example, the developers of Phillips Place in Charlotte, North Carolina, which includes separately financed apartment, hotel, and retail components, found that the retail portion of the project required substantially more equity than a typical retail development.

Although it was frequently possible to develop a project with little or no equity during the 1980s, more recent experience has required at least 25 percent equity capital in a deal to make it attractive to lenders. For mixed-use projects, requirements can often be 30 percent or more. In some cases, mezzanine financing is used to bridge the difference between what the developer and equity partners are willing to put up as equity and what the lender is willing to lend.

Longer Development Period. Mixed-use projects often require a longer period for development than single-use projects. Some multiphase mixed-use projects were started a decade ago and still are not complete. The number of developers, investors, and lenders with the ability to stay with a project for such extended periods is limited. The developer must have a solid reputation for completing long-term projects to attract interested

equity partners and lenders. Although all institutional investors and lenders carefully evaluate the feasibility of a proposed project before deciding to commit funds to it, they usually do not even begin that process unless they are first satisfied with the developer's ability to complete the project.

Numerous Uses to Be Underwritten. The mix of uses complicates the financing, as each use must be underwritten separately and some potential investors or lenders may be uncomfortable with one or more of the proposed uses. Thus, developers often seek and obtain numerous major equity partners and/or financing commitments from several lenders for a large mixed-use project. According to Peter Pappas of Pappas Properties in Charlotte, "Not many lenders will do a permanent loan on three or more products, which creates the need for bifurcating the product type so you can have multiple lenders in on the project."

Public Capital Markets. The growing importance and availability of real estate capital from public capital markets have made capital more readily available for large real estate investments, which can favor mixed-use projects, but much of this capital is targeted to specific property types. Real estate investment trusts (REITs), in particular, often are focused on specific types of property.

> Diversification by a REIT into a different property type raises yellow flags with the investment community. Will the REIT become distracted from its main line of business? Will it acquire and be able to integrate the management expertise needed for its investment in a new property type? REIT managers themselves may be wary of the risks of diversification. . . . The integration of land uses within a project adds complexity to the evaluation of the property's cash flows and the credit risks that different types of tenants within the project present.[4]

For example, two publicly traded REITs that have been active in mixed-use development—Post Properties and Federal Realty Investment Trust—recently pulled back from mixed-use development to focus on their core property specializations, apartments and retail, respectively.

On the debt side of the public markets, underwriters of commercial mortgage–backed securities (CMBSs) tend to prefer loans that are less rather than more complex, which does not favor mixed-use projects.

> Owners of mixed-use projects may have problems gaining access to the CMBS market depending upon the complexity of tenant types in the project. Combining different uses within a project presents the creditor with different types of credit risks and different real estate markets to consider. . . . Particularly [during times when there is a large volume of capital transactions taking place], underwriters and rating agencies have given first priority to transactions that are more easily and quickly underwritten—the plain vanilla loans.[5]

Risk Premiums. As a result of these and other complicating factors, investors and lenders frequently seek higher returns on mixed-use projects to offset the higher risk.

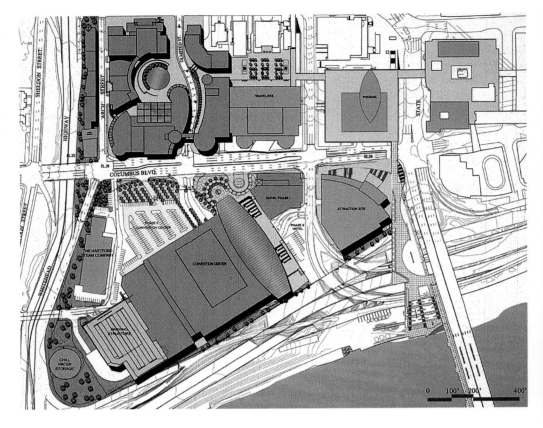

Led by the Capital City Economic Development Authority at the behest of the governor of Connecticut, Adriaen's Landing in Hartford involves both public and private financing. The project includes a convention center, hotel, retail space, and residential development in downtown Hartford along the Connecticut River.

"The complexity of developing and meshing multiple uses in a single development raises risk. . . . Complexity also tends to make each project unique, and lenders and investors generally attach significant return premia to nonstandard investments."[6] Moreover,

> higher risk leads to higher discount rates applied to cash flows. A standard discounted cash flow calculation indicates that, with a required rate of return of 18 percent, the present value of a dollar five years from now is only 44 cents; the present value of a dollar ten years from now is only 19 cents. High discount rates mean that cash flow in the longer-term future has little value to the typical lender or investor. Unless a project can generate sufficiently high cash flows in the early years (when its costs are also higher), it will not be perceived as financially viable.[7]

The frequent involvement of public financing and partnerships can add additional challenges. Developers must understand these issues and biases and effectively address them in the financial structure of the project if they hope to attract investors and obtain adequate financing at reasonable terms.

Sources of Equity Financing

Financing any real estate project begins with equity, and equity financing begins with a developer's own capital and that of the partners the developer can attract. Equity partner investors may include developers and private property companies, wealthy individuals and limited partnerships, pension funds, investment advisory firms using pension fund money, insurance companies, REITs, opportunity funds, investment banks, commercial banks

(especially in Europe), and other private investment entities. These investors all have different objectives for their investment.

Private Investors. Private investors in either general or limited partnership structures are typical financing sources for real estate projects of all types, especially for smaller and medium projects. Raising equity capital from private investors in the United States has traditionally involved developing partnerships with wealthy individuals interested in investing in private real estate ventures. A typical venture might involve a real estate developer as general partner and 20 to 50 wealthy individuals as limited partners.

In other situations, especially in Asia, numerous very wealthy individuals develop a partnership to undertake a development. One large international example is Suntec City, a mixed-use project on a 28.9-acre (11.7-hectare) site in the new, master-planned Marina Centre CBD of Singapore. The project comprises five blocks of office space, including one 18-story and four 45-story office towers, one of the largest international exhibition and convention centers in southeast Asia, a large shopping and entertainment center, two lower levels of parking for 3,200 cars, a landmark fountain, and other amenities.

Suntec City was funded entirely by a consortium whose 11 shareholders are among Asia's most successful entrepreneurs. Suntec's development cost totaled about S\$2.3 billion (about \$1.3 billion), but its appraised value upon completion was twice that amount. It was funded with an undisclosed shareholder equity contribution and approximately S\$1.5 billion in debt (\$844 million), with the balance funded from the sale of office space. The mixed-use complex occupies a 99-year leasehold acquired by bid from the Singapore government's urban redevelopment authority for S$208 million ($117 million).

Creating such partnerships with private investors is based in part on making contacts and establishing relationships over time with these equity partners and their financial advisers. As mixed-use projects grow larger, this approach can often be impractical in raising the bulk of the equity needed, and thus larger projects typically involve joint ventures between developers, private investors, and major sources of institutional equity, such as pension funds (or their advisers), insurance companies, and investment banks that create private equity funds.

Pension Funds. Pension funds, especially U.S. and European funds, are one of the major sources of equity capital for real estate, although they are more likely to acquire and own operating properties than engage in equity investing for development ventures. Thus, they generally agree to take a substantial equity position in a completed project once it reaches specific performance thresholds. They often invest in a project through advisers rather than directly.

Pension funds sometimes do invest in development deals as well. The Victory mixed-use development in Dallas, for example, involves a partnership of three private development entities—Related Urban Group, Hillwood, and Southwest Sports Group—and California Urban Investment Partners (CUIP), a joint venture between MacFarlane Partners (MacFarlane) and California Public Employees Retirement System (CalPERS), the nation's largest pension fund. CUIP has agreed to provide financing for Victory and will also fund future Related Urban Group development projects.

REITs. REITs and public real estate operating companies, as noted, are frequently focused in narrow property categories such as retail, office, or apartments. They have been major sources of equity capital for mixed-use projects, often through joint ventures and partnerships with other REITs or with private developers. Leading examples of projects built and financed through REITs and other public real estate companies include Federal Realty's Santana Row in San Jose and Bethesda Row in Bethesda, Maryland, and Post Properties's Riverside in Atlanta and Addison Circle near Dallas.

International Investors, Investment Banks, and Opportunity Funds. International investors, investment banks, and opportunity funds are often willing to take on challenging mixed-use projects if they can obtain returns that will adequately compensate them for their risk. Millennium Partners, a private development firm that builds urban mixed-use properties combining hotels, condominiums, retail space, and sports clubs, has arranged a consortium of international investors and private investment funds to finance its numerous projects, including German financial institutions, Goldman Sachs's Whitehall Fund, and George Soros's Quantum Realty Fund Limited.

Insurance Companies. Insurance companies also have been involved in mixed-use projects, although because of regulatory changes in recent years, they have not been major players on the equity side of the real estate market. Insurance companies were heavily involved as equity investors in such high-profile examples as John Hancock Center in Chicago and Prudential Center in Boston. Some insurance companies remain active on the equity side, however. For example, the primary equity investor for Atlantic Station in Atlanta, a huge redevelopment on the site of a former Atlantic Steel facility, is an insurance company. Atlantic Steel Redevelopment, LLC, the project owner and developer, is currently a joint business effort of Jacoby Development, CRB Realty, and AIG Global Real Estate. Jacoby and CRB are private real estate firms, while AIG is a large international insurance company.

Commercial Banks. Although banks are seldom equity investors in the United States, they are in Europe. In Austria, for example, a major mixed-use project is being undertaken by a consortium of banks and insurance companies. Vienna Donau City in Austria is a large mixed-use

Photographer: Steve Hinds; courtesy of Post Properties

Riverside in Atlanta was financed and developed by Post Properties, a publicly traded REIT.

project that combines living, working, recreation, and cultural facilities. The project, located on 42 acres (17 hectares) of land, offers about 5.4 million square feet (500,000 square meters) of gross floor area. The investment totals some $1.6 billion (€1.5 billion); the mix of uses includes 44 percent office space, 31 percent residential, 13 percent educational or other, and 11 percent culture and leisure. It is owned by Austria's largest banks and insurance companies, Nomura, and Wiener Holding AG.

Universities and Foundations. Nontraditional sources of equity for mixed-use projects include institutions such as universities and foundations, which look to invest to increase their endowments. Many now look for real estate investments in line with their institutional objectives, which for many include such issues as urban revitalization and smart growth.

For example, at University Park at MIT in Cambridge (see Chapter 8), MIT had been acquiring land for 25 years for the development of a corporate office and research park adjacent to its campus. The strategy was to invest portions of the MIT endowment in ways that would generate economic returns while also helping to accelerate the transfer of technology into the commercial marketplace. MIT chose Forest City as developer, structuring a deal whereby Forest City acquired each development parcel in the park through a 75-year ground lease, taken down at the start of construction. Base rent is calculated as a percentage of MIT's average basis in land value, adjusted for certain cost factors and for inflation. MIT was

responsible for the demolition of existing buildings (with the cost included in its basis), and both parties share equally in the cost of environmental remediation. Otherwise, the land is delivered as is; therefore, ground rent is net to MIT. This component of ground rent is senior to first-mortgage debt but is relatively small; hence, it has not impeded the securing of mortgage financing. In addition, MIT participates in the growth of income derived from the project over time, receiving 15 percent of cash flow above a base established when each building is initially 90 percent leased, as well as a 15 percent participation in net refinancing and sales.

Increasingly, foundations are also reconsidering how they invest to better align their investments with social objectives. "Many of the country's largest foundations, including MacArthur, Rockefeller, Surdna, Packard, Hewlett, Mellon, and Heinz, are focused on new urbanism, smart growth, and sustainable development. . . . By bridging the gap between the money-making side of the foundation and the programmatic grant-making side, foundations can make innovative real estate investments from the asset base of the foundation."[8] Arcadia Land Company, for example, has been able to attract $6 million in equity from the McCune Charitable Foundation, the largest foundation based in New Mexico, to form the Historic District Improvement Company for a mixed-use project in downtown Albuquerque.

Foundations are investing in numerous other smart growth projects in cities such as Baton Rouge, Jupiter,

Vienna Donau City in Austria was undertaken by a consortium of banks and insurance companies.

The developers of Santana Row in San Jose obtained debt financing from a consortium of banks from Europe, Canada, and the United States.

Florida, Pittsburgh, Portland, and San Diego. An organization formed in 1999—the Funders' Network for Smart Growth and Livable Communities—assists foundations in fostering and investing in smart growth.[9]

Sources of Debt Financing

Commercial banks, insurance companies, savings institutions, the CMBS industry, and, to a lesser extent, finance companies supply the major share of debt financing to the commercial real estate development industry. These institutions tend to specialize in certain types of transactions that vary from country to country, and developers should investigate the options available and then structure the best financing package that meets all funding requirements. The following paragraphs describe the financing usually supplied by private sources of financing (see Chapter 4 for government financing options).

Commercial Banks and Savings Institutions. Commercial banks and savings institutions specialize in both construction loans and longer-term mortgages. Banks are the major players in the debt finance business around the world; the role of savings institutions in the United States has greatly diminished since the savings and loan crisis of the late 1980s. Banks also make business lines of credit available that can be used to finance construction or predevelopment costs, especially on smaller or phased projects. Banks have traditionally been focused on short-term debt, but many are active in most types of real estate financing, both short and long term.

Banks often have a very formulaic approach to real estate finance and thus will need to be presented with financing for components or to be educated about mixed-use development. When making construction loans, they are also concerned about a source of permanent financing, and when undertaking longer-term mortgages, they are concerned about their ability to sell the loan to the secondary market. Thus, for construction loans their lending criteria are very much affected by the long-term lending criteria of takeout lenders such as insurance companies. When originating longer-term mortgages, they are concerned about the criteria and demands of the CMBS industry.

Generally, the banking industry is set up for financing single uses. Stephen Macauley, president of Macauley Properties in Marietta, Georgia, notes that "banks generally seek to finance each use separately and have difficulty with financing mixed uses." He notes they also consider unanchored retail space a risky investment. Bankers seriously consider where the industry is in the economic cycle and often will not take a chance on an unusual project when the economy is at risk, especially where many far simpler financing opportunities are available.

Banks also make intermediate-term loans, usually for five to seven years with a fixed or floating rate, and they hold long-term commercial mortgages, although increasingly they seek to sell these mortgages into the CMBS market to free up capital for more lending. U.S. banks seldom take an equity position in a project unless they are forced to take back a nonperforming loan. Banks may also provide gap financing to carry the development between the initial construction loan and the permanent loan.

Most major mixed-use projects involve bank financing, and some major mixed-use projects in the United States have sought financing from foreign banks as lenders. Federal Realty Investment Trust recently closed a $295 million construction loan associated with the development of its Santana Row mixed-use property in San Jose, California, involving Commerzbank AG as administrative agent, Fleet National Bank as syndication agent, Bayerische Hypo-und Vereinsbank AG as documentation agent, Bayerische Landesbank Bank, Landesbank Hessen-Thuringen Girozentrale, MidFirst Bank, and Bank of Montreal. Interest on the construction loan, initially set at LIBOR (London interbank offered rate) plus 212.5 basis points, will be guaranteed by Federal Realty. Both the interest rate and Federal Realty's guarantee of the loan are subject to step-down provisions based on the satisfaction of specified conditions.

Abacoa Town Center in Jupiter, Florida, used a finance company and an investment bank for debt and mezzanine financing.

Life Insurance Companies. Life insurance companies are leading sources of long-term debt but also are involved in other types of debt financing. They have the expertise and financial strength to meet most financing requirements for a mixed-use project. Often they supply construction, interim, and permanent financing; some even provide equity. The $275 million Gallery Place project in Washington, D.C., for example, being developed by a joint venture between two developers, has obtained financing from numerous sources, including debt financing from one insurance company and equity financing from another. Financing includes a $123.8 million construction loan from Union Labor Life Insurance Company, Ultra Fund of Amalgamated Bank, N.A., and BB&T Bank; a $58 million equity investment by Massachusetts Mutual Insurance Company and AFL-CIO Building Investment Trust; and $73.65 million in District of Columbia tax increment revenue bonds.

Commercial Mortgage–Backed Securities. The CMBS industry is now the big gorilla in long-term debt. Loan originators are increasingly seeking to sell their loans to the CMBS market, and to do so, the loans must conform to CMBS standard loan and documentation formats and be appealing to CMBS investors. Many loan originators now hesitate to make a loan if they believe they cannot sell it to the CMBS market.

CMBSs invest in pooled mortgages that may include a range of property types, but they often prefer that each individual loan be for a specific property type: "The process of pooling loans provides a mechanism for quality control. Mortgage sellers provide a lengthy set of representations and warranties [that] cover the qualitative aspects of the loan assets and the manner in which they are created."[10] In general, it is easier for these originators to provide warranties for standard single-use projects, which does not favor mortgages for mixed-use properties.

Investment Banks and Finance Companies. Investment banks and large finance companies are involved in both short- and long-term debt financing. Abacoa Town Center in Jupiter, Florida, for example, obtained $40 million in financing from such sources for its first phase. GMAC Commercial Mortgage provided construction financing of $32.5 million, and Lehman Brothers provide mezzanine financing of $7.1 million.

Structuring the Financing

Financial structuring is the process of matching a project's funding needs and the developer with the financial alternatives available in the marketplace. This process yields different answers for different projects, and it varies with conditions in the financial marketplace. The key questions involve the mix of debt, equity, and mezzanine financing; the mix of private and public financing; the use of construction and permanent financing; the number of financing sources that should be involved; the phasing of the development and the financing; and the packaging of project elements into financeable elements.

The issues must be considered at every stage of the financing process, from funding front-end costs to carry the project from conception through detailed planning and public review, to funding construction costs and operating/marketing expenses during construction and initial leasing, to permanent financing to carry the project through the long term. Developers of mixed-use projects need to work with many sources of funds to create a financing package that meets the needs of the project, the developer, the lender, and investors.

The key to success in structuring financing is ultimately determined in large part by how equity interests are managed. The wide range of investors in the market today and the range of financing structures and techniques increase the ability to structure a transaction to benefit each participant. The various players in real estate finance have different return criteria and time horizons, depending on their roles, preferred structures, constraints, volume, and so on. Putting together the right investors for the right deal is not easy, but the range of objectives and interests can be used to advantage in mixed-use developments.

Equity Structuring and Partnerships

In an ideal world, developers seek financing that is inexpensive, without risk, and simple. In the real world, however, what they can arrange is often just the opposite. The cornerstone to a private developer's approach is that he or she invariably seeks to develop the property to its highest and best use, maximize ownership interests in the property, and minimize the amount of equity at risk. This notion is particularly important in mixed-use developments because of the large sums involved, the number of investors frequently involved, and the importance of the developer to the success of the project.

In any joint venture or development partnership, the tradeoff usually involves some loss of control for the developer. A partner generally requires a hand in approving every major part of the development process, from contracts, design, leases, and additions to the development plan. Working with joint venture partners may involve delays or negotiation for unanticipated problems or modifications; this aspect cannot be underestimated.

The appeal of joint ventures and partnerships varies with the players involved, interest rates, tax laws, business cycles, and investment preferences of financial institutions, corporate tenants, and investors. Developers therefore need to communicate constantly with all parties in the transaction to determine the financial alternatives available for the project.

One innovative approach to creating equity partnerships is to package the equity into time tranches and target investors with longer-term horizons as equity investors. "The real goal is to connect appropriate investors with the appropriate investment. . . . Time tranches could be introduced to match investors who have different investment horizons with the appropriate 'piece' of an investment." Further, "time tranches imply that higher equity be invested in a real estate project than is normally the case for conventional projects. . . . Whether the increased equity comes from landowners, municipalities, or cash investors, at least a third of the total project costs need to be equity, as opposed to 20 percent for conventional development. Therefore, the way to break the logjam of financing progressive development is through increased equity by equity providers with a mid- to long-term horizon."[11] Foundations and universities are also possible sources for this kind of equity.

The public sector is likely to be a leading source of such capital, and the potential role of the public sector in financing a mixed-use development should be carefully explored. Public involvement can greatly assist the project's overall feasibility.

Partnership Options

Structuring the financing for a mixed-use project may involve numerous options: partnerships with landowners, partnerships with other developers, partnerships with lead tenants, partnerships with a variety of traditional equity investors, partnerships with nontraditional equity sources, alignment of financing sources with uses, mezzanine financing, selling land parcels to other developers, selling completed buildings to investors, phasing the project to reduce capital demands at a given time, and public/private partnerships (see Chapter 4). Many options are available, and no single formula exists for structuring financing. Developers must be creative and flexible. The project's financing structure must offer attractive investment options for all participants, requiring the expertise of a seasoned financial professional who can create the varying structures within an overall deal that makes sense for the project as a whole.

The traditional joint venture partnership is between a developer and a large equity investor. For example, at Bay Street Emeryville in Emeryville, California, which includes retail, restaurant, residential, hotel, and entertain-

Bay Street Emeryville in Emeryville, California, includes retail, restaurant, residential, hotel, and entertainment uses. The development team consists of Madison Marquette, an affiliate of international investment firm Capital Guidance Corporation, with the financial backing of California Urban Investment Partners, a $700 million joint venture of MacFarlane Partners and the California Public Employees Retirement System.

Pentagon Row in Arlington, Virginia, was developed through a partnership between Federal Realty Investment Trust and Post Properties.

ment uses, developer Madison Marquette, an affiliate of international investment firm Capital Guidance Corporation, obtained financial backing for the project from California Urban Investment Partners (a $700 million joint venture between MacFarlane Partners and the California Public Employees Retirement System).

In a joint venture, the developer may have to negotiate a deal in which the investor gets 50 percent or more ownership in the project, but the advantage is that the developer can obtain an ownership interest with minimal equity and risk and may also be able to collect development fees as well. By giving up one-half or more interest in the project, the developer reduces his equity requirement substantially. Moreover, having the institution as a partner provides the development with greater financial stability in the event of unforeseen delays, a soft market, or dramatic shifts in the capital markets.

In some cases, a joint venture or partnership is created between developers specializing in different proj-

ect components. These deals can be simpler in that each developer develops and owns his portion of the project and assumes the development risk involved. Pentagon Row in Arlington, Virginia, for example, involves a partnership between two REITs, Federal Realty and Post Properties. Paseo Colorado involved a similar joint venture between TrizecHahn and Post Properties.

When office space is a major component of a project, it may be possible to create a joint venture between the developer and a major tenant who wants to own the building and have the building reflect its corporate identity. Creating such a joint venture with a tenant early in the development process can generate additional cash and ensure a more fully leased building upon completion. Sony Center am Potsdamer Platz, for example, involved a joint venture with Sony Corp.

A third approach to joint venturing brings the developer together with a landowner. The developer avoids

The Denver Dry Goods Building involved the adaptive use of a historic six-story structure built in 1888. Located in downtown Denver, the building has been renovated for affordable and market-rate housing, retail space, and office uses. The building's 350,000 square feet (32,500 square meters) of space was subdivided into smaller condominium units and repackaged, using 23 different financing sources. The development was undertaken by the Denver Urban Renewal Authority (DURA) and the Affordable Housing Development Corporation (AHDC) of Katonah, New York.

Although large, unconventional adaptive use projects such as the Denver Dry may not be feasible when viewed as a whole, redefining the project into smaller components and packages may allow for a variety of development and financing options. Twenty-three separate sources of funding were pieced together to finance the several uses and phases of the project, including pension funds, state bond issues, tax increment bonds, U.S. Department of Housing and Urban Development (HUD) urban development action grants, the sale of low-income housing and historic tax credits, loans and equity investments from public agencies and private nonprofits, private bank loans, and developer equity.

The development of Phase I was split between two limited partnerships: Denver Building Housing Ltd. and Denver Dry Retail L.P. Denver Building Housing Ltd. was responsible for the development of 51 units of rental apartments and office space for the Denver Metro Convention and Visitors Bureau. This partnership was made up of two entities, the Federal National Mortgage Association (FNMA), which purchased the tax credits that provided the equity for the deal, and the Denver Dry

Development Corporation, a nonprofit 501(c)(3) corporation formed by DURA. The partnership selected AHDC and its president, Jonathan F.P. Rose, as the fee developer for these portions of the project.

The second partnership for Phase I, Denver Dry Retail L.P., was responsible for development of the entire second floor of the building, where a TJ Maxx store and office space for DURA were to be located. The Denver Dry Retail Corporation, an affiliate of AHDC, is the general partner of Denver Dry Retail L.P.

The development team for Phase II consists of a single limited partnership, Denver Dry Retail II, L.P., also an affiliate of AHDC. This partnership was responsible for the development of the Media Play store in the basement and first floor of the 16th Street building.

The key to the Denver Dry's resurrection was an echo of its past: just as the building was built in increments, so its reconstruction and reuse were accomplished piece by piece. The mammoth structure was broken down, figuratively and legally, into smaller condominium units to provide for more manageable and financeable packages of development. In smaller pieces, separate housing, retail, and office units could be planned and then bundled together into financing and construction packages.

■

---

having to buy the land, and the equity in the land assists in financing the project. This approach is complicated, however, in that the landowner may have to risk loss of the land to the lender if the project fails to perform. In other cases, the joint venture may proceed for only a short time until feasibility is determined and approvals are in place. At Phillips Place in Charlotte, for example, the developer worked closely with landowners during the early phases of the project; the deal that was struck offered landowners the option to contribute the land to the venture or cash out, and they eventually chose to cash out.

A fourth approach involving a public/private partnership is outlined in the accompanying feature box on the Denver Dry Goods Building. It provides a good example of the role that public financing can play in mixed-use development, highlights the complexity of the financing, and illustrates how a project can be packaged in financeable units. The role of the public sector

in mixed-use development is more fully described in Chapter 4.

Financing Upfront Costs

Equity is first required to undertake the initial planning and feasibility stages of the project that determine whether the project can feasibly be developed and financed. Equity is also the asset that a developer and other owners use in negotiations with lenders, and it may include land or property, the developer's capital and other resources, third-party capital, and so on. From the outset, the developer must carefully analyze the value and use of equity interests and design the ownership structure to maximize return on that equity.

The funding of front-end costs can be particularly problematic in mixed-use projects because of the high costs involved. Front-end costs can run into millions of dollars, and they thus entail a substantial risk for the developer and equity partners, as the money invested can be

Courtesy of TBA² Architects

The developers of Phillips Place in Charlotte, North Carolina, entered into a joint venture with a hotel developer for the hotel and sold the apartment land and apartment air rights to an apartment developer.

lost if the project does not proceed. Thus, usually only well-capitalized developers get involved in major mixed-use projects, as they have greater financial resources and can better afford to risk substantial mounts of capital. Moreover, if high front-end costs are likely, equity investors expect higher returns on the equity they invest.

Even the largest developers, however, would be hesitant to risk large amounts of their own cash on such front-end costs; thus, many mixed-use projects involve joint ventures or partnerships developed very early in the process, thereby spreading the risk among different investors. Such partners, however, often cannot be brought in until initial feasibility studies have been completed and the project is initially proved to have a potential for investment. In other situations, when the public sector controls the site and selects a developer in a competition, the public sector may provide some funds initially to cover the expenses of preparing a development proposal. For the most part, however, the developer must risk substantial equity at the outset to guide the project through the initial stages.

Equity can also be raised by selling land parcels to other development entities. A hotel, apartment, or office developer/operator, for example, may be interested in purchasing part of the land for developing his component of the project. At Phillips Place, for example, the developer entered into a 50/50 joint venture with a hotel developer for the hotel site and sold the apartment land

and air rights for apartments over retail space to an apartment developer. At Addison Circle, the developer sold office parcels to an office developer. Portions of a mixed-use project could also be presold to investors or sold after completion.

Multiple Financing Sources

The sources of financing for a mixed-use project depend on the size of the developer, the size of the project, the use or mix of uses to be financed, the amount of preleased or presold space, the credit rating of lessees, and the country or region where the project is located. In the case of government financing programs, location within a city can be an important consideration in deciding whether the project qualifies for public financing.

Because mixed-use projects are large and often quite expensive, numerous banks or other debt sources may be involved in financing a development. At Sony Center, total development costs for the project were roughly DM1.5 billion ($845 million). Nineteen banks put together the DM975 million ($549 million) nonrecourse debt package, which represented the largest real estate project financing scheme in German history. Dresdner Bank and Westdeutsche ImmobilienBank were the lead financial sources, and Sony was the major equity investor. At Mockingbird Station in Dallas, three banks—Comerica Bank–Texas, Union Bank of California, and California Bank & Trust—were involved.

In most cases, the developer should consider multiple equity and/or debt sources and financing programs. Although many projects during the 1970s and 1980s were financed through a single equity source and a single debt source, this approach is seldom followed today. A ULI survey conducted in the 1980s found that 33 percent of the mixed-use projects at that time were financed through a single source for the entire project. No data are available for projects being built today, but anecdotal evidence suggests that separate financing by component and/or phase is far more widely used today than it was in the 1980s. Mixed-use projects today are more likely to be phased and to involve more discrete components, facilitating this approach.

Although using numerous financial sources can complicate the development significantly, it is often the only method that will work. Even in tightly configured projects, separate financing or ownership of components is often used, which may create problems in the joint use or ownership of parking, energy or heating, ventilation, and air-conditioning (HVAC) systems, or other common areas. Good legal documents are necessary to spell out these arrangements in detail.

Construction Financing

Debt financing involves both short-term construction financing and long-term permanent financing. Construction financing is the riskier of the two, because the value of the proposal is yet to be verified and no income is available from the project to pay financing expenses. Construction lenders depend on the developer's expertise and ability to complete the project, covering that bet with an array of guarantees and protections. The lender also recognizes that market conditions can change before the building or buildings are ready for occupancy. What may look good on paper today may be a nonperforming asset 18 months from now when construction is completed.

Lenders generally employ standard measures such as debt coverage ratios and loan-to-value ratios, and they generally require a substantial amount of equity investment before they will lend money, usually around 25 percent. For example, of the $142 million in private financing that was required to finance CityPlace in West Palm Beach—which also included public financing—77 percent was provided by commercial banks, led by Key Bank for construction and miniperm financing, while the remaining 23 percent represents equity investment by the Palladium Company (now known as Related Urban Group) and an equity partner, a midwest pension fund.

Permanent Financing

Although construction financing is the first requirement, construction lenders will not lend on a project unless they know that the project's financial structure meets the requirements of long-term capital sources. Frequently for the developer, it means searching for a source of permanent financing before obtaining construction financing, as obtaining the latter is very difficult without permanent financing in place. Moreover, permanent loans are frequently sold into the securities market as CMBSs.

Three separate banks were involved in the financing of Mockingbird Station in Dallas.

The standards and criteria the CMBS sector uses to evaluate loans increasingly determine what is acceptable for originations, and thus banks and other financial sources in the business of making permanent loans that may be later sold into the CMBS market abide by these standards.

Arranging long-term financing has involved many approaches in mixed-use projects, and new approaches are being developed every day. Permanent financing is more often arranged separately for each component than is construction financing, but it ultimately depends on the nature of the project. Some projects that include numerous distinct structures can be financed principally component by component. On the other hand, a mixed-use tower is more likely to use a single source for permanent financing (although it is not a given). In general, notes Peter Pappas, "There is a small universe of permanent lenders that will do retail, multifamily, office, and/or hotel together."

In some cases, miniperm financing may be used, as was the case for University Park at MIT (see Chapter 8). The developer, Forest City, is a nonrecourse borrower. Each commercial building project was financed separately using conventional financing, and most financing was done on a miniperm basis (i.e., using small incremental mortgages that are converted to a master mortgage when further financing is no longer needed).

Mezzanine Financing

In addition to the simple conventional financing typically offered by commercial banks and insurance companies, mixed-use projects, because of their large capital needs and the fact they sometimes require more equity than single-use projects, use mezzanine equity and/or debt instruments. A mezzanine equity or debt investment is that part of the investment structure between the first mortgage and equity. With interest rates and borrowing costs below approximately 8 percent, high-cost mezzanine financing works for many projects that need gap financing.

For example, if a developer wishes to put in only equity representing 20 percent of the development costs and the lender is willing to lend only up to 70 percent of development costs, 10 percent of the costs may be financed through mezzanine financing, usually a loan at a higher interest rate than typical construction financing. Although mezzanine financing is technically debt, many lenders recognize that they are really in an equity position, because if the project fails to generate sufficient cash to pay debt service, their interest in the property is subordinate to the construction lender; thus, they get their money back only after the construction lender does, which may mean never.

Mezzanine lenders and investors active in the market seek equity-type returns through debt-type instruments. In certain instances, these investments take the form of a preferred equity investment in the ownership entity (the borrower). Mezzanine investments usually involve a preferred current return combined with a look-back return calculated on internal rate of return (IRR) and

may also include an additional share of profit above the look-back rate of return. Mezzanine financing is expensive debt, but it can be quite valuable in bridging the gap between debt and equity.

Flexibility and Financing

To facilitate financial structuring, the developer should allow for flexibility in the project's programming, design, ownership structure, phasing, and financing plan. Having the ability to adapt to unknown future conditions may mean the difference between a successful and an unsuccessful venture.

To evaluate that flexibility, the developer must answer certain questions: Can one portion of the project be sold without disturbing the ownership or financing of the remaining portions? How flexible is the financing package regarding refinancing? Is the construction schedule locked in, or can the timing or sequence be changed later? Are huge upfront expenditures for infrastructure involved, and how will they be financed? Can uses and their sizing be easily changed in future phases? Developers of mixed-use projects must be prepared for change.

Flexibility can be maximized through phasing, which is a critical technique for managing financing. Phasing the development of a project is a way to manage the capital needed from one source during a single time period, which can make financing easier. Once an initial phase is operational, it can be sold or can provide cash to help carry the undeveloped portion of the project. With phasing, developers have more freedom to decide on the timing and financing for other phases, to review the development plan and perhaps alter it, or to put the project on hold and wait for more favorable conditions later. Some very large projects have added phases a decade or more after the first phase was started. Thus, phasing breaks up very large projects into smaller, more manageable economic and financing units. The downside for financing is that carrying costs for the undeveloped land must be covered somehow in the financing plan.

Phasing also permits the developer to create different ownership structures and financing packages for each component of the project. Vesting ownership of different phases in different legal entities may enable the developer to sell part of the project more easily by creating separate financing packages that do not encumber other phases. This approach can complicate financing, however, and the tradeoffs should be carefully evaluated before proceeding.

Exit Strategy

The financial structure must also provide for a well-defined and carefully considered exit strategy; without such a strategy, investors are hesitant to put up their money. Thus, the developer must clearly explain the time frame for the investment, the hold period, the rules by which investors may exit, and the preferred window for exiting. Ownership plans that involve separate ownership of discrete uses and buildings are the simplest to exit, and developers thus frequently seek this approach

Brainerd Town Center in Chattanooga, Tennessee, will involve the transformation of a mall site into a mixed-use town center.

in structuring their deals. At WestEnd City Center in Budapest, for example, to facilitate the later disposition of elements in the project, different components are on separate parcels—a legal arrangement that does not detract from the functional integration of the center.

Well-designed projects and financing structures can even allow for exit strategies before the project is completed. One successful example of how a strong plan and phasing program can facilitate exit is Reston Town Center. The principal owner—Reston Land Corporation—sold the office and retail portions of the first completed phase of the project to Equity Office Properties, the hotel to Blackstone Group, and land for subsequent phases to Westbrook Partners. Westbrook's affiliate, Terrabrook, in turn brought in several new partners, including Boston Properties for the new office towers, Trammell Crow Residential for the residential component, and JBG Companies for the planned new hotel. Most uses are on their own land parcels. Development has continued to proceed under a master plan, and the separate owners are coordinating their efforts to maximize the project's overall performance.

Land Assembly and Purchase

Land for mixed-use developments can be acquired at many stages during the development process. In some situations, the developer is the long-term owner of the land, seeking to take advantage of a growing market and development opportunities. In other situations, the developer might purchase the land after determining that it has considerable potential for development but without having a specific program. In many traditional speculative ventures, a final agreement to lease or purchase the land often does not occur until much of the predevelopment analysis has been completed and the developer is confident enough to commit to developing the project.

Land for mixed-use projects must be assembled on a scale—and at a price and associated lease or purchase terms—that realistically reflects opportunities for development. Acquiring too much land can involve heavy carrying costs that are difficult to manage in the pro forma and can expose a developer to undue pressure to build faster than the market will bear. Acquiring too little land, on the other hand, can restrain effective design and programming.

Mixed-use projects characteristically play crucial roles in stimulating additional development and raising land values; accordingly, mixed-use projects warrant relatively greater attention to controlling adjacent land uses and values than other forms of real estate. For the developer, this interest may take several forms:

- a desire to discourage directly competitive developments in the immediate environs of the mixed-use project;
- a desire to encourage complementary development on adjacent parcels to achieve synergy or critical mass;
- a desire to discourage incompatible or deleterious uses around the fringes of a mixed-use project; and/or
- a desire to participate in rising land values and attendant development opportunities in adjacent areas.

Because land for mixed-use projects often involves relatively large sites—and often numerous landowners—land assembly can be more difficult than for single-use projects. For many downtown mixed-use projects, this process has been facilitated by the public sector, which often takes the lead, using condemnation proceedings if necessary, to acquire the land. If the public sector is not involved, the process is often more difficult, and the developer must first target the owners of key parcels, then diplomatically approach each one.

Market factors determine the land price, and developers must negotiate a land purchase price with a good understanding of how a proposed project will perform financially. In some cases, however, the developer may not be in a position to perform detailed financial analyses for the proposed project until he or she is relatively sure that all the necessary land can be assembled. Thus, the developer may have to negotiate land deals and prices without knowing precisely how much land value the anticipated development can support.

When the land is controlled by a single owner, frequently the case in suburban areas, the developer has more flexibility in arranging the purchase or lease of the property. This situation allows the developer to perform market analyses and preliminary financial analyses before purchasing the land or even before acquiring options on the land. It also allows the developer to arrange a phased takedown of the land to lower carrying costs.

Although land assembly can be a thorny problem in the United States, it can be even more complex in other countries where land interests are entrenched and land is not readily bought or sold. In Japan, for example, as-

sembling the site for Roppongi Hills, a $5 billion mixed-use project in Tokyo on 27 acres (11 hectares), took years and involved more than 600 separate negotiations. "We still are assembling it," notes Minoru Mori of Mori Building, the developer. "We are working on acquiring some corner lots, and we also have purchased the building next door." Originally, 600 landowners were involved in the project. Mori used his powers of persuasion to win them over. "I explained that by using density, they could actually share in the fruits of development," he notes. "I explained that the land itself doesn't have any value: it's what you create on it that has value. In the end, 200 landowners chose not to wait for the completion of Roppongi Hills and sold out to us. But we have 400 landowners remaining with the project."

In Roppongi Hills, the principal development entities are the Roppongi 6-chome Redevelopment Association, consisting of those 400 landowners or "rights holders," and Mori Building Co. Mori has signed a contract with

Market Square in Washington, D.C., consists of two mixed-use buildings, each with condominiums on the top floors, offices on the middle floors, and retail and restaurant uses on the ground floor. The buildings surround the Navy Memorial plaza. Land was assembled by the Pennsylvania Avenue Development Corporation.

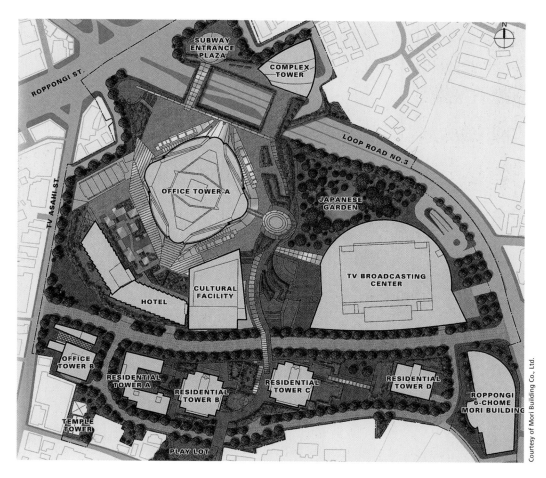

Land assembly at Roppongi Hills, located on 27 acres (11 hectares) in central Tokyo, involved negotiations with more than 600 property owners.

Courtesy of Mori Building Co., Ltd.

the association to actually construct the project. Although Mori Building acts as the driving force, the association itself is considered the principal of the project. This structure is key to Mori's urban development philosophy: rights holders who join a project should share in the profits from the value that the project adds to an area.

According to the association's plan, Mori Building Co. will purchase from the association about half the building space on the site. The project was projected to cost $1.8 billion. Mori raised two-thirds of the funds needed to complete construction through debt financing by government financial institutions and private banks, with the remainder coming from Mori's own fund. Later, says Mori, "We're thinking of securitizing the real estate."

Whatever the approach or situation, land costs are a critical factor in determining whether a mixed-use project succeeds or fails. In many cases, mixed-use projects can support higher land values than single-use projects, but the fact that land suitable for mixed-use projects is often very expensive means that a developer needs to have a clear understanding of the site's true potential for development before negotiating a purchase or land lease agreement.

3. See, e.g., William B. Brueggeman and Jeffrey D. Fisher, *Real Estate Finance and Investments*, 11th ed. (New York: McGraw-Hill/Irwin, 2002).

4. Clement Dinsmore, *The Impact of Public Capital Markets on Urban Real Estate* (Washington, D.C.: The Brookings Institution, Center on Urban and Metropolitan Policy, 1998), pp. 15–17+.

5. Ibid.

6. Joseph Gyourko and Witold Rybczynski, "Financing New Urbanism," *Wharton Real Estate Review*, Spring 2001, pp. 19–20.

7. Ibid., p. 22.

8. Christopher B. Leinberger, "Financing Progressive Development," *Capital Xchange*, May 2001, p. 17.

9. See Funders' Network for Smart Growth and Livable Communities, *Doing Well by Doing Good: Innovative Foundation Investments in Place-Based Smart Growth Development*, Real Estate Finance and Smart Growth Project, working paper, September 2002, www.fundersnetwork.org.

10. Commercial Mortgage Securities Association, *CMBS Basic Overview*, www.cmbs.org, accessed January 3, 2003.

11. Leinberger, "Financing Progressive Development," p. 17.

Notes

1. www.mccafferyinterests.com, accessed January 12, 2003.

2. The model was prepared by Patrick Phillips and David Versel from the Washington, D.C., office of Economics Research Associates.

4. The Public Sector's Involvement in Mixed-Use Development

The public sector often plays a pivotal role in mixed-use development through its activities in land use regulation, planning, urban design, economic development, redevelopment, capital improvements spending, and investments in civic and public facilities. This involvement can serve as both an impediment and a stimulant for mixed-use development.

The public sector's involvement ranges from zoning, public reviews, and approvals to assistance through a variety of means, including land assembly, public improvements, master planning, and championing the project before the public. The public sector may also provide any number of public financial investments or incentives, often participating as an active investor and developer in the project or portions of it, such as development of a city hall or a library. In many cases, the public sector is the prime mover behind the project, assembling land, developing plans, selecting a developer, investing in public improvements and public uses, and streamlining the approval process.

Indeed, mixed-use developments would not be so prominent as they are today without the active support and involvement of the public sector. The public sector has increasingly viewed mixed-use development as offering the opportunity for significantly improving the urban landscape in both urban and suburban environments. In pursuing a mixed-use development, it is criti-

cal that developers understand and appreciate the public sector's objectives and interests in the projects.

The Public Sector's Interests in Mixed-Use Development

Historically, the public sector and the public at large have been very wary of mixing uses, fearing that noxious uses such as manufacturing or other locally undesirable land uses (LULUs) in an urban or suburban setting will negatively impact other surrounding uses. Although this concern is still true, most public planners and planning officials have concluded more recently that the strict separation of uses can also create undesirable results if universally applied, resulting in a landscape with little or no urban vitality or sense of place.

Thus, creating more attractive urban environments is often the primary objective for most public sector involvement in mixed-use development. Because of their size, flexibility, and inherent potential to shape and activate urban space, mixed-use projects offer the public sector very attractive opportunities to create exciting new places. In urban districts, public objectives often involve a desire to enliven or redevelop an area that is underused or needs revitalization. In suburban or newly developing areas, objectives often involve a desire to create a sense of place and an identity for a community. Other objectives may include stimulating economic de-

Smyrna Town Center in Smyrna, Georgia.

velopment, increasing the local tax base, and creating more transit-friendly development and smarter growth.

Urban Revitalization

Many downtown and other urban business districts suffer from multiple problems—underused or blighted areas, crime, aging infrastructure, sterile office districts that are deserted at night, a lack of vibrant retail space, and/or a lack of attractive public spaces for people. Mixed-use developments can address these problems by bringing retail, hotel, residential, cultural, restaurant, or entertainment uses to an area that can help to revitalize and enliven blighted areas, nine-to-five office canyons, or the underused sites so prevalent in many urban districts. Even in strong downtowns, mixed-use developments offer the opportunity to bring new uses to the area and to shape attractive public open spaces that can further enliven and add a sense of place to a downtown setting.

And, by virtue of their scale, character, and impact, mixed-use projects can turn around blighted neighborhoods, stimulating additional new development. Many projects have been the initial and major force in revitalizing declining areas by creating exciting new, attractive, large-scale physical environments. Horton Plaza, for example, was a major catalyst for redevelopment in downtown San Diego; the mere anticipation of Horton Plaza's development caused land values to rise in neighboring areas. Seven of the ten case studies in this book involved the public sector's objectives to revitalize existing urban areas.

Revitalization through mixed-use development is a goal in cities throughout the world. In Liverpool, England, for example, the Paradise Street Development Area (PSDA) project is a major regeneration of the city center. A partnership of developer Grosvenor/Henderson, the Liverpool City Council, and Henderson Global Investors, it is a key element of Liverpool Vision's Strategic Regeneration Framework. The £700 million ($1.05 billion) mixed-use development is intended to reinvigorate the heart of

Liverpool, creating a vibrant city center in which to live, work, and relax. Covering a total of 42 acres (17 hectares), PSDA will incorporate 1.5 million square feet (137,000 square meters) of retail space, 236,700 square feet (22,000 square meters) of leisure space, and 409,000 square feet (38,000 square meters) of residential space. The development will be integrated into the existing fabric of the city center and link directly to other key areas, including Liverpool's CBD and waterfront.

Mixed-use development on a smaller scale can be used to revitalize smaller cities and towns as well. Notes Marilee Utter of Citiventure Associates LLC in Denver, "Smaller-scale projects are also transformational and can be phased or done by a variety of landowners/developers. Mixed-use is the best strategy of an incremental nature or when changes are needed in a smaller community that doesn't support a [large project]."

Suburban Place Making

In suburban areas, mixed-use projects can provide a focus for growth. Unlike single-purpose office parks, residential neighborhoods, shopping centers, or commercial strips found in most suburban communities, mixed-use projects can create new pedestrian-friendly places and districts that offer a strong sense of place, a focal point, and an identity for a suburban area that formerly had none.

Many suburban jurisdictions are now trying to create town centers that can provide a civic identity for newly developing suburban areas, such as Schaumburg Town Square in Illinois and Smyrna Town Center in Georgia. Others seek to redevelop or re-create existing main street areas into attractive mixed-use town centers, such as Birch Street Promenade in Brea, California. And in other more mature suburban business districts, infill development is being used to create new mixed-use districts with a strong identity and a pedestrian-friendly environment—Bethesda Row in Bethesda, Maryland, Renaissance Place in Highland Park, Illinois, or Fruitvale Village in Oakland, for example. Still others combine the need for redevelopment and suburban place making, as evidenced by CityCenter Englewood near Denver and Paseo Colorado in Pasadena, both of which involved public sector involvement in the redevelopment of defunct malls.

Smart Growth and Mobility

The typical pattern of suburban growth generally consumes farmland and open space at the fringe of metropolitan areas, generates long auto trips, and creates significant traffic congestion, air pollution, and related impacts. This sprawling pattern of land use does not encourage walking or biking, and it is not easily served by transit. Many jurisdictions, finding that these development patterns are not sustainable, are seeking ways to implement smart growth strategies that address these problems by—among other means—concentrating higher-density mixed-use development around transit stations.

> Smart growth supports the integration of mixed land uses into communities as a critical component of achieving better places to live. By putting uses in close proximity to one another, alternatives to driving, such as walking or biking, once again become viable. Mixed land uses also provide a more diverse and sizable population and commercial base for supporting viable public transit. It can enhance the vitality and perceived security of an area by increasing the number and attitude of people on the street. It helps streets, public spaces, and pedestrian-oriented retail again become places where people meet, attracting pedestrians back onto the street and helping to revitalize community life.[1]

Mixed-use development is compatible with and supportive of both transit and walking. Because of their relatively large size and higher densities, mixed-use projects tend to generate substantial travel demand that can reach tens of thousands of trips per day. Mixed-use developments also tend to spread trip demand throughout the day, because each use in the project has a different peak in terms of generating and attracting trips. Thus, a mixed-use development within walking distance of a transit station can be a significant source of riders throughout the day.

Concentrating such development around transit stations in attractive urban settings is viewed as a smart growth strategy, because it can increase densities at strategic locations, encourage walking and biking, reduce automobile use, reduce air pollution and traffic congestion, and alleviate some of the pressure to develop farmland and open space on the fringe of the urban area. Unfortunately, development at and around many transit stations has been frustrated in the past by opposition from citizens and/or poor planning by the public sector.

Although dense mixed-use development around transit stations can still draw opposition, many exciting projects are now being built around transit stations in cities such as Washington, D.C. (the Ballston area in Arlington, Virginia), Chicago (Arlington Heights), Atlanta (Lindbergh Station and other proposed projects), Dallas, San Francisco (Yerba Buena Center), and Portland, Oregon.

Federal, state, and local governments all seek to create more mixed-use and transit-oriented development. Such transit-oriented development is even more common overseas, including WestEnd City Center in Budapest and Sony Center in Berlin (see Chapter 8).

Economic Development and Tax Revenues

The desire to foster economic development and increase tax revenues is another reason for a public entity to want to become involved in a mixed-use development project. Mixed-use projects can stimulate the economy, generate jobs, and increase the tax base. For example, a project that includes a hotel with conference facilities can attract convention goers and tourists, creating jobs and new retail and hotel spending and providing a significant boost to the economy. New office space can attract new office jobs to the area while also boosting the property tax base. And new retail space can increase retail employment, the property tax base, and retail sales taxes.

> Mixed land uses can convey substantial fiscal and economic benefits. Commercial uses in close proximity to residential areas are often reflected in higher property values and therefore help raise local tax receipts. Businesses recognize the benefits associated with areas able to attract more people, as there is increased economic activity when there are more people in an area to shop. In today's service economy, communities find that by mixing land uses, they make their neighborhoods attractive to workers who increasingly balance quality of life criteria with salary to determine where they will settle. Smart growth provides a means for communities to alter the planning context that currently renders mixed land uses illegal in most of the country.[2]

In blighted or underused areas, large-scale mixed-use properties can significantly increase the property tax base and further increase the property values of surrounding property. Horton Plaza in San Diego, for example, has contributed more than $10 million per year to the city in property taxes since it was built in the 1980s, and sales

The proposed expansion of the Village at Shirlington in Arlington, Virginia, will include a county library.

Fruitvale Village is a neighborhood redevelopment project in Oakland that involved a public/private partnership initiated by a community development corporation (CDC). CDCs are quasi-public neighborhood-based organizations, generally nonprofit corporations serving a low-income community and governed by a community-based board.

The revitalization of Fruitvale has been spearheaded by Arabella Martinez, CEO of the Unity Council, a local CDC. "I want to infuse Fruitvale's established ethnic identity with a new social and economic vitality," she says. "I envision a complete connection among transportation and land use strategies and economic development for this community." To that end, the private/public partnership formed to revitalize Fruitvale has developed a plan that celebrates Fruitvale's ethnic diversity in a contemporary setting connecting community, retail, commercial, residential, and transit uses. The diverse development and financing team includes public, private, and non-profit entities and sources.

The project began in 1989, when Martinez began to explore ways to revitalize Fruitvale and regain some of its past luster. In 1993, a team of graduate students from the Oakland Metropolitan Forum of the University of California at Berkeley devised various ideas for improvements in Fruitvale, including creation of a pedestrian link from the BART (Bay Area Rapid Transit) station to the area's primary shopping/business district on International Boulevard, implementation of a building improvement program, more signage, and replacement of store awnings. Martinez credits the students' report as being the initial template for Fruitvale's redevelopment strategy.

Although funding to complete the changes was not available at the time, the Unity Council began to devise a strategy for forming a new neighborhood. When BART proposed building a stand-alone parking structure on a ten-acre (four-hectare) site in Fruitvale that, as proposed, would further separate commuters from the district, the Unity Council took action. The council quickly informed local residents of BART's plan, encouraging them to work together to propose other options. Community discussions prompted a number of alternative ideas for the parcel, and recognizing the need for community-friendly transportation, BART joined in the efforts. The Unity Council, in partnership with BART, developed a plan that includes 33,000 square feet (3,070 square meters) of retail/restaurant space, 40,000 square feet (3,700 square meters) for a health clinic, 40,000 square feet (3,700 square meters) for offices, a 12,000-square-foot (1,100-

Fruitvale Village in Oakland, initiated by a community development corporation, is intended to revitalize a community, foster economic development, and support smart growth and improved mobility in the region through transit-oriented development.

Courtesy of Fruitvale Development Corporation

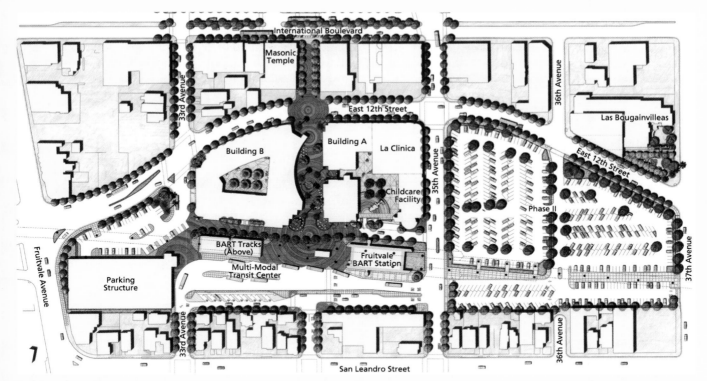

Site plan for Fruitvale Village, an urban village near a BART transit station in Oakland, California. The project includes retail/entertainment space, a health clinic, offices, a community center, a library, residential lofts, and a housing center for seniors.

square-meter) community resource center, a 5,550-square-foot (515-square-meter) library, and 47 residential lofts. The placement of these community facilities in the main plaza encourages residents of all ages to interact while providing much-needed services. Buildings will house retail stores on the first level, community facilities on the second level, and loft housing on the third. Construction began in January 2002 and is scheduled for completion in spring 2004.

Private investors initially feared the Fruitvale project, because Fruitvale had no money to support it. Martinez used her political muscle to secure more than $43 million in federal grants to date. "It takes a tremendous amount of time to make these inner-city redevelopment projects economically feasible and to receive the funding," Martinez notes. "After we secured the first $7.65 million grant, private investors began to support us. When they began to see improvements to the streets, even the shopowners on International Boulevard started to support the project; they have invested $2.3 million in their own community for redevelopment." One of Fruitvale's biggest supporters is the city of Oakland, which provided aid in financially supporting Fruitvale's improvement and facilitating the Unity Council's efforts.

A major private financial partner is Citibank, the sole conventional lender, which provided $27 million in construction and permanent financing. Citibank's Salomon Smith Barney Public Finance Division acted as project underwriter and marketed the tax-exempt bonds issued by the city of Oakland. Citibank's financing covered $19.8 million for the Unity Council's project and an additional $5.8 million to finance La Clinica de la Raza. In addition, Citibank's Social Investments Group provided $1.4 million in equity-like debt as a matching source for other fund providers.

According to Martinez, Fruitvale has blossomed since redevelopment started. Ten years ago, the vacancy rate on International Boulevard was 50 percent, crime and violence were high, and streets were dirty. Today, the vacancy rate is less than 1 percent, crime and graffiti have decreased, streets are cleaner, more than 110 new jobs have been created, and property goes for premium rates. With the area looking better, shopowners continue to invest in upgrading their properties. The results of the long-awaited improvements can be seen in residents' and shopowners' attitudes and the sense of pride in the neighborhood.

Sources: Ernesto M. Vasquez, "Bearing Fruit," *Urban Land*, July 2000, pp. 64–67; www.unitycouncil.org, the Fruitvale Transit Village Web site; Citigroup press release, December 16, 2002.

tax revenues have been substantial as well. It has become a major tourist attraction in itself, and both the retail stores and the hotel in the project are major sources of jobs. As a result of the project's success, land and property values have increased significantly in adjacent neighborhoods, and substantial development and redevelopment projects have followed, adding further to the city's developing economy, tax base, and municipal revenues. Pentagon Row, a mixed-use project combining retail, entertainment, and residential uses in Arlington, Virginia, was projected to provide Arlington County with nearly $90 million in increased tax revenue over a 15-year period while also generating close to 600 permanent jobs.

Roles for the Public Sector

The public sector's interest and participation in mixed-use developments have taken a variety of forms, from simple encouragement to active participation in development. The public sector can promote mixed-use development in several important ways:

- providing zoning incentives, possibly including the creation of a mixed-use classification;
- streamlining the approval process and championing the project before the public and various agencies;
- planning development areas as mixed-use districts, including providing specific land use and design guidelines;
- assembling land with powers of eminent domain or outright purchase;
- cleaning up brownfield sites for redevelopment;
- writing down land costs to make the project feasible;
- allowing for tax abatements and/or tax incentives;
- providing public financing, including the use of general city funds, tax increment funds, and state and federal funds;
- providing public infrastructure, such as street improvements, parking facilities, and transit stations;
- providing project components, such as a convention center, city hall, civic center, library, performing arts center, or museum;
- developing a specific mixed-use plan and program and then using a request for proposals (RFP) or request for qualifications (RFQ) for developing that plan and program;
- serving as master developer and/or actively directing the development plan and program;
- marketing, promotion, and public relations.

The appropriate role for the public sector depends in part on the need for public participation to make the project feasible, the sophistication and financial capability of the local jurisdiction, public objectives and needs, the potential impact of the project on the community, and the costs and benefits of alternative actions. Public/private development also varies considerably from country to country. An example of how the process has worked in England, for example, is described in the accompanying feature box.

Regulatory Process and Tools

Many single-use properties developed in the United States result in part from development regulations that mandate or encourage single-use development. In effect, land use regulations often inhibit or prohibit mixed-use development. If the public sector wishes to encourage mixed-use development, it must modify the regulatory and approval system to allow and encourage such development in a number of ways:

1. create new mixed-use and other more flexible zoning categories in the zoning code;
2. establish design guidelines that encourage effective design standards for mixed-use development;
3. modify and streamline the approval process for desirable mixed-use projects, reducing the developer's risk; and
4. use public meetings and charrettes to build a vision and consensus for new mixed-use development in areas where it is appropriate.

Most important, the public sector must promote and champion mixed-use concepts and look for ways to encourage and facilitate mixed-use development. To do so must frequently involve a prominent elected official who is willing to strongly and consistently champion mixed-use projects before the public and the various administrative bodies that will need to approve it.

Zoning Background

Historically, zoning has attempted to predesignate the purposes for which land can be used, in so doing segregating uses into assigned geographic areas. The underlying assumption that different uses should be segregated, however, has increasingly been called into question in recent decades. In the 1960s, Jane Jacobs, an author and early critic, attacked conventional zoning, arguing that cities needed instead "a most intricate and close-grained diversity of uses that give each other constant mutual support, both economically and socially."[3]

In the 1970s and 1980s, critics began to point out that mixing land uses and more compact development can also make sense for the environment. ULI was a leading participant in the Council on Development Choices for the 80s, which issued a report recommending regulatory reform to allow more mixed-use development.[4] A principal objective of that group—"to encourage a greater mix of uses in new projects, in neighborhoods, and in communities"—is as relevant today as it was then. Today's smart growth and new urbanist advocates are still seeking to overhaul zoning ordinances to allow mixed-use development more easily; they have been increasingly more successful in recent years.

Zoning historically has been almost entirely negative—defining what cannot be done but seldom providing incentives for what should be done. In many districts, for

Gloucester Green is a mixed-use development in the center of Oxford, England, that includes retail shops, restaurants, private flats, offices, a refurbished arts complex, a bus station, an underground park structure, and public open space. The project was built in the late 1980s but involved a long planning and development period.

Before development, all that marked the location at Gloucester Green was a parking lot, a small bus station, and a few minor buildings. The Oxford City Council decided in 1978 to regenerate the site at the heart of its central conservation area and to prepare a document for public consultation and debate.

The resulting Gloucester Green discussion paper proposed several options that ranged from a complete overhaul to smaller-scale infill. Opinion was in favor of general redevelopment to include a larger bus station and a piazza planted with trees, leading to five financial evaluations of the 50,000-square-foot (4,650-square-meter) plot with a combination of uses, including housing, shops, offices, and public space. The council rejected an alternative scheme because it favored retail and was not spatially well organized.

Reflecting this rejection and a change to the Labour-controlled council, a stricter design brief included guidelines on land uses, their arrangement, their aesthetics, and reinstatement of the royal-chartered market. It was referred to the Department of the Environment because it proposed to demolish two historic buildings. Two years later, an explicit brief had been finalized. The facilities were to include an arts center, retail outlets for specialty shops, a cleaning depot, and facilities for the bus station; the piazza was to accommodate 150 market stalls, and the residential units were to include local authority tenants as well as private owners. The site was to house these requirements in two mixed-use buildings with the shops at ground floor, some offices on the first floor, and the remainder as residential units. The scheme went to a competition in 1983 to allow for a range of spatial and aesthetic options to be examined. Six teams were asked to exhibit their schemes, which were publicly displayed while the council studied the submissions.

Gloucester Green is a mixed-use development in the center of Oxford, England, that includes retail shops, restaurants, private flats, offices, an arts complex, a bus station, and public open space. The project was initiated by the Oxford City Council.

The team chosen included local architect Donald Kendrick, local builders Benfield and Loxley Ltd. and Dimsdale Developments Ltd., and surveyors Moult Benn and Co. With the highest overall yield and a high premium, their proposal was also the most popular with the public, although the council was not entirely happy with some of the architectural detailing. Following a number of problems with finance and difficult relations between the developers and the council, Guardian Royal Exchange took over. The project was completed in 1989 to 1990, by which time most of the offices and residential accommodations had been leased. Renting out the retail units proved considerably harder.

Source: Resource for Urban Design Information, www.rudi.net.

example, regulations often specify permitted uses, the maximum height of a building, and the required dimensions for front, side, and rear yards. Taken together, such limitations defined what is frequently called the *zoning envelope*, an invisible box that a building could completely fill but out of which it could not protrude in any direction. The visual effect of this approach is evident in the monotony of much of the built environment across the country today.

Recent thinking seeks to remedy the deficiencies of traditional zoning in two respects: 1) by moving toward a more beneficial, well-planned integration of different land uses at a proper scale; and 2) by emphasizing incentives for better design, amenities, affordable housing, and other public purposes. Numerous regulatory techniques have been devised to accomplish these suggestions, including floating zones, overlay districts, performance zoning, special-purpose districts, and mixed-use zoning. Figure 4-1 discusses the pros and cons of several of these techniques. Increasingly, special zoning ordinances are established to encourage mixed-use development zones, including mixed-use ordinances, planned unit development ordinances, or traditional neighborhood development (TND) and smart growth ordinances. Moreover, many jurisdictions are developing specific plans for specially designated areas that outline specific uses and design guidelines.

Mixed-Use Zoning

Mixed-use zones are different from most other techniques such as PUD ordinances and special-purpose districts, primarily because they not only permit a mix of uses but also encourage or even require such mixing. According to the American Planning Association, "Many cities in the United States already have zoning categories that specify certain combinations of land uses; for example, a community may permit multifamily housing in

figure 4-1

Zoning Tools for Encouraging Mixed-Use Development

	Overview	Pros	Cons
Mixed-Use Zoning District	Zoning district that allows different types of uses (such as housing, shopping, and offices) to locate in the same district, provided these uses are reasonably related and compatible.	Encourages creation of vibrant, pedestrian-oriented community and neighborhood centers. Specifies future locations of mixed-use development, so neighborhood opposition can be addressed in advance.	Requires qualified staff to administer.
Overlay District	Mapped area where special regulations promoting and managing mixed-use development are applied. An overlay is typically superimposed over conventional zoning districts but may also be used as a stand-alone regulation to manage mixed-use development in desired areas of the community.	Encourages creation of vibrant, pedestrian-oriented community and neighborhood centers. Specifies future locations of mixed-use development, so neighborhood opposition can be addressed in advance.	Can add complexity to local development regulations. Requires qualified staff to administer.
Planned Unit Development	Revised land development regulations to encourage developers to propose planned mixed-use developments for sites they choose in the community. Developer's plans are approved only if they meet specified community standards.	Eliminates need for developer to go through burdensome rezoning process. Enables developers to create vibrant, pedestrian-oriented community and neighborhood centers.	Neighbors frequently oppose new planned developments. Requires qualified staff to administer.
Specific Plan	Detailed plan that indicates exactly how a particular area of the community should be developed, down to the location, size, and use of particular buildings. Can be used to promote mixed uses simply by locating different uses close together in the plan.	Gives developers maximum flexibility in designing creative, vibrant, new mixed-use development projects.	Neighbors frequently oppose new planned developments. Can be rather complex to administer, as plans are negotiated project by project.
Performance Standard	Regulation of development based on whether it meets predetermined measures that are usually related to the development's impact on neighboring properties, the environment, or local public service capacity. Does not require separation of uses: a particular use can locate anywhere so long as it meets established performance standards.	Very effective way to manage impacts of development without requiring separation of uses (zoning). Gives developers considerable flexibility in designing creative, vibrant, mixed-use development projects.	Requires qualified staff to administer. Opposition may arise as a result of the uncertainty about particular uses that may locate nearby. Somewhat complex— may be difficult for the average citizen or developer to understand.

Source: Georgia Department of Community Affairs, *Encouraging Mixed-Use Development.* http://www.dca.state.ga.us/toolkit/toolkit2.asp?ID=14, accessed October 4, 2002.

an office district. This 'permissive' approach, however, is not likely to result in truly integrated uses. . . . If a community wishes to encourage a mixture of land uses, it must do more than permit residential uses: it must actively promote them."[5]

One of the earliest examples of a zoning ordinance that provided incentives for mixed-use development was a 1974 amendment to the zoning code in Washington, D.C., that designated several areas as CR (commercial/residential) mixed-use districts. The new mixed-use zoning provided incentives and bonuses for the provision of various uses or amenities (moderate-income housing, areas devoted to pedestrians or bicyclists, retail or service space contributing to the creation of evening activity centers, and preservation or enhancement of places or structures of historical importance). It was one of the first true mixed-use zoning districts in the United States.

In setting up a mixed-use zoning category, the Georgia Department of Community Affairs recommends involving stakeholders (neighborhood organizations, property owners, developers, government officials) in the process and focusing on appropriate areas for mixed-use zoning districts as the first steps. To determine the mix of uses:

> . . . It is quite likely that more than one type of mixed-use district will be identified through this process. For example, you may identify the need for a mixed-use district that is primarily residential in nature, with only limited commercial development permitted, while other areas of the community may call for a mixed-use district that is primarily commercial with higher-density apartments mixed in. In addition to defining the allowed uses, other specific requirements should be defined, including specific lot size minimums, building setbacks, and other development restrictions to apply within each type of mixed-use zoning district. Use visual images or examples to help stakeholders grasp concepts being discussed. Remember that the purpose of mixed-use zoning is to develop vibrant, walkable areas in your community.[6]

Another example is a zoning ordinance proposed for Anne Arundel County, Maryland, that creates "four mixed-use development districts— . . . primarily residential, primarily commercial, employment, and transit oriented. They are 'floating zones' to be requested as options to the zoning otherwise in place and only in areas designated on small-area plans for mixed-use development. As an incentive, they allow considerably greater density than underlying zoning."[7] In Charlotte, North Carolina, mixed-use district zoning involves "an overlay district that is designated for certain areas intended as future activity centers, including areas around proposed rail transit stations. Unlike the proposed Anne Arundel County ordinance, for which special reviews and hearings are required, Charlotte's allows mixed uses by right provided they comply with detailed design provisions."[8]

Colorado Examples. One of the most prominent features of the Colorado Springs, Colorado, comprehensive plan adopted in 2001 is the emphasis it gives to developing centers of activity that mix different uses, similar in many ways to the Downtown and Old Colorado City

One of several mixed-use buildings that has been developed in the West End of Washington, D.C., as a result of flexible zoning, 2401 Pennsylvania Avenue includes retail, office, and residential uses.

areas. The city is now working to change its regulations to help achieve the development of these mixed-use centers and to update elements of existing zone districts, using a City Council–appointed task force, private consultants, and staff to write new rules to achieve new patterns of development.

A recent diagnosis of mixed-use zoning and street standards in Colorado Springs by city staff and Clarion Associates found:

> . . . there is very little in the current zoning and subdivision codes to address mixed-use development, and some existing regulations may actually hamstring and discourage [mixed uses]. Ultimately, a new set of zoning development and design standards and guidelines will be needed to guide and manage future mixed-use development in Colorado Springs. . . . The diagnosis discusses the following alternative approaches to applying new mixed-use standards and guidelines, including each approach's advantages and disadvantages: 1) create new zone districts to facilitate development of mixed-use centers as defined in the comprehensive plan; 2) add new uses in existing zone districts to encourage mixed-use development; 3) create new development standards for "activity centers"; 4) create new development standards for all new nonresidential development; 5) create regulatory incentives for mixed-use [development].[9]

The diagnosis goes on to recommend the creation of five new zone districts that align with the different types of activity centers described in the comprehensive plan.

Denver has adopted mixed-use zoning to build more community- and pedestrian-oriented neighborhoods where people can live, work and shop in one place. The mixed-use zoning will be used to shape new development in areas such as Gateway and Stapleton. For example, consistent with the values of the Stapleton Development Plan, the new RMU20 zoning permits a mix of different housing types and small, neighborhood-scale retail stores in select locations, facilitates more efficient development,

Denver recently adopted mixed-use zoning to build more community- and pedestrian-oriented neighborhoods. This new zoning is being used to shape the new Stapleton community—including a town center—being built on the site of the former Stapleton airport.

fosters more transit ridership, and provides a broad mix of community residents.

Plan review processes included in the language and the associated rules and regulations ensure that adjacent uses will be compatible and that design will be of a high quality. The mixed-use districts provide more design review than is required by any of Denver's existing zone districts.[10]

The zoning has allowed for an innovative plan at Stapleton that includes several mixed-use town centers. East 29th Avenue, Stapleton's first town center, includes a broad mix of uses:

- a full-service grocery store as well as a variety of neighborhood stores and restaurants;
- a traditional 2.5-acre (1-hectare) green (Founders' Green);
- Main Street Flats, with 66 one- and two-bedroom rental flats above the ground-floor retail shops;
- Main Street Office Suites, with 30,000 square feet (2,800 square meters) of executive offices overlooking 29th Avenue;
- the Town Square Building, a five-story office building bordering the north side of Founders' Green;
- the Town Green Apartments, with 232 one-, two-, and three-bedroom rental flats, townhouses, and live/work lofts with attached garages just south of Founders' Green;
- Clyburn at Stapleton, with 100 units of affordable apartments for seniors at 26th Avenue and Quebec.

East 29th Avenue will open in fall 2003.

Oregon Examples. Several states are taking the lead in fostering the creation of new mixed-use zoning ordinances; Oregon has been a leader. The Oregon Transportation and Growth Management Program recently developed the *Commercial and Mixed-Use Development Code Handbook*—a guide to encouraging "smart" commercial and mixed-use development through public policy and land use ordinances, including a model ordinance. The ordinance describes five different zone districts—a downtown/main street district, a small neighborhood center district (one to three acres [0.4 to 1.2 hectares]), a large neighborhood center district (up to ten acres [4 hectares]), a community commercial district, and a corridor commercial district—and outlines the uses and development standards permitted in each. It also articulates guidelines and standards that are intended as discretionary approval criteria and meant to be flexible, recognizing the wide range of commercial needs in the community and the creativity of the market: compact development; mixed land uses; pedestrian access, safety, and comfort; street connections; crime prevention and security; parking and efficient land use; creation and protection of public spaces; and human-scale building design. The applicant must demonstrate how the proposal conforms to all the guidelines, and the decision-making body must find that the proposal satisfies the guidelines.

In some cases, the developer can work with the local community to establish new, tailor-made zoning for a specific site, such as Orenco Station in Hillsboro, Oregon, a suburb of Portland. Orenco Station is a pedestrian-oriented, mixed-use community planned by master developer Pacific Realty Associates, L.P. (PacTrust) for 1,834 housing units, and retail and office space. The compact design includes a wide range of housing types, among them single-family detached houses, accessory units over garages, live/work lofts, and townhouses over retail shops.

The site originally was zoned for industrial use and later for subdivision housing; development of the present community followed the site's designation as a town center in the Portland Metro Region 2040 Plan, which established a gradient of residential density targets at varying distances from the Orenco light-rail stop and mandated mixed-use development. With little precedent for either higher-density *or* mixed-use development in the area, PacTrust assembled a team of designers and engineers and a homebuilder to explore the uncharted waters.

A market survey of employees in the surrounding high-tech facilities established the preferred design and housing and defined affordability. The survey and subsequent focus groups revealed respondents' affinity for the look and feel of the older Portland suburbs, with their Craftsman and cottage-style architecture, picturesque rose gardens, and neighborhood shops. The research reflected a somewhat nostalgic bent but one that fit well with the concept of more densely developed and livable transit-oriented development.

Two years of discussions, design studies, and negotiations with city, state, and transit officials culminated in a zoning ordinance customized for Orenco Station, which was dubbed a "station community residential village." The new zoning established design guidelines to allow for—and ensure—a heterogeneous, urban mix of housing types and land uses not typically found in the suburbs.

Hong Kong Example. Mixed-use zoning is also found in Hong Kong. The Town Planning Board of Hong Kong in 2002 agreed in principle to a package of proposals for further streamlining the planning and development process and providing greater flexibility in the use of land or buildings. A major proposal is the introduction of broad terms to provide greater flexibility to change use. The board considered that some of the existing terms in the Notes of Outline Zoning Plans were too specific, rendering planning control in that respect very rigid. "Although 'retail shop' and 'barber shop' have similar planning implications, they are regarded as two types of uses at present because they are separately listed in the Notes," a spokesman for the board explained. "With the introduction of broad terms—e.g., 'shop and services' —all uses in the same broad use could be interchangeable, which would significantly reduce the need to apply for planning permission."

A new mixed-use zoning mechanism was also introduced to meet changing needs. Under the concept of mixed-use zoning, a mix of uses in a spatial area (i.e., a horizontal mix) or in a building (i.e., a vertical mix) would be allowed. The mixed-use zoning is intended to replace the existing commercial/residential (C/R) zoning, under which the location of residential and commercial uses on the same floor may generate nuisances to the residents. The new zoning could maintain the flexibility of C/R land use while providing better planning control.[11]

PUD Ordinances
PUD ordinances have been used for many years to allow more creative approaches to development, particularly in suburban communities. Often embodied as part of the local zoning ordinance, they increase flexibility in the design and siting of development.

> The PUD process allows a much freer placement of buildings on the land than conventional lot-by-lot systems. The total parcel rather than a single lot is the unit of regulation, and controls apply to entire developments. Densities may be calculated on a project basis, allowing the clustering of buildings to create useful open spaces and preserve natural site features. Increased flexibility allows project elements—housing, transportation systems, open spaces, nonresidential uses—to be interrelated with one another. Traditionally tight controls over use districting are also relaxed, permitting mixtures in dwelling unit types and land uses within the same project.[12]

Typically, negotiations between the developer and the local planning board, working within broad legislative guidelines, help to establish a specific plan. This process can afford developers substantial advantages: higher densities, a more flexible design, savings in construction costs, and improved marketability. For a community, the PUD ordinance can offer greater control over development (for example, by negotiating flexibility or greater densities with developers in return for more amenities) and ultimately preserve open space and reduce costs typically associated with sprawling development.

If properly devised, a PUD ordinance can be sufficiently flexible to allow for mixed-use developments.

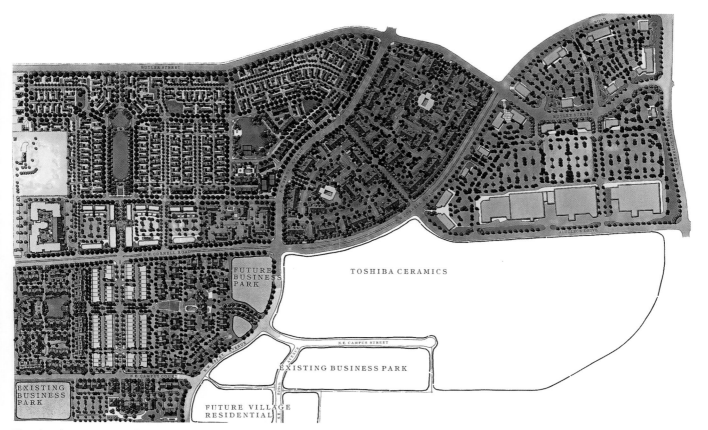

Site plan for Orenco Station, a new urbanist community near a transit station in Hillsboro, Oregon, that includes a mixed-use town center. A customized mixed-use zoning ordinance was developed for the project, dubbed a "station community residential village."

Reston Town Center was developed under a PUD ordinance that was established for the entire Reston community.

Frequently, PUD ordinances are oriented toward suburban residential developments, allowing flexibility to arrange uses, density, and open space in an innovative plan and often allowing for the creation of areas of more intense mixed-use development. Many of the mixed-use town centers being developed in planned communities —such as Reston Town Center in Reston, Virginia, and Valencia Town Center Drive in Valencia, California— are being developed under PUD ordinances.

In some cases, PUD ordinances are combined with specific plans in redevelopment areas as well. In Cambridge, Massachusetts, the city commissioned a planning study of its 60-acre (24-hectare) waterfront area, culminating in the East Cambridge Riverfront Plan. Guidelines specify preferred land uses; scale, location, arrangement, and massing of buildings; traffic and circulation patterns; and design details. To enforce the plan, the city adopted a PUD zoning district to replace the neighborhood's industrial zoning, slashing floor/area ratios (FARs). Developers who opted to follow the plan's design guidelines and community-sensitive approval process, however, could double densities. CambridgeSide Galleria, a retail/office/residential mixed-use project, was one of the last projects planned and developed in the area. The Riverfront Plan stipulated that the site be developed as a 24-hour, pedestrian-oriented, mixed-use complex, including an 800,000-square-foot (74,350-square-meter) shopping center.

TND and Smart Growth Ordinances

More recent regulatory tools—traditional neighborhood development and smart growth ordinances—are being adopted in many regions of the United States, often in parallel with more conventional zoning. These ordinances frequently focus on development standards, especially for single-family housing, for the larger community but also are quite specific about encouraging and integrating a mix of uses.

CambridgeSide Galleria in Cambridge, Massachusetts, was developed in the East Cambridge Riverfront Plan area; to enforce the plan, the city adopted a PUD zoning district to replace the neighborhood's industrial zoning.

The Specific Plan for the Third Street Promenade in Santa Monica allowed the developers of Janss Court to increase the overall density of the project if they provided strong pedestrian connections between the promenade and the public parking structure.

For example, the TND ordinance for the city of Belmont, North Carolina, has the following intent:

The purpose of this district is to allow for the development of fully integrated, mixed-use pedestrian-oriented neighborhoods. The intent is to minimize traffic congestion, suburban sprawl, infrastructure costs, and environmental degradation. Its provisions adapt urban conventions [that] were normal in the United States from colonial times until the 1940s and historically were based on the following design principles:

- All neighborhoods have identifiable centers and edges.
- Edge lots are readily accessible to retail and recreation by nonvehicular means (a distance not greater than one-quarter mile [0.4 kilometer]).
- Uses and housing types are mixed and close to one another.
- Street networks are interconnected and blocks are small.
- Civic buildings are given prominent sites throughout the neighborhood.[13]

The ordinance includes design standards for general, public, and civic uses, shopfronts, attached houses, detached houses, and businesses. The ordinance permits and controls a range of uses through a variety of very specific stipulations:

- The entire land area of the TND shall be divided into blocks, streets, and lots, and optional natural or greenbelt areas.
- Similar land categories shall generally enfront across streets. Dissimilar categories shall abut at rear lot lines. Corner lots [that] front on streets of dissimilar use shall be set back the same as the adjacent use with the lesser setback.
- Large-scale single uses (conference spaces, theaters, athletic facilities, etc.) shall occur behind or above habitable streetfront space.
- Land designated for shopfronts shall contain residential and commercial uses.

The ordinance can be used for land parcels of 40 to 200 acres (16 to 80 hectares), with larger parcels processed as separate 200-acre (80-hectare) parcels. Maximum permitted densities and total number of dwelling units are established during review of the site plan.

TND and smart growth ordinances are generally quite flexible in terms of allowing a variety of uses but highly prescriptive regarding how these uses are arranged, designed, and developed. They are generally much more prescriptive than most PUD ordinances and are used essentially to allow a mix of uses as well as to prescribe preferred urban design patterns.

Specific Plans and Design Guidelines

Mixed-use projects are often developed to conform to specific plans established by the local government for certain areas or on redevelopment sites where the public sector has control and can establish strict guidelines for use and design of the development. Plans and guidelines that are effectively crafted and in line with market demand add a level of predictability to the approval process.

California. In Santa Monica, for example, the city's Specific Plan for the Third Street Promenade designated maximum FARs for each privately owned parcel. Certain parcels (such as the Janss Court site, a mixed-use property) that back up to city-owned parking garages were eligible for a density bonus if a 20-foot-wide (six-meter) pedestrian connection was made between the parking structure and the promenade. The base FAR permitted for the Janss site was 3.0; agreeing to provide the passage permitted an increase in the FAR to 3.5. Providing housing instead of commercial uses enabled the additional 0.5 FAR because the Specific Plan allows housing to be counted at half its actual density.

The Specific Plan also required that new buildings fronting the Promenade be stepped back, beginning at the third floor. The intents were to maintain a cornice line at about 35 feet (10.7 meters) consistent with the original buildings lining the Promenade and to preserve the human scale of the street.

In San Francisco, perhaps one of the best examples of a mixed-use development that was developed under a specific plan is Yerba Buena Center (see Chapter 8), which involved a long and involved public planning process for a downtown redevelopment area.

Massachusetts. The 12-story Heritage on the Garden in Boston was the product of a design competition in the early 1980s, in which the city awarded development rights to the Druker Company, a Boston-based developer.

In the early 1970s, the city declared the site that now contains the Heritage an urban renewal area and held a competition for its redevelopment. The developer who was initially selected to develop the site proposed a project consisting of six 40- to 60-story contemporary office buildings; citizens from Back Bay and Beacon Hill vigorously opposed the proposal, protesting both the huge scale of the project and its shadowing of the adjacent public garden. After years of rancorous opposition, the citizens prevailed. They eventually formed the Park Plaza Civic Advisory Committee and worked with the city to establish design guidelines for the site.

The guidelines called for a smaller-scale mixed-use project with retail on the ground floor, residential above, and ample setbacks to avoid casting a shadow over the public garden. In addition, the building had to blend architecturally with the Back Bay. In 1982, nearly a decade after the ill-fated first project was proposed, the city held a second competition. In late 1983, the Druker Company was awarded the development rights, and it immediately began to assemble the site. Over the next two years, Druker successfully negotiated the purchase of property from eight of the site's nine owners. For the lone holdout, the city exercised its power of eminent domain to obtain ownership and complete the site's assembly.

Druker was selected over other bidders for several reasons. It proposed a building that had a lower FAR than was allowed for the site, and, through the creative use of setbacks and belvederes, the company avoided creating the monolithic wall of offices that citizens decried. In many instances, Druker offered more than was required in the city's RFP. For instance, where the guidelines called for donating $50,000 for maintenance of the garden, Druker offered $75,000. The company also contributed a linkage fee of $1 million, payable over 12 years, which the city is using for affordable housing. Working with citizen groups during design can result in a better product and, by addressing potential opposition upfront, help avoid costly delays.

At University Park at MIT in Cambridge, existing zoning ordinances could not accommodate the desired objectives and mix of uses; the solution was to develop a master plan and to zone the property in conformity with the plan. This planned district zone—the Cambridgeport Revitalization Development District—establishes the overall parameters for the project. It sets the maximum total gross building area (GBA), limits the amount of retail

Steve Rosenthal

Development of Heritage on the Garden in Boston—which includes office, residential, and retail uses—involved a design and development competition with considerable public involvement. The winning proposal offered a lower floor/area ratio than was allowed on the site.

To clear a path for the development of CityPlace, the city of West Palm Beach overhauled its planning and regulatory codes and developed a new master plan for the downtown.

Courtesy of Elkus/Manfredi Architects Ltd.

space, and specifies a minimum amount of GBA to be devoted to housing. It also specifies the construction of a minimum number of low-income housing units and establishes the minimum amount and general location of open space. It specifies FARs and height limits for various portions of the site and establishes some timing requirements for the completion of the housing units and open space. Finally, it sets a requirement for the submission of a master plan and design guidelines, and procedures for incremental approvals.

The design guidelines, comprising both text and graphics, is a 25-page agreement among the three parties to the agreement—Forest City (the developer), MIT (the landowner), and the city of Cambridge. These guidelines embody the developer's master plan, in many cases refine or modify the specifics of the zoning district, and establish the ground rules for specific approvals as development proceeds. Among other things, they set forth the primary use patterns and general plan, and standards of quality for open space and the streetscape, building design and height, parking, and pedestrian and traffic circulation.

Texas. A higher-density, mixed-use residential neighborhood was first suggested in the 1991 comprehensive plan for Addison, Texas, and more recently in a community-based "visioning" program (Vision 2020). The developer and the city undertook a series of steps to formulate the program and design for Addison Circle, to educate the public regarding the benefits of the design, and to establish the terms of the public/private partnership.

Eventually, a set of design and development standards was hammered out with the town and codified in a Planned Development District approval, covering such items as density, lot coverage, exterior building materials, setbacks, and the streetscape. The developer also identified gaps in funding that needed to be resolved to provide the infrastructure and level of quality the town and the developer wanted. The final agreement with the town of Addison committed the town to spending a total of

$9.5 million from its general fund over the life of the project: $5.5 million upfront on infrastructure, street, and open space improvements and the remaining $4 million during the second phase of development.

Germany. In Berlin, a competition was held in 1991 to develop an appropriate plan for the entire Potsdamer Platz district. The resulting plan provided the basis for the subsequent competitions that were used to select the development and architectural teams that would fill out the district plan with detailed designs for each building site. The plan specified, among other things, dimensions of sites at Potsdamer Platz, layout of streets, and height and massing of buildings. It did not, however, address the uses that would be permitted or the architectural form of the new buildings. The sale contract for Sony Corporation's purchase of one property specified conformance with the plan as well as certain other obligations for Sony, including the on-site preservation of the former Hotel Esplanade as a historic structure and provision of a permanent home for the *Filmhaus,* an important organization in the German film industry.

The Approval Process

Whatever zoning is in place, the approval process for mixed-use projects in many jurisdictions is often difficult and time-consuming, often discouraging rather than encouraging mixed-use development. If public officials wish to change land use planning to favor more mixed-use development, they need not only to create mixed-use zoning districts but also to streamline the process to allow approval of mixed-use developments in a reasonable time period. For the developer, the approval process is fraught with uncertainty and is often very time-consuming, resulting in higher risks and costs. Reducing uncertainty and the time it takes to receive approval will go far toward enhancing the feasibility of desirable mixed-use developments.

When projects of major importance to the local jurisdiction are involved, a proactive public process helps to

To facilitate development of Downtown Silver Spring in Maryland, the Silver Spring business district was designated a State of Maryland Enterprise Zone. The first phases of the development are complete, including retail space and restoration of the Silver Theater for the new home of the American Film Institute.

smooth approval and development in a variety of ways. For example, at CityPlace in West Palm Beach (see Chapter 8), the city's planning regulations and zoning made it very difficult to build attractive, exciting, mixed-use urban places; to clear a path for redevelopment required the overhaul of the city's planning and regulatory codes and the appointment of new staff and commissions receptive to change. A new downtown master plan using new urbanist principles was created and an RFP issued for redevelopment of the 72-acre (29-hectare) site. The city also took on all the permitting work for the project to ensure that the regulatory process did not impede the development.

The approval process varies with every development and jurisdiction; the range of problems to be overcome and solutions that have been proposed or enacted are many, ranging from variances and conditional rezoning to neighborhood engagement and "green taping."

Variances and Privatization. The straightforward approach to gaining approval for a development that does not strictly conform to regulations is through variances and/or privatization of nonconforming components. At Miami Lakes Town Center in Miami Lakes, a large master-planned community in Florida, the entire 90-acre (36-hectare) site for the town center was zoned BU-2 (business use), which is permissive in its range of permitted uses. Specific development proposals in this zone, however, must be reviewed and approved in a public hearing by the county's Zoning Appeals Board. During the hearing process for the town center, the county raised several issues, including the design and width of Main Street. As it was proposed and ultimately built, the street has one 12-foot (3.6-meter) lane in each direction, 45-degree angled parking, and a minimum three-foot (0.9-meter) landscaped median—just large enough for a row of live oak trees. The design does not meet county street standards and thus was required to be privately owned and maintained. All other streets are public and built to Dade County standards.

Street design standards are a frequent problem for mixed-use town centers. A similar approach was used at Valencia Town Center Drive in Valencia, California, for the same reason. In general, notes David Leland of Leland Consulting in Portland, "Engineering standards are a huge problem in many cities, and new developers must find strategies for overcoming archaic regulations that can be very costly and detrimental to their projects."

Other design and development issues at Miami Lakes included numerous building setback reductions, reduced easements, and shared parking. Eventually, the necessary variances were granted in recognition of the special development concept proposed. The county supported the overall concept; Main Street clearly could not have been possible with strict adherence to zoning standards. Obtaining approvals was made somewhat less difficult as a result of the developer's excellent working relationship with Dade County for nearly 30 years.

Conditional Rezoning. Conditional rezoning is sometimes used where no other mixed-use zoning techniques are in place. At Phillips Place in Charlotte, for example, developing a mixed-use project on the property required rezoning. In the South District Plan, the site was recommended for multifamily housing at a density of 22 units per acre (54 per hectare). This density would have allowed potentially 800 units, which would have generated significant traffic during peak hours. The developers sought to amend the plan to incorporate nonresidential uses, which they successfully argued would reduce peak traffic, avoid placement of residential housing adjacent to high-tension power lines, and provide retail stores not presently in the Charlotte market and public spaces that would be an amenity for the surrounding area, while still providing for the multifamily housing originally targeted by the plan.

To complicate the rezoning approval process, the county had no mixed-use zoning classification. Thus, the developer had to apply for an amendment to the General Commercial zoning category to allow residential above retail uses, further lengthening the approval process, even though city staff and elected officials supported the project. The conditional rezoning plan required sensitivity to the surrounding land uses and residents, as it involved achieving residential densities higher than those previously approved for the area.

Green Tape Permitting. Some local jurisdictions take a proactive approach to ensure that the quality mixed-use projects favored by the jurisdiction are encouraged rather than discouraged during the approval process. For example, as part of the county executive's plan for the redevelopment of Downtown Silver Spring in Maryland, which includes a diverse mix of uses, the Silver Spring Business District was designated a State of Maryland Enterprise Zone. This designation provides a number of incentives to attract and retain businesses in the enterprise zone.

As one of these incentives, the Department of Permitting Services created a "green tape" permitting and inspection program to expedite the land use and building permit processes for prospective businesses in the enterprise zone. The mission of the green tape program is to facilitate the issuance of building permits for commercial construction in the enterprise zone involving new construction, additions, structural alterations, or changes in use. The Green Tape Team, headed by a "permit technician" caseworker, assists an applicant with the various filing requirements, regulatory reviews, and inspections, including predesign consultations and assessment inspections. The permit technician works with other team members to ensure, to the greatest extent possible, a seamless permitting and inspection process. Technical staff on the team include engineers, plan analysts, inspectors, and managers with expertise in building, electrical, fire, mechanical, accessibility, zoning (including signs), sediment/stormwater management, and subdivision plan review and inspection codes and standards.

The Green Tape Team works closely with the Silver Spring Regional Center to identify qualifying businesses and coordinate green tape services. The Department of Permitting Services maintains information in its database that flags potential green tape properties to make it easier to notify the regional center about potential green tape customers.

Establishing Explicit Requirements. Montgomery County, Maryland, has also sought to establish a strong framework for redevelopment as one way to facilitate the approval process, but even here problems often crop up. In the redevelopment of Bethesda, the county sought to make public requirements very explicit upfront to allow the developer to craft a project that conforms to the guidelines, making the approval that much easier.

At Bethesda Row, for example, Montgomery County's master plan for downtown Bethesda established the framework within which Bethesda Row was developed. Although this plan generally encourages mixed-use developments with an urban character, it also created some barriers that had to be overcome, chiefly with regard to transportation and to the developer's proposed streetscape improvements. The county's traffic model indicated that road capacity was insufficient to support the proposed development, although the model itself conflicted with the county's land use goals, which called for just the kind of development that Bethesda Row represented. As a result, Federal Realty—the developer—had to spend considerable time working with the county to change its traffic standards and to address its traffic concerns.

The county also had very specific guidelines for streetscape concepts for the downtown area that regulated everything from paving materials to trash containers. Federal Realty had to convince the county that its development concept would create an attractive streetscape that would be acceptable to the regulators and in line with market demand. Numerous details were negotiated, such as the appropriate height of street trees and the percentage of sidewalks that could be paved with brick, and Federal Realty was able to gain approval from the forward-thinking county administration for some rather interesting design

At Bethesda Row in Bethesda, Maryland, numerous streetscape details were negotiated with Montgomery County, including placement of seating for the outdoor café next to the roadway rather than the building, thus keeping pedestrians closer to the store windows.

features. The most notable was placement of seating for outdoor cafés. Rather than the usual configuration of seating immediately next to the restaurant, outdoor tables at Bethesda Row are placed next to the roadway (and the on-street parking spaces), keeping the pedestrians where the retailers want them—right next to their store windows.

Today, Bethesda Row is very popular with local residents, providing them an enjoyable environment for shopping, dining, or simply visiting. They also appreciate the fact that Bethesda Row is a major improvement over what previously existed on the site, although when it was first proposed, many residents were concerned about the impact Bethesda Row would have on the community. In particular, they were worried that the project would drive local retailers out of business, replacing them with the same national retailers that could be found at any mall. Federal Realty addressed these concerns by meeting with residents to discuss their ideas for the development and by demonstrating through its leasing strategy that their fears were unfounded. Indeed, Federal Realty has managed to attract an interesting mix of local, regional, and national retailers that generate considerable customer traffic while still providing a special shopping experience. Bethesda Row was fortunate to have the political support of several leaders in the community who were eager to see an innovative addition like Bethesda Row to their downtown.

Streamlining through Information Technology. The city of Emeryville, California, near San Francisco, has sought to streamline its mixed-use approval process through better information technology. At EmeryStation Plaza, being developed on a brownfield site adjacent to an Amtrak Station, city planners coordinated a risk-based assessment with Westinghouse (the former industrial user of the site), Wareham Development (the developer), and the regulatory agencies to facilitate redevelopment of the site. Westinghouse used a "one-stop shop" to refine site assessments. The one-stop shop is a Web application that allows landowners, developers, residents, and other interested parties to access land use zoning, property ownership, and environmental information on any parcel in the city of Emeryville. It is an interactive informational tool for residents and developers that simplifies and speeds up information gathering.

The creation of the one-stop shop was funded by the EPA's Brownfields Pilot Program. Currently, the city is assisting with acquisition of adjacent property to widen access into the commercial development. In consideration of the infrastructure improvements and community amenities that Wareham is contributing, the city will convey an adjacent two-acre (0.8-hectare) site for the construction of affordable housing and a parking structure. Portland also has a similar Web-based system.

Multijurisdictional Approvals. One of the most difficult situations affecting the approval process involves high-profile projects that require approvals from various levels of government, greatly complicating the process and taking it well beyond that of the local jurisdiction. Such

Tax credits for historic renovation of Tower City Center, a designated historic landmark in downtown Cleveland, were important to the project's financial feasibility.

projects require considerable patience and resources to succeed.

At Tower City Center, for example, a major downtown redevelopment project in Cleveland, the complex was designated a historic landmark (tax credits for historic renovation were important to the project's financial viability). The developer had lengthy discussions with the Ohio State Preservation Office and the National Park Service, both of which must approve any changes to historic structures and elements, and the Federal Advisory Council on Historic Preservation, which advises the National Park Service.

The developer, for example, had to obtain approval to replace the steep pedestrian ramps that led to the transit station, to redesign the old transit waiting room as an integral part of the arcade, and to alter some shopfronts in the arcade. Approvals also were necessary for the restoration of the post office building, which retained the 1930s art deco look of the lobby section. The post office building received tax credits, but the National Park Service denied tax credits for the central concourse, where designers replaced the old, narrow corridors to the transit stations with an atrium covered by a skylight.

Neighborhood Engagement. The thorniest problem in gaining approval is frequently related not to regulations but to public opposition. Success for many mixed-use projects often requires that both developers and local government engage local citizens in the process.

For example, at Prudential Center in Boston, a mixed-use project first begun in the 1950s and then expanded and redeveloped in the 1990s, the initial proposed redevelopment, because of its size and potential impact on neighborhood life, outraged members of the adjacent communities.[14] Kevin White, Boston's mayor at that time and a champion of the neighborhoods, scrapped the plan and recommended a fresh approach that included the participation of 22 neighborhood, civic, and business groups to assist in the development of a new plan and its review. This approach empowered an appointed citizens group, Prudential Property Advisory Committee, to establish guidelines, evaluate design concepts, and assess overall project mitigation impacts as physical planning began. The developers also reconstituted their team, seeking planners and architects recognized for their inclusive design processes, to develop a politically acceptable plan that would make developmental sense as well.

The mayor, the Boston Redevelopment Agency, and Prudential put the team in play, yet it was up to the members themselves to find a way to collaborate. The group invited a facilitator, who kept the dialogue open and helped to create a process that has since proved to be applicable to other development approvals. Prudential's goal was to increase the value of the center by expanding its asset base. The new plan accomplishes the objective, albeit on a smaller scale. At the same time, it adds value by fostering connections with adjacent areas and strengthening existing assets. In the end, the consensus-based process garnered support from all interested parties. The final expansion plan included the addition of 1.8 million

Courtesy of CBI Inc.

Redevelopment and expansion of Prudential Center in Boston involved strong citizen involvement and a collaborative process instrumental in shaping the redevelopment plan.

square feet (167,300 square meters), comprising several office buildings, more residential buildings, and a new retail area.

Twenty years ago, the Prudential Center was the image of anachronistic urban thinking. Today, it has evolved into an active retail, office, and residential district. This transformation is attributable partially to citizens who were willing to get involved in a long, sometimes thankless effort to protect and enhance the quality of life in their neighborhoods.

Charrettes. Increasingly, developers and local governments are employing new processes that can better facilitate the approval process by encouraging community input that allows the community to help shape and buy into a vision for a particular site and development. Both developers and local governments are increasingly aware that to ensure support for innovative quality projects, they need to involve community residents in a constructive manner. This approach requires more than just listening: developers and local governments also must demonstrate their willingness to compromise and adjust the features of the project to accommodate those concerns.[15]

One method of engaging the public in the process is through *charrettes*. The National Charrette Institute (NCI) has formalized a process for using charrettes in developments:

> The NCI charrette is a collaborative process for empowering people who are important to a project to work together and support the

One of the city of Chattanooga's most recent re-vitalization projects is not urban at all. After years of successful downtown redevelopment, Chattanooga has broadened its focus with a project to revitalize four square miles (10.4 square kilometers) in the inner suburban ring anchored by Eastgate Mall, the city's oldest suburban mall and long in decline.

The mayor requested that the Chattanooga–Hamilton County Regional Planning Agency develop a plan to re-vitalize the area. A consulting team was selected for a planning study to be managed by the regional planning agency but funded primarily by the stakeholder group the agency assembled. The winning proposal was submitted by Miami-based Dover, Kohl & Partners Town Planning. Private sector stakeholders funding 80 percent of the study included 40-percent-leased Eastgate Mall, fully leased Brainerd Village strip center next door, Osborne Office Park adjacent to the mall, and other businesses and banks in the area.

After preliminary field evaluation and market research, a public design charrette was held by the regional plan-ning agency that drew 300 residents and business owners to help create a new vision for the mall and the surround-ing area. The heart of the week-long process was a six-hour "designing in public" event in which 150 community members gathered in an empty storefront inside the mall and broke into groups to create separate plans for the area. Over the next few days, elements of these plans were evaluated and combined to form a composite draft plan that was presented at the end of the week to an audience of about 250. The high level of participation in the char-rette and participants' positive emotions surrounding the failed mall surprised planners, local officials, and mall owners.

Victor Dover, of Dover, Kohl & Partners, noted that the plans created by 11 groups of "citizen planners" all had a prodevelopment theme. "They envisioned more devel-opment, building their way out of the problem instead of downsizing. That was interesting, because in some com-munities the reaction to development is much cooler. In many other places, folks have given up on the idea that development can make things better and have adopted a NIMBY [not in my backyard] attitude," he said.

Norie Harrower, who leads Eastgate Mall, LLC, the Hart-ford, Connecticut–based investment group that had re-cently purchased half the mall, approached the charrette process with considerable skepticism. "I tend to believe a lot of those things are exercises in futility," he said.

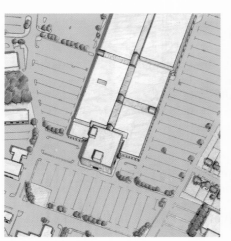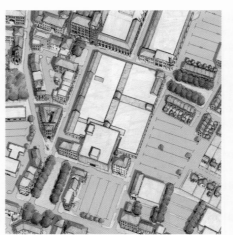

Courtesy of Dover, Kohl & Partners

The plan for redeveloping Eastgate Mall in Chattanooga, Tennessee, into Brainerd Town Center involved a public design charrette that drew 300 residents and business owners to help create a new vision for the mall and the surrounding area. Plans involve a long-term transformation that will play out over several decades.

results. . . . The NCI charrette is a rigorous and inclusive process that produces the strategies and implementation documents for complex and difficult design and planning projects. It is cross-disciplinary, collaborative, and values and vision driven. It is a con-tinuous effort of at least four days long and uses continual feedback loops as leverage for change. . . . In an environment of increasing difficulty and complexity for public and private planning initiatives, charrettes are becoming a key resource in a professional planner's toolbox. The . . . charrette is one of the most effective methods of getting public support for the most challenging planning issues such as increasing density, integrating a mix of uses and a diversity of residences, and creating a healthy public realm. The charrette helps forge strong partnerships between public and private enti-ties, and the process fosters genuine civic spirit.[16]

The accompanying feature box shows how a charrette was used in Chattanooga to facilitate the redevelopment of a defunct mall site into a mixed-use development.

"Everybody gets all excited, and the visionaries come into town and spin the wheel and then leave. Nothing happens—and it costs a lot of money."

When the mayor told the new mall owner that he was integral to the kind of comprehensive revitalization of Eastgate that the city had accomplished earlier downtown, Harrower was not enthusiastic. He had expected only to improve the mall property and sell it for a modest profit. But at the urging of the mayor and other local officials, Harrower agreed to host the charrette in the mall.

"That was when I got hooked because all of a sudden I saw hundreds of people. I thought 20 or 30 irate citizens would show up and say, 'Tear the damn place down.' I saw some real articulate people coming in who cared. What I picked up on first was the emotion," he recalled. "And the mayor was there. I began to see that the city was really behind this process. It is important to a developer to have a city behind you," adds Harrower. "The citizens were behind it. They didn't want to tear it down. They actually wanted us to revive it. [And] that was what we wanted to do."

A draft plan was presented in public at the end of the week-long charrette. Harrower had worked extensively with the consultants as they created the composite plan from designs proposed by the citizens. What he asked for in exchange, he says, was that "whatever we came up with had to be doable. It had to be achievable."

Over the next few weeks, the plan was polished, and the realities of funding, traffic engineering, and the real estate market were considered. The plan did not change substantially from the initial draft, but it gathered so much support from the city, the mall, and prospective tenants that the final public presentation in April—made soon after Harrower's group acquired the rest of the mall in a second transaction—included not only the finalized plan but also announcements of the first projects to implement the plan.

The new plan calls for creating a town center by turning the mall literally inside out and embedding it in a street grid with new office, retail, and residential construction. The mall's exterior will be refaced with new outward-facing storefronts in one- and two-story urbanist designs. Much of the 50 acres (20 hectares) of parking will be used for new housing, parks, civic buildings, and a town square.

With strong public input, a visionary plan was created for the future town center that guides its physical design and economic development. Partnerships and working relationships were established among local government officials, planners, and business owners.

Dover cautions that the vision is just the first step in a long transformation. "We can't predict everything that will happen. The vision should allow you to do anything at any size and know that your piece of it will fit the greater whole that we're attempting to build over time. A single property owner, a mall developer, or a subdivision developer can do that with great confidence because they control all of the land. But here, with a variety of property owners, small and large, the only common manager of the whole process is the community, the city. That's why the city is involved in the planning, because no one else is responsible for the big picture."

Source: Adapted from Richard Bailey, "Mall Over," *Urban Land,* July 1998, pp. 46–49+.

Development Incentives and Tools

A wide variety of development incentives and tools, ranging from land assembly and writedowns to provision of public infrastructure and public financing, can be used to encourage mixed-use development. From the public sector's standpoint, the appropriate strategy depends on many factors; it may incorporate one or all of the special tools available to it, and it may range from passive to active involvement in the development process. This section provides only a brief overview of how some of these tools are being used in mixed-use development. Whatever the tools that are used and where mixed-use developments are appropriate, however, planning agencies should nurture a political, planning, and civic environment that makes mixed-use development feasible and an attractive alternative to single-use projects.

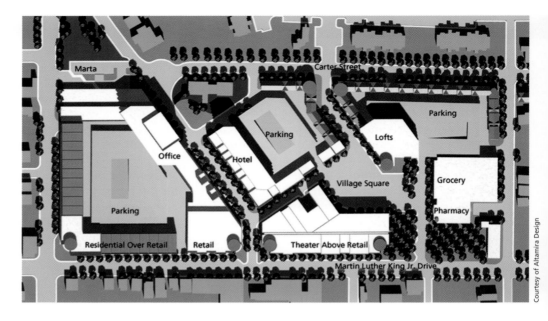

Historic Westside Village in Atlanta is located in a HUD empowerment zone; thus, businesses within the zone can take advantage of wage credits, tax deductions, bond financing, and reductions in capital gains taxes.

Courtesy of Altamira Design

Land Assembly, Land Writedowns, and Tax Incentives

In many cities, the major obstacles to revitalization and subsequent mixed-use development are problems related to land assembly, land costs, and land preparation. Efforts by private developers to assemble parcels large enough for successful mixed-use development are often unsuccessful or involve exorbitant costs when owners hold out. Some brownfield sites require cleanup that is extremely expensive, making it infeasible to develop the land without public involvement.

Land Assembly and Preparation. Local governments can help facilitate development by taking steps to alleviate problems associated with land acquisition. Eminent domain, the key tool, provides local governments with the power to take private land for public use, with reasonable just compensation to the owner or owners. This technique considerably reduces the time required to assemble and develop mixed-use sites. It also allows the implementation of a large-scale redevelopment scheme to proceed under the coordinated guidance of one agency that controls the land. A good example is Yerba Buena Center, which was undertaken by the San Francisco Redevelopment Agency (see Chapter 8). Local governments can also assemble land through simple fee acquisition, without the need for using eminent domain, where market conditions are favorable.

Brownfield cleanup is another way to create a viable site. Brownfields, often existing as a parcel under one owner, are often worthless from an economic point of view, because the cleanup costs can exceed the underlying land value. The only way to bring the land back into use is through some effort from the public sector, usually involving federal funds, to cover the costs of cleanup. Two of the more prominent examples underway today are Atlantic Station in Atlanta, where the EPA is involved in redevelopment of the Atlantic Steel site in Midtown, and Victory, adjacent to downtown Dallas.

Other techniques to facilitate land assembly include land exchanges or swaps between the public and private sectors and relocation assistance from the public sector for space users in the property slotted for redevelopment.

Land Writedowns and Tax Incentives. In addition to assembly and/or cleanup, the public sector often must write down the land that it owns or acquires to make a major project feasible—which means selling the land for less than the government has invested in it, including acquisition, legal, infrastructure, and/or cleanup costs. It might also mean phasing the sale of the land to the developer over time to eliminate carrying costs for the developer.

Tax incentives may include simple tax abatement (forgiving the property tax altogether for a certain period of time), freezing the tax for a certain period of time at a low rate, or tying the tax rate to the project's income stream rather than its assessed value. Peabody Place (see Chapter 8) benefited from tax incentives in downtown Memphis.

Historic Westside Village in Atlanta is located in a HUD empowerment zone. Empowerment zones are used to encourage economic development in distressed areas; designation as an empowerment zone means that businesses locating in these areas can take advantage of wage credits, tax deductions, bond financing, and reduced capital gains tax to stimulate economic development and job growth. Each incentive is tailored to meet the particular needs of a business and offers a significant inducement for companies to locate and hire additional workers. Historic Westside Village is a pedestrian-friendly, transit-oriented, mixed-use development on 17.5 acres (7 hectares). The project, being developed by the Harold A. Dawson Company, will serve as a catalyst to redevelop this historic intown neighborhood. The development will include 200,000 square feet (18,600 square meters) of retail, including a grocery store, two 150,000-square-foot (14,000-square-meter) office buildings, 100 apartments, 200 for-sale loft and condo units, and 35 townhouses.

Several case studies in this book, including CityPlace, Peabody Place, Sony Center, and Yerba Buena Center, have used land assembly, writedowns, or tax incentives.

Providing Infrastructure Improvements

Yet another form of the public sector's support of private development is provision of some public infrastructure for the project—improving streets or roads, providing open space or parks, and/or paying for new public parking structures. At Sony Center am Potsdamer Platz in Berlin, for example, the city government, the federal government, and the German railway company collectively invested more than DM4 billion ($2.2 billion) in infrastructure improvements in and around Potsdamer Platz, the area of Berlin where the Berlin Wall formerly stood.

In the United States, tax increment financing is a principal means of financing infrastructure improvements. Tax increment financing allows local governments to create special tax districts, plan public improvements in those districts, issue bonds to pay for the improvements, and subsequently pay off the bonds with monies derived from any increase in property and/or sales taxes in the district that result from the public improvements.

Tax increment financing is being used, for example, at the 138-acre (56-hectare) Atlantic Station project in Atlanta to pay off $110 million in revenue bonds; the bond money will be used to build water and sewer lines, streets, and other infrastructure improvements, and to clean up environmental problems on the former industrial site. The tax allocation district, administered by the Atlanta Development Authority, will remain in place until the bonds are paid off through the increased revenue stream, in approximately 25 years.

At CityPlace, $55 million in tax increment financing was used to pay for 30 percent of the parking deck construction, and for landscaping, fountains and artwork, lighting, and public space improvements.

A parking district created by the county was essential to the financial feasibility of Bethesda Row in Bethesda, Maryland. The county built the 1,000-space garage at the center of the development site. Nearly all the parking for the development is provided in the county-owned garage and on county-owned surface lots or metered on-street parking; 3,376 parking spaces are available within 500 feet of Bethesda Row. The county established a parking lot district for the Bethesda CBD years ago, building parking facilities that users would pay for hourly or daily. The facilities also are supported by a surtax on property tax assessments for properties that do not provide their own parking, allowing owners of smaller buildings to avoid having to provide their own on-site parking and ensuring that all the parking in the area is operated and managed efficiently.

Public Components, Ownership, and Financing

In many situations, the public sector chooses to invest in a project as one of the owners through a ground lease,

At Addison Circle, the city of Addison provided $9.5 million for infrastructure, street, and open-space improvements.

Courtesy of RTKL.

participating agreement, public financing, or provision of a major public facility such as a convention center, arena, cultural facility, city hall, or library. The public sector generally enter into such deals when it has a very strong economic or civic interest in a prominent site.

Public financial investment is generally directly tied to a commitment of much larger private investment; that is, the public investment is intended to leverage private investment. By requiring that public funds be leveraged, public agencies ensure that public investment generates known and immediate short-term benefits and aids projects that require small amounts of public assistance to make them an attractive private investment. Leveraging tends to preclude highly speculative and costly public investments that do not result in significant private investment.

The public sector may wish to maintain some form of financial participation or ownership interest in the project, which could involve a complex equity participation agreement and/or ground lease. Rowes Wharf illustrates how one public/private deal was structured to allow for ongoing public ownership. Other public financing may come from numerous sources—industrial revenue bonds, mortgage revenue bonds, general revenue bonds, federal grant programs, state programs, or various other means.

Several case studies in Chapter 8 provide examples of public ownership of mixed-use project components. Yerba Buena Center in San Francisco, for example, includes numerous publicly owned components, starting with the Moscone Convention Center, the original impetus for the project. Other prominent examples of developments with significant public ownership include Smyrna Town Center in Smyrna, Georgia; Fairview Village near Portland; Cathedral City Downtown, California; and Cornelius Town Center in North Carolina (see also the section on public, civic, and transit uses in Chapter 2). Other examples of financial participation or public ownership are outlined below.

Hollywood & Highland. The city of Los Angeles is a significant owner participant at the recently opened Hollywood & Highland development in Hollywood, California. This $615 million urban entertainment/retail/hotel "only in Hollywood" destination includes 640,000 square feet (59,500 square meters) of one-of-a-kind shops, restaurants, entertainment venues, studio broadcast facilities, cinemas, a hotel, and a live broadcast theater to be home for the Academy Awards®. The project is located on Hollywood Boulevard adjacent to the historic Grauman's Chinese Theatre and across the street from the historic El Capitan Theatre. It also sits atop a subway station that runs from downtown Los Angeles through Hollywood and on to Universal Studios in North Hollywood. The hotel, already located on the property, was expanded to the 640-room, four-star Renaissance Hollywood Hotel. The project also includes a transit center with a Metro Rail portal, an MTA bus transfer station, tour bus and shuttle dropoff facilities, a drop-and-ride zone, and a parking structure for 3,000 cars.

Cornelius Town Center in North Carolina. The town of Cornelius has been instrumental in developing the town center, including provision of a town hall and other public components.

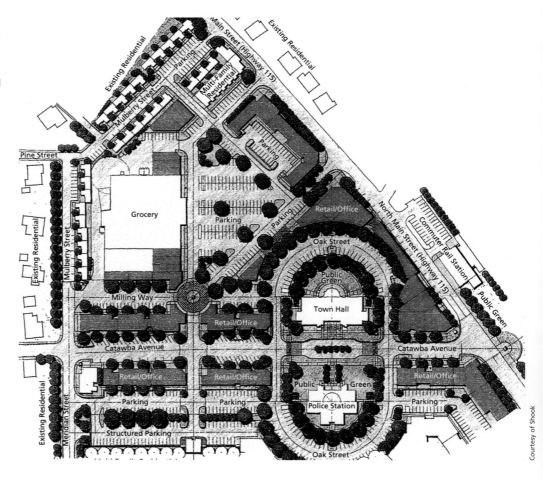

The city of Los Angeles is a significant owner/participant in the Hollywood & Highland development, owning both the theater and the parking structure.

Courtesy of Bragman Nyman Cafarelli

The public/private partnership involved a business deal with the city of Los Angeles that gives the city ownership of assets. The city will own the theater and parking structure in return for its $90 million investment—$60 million for parking and $30 million toward the theater's cost of $70 million.

The project received solid support from Mayor Richard Riordan, the city council, the Community Redevelopment Agency, and the Metropolitan Transportation Authority. It also received enthusiastic backing from the Hollywood business community and most nearby homeowner groups; it moved rapidly through the city approval process as a result of the high level of cooperation from all the city agencies.

Economic benefits were projected to be substantial. One independent analyst has estimated up to $265 million in economic impact, including $7.7 million in new tax revenues that will go to the city and an estimated $22 million annually in new spending rippling through Hollywood and neighboring areas. The project also created 836 construction jobs per year during its two-year construction period, and early estimates projected it would create 2,430 permanent jobs when in operation.

Tower City Center. At Tower City Center in Cleveland, a transit station is a major component. Early in the development process, the city's rapid transit agency agreed to give the developer management responsibility for the rail transit reconstruction to ensure its coordination with the construction schedules of the other parts of the proj-

ect. The redesign and reconstruction of the transit station necessitated extensive negotiations and cooperation with the Greater Cleveland Transit Authority, which owns the station and tracks. The Ohio Department of Transportation and the Urban Mass Transit Administration (now the Federal Transit Administration) contributed financial support for renovations and oversaw administration of the project. A substantial part of the renovation and construction costs of transit passenger accessways was funded by the Federal Transit Administration. Additional funding came from federal sources through the city of Cleveland. The complete rebuilding of the rail transit station and the concurrent expansion of activities around the station have reinvigorated rail transit travel in Cleveland. At the same time, the station has proved a boon for workers and shoppers in the project.

Sugar Land Town Square. At Sugar Land Town Square in Texas, which will include retail shops, office space, residential lofts, and a hotel, the city of Sugar Land is providing a conference center that is part of the new hotel for the project and a portion of the parking structure. The city sold $19 million in bonds for its portion of the hotel project—the 60,000-square-foot (5,600-square-meter) Sugar Land Conference Center and 360 spaces of an adjoining 525-space parking garage. The bonds funded $18 million toward design and construction and $900,000 in issuance costs and debt service reserves.

The city funded $10 million of the $19 million in bonds, with the Sugar Land 4B Corporation participating in the project at $9 million. Voters created the 4B Corporation in 1995 to collect a quarter-cent sales tax for development in the city. "The conference center/garage will be self-funded," says City Manager Allen Bogard. "Revenues from the hotel occupancy tax will fund $10 million and the remaining $9 million in debt will be funded from sales tax generated from the Town Square project." The conference center will be leased to the hotel operator.

Rowes Wharf. In the 1960s, the Boston Redevelopment Authority acquired the dilapidated Rowes Wharf property as part of the Downtown Waterfront Urban Renewal Plan. The Rowes Wharf parcel was the last gap on the harbor in the financial district. In 1982, the redevelopment authority issued strict guidelines for evaluating development proposals, including specific requirements for building height (165 feet [50 meters] maximum), density (FAR of 4.0), uses (residential, commercial, retail, and below-grade parking and servicing), and public amenities (harborfront walkways and a ferry terminal). In addition, the redevelopment authority imposed controls to preserve view corridors to the harbor from adjacent streets, to provide open space equal to at least 50 percent of the site, and to guarantee that the architecture would reinforce the character of the Boston waterfront in its massing, building type, materials, and details.

In the first stage of the redevelopment authority's competition for selecting a development team, seven proposals were narrowed to three. The redevelopment authority chose Rowes Wharf Associates—a joint venture of the Beacon Companies and Equitable Real Estate—and its architects, Skidmore, Owings & Merrill, who then began a two-year design review in accordance with the redevelopment authority's practice. Throughout the process, which covered all phases of the architectural work from concept design to contract documents, the original proposal was refined and improved with the assistance of an advisory team from the Boston Society of Architects, including the addition of a domed space with a public observatory and the six-story-high arched courtyard.

In fact, three separate programs were put forward in the course of the development process. The first involved primarily residential and office uses, the second added the hotel, and the third reduced the amount of residential space while increasing office uses. The last change affected the central wharf; originally programmed for residential condominiums, it was changed to office uses to prevent the wharf areas from becoming too private in their orientation. Residential uses in this location could also have been adversely affected by the noise of the water shuttle, ferries, and commuter boats operating in south wharf areas.

The business terms of the deal are especially complex because of the redevelopment authority's desire to maintain an ownership interest in the project. The project was undertaken pursuant to a single ground lease between the redevelopment authority and Rowes Wharf Associates. Once the shell was completed, the project was converted from a ground lease to a condominium project created by a master deed in which the redevelopment authority as landowner and Rowes Wharf Associates as building owner are codeclarants. The condominium contains an office/retail unit, a hotel unit, and a reserved (residential) unit. Rowes Wharf Associates acquired, through purchase money notes, the fee ownership of the reserved (residential) and hotel units, but the office/retail unit will remain as a leasehold between the redevelopment authority and Rowes Wharf Associates until 2065.

The office leasehold agreement requires a base annual rent of $1,282,400 and 10 percent of net cash flow from the office/retail unit after a return of 12.5 percent on total project costs. The condominium arrangement was used to ensure that both the hotel and residential portions could be owned in fee simple. The hotel could not have been financed using a ground lease, and the residential units could not have been marketed effectively if they were developed on leased land. In addition, part of the deal with the city involved a $2.1 million contribution from

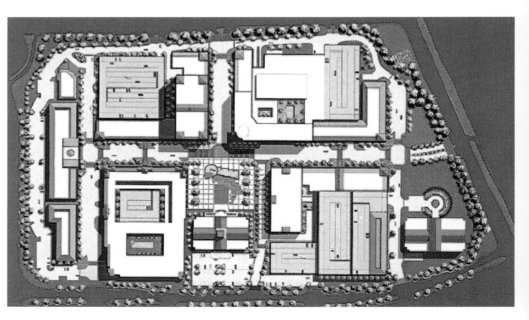

The city of Sugar Land used bond financing to provide a conference center and a portion of the parking structure at Sugar Land Town Square in Texas.

The development of Rowes Wharf in Boston involved a ground lease and complex ownership agreements between the Boston Redevelopment Agency and the developer, Rowes Wharf Associates.

Courtesy of Skidmore, Owings & Merrill

the developer to a fund to support low- and moderate-income housing, part of the Boston linkage program.

The project involves no public financing, and the leasehold interest was acquired at fair market value. The project was financed through a 50/50 joint venture between Beacon and Equitable, with Equitable providing the construction financing. Permanent financing has been obtained from Bank of New England.

Public Development Entities

As highlighted in previous examples, local governments have become principal owners and/or master developers of projects; they can undertake such development through a variety of public development entity structures. Special development and redevelopment authorities, commissions, and corporations are frequently used to undertake large-scale mixed-use development, and are empowered to use many of the tools already described. These entities exist in both central city and suburban locations; they often take on primary leadership for the area, focusing a variety of tools and resources with the single objective of successfully redeveloping the area into a vibrant new mixed-use district or community. Numerous other public development entities, such as transit agencies, may also be involved.

A Redevelopment Authority in Cincinnati. Central city and/or downtown redevelopment authorities are a common type of public organization involved in mixed-use development. They initiated many early mixed-use projects in the 1960s, and they are still active today in many cities.

In Cincinnati, the creation of a new authority was recommended to foster mixed-use development in the area of downtown between two new sports stadiums called "the Banks." The recommendation from the Riverfront Advisors Commission concluded that the city and county should jointly create the Riverfront Development Commission (RDC) to oversee the development and ensure implementation of the vision for the Banks.

Generally, the RDC is charged with coordinating public and private development at the Banks to ensure implementation of the vision as articulated in planning documents. This group has authority to make decisions and has the support of the city and county to ensure cooperation among the many parties involved.

The RDC was envisioned to have four responsibilities: 1) review developers' proposals and assist with the selection of one; 2) serve as the developer's advocate with the many entities involved; 3) participate in amending Cincinnati's zoning code; and 4) ensure ongoing operational management. The RDC would work with the city, county, and the developer to establish an entity that has the capacity for ongoing management of the Banks. This entity would ensure that the development is a safe, clean, and inviting place for residents and visitors alike. It would also ensure strong transportation links and effective, aggressive marketing of the Banks as a destination, and would leverage marketing dollars with other organizations involved in conventions, tourism, entertainment, and economic development.

The City as Developer at Smyrna. A mixed-use project in a small city may be undertaken by the city itself through one of its agencies, as was the case in Smyrna, Georgia, for the Smyrna Town Center. Consumed in Atlanta's urban sprawl, Smyrna, a city of 30,000, had lost its identity. By 1988, its downtown had essentially ceased to exist. Except for a few marginal businesses operating out of dilapidated structures, there was no life or activity in downtown Smyrna. That year, realizing that strong action was needed if Smyrna were to survive, city officials developed a plan and design for a new library and community center and subsequently decided to use those civic buildings as leverage to create an entirely new town center.

The 29-acre (11.7-hectare) site is located one block from the existing main street. It was planned to contain most of the town's civic and community buildings, a town green, a three-acre (1.2-hectare) park and duck pond, and land for private high-density commercial and residential development. A loop road can be closed off to traffic during festivals on the main street. Design guidelines control future development.

The city assembled and purchased the land, financed the planning process, and installed sidewalks. Although public funds were committed to the project without a public referendum, local citizens participated in the planning process in several ways: formal town hall meetings, downtown development task forces, and informal neighborhood meetings with city council members, for example. Many local organizations and private sector companies also became involved in the project.

Completion of the community center and library in 1991 sparked the development of 22 cottage houses (at seven units per acre [17 per hectare]), which sold out instantly, and 40,000 square feet (3,700 square meters) of retail/office space on land that the city sold to private developers—with payments due only after housing sales began. Encouraged by the private development, a second phase of three additional public buildings—a city hall, a public safety facility, and a seniors' center—was built.

Private development has continued with construction of a drugstore, a new branch bank, and an office for Post Properties. Later phases of public development involved relocating a historic restaurant to the downtown to serve as a welcome center and building a replica of the city's old train station as a museum. A privately developed and financed retail/residential project is the most recent addition.

Today, Smyrna's town center is a busy place and a popular venue for festivals. The city's public buildings have been geographically consolidated. Land costs were reduced by the sharing of a frontyard—the town green—and parking, and the savings were added to the design and materials budgets. The initial economic results were impressive. Annual building permit values increased 250 percent in 1996 and 1997. The average sale prices of houses increased from $139,000 in 1990

The Riverfront Development Commission, charged with coordinating public and private development to ensure implementation of the vision for the area, was created to oversee development of the Banks in Cincinnati.

Courtesy of Riverfront Development Commission

The city of Smyrna, Georgia, served as master developer for the new Smyrna Town Center, including development of the Smyrna Community Center.

to $250,000 in 1997. The tax base has grown to more than cover the $25 million in public costs; the tax rate has been lowered each year and is now one of the lowest in the state. The city bond rating has been upgraded to AA–. Most important, the city of Smyrna has a new identity.

Smyrna and the other examples above highlight the importance of strong public leadership in mixed-use development. In many cases, whether downtown or suburban, the best mixed-use projects involve public development entities that create, nurture, sustain, and invest in a public vision for a new mixed-use development and public realm that will play an important role in the civic life of their community.

Notes

 1. Smart Growth Network, www.smartgrowth.org, accessed October 4, 2002.

 2. Ibid., accessed October 6, 2002.

 3. Jane Jacobs, *The Death and Life of Great American Cities* (New York: Random House, 1961), p. 14.

 4. See Council on Development Choices for the 80s, *The Affordable Community: Adapting Today's Communities to Tomorrow's Needs* (Washington, D.C.: ULI–the Urban Land Institute, 1982).

 5. Teresa Zogby, "Mixed-Use Districts," American Planning Association Planning Advisory Service Memo, November 1979.

 6. http://www.dca.state.ga.us/toolkit/printable.asp?ID=14, accessed November 11, 2002.

 7. Ibid.

 8. Ibid.

 9. http://www.springsgov.com, accessed November 12, 2002.

10. http://www.denvergov.org/Planning_Services/template16763.asp, accessed November 13, 2002.

11. Press release, July 4, 2002, www.info.gov.hk, accessed November 13, 2002.

12. American Society of Planning Officials, *Planned Unit Development Ordinances*, Planning Advisory Service Report No. 291, May 1973, p. 1.

13. www.ci.belmont.nc.us/tnd.htm, accessed November 18, 2002.

14. The following discussion of Prudential Center was adapted from Charles N. Tseckares, "The Politics of Development," *Urban Land*, September 2001, pp. 78–81.

15. See Steven C. Ames, editor, *Guide to Community Visioning*, rev. ed. (Chicago: APA Planners Press, 2001).

16. www.charretteinstitute.org, accessed November 4, 2002.

5. Planning and Design

Compared with most real estate projects, mixed-use developments involve very complex designs, requiring not only good architecture but also superb land use planning and urban design. A sense of place, public spaces and streetscapes, the interrelationship and identity of elements, pedestrian circulation and amenities, and parking are just a few of the issues and elements crucial to the economic success of a mixed-use project. These design issues must be carefully, creatively, and successfully addressed, or the project will suffer. Although mediocre design will not necessarily doom a single-use project, mediocre design will likely lead to failure for a mixed-use development.

Most mixed-use projects pose a special set of physical planning challenges that go far beyond the architectural and engineering concerns of other types of real estate projects:

- To design and position each use to achieve its maximum potential and at the same time combine the uses so they perform as a whole and benefit from one another;
- To provide an efficiently functioning infrastructure (parking, services, utilities, and effective mechanical, electrical, and structural systems) capable of servicing each project component's differing demands;

An evening celebration at Southlake Town Square in Southlake, Texas.

- To maximize the benefits of a well-integrated transportation, vehicular, and parking program/plan to facilitate vehicular and pedestrian access to the various uses;
- To provide easy and effective pedestrian access to project components and to relevant adjacent areas by positioning the components and by designing attractive pedestrian areas and horizontal and vertical pedestrian movement systems;
- To include amenities and attractions that cannot easily be provided in single-purpose projects, such as exciting people-oriented spaces and a public realm that can capitalize on the synergy of diverse uses and activities in the project, and to do so in a way that uncovers and features the singular location and opportunity;
- To mass individual components in the project so as to create a harmonious, distinctive architectural character for the project;
- To make the development part of the existing community and create an appropriate internal and external human and urban scale, particularly when typical density, building mass, and architectural image of a mixed-use project are often quite different from surrounding areas;
- To plan each building phase of a staged development program as a self-sufficient entity while allowing for effective integration of subsequent elements;
- To design for and accommodate the operating cycles of the various uses in projects with elements that have

greatly differing activity cycles while keeping common areas open and basic services operating;

- To manage a design process that often involves multiple designers—including urban designers, landscape architects, engineers, and architects for each separate project component—as well as input from building operators and a variety of other sources.

Ultimately, the design process for a mixed-use project is an exercise in place making and city building, not just real estate development, requiring a vision for the place to be created. The vision can come from many sources—developers, urban designers, public sector leaders, key tenants, hotel operators, community members—but in the end it should be a shared vision. Increasingly, charrettes and planning meetings open to the public are instrumental in shaping the vision, and frequently public involvement early in the process benefits the project down the road when approvals are needed.

The Design Process and Design Team

Planning and design for mixed-use projects involve a long process that begins with general conceptual design and then moves into greater detail as the project concept is refined. The plan and the design need to respond to numerous factors that will push and pull the design in numerous directions, but ultimately the design should be driven by a well-informed vision. Like most complex decision-making processes, design proceeds through a series of tentative solutions in response to the project's critical building, site, and program requirements. The multiple designers and uses involved frequently entail a collaborative process that requires strong team leadership from the lead designers and the developer.

The Design Process
Although no project is designed in quite the same series of steps as another, any design process has three major

A critical element of the design process is the creation of a compelling vision for the new development. Pictured is a conceptual rendering of an office street at Brainerd Town Center in Chattanooga, Tennessee.

Courtesy of Dover, Kohl & Partners

Some developers tightly manage design and construction by establishing strategic working relationships with specific architects and construction firms. McCaffery Interests, for example, has worked closely with the architectural firm Antunovich Associates on numerous projects, including the Market Common Clarendon II in Arlington, Virginia.

Courtesy of McCaffery Interests

The town center design for Birkdale Village in Huntersville, North Carolina, features a main street with residential over retail, using wood-frame construction.

Courtesy of Crosland and Pappas Properties

phases: preliminary conceptual design, design development, and design documentation. During conceptual design, the fundamental shape and massing are determined—including the arrangement of the circulation armature and the character of the public spaces—so that design criteria and general performance specifications for the project can be established. This process is iterative and involves studying numerous alternatives. Preliminary cost estimates and unusual contract or material requirements are also defined.

Based on an approved concept developed during the preliminary design phase, design development includes the more detailed design and development of all project components, including selection and design of the structural and mechanical systems; design of building components, including development of floor plans, building elevations, selection of materials, and development of applicable typical details; preparation of outline specifications; preparation of renderings and final presentation materials to aid the developer in negotiations with financial institutions and public officials; and preparation of an updated estimate of construction costs and construction schedule (preferably with input from a contractor or construction manager).

Working drawings and specifications are prepared during the documentation phase. They are the basis for construction contractors' bids, contract award, and actual construction, and they must therefore be quite detailed. The parties also confirm budgeted costs and provide a preliminary construction schedule.

Managing Multiple Designers and Contractors

Mixed-use projects invariably involve numerous designers. A typical approach is to use one urban design and planning firm to develop a master plan that arranges the various uses and elements on the site, a variety of architects to design the specific buildings and components, and landscape architects, engineers, and other specialists to design important details and provide technical design services. In many cases, developers deliberately use a variety of architects to arrive at a design that incorporates a variety of styles akin to what is found on typical downtown city streets.

A design group that worked on the project during preliminary design may not continue with the project during design development. Such a change could occur for several reasons. For example, planning skills required for preliminary master planning emphasize conceptualization of an overall program and organization of elements rather than design of individual buildings and public spaces. In other cases, one set of designers may be retained by the public sector to develop an overall scheme, and then specific developers bring other designers to develop specific buildings or projects. In most cases, however, a master plan designer should have a continuing overview role.

Some developers prefer a strong partnership with a design firm that is used for numerous projects, as this approach can create a strong team and highly efficient design and construction. For example, McCaffery Interests, a retail and mixed-use developer with projects in Chicago, Minneapolis, Washington, and other cities, has established an approach that allows them "to respond quickly to the needs of its partners and tenants through the internal management of design, construction, and tenant coordination. In addition, the company has established strategic working relationships with Plant Construction Company and Antunovich Associates architects; these two firms have adopted a greater awareness of McCaffery Interests's typical project characteristics and a sense of loyalty to the company's efforts. They are attentive and committed to design and construction needs and success."[1]

Collaboration and Leadership

Although physical design is primarily the responsibility of urban designers, architects, engineers, and planners, collaboration with the developer and other key team members is necessary to ensure that physical plans are

Certain issues concerning mixed-use development are universal, but what works in the United States does not always work in other nations. In mixed-use design that involves a foreign architect, involving local architects and engineers in projects is imperative—not only because most foreign designers are not licensed in every country where they work but also because local professionals know the pitfalls of local design and construction. Typically, three categories of design service can be used for mixed-use projects: one-source design, concept designer and construction architect, and design architect and construction architect.

Some clients prefer one-source design; that is, they buy the services of an international designer to create the project from concept through construction documents. Under this scenario, local professionals are brought in to review and approve the drawings and then serve as the architect of record. If local professionals have not been part of the decision-making process with the international designer during the conception of the design, however, they are less able to deal with the many issues that arise during construction. Further, they have no vested interest in the project and its design. This method can have disastrous results in a country where local professionals have rights of approval over the design.

The method by which an international designer conceives the design—and a local architect develops and documents it—can be equally dangerous for the owner. Given that the client wants the designer's ideas but does not want to pay for design development and given that the architect is not attuned to the intricacies of the project, the result may not be satisfactory to anyone.

The most successful design team approach involves an international designer who provides a detailed project design and then turns the project over to a local architect to create construction documents. This approach is most effective when the local architect is included in the design process from the beginning, making possible speedier documentation and construction. With this method, the architect of record has a vested interest in the project, having been part of the decision-making team throughout the design process.

Source: Adapted from Raymond Peloquin, "Into the Fabric Woven," *Urban Land,* April 1999, pp. 77–79+.

reasonable, functional, and cost-effective from a variety of perspectives. Because the various uses in a mixed-use development have complex and conflicting needs and because the uses chosen for the project strongly affect design, the developer often plays a much stronger role during design than for a single-use project. The developer's understanding of the marketing needs of each individual land use and the tradeoffs between integration and separation of uses is critical. The role of an experienced project manager working for the developer is essential.

The master developer's basic role is one of team leader, bringing in and coordinating the efforts of all team members from the very beginning. During the design phase, input is required from a variety of sources, including the leasing agents and operators for each part of the development—offices, retail, hotel, residential, parking garages, and so on—financing experts, market experts and marketing consultants, major retail tenants, major office tenants, development partners such as apartment developers or hotel developers, construction contractors, and public officials. Each participant's input should relate not only to a specific use or issue but also to the overall project concept and operation. This collaborative team approach can be one of the most important aspects of the design process, because no one person is likely to have a complete understanding of the detailed design and operational issues for all the project's uses and elements.

To ensure constructibility and cost-effective design, it is especially important that the general contractor participate on the design team during the early stages of design. A contractor in the role of construction manager will be able to quantify the costs of design decisions, such as stacking residential on top of retail or a hotel on top of residential. The transition from one type of function to another can be expensive, and these issues need to be addressed and/or quantified early in the process.

Because of the complexity and collaboration involved with mixed uses, the design fees and expenses for mixed-use developments can be considerably higher than for single-use buildings. More parties are involved, and thus more coordination of effort is required; one master planner or architect often orchestrates the whole process.

Location and Site

Design for a mixed-use project begins with the distinctive character of the location and the site and a vision for what can be built on that site. The most important location and site conditions affecting design, apart from market issues discussed earlier, include the location and size of the site, allowable density and land costs, topography and site conditions, site access and proximity to roadways and/or transit, and the nature and condition of surrounding uses.

Location and land prices dictate density and thus affect configuration. For example, a compact urban site

where land is expensive might dictate the need for one large vertical structure, such as those found along North Michigan Avenue in Chicago or downtown Shanghai, sites of numerous mixed-use towers. A larger, less expensive suburban site allows for more horizontal development, such as that found in a great many lower-density mixed-use town centers in the United States.

Location and Site Size

Location and size of the site are fundamental in shaping design. Mixed-use developments have been built on sites of all sizes, ranging from less than one-half acre to more than 100 acres (0.2 to 40 hectares). They have been developed in locations ranging from high-density downtowns to suburban business districts to master-planned communities and resorts (see Chapter 2).

Downtown sites are traditionally at the smaller end of this range. Of the case studies in this book, the sites range from approximately six acres (2.4 hectares) for Jin Mao

Tower and Sony Center am Potsdamer Platz to nine acres (3.6 hectares) at Peabody Place, 14 acres (5.7 hectares) at West End City Center, and 87 acres (35 hectares) at Yerba Buena Center. Projects built today on small downtown sites within an existing street grid, for example, must respect that environment if they are to succeed. Market Square in Washington, D.C., for example, is located on a two-block site in downtown Washington that was originally bisected by a street. The developers won approval to close the street, but the street vista remained; the street was transformed into the U.S. Navy Memorial plaza, which is now surrounded by two freestanding mixed-use structures, each containing several floors of residential over office space, with retail uses at ground level on most sides of the buildings. Projects built on larger sites, such as Yerba Buena Center in San Francisco (see Chapter 8), also need to respect their context, but they are also about creating a new context and thus are much more exercises in city building.

Suburban sites are often much larger, offering more flexibility and allowing for the creation of their own interior street and public open-space system. In some sense, these size and location features allow suburban mixed-use developments to create oases in a hostile, auto-oriented landscape. Projects such as Phillips Place in Charlotte, located in a low-density suburban business district, and Valencia Town Center Drive, located in the master-planned community of Valencia, California, have been designed to create their own new urban place, but there is little in the surrounding environment that they can be integrated with; thus, they are focused on their own internal main streets. (Chapter 2 has a more thorough treatment of the types of sites suitable for mixed-use projects.)

Allowable Density and Land Costs

Allowable density and land cost go hand in hand with location, but they are an issue in their own right. Prime locations with few restrictions on density, and thus high

Chicago's 900 North Michigan Avenue is a 66-story mixed-use tower located on a street with numerous high-rise mixed-use developments.

land costs, inevitably drive the design into a vertical configuration. Perhaps the best examples of how small, expensive sites with large allowable densities can affect mixed-use developments are on North Michigan Avenue in Chicago, an area with some of the highest land prices and allowable densities in the United States. Mixed-use developments that have been developed within roughly ten blocks along that thoroughfare include North Bridge, Park Tower, the John Hancock Center, Olympia Centre, Water Tower Place, 900 North Michigan Avenue, and One Magnificent Mile. The sites range from under one to just over two acres (0.4 to 0.8 hectare), and the GBA of each development is around 1 million square feet (93,000 square meters). Each project is primarily vertical, with high-rise towers ranging up to 100 stories. Land prices, market conditions, and allowable densities clearly dictated the necessity for high-rise structures in each case.

Suburban sites, on the other hand, usually involve lower land costs and lower allowable densities, allowing for a more flexible design and resulting in highly varied development patterns and designs. At Valencia Town Center Drive, for example, the land was part of a large master-planned community that had been under development for several decades, and the site for the mixed-use town center was chosen because of its strategic location in the community that would allow it to provide an important sense of place and civic identity. Although it is one of the densest portions of the community, its overall density is quite low compared with central city or suburban downtowns.

Topography and Existing Site Conditions

Site conditions that can play a role in design include topography, soil conditions, and existing buildings or uses on the site. At CityPlace in West Palm Beach, for example, an existing church on the site became a focal point and an important place maker for the site. At Phillips Place in Charlotte, a site that sloped downward from front to back allowed for a two-level parking structure providing at-grade parking on the upper level for the retail stores and at-grade parking for residences on the lower level. Each parking level is accessed from a different point, but each is entered at grade, with no need or option to move from one level to the other.

Peabody Place in Memphis (see Chapter 8) is a prime example of how existing buildings and street layouts can strongly affect the design. In this case, numerous historic structures on a multiblock area in downtown Memphis divided by city streets were designated for rehabilitation. Several new buildings were developed to fit into the existing fabric, but the overall development plan was driven largely by the need to enhance and redevelop the site and buildings within the existing street fabric of the downtown.

Greyfield sites involving large defunct commercial or retail properties often present interesting challenges involving the reuse of existing buildings that can shape the design; such sites and developments frequently involve the reconfiguration of an existing center rather

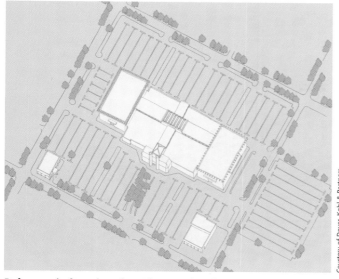

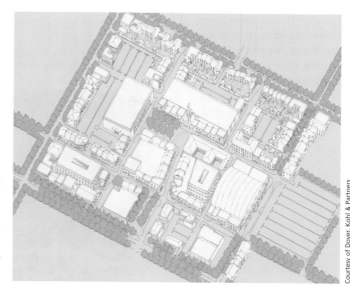

Courtesy of Dover, Kohl & Partners

Before and after plans for Winter Park Village, a mixed-use town center on the site of a failed mall in Winter Park, Florida.

than total demolition. At Brainerd Town Center in Chattanooga, the chosen phased approach replaces the mall incrementally, an approach that involves numerous design and operational challenges.

Site Access and Proximity to Roadways and/or Transit

Providing access to the site via roadways or transit is fundamental as well, but the design need not be a slave to the roadway, as has been the case with many suburban strip shopping centers. Site access begins with visibility and an identifiable image and then proceeds to entry points and internal circulation.

Attractive mixed-use designs frequently do not put everything they have on display to the surrounding arterials or highways; rather, they are designed to entice and lure the driver through the creation of attractive facades and vistas, and even a little mystery. This effect is sometimes achieved by creating a main street with well-designed entry features that is perpendicular to a high-traffic arterial. This approach was used at Abacoa Town Center in Jupiter, Florida, and CityPlace in West Palm Beach. Once the driver is curious, entrances into parking lots and structures can be strategically placed off surrounding roadways.

When transit is available, access for pedestrians from the transit station must be a top priority in the design. At Atlantic Station, for example, the developer is spending millions of dollars on a bridge that will connect the project to a nearby transit station. At Mockingbird Station in Dallas, a pedestrian bridge connects the project with the adjacent transit station. The design of the project, which includes the adaptive use of an existing industrial building, is reminiscent of railroad station architecture, and the industrial construction and stylized use of stained glass at the transit station are major influences on both architectural plans and the design of marketing tools.

The developer of Atlantic Station in Atlanta is spending millions of dollars on a bridge that will connect the project to a nearby transit station and neighboring districts.

Courtesy of Development Design Group, Inc.

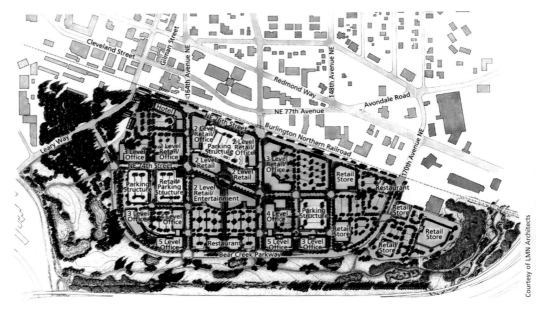

The plan for Redmond Town Center in Redmond, Washington, highlights pedestrian-friendly streets and public open spaces.

Surrounding Uses and Context

The nature and condition of surrounding uses—and the larger surrounding community—are critical design issues, particularly for infill mixed-use projects. To maximize a positive effect on the community for which it is planned, a mixed-use development should reach out as much as possible to the surrounding community. The best designs to achieve this objective are those that provide a sense of place and an appropriate form, adding to rather than detracting from the surroundings. The project should involve a design that surrounding communities will want to connect to—if not immediately, then over time.

Contextual design is often very different for suburban developments and urban mixed-use developments. In an already developed urban environment, the project design will likely be contextual, and, if it is successful, the project will become an extension of the existing urban fabric. In the suburbs, however, the fabric may not exist in the same way, and the surroundings may not offer a pedestrian environment to connect with and enhance. In this situation, the mixed-use development may need to exist as a pedestrian-friendly island or oasis in a largely auto-dominated setting. Moreover, in suburban settings external relationships are driven more by visibility from roadways and easy auto access, because they are key forces in suburban markets.

Urban Design and Place Making

Ideas about urban design have changed dramatically over the past two decades, and as a result, many mixed-use projects designed and built today are completely different from their counterparts of 20 years ago. The latest designs frequently use very different architectural styles and materials, with far less glass, more brick and textured surfaces, more traditional architecture and frequent historical references, and greater attention to design details where pedestrians pass by. These designs are also more horizontal in nature, with a much higher percentage of low-rise buildings than in the past. Most important, these new designs rely much more on open-air public spaces —streets, squares, greens, and parks—as central organizing elements, than on enclosed atriums, malls, or underground concourses. As a result, the latest designs are much more likely to be perceived as a district than a complex, a place instead of a project.

Even with this change, the urban design concept must respect certain basic precepts that apply to the design and layout of all types of mixed-use designs. Mixed-use projects require countless connections—horizontal and vertical—between uses. Such connections can be facilitated not only through proper placement of uses but also through strong visual connections and sight lines, a well-thought-out pedestrian circulation system, well-placed escalators and elevators, good signage, an attractive streetscape and landscaping, and careful placement of parking. All these elements should be used to facilitate visitors' ability to find their way, allowing users to easily know where they are and how to get where they are going, and encouraging visitors to stroll and wander without fear of getting lost. The design must also effectively address such issues as connections with surrounding uses, the identifying architectural features of each individual component, building systems and infrastructure, building materials and finishes, and the project's architectural profile.

The Urban Design Concept

Perhaps the best place to start the conceptual design of a mixed-use development is with the public spaces and the circulation system—what Walt Niehoff of LMN Architects in Seattle calls the "central armature" of the project or the "negative space." To do so means defining the nature of the space between the buildings—streets, pedestrian pathways, town squares or plazas, atriums, retail pathways, for example. Such space, if properly designed, defines an attractive public realm that will attract users, help orient them to the project's various components, and establish the project as a special place. (See "Public Spaces and People-Oriented Places" later in this chapter.)

Fundamentally, the design must address the issues of streets in central public areas that allow cars, open-air pedestrian areas where cars are not allowed, enclosed atriums and galleria, or some combination of them. The answer is partially driven by the nature of the site and the requirements of the program, but the design philosophy is equally important.

Central Organizing Elements. Projects that use streets are of two types—those designed around existing streets and those that create new streets. Projects that use existing streets are usually in downtown redevelopment areas, including, for example, Bethesda Row in Bethesda, Maryland, Peabody Place in downtown Memphis, and Yerba Buena Center in San Francisco. Projects that create new streets are usually on large undeveloped parcels or involve redevelopment of shopping centers or industrial properties, such as, for example, Valencia Town Center Drive at the heart of the new community of Valencia, California, Santana Row on a shopping center redevelopment site in San Jose, and Legacy Town Center in the Legacy business park in Plano, Texas.

Projects that use open-air plazas and pedestrian areas without streets are often located on smaller parcels. They may include streets along the edges of the project, reserving internal open spaces for pedestrians only. Market Square in Washington, D.C., for example, includes two separate mixed-use buildings surrounding the U.S. Navy Memorial plaza; the project is surrounded by public streets, but a central street that previously bisected the site was closed to allow for the creation of the plaza and memorial. Canal City Hakata in Fukuoka, Japan, uses a dramatic open-air retail pedestrian promenade as the public realm, Rowes Wharf in Boston uses dramatic archways and waterfront walkways, and Sony Center am Potsdamer Platz in Berlin uses a covered but not fully enclosed plaza as a central organizing element.

Projects that use enclosed atriums, galleria, or malls as central organizing elements were the standard in the United States during the 1970s and 1980s, and although they are less popular today, they are still a preferred approach in many situations. Examples from the United States include Pentagon City in Arlington, Virginia, which uses a four-level mall anchored at both ends by department stores, 900 North Michigan Avenue and North Bridge in downtown Chicago, and AOL Time Warner Center in New York. Pacific Place in Hong Kong uses a high-end, multilevel shopping mall as the main pedestrian circulation system connecting the uses, Jin Mao Tower includes a large retail atrium, the recently completed JR Central Towers in Nagoya, Japan, includes office and hotel towers rising from a 20-story podium containing retail stores above a transit station, and West End City Center in Budapest uses a mall as a central organizing element and pedestrian circulation system.

Level of Integration. In addition to the central organizing elements, the general configuration and approach toward the integration of uses should be established at the outset. When evaluating various choices for configuration, designers should keep in mind that constructing two or three different uses in one structure, one on top of another, is almost always more complicated and more expensive than dividing the uses into separate buildings.

The complications are related to both structural costs and marketability. The most significant complications relate to the building structure and systems, including column spacing, plumbing, HVAC, entrances, and circulation systems. If the components are in separate buildings, those issues become as straightforward as in single-use buildings, and the design issues occur only at the lowest levels of the buildings where the uses must connect.

The issue of marketability is also important for mixed-use buildings. Stacked uses raise issues with tenants. Certain types of office tenants may not wish to be lo-

A Metro transit station and the U.S. Navy Memorial plaza are central organizing elements at Market Square in Washington, D.C.

Santana Row in San Jose is driven by an urbanist design philosophy that emphasizes pedestrian-friendly retail streets as a fundamental organizing element.

cated above retail or entertainment uses, and the same may be true for residents or hotel operators. These issues should be carefully assessed when configuring the project.

Design Philosophy. Although the initial design concept is driven by many of the site factors mentioned earlier, it also is driven by the design approach and philosophy of the master planner and urban designer. One need only review the wide range of approaches proposed for rebuilding the World Trade Center in New York to see how different architects and urban designers come up with very different design concepts using similar programs.

Designers and developers have debated for decades the pros and cons of various design philosophies— modernism, postmodernism, contextualism, and new urbanism—and what design philosophy works best and where. Frank Lloyd Wright once said of tall buildings that they should be sited so that each could "cast its own shadow," reflecting a previously long-held view among designers and developers that a good design is one that makes a distinctive, "freestanding" statement—drawing attention, being a landmark, dominating the skyline, becoming a magnetic force. Until the late 1970s, this philosophy dominated the design of major buildings and projects. Beginning in the 1980s, partly because of the rising interest in historic preservation and cultural heritage, "contextual" design has been the banner of many urban designers, who began equating good design with harmony, scale, a sense of history, and a balance of new and existing.

Both these extremes are quite visible in mixed-use development today. The dramatic high-rise designs of AOL Time Warner Center in New York and Kuala Lumpur City Centre have had a powerful effect on the development of their respective city neighborhoods. In contrast, the quiet introduction of University Park at MIT into the urban fabric of Cambridge or Renaissance Place into the fabric of Highland Park, Illinois, were successful designs without making a highly visible architectural statement.

The architect's design philosophy is a fundamental driving force in shaping a general framework that arranges uses, densities, buildings, infrastructure, and open space on the site to create a workable whole and a sense of place for the development. Thus, it is critical for the developer to choose an architect and/or urban designer whose vision is likely to be compatible with his own.

Connection with Surrounding Uses

Location, context, and climate are key factors in determining the character of the design concept. The use of an enclosed plan and/or an inward orientation versus a more open plan is often driven by context and location. Enclosed and inward-oriented projects in downtown areas were popular during the 1970s and 1980s, but most recent downtown projects have moved away from this approach. Even internal malls—such as the one at North Bridge in Chicago—increasingly seek to engage pedestrians at the street level as well.

As part of site planning at Southlake Town Square in Southlake, Texas, David Schwarz, the project designer, superimposed the historic grid of downtown Fort Worth on the Southlake property to reveal the scale and potential of the site. Working from this starting point, Schwarz transformed the seven single-use islands of the original plan into 12 blocks with mixed uses focusing on a large town square and all interconnected by a bent grid street network.

The developers questioned the approach, requiring evidence from Schwarz that the 24-plex cinema and big-box retail uses originally envisioned for the project could be incorporated into the proposed block and street pattern. Schwarz responded with drawings and plans illustrating the adaptability of the proposed urban fabric; he began presenting slide shows of historic town centers and traditional types of urban public gathering spaces to the developers and later the public.

The developers approved the concept of an open-air town center that reserved the northern portion of the site for the potential inclusion of a large cinema and big-box retail stores. The design team then worked through the final plan, first delineating the public spaces, then the blocks (which were made large enough to contain

parking lots or garages at the interior of each block surrounded by buildings), and then the mapping of uses. The largest block is 350 feet (107 meters) long, somewhat longer than the designers would have preferred for pedestrians' comfort but necessary to accommodate parking garages.

The designers created shorter walking distances between the parking areas and the commercial streets by incorporating mid-block breaks along each block face. This technique works particularly well around the town square, which is also broken up into three segments, creating a network of short block segments, streets, passageways, and a variety of public spaces. It becomes less effective on the side streets away from the square, where the street wall gives way to parking areas on at least one side of the street, creating a less attractive pedestrian environment. Future plans call for the construction of shallow liner buildings, up to 80 feet (24 meters) deep, that will wrap around and help mask these parking areas and create building fronts on both side of the street.

The site plan established a hierarchy of streets in a bent grid pattern that emphasizes the intersections between the streets. In doing so, Schwarz notes, "we identified which ones were important and why, not just in terms of

Courtesy of Cooper & Stebbins

Southlake Town Square in Southlake, Texas, is a town center organized around a large central green used for a variety of events during the year. A courthouse is located at the back of the square.

how they look but what they do." The streets surrounding the town square were designed as traditional downtown shopping streets with on-street parking and pedestrian amenities. Two of these streets provide the main entrances to the project, running north from Southlake Boulevard along either side of the square. At the northern end of the square, the views down both these streets are terminated by buildings at the corners of the block, providing a strong sense of enclosure to the space. The extension of Grand Avenue, yet to be developed, will act as a long promenade and the sole streetscape connecting the square and the northern section of the project. All other streets act as short connectors that provide alternate travel paths for movement within the site or as throughways that pass completely through the site and connect to major arterials.

One large difference between Southlake Town Square and other town center projects is that all the project's streets are public. Doing so created challenges in terms of reducing the 70-foot (21-meter) right-of-way on public streets, which Schwarz met by adding generous sidewalks, rows of street trees, and angled parking on both sides of the primary pedestrian streets and "necking down" intersections to decrease the walking distance when crossing streets. Although this arrangement slows traffic and improves the pedestrian quality of the streets, 70-foot (21-meter) rights-of-way with 14-foot (4.3-meter) sidewalks on blocks surrounding the three public blocks and 11-foot (3.3-meter) sidewalks on all others create a space that some consider too open to establish a strong sense of enclosure with Southlake's two-story buildings. The size of the open space will be scaled down, however, as street trees mature and create a canopy around the square.

Schwarz describes the urban fabric as a pattern of street–building–alley–garage–alley–building–street, which allows most parking, delivery areas, and services to be located behind buildings to maintain the street wall and enclosed spaces. Schwarz notes that, although an individual developer cannot control what might occur on adjacent properties, the interconnected blocks and street grid make Southlake Town Square a "very attachable fragment of urbanism."

Schwarz considers parking the most important element of the design, however. "Parking controls everything," he says. "It's the driving force." In addition to the angled and parallel on-street spaces, the plan incorporates parking decks and surface lots. Decks are freestanding except where the topography enabled liner buildings to be easily added to conceal the garage.

Although the construction of parking decks was required to support the amount of commercial space permitted, the developer was allowed to calculate parking needs block by block. By phasing the development so that partial blocks were completed on opposite sides of the street and square, the developer was able to delay the requirement to build the garages until after substantial amounts of commercial space were operational. Thus, development could be completed on two sides of each block without triggering construction of the parking deck. This phased development also made sense from the perspective of place making, which calls for creating two-sided streets and enclosed spaces early in the project to establish a sense of place.

Source: Adapted from Charles C. Bohl, *Place Making: Developing Town Centers, Main Streets, and Urban Villages* (Washington, D.C.: ULI–the Urban Land Institute, 2002). ∎

A corner building at Southlake Town Square, with retail below and office above.

Courtesy of Cooper & Stebbins

In the past, siting, inward orientation, and lack of integration with their surroundings of projects like Omni International in Atlanta (now called CNN Center) and the Renaissance Center in Detroit were, to a large extent, responses to attitudes about the surrounding downtown. These projects were designed in part with the notion that projects must provide shelter from the inhospitable cities. Thus, the designs provided plans where pedestrian activity was enclosed and internalized rather than located in open areas or out on the street. The inward orientation was partially a response to the perceived danger of the urban areas where they were built. Building a mixed-use development in downtown Detroit or Atlanta was considered a proper step toward revitalization, but the years have taught developers and downtown planners that such enclosed and inward-oriented developments are not effective solutions for revitalizing downtowns.

More recent downtown projects of the 1980s and 1990s, such as Market Square in Washington, D.C., and Rowes Wharf in Boston, offer outdoor public spaces as their focal points. Projects of the 1990s and later, such as New Roc City in downtown New Rochelle, New York, and Salt Lake City Gateway often go a step farther by making the street the focal point of activity. These projects embrace the urban context and add to it in positive ways.

The suburbs often have little in the surrounding landscape with which to connect, and thus a certain internal focus often prevails. It is not necessarily bad, as suburban mixed-use projects are more in the business of creating a place and an urban fabric that can ultimately establish an expandable urban design as new developments are "attached" to it. Both Mizner Park in Boca Raton and Reston Town Center in Reston, Virginia, for example, are focused around internal main streets and public spaces, but the street is public in nature and easily accessible by car or on foot. The exterior of both projects includes parking structures, although these exterior sites also include substantial housing that enhances the surrounding context. Both have succeeded in creating an internal place and street while also improving and stimulating the creation of a larger surrounding urban environment.

A key problem that most suburban projects must face is the need to find a place for large, easily reached parking structures near the periphery of the site. Using ground-floor retail in these structures or surrounding them with residential buildings or other uses is one approach to solving the problem. Mizner Park, for example, includes townhouses that surround the parking structures, thus creating an attractive residential street. Addison Circle lines its parking with residential lofts to screen it from public view. Reston Town Center uses retail spaces on the ground level of some of its parking structures.

The exterior design and profile of the development must always balance numerous issues. Certainly the project must provide the strength of image, presence, and identity needed for success, but those factors must be balanced by the need for the mixed-use development to contribute to the overall community. The design of

Bethesda Row connects with surrounding uses by fitting into and respecting the existing street fabric. The project is an infill mixed-use project that includes both restored and new buildings.

mixed-use developments should avoid creating fortresses and monuments and seek to create a place that can serve as a bridge and connector between different areas and uses within the community.

Establishing Internal Relationships

The positioning of uses to optimize internal relationships must take into account the identity and security of individual components, the importance of links between the various components, and any central space around which the components will be arranged. Specific issues regarding individual uses are discussed in the following section, "Positioning and Designing Primary Uses."

Because the relationship between uses is such an important aspect of a mixed-use development, the design of the project must reflect and promote the interconnections that can occur yet maintain an identity for each use as well as strong connections to the surrounding environment. Internal circulation systems must allow users to differentiate between each use yet visualize and understand connections between them. Designs that do not provide such differentiation are often confusing and can create unpleasant experiences.

Although experience over the years has downplayed the importance of market synergies and taught that project components should be able to draw primarily on substantial markets from outside the project, the different uses should be spatially related to help maximize synergy among all components of a mixed-use development. Both design and marketing should shape uses that complement each other. For example, at Phillips Place in Charlotte, North Carolina, a limited-service hotel with no restaurant was located at one end of this main street–oriented project, the Palm Restaurant directly adjacent to it on the street. This arrangement provided for a top-quality restaurant for the hotel without the need for the hotel to provide or operate it as well as a built-in market for the restaurant. The restaurant also takes advantage of the significant market generated by the multiplex cinema in the project as well as the considerable on-site residential population.

Whatever the configuration of public space used, careful placement of uses to create strong internal relationships between uses is critical to the success of the development. This configuration often begins with the retail space, which is usually fundamental to the design of public spaces. The successful treatment of the retail zone can be critical to the long-term viability of not only this project element but also the entire development. Generally, retail is the most public use and is often used to link the other uses. The retail element can also spread out to the edges of the project to connect it with the exterior environment, including streets along the edge of the project.

The retail element is not always a defining element in the public realm. In some cases, public greens or parks and public buildings shape the public space, with little or no retail involved. For example, at Smyrna Town Center in Smyrna, Georgia, several public buildings surround a town green, creating a strong civic space that is the primary identity of the project. At University Park at MIT, a campus-like green is the central element of the project. Waterfront promenades serve this function at Rowes Wharf in Boston.

Visual Orientation and Pedestrian Circulation

Strong visual connections and sight lines can be achieved by well-designed central open spaces that facilitate spatial orientation. The use of a main street or a central park or plaza is an excellent way to achieve this aim. In a well-designed mixed-use project, it should be easy to find the center of the project and then identify all or most of the major components. For example, at Yerba Buena Center, a central park provides easy visual identification of most of the major uses surrounding the park. At Mizner Park, the main street is two blocks long and includes a linear park down the center, affording both strong sight lines down the street as well as a compelling pedes-

trian environment that invites exploration; it also has a fountain and restaurant court at the center of the park and main street. At University Park at MIT, three separate commons/public open spaces are used to enhance visual orientation.

Pedestrian circulation in a mixed-use development generally works best when the primary pedestrian spine is not too long, preferably 1,000 to 1,200 feet (305 to 365 meters). Notes Robert Simpson, director of community development for the city of Englewood, Colorado, "The theory is that shoppers and pedestrians will walk about a quarter mile [0.4 kilometer] if it is interesting. This length can be extended to one-half mile [0.8 kilometer] *if* it is really interesting with activity, windows, shops, art, and so on." Some mixed-use projects, such as CityPlace in West Palm Beach, have successfully used two major spines, but usually one dominates.

Other streets, corridors, squares, and spaces can be attached to this major spine to broaden its reach and enhance connections, but there should be little confusion between the primary spine and secondary connections. For optimum circulation and connectivity, this central spine should also have a central gathering place to enhance visual orientation, such as in Mizner Park. Notes Paris Rutherford of RTKL Associates in Dallas, "It is important to establish a clear hierarchy of streets, paths, and open spaces to create visual/experiential interest and not rely on an overly simple and abstract design. Many main street projects rely on the main street alone and are ultimately positioned poorly, as they do not offer the complexity necessary to foster community."

When the spine is a street, many designers believe it is important to break the street into short blocks of about 300 feet (91 meters). Even shorter blocks may be desirable; much of downtown Portland, for example, includes blocks of only 200 feet (60 meters), providing more connections, more vistas along side streets, and many options for pedestrians. Richard Heapes, a principal designer of Mizner Park when he was with the firm Cooper Carry

Market Commons Clarendon is organized around a U-shaped street that surrounds a small park with fountains, landscaping, and a playground. Several passageways afford access from the surrounding townhouses and residential neighborhoods. The space provides a sense of enclosure and safety while also maintaining strong sight lines between the various buildings along the street.

Architects, notes that one of the things he would do differently in the design of that project is to create more side streets that feed into the main street.

Reston Town Center provides a good example of how these issues can be handled. The project uses both a major spine as a main street as well as perpendicular and even parallel streets that have become active retail and pedestrian areas, including a parking garage on a parallel street that includes ground-level retail space.

Vertical connections are another important concern. Many mixed-use developments that use retail areas as the primary internal circulation network—especially projects that include retail malls—attempt to minimize walking distances by building on multiple levels. The theory is that shoppers resist walking horizontally more than three city blocks—1,000 to 1,200 feet (305 to 365 meters)—and that creatively designed vertical space can be effectively employed to market retail merchandise on a small site. Elevators, escalators, and other people movers transport shoppers from one level to another. Such applications are employed primarily when major retail malls are included, such as at 900 North Michigan Avenue in Chicago or Pacific Place in Hong Kong, both of which include multilevel shopping centers served by both elevators and escalators.

Second-level retail space is seldom used in main street settings unless it is internal to a single store, such as a two-level bookstore. Restaurants and cinemas are sometimes effectively placed on second levels, however, such as at CityPlace in West Palm Beach, Market Common Clarendon in Arlington, Virginia, and Paseo Colorado in Pasadena. These uses frequently function as destinations and do not depend on exposure to pedestrian traffic and impulse spending, which many retailers rely on for business.

Vehicle Circulation

The effective design of internal circulation for vehicles is important for drawing auto users to the project, making certain that both auto and pedestrian users have a productive and pleasant experience, and ensuring that all uses are well served by the parking. An effective design does not necessarily mean that auto and pedestrian traffic must be strictly separated. At Mizner Park, for example, one of the main auto entrances draws autos down the main street of the project, where parking is located on both sides of the street. If parking spots are not available there, signs direct visitors to various parking structures on the property. At Addison Circle, a major traffic circle provides a central place for visitors, both auto and pedestrian traffic, to orient themselves.

Access for service and deliveries must be carefully planned during design and layout. Loading ramps are by nature unattractive, but they are essential and must be carefully planned for. For higher-density mixed-use projects such as mixed-use towers and/or integrated mixed-use structures, underground truck access and service areas are often the best solution. Mixed-use town centers, on the other hand, will more likely use well-

The main street at Mizner Park in Boca Raton, Florida, is two blocks long and includes a linear park at the center, affording strong vista lines down the street and a pedestrian environment that invites exploration.

hidden and -screened alleys or service courtyards. At CityPlace, two service roads are located parallel to the main retail street (Rosemary Avenue) and behind stores. Both can be accessed from nearby arterials or from secondary streets in the development, keeping truck traffic off the main retail street. Several other short side streets also provide service access for trucks. Notes Paris Rutherford of RTKL Associates in Dallas, "There are many current examples where alleys are combined with large parking garages; not thinking through the impact of this design on residential units creates a negative community experience."

Landscape and Streetscape

Attractive pedestrian landscapes and streetscapes are also of critical importance, and careful attention should be given to issues such as the size and type of shade trees, the design and placement of benches, the width of corridors, sidewalk materials and widths, the character and placement of water features and sculptures, the use of lighting, and the use of signage (see following section), all of which should work together to invite pedestrians to explore the project and allow them to enjoy finding their way around the setting.

Some of these landscape elements are fundamental to the urban design, such as street and sidewalk dimensions, while others are essentially details. At Addison Circle (see Chapter 8), for example, an urban village–style project, the design reverses the typical suburban norm of deep building setbacks and narrow sidewalks; the residential building facades at Addison Circle are close to the street, and sidewalks are generous. Sidewalks are 12 feet (3.6 meters) deep on residential streets, and buildings are set just six feet (1.8 meters) back from the sidewalk (18 feet [5.5 meters] from the curb). The six-foot (1.8-meter) setback allows for a landscaped buffer, entries, and stoops between sidewalk and building. On boulevards, the sidewalk is 14 feet (4.2 meters) wide, and buildings are set back 24 feet (7.3 meters) from the curb,

Landscape features—brick sidewalks and planters, benches, a central fountain, flowers, and trees—in front of the Community Center at Smyrna Town Center in Smyrna, Georgia, create a comfortable environment.

The developers of Santana Row in San Jose have incorporated a rich landscape that includes hundreds of trees and several green open spaces.

allowing for a ten-foot (three-meter) zone for landscaping or outdoor dining.

Lighting requires special attention in outdoor settings, because nighttime activity is usually an important aspect of successful mixed-use projects. Lighting is a principal determinant in establishing the nighttime atmosphere. At Phillips Place, the streetscape and lighting were emphasized to ensure that the pedestrian experience, during the day or in the evening, would be pleasant and safe. Brick sidewalks and outdoor seating encourage people to relax and enjoy themselves. Decorative street signs are mounted in all areas of the project. The general lighting level is less intense than that typically found in shopping centers, but it gives pedestrians a sense of safety and invites strolling. The glow of the subdued lighting also enhances the romantic nighttime mood of Phillips Place. Special attention was given to the lighting of the fountains, the theater marquee, and the hotel porte-cochere to give them the necessary presence along the main street.

Plantings and greenery should be used to create a compelling natural setting, such as a park or green, and to enhance unnatural ones, such as streets, parking lots, or internal malls. At Santana Row in San Jose, the developers have taken great care to incorporate a rich landscape that includes hundreds of trees and several green spaces. The development is focused around a lush town green. During initial clearing of the site, the developers were able to save 14 40-year-old oak trees and 26 palm trees from destruction. At Phillips Place in Charlotte, the main street includes angled parking with landscaped dividers between every two spaces, adding greenery to the street and parking. At CityPlace, individual plantings were selected to match the architecture rather than a uniform pattern of identical trees and plants.

Landscape details are endlessly variable, and no formula exists for good landscape design other than to hire a talented designer and then work closely with him or her to achieve the desired results. Many landscape designers employ a thematic or storytelling approach to landscape design in mixed-use projects. "Public Spaces and People-Oriented Places" further discusses landscape issues and provides more examples.

Signage

Well-designed signage can not only contribute to an effective circulation and landscape plan for a mixed-use project but also be important in establishing a strong project identity and brand. To provide orienting clues important to users of a mixed-use development, locational, directional, and tenant signage is extremely important. Consistent directional and orientation signs throughout the development enhance users' experiences, helping them find their way and providing them with a positive image of the development. Prominent tenant signage is critical to marketing the development and in attracting visitors.

In general, the overall design concept for the development strongly affects signage. If the project is in an urban area with streets as primary pedestrian open spaces, signage often is minimal and in keeping with signage on surrounding streets. In fact, for such a project and context, too much signage, especially directional signage, can be detrimental to the project's success. The best approach to directional signage in such a situation may be to minimize it to maintain the "messy" urbanism that prevails in the area.

For most projects, however, especially enclosed projects with numerous components or large mixed-use districts, signage is critically important and should be given significant attention in the overall design. In developments that involve numerous streets or pathways, good signage is a necessity or a visitor can get lost. Well-placed signage that displays a map highlighting all the major uses and pedestrian pathways should be placed at entrances and other strategic locations to ensure that visitors understand the scope of the development and are not discouraged or confused.

A signage program should provide separate messages for drivers and pedestrians. For many developments, the signage begins with roadway entrance signs featuring the name of the project and clear directions to parking areas. Often such entrance signs feature tenant signage as well, highlighting some of the major retail, hotel, and office tenants in the development.

Ensuring that tenant signs can be seen from nearby roadways is important, especially in the suburbs, but suburban projects sometimes face unusual problems in featuring or presenting this signage. For example, Phillips Place in Charlotte (see Chapter 8) features a retail main street that is parallel to the adjacent thoroughfare (Fairview Road), with some stores also having back entrances that face the thoroughfare and parking area. Contrary to standard suburban retail design, the storefronts along this internal street are not visible from the adjacent thoroughfare, although some of the larger stores have signage that is visible and some also have back entrances that face the thoroughfare. The development team considered the layout essential to the success of the pedestrian environment they were seeking. To mitigate the lack of visibility from the thoroughfare, tenants without signage on Fairview Road are given prominent positions on two featured entrance signs.

Pedestrian-level signs begin at both the parking lot and at pedestrian street entrances and should also be located at central gathering places. Frequently signage includes maps highlighting the publicly accessible uses in the project. (Private residential uses and entrances are often not emphasized on these signs, as they are not generally publicly accessible.) A certain predictability as to the location of signs is an important factor in efficient information processing; if people do not find signs where they expect them, they will get frustrated.

The amount of information on a sign can significantly affect its usefulness. Even though pedestrians presumably have time to stop and read a sign, they prefer to keep moving. Thus, signs with a long list of information, while often necessary, are much less useful than those with just a few items that can be understood quickly. Strong graphics are thus important in conveying information quickly. Continuity and consistency are also essential. People assume that if no sign is visible, they should keep going until they see a sign. Additional signs to reassure pedestrians that they are on the right path are generally welcome.

In many situations, signs are often difficult to see because they are poorly designed, inconsistently placed, or poorly lit. The problem is accentuated in complex settings where information overload is possible. To be easily perceived and understood, information on a sign must be divided into small information packages and structured according to content. Messages should be clear and unambiguous in meaning and about their intended audience.

Tenant signage is also important. Customary approaches to controlling tenant signage in shopping malls can be used in mixed-use projects with malls, but many mixed-

Entry signage at Phillips Place in Charlotte, North Carolina, takes on architectural qualities.

use projects with open-air configurations, especially main street projects, are allowing for and encouraging considerably more flexibility and self-expression than most malls or strip shopping centers. Developers and designers of mixed-use projects often look for an unusual urban and nonmall image, and thus tenant signage should not be excessively controlled. Many tenants now prefer main street locations because they can better control the look of their signage and storefronts, and developers and designers should respect such preferences.

Finally, signage must be integrated and consistent with the overall landscape design for the project. When enclosed malls are central elements, signage typically found in malls is appropriate. Enclosed projects generally require more extensive signage, as they often are visually more difficult to understand and navigate. Such projects should include maps highlighting the entrances to hotels, office buildings, cinemas, bathrooms, and all retail locations.

Open-air and town center configurations require less directional signage, but signage is still an important element. For example, at Phillips Place in Charlotte, which is primarily configured as one long main street, all the public portions of the project are visually easy to see from the street: the hotel is at one end, the cinema at the other, and retailers are placed along the street in between, with residential uses above the retail. Such a configuration is easily understood and thus does not require much pedestrian-level directional signage. Town centers still,

however, require signage to help visitors locate tenants and specific entrances. Location maps for retail and other uses in a town center should fit that image and not resemble signage typically used in malls. Street signs, for example, should be featured elements in the streetscape in a town center.

Signage programs usually involve some level of uniformity throughout the development, but some designers believe that selectively varying the signage from one area to another can be effective as well. According to Howard Elkus of Elkus/Manfredi Architects, "Signage can be uniform throughout a project or can vary to accentuate different streets, zones, places, and uses. I think of Rome's shopping district, where street merchant associations have created their own signage, some with decorations."

Architectural Profile and Image

In the end, the entire mixed-use development must also present an attractive and coherent urban design image and architectural profile. This image should provide identity for each component while also providing a cohesive and understandable overall image. In large projects with many designers, design guidelines can play an important role in articulating the intent of the design philosophy or story.

An excellent example of mixed-use design that provides identity for each use in a single unified and attractive architectural statement is Riverside in Atlanta. The plan is organized around a central green surrounded by retail space on the ground level, residential space above the retail on one side in low-rise structures, and office space above retail on the other side in a higher-rise structure. Each element has its own distinct character, yet the whole is a very harmonious design that also offers a wonderful public realm at the center, which enhances the viability of all the uses.

Although the overall design must connect the uses, varied treatment of the facades is a preferred way to provide identity for separate components. Each use should have its own architectural identity. Depending on the context, it often involves the use of different architects. In many cases, mixed-use projects involve master plans whose design guidelines establish a direction for the design of individual buildings or allow for the master planner to oversee the direction taken by multiple architects. If a true urban look is desired, some developers and master planners even go so far as to develop general guidelines but not allow individual architects to see what other architects are doing with specific building designs, on the theory that this approach allows for a design that looks more like it grew up over time and avoids a look that is too planned and designed. Market Street at Celebration in Florida, for example, was designed by numerous prominent, internationally known architects, including Philip Johnson; Robert A.M. Stern; Venturi, Scott Brown and Associates; Michael Graves; and Cesar Pelli. Numerous firms were used to give each building a distinctive character and provide the variety

This directional sign at Reston Town Center is a useful tool for visitors as well as an attractive piece of street furniture.

Riverside in Atlanta presents a unified and compelling architectural profile that creates a distinctive image for the overall project.

Market Street at Celebration near Orlando, Florida, includes a variety of buildings designed by numerous prominent, internationally known architects, including Philip Johnson and Michael Graves.

of style found in other towns that have evolved over the years.

The architectural profile for each use should be carried through to a street-level identity for that use. When the uses are closely integrated, separate access to each use is essential, and the entrances should have their own distinct image. Retail entrances should be highly visible; they can be colorful and even loud. Residential entrances are frequently quiet and unobtrusive. Office and hotel entrances should be obvious but refined. Even when all the uses are in one integrated structure, successful designs provide identity for each component from the outside, giving tenants and customers a strong sense of place and orientation. (Entrances and identity for individual uses are discussed in greater detail in "Positioning and Designing Primary Uses.")

The use of different architects for each use is one way to ensure a distinct look for each. At Bethesda Row

Encompassing hotel, office, residential, marine, and retail uses in a distinctive waterfront setting, Rowes Wharf is a landmark addition to the skyline and urban fabric of Boston. Located on the harbor and next to the financial district, the 1.1 million-gross-square-foot (102,200-square-meter) mixed-use development weaves together its numerous uses in three separate buildings. The project is exemplary in both its contextual design and the quality of its public spaces and waterfront promenades.

Rowes Wharf is designed in the shape of an "E," with the fingers (wharves) extending into the water. At its highest point, the project rises to 15 stories and includes 330,000 square feet (30,700 square meters) of office and 12,500 square feet (1,160 square meters) of retail net rentable area, 230 hotel rooms, 100 residential condominiums, 38 marina slips for residents and transients, a water shuttle, docking and terminal facilities for commuter and excursion boats, and 700 underground parking spaces.

The project sits astride what was once two wharves—Rowes and Foster's Wharves—built in the early 1760s and is located near the center of the downtown financial district. After thriving for nearly 200 years, the Boston waterfront began to show signs of decay in the 1930s and in the 1960s was designated an urban renewal area.

The site, located directly on the harbor, was separated from the heart of downtown to the west by an elevated interstate highway, which more recently has been placed underground. To the north is Harbor Towers, a high-rise residential project, and beyond that the New England Aquarium, more wharves, and parkland. To the south are numerous office and warehouse buildings and a bridge that connects downtown Boston with Fan Pier, a large redevelopment area, and the areas beyond it that line the outer harbor.

The developers and architects shared a goal in planning the project: to design a building compatible with and complementary to the historical characteristics of its environment while serving an urban mixed-use project's thoroughly modern marketing and operational needs. The project is laid out in three principal structures. The L-shaped first building, which extends on a north/south axis along Atlantic Avenue and incorporates the southernmost wharf, is the primary structure of the complex (referred to as the Atlantic Avenue Building or AAB). The building is divided near its center by Foster's Court. This building incorporates all four uses as well as a structurally daring arch; it consists of offices on the second through seventh floors, hotel rooms on the eighth through 15th floors on the south side of AAB, corresponding restaurants and meeting rooms on the first two floors, a major health club on the lower level, and 27 condominium units on the 11th through 15th floors on the north side of AAB.

The main lobby entrance for the hotel is located on the South Atlantic Avenue side of AAB, the lobby for the office space is on both sides of Foster's Court, and the lobby for the condominiums is on the North Atlantic Avenue side of AAB. AAB also offers street-level retail facilities.

The site plan for Rowes Wharf arranges a mixture of residential and commercial buildings amid open spaces along the harbor in Boston.

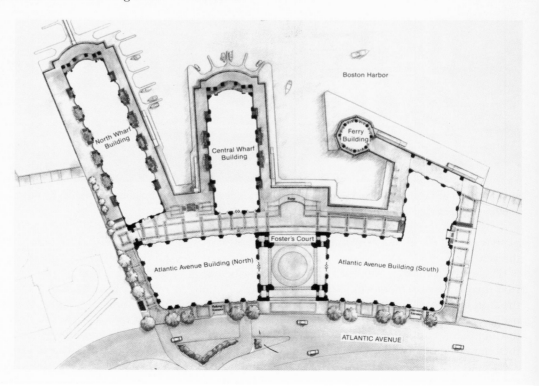

The remaining two wharf buildings are the eight-story North Wharf Building with 73 residential condominiums and the six-story Central Wharf Building with 70,000 rentable square feet (6,500 square meters) of office space.

Public walkways and open space areas integrate the entire development. Landscaped areas include trees, shrubs, and flowers, and custom-designed fixtures provide lighting. Extensive paving throughout the site is of brick and granite, including pedestrian crossings to the financial district. The perimeter walkway along the waterfront combines brick and wooden decking. In addition to the numerous walks, promenades, and plazas, other public amenities are located along the waterfront areas, including 38 marina slips, a dinghy dock, and an enclosed ferry terminal and pavilion. Five levels of underground parking provide 700 spaces.

Architectural elements—from fenestration patterns to the curve of the main building—were drawn from Boston's historic architecture to integrate the project with the existing city fabric. The moderately scaled 15-story towers of the AAB relate to the office towers of the business district; a series of setbacks, stepping down to nine stories, responds to the historic scale of older buildings near the waterfront. Projecting into the harbor, the six- and seven-story pier buildings are related in scale to Boston's traditional wharf structures and gradually step down to only three stories at the water's edge. The facades are of brick and highly detailed precast concrete that has the density and feel of carved limestone. Slate and copper roofs and painted wood accents enhance the building's traditional character.

Foster's Court, a monumental 10,000-square-foot (930-square-meter) courtyard topped by a vault of four intersecting arches, is the project's focal point. Its visual and physical openness provides a dramatic passage from the city to the harbor. Within the arches, an ornate glass dome reveals the sky. Above the court, under a 150-foot-high (45-meter) copper-clad dome, sits Foster's Rotunda, an observatory and reception area providing striking vistas of downtown and the harbor.

The project was designed first to fit its site and surrounding environment; the interior spaces were designed after that. The one landside building and the three wharf buildings form a cohesive whole on the outside, yet inside, offices, residences, and a hotel function independently. In planning the project, the developer assigned separate teams to represent the different uses, ensuring that every component was fairly represented.

Facing the challenge of building the project on a narrow land and water site, the developer chose the up/down construction method to allow for the simultaneous exca-

Courtesy of Skidmore, Owings & Merrill

A featured element of the design for Rowes Wharf is Foster's Court, a grand central archway that runs through the main building and links the downtown with the waterfront.

vation and construction of the below-grade levels and the erection of the steel superstructure. The method economizes on time and space, saving as much as one-third of the total time for below-grade construction before the superstructure is started, compared with the time it would take with more traditional building methods, and more than offsetting the generally higher cost of this construction technique. This method trimmed six months from the original construction time frame.

in Bethesda, Maryland, for example, to achieve the look it was aiming for, Federal Realty hired three local architectural firms to collaborate with Cooper Carry Architects on designs for the different phases of the project. The multiple ideas generated successfully hid the fact that the rather large buildings at Bethesda Row were all redeveloped at the same time. Individual retail tenants also were encouraged to design facades for their stores. For example, a skateboard shop has a stainless steel facade with bold lettering and lighting, while a nearby upscale market has a storefront featuring an expanse of windows and softly colored tiles. The attention to design has worked to create a successful urban environment.

Finally, the overall image should not be too perfect or overplanned. Some incongruity is permissible and adds authenticity to places. Reston Town Center is a notable example. It is a large mixed-use town center that has been phased over time to become a large mixed-use district reflecting fairly diverse architectural styles in its various phases; when eventually completed it should result in a district that looks like it grew up over time, not overnight or all at once. Its incongruities in design are similar to those found in many big city downtowns, giving it an authentic urban atmosphere through a carefully thought-out set of development guidelines that offer flexibility where warranted but are quite restrictive when necessary.

Positioning and Designing Primary Uses

The urban design concept sets the framework for positioning various uses, but positioning also depends on the marketing and operational needs of each individual use in the project. Offices without the "proper" address, setting, identity, and access will not achieve the desired occupancy or lease rates. A retail center that cannot be easily identified, that is not visible, or that is not laid out effectively for tenants and shoppers will not draw the necessary tenants or customers. A hotel that is not placed in an accessible or visible setting or an apartment building that offers poor views or little ambience will underperform compared with the competition.

Strategically positioning uses in the mixed-use development can make the difference between a successful and an unsuccessful project. One use that becomes weakened because it is poorly positioned within the overall design can undermine the benefits of providing several uses in one project. Positioning must take into account issues such as access and entrances, address, identity and visibility, security, marketability, connections to other uses, ownership, and the importance of the component to the project's success.

Planning Retail/Entertainment Space

If retail is to be a central component in a mixed-use project, then the design and layout for the overall project need to go hand in hand with the design for an effective and attractive retail component; retail is a principal

Reston Town Center effectively combines and positions main street retail with office and hotel buildings.

defining element in the creation of a public realm and a circulation system, which the entire project must draw on for strength. If the design of this public realm does not work for the retail, the poor performance of the retail element will cast a pall on the project as a whole. Thus, designing the retail environment and the larger public realm is a fundamental starting point in the design of the overall mixed-use project.

In some mixed-use projects, the retail component is poorly planned, often placed and designed as an afterthought. In some cases, architects and developers have neglected the retail space until after the basic building plan has been finalized. The layout of the retail space at Renaissance Center in Detroit, for example, is a classic example: retail space was located around the edges of an internal atrium on various levels. It was located intermittently around the periphery, the space was confusing and disorienting, and movement between levels was difficult, leading to poor performance for the retail space.

A lack of attention to fundamental principles of retail design can create circulation problems, awkward areas to lease, poor exterior visibility, and poor performance for the retail space.

Retail Placement. Retail space is usually located centrally for two reasons. First, an architecturally attractive retail center with a creative mix and positioning of tenants, especially restaurants, can serve as a stimulating amenity for all the other uses; thus, retail should be designed to provide good access from all internal uses. Second, retail establishments thrive on pedestrian traffic, and one of the best ways to generate such traffic is to position and design the retail area so that pedestrian traffic can easily pass through the retail area on the way to other destinations.

When retail space is not centrally located, problems can occur. At Jin Mao Tower in Shanghai (see Chapter 8), for example, poor retail performance can be attributed in part to the design and configuration of the project, which placed retail stores in a six-story pavilion adjacent to the office/hotel tower. The placement did not take advantage of or enhance pedestrian flows within the project or the broader neighborhood; this placement problem, combined with the fact that the retail component was too large for the market at the time, resulted in substantial retail vacancies on the upper levels.

Locating the retail component centrally should not result in isolating it from surrounding areas, as retail must draw from the larger market as well to prosper. In general, inappropriately positioned retail space is no longer as common as it once was, because retail space has become a more fundamental element in mixed-use developments and an important means of attracting various markets. Moreover, developers who undertake such projects usually have a strong background in retail, or they bring in partners who do. Nevertheless, retail is still the use that is most often mishandled in design of a mixed-use project.

Visibility, Identity, and Access. Although visibility, identity, and access are critical issues for a major retail facility of any kind, they are especially important in a mixed-use development because of the proximity and competing interests of other uses. The exterior signage for and architectural design of the retail component should boldly identify the facility as a shopping area. For example, the primary entrance to Abacoa Town Center is located on the corner of a major intersection and features a park with fountains as well as a theater green and stage, all located in front of a series of stores that face onto the park and the intersection beyond; a retail and residential main street extends into the project from this front door.

Readily available parking and easy auto access are also critical, especially for suburban mixed-use projects that must compete with more conventional retail venues offering large surface parking lots in front of the stores. At Birkdale Village in Huntersville, North Carolina, the plan provides high visibility and ample parking for major big-box tenants that face toward the nearby roadway, but it

The site plan for Birkdale Village in Huntersville, North Carolina, provides high visibility for major big-box retail tenants that face toward the nearby roadway as well as inviting vistas and access roads to the interior main street retail area.

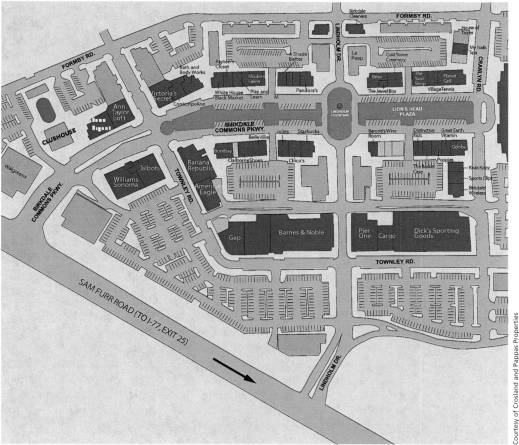

Courtesy of Crosland and Pappas Properties

The primary entrance to Abacoa Town Center in Jupiter, Florida, is located on the corner of a major intersection. A park with fountains, a theater green, and a stage is located in front of a series of stores that face onto the park; a retail and residential main street extends into the project from this front door.

also provides inviting vistas and access roads to the interior main street retail area, where additional parking is provided.

Retail uses in mixed-use projects need not strictly emulate the competition to succeed. Adequate parking is necessary, but negative visual impacts can be addressed through the use of smaller parking courts, landscaping, separate parking structures, and other uses around the parking lot. For example, at Mizner Park in Boca Raton, which is organized around a main street with a pedestrian park down the middle, parking for retail and restaurant patrons is provided on both sides of the two one-way streets and in parking structures. Auto traffic entering the project can go directly to the parking structure or can traverse main street first.

In downtown projects where parking is often provided in city parking structures, strong links must be established between the retail facilities and the off-site or public parking. Equally important in downtown mixed-use developments, retail uses and entrances must be located on strong retail streets.

Many retail uses in projects of the 1960s and 1970s have suffered from poor visibility and access. Many such developments—L'Enfant Plaza in Washington and Renaissance Center in Detroit, among them—placed the retail facilities in interior concourses or atriums with little visibility from surrounding areas. As a result, they often experienced substantial vacancies and/or became simply service areas for the project, with little appeal to off-site markets.

Main Street Retail Design. The trend in recent years for mixed-use retail is to create a traditional main street retail setting. This approach requires a design that allows for streets, autos, and streetfront parking, with no pedestrian-only zones.

In effect, the overall project must be designed as a district divided by streets, not an integrated structure. Projects such as Reston Town Center in Virginia, Phillips Place in Charlotte, Valencia Town Center Drive in California, and Redmond Town Center in Washington, all use a main street model that not only provides an attractive and effective retailing environment but also creates an attractive mixed-use setting for all the uses.

In these main street settings, it is traditionally difficult to make second-floor retail space work, following the old adage that first-floor space is rented and second-floor space is given away. But some developments have overcome these challenges. Second-floor commercial uses can be successful, but access is critical. Restaurants and cinemas are often the most suitable tenants for second-floor space. At Paseo Colorado, for example, access to second-level restaurants is achieved by several grand stairways, visible second-level plazas, and multiple elevators and escalators throughout the project. City-Place in West Palm Beach uses its adjoining parking structure for direct access to a second level of restaurants overlooking the central plaza and a grand staircase to provide access to the Muvico Theaters on the second level.

Storefront Design. The design of retail storefronts, especially for main street retail stores, is also an important issue to consider, and some criteria are essential for storefronts and tenants. Some developers and designers have sought to carefully control storefront designs, especially in malls, but main street environments often allow retailers to express themselves with fewer constraints. One of the reasons retailers like main street environments is that they have greater flexibility to express themselves through storefronts. Thus, too much control squelches this advantage and puts retailers off. On the other hand, working with tenants to express an overall design theme can be beneficial for the development.

The concept for Paseo Colorado in Pasadena, for example, sought to re-create the more intimate scale and the textures and materials of the adjacent Old Pasadena. Two very detailed tenant criteria documents convey this concern for appropriate materials to prospective tenants. The first, *Athens of the West–Pasadena Style*, is a coffee table–style book with full-color images on glossy paper detailing Pasadena's heritage, design objectives for each of Paseo Colorado's "neighborhoods," and development standards for storefronts, signage, and similar elements. The second publication, a paperback titled *Craftsman's Journal*, provides additional technical criteria and contacts for artisans and artists. The introduction to *Craftsman's Journal* describes Trizec's philosophy and objectives: "The creative contributions of individual tenants are critical to Paseo Colorado's success in creating an environment where the visitor feels a tangible sense of place. Each merchant will be required to creatively alter or adopt predetermined design concepts to meet the specific existing conditions."

Planning Residential Uses

The principal factors in positioning and designing residential uses are security, privacy, amenities, style, and views. Residential uses are the least public of the four major uses usually found in mixed-use developments, and for this reason residential uses have often been positioned to emphasize security and privacy in the plan but also views and lifestyle amenities. Residential can be configured in a variety of ways in mixed-use projects, ranging from the top of a mixed-use tower to residential over main street retail to a freestanding apartment building or townhouses.

Separate Residential Buildings. Placing residential uses in separate buildings is clearly the simplest approach; it is more cost-effective to construct, minimizes potential conflicts, reduces building and fire code requirements, and is easier to finance. Lenders and investors generally prefer buildings with a single use, because mixed-use buildings may limit exit strategies and therefore the number of entities that want to own such a combination of uses. This configuration also results in less integration of uses and complicates the design of main streets, because without residential or some other use on the upper floor, buildings on main street do not have enough height to effectively frame an attractive public realm.

The simplicity of separate buildings is compelling from a financial perspective. At Valencia Town Center Drive in Valencia, California, for example, the residential apartments are located at one end of the main street, in an area quite separate from the office and retail areas. Reston Town Center in Reston, Virginia, also places the residential uses at the ends of the main street. University Park at MIT includes both loft housing in a converted warehouse and new wood-frame walk-up apartments. At Legacy Town Center in Plano, Texas, the parcelization and phasing plan horizontally blends residential and other uses and avoids a costly layered approach. McKenzie Towne in Calgary, Alberta, and Pentagon City in Arlington, Virginia, also place residential uses in separate buildings.

Residential over Retail. The notion of placing residential uses over retail uses was long held unworkable in mixed-use projects, even though this configuration is common in many downtowns. But ideas about the

Reston Town Center includes a variety of residential housing types, including townhouses and apartments, in distinct residential neighborhoods within and adjacent to the town center.

Residential uses at Legacy Town Center in Plano, Texas, are principally located in separate residential buildings.

Residential over retail at CityPlace in West Palm Beach, Florida.

appropriate placement and configuration of residential uses have changed significantly in recent years. In fact, the concept of residential over retail uses has become a standard configuration in many mixed-use town centers and urban villages. At Phillips Place in Charlotte, North Carolina, for example, the highest apartment rents per square foot in the project—which includes freestanding apartment buildings—are achieved in the residential units overlooking main street. These units are especially attractive to young singles and couples who are looking for a lively and interesting urban experience. Most of these residential over retail projects involve rental apartments and not condominiums.

The chosen configuration is also sometimes the result of public pressure. At Paseo Colorado in Pasadena, the city was not willing to approve the redevelopment of the mall site without the inclusion of residential, resulting in apartments' being added on the upper levels of this open-air retail and mixed-use plan. Numerous other recent mixed-use town centers that have placed residential over retail with some success include Pentagon Row and Market Common Clarendon in Arlington, Virginia, CityPlace in West Palm Beach, Birch Street Promenade in Brea, California, and Addison Circle in Dallas.

From the perspective of urban design, the residential use also adds height, helping to create a more compelling public realm for the overall project. Notes Howard Elkus of Elkus/Manfredi Architects in Boston, "Architecturally, the additional stories help the design by providing the height and mass necessary to effectively define the important public spaces that are critical in defining the urban sense of place that are the project's signature."

The relationship between the residential and commercial areas is of particular concern for residential over retail. At Paseo Colorado in Pasadena, this relationship has been carefully controlled. Three residential lobbies have been created at the street level (two for the luxury apartments and one for a loft-style building), separated from the access to the retail and commercial areas. To facilitate access from the apartments to the restaurants and other areas of Paseo Colorado, however, stairs with electronically controlled gates are provided from the lower level of the housing to Fountain Court and Euclid Court.

Residential in Mixed-Use Towers. Residential uses are also frequently included in mixed-use towers, especially in the downtowns of major cities. In a mixed-use tower, the residential component is usually placed at the highest point of the project to take advantage of views—which can add significant value to units in strong downtown markets such as New York, Chicago, and San Francisco—and to remove residents from street noise. Views are especially important for luxury condominiums such as AOL Time Warner Center and Trump Tower in New York and Park Tower and 900 North Michigan Avenue in Chicago.

For most mixed-use towers, highly visible entrances for the residential are not necessarily important or even desirable. In fact, a low-key entrance is often preferred so as not to attract unwanted attention to these private residential buildings; they are sometimes more secure if they are less visible. Thus, residential entrances are often placed on quieter streets away from the main commercial areas, or they are located off quiet courtyards set back from the busier commercial areas.

Mixed Configurations. Mixed-use projects frequently include a mixture of residential configurations, often mixing housing over retail with other housing types. At Market Street at Celebration, for example, the business district/town center in Celebration, Florida, was inspired by traditional downtown areas in small American towns. The 18-acre (7.3-hectare) site is built around a lake and includes community facilities (bank, post office, town hall), residential, retail, and office space, restaurants, and a cinema. Apartments are located above retail space and around the downtown area to help create a vibrant atmosphere. Four buildings contain 78 apartments plus an additional 45 apartments located above retail space. The

The residential entrance to the condominium lobby at Park Tower, a mixed-use tower in Chicago that also includes hotel and retail uses.

Orenco Station in Hillsboro, Oregon, includes live/work townhouses as well as lofts over retail space.

apartments range from 640 to 1,516 square feet (60 to 140 square meters).

At Orenco Station, the town center incorporates retail at street level and offices and residential lofts above. Live/work townhouses feature an art gallery, high-tech businesses, and professional offices looking onto pleasant terraces just off the street. Above, brownstone-style stairways lead to classic townhouses overlooking a stately park. (See the accompanying feature box for another example.)

Among the notable recent mixed-use projects with a large residential component is Riverside in Atlanta. The project includes 527 apartments, 220,000 square feet (20,450 square meters) of commercial office space in a nine-story office building, and 25,000 square feet (2,325 square meters) of ground-floor retail space with a restaurant, corner grocery, hair salon, and other establishments. The developers have marketed the project as offering a "resort-like lifestyle within the framework of a small town" and "a pedestrian-oriented environment with a sense of neighborhood and security, much like many European villages." Residential units include one-bedroom, two-bedroom, three-bedroom, and four-bedroom apartments, studios, lofts, and townhouses/carriage homes.

In developing the concept, Post executives and representatives from local civic and community groups participated in a week-long brainstorming session, known as a charrette. The firm of Duany Plater-Zyberk led the charrette, which was used to jump-start creative juices, give shared authorship to interested parties, and generate valuable feedback to the designers and architects. The plan that was ultimately developed involved a centrally located, lush town square surrounded by the office and residential buildings, which serves as the community's focal point.

The community's apartment houses are located in the Pittman and Princeton buildings overlooking the town square. Apartments are available in 19 floor plans ranging from 705-square-foot (65-square-meter) one-bedroom units to 3,000-square-foot (280-square-meter) "super units." Most of the initial 203 apartments are located above retail outlets, but several units are available with entrances opening directly into the town center. Each is equipped with wiring for high-speed access to the Internet and apartment-wide surround sound. Other features include designer kitchens, hardwood floors, and ten- to 12-foot (3- to 3.6-meter) ceilings.

The three-bedroom, 3½-bath units have many of the amenities of a custom-built home, including crown molding, Corian countertops, elevated marble vanities, and cherry cabinetry. Renting for more than $4,500 per month, these units attract renters by choice, who eschew homeowner-

Photographer: Steve Hinds; courtesy of Post Properties

Residential entrances at Riverside in Atlanta.

ship. Other amenities include a swimming pool, lit tennis courts, easy access to the Chattahoochee River Recreation Area, covered parking decks, social gatherings and a business center for residents, controlled access, an automated teller machine, and a resident activity center with a grand piano.

Source: Adapted from www.postproperties.com, accessed October 30, 2002. ∎

Planning Office Space

First-class office buildings, whether freestanding or in a mixed-use project, must have a distinct identity if they are to achieve their maximum potential. In general, the best ways to achieve identity for an office building are through prominent placement, good architecture, height, and strong entrance features.

Placement and Identity. Office space is generally less publicly oriented than retail or hotel uses and is thus often placed to achieve a prominent but somewhat separate position in the overall internal design. Office space should be positioned and designed to heighten the identity of the office space yet still provide a close link with the hotel and retail areas, which can be primary amenities for office tenants. Moreover, office tenants are one of the prime generators of retail and restaurant activity, and therefore offices should be located to strengthen that relationship.

If the office building is located in a main street or urban village setting, then it must fit in while also creating an attractive office lobby space and building setting. For example, at Reston Town Center in Reston, Virginia, the two initial high-rise office buildings are set behind a curved plaza and fountain, with distinctive architectural features and design elements that set the buildings apart from the rest of the retail street. They also fit in with the retail portion, however, and in fact include ground-level retail uses. Other more recently added office buildings in the project are taller and offer even more distinctive architectural profiles.

In some cases, however, especially when it is not deemed a cornerstone use, office space may be located in less prominent or distinctive positions. At Mizner Park, for example, office space was not a major element and does not have a strong identity within the project; it is located on several floors above the retail space on one side of the main street, and office entrances are not given much prominence in the design. At Valencia Town Center Drive, courtyard entrances are used in front of some office building lobbies set along a main street, with plentiful parking in the rear and separate entrances at the back of the buildings to reach that parking. Rear facades use a more conventional glass wall to create a stronger office image from the rear, while main street frontages use more fanciful facades.

In mixed-use towers, the mix of uses can sometimes detract from the individual identity of the office space, but this problem can be offset by the overall height and size of the entire building, which will add prestige to the office address. Prominently placed office lobbies at ground level can give the impression that the entire building is devoted to office space when in fact only a portion of it is.

The placement of office space can also be affected by the street address itself. At Tabor Center in downtown Denver, the office space is located on 17th Street, a more prestigious office address than 16th Street, where the retail facility was located. The street address is generally much more important in downtown locations than in suburban areas, where location in a general area and proximity to major roads are more important than the actual address.

Entrances. Because offices should be easy to locate and carry an address with some prestige, the entrance to the office portion of a mixed-use development must be easily identified from the exterior of the building and should be located on an attractive, prominent street. In some early mixed-use projects, the entry to the office space was provided from an enclosed retail mall, making the entrance hard to find and detracting from a desirable corporate image that office tenants usually want.

If an office building is connected to a mall, it ideally should have one entrance from the street and one from the mall. This configuration is used at Liberty Place, for example, which includes two large and distinctive skyscrapers on a single block in downtown Philadelphia, with a ground-level retail facility linking the buildings. In mixed-use projects that include malls, the nature and number of the connections to the mall vary depending on the developer's and tenants' preferences. At Pentagon City in Arlington, Virginia, for example, the original plan included office building entrances and exits from numerous levels of the mall, but the lead tenant in the building preferred to restrict access to the offices from the mall and thus several of these entrances were closed.

If the office space is in a town center or other open-air configuration, it should have its own enclosed lobby with distinct street entrances from both the main street and from adjacent parking structures or side streets where parking is located. Such a design provides it with a strong corporate identity on one side while also integrating it with the pedestrian and retail life of the project. Reston Town Center, for example, includes two entry areas, one a ceremonial entry in the retail and fountain court off main street and the other a functional day-to-day entry on the opposite side adjacent to the parking garages.

A small green creates a strong entrance identity for the offices at Gateway Village in Charlotte.

The entrance to the free-standing office building at Mizner Park in Boca Raton, Florida. Other offices in the project are located above retail and have entrances from the retail main street.

The placement of offices around attractive parks and public spaces can further enhance entry features and is a natural arrangement that will enhance value. At University Park at MIT in Cambridge, for example, numerous office and R&D buildings have been placed around campus-like quads and greens.

Whatever the configuration, the design should discourage or restrict non-tenant-related pedestrian traffic through the lobby. At Prudential Center in Boston, office buildings are centrally located, with retail galleries passing in front of the lobbies. In the case of the original Prudential Tower, the retail corridor passes directly in front of the lobby entrance, but no retail is located in this immediate area, maintaining a strong corporate image for the base of the building while also allowing for a busy urban atmosphere. A new office building, 111 Huntington Avenue, was recently added that uses a similar set-back lobby off the retail corridor while also

creating lobby areas and entrances from the street and from a new winter garden.

Planning Hotels

Four primary concerns for positioning and designing hotels in mixed-use projects are visibility, entrances, security, and signage. A strong and separate building identity for the hotel is preferred but not required in all circumstances. For example, hotels in mixed-use towers and/or integrated structures can do well so long as they have strong signage and prominent entrances. In suburban locations, however, visibility from roadways (especially the brand and its signage) is essential for the hotel to succeed. Internal visibility is also important, and the stronger the brand, the stronger the visibility should be, as the brand creates a strong image for the overall project.

Placement and Visibility. Similar to residential uses, hotels should be placed and oriented so that they are visible and can take advantage of views—a major selling point, especially for downtown facilities. At Yerba Buena Center, the Marriott Hotel is placed adjacent to the principal open space, offering views of downtown San Francisco. At Jin Mao Tower in Shanghai, the hotel is marketed as the highest hotel in the world by virtue of its location near the top of this skyscraper, one of the world's tallest buildings; it offers spectacular views of the city.

In mixed-use town centers and urban villages, hotels are sometimes used to anchor one end of the street. At Phillips Place in Charlotte, North Carolina, for example, the hotel anchors one end of a main street, and the other end is anchored by a cinema complex. Reston Town Center also places the hotel at one end of the street. At CityPlace in West Palm Beach, the hotel is planned for a site across a major arterial, where it will be located next to a major conference center. Strong pedestrian design elements will be used to ensure that pedestrians can move easily from the hotel to the main project.

Other town centers and urban villages have used a more central location for the hotel. At Valencia Town

An entrance to one of the newest office buildings along a street-front at Reston Town Center in Virginia.

The Doubletree Hotel at Legacy Town Center was among the first buildings completed in the project. The hotel is a centerpiece in the overall design and is prominently located next to the town square and lake at the center of the project.

Center Drive in Valencia, California, the Hyatt Valencia is placed near the middle of the main street and along a major arterial that bisects the main street and the overall project, which also includes retail, office, and residential uses. At University Park at MIT, the hotel is near the center of the development plan.

Entrances and Lobbies. Wherever the hotel is placed, the entrance to the hotel should be very prominent and located on a secure street so that hotel guests can feel comfortable and safe. The entrance must provide for auto access, arrivals, taxis, and dropoffs, and it will likely take up a considerable area. It should be positioned and designed so as not to invite local pedestrian traffic and generally should not serve as a primary passageway to the project's other components such as retail space or a convention center, because doing so will attract unwanted traffic, detract from the atmosphere of the hotel lobby, and create a security problem. At 900 North Michigan Avenue in Chicago, for example, the hotel is part of a

mixed-use tower, and an entrance and ground-level lobby provide identity at the ground level, with the main lobby and guest rooms located on the upper levels.

Major problems can develop for the hotel when entrances and lobbies are confused with other uses. The original configuration at the Renaissance Center in Detroit, for example, placed the hotel at the center of this large enclosed project. The hotel was surrounded by an atrium on all sides as well as four office buildings and retail space, creating an identity problem for the hotel, even though it was a large and prominent structure at the center of the project. The hotel entrances and lobbies were recently redesigned to address these problems, but at considerable expense.

Although hotel lobbies have been used as major public spaces in mixed-use projects, such as the atrium hotels at Embarcadero Center in San Francisco and Peachtree Center in Atlanta, hotels in mixed-use projects have been moving away from this role of providing a public realm

The hotel at University Park at MIT is placed centrally and near the main entrance to the project.

The entrance to the Park Hyatt Hotel at Park Tower in Chicago.

Design fundamentals and standards can vary considerably from one country to another.

Office Design

Although a typical office floor plate in the United States measures from 20,000 to 30,000 square feet (1,860 to 2,790 square meters), international floor plates are half that size, or smaller. International tenants typically require 1,500 to 3,000 square feet (140 to 280 square meters), again half the size of typical office tenants in the United States. Building codes can restrict the size of floor plates. In Germany and many European Union countries, "right to light" regulations restrict the depth allowed from the building core to the exterior, discouraging high-rise buildings and encouraging longer, lower-scale buildings. In many countries, a common kitchen is provided on each floor as part of the base building core. A larger tenant amenity package, including such offerings as a health club and business center, are a priority with international developers wanting to attract large corporate tenants.

Hotel Design

With public space requirements for international properties in Asia and the Middle East substantially greater than those for equivalent U.S. properties, an international four- or five-star hotel may have up to ten separate restaurants because of the lack of local high-quality dining venues. In Europe, where upscale restaurants and experienced restaurateurs abound, the hotel restaurant program is smaller.

Expanded meeting facilities and sizable business centers also are required in Asia and the Middle East. Hotels increasingly provide business facilities for guests. It is becoming standard for hotel rooms to be equipped with or have access to fax machines, international telecommunications, satellite TV, and the Internet. Hotel room sizes vary, depending on the region of the world. On average, hotel rooms in Asia are larger than rooms in comparable U.S. hotels, while a European hotel room tends to be smaller than its U.S. counterpart.

Residential Design

Residential units in mixed-use developments are geared toward the higher end of the market because they are expensive to build. Although sizes of apartments vary greatly among geographic locations, serviced apartments typically require less area per unit and lower interior costs than an equivalent standard apartment. In many countries, an additional maid's room is a standard amenity for a small percentage of both types of apartments. Security is always an issue, but not necessarily because of crime. Many apartment dwellers simply want to be assured of privacy from activity in the project.

Retail and Entertainment Design

International shop sizes and retail tenant mixes vary significantly from those in the United States. Although smaller shops and mom-and-pop outlets are standard, as increasing numbers of U.S. "brand" retailers move into the international market, a greater mix of shop types and sizes can be expected in the future.

In U.S. stores in the 1980s, a 100-foot-deep (30-meter) tenant space in a regional center was acceptable, while in the global marketplace, 30 feet (nine meters) was closer to the norm. Now that the need is less to hold large amounts of inventory on site, the depth of U.S. stores is decreasing. With larger numbers of retailers

and increasingly are becoming more private places located at the edges of the project. More recent projects have generally chosen not to create major public spaces in the hotel itself and have sought instead to minimize pedestrian traffic through the hotel lobby, imbuing it with a sense of quiet privacy for travelers.

Public Spaces and People-Oriented Places

As the previous sections emphasize, designing an attractive public realm is fundamental to the success of a mixed-use development. People-oriented spaces, whether open or enclosed, large or small, greenscape or hardscape, should be designed to create a strong image and sense of place for the development. Such spaces significantly shape the development's relationship with the surrounding environment, the interrelationship of uses within the project, and the visual connections between spaces, and provide an overall theme and sense of fun and excitement (or lack of it) for the entire mixed-use development.

Although attractive public spaces and people-oriented places have been successful in single-use projects, the nature of a mixed-use development—including size and critical mass, numerous buildings and uses, and sizable development budgets—makes it possible to create and justify larger, more dramatic, and more exciting public spaces and people places. In some cases, these spaces take on such importance that they become almost separate uses in themselves—components that live in people's minds more than any single use.

Public and people-oriented spaces in mixed-use projects come in various shapes, sizes, and configurations that have changed considerably over the past several decades. They include streets, urban plazas and squares, town greens, parks and gardens, promenades and courtyards, canopied outdoor spaces, and atriums and galleria. Fre-

moving into the international market, however, store depths in other countries are increasing (though they are still no deeper than 65 feet [20 meters]).

The decreased depth of stores tends to push a retail center's configuration into a racetrack. A circular common area creates a continuous loop of storefronts, allowing more small shops to front on the mall. This configuration provides a very different shopping experience from the linear U.S. model.

In the United States, more than two levels of retail shops is considered risky, but in many countries, four to six levels of retail space are common. Internationally, anchor stores also are smaller, with the maximum amount usually about 10,000 square feet (930 square meters); however, larger anchors containing 20,000 to 25,000 square feet (1,860 to 2,325 square meters) are beginning to appear. In Asia, the department store still reigns supreme, with freestanding eight- to ten-story properties common.

Place Making

Designers and developers must keep three issues in mind: the creation of place, integration of the project into the urban fabric, and the local culture and context. Most important is the creation of place. Whether in the United States or internationally, the density involved in mixed-use projects makes it necessary to create breathing spaces where people can relax and spend time. Civic spaces and public plazas can create a friendly, welcoming atmosphere. Such spaces also allow the developer to expand the daily life of the project through promotions, shows, and tourist events—and to promote the project as a center of activity for the local population.

A 2 million-square-foot (186,000-square-meter) mixed-use development by its very size commands a significant presence in a city. Thus, it is of primary importance that it be integrated into the fabric of the city. Because of privacy, security, or exclusivity, some international developers may elect to build a project that is internally focused. This shortsighted approach could create islands of activity that are isolated from the city itself.

International developers frequently want to bring an American style of architecture and design to their projects; unfortunately, the project may become a victim of fashion, which likely will change even before the mixed-use project is completed. If an international project is truly to succeed, it must speak to the local culture, context, and community. It is the permanence of the idea that grounds a project in its location. Styles come and go, but good ideas remain strong throughout time.

Source: Adapted from Raymond Peloquin, "Into the Fabric Woven," *Urban Land,* April 1999, pp. 77–79+.

■

quently, several types of these spaces are combined in one project. For example, some mixed-use town center projects combine a mall galleria with outdoor main street environments. Valencia Town Center in Valencia, California, includes both a main street and an enclosed skylighted mall, and Easton Town Center in Columbus, Ohio, includes both main streets and an enclosed retail galleria. Mixing attractive indoor and outdoor public spaces allows the project to minimize the impact of weather and climate and adds variety to users' experience.

Although atriums and galleria were prominent people places in the early mixed-use developments of the 1970s and 1980s, today the trend in mixed-use design is clearly toward creating an open-air public realm focused on streets, squares, and greens. Whatever their exact nature, public spaces need to be surrounded by attractively designed buildings and uses that effectively shape and energize the open spaces, creating a compelling public realm that becomes a focal point for activity.

Streets

Whatever the nature of the development, even if it is a mixed-use tower, the design in most cases needs to engage the street at some level. Increasingly, developers and designers are using the street itself as the primary open space in a mixed-use development, especially in town center and urban village projects. Early examples that effectively used the street as the connecting open area for the project include downtown projects such as South Street Seaport in New York and Waterfront Place in Seattle. Pioneering early suburban projects include Miami Lakes Town Center in Miami Lakes, Florida, Princeton Forrestal Village in Princeton, New Jersey, Reston Town Center in Reston, Virginia, and Mizner Park in Boca Raton, Florida.

Mizner Park has been especially effective in using the street, because it combines the street with a long linear park that runs down the center and length of the street. It effectively creates a configuration that allows the street

Courtesy of RTKL Associates

Birch Street Promenade includes residential over retail along a main street in Brea, California.

and the park to reinforce each other, with one an active pedestrian and traffic corridor and the other a quieter space that adds an important visual identity to the street environment.

Using streets as a primary element in the open space system provides for active and pedestrian-friendly environments that both pedestrians and drivers can easily view and access. In downtowns, using streets allows for excellent integration with the surrounding urban areas, showing an inherent respect for the integrity of the urban

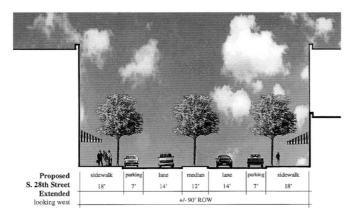

Proposed S. 28th Street Extended looking west	sidewalk 18'	parking 7'	lane 14'	median 12'	lane 14'	parking 7'	sidewalk 18'
	+/- 90' ROW						

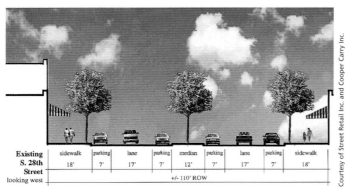

Existing S. 28th Street looking west	sidewalk 18'	parking 7'	lane 17'	parking 7'	median 12'	parking 7'	lane 17'	parking 7'	sidewalk 18'
	+/- 110' ROW								

Courtesy of Street Retail Inc. and Cooper Carry Inc.

Street sections and dimensions for existing and proposed streets at the Village at Shirlington in Arlington, Virginia.

environment. In suburban areas, using streets as the primary open-space system allows the development to create a town center atmosphere that is sorely lacking in most suburban areas; it also allows for other new developments to be easily connected to the project, extending the urban pattern in an orderly and attractive manner.

The use of retail main streets in mixed-use projects can provide animated and active open spaces and a strong thematic focus that can establish the framework for a strong public realm. At Orenco Station near Portland, for example, the design of the main street echoes the nearby small community of Orenco with brick facades and bay windows and balconies extending over the street. The resulting strong urban enclosure frames the open space of the main street retail area and provides 24-hour "eyes on the street."

Retail stores, which line the ground floor on both sides of the half-block area, include a coffee shop, two restaurants, and a wine shop as well as other specialty stores and services. Townhouses are located above, except on the corners, which have commercial office space above. Parking is located behind the retail as well as on the street. The retail buildings in some cases have roll-up garage-door fronts to allow for outdoor dining along the extra-wide 17-foot (5-meter) sidewalks. The mixed-use town center, within easy walking distance of a transit station, includes 24,000 square feet (2,230 square meters) of mixed-use retail, 32,000 square feet (3,000 square meters) of office space, 20,000 square feet (1,860 square meters) of residential lofts over retail space, and 70,000 square feet (6,500 square meters) of live/work townhouses.

Some developments have used existing streets and then expanded them through the creation of pedestrian squares and small streetfront enclaves just off the main street. The Market Common at Clarendon, for example, involves retail space arranged along both existing streetfronts and a newly developed U-shaped street and a small green. Numerous large retail tenants, including Crate & Barrel, Pottery Barn, the Container Store, and

Although Easton Town Center in Columbus, Ohio, is principally arranged around streets and outdoor spaces, it also includes a large pavilion.

Market Common Clarendon includes retail along both existing streetfronts and a newly developed U-shaped street and small green.

Barnes & Noble, have located in the project, with apartments located on upper floors. This configuration creates strong visibility from surrounding well-trafficked roadways while also creating a more protected main street atmosphere for pedestrians.

Landscaping can make a fundamental contribution to the overall character of street open-space systems. As noted earlier, the street can become a parklike setting in itself if it includes street trees and well-designed greenery and landscape elements.

Streets are fundamental elements of the open-space system at seven of the ten case studies in Chapter 8. Peabody Place and Yerba Buena Center are built in downtown environments where the streets in the development are integral to the urban street system already in existence. Addison Circle and University Part at MIT are new projects that use new and fairly quiet streets as integral elements of the open-space system. And CityPlace, Phillips Place, and Valencia Town Center Drive create

and use active retail main streets as fundamental organizing elements and public spaces in their urban design.

Urban Plazas and Squares

Urban plazas and squares, one of the most common forms of public spaces in mixed-use developments, have been developed with varying degrees of success. They differ from town greens in that they are largely hardscape designs, although they often do include some green space as well. Among the critical planning factors for a successful urban plaza or square (one that is active and draws people) are well-defined edges, surrounding uses that animate the space (such as retail shops or restaurants), adequate sun exposure, and attractive landscaping, including trees, water and fountain elements, and seating.

If one recalls the image of the empty windswept plaza often associated with a freestanding office building, it is easy to see how the design and placement of plazas can be problematic. Successful plazas and squares require careful planning to avoid the unappealing spaces that can sometimes result; perhaps the most important factor affecting the success of a plaza or square is its relationship to surrounding buildings and streets. Many early examples of plazas in mixed-use projects were not effectively shaped by surrounding buildings, and others were on upper levels away from surrounding streets and pedestrian activity; either of these features can significantly detract from the success of a plaza.

Westmount Square, designed by Mies van der Rohe after the international school, is an early example of the use of a plaza in a mixed-use development. The plaza is located above street level and on top of a retail concourse; it is surrounded on three sides by buildings but has no substantial retail activity at the plaza level because the main retail concourse is below. Landscaping and seating were not abundant in the original design. This kind of plaza is typical of the international style and has been used less and less frequently in mixed-use developments as designers seek to create more lively and animated public open areas. In the case of Westmount Square, the retail concourse, not the plazas, is the central people-oriented place for the project.

More recent mixed-use projects have used plazas as "urban squares," that is, plazas surrounded by buildings and animating uses. Urban squares need not be square (they frequently are irregular in shape), but they are usually very active, surrounded by buildings on three or four sides, well defined at the edges, faced on one or more sides by retail or restaurant uses, and located at the heart of commercial and civic activity.

Reston Town Center was one of the earliest examples that used an urban square in a mixed-use project. Phase I of the project used a small square that featured an ice rink in winter and an informal performance area in summer; the space became so popular that a special glass canopy was added that provides shelter as well as an important architectural identity for the space. The square is faced by a hotel on one side, offices on a second, and a retail/restaurant building on a third; all these buildings contain ground-floor retail and restaurant uses.

Pentagon Row in Arlington, Virginia, includes an urban square with a tight configuration of buildings surrounding the square, creating an intimate social atmosphere. The square is surrounded on three sides by retail at the ground level and residential uses above, and is open to a street on the fourth side. It is strategically placed on the path to the nearby Metro station. Pedestrian connections at the corners of the square connect to other portions of the development. An ice skating rink operates in the square during the winter, and restaurants with outdoor seating open onto the square for al fresco dining during warm weather.

One of the best recent examples of an urban plaza is CityPlace in West Palm Beach, Florida, highlighting the importance of fountains, retail and restaurant uses, historic buildings, and cultural uses as factors in successful urban squares (see Chapter 8). CityPlace provides a European-style urban town square surrounded by retail

Courtesy of Elkus/Manfredi Architects Ltd

Night lighting of the plaza at CityPlace in West Palm Beach creates a compelling evening atmosphere.

Southlake Town Square includes a large public green that is surrounded on two sides by retail/commercial buildings and on a third by the town hall.

Courtesy of Cooper & Stebbins

buildings and featuring a historic former church. The church plaza in front of the restored church—now the Harriet Himmel Gilman Theater—is the center of gravity for the development, providing a grand public room. A dramatic fountain in the church plaza stands as civic art during the day and provides water, light, and fog shows choreographed to music each night.

The CityPlace development team was careful to preserve the dramatic views of the church building through the careful design of the Italian-style plaza in front of the church and by curving the commercial streetfront to open up around the plaza. The church and the plaza are located near the intersection of two principal pedestrian-friendly streets; together, the plaza and these two streets define the central core area and public spaces of the town center.

Town Greens and Squares

Town greens and squares are increasingly popular in mixed-use projects and often go hand in hand with town centers, main streets, and other street-oriented designs. Town greens and squares can be both green and park-like, such as the large green square at Southlake Town Square in Southlake, Texas, or use a mix of green and hardscape, such as that found at Riverside in Atlanta or Princeton Forrestal Village in Princeton, New Jersey. Town greens and squares differ from urban plazas in that they are greener and often larger than urban squares, and they are generally less urban and frequently surrounded by lower-scale buildings than would be found around an urban square. Like urban squares, they frequently include fountains and other water features and are faced by retail uses to enliven the space. In some cases, they are quite small and village-like, such as that found at Haile Village Center in Gainesville, Florida. Town greens are similar to urban squares in that they require many of the same elements to succeed—well-defined edges, the right surrounding uses to animate the space, and attractive landscaping.

Town greens and squares frequently have a civic identity in the community, even when they are private spaces. At Southlake Town Square, for example, the town square is the centerpiece of the project, the center of gravity around which the buildings and activities revolve; it is faced on one side by a major civic building. In this case, the square is actually a series of three half-block panels: the first is occupied by a pond and pavilion adjacent to a nearby arterial, the middle panel (the central square) is crisscrossed by walkways that meet at a central fountain, and the northernmost panel is occupied by the town hall building. Each provides a variety of public gathering spaces that take on an increasingly urban character moving from the arterial toward Town Hall.

The town square is integral with surrounding streets, providing a network of pedestrian space that extends the public realm from the square to the new post office block, up the Grand Avenue promenade, and across the site to the residential neighborhood. Including the town square, the project includes a total of 13 acres (5.3 hectares) of public parks and open space. A second "Olmstedian" park, located just one block from the square, is a large park encompassing an entire block of meandering trails and the largest cluster of mature trees on the property.

Town greens frequently include a variety of landscape design elements. The Town Square at Southlake is oversized in relation to the two-story buildings surrounding it, but the addition of the four-story Town Hall has scaled down the space, and the trees planted along the streets and around the square will continue to enhance the human scale of the space as they mature. A combination of tall light posts and short, lighted bollards also provides a more intimate scale in the square at night. Landscaping and outdoor furniture were carefully chosen to avoid a contrived atmosphere.

The square is not enclosed by buildings on all sides, partially because of a shift in the plan to accommodate the town hall. In return for locating the new town hall

in Southlake Town Square, the city required the developer to leave the square open to provide a view of the building from the busy four-lane arterial on the south side of the square.

At the new Cathedral City Downtown, a new town center that will incorporate a number of uses in a cohesively planned urban environment in this California desert community, plans for the new town square combine civic uses with a community gathering place for events. The one-acre (0.4-hectare) town square will include an amphitheater, a sculpture courtyard, a children's rock garden, and an interactive fountain. It will be surrounded on all four sides by civic and other buildings, including a 68,000-square-foot (6,300-square-meter) civic center. The project has a desert-inspired Mediterranean theme with open courtyards, covered walks, colonnades, and arcades. Walkways are marked by dynamic paving, splashing fountains, and appropriate desert landscaping. Restaurant seating and shops open out into the walks, welcoming shoppers in a lively European fashion.

Gateway Gardens at Gateway Village in Charlotte, North Carolina, opens onto West Trade Street with a cascading landscape and hardscape of greenery, seating areas, stairs, and a fountain. Intended as a grand civic space providing a nucleus for the entire project, the space includes a curving, tree-lined walk that encompasses an expansive lawn designed for both public space and private gatherings. The gardens are divided into separate "garden rooms": the water garden, which contains the fountain and the water wall; the terrace garden, which has outside tables with umbrellas for the Gateway Café; and the central green, which is designed to seat up to 1,500 people for outdoor concerts and events.

Although many greens are intended to be quite active, they can also be quiet places. University Park at MIT, near the MIT campus in Cambridge, uses a green more akin to a university quad or common. The green is a place for quiet repose, as few retail or restaurant tenants are located in the development. The green includes several

sculptures that highlight the industrial history of the site. The design places the green at the center of the project; the edges of the green are defined by the street and mid-rise buildings beyond the street on one side and low- and mid-rise buildings on the other three.

Town greens and squares need not be square, and they often come in a variety of shapes—circular and oval at CityCenter Englewood in Englewood, Colorado, and Smyrna Town Center in Smyrna, Georgia, for example, and long and narrow at the center of Mizner Park in Boca Raton.[2]

Parks and Gardens

Parks and gardens, although sometimes quite similar to town greens, are considered, in this book, generally larger than greens, less tightly enclosed by surrounding buildings, and less active and animated. In some cases, parks are quite large, such as the 50-acre (20-hectare) park at Kuala Lumpur City Centre (see Chapter 2) or the 35-acre (14-hectare) park at Diagonal Mar in Barcelona. The latter park, a public park for the city, features lakes, pedestrian walkways, bicycle and skating paths, children's play areas, a dog-walking area, and multiple water features.

When considering including a large park, developers should be aware that retail stores generally do not do well next to large parks unless they are carefully merchandised and in a "single-loaded" configuration (where retail is on only one side of the street or pathway). Large parks are often designed as a place for escape or quiet repose in an active urban environment and generally are not prime retail streetfront retail settings.

Among mixed-use developments that feature a park is Yerba Buena Center in San Francisco (see Chapter 8). The park and garden area in the development are central to the design and marketing of the project. The central feature of the plan for Yerba Buena is the Esplanade Garden, located atop the Moscone Center North. The garden contains several smaller theme gardens and areas,

The plan for the village center at Baldwin Park near Orlando, being built on the former site of the Orlando Naval Training Center, provides a variety of public spaces, including a waterfront park.

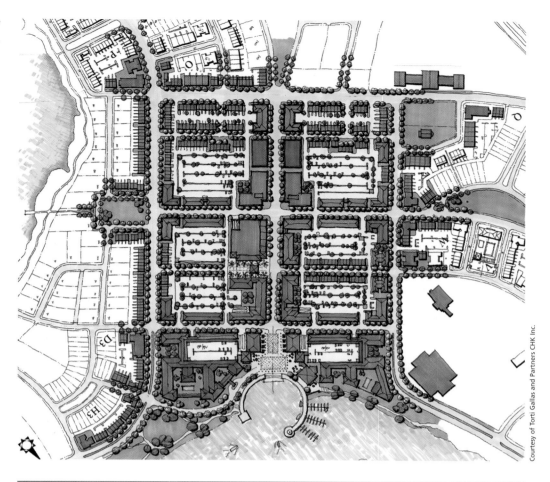

Courtesy of Torti Gallas and Partners CHK Inc.

Diagonal Mar in Barcelona includes a 35-acre (14-hectare) park.

Courtesy of Hines Inc.

cafés, and offices for the nonprofit Yerba Buena Alliance and the garden's management. Esplanade Garden is the location of organized events programmed by Yerba Buena Alliance as well as informal activities. Adjacent to Esplanade Garden, between the two Center for the Arts buildings, is the more intimate East Garden.

Esplanade Garden is also connected to children's facilities on an adjacent block via a pedestrian bridge. The development also includes several public plazas. The strategy of the Yerba Buena plan is to use this open space as the common link between the various uses and structures in Yerba Buena Center. Because of a high water table, the Moscone Center could not be built completely underground, and as a result, Esplanade Garden is raised up to four feet (1.2 meters) above grade in places, making the pedestrian connection between the street and the garden less than ideal. Efforts have been made to mitigate this condition by installing the East Fountain and park along the street edge, intended to announce the gardens beyond.

Funding and motivation for the park and garden at Yerba Buena Center came from the San Francisco Redevelopment Agency, but such parks have pure economic value as well. The developers of Atlanta Galleria chose to develop the park on their own land with their own money. Galleria Gardens is a linear, five-acre (two-hectare) park that includes a central walkway, several water features, and numerous trees and seating areas. The park is surrounded by five office buildings and a hotel/retail complex at one end, and it provides an attractive visual amenity as well as a central public area for all the other uses. This kind of plan is a refreshing alternative to the typical suburban office park.

In some cases, parks and gardens are placed atop other uses on a second level above grade. At WestEnd City Center in Budapest (see Chapter 8), the primary public open space for the development and an amenity that all users of the project can enjoy is the 237,000-square-foot (22,000-square-meter) roof garden, which sits atop much of the retail space. Featuring abundant natural grass and an array of trees and flowers, the garden offers a welcome respite from the urban activity below. Futuristic light standards make the garden usable at all hours, and workers or shoppers can have lunch or relax at the many tables and benches. The developer has paid careful attention to maintenance of the roof garden, and despite its location, no problems have occurred with viability of the plantings or damage to the roof below.

Small, quiet "pocket parks" have also been used in mixed-use projects. At Pacific Place in Hong Kong—which contains three hotel towers ranging from 50 to 61 stories and a 40-story office tower, all built over a podium containing a shopping center—the sloping site allowed for the creation of a quiet park that is at grade with the street on one side, but above grade on the other. The park, which allows views down to the automobile entry at the center of the project, is landscaped with plants and walkways and flanked by two curving towers.

A retail promenade at CityPlace in West Palm Beach, Florida.

A private residential courtyard at Phillips Place in Charlotte, North Carolina.

It is generally a quiet park with no adjacent retail or entertainment uses.

Promenades and Courtyards

Many mixed-use projects include internal open-air promenades and courtyards that are quite separate from surrounding streets and traffic. Courtyards are generally small quiet spaces of varying shapes, generally surrounded by other buildings and located away from surrounding street traffic. Promenades are often linear and can be quite large and/or long; they may include open-air shopping areas or substantial waterfront walkways. Such internal pedestrian areas can provide attractive public realms that provide an escape from the noise, traffic, and fumes associated with streets and auto traffic.

The open-air spaces at Paseo Colorado, for example, have both courtyards and pedestrian-only promenades, including the new Garfield Promenade, as well as retail along existing streetfronts. The project includes two promenades that form a cross, one running the length of the rectangular-shaped project and the other bisecting it in the middle. The latter is a former street that has been closed to auto traffic, while the former is much narrower and provides an open-air shopping arcade and intimate walkway through the village, inspired by the alleyways of historic Pasadena. The areas are connected at the center and are enlivened with retail shops and restaurants, creating a pedestrian-friendly environment. A second-level courtyard on the western edge of the project is accessed through featured stairways and provides outdoor seating for diners as well as attractive spaces for receptions and parties. Private courtyards are also provided for residents. The project includes 560,000 square feet (52,000 square meters) of retail/entertainment space, 400 residential apartments, and offices.

Smaller courtyards can also be placed between buildings to create intimate outdoor settings. Vancouvercenter in Vancouver, Washington, uses courtyards to create attractive narrow open spaces between office and apartment buildings on this one-block site in downtown Vancouver. The buildings abut street frontages, and courtyards pass through the block in both north/south and east/west directions.

Major promenades have also been used in mixed-use projects, frequently together with waterfront areas. One of the best known and most elaborate is the South Street Seaport in New York City, which features retail and cultural uses as well as several working piers along New York's East River. Another is Rowes Wharf in Boston, whose plan includes a pedestrian promenade that begins at the street and proceeds through a grand arch at the center of the project, then opens up to a waterfront promenade along Boston harbor. The waterfront promenade stretches the length of the project and includes areas on two wharves where residential uses are located. A third is Canal City Hakata (see feature box), which includes an internal walkway and promenade along a canal.

Lakes and rivers can also be used for promenades. At Market Street at Celebration, many of the buildings are situated along a wide promenade circling a lake. The outdoor spaces include a dock on the lake, a bridge, fountains, courtyards, and a park.

Other mixed-use developments that have taken advantage of waterfront locations to create attractive promenades and waterfront spaces include Washington Harbour in Washington, D.C., Queensway Bay in Long Beach, California, Tualatin Commons in Oregon, Schaumburg Town Square in Schaumburg, Illinois, the Woodlands Waterway in the Woodlands, Texas, RiverPlace in Portland, and Bryant Street Pier in San Francisco.

Enclosed Public Spaces and Atriums

When John Portman created the modern atrium hotel in the Hyatt Regency at Peachtree Center in the late 1960s, a trend toward developing large atriums in hotels and mixed-use developments was born that continued for two decades. Although the popularity of large atriums and enclosed public spaces has waned over the past decade

Several types of public spaces are used at Canal City Hakata in Fukuoka, Japan, including a canal flowing through a canyon at the center, accompanying pedestrian walkways, balconies, and a dramatic central amphitheater space at the heart of the project. The unifying element for the project is the canal. Echoing both the merchant bustle of old Hakata and the river valley beyond the city, this new canal, with its bordering walks and bridges, functions as both a decorative pool and a main street. Open to the sky, it cuts a curving path through the "geologic" layers of earth-colored balconies that serve the office and hotel levels above. Along this route, garden courtyards and other spaces open up to celebrate the story of nature—stars, moon, sun, earth, sea—each distinctively symbolized by one-of-a-kind spatial enclosures, pavings, plantings, fountains, lighting, graphics, and artwork.

Courtesy of FJUD

Several types of outdoor open spaces are used at Canal City Hakata in Fukuoka, Japan, including walkways along a canal and a dramatic central amphitheater.

Plants, while relatively confined in the central paved areas, expand at Canal City's perimeter into a canopy of trees. Canal City is a dramatic oasis in the hard modern city, but it also extends toward neighborhood streets that may some day be lined with trees as well. The link from the shopping street to a conventional park outside the walls is quite popular, confirming that for all its flamboyance, Canal City really is becoming integrated into its community.

Completed in 1996 but still evolving as tenants and uses change, Canal City Hakata is both a consciously designed catalyst for downtown revitalization and the supplier of a large chunk of new development in itself. In fact, according to its primary developer, the Fukuoka Jisho Company, it is the largest private retail project in Japan's history. Its 2 million square feet (186,000 square meters) of shops, restaurants, and offices include a 13-screen AMC cineplex, a Japanese legitimate theater, a miniamusement park, an Opel showroom, and two major hotels, the Washington and the Grand Hyatt.

Although strategically linked with three existing dense urban neighborhoods that intersect at Canal City and with the historic Hakata riverfront, the Canal City site itself was a featureless, nine-acre (3.6-hectare) former factory compound. As it happened, both the developer and city shared an interest in creating a park and gathering place as well as a retail and commercial magnet. The notion of combining a park with a marketplace led to the project's most daring decision: that this bustling, tightly packed urban environment would become an artistic metaphor not just for Hakata's commercial past but also for its natural environment.

Source: Adapted from Robert L. Miller, "Narrative Urban Landscapes," *Urban Land*, February 1998, pp. 62–65+.

in the United States, a few are being developed today, and atriums and malls are still in vogue in many international settings, especially in Asia but also in Europe. Large enclosed malls are still relatively new and unusual concepts in many of these international settings and thus can tap into underserved demand for this kind of retail experience. Atriums and gallerias have been used as separate components and as a central organizing element for mixed-use projects.

Hotel Atriums. Several mixed-use developments have used hotel atriums as central focal points and people places, among them Embarcadero Center in San Francisco and more recently Espirito Santo Plaza in Miami, which includes a ten-story landscaped atrium in the hotel on the upper floors of this mixed-use tower.

A hotel atrium can incorporate various levels of drama to regulate the amount of public attention it creates. The Hyatt Regency at Embarcadero Center has one of the most well-known and dramatic atriums in North America, serving to create a positive image for the entire center. It comprises a triangular space with one wall cascading out from one side to cover the space at the top. A fountain, sculpture, restaurants, and retail facilities are included at ground level, and entertainment is programmed there regularly. Because of the nature of the hotel, which does substantial convention business, the active lobby area is acceptable and desirable, even though it makes regulating access to rooms difficult. The space also works to create a sense of place for the entire project. In general, however, hotel atriums can create problems for the hotel by attracting people to a space that needs to remain quiet and secure, and thus they have been used infrequently in recent years.

Atriums and Galleria in Malls. Shopping center atriums and galleries have also been traditional public spaces in many mixed-use projects. Shopping centers are almost by definition primarily horizontal, but in several modern mixed-use developments, they have been designed in a vertical configuration. One of the best ways to link the various levels of a vertical shopping center is through a central atrium, allowing shoppers to make visual connections between various levels as well as providing an attractive central place. One of the earliest examples is Water Tower Place in Chicago, which includes an eight-level shopping center surrounding a central atrium that also houses the elevators for the retail center. Trump Tower in New York and 900 North Michigan Avenue in Chicago use a similar concept.

Galleria designs are frequently chosen for more horizontal enclosed malls in mixed-use projects. Galleria are usually characterized as elongated shopping arcades covered by a vaulted and/or skylighted ceiling. This concept was pioneered for shopping centers at Eaton Center in Toronto and at the Houston Galleria in Houston, both of which feature a multilevel shopping center covered by a glass vaulted ceiling. More recent examples include

Located between the two Petronas Towers at Kuala Lumpur City Centre is the six-level Suria shopping center and atrium. This development also features a large park, which the Suria overlooks.

Photographer: Jeff Goldberg, ESTO Photographics Inc.; courtesy of Cesar Pelli & Associates

Photographer: Jeff Goldberg, ESTO Photographics Inc.; courtesy of Cesar Pelli & Associates

The Forum, the atrium at Sony Center am Potsdamer Platz in Berlin, is the centerpiece of the project. Although the Forum is surrounded by buildings and covered by a glass canopy, it is not fully enclosed.

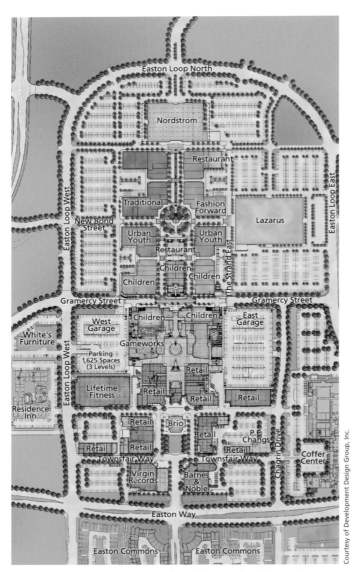

Parking at Easton Town Center is a mixture of surface and structured parking located at the outside edges of the development, which is oriented around internal streets.

the Fashion Centre at Pentagon City in Arlington, Virginia, and Copley Place in Boston. At Pentagon City, the galleria and mall link a multilevel parking structure on one side of the mall with hotel, office, residential, and transit uses on the other.

One of the finest recent examples is the addition of a glass-covered shopping galleria/arcade to the Prudential Center in Boston. This addition helped tie the project together, allowed for additional retail space, and replaced many windswept plazas that were not functioning well as public spaces. Another recent example is the two-block-long gallery and central space at the new AOL Time Warner Center in New York.

Atriums as Grand Central Space. Early examples of nonmall atriums as the central organizing element for a large mixed-use project include Plaza of the Americas in Dallas, which was formed by enclosing the space at the center of a group of two office towers, a hotel, and a parking garage, and Renaissance Center in Detroit, which includes a central hotel tower surrounded by four office towers and a central atrium that connects them. One of the finest early examples is Crystal Court in the IDS Center in Minneapolis, formed by enclosing the ground-level space between a major office tower, a hotel tower, and a two-story retail structure. The entire public space in the atrium is connected to various adjacent blocks by skywalks. The atrium itself features a multifaceted glass ceiling that allows an outstanding view of the IDS tower rising above it and includes a central open area that provides space for circulation and programmed events. Because of its location and superb design, the Crystal Court has become a central focal point for the downtown and has made a major positive contribution to the life of the city.

A more recent example of atriums as central organizers is found at Sony Center am Potsdamer Platz in Berlin (see Chapter 8), which features the Forum, a 43,000-square-foot (4,000-square-meter) public space enclosed by the buildings of the Sony Center and capped by the signature Forum roof that creates an endless play of light and shadow in the space below. This un-air-conditioned space includes open entrances to surrounding streets from numerous directions.

The best of these atriums and galleria create a sense of place, a central focus, a space that is fun to be in. Most developers and designers are discovering, however, that open-air spaces work better to create a sense of place; thus, atriums and enclosed spaces are becoming less central, more peripheral, or nonexistent in most new mixed-use projects.

Parking Design

"Form follows parking" is the increasingly used mantra in urban design. The phrase acknowledges one of the major problems in urban and mixed-use design: what to do with all the cars. Parking is often the largest user of land and/or building space in a mixed-use development, and effectively incorporating large amounts of parking into an attractive and functional urban design is a major challenge.

Parking is an integral component of most mixed-use developments and can significantly affect the project's overall operational efficiency, image, and success. The parking component of a mixed-use development should be carefully planned and designed by an experienced team comprising an urban designer, a traffic/parking consultant, an architect, and a parking operator. Parking facilities in mixed-use developments must not be treated as subordinate uses but as legitimate elements that can enhance the entire project. The parking component must be carefully planned and designed, not simply worked into the development pro forma.

Planning and design of a parking facility begins with an assessment of demand and the opportunity for shared parking (see Chapter 2). Once this analysis has been completed, the following issues should be thoroughly evaluated:

- the physical structure of the parking—surface parking, below-grade structured parking, or above-grade structured parking—and the associated costs and benefits of each;
- the substantially different parking needs and characteristics of different land uses;
- placement of parking on the site and design of the pedestrian system;
- design and capacity of entrances and exits;
- design of internal circulation system, sight lines, stalls, and interior finishes;
- directional signage;
- security and safety, including lighting and parking control systems;
- exterior design and materials;
- payment systems and separation of users.

Parking facilities in mixed-used developments may vary from a single parking structure with one entrance to multiple structures and lots to on-street spaces. They may have a variety of entrances, some with fees and some without, some restricted and others not. Projects with multiple facilities offer many options, but these options can confuse the visitor if not properly planned, especially when some lots are dedicated to specific uses.

As discussed in Chapter 2, shared parking is also a critical issue in mixed-use design. When properly designed and managed, shared parking can reduce the maximum number of parking spaces required. Good mixed-use design and programming can also reduce demand for parking by increasing pedestrian trips. For example, a restaurant or delicatessen within walking distance for office workers requires fewer parking spaces than a restaurant that can be reached only by auto. Office space located within easy walking distance of a hotel may require fewer parking spaces for visitors than office space without such proximity, because business guests staying at the hotel will be able to walk to the office.

Courtesy of Kohn Pedersen Fox

The parking structure at Espirito Santo Plaza in Miami is a substantial building in itself. Topped with a health club and roof garden, it is connected to the other components by a dynamic atrium and pedestrian walkway.

Structured versus Surface Parking

A fundamental decision that must be made in planning parking facilities for a mixed-use development is whether to provide structured above- or below-grade parking, surface parking, or a combination. Whether to develop structured or surface parking is largely a function of economics, available land, and aesthetics. The cost of structured parking is always much higher than the construction of surface parking, and the cost of underground structures is nearly double the cost of aboveground structures.

Structured parking is usually the necessary alternative if the cost of land is high or if insufficient land is available to meet the estimated parking demand with surface parking. Some amount of structured parking has been required for most recently completed mixed-use developments, including all the case studies in Chapter 8. Surface parking could likely meet some or all of a suburban mixed-use development's parking needs in a phased program, but successful suburban projects eventually develop parking structures as the project matures and is built out

Economics, however, should not be the sole basis for making this decision. Market factors, project design, and other practical matters also need to be considered. The convenience of structured or surface parking for patrons of the mixed-use development must also be carefully evaluated. Structured parking can result in greater convenience for patrons, minimizing walking distances

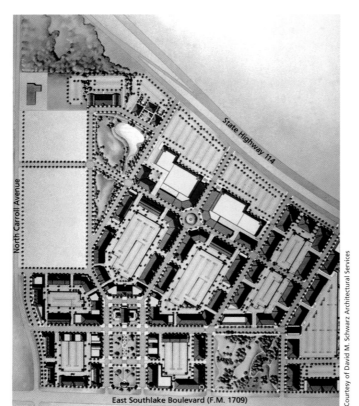

The plan for Southlake Town Square in Southlake, Texas, places most of the parking at the center of blocks surrounded by buildings.

between the facility and the patron's destination, but the market may prefer surface parking. Some drivers may resist garages, where they could encounter problems maneuvering their vehicles; others do not feel secure in such facilities. And in some markets, structured parking in a suburban setting is unusual and might thus detract from the project's market image. Despite the advances that have been made in the security of parking structures, individuals who are unaccustomed to using them

might perceive them as unsafe or less safe than surface parking. These noneconomic factors must also be weighed in deciding what kind of parking to include.

In addition to a more intensive use of land, structured parking can also be used effectively to support multi-level retail space. The multilevel entertainment center at Peabody Place in Memphis, for example, benefits greatly from the fact that customers can reach the center directly from numerous levels of the adjacent parking garage.

Parking Design for Primary Land Uses

The design of the parking facility for a mixed-use development must fully address the substantially different and sometimes conflicting parking needs and characteristics of the project's different users. Developers, architects, and traffic/parking consultants must be aware of the differences and arrive at an efficient parking design that works for all uses while also positively contributing to the overall urban design. Efficiency and practicality, while important, are not the only things to consider in design of a parking facility for a mixed-use project. Designers should take a real interest in patrons' perception of the parking facility. Does it work for the parker as driver? Does it work for the parker as pedestrian?

Moreover, while accommodating the needs of all land uses in the project as much as possible, the design of the parking facility must recognize the importance of the predominant use, if there is one. The design of a parking facility for a mixed-use development dominated by retail space will be different from that of a project dominated by office or residential space.

Major retail components in mixed-use developments generally seek a parking design that can accommodate nonexclusive, high-turnover parking. Typically, major retail tenants today require a parking management plan in their leases. Such a plan defines everything from the number of entrance and exit lanes to parking rates and often requires two or more hours of free parking for

The parking plan for Mizner Park includes on-street parking, freestanding structured parking, and structured parking with buildings above.

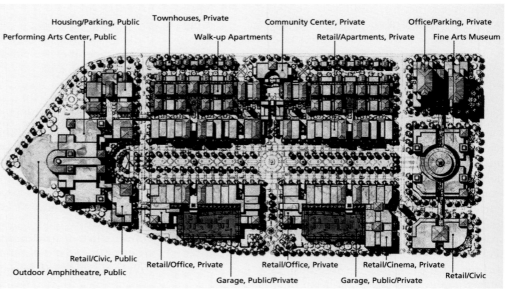

patrons. Incentive parking rates are also sometimes required for retail patrons. For example, the rate for under three hours might be $1.00 per hour, with the rate increasing substantially for the fourth and fifth hours.

Office tenants, in contrast, seek exclusive, monthly parking and assurances that their spaces will not be used by hotel guests or shoppers during working hours, particularly if the office worker leaves and returns later in the day. Hotels often seek a facility that can accommodate valet parking. Residents of a mixed-use development often expect exclusive, assigned spaces. The design and operation of parking facilities in a mixed-use development must address these differing needs and reconcile them to the maximum extent possible.

Parking Placement and Pedestrian Connections

The placement of parking is critical not only for the parking and the uses served but also for the overall design of the development. Parking must be well placed and accessible from surrounding roadways as well as from the uses being served, but it also should be as unobtrusive as possible so that it does not detract from the urban environment sought. The strategic location, design, and programming of parking areas and structures can also create or enhance attractive, well-traveled pedestrian links that can reduce demand for car movement and thus parking spaces. Numerous techniques are being employed to creatively place and design parking structures in today's mixed-use projects.

One technique is the liberal use of on-street parking, which can be used effectively to provide attractive and functional parking arrangements in retail areas. Many main street and town center projects, including Phillips Place (see Chapter 8), use parallel or angled parking on their main streets to provide convenient parking for retail tenants. In some cases, on-street parking requires special efforts to overcome local codes. At Valencia Town Center Drive (see Chapter 8), the developers wanted a 53-foot-wide (16-meter) main street with on-street park-

ing, but traffic codes demanded a four-lane 64-foot-wide (19.5-meter) street that prohibited on-street parking. Fortunately, the company owned the site and chose to develop the street as a private 53-foot-wide (16-meter) roadway with one lane of traffic in each direction and angled curbside parking.

Another technique is the use of smaller parking lots scattered throughout a site. Although it is generally not optimal or cost-effective to create small parking garages, surface lots can be relatively small.

> Developers can avoid the negative effects created by a sea of parking by dividing large parking areas into many smaller lots—which can be more easily concealed by the placement of buildings, site topography, and landscaping—and distributing them throughout a site. The largest lots can be concentrated along the least desirable borders of a site (often near a busy highway), but at least one side of the town center should always be bordered by something other than a parking lot, preferably something that connects it with a neighborhood.[3]

The use of ground-level space in parking structures for retail and service uses, now commonly used in mixed-used development, results in a more attractive streetscape and pedestrian environment.

Surrounding the parking (surface lots or structures) with other buildings is also a common method. Parking structures are surrounded by residential and retail uses at CityPlace in West Palm Beach and Addison Circle in Addison, Texas, and Pentagon Row in Arlington surrounds a surface parking lot in a similar fashion. The other uses may include relatively small buildings, thus minimizing the negative impact of these structures for the surrounding streetscapes. Mizner Park in Boca Raton uses townhouses to hide the parking structures.

The creative use of grade changes can hide a parking structure. At Phillips Place, for example, the slope of the site allowed for the creation of a two-level parking structure that looks like a surface lot for the retail users

The atrium at Espirito Santo Plaza connects the tower with the parking structure.

Courtesy of Kohn Pedersen Fox

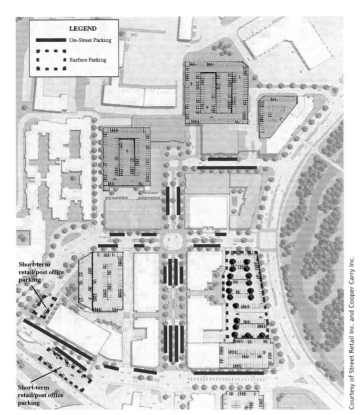

The parking plan for the proposed expansion of the Village at Shirlington in Arlington, Virginia, includes on-street parking, surface lots, and structured parking.

but contains a second level accessible to residents further into the site.

Parking structures can sometimes be placed in locations where most other uses would not work well. For example, at WestEnd City Center in Budapest, 1,500 parking spaces are provided in both underground garages and a multilevel parking structure built above a section of active railroad tracks leading to the nearby Nyugati station.

The ultimate method for minimizing parking structures' obtrusiveness is the use of underground parking, which is expensive but may be cost-effective if land values are high enough. At Jin Mao Tower in Shanghai, 800 of the 900 parking spaces are provided in an underground garage. Sony Center also has an underground parking structure with 980 spaces. Such structures effectively minimize the amount of street frontage devoted to parking lots and structures, ultimately enhancing the quality of urban design and the experience for pedestrians—increasingly important goals in mixed-use projects.

Convenient and safe pedestrian connections between the parking facility and the uses in the mixed-use development are essential and must be carefully planned. Walking distances from the parking facility should be kept to a minimum. Pedestrian connections can take a variety of forms—bridges, sidewalks, elevators, escalators, or concourses—between the parking facility and major project components, but increasingly they involve surface sidewalks. When parking is below grade, separate elevators to different uses may be necessary.

Considerable attention should be given to the design of the pedestrian experience to ensure that it is as pleasant and inviting as possible. Entrances from the parking structures are often used more heavily than street-level pedestrian entrances and in effect serve as the main entrances to the project. Entrances to the mixed-use development from parking areas should thus not be back doors but second front doors.

Entrances and Internal Design

One requirement for an effective parking facility is adequate capacity for the entrances and exits. In a mixed-use development, it is often preferable to provide separate entrances/exits for specific uses in the project. To prevent conflicts with street traffic, entrances should provide adequate reservoir space and should not be located close to street intersections. In general, the design of the facility and the placement of entrances and exits should favor entering rather than exiting traffic to expedite the movement of traffic from the street into the parking facility. Specific requirements for the design of entrances and exits are often included in local ordinances, but the needs of a mixed-use development may be different from those set by ordinances and should be carefully assessed.

Simplicity and ease of circulation and parking should be the primary considerations in the design of the internal circulation system for a parking facility. A driver should be able to move easily and confidently through the parking facility, even without ever having used it before. The design of the internal circulation system for a parking facility, whether a straight run or circular or some combination of the two, is dictated by the size and topography of the site, the size of the facility, and conventional practices in the area.

A shared parking facility serving a mixed-use development can have significant inbound and outbound traffic flow at numerous "peak" periods of the day. Accordingly, the design of the access and circulation system should accommodate bidirectional movement in certain lanes without significant conflict and should be easy to use and understand.

Categories and sizes of the various uses in the project are important factors in selecting stall sizes. If the project includes a major retail component and turnover will be comparatively high, it may be appropriate to provide only (or primarily) standard-size stalls. In a mixed-use development containing a major office component (and thus a substantial percentage of all-day parkers), a percentage of smaller stalls may be feasible. If compact spaces are provided, they must be well marked, easily distinguished from standard spaces, and strategically located throughout the facility.

When parking is separated by uses, internal controls may be needed to ensure separation. At Addison Circle in Addison, Texas, all vehicles access the parking garages from the same entry points. Commercial tenants, patrons, and residential visitors park without charge on the ground floor in an unsecured area; residents proceed through a security gate to park on the upper floors.

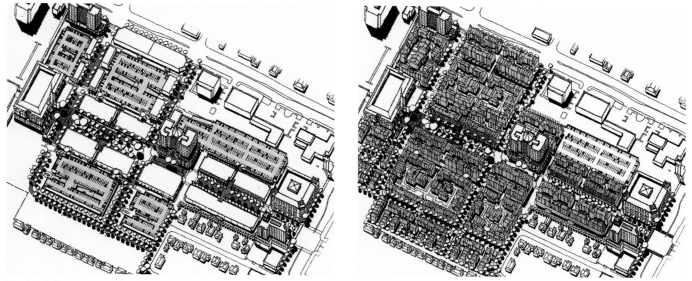

Much of the structured parking at Santana Row has residential units above.

Well-conceived signage is vital to the success and efficient functioning of any parking facility, but it is especially important to the success of parking facilities serving a mixed-use development. Signage should include:

- Directional signs at the entrances to the development from the public streets;
- Signs at the development's exits giving directions to the streets surrounding the site;
- Internal signs directing parkers to parking areas serving specific uses;
- Internal signs directing drivers to available parking spaces, including, in larger, more complex facilities, electronic signs to identify areas with vacant spaces;
- Information directing parkers to and from their destinations, using graphics and color coding effectively.

Signs should help drivers make a quick decision, and be easily readable, located so that they are clearly visible, and few in number so that a driver is not faced with multiple decisions to make at once. Signs in garages should also direct pedestrians to the elevators/stairs and exits.

The design should also emphasize sight lines and pedestrian access to elevators and stairs, and interior finishes, paint colors, and lighting should make the pedestrian feel comfortable and safe. Because parking in mixed-use projects often operates 18 or more hours per day, safe day and night operation must be ensured; thus, electronic security systems and other security devices and monitoring may be necessary.

Exterior Design and Materials

Because parking is a major component of most mixed-use developments, it is essential that the parking facility be designed to be compatible with the project's overall image and character. The parking facility must be integrated with and add to, not detract from, the project's total aesthetic appeal. If structured parking is provided,

This parking structure at Reston Town Center includes ground-level retail space along a secondary retail street.

At Park Tower in Chicago, where condominiums are stacked atop a hotel, the exterior design and fenestration pattern change substantially at the transition point from hotel to residential.

the exterior materials of the structure should conform to the project's overall design and be aesthetically pleasing. If the garage is prominently placed, quality exterior design and materials should be used for the garage exterior. If the garage is hidden behind other buildings, exterior design becomes less important. For surface parking, the creation of an attractive landscape design that includes substantial greenery is important.

In general, the design of the parking facility and the parking experience can be crucial to the image of a mixed-use development. Many parking garages are uninspired, often ugly spaces leading to cold and unpleasant entrances to the building. Many parking lots are poorly landscaped and not friendly to pedestrians. Focusing a little more time and money on creating a pleasant parking experience can pay dividends. Because so many people arrive at a mixed-use development by car, it is important to consider carefully the desired image of the development from the auto user's point of view.

Structural and Engineering Issues

Structural design of a mixed-use development is complicated by the fact that each use has different structural requirements that will affect placement and by the fact that mixing or stacking these uses may involve difficult transitions and structural challenges. This complexity affects construction costs and may also lead to special design solutions to meet building and fire codes. For example, the fire department approved the Santana Row project in San Jose but with extra safety requirements in place such as metal stairwells, extra-strength fire walls, and extensive sprinkler systems. The project subsequently experienced a devastating fire during construction that destroyed a residential building. Notes Paris Rutherford of RTKL Associates in Dallas, "Mixed-use development often requires innovative structural advances not allowable by most building codes. As such, we often collab-

orate with building officials to be able to complete the project."

Structural Issues

The structural configuration that presents the greatest complexities for engineering and design is stacking uses vertically, especially in a high-rise building. For example, mixed-use towers frequently include underground parking, retail on the lower levels, offices above the retail, and residential and/or hotel uses on top of office space; the differing requirements of those uses, especially residential or hotel over office, create the greatest design problem. The differences involve shape and size of the floor, the building core and the distance from the core to exterior walls, placement of plumbing and other building systems, column spacing, floor-to-floor dimensions, and floor loading.

Floor Size and Layout. Typical office buildings can accommodate a variety of floor shapes but often use a square shape that leaves a substantial area at the center of the building that is some distance from the perimeter. This space can easily be used for the core of the building and for interior offices that do not need windows. Residential and hotel towers, on the other hand, are often long and narrow, because every unit must be placed along the perimeter of the building to provide exterior window space and to provide a reasonable layout for each unit.

The size of the building's core is also an issue. Because office buildings generally use large core areas where elevators, HVAC equipment, wiring risers, stair wells, and restrooms are centralized, they can better use larger central areas. Residential buildings usually have fewer elevators per square foot of gross building area and no central restrooms, resulting in a smaller core and certain limits on the optimal depth of a building.

In short, a large square floor space is suitable for office space, but smaller square floor plates and/or more rectangular floor layouts are more suitable for residential or

The residential floor plate at Park Tower in Chicago is smaller, has more corners, and has a core that is arranged differently from that in the hotel. Although column spacing is largely the same for both uses, subtle differences exist here as well.

hotel uses, leading to inherent conflicts and compromises in a mixed-use tower.

When uses are stacked in a single structure, the problem is often solved in one of several ways. One is to make floors smaller at the upper levels where residences or the hotel is located. This strategy was used in three mixed-use towers on North Michigan Avenue in Chicago. The John Hancock Center and Olympia Centre narrow gradually as they rise, while at Water Tower Place, a single narrow tower of hotel and residential uses rises from a very large 12-story base structure containing retail and office uses.

A second method is simply to combine uses that are structurally compatible. At Park Tower in Chicago, which uses a roughly rectangular and relatively small 8,000-square-foot (745-square-meter) floor plate, retail uses are located on the lower levels, the hotel and condominiums above. The condominium and hotel floor plates are similar in size and shape and use similar column spacing, minimizing the problems in stacking uses.

A third solution is to place the residential/hotel uses at the top of a structure surrounding a central open space, recreational area, or atrium. Some units or rooms can thus be oriented outward, some inward, and swimming pools, tennis courts, and courtyard areas can be centrally placed. This design solution was chosen for Espirito Santo Plaza in Miami and Market Square in Washington, D.C. The former includes an atrium hotel atop an office tower, the latter residential uses that open both inward onto courtyards and outward over a retail building.

Column Spacing and Structural Issues. The actual structural requirements of the different uses—column spacing, floor-to-floor dimensions, and floor loading requirements—are also issues of concern. Column spacing can vary considerably between uses, especially between office and residential uses. Both exterior and interior columns can become factors to varying degrees, depending on the structural system used. For example, optimal design solutions usually call for different fenestration

patterns for office and residential uses, which can affect the placement of exterior columns. For interior columns, the optimal layout and number of supporting columns may be different for residential and office uses, leading to compromises that can increase costs or reduce efficiency. In addition, different uses often use different structural systems entirely, for example, concrete for residential in many parts of the country and steel for offices.

One innovative structural approach used at Paseo Colorado addresses several of these issues. The project involved demolition of an existing mall and the addition of new retail and residential facilities on top of an existing concrete parking garage, maintaining to the greatest extent possible the same structural grid as the garage. Above the two new levels of retail construction, the residential portion sits on its own concrete base, which is raised four feet (1.2 meters) above the retail roof. This separation allows for the horizontal routing of utilities in the four-foot (1.2-meter) plenum space; plenum space is often used for this reason in mixed-use projects. In addition, courtyards and paseos run throughout the project, allowing residences to open both outward to the street and inward to the courtyards and plazas.

A slightly different approach is to use an entirely new structural system that simply rests on top of the lower-level structure. At Janss Court in Santa Monica, the residential uses are wood-frame structures built on the roof of the office building, with entirely different structural systems and building footprints. The special technique allowed for Type V (Uniform Building Code [UBC]) fully sprinkled and fire-treated wood-frame construction for the apartments located on the top three floors, above four levels of office and retail space. The apartments sit on 6.5 inches (16.5 centimeters) of concrete over a three-inch (7.5-centimeter) metal deck. The composite deck has a two-hour fire rating. The first four floors of the building feature Type I (UBC) steel-frame construction; the seismic load of the wood-frame apartments is transferred to the steel-frame commercial building below.

The wood-frame construction provided substantial cost savings to the residential component of the structure and gave the top three floors of the building a distinctly residential look. This construction technique was not permitted in jurisdictions (such as neighboring Los Angeles) where the UBC is more strictly interpreted; for fire-fighting requirements, the UBC does not permit wood-frame construction above 55 feet (16.7 meters). In Janss Court, however, the city considered the first level of residential the equivalent of the ground level because fires would be fought from the terrace and not from the street level.

In larger towers, more advanced structural engineering solutions are sometimes used. At One Magnificent Mile, a mixed-use tower on North Michigan Avenue in Chicago that contains 1,026,536 square feet (95,400 square meters) of gross building area, a "bundled tube" was configured for the building's structure, including three reinforced concrete tubes rising 21, 49, and 57 stories.[4] The structure allows for flexible interior space to accommodate the varied layouts for the different uses. The development includes 69,398 square feet (6,450 square meters) of combined retail, restaurant, office, and mechanical space on the first through third floors; 352,028 square feet (32,720 square meters) of office space on the fourth through 19th floors; 5,023 square feet (465 square meters) of swimming, club, and mechanical facilities on the 20th and 21st floors; 465,287 square feet (43,000 square meters) of residential space (181 units) on the 22nd through 56th

floors; and 75,289 square feet (7,000 square meters) of underground parking (181 spaces).

Concrete was chosen over steel, because flat plates are more suitable for condominium floors, eliminating the need for a suspended ceiling and decreasing the floor-to-floor space. The condominium floors are only nine to ten feet (2.7 to 3 meters) from floor to floor, while the offices are twelve feet, six inches (3.8 meters) from floor to floor. The concrete tubes also allow more varied exterior wall openings. For example, the office floors have a uniform exterior grid of columns on 10-foot (3-meter) centers, while the grid on the condominium floors ranges from two feet, six inches to nine feet (0.8 to 2.7 meters) as a result of the location of various rooms. With a punched wall tube, these variations could be accommodated by modulating the spandrel depths to transfer loads appropriately.

Although each tube is similarly shaped, interior column placement and spacing differ in each. The 21-story west tube, which includes only offices, contains only four interior columns with 30-foot by 30-foot (9-meter by 9-meter) spacing. In the 57-story central tube, containing both office and residential uses and the elevator core, the spacing of interior columns is somewhat irregular and is based on the optimal layout for the residential floors. In the 49-story south tube, six columns are staggered in a 20-foot by 30-foot (six-meter by nine-meter) pattern, which was deemed the optimal configuration for residential, office, and parking uses contained in the tower. Floor

This six-story mixed-use building at 510 Glenwood in Raleigh, North Carolina, includes ground-level retail and restaurant space, two levels of office space, and three levels of residential space, all of them evident in the fenestration pattern of the facade.

construction also varies, with flat plates used in the condominium floors and flat slabs with drop panels used in the office and retail levels.

To accommodate differing structural requirements often means paying a higher construction cost per square foot, because the structural system must be able to accommodate all uses, often more expensive than a structural system for one single use, and because engineering the transitions between the uses, especially between office and residential/hotel, can also be expensive. Structural choices depend on many factors, but in general, the greater the vertical integration of structural components, the higher the construction cost per square foot. One of the most difficult combinations is to stack residential or hotel over office. The most common vertical mixing usually involves office or residential over retail, which is usually not problematic for small retail tenants but can be quite problematic when large retailers—with large open-floor requirements—are involved. Hotel and residential uses can generally be stacked without substantial problems.

Building Systems

Mechanical and building systems also require a different approach from those for single-use projects. HVAC, building control, and telecommunications systems all present both problems and opportunities.

Plumbing. One of the major system problems encountered when stacking uses is engineering the plumbing system so that the transition is smooth from the central plumbing of an office building to the dispersed plumbing in residential and hotel structures. Office and retail space need relatively simple plumbing compared with residential buildings or hotels. Offices usually include centrally located restrooms on each floor stacked vertically in the core and perhaps two or three kitchens per floor, depending on the size of the floor and the tenants. Retail stores generally have modest restrooms and plumbing near the rear of the store, although restaurants have more substantial needs. Residential and hotel structures, on the other hand, do not need central restrooms on upper floors and must provide for restrooms and/or kitchens in every residential unit or hotel room. Engineering the transition from a central-core plumbing system to a dispersed system can add significantly to the project's cost.

HVAC Systems. A mixed-use development can theoretically save significant amounts of money on the construction and operation of building HVAC systems, as it is often economically efficient to build one energy plant for the entire complex. With a central plant, energy use can be balanced throughout the day if peak power demands for each use occur at different times of the day. Although hotels and residences have their biggest draw at night, offices have their biggest draw during the day. Often retail space uses the most energy on weekends. Nevertheless, a well-designed and -integrated HVAC and energy system can be significantly more economical than that for a single-use building.

The huge Kuala Lumpur City Centre, with 8 million square feet (743,500 square meters) of office space (including the two Petronas Towers, tallest in the world), a hotel, a shopping center, and cultural facilities, is served by a 30,000-ton chilled water plant.

At Riverplace in Minneapolis, for example, the entire development shares a central boiler and cooling towers, which feed water to heat pumps and use the heat generated by the shops and restaurants to heat the apartments and offices. The system at Riverplace is based on a hot water core system that circulates water throughout the entire development. The water is used as a heat sink and allows for both heating and cooling during the entire year. At each place where heating or cooling is needed, an individually metered heat pump is used. An individual meter on each heat pump measures the amount of energy removed from the core water supply. On the basis of that use, the energy company, which is owned by the partnership that owns Riverplace, charges users.

This kind of system could work for many mixed-use developments. It includes a large boiler that is amortized over the many uses, a 14-inch (35-centimeter) pipe that goes through the entire development and gets smaller at the extremities, and individual heat pumps for each end use. A major disadvantage of the system is the relatively expensive maintenance on a great number of heat pumps (850 at Riverplace), each with an individual compressor that could break down. An advantage is the extreme flexibility for both heating and cooling and the potential economies when an energy management system is used.

At the huge Kuala Lumpur City Centre development, which includes 8 million square feet (743,500 square meters) of office space (including the two Petronas Towers, tallest in the world) as well as a hotel, shopping center, and cultural facilities, the development is served by a 30,000-ton chilled water plant, which is an optimized combination of natural gas–driven cogeneration equipment in concert with steam turbine–driven chillers and electric chillers. The development was the first in Malaysia to be served by the district cooling that uses natural gas as the primary energy source for its air-conditioning system.

Shared energy systems can create certain problems of management, however, especially in allocating charges equitably between uses that generate heat and those that use it. Moreover, when separate financing is used for individual components, it is often desirable to keep all building systems separate.

Telecommunications Systems. Advanced telecommunications and intelligent community systems are also being included in new mixed-use developments. Santana Row in San Jose, for example, teamed up with Cisco Systems and HP to create a sophisticated intelligent community that includes an end-to-end converged Cisco IP network providing high-bandwidth Internet access to every resident, retail outlet, and hotel guest via Category 5 cable. To initiate an Internet connection, users simply plug their computers into the data connection at their residence, office, or hotel room and launch a Web browser. The developers also wanted to deliver Internet access throughout the open spaces and public areas of the project, so

Santana Row in San Jose includes an advanced telecommunications and intelligent community system.

the system includes a wireless local area network. Santana Row placed access point antennas to provide coverage from many of the community's park areas as well as several public areas in buildings, including outdoor dining areas in restaurants, coffee shops, cafés, and hotel lobbies. The antennas are fully enclosed in the buildings.[5]

Redevelopment and Historic Preservation

Redevelopment, historic preservation, and adaptive use continue to be important elements in mixed-use development. Historic buildings generally offer a certain identity and character that may serve to create a valued link with the past, adding richness, continuity, and image to a mixed-use development.

Redevelopment and historic preservation, for purposes of this book, are grouped in two broad categories: 1) preservation and/or adaptive use of an older building in a mixed-use development; and 2) reconfiguration or addition of new space to a large existing project or district. Objectives for these kinds of projects can vary widely, ranging from a desire to incorporate historic character and charm into a new project to revitalizing an existing building or district to respond to the public's desire for preservation.

Using Older Buildings in Mixed-Use Developments

Old and often historic buildings are often used as featured components and signatures for mixed-use developments. In some cases, an isolated historic building is preserved, while in others, several historic buildings are involved. Occasionally, single historic structures have been transformed into mixed-use structures. And increasingly, older buildings that are not historic are being reused in mixed-use schemes.

Often the preservation of older buildings is a source of tension during the development process for many mixed-use developments, especially when numerous buildings of varying historic quality are involved. The decision about which buildings should be preserved and which should be destroyed and the tradeoffs between historic character, modern functionality, and optimal design are often hotly contested by developers, public officials, preservationists, and community groups.

Preserving buildings is particularly important and sometimes problematic in mixed-use design, because these buildings are already in place and usually cannot be moved; they often serve as a focal point around which the design revolves, but they also must be incorporated into a plan and design that positions the various uses to best advantage, in some cases creating thorny problems for the developer and in many cases fundamentally shaping the plan.

In several recent examples, the historic buildings became centerpieces and focal points for the projects. At CityPlace in West Palm Beach (see Chapter 8), for example, a historic church was transformed into a performing arts theater surrounded by a central plaza and fountain, all of which serve as the central place and signature space for the development. Originally the First United Methodist Church, this 51,786-square-foot (4,800-square-meter) structure is one of the finest examples of Spanish Colonial Revival architecture of its time. The interior of the three-story facility is architecturally significant because of details like original open-truss cypress ceilings, a tiered mezzanine, and large divided windows overlooking the main floor. The structure of the building comprises steel columns and beams. Exterior walls are hollow clay with a moderately textured stucco surface. Cast concrete ornamentation is present on all facades. Only minor alterations have been made to the building since 1926. Over the years, many of the windows on the ground floor were enclosed and covered.

The former church is now named the Harriet Himmel Gilman Theater for Cultural and Performing Arts in honor of Mrs. Gilman's generous gift to complete its

The owner of Cabin John Center in Montgomery County, Maryland, is pursuing a plan to transform the strip shopping center into a mixed-use town center by adding additional retail, a main street, residential uses, and parking structures.

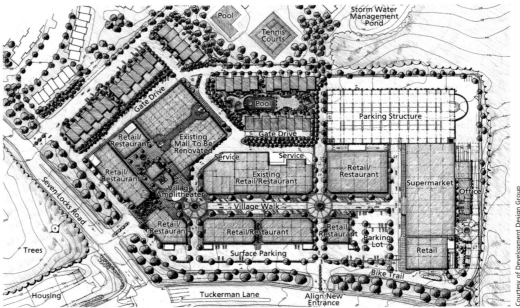

restoration. The Harriet is the centerpiece of CityPlace, and its architectural style is an important model for the basic design philosophy of the entire development. The venue offers a wide variety of cultural programming, including music, dance and theater. It is also available for special events, receptions, banquets, meetings, and other activities. The performance hall is 11,000 square feet (1,020 square meters) with retractable seating that can accommodate 400 to 850 people for theater performances, 900 guests for receptions, banquet-style seating for 600, and up to 60 units for trade show exhibitions.

Old industrial buildings can also serve as signature elements. The Ritz-Carlton Hotel and Residences Georgetown, located in the heart of historic, vibrant Georgetown in Washington, D.C., is an upscale mixed-use development that incorporates several historic buildings. The $150 million, 500,000-square-foot (46,500-square-meter) development includes a 93-room Ritz-Carlton Hotel, 30

luxury residences, a multiplex theater, 10,000 square feet (930 square meters) of retail shops, and more than 600 parking spaces. The various components of the development are arranged around existing streets and a series of landscaped courtyards in a diverse community of uses, well integrated into the fabric of the neighborhood.

A central feature of the development is the former municipal incinerator building, constructed in 1932 and operated as the neighborhood incinerator until 1971. This red brick, industrial, art deco–style building, which includes a landmark brick smokestack that is one of the tallest structures in Washington, is the centerpiece of the project and has been restored to serve as the central lobby of the complex. In addition, the developers ensured the careful preservation of three historic homes on the site, including the Brickyard Hill House, built in 1800 and owned by the first mayor of Georgetown. The house was temporarily moved off the property to prepare the land for development and then returned to the property, where it was restored and incorporated into the project's design.

In some cases, existing mixed-use projects have embraced the redevelopment of adjacent historic buildings and integrated them into the overall development concept. For example, the newest (yet oldest) structure at Embarcadero Center (which first opened in the 1970s) in San Francisco is the old Federal Reserve bank building, recently reborn as an office building and spectacular venue for special events. Originally completed in 1924, the landmark building was acquired by the Embarcadero Center owners in 1982 and fully restored to its original splendor; it is now included in the National Register of Historic Places. Eight of its nine floors are used for office space, but the historic banking hall on the main floor is now the setting for private parties and corporate events, and the space has become a signature venue for the development.

Among the case studies in this book, WestEnd City Center involved the restoration of a historic customs house now used for office space. The building, considered a historic structure, had fallen into disuse. The developer—TriGranit—agreed to restore the building as a condition of allowing new development on the remainder of the site. TriGranit absorbed the cost of the renovation, and today the building, with a lofty atrium flooded with natural light, houses some of the offices of TriGranit staff, with additional space available to other users.

University Park at MIT involved the restoration and adaptive use of two historic buildings. The Jackson Building, a five-story industrial loft building that was once a Sears shoe factory, was renovated for R&D use. And the F.A. Kennedy Steam Bakery, where Fig Newtons were created, was converted into the Kennedy Biscuit Lofts rental apartment units and the Bright Horizons Child Care Center.

Buildings that are old but not particularly historic have also been incorporated in mixed-use developments. At Mockingbird Station in Dallas, the existing telephone company switching warehouse on the property was structured in a manner such that four levels could be added above the existing warehouse at minimal structural cost. And the proposed redevelopment plans for the Cabin John strip shopping center in Montgomery County, Maryland, involve building new residential, office, and parking structures—around the existing retail buildings—on parking lots and other underused land.

Single buildings can also be transformed into mixed-use structures, but developing a mixed-use project in a single existing building can present substantial challenges —and pitfalls—and not many have been completed to date. Preserving and modernizing an older building for only one use can be very difficult: costs are difficult to estimate because of unforeseen structural problems, and older buildings are often not optimally efficient by today's standards, even after renovation. To make a mixed-use project work in an existing structure, it is usually neces-sary to substantially alter the structure, especially the interior, to accommodate new uses.

Some adaptations of single buildings have involved new construction atop old buildings. Queen's Quay Terminal in Toronto—originally a terminal warehouse on the Toronto waterfront—was converted into a mixed-use building with a major specialty retail center of 100,000 square feet (9,300 square meters) on two levels, nearly 400,000 square feet (37,000 square meters) of office space on six levels, and 170,000 square feet (16,000 square meters) of luxury condominiums on four newly constructed levels atop the eight-story structure. Numerous atriums in the poured concrete structure create a functional contemporary design. The very attractive project has become an important focus of urban activity in Toronto.

To create a true mixed-use development within an existing building, the building must be large and flexible. In some cases, it is better if the building is relatively undistinguished so that substantial alterations to the structure can proceed without major opposition. At the same time, the building must be essentially structurally sound with some historic character that contributes to the identity of its context to make preservation and adaptive use worthwhile. Other examples of converting a single building into a mixed-use facility include ASQ Center in Milwaukee, which includes office, hotel, and retail uses in a historic department store, and the Denver Dry Goods Building (see the accompanying feature box).

Redeveloping Existing Districts with Mixed Uses

Many existing urban districts are to varying degrees mixed-use districts, but in many cases cities and developers undertake plans and projects to strengthen them, which often results in the creation of mixed-use developments within mixed- or multiuse districts. In this situation, the principal development and design problem becomes one of creating links, filling gaps, and expanding the existing configuration.

Urban and historic districts can provide excellent opportunities for mixed uses because they often contain diverse uses and building types and because they often need full-scale revitalization. In some cases, the urban fabric is so deteriorated that it can be mended only by providing a full complement of uses and services. Moreover, such areas often have a special character and sense of place that can support quite diverse activities and uses.

One early example of such an effort is the South Street Seaport in New York City, a collection of old buildings and piers configured on several blocks along the East River. This mixed-use development included the renovation and adaptive use of numerous historic structures and piers for office, retail, residential, museum, and recreational uses and the construction of several new retail and office buildings. At the time it was established, the primary purpose of the Special South Street Seaport District, within which the project was developed, was to encourage the preservation, restoration, and rede-

For nearly 100 years, the Denver Dry Goods department store served as the retail heart of downtown Denver. Built in 1888 and added onto three times over the years, the 350,000-square-foot (32,500-square-meter) Denver Dry was the city's premier department store for generations of Denver residents. But fortunes change, and in 1987 the building was sold and the store closed.

The Denver Dry Goods Building occupies the entire frontage of California Street from 15th Street to 16th Street. The building is located strategically: it sits where the 16th Street Pedestrian/Transitway Mall joins the light-rail system, which began operation in fall 1994. The Denver Dry also links the convention center, retail business district, and downtown hotels.

The Denver Dry Goods Building was erected in 1888 as a three-story structure occupying half the California Street frontage closest to 16th Street. The red brick, sand-stone, and limestone structure was designed by Frank D. Edbrooks, the architect of several notable Denver buildings, including the historic Brown Palace Hotel. In 1898, a fourth story was added to the original structure, and in 1906, a six-story addition was constructed on the 15th Street side of the original building. In one last expansion, in 1924, an additional two stories were constructed on top of the original building, which became the location of the Denver Tearoom.

With the beloved Denver Dry facing destruction, the Denver Urban Renewal Authority (DURA) stepped in and purchased the building in 1988. After several false starts, DURA selected the Affordable Housing Development Corporation (AHDC) as project developer, and together, DURA and AHDC have managed to resurrect the Denver Dry, fashioning it into a vibrant mixed-use project of affordable and market-rate housing, retail, and office space. Ultimately, the key to the Denver Dry's resurrection was an echo of its past: just as the building was built in increments, so its reconstruction and reuse were accomplished piece by piece. The mammoth structure was broken down, figuratively and legally, into smaller condominium units to provide for more manageable and financeable packages of development. In these smaller pieces, separate housing, retail, and office units could be planned and then variously bundled together into financing and construction packages.

The plan that ultimately took shape provided for three development phases. Phase I consisted of 51 units of affordable and market-rate housing, 73,370 square feet (6,800 square meters) of retail space, and 28,700 square feet (2,700 square meters) of office space. Phase II consisted of an additional 42,000 square feet (3,900 square meters) of retail space, and Phase III added 66 for-sale residential units in approximately 77,000 square feet (7,100 square meters).

The first phase of development, completed in October 1993, concentrated on the 15th Street building and one floor of the 16th Street building. Waxman's Camera and Video took over the first floor and basement of the 15th Street building. National retailer TJ Maxx committed to taking most of the second floor of the 15th Street and 16th Street buildings with the proviso that an escalator be installed to provide direct access from the street to the second floor. The remainder of the second and third floors of the 15th Street building was improved for office use, and the top three floors of the building were renovated for housing. The housing use takes advantage of its

The Denver Dry Goods Building is a landmark department store in downtown Denver that has been reborn as a mixed-use development with office, residential, and retail uses.

height and the building's large windows to afford spectacular views of Denver and the Rocky Mountains beyond. Construction of this phase lasted ten months.

During Phase II, the first floor and basement of the 16th Street building were converted to retail space and leased by Media Play. Phase II took seven months to complete. The remaining portions of the 16th Street building, floors three through six, were renovated as for-sale housing.

Renovation to the exterior of the building included the removal of more than 30 layers of white lead-based paint to expose the original orange-red brick, sandstone, and limestone surface of the building. This process took eight months to complete and cost $800,000. The original wood windows were renovated and retrofitted with double-pane glass. In addition, new canopies and signage were installed.

The interior of the Denver Dry Goods Building was gutted except for historic elements to allow building in phases. Architectural plans for the reconfiguration of the approximately 50,000-square-foot (4,600-square-meter) floor plates provided for separate, dedicated elevators for the housing and office uses, reusing the existing department store elevator banks. New, direct access was provided to the second-floor retail space.

Significant fire and life safety improvements were made all at once for the entire building. In addition, new HVAC and electrical systems were installed. Evaporative coolers were installed in lieu of central air conditioning in the apartments, and city steam was used for heating.

For the housing component, the challenges for designers were to use the deep bays of the existing space and to bring light to these deep interiors. Solutions included wide hallways with adjacent leasable storage units and the provision of clerestory windows to light interior bedrooms.

For the office space, the greatest challenge was to provide space for new HVAC systems while respecting the high window openings of the historic structure. Designers decided to construct dropped soffits in part of the space while maintaining the original 18-foot-high (5.5-meter) ceilings along window walls and other significant areas.

■

South Street Seaport is a historic seaport area of New York that has been transformed into a lively mixed-use district with office, retail, residential, museum, and recreational uses.

velopment of properties and buildings in the area. The district was targeted to be a type of "museum"—an area of the city with special cultural, recreational, and retail activities.

Another example is Waterfront Place in Seattle, a mixed-use development that combines six historic buildings with four new structures in the redevelopment of a six-block neighborhood in Seattle's central waterfront district. The development's mix of rehabilitation and new construction was carefully planned to create an urban neighborhood that would fit into the existing fabric of downtown Seattle. The six existing buildings that were restored are included in the National Register of Historic Places. The scheme was to create a mixed-use development that is integrated into the existing streetscape and street fabric and that preserves and enhances the neighborhood's diverse urban character. Rather than being extended to the maximum allowable heights, the new buildings were constructed to the scale and architectural character of the existing mid-rise structures. Among the case studies in this book, Peabody Place in Memphis (see Chapter 8) provides a good example as well, and Tower City Center in Cleveland (see the accompanying feature box) provides an example of the restoration and redevelopment of a historic district that was in fact developed from the start as a mixed-use development in the 1930s.

Perhaps the most common present examples of redeveloping existing districts are the restoration and redevel-

Tower City Center is a downtown mixed-use project that incorporates much of the original Cleveland Union Terminal mixed-use project, first built in the 1930s. The complex includes numerous large older structures and existing facilities, including the landmark Terminal Tower and a transit station. The redeveloped complex includes more than 360,000 square feet (33,500 square meters) of redeveloped and expanded retail shops on three levels, an 11-screen cinema complex, more than 1 million square feet (93,000 square meters) of office space in three historic buildings and two new buildings, a 208-room luxury hotel, new transit station waiting areas and accessways, and 3,150 parking spaces. It is physically connected to Dillard's department store, a newly renovated 500-room hotel, two additional office buildings, and the city's new stadium and arena. The Terminal Tower, a landmark in downtown Cleveland, furnishes an important entranceway into the complex but is under separate ownership.

The project acts as an important central activity point for all of downtown Cleveland, linking the busy transit station, central business and shopping activities, and major public sports and cultural facilities. With other significant private and public investment in downtown, it has been a catalyst for revitalization of the city's CBD. The developer worked with RTKL Associates to design a functional and attractive retail space in the cramped, dark, stodgy setting of the historic buildings. Together, they spent considerable effort in determining building components and spaces that could be preserved and negotiated major changes in the existing transit station areas and accessways.

The project site occupies 34 acres (13.7 hectares) centered in a triangular five-block section of Cleveland's downtown. When acquired by Forest City Enterprises, the structures consisted of the Terminal Tower, the abandoned rail terminal, including a 50,000-square-foot (4,600-square-meter) retail arcade stretching from the Terminal Tower through the rail terminal, and the foundation structure, including a number of bridges for city streets and foundation supports constructed in the 1920s for buildings never developed.

Although the Terminal Tower was in fairly good condition and had a number of attractive features, including a handsome entrance portico with a decorated barrel-vaulted ceiling and wall murals, the remainder of the space presented many design problems. The two-level retail arcade was drab and dark. The rail terminal building contained no grand spaces such as those in the Washington, D.C., and St. Louis terminals—just a modest waiting area with faux classic columns around the walls and a vast area of back-of-the-house office and storage space. The station platforms were reached from three concourses that split the retail space. The platforms themselves were dark and uninviting.

The planners and architects set out to design an attractive retail mall that would retain as much of the historic structures as feasible, given the change in building use. Working within the existing axes of the site and buildings, the designers created a series of three grand spaces for the retail mall. The first, Tower Court, is between wings of the Terminal Tower. The second, Station Court, located under Prospect Avenue, surrounds the transit station entrances. The Skylight Concourse, the third and largest of the spaces, faces the river and is covered by an arched glass skylight reminiscent of old railway stations. At the riverfront edge of the Skylight Concourse, a two-level food court sits above a two-level underground parking structure in space formerly occupied by train tracks. In all

Tower City Center involved the redevelopment of the Cleveland Union Terminal complex, a historic mixed-use development and district built in the 1930s that is a landmark in the heart of downtown Cleveland.

Courtesy of Forest City Enterprises

three spaces, fountains and decorative art and sculpture create interesting centers of activity. The retail arcade connects through restored portals with the adjacent hotel and Dillard's department store.

Beneath the new retail mall, the transit-related renovations included moving the old station nearer the center of the project, building new platforms and waiting rooms, improving track and escalator systems, designing pedestrian access through the retail spaces, and constructing an atrium to open up the transit space to the retail arcade. These major alterations in the original transit configuration created more compatible and convenient spaces for both transit passengers and retail shoppers.

On either side of the Skylight Concourse on the south side of Prospect Avenue, the architects used the old foundation columns as bases for a new 360,000-square-foot (33,500-square-meter), 13-story office building and a 208-room Ritz-Carlton Hotel with four additional floors of office space. Both can be entered directly from the retail arcade, although the hotel lobby on the sixth floor is accessed by elevators. The developer created a new passage under West Third Street into the former post office, now the MK-Ferguson Plaza building, where the designers refurbished the lobby's art deco marble floor, transaction windows, and writing desks and carved out two large atriums from the massive floor plates to bring natural light to interior office spaces.

Significant design elements of the historic structures have been incorporated in the redeveloped complex. The small retail arcade in the old central concourse was largely retained in its original layout. The decorated ceiling and wall murals in the Terminal Tower entranceway were cleaned, regilded, and repainted. Lighting fixtures in the rail terminal building were restored and rehung, some in their original places. Large decorative medallions from the former arcade railings were incorporated in the new balustrades throughout the project. Classic columns in the old waiting room were retained in the Skylight Concourse of the new arcade. Doorways to public streets were retained and restored.

Construction began in 1988, and the retail mall opened in March 1990 to wide acclaim and interest. The office buildings and hotel also proved successful, even during the recession of 1990 and 1991.

■

Historic Westside Village in Atlanta involved renovation and new development within the existing street fabric to create a new urban village.

Courtesy of Altamira

opment of existing main streets into mixed-use districts and town centers. These projects generally retain the existing street fabric but often include the addition of new low-rise retail and mid-rise office or apartment buildings. One recent example is Historic Westside Village in Atlanta, which will involve both new development and historic buildings but will work largely within the existing street fabric to create a new mixed-use urban village. The plan calls for a grocery store, movie theaters, restaurants, townhouses, condominiums and lofts, and shops.

Another is Bethesda Row, a multiphase mixed-use redevelopment project in the heart of Bethesda, Maryland. Four phases have been completed, and future phases are in planning. Together, the first three phases feature 110,000 square feet (10,200 square meters) of office space, 190,000 square feet (17,600 square meters) of retail space, and 40,000 square feet (3,700 square meters) of restaurants; the fourth phase includes a new office building with ground-level retail. The project has helped to turn this formerly neglected part of Bethesda's downtown into an attractive and vital part of the community. During Phases I and II, the development team renovated existing structures; during Phase I, it also built a new structure to house Barnes & Noble. Phase I involved structural renovations and facade improvements to the existing two-story building and streetscape improvements, including a new fountain and plaza on the corner of the site. Phase II involved the renovation and retenanting of the existing low-rise building on the site. Both Phase III and Phase IV involved exclusively new construction. From very early in the development process, Federal Realty's goal was to develop a distinctive project with an urban character. The development team traveled to other successful main street projects around the country to try to identify the characteristics and qualities that made them successful, concluding that it was a mix of variety, vitality, and visual interest that made them what they were.

Redesigning and Renovating Existing Mixed-Use Projects

Mixed-use properties, like all real estate, require periodic renovation and updating to remain current—in some cases, substantial redesign and reconfiguration. In fact, many of the mixed-use properties developed in the 1960s, 1970s, and 1980s, it is now quite evident, were to varying degrees poorly configured. There is considerable room for improving the sense of place and performance of these assets through redesign and redevelopment.

Many of these early projects are megastructures, monolithic, and/or not well integrated with the surrounding urban environment. They are usually enclosed, often focused around a mall or retail concourse, with few quality outdoor public spaces. Most important, the pedestrian experience is poor in many of these projects.

The solutions vary greatly, but a few recent prominent examples are instructive. One is to refine and open up an enclosed project, illustrated by the Renaissance Center (see below). A second is to add a sense of place by creating a main street to a parcelized project connected by concourses, illustrated by Crystal City. A third is to transform a development connected by windswept plazas by filling in empty spaces and adding a retail galleria that connects the various uses under skylights, illustrated by the regeneration of Prudential Center, described on the facing page.

In some cases, the renovation does not involve a major redesign, just an update. Mixed-use towers, for example, are not easily modified, but they do not necessarily require major modifications except at ground-level pedestrian areas. For example, at the John Hancock Center in Chicago, a recent $22.5 million redevelopment of a mixed-use tower first built in the 1960s has successfully revitalized the structure that launched Michigan Avenue into the Magnificent Mile. When awarded the assignment in late 1992, U.S. Equities recommended modify-

The Renaissance Center in Detroit, now known as the GM Renaissance Center, has been reconfigured to make it more pedestrian- and user-friendly, including the redesign of both streetside and waterside entrances and the addition of a waterfront promenade and a glass-enclosed winter garden.

ing the approved plans to include enhanced Michigan Avenue retail space, dedicated observatory and office entrances and elevator lobbies, an expanded parking facility, and a redesigned plaza. Following the redevelopment, office occupancy levels increased from 47 percent at the end of 1992 to 91 percent in 1999. The redesign of the building's retail space, which had been largely vacant for several year, achieved 98 percent occupancy following the renovation.

Reconfiguration of Enclosed Space at Renaissance Center
Perhaps the most prominent example of the problems that many older mixed-use projects face is the Renaissance Center in Detroit, which was recently substantially redesigned and redeveloped. Purchased by General Motors Corporation (GM) in October 1996, the 5.5-million-square-foot (511,000-square-meter) Renaissance Center (Phase I) is located in the heart of downtown Detroit. GM engaged Hines to lead the redevelopment and asset and facility management for the complex. Renaissance Center includes four 39-story office towers totaling 2.6 million square feet (242,000 square meters) that surround a 74-story, 1,342-room hotel. The top-to-bottom renovation of the Renaissance Center is one of the largest renovations of its kind anywhere in the world.

Much of the redevelopment has been focused on the first five levels (400,000 square feet [37,000 square meters]), including creation of the five-story, glass-enclosed winter garden; reconfiguration of the retail space to create 150,000 square feet (14,000 square meters) of retail and professional service space, including more than 20 retail tenants plus 18 restaurants and specialty food stores; creation of a 35,000-square-foot (3,250-square-meter) GM museum and a 40,000-square-foot (3,700-square-meter) exhibit space; and creation of a 12-foot-wide (3.6-meter) glass circulation walkway accessible from all four office towers. Entrances and parking have also been improved.

Redevelopment included several other key elements:

- Front Entrance and New Grand Gallery—The updated plan includes a new front entrance for GM world headquarters. The cement berms on Jefferson Avenue have been removed and replaced by a glass and steel entry leading to the grand gallery and multistory welcoming center. The state-of-the-art facility includes a spacious, expansive, curvilinear design.
- Winter Garden—The new enclosed glass atrium provides a panoramic view of the Detroit River and Canada. The soaring, five-story structure includes sculptures, flowering plants, and trees, and includes indoor and outdoor cafés and restaurants and new retail outlets in an outer perimeter area. The atrium faces the new riverfront promenade alongside the Detroit River. The pedestrian walkway will be enhanced with trees, potted flowers, and benches.
- Renaissance Center Towers—The four office towers of Renaissance Center have been renovated as well. Each tower features new floor plans, updated eleva-

tors, and new furnishings. At least 7,000 GM employees will be located in the four Class A office towers. A new circular glass walkway was constructed around the hotel's second level to provide office workers and visitors with better circulation and accessibility among the towers.
- GM University—The automobile manufacturer has created a virtual university on the second level between Towers 200 and 300. More than 1,400 courses are offered to salaried employees through GM University. The facility includes classrooms with computers, meeting rooms, and a lounge.
- Detroit Marriott Renaissance Center—The 1,342-room hotel, America's second tallest, has undergone a $100 million transformation. The hotel, formerly known as the Westin Hotel Renaissance Center, features a new third-floor lobby with restaurants, cocktail lounges, and concierge service. The existing lobby has been transformed into a baggage area. The Summit, the hotel's revolving 71st-floor restaurant, has been completely transformed to a fine dining venue. The Riverfront Ballroom has been converted into a 350-seat, full-service restaurant and a new grand ballroom built in its place. Other existing ballrooms and meeting rooms and the hotel rooms have also been renovated. Renovations were completed in 2001.
- Parking Structures—The GM world headquarters features three new parking structures. The Franklin Street garage was constructed east of the Renaissance Center in 1998 and can accommodate 600 vehicles on five levels. The second parking structure, a 2,000-vehicle garage completed in 2000, includes commercial space on the first two levels. A third parking structure was completed in 2001.[6]

Addition of a Main Street to Crystal City
Crystal City in Arlington, Virginia, is an expansive mixed-use district that includes offices, apartments, a hotel, a transit station, and retail facilities. Although it consists of a large number of freestanding buildings, it has few compelling public spaces, and most of its retail space is located in underground or internal concourses. Most of the space in the project has performed very well over the years, and vacancies remain low, but the developers believe they can improve the project's performance by strengthening its sense of place through the creation of a main street for the project. Planning is now in progress.

Developer Smith Commercial Realty and designer Cooper Carry developed a master plan design that converts the complex from a 1960s, internally oriented, office superblock to a street-oriented, 18-hour office/retail environment. Beginning with realignment of the infrastructure, the plan calls for converting a one-way, commuter-oriented traffic pattern to a two-way, pedestrian-friendly system that reconnects primary corridors, simplifies intersections, and normalizes the sense of orientation. Among the 7 million square feet (651,000 square meters) of commercial office space, the plan proposes a new streetfront of cutting-edge, complementary architecture

Crystal City, a large multi-building mixed-use project in Arlington, Virginia, is connected by an enclosed retail concourse. The streetscape along Crystal Drive is being reconfigured to create a new retail main street.

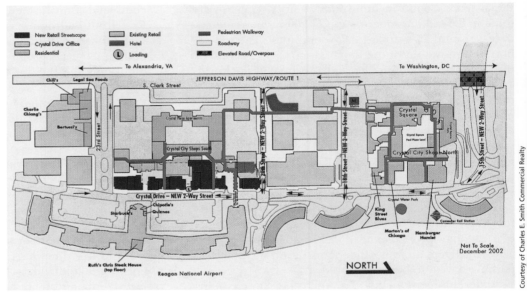

containing office lofts, a performing arts theater, an urban grocery, theme restaurants, and retail anchors.

The initial focus for redevelopment will likely be the creation of a pedestrian-scale destination retail environment along the west side of Crystal Drive from South 18th Street to South 23rd Street. "This is precisely what the Board is looking for in Arlington," says Jay Fisette, County Board chair. "Street-level retail will make the area more attractive for pedestrians and will create an atmosphere of community in this highly developed portion of Arlington."

Smith Commercial Realty will demolish an existing parking structure and develop 134,050 square feet (12,500 square meters) of ground-floor retail space with up to 84,034 square feet (7,800 square meters) of second-floor office or retail space. The amended site plan also includes significant pedestrian space with new sidewalks and street trees along the north side of 23rd Street and the west side of Crystal Drive as well as 13 additional crosswalks.

A major crossing with a pedestrian-activated signal will be constructed mid-block between South 20th and 23rd streets across Crystal Drive. Smith also plans to enhance the existing park on the east side of Crystal Drive at the mid-block crossing to improve the connection to the new plaza proposed for the new retail section on the west side.

Reconfiguration and Infill Development at Prudential Center

It took ten years to complete the initial 7 million square feet (650,000 square feet) of Prudential Center, one of the first large-scale mixed-use projects to be conceived and developed during the postwar urban redevelopment period. City government and the Boston Redevelopment Agency encouraged the development with tax breaks. Standing 52 stories high, its central tower became Boston's tallest building, serving as a catalyst for the revitalization of the city in the 1960s.

When the first of the Pruden- tial Center's towers opened in 1964, it was the tallest tower in North America outside New York and one of the most fa- mous in Boston. In the recent redevelopment, many buildings were added to the project, in- cluding a 36-story office tower, an 11-story office building, residential buildings, and 90,000 square feet (8,400 square meters) of additional retail space.

Although the office and residential components of the project were commercial successes, the original com- plex failed as urban design. Built over former railroad yards and an extension of the Massachusetts Turnpike, the center sits on an elevated platform above the street plane where the Back Bay and South End grids converge. But the reigning design concept of the era—a tower on an open plaza—was inconsistent with the traditional development patterns of the city. As a result, the wind- swept plaza was isolated from the surrounding neigh- borhoods. Retailers suffered. The original site plan featured a ring road that isolated the center from the surrounding streets, discouraging pedestrian circula- tion and access.

In the 1980s, thanks to a new economic cycle, Pruden- tial Development realized that a major redevelopment was feasible. The addition of more than 3 million square feet (279,000 square meters) would help to transform the aging center into a contemporary destination that

could compete with Copley Place, its successful, newer mixed-use neighbor.

In the late 1990s, as the resurgent economy made Boston one of the hottest markets in the country, Boston Properties bought the commercial components of the center and acquired the as-yet-unbuilt development rights to the complex. The existence of the master plan, for which the firm assumed responsibility as part of the sale, facilitated the current wave of construction, including major improvements and new buildings: a 36-story, 850,000-square-foot (79,000-square-meter) office tower; a 130,000-square-foot (12,000-square-meter) residential building; an 11-story, 200,000-square-foot (18,600-square- meter) office building; a 70,000-square-foot (6,500-square- meter) neighborhood market; a 400,000-square-foot (37,000-square-meter) mixed-use building with a large residential component; 90,000 square feet (8,400 square meters) of additional retail space; and a 20,000-square- foot (1,800-square-meter) enclosed pedestrian walkway that connects to the existing second-level retail arcade. Estimated costs for the acquisition, construction, and complete repositioning of the center put Boston Properties's total long-term investment at nearly $1 billion.

The remaking of the Prudential Center relies on a variety of design interventions intended to integrate the project into the surrounding neighborhoods and help create a lively, accessible mix of uses on the plaza level and a memorable icon that can be seen across the city. An overall goal of the redevelopment is to connect the isolated center with adjacent residential neighborhoods. New buildings are sited at the edges of the complex, and a system of pedestrian circulation and retail corridors, and links to transportation were integrated to increase access through and to the center. These new uses also respond to the surrounding communities' desire for more public space and the everyday needs of office and residential tenants.

The cornerstone of the new development—111 Huntington Avenue—updates Prudential's identity. The low-rise portion of the building, quiet in its expression, is clad in traditional materials—precast concrete, glass, and aluminum—that harmonize with the surrounding commercial avenue. In contrast, the aluminum and glass tower makes a dramatic architectural statement in the immediate area and on the city's skyline.

The new winter garden improves pedestrian connections with the Back Bay and South End neighborhoods. An indoor linear park, which combines open space and paths for circulation, is 50 feet (15 meters) wide and has a 35-foot-high (10-meter) ceiling. It also creates a grand entrance to 111 Huntington and provides a new connection to the subway station below. Lined by retail shops on one side, the winter garden includes abundant seating areas and serves as an extension of a new 1.2-acre (0.5-hectare) outdoor park. Numerous other buildings and uses have been added to enhance the mix and design.[7]

The Importance of Design

In the end, mixed-use design is about creating a sense of place while efficiently and effectively meeting the design and program needs of all uses in the development. To do so takes considerable effort and attention from designers, developers, and numerous other team members. Good design can create compelling and memorable spaces and places for a variety of markets and users that should create premiums for the owner and the larger community. Bad design will squander the advantages offered by mixed-use development and may lead to compromises or conflicts between uses that can ruin the project. Failing to provide well-thought-out design solutions will create operational problems that will be difficult to solve and sometimes remain long after construction is finished. Good mixed-use design takes time, money, and considerable talent, none of which should be short-changed during the development process.

Site plan for the Prudential Center in Boston.

A street scene at Salt Lake City Gateway in Utah.

Notes

1. www.mccafferyinterests.com, accessed January 11, 2003.

2. For more information about urban parks and greens, see Alexander Garvin, et. al., *Urban Parks and Open Space* (Washington, D.C.: ULI–the Urban Land Institute, 1997); and Peter Harnik, *Inside City Parks* (Washington, D.C.: ULI–the Urban Land Institute, 2000).

3. Charles C. Bohl, *Place Making: Developing Town Centers, Main Streets, and Urban Villages* (Washington, D.C.: ULI–the Urban Land Institute, 2002), pp. 291–292.

4. Material on One Magnificent Mile adapted from Christopher Olson, "A New Gateway to Chicago's Michigan Avenue," *Building, Design, and Construction,* October 1984, pp. 78–83.

5. *Santana Row: Building an Advanced Networking Community.* White Paper (San Jose and Palo Alto: Cisco Systems and HP). www.cisco.com, accessed January 30, 2003.

6. Adapted from www.ci.detroit.mi.us and www.hines.com, accessed September 30, 2002.

7. Adapted from Charles N. Tseckares, "The Politics of Development," *Urban Land,* September 2001, pp. 78–81.

6. Marketing and Promotion

Marketing for a mixed-use project should begin early in the development process with a strategy for the overall project. This umbrella strategy recognizes that, although the marketing for each component of the project tends to follow a "best practices" marketing strategy for that specific product, the market advantage of location in a mixed-use development needs to be part of the marketing strategy for each component. This chapter focuses first on the overall marketing of a mixed-use development and then on marketing relationships and methods for each of the most common components.

The marketing strategy for a mixed-use project begins to evolve as the project is conceived. When a land use is considered for inclusion in the project, its potential to add to the marketability of the overall project needs to be determined. Likewise, its inclusion in a mixed-use project should also be examined to determine whether association with a mixed-use project will improve its marketability. Ideally, every use in a mixed-use project does both, but developers frequently report that the synergy among uses in mixed-use projects did not meet their expectations. A superior marketing strategy defines and builds on potential synergistic relationships while making sure that each component stands on its own merit.

An office building entrance at Mizner Park in Boca Raton, Florida. Public sector involvement and a pioneering town center concept generated considerable interest in the project.

Potential synergistic factors are identified in the market and feasibility analyses conducted initially and then updated as planning and design for the project are undertaken. The objective of an overall marketing strategy for a mixed-use project should be to aggressively market these synergistic factors to the benefit of the project's overall success.

Initial Marketing Strategies

The earliest marketing efforts occur before the project is even committed to or formally announced; they are oriented toward attracting major tenants for the office and retail components and a major hotel operator for the hotel if one is contemplated. In many cases, the financial feasibility of the project hinges on having letters of intent from key tenants. Because residential marketing does not seek major tenants, promotion of the residential component generally begins closer to when the residential component starts construction.

Developing a Marketing and Promotion Strategy
The size of the overall marketing budget should be commensurate with the size of the mixed-use development, the number and scale of the components, and the competitive market where the project will be undertaken. The marketing strategy for every mixed-use project is different from the separate marketing strategy for any

A rendering of the development concept for Cathedral City Downtown in Cathedral City, California, a publicly initiated town center that includes civic, commercial, and residential uses. Renderings can be important tools in the early marketing and promotion of a mixed-use project.

component. Thus, the overall marketing budget needs to provide sufficient funds to support opportunities for more varied and innovative marketing approaches than are needed for a single-use project.

A Balanced Approach. The challenge is to devise an approach that balances the need to promote the project as a whole while also actively marketing each component as a distinct entity. For the project, marketing should focus on creating a sense of place and image that will result in high name recognition and an association with superior quality and therefore garner a premium in the marketplace. Marketing for each component can then build on the project's reputation in the marketplace.

The scale of a mixed-use project, with rare exceptions, requires an in-house marketing staff. The complexity of most mixed-use projects, however, also requires the use of various sources of outside expertise. In many cases, the in-house marketing staff coordinates the activities of the various marketing consultants and brokers. Regardless of how the marketing function is structured, the activities undertaken will include naming the project, naming the project's components, leasing and selling space and units, advertising, public relations, operating a marketing center, developing visual presentations, and programming marketing events. Each activity plays a different role for the mixed-use project, for each use within the project, and for each stage of marketing and development.

In the overall development process, a series of strategic marketing decisions are made as the project is planned: the way the project will be announced, and planning for a marketing center location, including its features and scale at initiation and during buildout of the project. At this time, a preliminary decision is made as to which marketing functions will remain in house and which will rely on outside contracted services or other arrangements. At this juncture, the developer might have already secured the services of marketing specialists to assist in making this determination.

At Tabor Center in Denver, Colorado, the marketing strategy began with a strong public relations program aimed at gaining support from and integrating the project with the community. Efforts ranged from early involvement of civic groups to naming the hotel's meeting rooms after prominent local citizens and, ultimately, naming the project after a famous 19th-century Denver silver miner. One person from the Williams development organization acted as the public relations contact for all the project's uses and worked closely with the Rouse Company (the retail operator) and the Westin Hotel to determine their needs and marketing styles. As a result of this strategy, the community perceived the project as a single entity rather than a collection of separate uses. A shared marketing center was established, and a slide show, which described the project as a whole, was put into use three years before the project opened. Managers of individual components, however, handled direct marketing of space. Rouse was responsible for leasing and promoting retail space, Westin for promoting hotel rooms and meeting facilities, and Williams for leasing office space.

Initial Promotion. Announcement of the project is a key focal point of early marketing efforts and can range from high key to low key in magnitude. A dramatic early announcement can prove advantageous to all follow-on marketing if the momentum it creates can be maintained. A less dramatic announcement might be more appropriate if the initial announcement is being used to attract key tenants needed for project feasibility, financing, or public approvals.

The announcement can take the form of a well-placed news article in the real estate section or advertisements in local, regional, national, or international trade publications or business magazines. Full-page, four-color announcements and "tombstone" ads announcing financing by the principal lender are common. Community events, comments and speeches from elected officials, and parties can also be effective tools in promoting the project at this state.

Firm commitments from key office tenants or for partnerships or participants in components such as a hotel or shopping center are news items that can be exploited. The early announcement of a tenant from a booming business sector such as the high-tech sector of the 1990s or a prominent company or institution can induce other users from that sector to consider locating in the project.

One critical discussion at this juncture is the need for and scale of an off-site marketing center or, in some instances, the necessity for an on-site center preceding the first phase of construction. At the Carlyle Urban Village in Alexandria, Virginia, the marketing center was located on a major thoroughfare on one edge of the site where both residential and commercial buildings could be marketed while the buildings were being constructed.

A preconstruction marketing center might also be located at the developer's offices or at a location near the project site or in conjunction with a brokerage firm that has an exclusive marketing agreement. Wherever it is located, it might have a scale model, site plans, artist renderings, design video, and/or a virtual reality tour in addition to the more conventional print materials. In a few instances, a full-scale model unit has been created in a prefabricated module for high-rise residential projects. Whatever the characteristics of marketing centers, they must be an economically justified element of a cost-effective marketing strategy. Such centers can be quite expensive, with models themselves sometimes exceeding $100,000. The key goal here is to create a vision of what is coming so people know what they are getting.

Early development of a Web site can also be helpful in initial promotion and public relations. Miramar Town Center, for example, is a proposed mixed-use town center in Miramar, Florida, that has been initiated by the city of Miramar; much of the initial promotion of the project has come from the city, including a section of its Web site devoted to the project.

Branding. The concept of branding is also increasingly used to drive the process. Notes Marilee Utter of Citi-venture in Denver, "Branding involves ensuring that the entire concept, design, name, and marketing for a project are cohesive." The Roppongi Hills development in Tokyo, a major mixed-use project being completed in 2003, exemplifies the importance of branding for this major office, retail, residential, and hotel complex in the heart of Tokyo. The developers of this project, Mori Building Co. Ltd., are so committed to their brand identity that they have produced a small booklet, *The Roppongi Hills Brand Book,* to set forth their brand concept in detail.

The most important marketing objective of any predevelopment activity is to establish the project as the most significant new real estate development on the horizon—a special place with special amenities and special locational advantages. Images of quality, prestige, convenience, and added value set the project apart from any competitive freestanding components and, ideally, any competitive mixed-use developments. The potential synergism of uses should be featured—live, work, and play—or the synergism between tenants from a specific business or professional sector who benefit from proximity to each other. These early impressions are then reinforced by the ongoing marketing of the project and its components as development proceeds.

Naming the Project

Naming a mixed-use project is one of the earliest and most critical steps in marketing. The project's name can become an important value-added asset. Rockefeller Center, Embarcadero Center, Peachtree Center, and Illinois Center are all well-recognized names that are memorable, have a degree of geographic identity, and evoke an image of importance. A well-selected name is the cornerstone of a successful marketing strategy for a mixed-use project. The naming process must consider names for individual components as well.

Naming Ideas and Sources. From the perspective of marketing a mixed-use project, the critical question that needs an answer is what characteristics of the site, its lo-

Miramar Town Center is a mixed-use town center initiated by the city of Miramar, Florida. It includes a city hall, cultural arts center, library, and education center. Initial plans also call for 437 apartments, 89 townhouses, 101,000 square feet (9,383 square meters) of retail space, and 78,000 square feet (7,246 square meters) of office space. Initial promotion of the project came from the city; a section of its Web site is devoted to the project.

Courtesy of Torti Gallas and Partners CHK Inc.

The Roppongi Hills Brand Book is small, roughly four inches by ten inches (10 by 25.5 centimeters), and includes both Japanese and English text versions fused back to back. It is written, designed, and laid out somewhat like a book of poetry, using short sentences and rhythmic phrasing; several pages include only one line of text. The text of the book explains the Roppongi Hills brand using a literary style with no graphics except for project logos. The first several pages of the text are shown below:

The book goes on to present and describe three different logos for the project, discusses the Roppongi Hills philosophy, describes the project as a workplace, a place to live, and a cultural capital, and discusses the developer's role.

Source: Mori Building Co. Ltd., Roppongi Hills Management Office, July 1, 2002. ∎

Page 1

> Roppongi Hills is a city within a city: indeed, it's a "town."
> What does it mean for a "town" to become a brand?
>
> Roppongi Hills was created as a redevelopment. There was already a town, and already people living here.
> Together, we decided to make a new town, which involved many people over a very long time.
> It is our mission to nurture this town, to develop it thoroughly and continually.
>
> What is Roppongi Hills?
> By making this little book and by repeatedly sharing and confirming the same concept,
> Roppongi Hills will become a "brand" with one consistent story. It is a place that will certainly involve people in a consistent way.
> The goal is for our town to become an indispensable place for the people of Tokyo and from around the world for a long time to come.
> This will be the great challenge for all of us.

Page 2

> Brand positioning: What is Roppongi Hills ?

Page 3

> Roppongi Hills: The city where new ideas are born

Page 4

Brand purpose: The reason for being

Page 5

Roppongi Hills is a city that nurtures people with open-minds.

It is a center for global players. From the heart of Tokyo, Roppongi Hills will lead the nation and the entire
Asian region in open conversations with the world. Shaping our future.

Roppongi Hills logo.

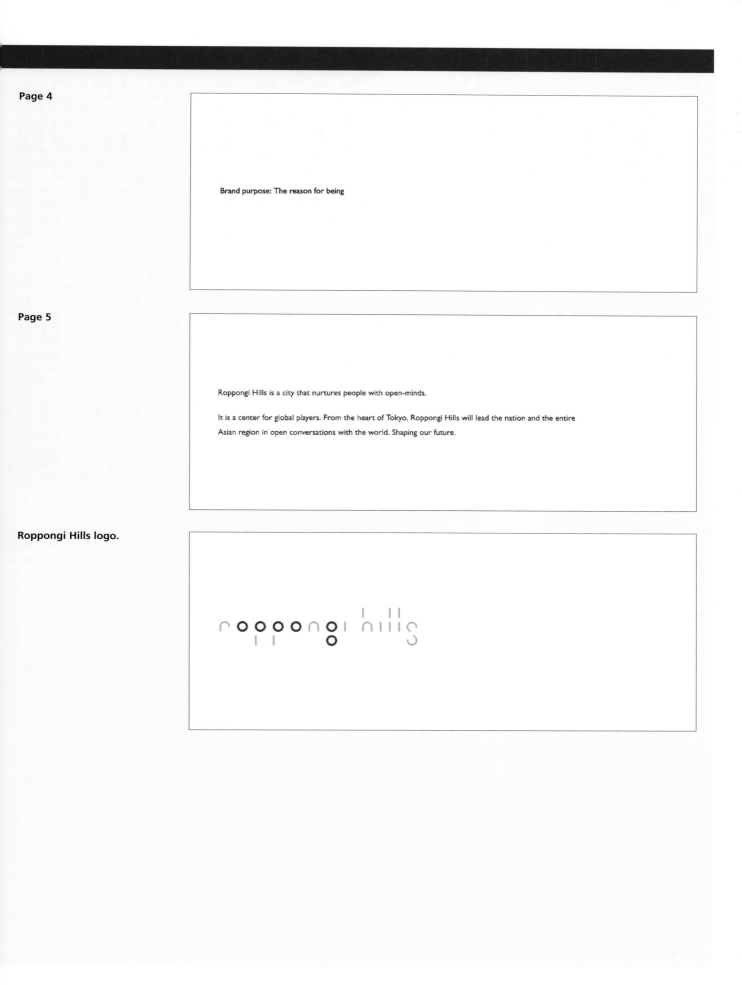

CambridgeSide Galleria in Cambridge, Massachusetts, is the name of both the retail mall and the overall mixed-use development, which also includes residential and office space.

cation, its committed major tenants, its historical background, and its intended market can be combined into a name that will be memorable and have marketing value. The advertising pitch that "image is everything" is very good advice.

A review of almost 40 mixed-use projects developed in the 1980s and 1990s shows that a geographic association with a central place, city, or state was the preferred choice for most mixed-use developers—Oakland City Center, for example. Association with a historic building or place was second: Heritage on the Garden is a subtle reference to both history and a location on the Boston Public Garden. A new development in Washington, D.C.—Terrell Place—was named to commemorate Mary Church Terrell, a life-long activist for equal rights who led a successful campaign to desegregate Washington's dining establishments. One of Terrell's most famous protests occurred in front of the old Hecht's department store on Seventh Street, which will be part of the new Terrell Place mixed-use development.

Association with a waterfront was third; waterfront names and themes can evoke a special sense of place. For example, a name like Rowes Wharf in Boston or Waterfront Place in Seattle immediately says where the project is located and associates the project with water. Water has always had a favorable marketing association for any type of project.

Some projects have been named after major corporate tenants with status in the marketplace or for an adjacent use or important institution. The Sony Center in Berlin is a clear example of an internationally known corporate identity. University Park at MIT seeks to gain identity and value from its association with the Massachusetts Institute of Technology. In a few instances, projects have been named after the developer or the development entity; such naming strategies are a desirable marketing strategy only if the developer's name, the institution, or the tenant's brand name would be powerful attractions for other tenants or investors. Association with a city or state such as Illinois Center or California Plaza might be a good strategy for a project that seeks a national or international market. Whatever the project's name, it should evoke a strong and positive image for the project.

Rarely does the developer of a mixed-use project forgo an overall name for the entire project and rely on naming individual components for project identity and marketing. In fact, if this approach were the logical conclusion of naming, one could also conclude that the project does not fall within the definition of a mixed-use project and is rather merely a group of unrelated development components that happen to be physically close. An exception is the Ritz-Carlton Hotel and Residences in Georgetown (Washington, D.C.), where the hotel's exceptional name status provides the desired cachet to the project.

And other names seemingly are derived from a variety of other sources. Suntec City in Singapore, Malaysia, for example, comes from the Chinese words *xin da,* which

Naming a Mixed-Use Development

Association with a Central Place, City, or State
- Abacoa Town Center, Abacoa, Florida
- Addison Circle, Addison, Texas*
- *Bethesda Row, Bethesda, Maryland*
- California Plaza, Los Angeles, California
- CambridgeSide Galleria, Cambridge, Massachusetts
- Celebration Town Center, Celebration, Florida
- *Charleston Place, Charleston, South Carolina*
- Hollywood & Highland, Hollywood, California
- Mashpee Commons, Mashpee, Massachusetts
- *Miami Lakes Town Center, Miami Lakes, Florida*
- Oakland City Center, Oakland, California
- Redmond Town Center, Redmond, Washington
- *Reston Town Center, Reston, Virginia*
- Smyrna Town Center, Smyrna, Georgia
- Valencia Town Center Drive, Valencia, California*

Association with a Historic Name, Building, or Place
- Battery Park City, New York, New York
- *Belmont Dairy, Portland, Oregon*
- *Denver Dry Goods Building, Denver, Colorado*
- Heritage on the Garden, Boston, Massachusetts
- Liberty Place, Philadelphia, Pennsylvania
- *The Mill at Glenville, Greenwich, Connecticut*
- *Mizner Park, Boca Raton, Florida*
- Peabody Place, Memphis, Tennessee*
- *Pentagon City, Arlington, Virginia*
- *Pioneer Place, Portland, Oregon*
- Santana Row, San Jose, California
- *Tabor Center, Denver, Colorado*
- Terrell Place, Washington, D.C.
- *Tower City Center, Cleveland, Ohio*
- *Truman Annex, Key West, Florida*
- *Village at Shirlington, Arlington, Virginia*

Association with Waterfront
- *Fisherman's Terminal, Seattle, Washington*
- Harbor Town, Memphis, Tennessee
- *Rivercenter, San Antonio, Texas*
- *RiverPlace, Portland, Oregon*
- *Rowes Wharf, Boston, Massachusetts*
- Waterfront Place, Seattle, Washington

Association with Institution, Company, or Principal Tenant
- *Audubon Court, New Haven, Connecticut*
- *Princeton Forrestal Village, Plainsboro, New Jersey*
- Prudential Center, Boston, Massachusetts
- Ritz-Carlton Hotel and Residences Georgetown, Washington, D.C.
- Sony Center am Potsdamer Platz, Berlin, Germany*
- *University Park at MIT, Cambridge, Massachusetts*

Association with Developer or Landowner
- *Crocker Center, Boca Raton, Florida*
- *Janss Court, Santa Monica, California*
- *Palmer Square, Princeton, New Jersey*
- *Phillips Place, Charlotte, North Carolina*

Note: Detailed profiles of the projects in *italics* are available in ULI's Development Case Studies at www.uli.org. Projects noted by an asterisk (*) are described in case studies in Chapter 8.

■

---

mean "new achievement," and the Crescent in Dallas, Texas, is based on building design.

Focus groups are frequently used in developing a marketing program and naming a project. Focus groups can provide quick and valuable feedback regarding which names resonate with the community and the market and which ones do not.

Naming Individual Components. After the project is named, the next task is to name components. Maximizing the synergism between components and the whole can be achieved if the name of each component is closely associated with the name of the mixed-use project and still maintains its own identity. The objective should be to create a name that can be used by each component in some distinct way. Certainly, if the project will have a hotel, the hotel chain will require use of the brand name, such as Hilton or Hyatt. A top brand tied to the name of the project can also serve to enhance the stature of the project, for example, "*Brand* Hotel at *Name* Center,"

or some variation. Although the strategy for a hotel component is obvious, the derivations of names for other components vary widely.

The office component in a mixed-use project might gain address status and locational clarity by being identified as One, Two, or Three *Name* Center. For example, the principal office building at Addison Circle is named One Addison Circle. If a major tenant preleases a building, the building is frequently named after the tenant. Sometimes an office building is given its own distinct name but frequently takes on other associations; for example, the official name of the office building at Pentagon City in Arlington is Washington Tower, but it is frequently referred to as the Pentagon City Tower.

Retail and hotel elements are frequently named after the overall project because their identity clearly benefits by association with the overall development, for example, *Fashion Centre at Pentagon City* and *Ritz-Carlton, Pentagon City.* When an effective name association exists, retail ad-

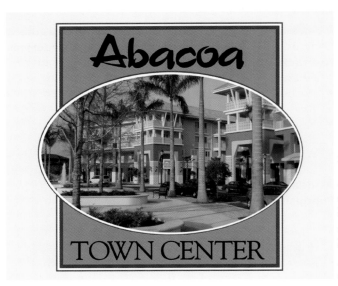

The logo for Abacoa Town Center in Jupiter, Florida, which is named after the planned community of Abacoa.

vertising continually reinforces the name of the development in the marketplace. The reverse may be true as well, however. Many projects have derived their name in part from the retail component, such as *CambridgeSide Galleria* in Cambridge, Massachusetts. When the name of the development has an appellation like "town center"—Reston Town Center or Miami Lakes Town Center, for example—the retail component's name is usually the same as the name of the overall mixed-use development.

To market residential components in mixed-use projects usually requires more distinctive names, especially if the development has a dominant retail or office component. Such a strong and distinctive name can both stand on its own and be associated with the overall project name. For example, the name of the freestanding apartment building at Pentagon City is the Metropolitan at Pentagon City, which is often referred to simply as "the Metropolitan." If the dominant use in the project is residential, then use of the overall project's name is often preferred. Some apartment developers also prefer to use their brand names in the project, as in Post Addison Circle.

Unusual or historic residential buildings often require unusually distinct names, especially when they are in a largely commercial setting. For example, Kennedy Biscuit Lofts at University Park at MIT is named after the bakery that once occupied the building. If the residential component is developed by a subcontractor that has a naming strategy associated with its development reputation, the component could have greater marketing value than the project. In any case, the residential component will always have a name, not just an address, and it will most often be tied to the image that the residential product wishes to convey to the market.

Initial Marketing to Major Tenant Prospects

Marketing efforts rely heavily on the developer's well-prepared presentations. For both the hotel and retail space, these efforts are highly targeted. Most developers of mixed-use projects focus on attracting one of the major hotel chains, thus limiting marketing to five to ten different well-known hotel operators or chains. This effort is critical, as the quality of the hotel operator makes the difference between low and high occupancies for the hotel and the hotel brand conveys a price point for the entire project.

Some mixed-use projects have not been able to attract the right brand hotel operator until well after the project is completed, and the developer has built the hotel and operated it independently. This approach can lead to low occupancy rates, poor economic performance, and a poor image for the project as a whole.

In special circumstances, an unaffiliated hotel can succeed, such as a historic hotel with a well-known name. Peabody Hotel at Peabody Place, for example, was a historic hotel in downtown Memphis that has been refurbished; the hotel name in that market is so strong that the entire project was named after the hotel. The hotel is managed by the Peabody Hotel Group, a subsidiary of Belz Enterprises (the project developer), which owns and operates another Peabody Hotel in Orlando, Florida, and nine other hotels throughout the country.

Large-scale retail requires very specialized development. If the retail component is the size of a regional shopping center, initial marketing may involve a search for a shopping center developer as a joint venture partner—or a primary shopping center developer who is seeking others to develop one or more of the nonretail components. Attracting quality anchor tenants, whether major department stores, a restaurant, a multiscreen cinema, or another high-profile retail establishment, that can serve as an anchor is critical. The retail component usually cannot be financed without the commitment of anchor tenants. If retail is a minor component, however, marketing the space will likely follow the leasing of the other uses. In general, retailers respond to the demographics of the market and the strength of the overall project and retail concept.

Attracting a major tenant for the office component involves a much less targeted effort, as the number of possible major tenants is far more numerous. The developer must understand the marketplace and potential growth sectors in the office market. In any given market, only a limited number of major new leases are written in one year, and the developer must find and target those firms. A close relationship with local brokers is most helpful, because such tenants often use a favored broker to help them select new locations. At University Park at MIT in Cambridge, Massachusetts, for example, the developer established an exclusive marketing relationship with a premier Boston brokerage firm for the nonresidential uses but marketed the rental units through its own subsidiary, Forest City Residential, operating out of the headquarters office in Cleveland. Notes Marilee Utter of Citiventure in Denver, "A branded concept is important to office tenants, and their identity should be reflected."

In a rapidly growing market experiencing an influx of companies seeking new national or regional headquarters, the marketing search might go national or international. In this case, working with brokers who have national or worldwide offices or affiliates is a likely strategy. Many large companies seeking a location for a major new office use their favored broker in their headquarters city to search for possible projects under development while the projects are still in the initial phases of feasibility analysis.

Marketing Tools and Strategies during Development

Once the project is announced and development begins in earnest, the focus of marketing involves the development of marketing materials, site-based marketing, leasing, and promotion and public relations. The marketing should use a multifaceted approach, promoting the project as a whole while also highlighting the various components, providing descriptive materials and renderings to establish the development as a new "place" in town, aggressively marketing and leasing individual uses, and promoting the project to the press and the community to create and attract positive attention.

Brochures and Marketing Materials

Attractive brochures can be highly effective tools for conveying the development's overall concept. Brochures are generally four-color publications that include site plans, renderings of the exterior and interior, floor plans, and descriptions of the project and its components. The brochure for a mixed-use project works best if it is designed to be part of a folder with a variety of inserts that can be tailored to the particular potential tenant: an office, national chain tenant for the retail, or the purchaser of a condominium. Thus, each component of the mixed-

This image of AOL Time Warner Center presents a compelling vision of the project concept. The development originally was named Columbus Circle after its location in New York, but it was given its current corporate name after AOL Time Warner committed to leasing much of the office space in the project.

use development can have its own special package of marketing information while benefiting from the added value of its location in a mixed-use project. This format can also be easily updated with new inserts.

Some developers use separate brochures for the separate components, especially for office and residential uses, but this approach works well only when they are tied to the overall marketing for the mixed-use development. With a separate brochure, a component can lose any advantage it has over other similar products that do not have the advantage of the amenities and reputation associated with a mixed-use project.

The marketing brochure for Lindbergh City Center in Atlanta, for example, is flexible enough so that it can be tailored for each component, potential tenant, or purchaser and still be a unified design that each can build on for its targeted marketing. Lindbergh Center's location at a MARTA train station is its market advantage. Thus, the key graphic element, a train streaming though the name, ties all the marketing pieces together and to that market advantage.

Site-Based Marketing

Throughout this stage before the project is completed, visual presentations, models, and marketing centers also play a critical role. Because most mixed-use projects involve several buildings, models are important tools for conveying the overall concept and plan for the development; they can highlight not only the individual uses but

Courtesy of Carter & Associates

The cover and logo for a Lindbergh City Center marketing piece. Lindbergh City Center is a large-scale mixed-use development being built around a transit station in Atlanta. The importance of the transit station in the positioning of this development is clear from both the name and the marketing line on the cover.

also their interrelationships and the open spaces, amenities, and people-oriented places. A marketing center is one of the best places to display such a model as well as other visual presentations such as architects' renderings and video/slide shows. Especially for a large project, such a marketing center can be very cost-effective. A recent new marketing tool is the use of computer simulations and visualizations.

The advance strategy for marketing Lindbergh Center in Atlanta is to have one marketing center on site for the office, retail, and condominium components. The apartment development is not initially planning to participate. One model was planned for the entire project, but marketing center plans are being designed so that each component has a separate entrance. This approach allows the maximum variety of marketing tools.

At Sony Center am Potsdamer Platz, the developer, Tishman Speyer, recognized early that this large redevelopment area faced fierce competition from other more established locations in Berlin. Tishman Speyer undertook a major marketing effort more than five years before the opening of the project, including the InfoBox, an information center where visitors to Potsdamer Platz could learn about the area and the development projects underway. It attracted more than 2 million visitors a year.

Outdoor signs with descriptive information and renderings at the construction site raise the curiosity of those living and working in the area, particularly those who are part of the target market for the project. Construction site–watching is a national pastime that can be used to additional advantage. For an urban site, the fence around the project can be both a marketing tool and a way to reach out to the community. For example, a mural depicting themes associated with the history of the site painted by students from nearby schools can be an attraction during construction and can minimize unwanted graffiti. On a more suburban site, the early development of a landscaped entrance along with informational signs and graphics can be very effective in promoting a quality image for the project.

Marketing and Leasing Specific Uses during Development

For office space, the period before completion of the project is particularly critical, and the time required to lease an office building is generally a good measure of that building's financial success. Brochures and audiovisual presentations, widely used during preleasing, can provide the most comprehensive description of the project and the environment that the developer is trying to create. PowerPoint or other computer-based presentation software has largely replaced the slide presentation of the past; moreover, it can be easily tailored to the needs of a targeted tenant. The greater the amount of office space preleased, the greater the building's profitability. The use of brokers or an in-house leasing team generally depends on the developer's management style and experience in the local marketplace, but the use of an aggressive leasing team and well-planned advertising and public relations is indispensable throughout the process.

Models and computer-generated three-dimensional imagery can be very effective on-site marketing tools. This model of Atlantic Station in Atlanta highlights the cinema and public spaces.

The sales campaign before the project is completed is critical for residential uses as well. Because of high carrying costs, the quicker the residential space is rented or sold, the larger the profit and/or the smaller the risk. Residential marketing does not normally begin until the developer is committed to this component, however, because it is not necessary to attract anchor tenants. Print media again are very useful, especially the real estate sections of local newspapers. Radio and television advertisements can also be very effective, as the potential market for residential space includes a much broader segment of the population than for office space. Two key issues in marketing for-sale units that do not apply to other uses are floor plans for the various units and the need to make attractive financing available for potential buyers.

Unlike office and residential uses, retail and hotel uses require a somewhat more multifaceted approach to marketing; marketing these components begins very early and continues at a very rapid pace throughout the life of the project. Promotional efforts before opening are only the first stages of overall promotion.

Marketing the retail component before completion of the project must focus on two primary marketing efforts: attracting quality tenants and building interest and curiosity among the general public. A retail center, unlike an office building, must be substantially leased before opening if the center is to be successful. Most centers are planned to open after a minimal acceptable occupancy level is achieved (usually at least 60 percent). Without this level of occupancy, the public will view the center as somewhat of a failure—an image that will be very difficult to overcome and will negatively affect the project's overall image. General promotion of the retail center as a whole before opening is also critical, because broad public awareness and interest are necessary throughout that period. If the retail component is planned to provide service and convenience uses, it is probably desirable to have those retail tenants open as offices are occupied.

Marketing and promoting the hotel before the project is completed is more complicated than for other components, as it involves three major marketing efforts. The first is to attract a reputable hotel brand and operator to manage the hotel. The second, similar to that for retail space, seeks to create general public awareness so that when the hotel opens, various sectors of the local economy and population will generate demand for rooms. The third is marketing directly to corporations, associations, and other businesses that might generate room-night demand and/or hold meetings in the hotel. Especially for a major convention hotel, marketing to major convention sponsors must begin years in advance of the scheduled date of the event. The hotel operator again plays a critical role, which is all the more reason to line up the hotel operator very early in the development process. Marketing for the hotel requires a much broader effort, one that reaches well beyond the local market.

Public Relations and Promotion

Mixed-use projects can very successfully attract press and public attention if they are effectively promoted. Press releases and other public relations tools can help obtain free print or television coverage for major events, such as the project's formal announcement or ground breaking. Other promotional methods include attracting local celebrities, such as sports figures, to move into the project.

Every mixed-use project has newsworthy features: the unusual planned mix of uses, site features, building design, key tenants, public/private joint venture arrangements, and others. They are the makings of feature stories in various print media. For example, marketing professionals should develop a good working relationship with the real estate editor of general-circulation newspapers in the region and provide not just facts and figures but also access to the development principals to humanize a story. A mixed-use project can be front page news, at least in the real estate section. Visuals that are simple and color-ful and can be easily reprinted in local publications—site plans, maps, and renderings—are especially useful.

As the project progresses, promotion continues to focus on the project as a whole but highlights major events, such as topping-out ceremonies and the completion and opening of various components. Promoting and leasing or selling the various uses in the project, however, should have the greatest emphasis. Effective marketing strategies for each component that create some momentum will impact the project's overall success.

Marketing at this stage should also convey the concept and create a positive image in the surrounding community. At Paseo Colorado, developers sought to build and convey a "village experience." The developer worked to create a "marriage between retailers and residents," not unlike the friendly, first-name-basis lifestyle of a traditional village. To that end, community teas were held during the planning stages to acquaint people with the developer's concept. The results of the teas were shared with

Strong design images and land use plans—such as these for Abacoa Town Center in Jupiter, Florida—are especially important in marketing the retail space to prospective retail tenants. Retail tenants look for clear and compelling development concepts, design imagery, and plans—as well as the usual market data—before they commit to a new or unusual concept.

Courtesy of de Guardiola Development, Inc.

At Paseo Colorado in Pasadena, California, the developers sought to build and convey the concept of a "village experience."

Courtesy of Trizec Properties

prospective tenants to make sure they understood and would advance the broader objectives of the project.

At Mizner Park in Boca Raton, Florida, considerable attention in the press greatly helped to market the residential component of the project. Of the 136 apartments in the initial development, 50 percent were rented before construction and even before furnished models were available for tours. All the apartments were leased before opening day. This outcome was largely accomplished with little marketing effort, as the press generated by the redevelopment and by the referendum gave the residential units tremendous visibility in the marketplace. Current marketing materials use the phrase "Mizner Park: A Village within a City."

Office Marketing and Leasing

Each mixed-use project involves marketing and leasing or selling issues unique to each component. Although marketing or leasing practices for office, retail, residential, or hotel uses start with the normal practices for those components, some potential differences exist as to how marketing should proceed for each component when it is part of a mixed-use development.[1]

Office Marketing Strategy

Early in the overall marketing strategy for a mixed-use project, the marketing team must determine the degree to which an office location in a mixed-use project is a marketing and leasing advantage. To what extent does location in a mixed-use project lend status that will enhance rent premiums or at least provide a competitive advantage in the market? How should the marketing strategy exploit these advantages?

If the project has multiple office buildings, a connective marketing strategy must be developed so that marketing for the first building flows seamlessly into that for the next building. This is the point where the overall naming strategy for a mixed-use project can come into play. Even though the objective should be to have a strong association with the overall project, the office component, particularly multiple buildings, should maintain some individual identity. The marketing team should have input into building design, potential naming rights, and construction sequencing, particularly as it relates to provision of parking, tenant amenities, and site improvements needed to attract tenants. Here is where a brochure for a mixed-use project that tells the whole story can be tied to the marketing piece for each phase of office development and where customized pieces can emphasize project features that set this address apart from the competition for specific tenants.

Early marketing that identifies a tenant with a highly visible name who might want naming rights for the building it occupies could affect the strategy for naming the project or various other components. A name brand tenant may be useful in attracting other big tenants from

At Mizner Park in Boca Raton, considerable press attention greatly helped in marketing the residential component. Of the 136 apartments available in the initial development, 50 percent were rented before construction was started, and all were rented by opening day.

the same business sector or tenants that might feed off the presence of that tenant. In Berlin, a topping-out ceremony for the Sony Center was used to call attention to this mammoth project and its lead tenant. At the same time, the overall image of a project with multiple uses and multiple office buildings might be distorted by the presence of a dominant tenant. This potential should be considered in initial discussions about naming the project and its components and a determination made about the positive or negative effects that might result.

Leasing

The other major issue that needs careful consideration in marketing the office component is whether to use outside brokers, an inside leasing agent, or some combination. Outsiders who market office space in a mixed-use project may not have the emotional commitment or knowledge of the mixed-use concept to effectively tell the project's story. The right decision for each project is determined by the circumstances. A project with a nationwide or worldwide market might need a different approach from a project that is targeted to the regional market. The critical question is which structure will give the project the best access to the desired mix of potential office tenants and will best leverage the advantages of location in a mixed-use project. One factor that may come into play is the scope of the developer's local, national, and international operations; another may be the focused effort required for preleasing in a competitive market.

At University Park at MIT in Cambridge, Massachusetts, a relationship was established with Meredith & Grew, a premier Boston brokerage firm well known in the area, to participate in planning and to market the project. Anyone looking for space in the Boston region consulted Meredith & Grew. Thus, Forest City did not advertise locally or nationally. On the other hand, office leasing at Rowes Wharf in Boston, with its special waterfront location, was handled in house, mostly to tenants needing less than 50,000 square feet (4,650 square meters).

After the project is completed, the issue of how to re-lease office space must be considered during post-development management of the project (see Chapter 7). The expectation is that the project's reputation will allow higher rents as leases expire and are renegotiated.

Retail Marketing and Leasing

Retail marketing begins with retail positioning (see Chapters 2 and 5). Most positioning strategies involve both local and national tenants. Other issues to be determined include partnering with retail developers for marketing and promotion and whether to use in-house or outside brokers.[2]

Retail Marketing Strategy

The scale of the retail component largely dictates the approach taken for retail marketing and leasing. If the retail component is small and comprises primarily service and convenience uses, the developer is likely to call on an outside broker who specializes in retail leasing and who has contacts with potential tenants. An alternative for a large development organization with retail leasing expertise is to handle this activity with in-house staff.

In some cases, the responsibility for pursuing local or national and international tenants might be divided between two distinct entities. At WestEnd City Center in Budapest (see Chapter 8), all marketing and leasing were handled in house by TriGranit, but expatriate staff from TrizecHahn worked on leasing with international tenants while Hungarian staff worked with local tenants. Although a number of western retailers can be found at WestEnd City Center, Hungarian tenants predominate.

When the retail component is large, it is likely that the project's master developer is a retail developer or has entered into a joint venture with another developer experienced in shopping center development, leasing, and operations if it does not have that capacity itself. When a separate entity is involved or shopping center development is handled by a separate division of a large development group, responsibility for marketing and leasing the retail component falls to the shopping center development entity.

If the retail component is to be developed and managed somewhat independently, it is important that representatives of it be part of the management team and be involved early in the development process. At that point, the planned character and quality of the retail component are articulated and defined by the agreements between the various entities. It is also when the naming relationship between the retail and other components is determined. If the retail component is of any significant scope—even if it is largely support retail—it is the glue that holds all the other components together. It is the most visible use in the development for the nearby community, and marketing of it never stops. A poor rep-

utation or business failure in the retail component always has some negative impact on the rest of the development; thus, its marketing efforts need to be closely intertwined with and consistent with the image and reputation sought for the development.

The retail component always has its own independent marketing tied to seasonal retail sales, but it may be desirable to have jointly funded and well-coordinated promotional activities and seasonal events for the entire mixed-use project. For example, Santa's arrival at the development and at the retail component during the Christmas holiday season might be coordinated, and special events like an outdoor concert or caroling can be tied to hours when the center is open.

The retail component might also have special early or late shopping hours and personal shoppers for center tenants. Food service units in the retail component might provide catering, and the retail area might have a community space for parties during or after hours. Opportu-

A rendering of Zlote Tarasy in Warsaw, Poland, creates an exciting image for the development. The project is planned to include retail, office, and hotel uses.

Winter Park Village is a town center and main street development on the site of the former Winter Park Mall. Retail is marketed as "a bold new entertainment and fashion center" in "an inviting urban village environment."

nities are endless and must be thought through, even as early as the design stage for the retail component.

Most retail centers should include a marketing fund to pay for joint promotion and events. At Phillips Place in Charlotte, the retail center does not have a marketing fund, which has limited the center's ability to sponsor events and promote the center broadly. The project developer does, however, contribute annually to several events and advertising.

Tenanting and Leasing

In general, marketing the retail component should include clear, comprehensive data about demographics and the competition. Retailers are also very interested in the site plan and the store layout plan and how parking is handled, so a site plan with parking must be included. They want to know how common area maintenance (CAM) charges are handled and what those charges will be. They also want to know about rules and plans for signage. Finally, they want to know which other tenants will be locating in the center.

The International Council of Shopping Centers (ICSC) is quite helpful in pursuing national tenants.[3] ICSC is devoted exclusively to the development and management of shopping centers, and at its conventions and trade shows, tenants seeking locations and centers seeking tenants gather to make deals. Moreover, many vendors of specialized marketing techniques are represented. ICSC can be a prime source for a mixed-use project developer seeking tenants or a joint venture partner.

Targeting the right class and mix of tenants is critically important, especially for smaller specialty retail centers seeking to offer something different. At Phillips Place in Charlotte, North Carolina, for example, careful attention was paid to attracting national tenants not currently in the Charlotte area to provide Phillips Place with a distinctive collection of tenants. The project was marketed to prospective tenants as a regional destination, and the town center concept—with its specialty retail and entertainment attractions—helped draw desirable nationally known retailers to the project.

At Tower City Center in the center of downtown Cleveland, the retail leasing program was originally targeted to high-profile, middle-market, and upscale national tenants such as Gucci, Fendi, Barneys, Disney, Liz Claiborne, the Limited, and Victoria's Secret. Several tenants were one-of-a-kind stores in the Cleveland region. But in this case, the developer's attempts to bring in too many high-end retailers to occupy large spaces proved to be an error, given the strong market of middle-income shoppers. The tenant and space mix had to be adjusted toward retailers more consistent with a middle-income market.

At Mizner Park in Boca Raton, Florida, the retail leasing strategy started by targeting local tenants, then moved on to regional and then national prospects. The focus was on high-end specialty retailers, primarily fashion stores and art galleries drawn from the Palm Beach/Broward County area. All leasing was kept in house, because the development firm enjoyed a considerable presence in the regional commercial leasing market.

At WestEnd City Center in Budapest, TriGranit handled all the marketing and leasing in house. Unlike some of the other centers in the Budapest market, all the retailers at WestEnd City Center are well established and have extensive experience in the market. A number of local firms conducted market studies, and when the shopping mall opened, it was 100 percent leased.

Courtesy of Cooper Carry Inc.

At Mizner Park in Boca Raton, the retail leasing strategy began with local tenants, then moved to regional and then national tenants. All leasing was handled in house by the developer, which has strong expertise in retail leasing.

The path to the residential leasing office at Fairview Village near Portland. The use of on-site marketing centers and model units is a prerequisite for most successful residential marketing programs.

Courtesy of Holt & Haugh, Inc.

One special characteristic of retail leasing is percentage leases, in which the landlord has the potential for increased rental income if retailers reach certain sales thresholds. This leasing approach is most common in large regional shopping facilities and less likely for service retail. As a leasing and operational strategy, it requires a sophisticated knowledge of the retail industry.

Residential Marketing, Leasing, and Sales

The strategy for a residential component differs, depending on whether that component is for sale or for rent. If the units are rentals, how they are marketed depends on whether they are planned for conversion to condominiums at some later date. For-sale units in mixed-use projects are likely condominiums, although less frequently they might be townhouses on land parcels or cooperatives.

Marketing For-Sale Units

For-sale units can benefit from a location in a mixed-use project, particularly if the project has a special identity or location. At Rowes Wharf on the Boston waterfront, the residences were marketed first, and all 100 units were sold 100 days after they went on the market. The buyers for the units were largely empty nesters. Unlike the office and retail uses that were marketed in house, an outside firm handled the residential marketing. At Market Square in Washington, D.C., the residential condominiums are named the Residences at Market Square to tie them to the prestige of the overall project, home to the U.S. Navy Memorial.

Marketing of high-end condominiums can greatly benefit from association with a premier hotel brand. Millennium Partners, for example, positions and markets most of its high-end condominium projects with Ritz-Carlton or Four Seasons Hotels, which has allowed it to request very high sale prices for many of its condominium units.

The sale of for-sale units is a one-time event, with resales occurring sporadically. When a resale does occur, the unit owner has the right to choose its own selling agent, and it is that agent's skill that determines how well location in a mixed-use project brings added value to a particular sale. The overall project management entity should be prepared to assist the marketing of resale units with brochures and information that the broker can give to prospective buyers.

Marketing Rental Units

The marketing of residential rental units is very different from that for for-sale units or, for that matter, for any other component. Unlike office space, where tenants may take anything from small to large floor areas and buildout varies from tenant to tenant, or retail, where store size and positioning in relation to entrances and other complementary tenants may be the most important factors, the size and floor plans for rental residential units are for the most part predetermined by the market analysis. They are delivered ready for occupancy.

Locational choice is first come, first served, with top-floor, corner, and view units priced at a premium. The finishing standard is dictated by the market segment targeted, with marketing emphasizing the unit's features, security, locational advantages, proximity and availability of neighborhood retail shops, access to transit, parking, and price. The hope is that demand will allow rents to build during lease-up so that as leases come due, rents on the earliest rented units can be increased.

Here is where location in a mixed-use project can be a major asset in marketing rental residential units. The premier status of mixed-use projects in their market tends to rub off on residential units, which should, with effective marketing, result in additional rental premiums and rapid lease-up. To achieve premium rents, the initial planning for rental units in mixed-use projects must determine whether potential quality of the rental residential portion and market potential of the other components

Marketing residential units at Legacy Town Center in Plano, Texas, emphasized both town center amenities and proximity to adjacent and nearby employment centers.

match. When it does, the naming association can be a major marketing advantage.

General rental marketing practices are available from a variety of sources.[4] Depending on the rent range, available units can be initially and on an ongoing basis marketed to tenants and employees of other components in the mixed-use project. The range of specialized marketing opportunities is significant. Moreover, because turnover is a cost of operations after initial occupancy, the potential exists for reduced turnover using marketing techniques that offer benefits to tenants for the use of facilities in other components of the project. For example, tenants can be offered discounts when housing guests in the hotel, or they can receive dining discounts when using restaurants in the project. The marketing team might need to identify some of these ideas early in the process if they require some form of formal agreement among various parties.

Residential Marketing Tools

The marketing literature for residential uses generally focuses on units first and then amenities, but in mixed-use projects, marketing place and address frequently takes precedence. The value of living in a well-designed mixed-use project with retail amenities and attractive public spaces can attract interest in a residential building. Here is where marketing "live, work, play" can be most valuable.

The use of model units is a prerequisite for almost any successful residential marketing program. Model units may be located in unusual locations before construction of the building. For example, a full-scale condominium unit or typical rental apartment might be a part of a marketing center. Models might be set up in an office building ahead of residential construction, or a residential marketing center might be located in the retail component.

At Heritage on the Garden in Boston, the Druker Company opened a sales office in a rented storefront across from the Heritage while construction was still in progress. There it displayed a miniature replica of the entire building and an $80,000 full-scale, fully furnished model of a bathroom and kitchen for the residential condominiums. Samples of woodwork, paneling, tile, and other features were also on display for would-be buyers to examine. When the condominiums finally went on the market, sales were brisk and all 87 units sold in three months.

Residential Target Groups

Target groups for residential marketing generally include a variety of households without children—singles, young couples, young and old same-sex couples, empty nesters, and divorced individuals. Condominiums are generally aimed at an older and more affluent market than rental units, but the rental market also includes affluent demographic segments that are drawn to mixed-use environments.

Post Properties, for example, is marketing Addison Circle (see Chapter 8) as a sophisticated urban lifestyle community and is targeting those who rent by choice, not from necessity. Paris Rutherford, one of the project's designers with RTKL/Dallas, notes that these renters are often "double-income couples with no children, empty nesters, and young professionals, typically between 30 to 55 years old. They rent by choice, preferring the urban lifestyle Addison Circle affords." Quality of life is a key issue for this market segment, and amenities such as

The interior atrium in the Grand Hyatt Shanghai at Jin Mao Tower. Hotel marketing emphasizes luxurious accommodations and panoramic views.

If a hotel is planned for the project, marketing the development concept to a prospective hotel brand or operator will likely involve a short list of five to ten brands that fit with the market image of the project. Pictured is the entrance to the hotel at the Ritz-Carlton Hotel and Residences Georgetown in Washington, D.C.

pools and health clubs are only a starting point; convenience, community, entertainment, and culture are increasingly sought.

One additional target market for both for-sale and rental units is corporate units. If the office component has a significant number of national or multinational firms as tenants, the opportunity may exist to market for-sale or rental units to these firm for their employees' use during extended stays. This opportunity should be carefully examined before a decision is made to aggressively pursue it, however. Such units essentially become "hotel" units and may not be compatible with other retail tenants or owners, although the problem is probably less with rental units; lease terms could be used to control patterns of use. When the presence of residential units is intended to bring street life to the development, the transient nature of corporate personnel may be counter to other objectives of the project as a whole.

Attracting Hotel Operators and Hotel Marketing

If market analysis determines that a hotel is a likely component of the project, the search for one begins as soon as the preliminary master plan for the project has been developed. Because hotels range from luxury to budget, the search should target those that would fit the quality being considered for the project.[5]

Matching the Hotel with the Overall Concept
Perhaps the most critical issue in seeking a hotel operator is finding the right brand match for the project. If the mixed-use development is targeting the high end of the office and retail markets, then the hotel needs to have a high-end brand name. Likewise, if the project's target market for office tenants is in the middle range, then planners should seek a mid-priced hotel operator. For example, the price point for a project that is closely associated with a

university or medical complex in an off-center location is different from that for a center-city mixed-use project that caters to high-end business travelers and tourists. If the project includes or is located near a major convention center, its hotel must be competitive with other nearby hotels seeking to tap the same market.

An unusual example that makes the point of finding the right fit is that of a hotel that will feed off a medical complex. The site has a mix of potential markets: patients and their families coming for evaluation and/or treatment, top medical professionals coming for meetings, mid-level professionals coming for training, and pharmaceutical and medical equipment sales representatives, to name a few. Persons in each category might require somewhat different room prices. Thus, several types of hotels, from extended-stay to those catering to business travelers, might be considered. The choice depends on the other uses in the project and the depth of the market for a specialized type.

Boutique hotels are also making inroads in the hotel market and may be good fits with mixed-use projects. Santana Row in San Jose, for example, includes the 213-room Hotel Valencia boutique hotel as well as luxury and lifestyle retailers and luxury apartments in an urban village/town center.

At University Park at MIT, Forest City Enterprises considered a hotel sufficiently important to the success of the project in a pioneer location that it developed the hotel itself and then negotiated a management agreement with Hilton as an unaffiliated house.

Attracting and Working with Hotel Operators
Some developments have sent RFPs to all possible hotel operators/developers with a market analysis that predicts the number of rooms that might be supported by a range of room values. Rather than take the best offer, the developer preferably should meet with the most likely two or three operators for further talks before selecting one.

Before selecting any hotel name or operating company, the developer should ascertain the company's:

- responsiveness to the market orientation of the mixed-use project;
- responsiveness to the developer's objectives;
- reputation with the public, with other owners and developers, and with lending institutions;
- record of experience, competence, stability, and continuous growth;
- ability to provide complete and reliable marketing services, operational controls, financial reports, and preopening management and technical services;
- development expertise;
- operating experience in other mixed-use projects;
- financial objectives and financial commitment as it relates to the project; and
- standard operating agreements.

Once a hotel operator has been confirmed, the project developer works with that operator to define market relationships with other uses in the project. For example, a significant office component in the project might be an excellent target for business travelers for both short- and extended-term stays. Likewise, the hotel can be a major source of meeting and function space. A favorable pricing structure for tenants of the project might be worth exploring as a bonus for taking advantage of office space in the project. As mentioned earlier, the naming of the hotel can provide a marketing advantage for both the hotel and the other uses in the project if uses and market segments are highly compatible.

Events and Promotion after Project Completion

The official opening of a mixed-use project, which may not coincide with effective opening dates for individual components, affords an excellent opportunity to promote the project that goes well beyond the opportunities for any single-use project. A large mixed-use development may have several phases extending over many years. Thus, "completion" can be hard to define. Opening may come only after completion of one or more components.

New marketing and promotion themes can be introduced once the project opens and as it matures. At Reston Town Center in Reston, Virginia, for example, the marketing theme is "The Heart of the Action. Reston Town Center." The theme builds on the project's tremendous success, especially its retail, restaurant, and entertainment components, events, and activities. Reston Town Center continues to offer a strong pedestrian-friendly urban experience in a very suburban location, drawing visitors from a wide area to its events, restaurants, cinema, and shops.

Opening Events
The project's opening can be planned as a major event, involving prominent local political and business leaders,

Courtesy of Hold & Haugh, Inc.

Mixed-use projects with main streets, such as Fairview Village near Portland, Oregon, are well suited to old-fashioned parades.

entertainment, fireworks, and numerous other activities. Such promotional activity reinforces the project's sense of place, which in turn increases each component's visibility and marketability. Heavy advertising in local newspapers is critical at this time, and radio and television advertising is appropriate when these media are cost-effective. The project's opening is the time when public relations efforts should be at their peak.

Paseo Colorado in Pasadena, for example, officially opened on Friday, September 28, 2001, with a series of events that brought out thousands of local residents. At 9:00 a.m., hundreds of residents and dignitaries crowded Colorado Boulevard for a ribbon-cutting ceremony that included a performance by acrobat Trent Sherrell, a Flying Chiffon aerialist formerly with Cirque du Soleil. As Sherrell flew through the air performing a series of acrobatic stunts, several dignitaries, including Pasadena Mayor Bill Bogaard and TrizecHahn's President and Chief Executive Officer Lee H. Wagman, pulled a ribbon, causing a 30-foot-high (nine-meter) drape covering Paseo Colorado to dramatically disappear within a matter of seconds. As Paseo Colorado was unveiled, cannons shot rose-petal-shaped confetti into the air, and the restored view corridor along Garfield Avenue was visible for the first time.

The event included numerous speeches that also drew attention to the project. "Paseo Colorado is a wonderful new addition to the city of Pasadena. This project has not only created a new destination for residents but has also contributed to a beautiful new civic center with the restoration of the Garfield view corridor," said Mayor Bogaard.

On Friday evening, an estimated crowd of 15,000 people gathered at Paseo Colorado lining the Garfield Promenade for a free concert by the Pasadena Symphony and a ceremony in honor of the victims of September 11. Thousands stood together in a moment of silence, which was followed by a candle-lighting ceremony and a medley of patriotic anthems.

At Santana Row, the grand opening spanned four days, beginning with an opening-day ceremony in which a 40- by 72-foot (12- by 22-meter) curtain opened to reveal the retail portion of this main street–oriented mixed-use project. Throughout the opening weekend, a mix of street performers, children's groups, and community-based entertainers provided entertainment, and food samples from the restaurants in the development were available for a nominal fee. The following days included a lifestyle showcase of brands, products, and services; a showcase of technologies; a fashion show; and a farmers' market. The farmers' market is open twice weekly and features more than 80 vendors; it is a continuation of a market that was begun ten years ago on the site, formerly a mall.

And at CityCenter Englewood in Englewood, Colorado, a multimedia performance of music, dance, art, and film highlighted a special evening planned to celebrate the opening of the center and the grand reopening of the Museum of Outdoor Arts. The program featured Vivaldi's Four Seasons and music by Up Close and Musical (musicians from the Colorado Symphony Orchestra), dance by the David Taylor Dance Theatre, live performance art by artist Lindy Lyman, and a film interpretation of Vivaldi's music. The celebration was held in the outdoor plaza, home to the new Englewood Civic Center, which houses the city administration, Englewood Public Library, Englewood Municipal Court, and the Museum of Outdoor Arts. Numerous other retail and residential components were in the planning or early development stages at the time of this event. Fun for children, concessions, displays, and information booths about the current and future elements of CityCenter Englewood were also included in the event.

Ongoing Events

Beyond the grand opening, other events can be used to promote the project as a whole on a continuing basis. For example, at Miami Lakes Town Center in Florida, the developer sponsors five major events throughout the year, including an arts and crafts show, a jazz music festival, and a festival of lights at Christmas. The retail component is promoted through print and radio advertisements funded in part by a merchants association fee of $1.50 per square foot ($16.00 per square meter). All advertising campaigns use the tag line "Taking It to the Street" to promote the open-air main street experience.

At Valencia Town Center Drive, a very suburban location, the developer uses events to emphasize how much fun a pedestrian-friendly mixed-use environment can be compared with an enclosed consumer-oriented mall. Newhall Land encourages events, from a jazz festival to a concert series to family activities such as the Italian Street Painting Festival, to lure people to Town Center Drive.

The program for the first half of 2003 at Reston Town Center in Virginia includes seven to 11 events per month, with events shifting with the seasons. March events included an art show in an office lobby, a Girl Scout cookie sale on the plaza, a St. Patrick's Day celebration at Clyde's Restaurant, a blood drive, and a special free movie and social event for seniors; June events included Concerts

on the Town each Saturday night, a bicycle fundraiser for the American Diabetes Foundation, and the annual Taste of the Town food extravaganza.

Modest, simple events can also be effective marketing and management tools—and can even create income. At University Park at MIT, the management team programs activities in the common areas—festivals, tenants' use of open spaces (for a fee) for their own special events, tenant appreciation days (with ice cream), and seasonal activities and decorations. Any revenues generated by these activities are used to offset assessments.

In public/private developments, the public sector can also play a strong role in supporting events. At Addison Circle (see Chapter 8), the overall marketing of the project has benefited from the public/private partnership with the town of Addison, resulting in substantial positive press and public relations for the development. Events have drawn much interest from the surrounding community. For example, all Addison residents, businesses, and employees were invited to the grand unveiling in April 2000 of *Blueprints at Addison Circle,* a piece of public art paid for in part by the town of Addison that is located in the circle and celebrates Addison's history and its future.

Managing an extensive events program requires considerable time, talent, and budget. For managing large special events, firms are available that specialize in the creation of events and ongoing activities for a center, and they can assist with planning and management in coor-

A special annual event at Valencia Town Center Drive in Valencia, California, is the Italian Street Painting Festival.

dination with the property manager and marketing staff. A combination of on-site management and outside event managers and consultants can be very productive in establishing and maintaining a successful events program.

Marketing Components after Completion

Marketing following completion of the project seeks to achieve full occupancy at maximum rents to achieve an attractive stabilized income stream. Completion also affords somewhat different opportunities for marketing individual components. For the overall project, a series of planned tours for brokers, office space planners, residential interior decorators, public officials, business leaders, journalists, and so on can stimulate another round of interest in the mixed-use development. The emphasis also shifts for components. For example, marketing office space shifts from models, renderings, and brochures to the actual product, which makes the leasing agent's job easier—or more difficult—than before completion, depending on the quality of the final product and its actual state of completion. When a project is phased, the leasing agent may need to focus on convincing potential tenants that the project's other components will be completed as planned. Such phased and "unfinished" components offer special challenges. The agent must sell something that currently exists in the context of an environment that does not yet exist.

This one example shows why marketing must be represented in the planning stage of a mixed-use project. The decisions about what common elements and overall amenities and design features should be completed in Phase I may be critical to effective marketing and absorption rates for offices, residential sales or rentals, and the signing of retail tenants as development proceeds.

Even more than for office space, residential units must be completed to sell or rent units, as the interior layout and atmosphere of residential units are very difficult to convey in two dimensions; the actual product is a much more effective tool for selling or renting the space. Pro-

moting residential space is thus at its peak just before and within a year or two of the project's opening. During that time, heavy print, radio, and television advertising and referrals are the most effective tools. The image and success of the service retail space also plays an important role in selling or renting residential units.

Once the hotel is operational, most marketing activities for it are controlled by the hotel operator, including the on-site marketing staff and the hotel's national and international marketing and reservations staffs. More than for other uses in the project, the hotel's marketing efforts are oriented toward establishing a distinct identity for the hotel. Marketing must go well beyond the local area, requiring a separate staff and approach for promoting the hotel. Unlike marketing of the office and residential uses, promoting the hotel is a much more continuous activity. Here again, a location in a mixed-use project can be a distinct marketing advantage. If the mixed-use development achieves notable stature as a place, it rubs off on the hotel property. Moreover, tenants in the office component can be a reliable source of repeat business.

Promoting a large retail component is also a continuous activity. Retail space needs to be promoted as a whole, even though individual merchants will promote themselves. The two mechanisms that have been generally used for promoting a retail center are merchants associations and the marketing fund. A merchants association, the more traditional approach, is largely controlled by the merchants themselves, although the developer must also play a role and contribute financial resources. Marketing funds are a more recent innovation; they are totally controlled and administered by the developer/owner of the center. The advantage of marketing funds is that they free the center's marketing director from the many organizational details and internal politics of a merchants association, allowing him or her to concentrate on marketing and promotion rather than on management of the association.

Arts Night at Southlake Town Square in Southlake, Texas.

The central plaza at CityPlace in West Palm Beach, which draws people throughout the day and evening, is a major marketing benefit for the project.

Photographer: C.J. Walker; courtesy of Elkus/Manfredi Architects Ltd.

In some instances, a center has both a merchants association and a marketing fund, allowing merchants to focus their marketing efforts to their liking and the center's managers to focus on a broader and perhaps longer-term strategy. In any case, a marketing fund may work better for the retail component of a mixed-use project, as the center's management can concentrate more on overall marketing for the project without having to receive the agreement of a merchants association that might not be sophisticated enough to work jointly with the project's management.

In either case, tenants are assessed fees to help support the fund, and some funds are provided out of rents; the marketing entity is charged with promoting the retail component as a whole and with organizing promotional events. Most retail managers have found it helpful to focus on five or six major promotions during the year and to supplement them with appropriate smaller events. Promotional activities must be oriented toward sales rather than simply attracting people to events. Some retail centers have avoided using major special events, focusing instead on advertising in the local media. Few hard and fast rules exist about the appropriate advertising mix; promotional advertising generally relies on newspapers and a mix of other media appropriate for the center and the general location.

Notes

1. See Jo Allen Gause, et al., *Office Development Handbook*, 2nd ed. (Washington, D.C.: ULI–the Urban Land Institute, 1998), pp. 187–207, for basic marketing and leasing strategies; and Building Owners and Managers Association International and ULI–the Urban Land Institute, *What Office Tenants Want: 1999 BOMA/ULI Office Tenant Survey Report* (Washington, D.C.: BOMA International and ULI–the Urban Land Institute, 1999), for useful marketing strategies.

2. See Michael D. Beyard, W. Paul O'Mara, et al., *Shopping Center Development Handbook*, 3rd ed. (Washington, D.C.: ULI–the Urban Land Institute, 1999), pp. 221–227, for information on marketing shopping centers; and Michael D. Beyard, Raymond E. Braun, Herbert McLaughlin, Patrick L. Phillips, and Michael S. Rubin, *Developing Urban Entertainment Centers* (Washington, D.C.: ULI–the Urban Land Institute, 1998), for useful insights into the highly specialized concept of urban entertainment retail.

3. ICSC, 665 Fifth Avenue, New York, New York 10022.

4. See, e.g., Adrienne Schmitz, et al., *Multifamily Housing Development Handbook* (Washington, D.C.: ULI–the Urban Land Institute, 2000), pp. 163–180.

5. PKF Consulting, *Hotel Development* (Washington, D.C.: ULI–the Urban land Institute, 1996). Although this book does not focus specifically on marketing hotels, it does detail market segments and various types of hotel products; an appendix includes a list of major hotels with addresses of the headquarters office as of publication in 1996.

7. Operations, Management, and Maintenance

As large-scale mixed-use and joint public/private developments have evolved and matured in recent decades, they have also been the testing grounds for a variety of operations, management, and maintenance techniques. Early mixed-use projects tended to be much less complicated in ownership structure and therefore required less complicated approaches to issues of operations, management, and maintenance. Likewise, some of the early strategies, having been tested and found less than optimal, have been replaced or refined to meet current characteristics of the projects they must support. Thus, no simple formula exists for the design of operations, management, and maintenance structures for mixed-use properties. Rather, structures must reflect the particular nature of each project and the objectives of major participants.

This chapter examines some of the common operations, management, and maintenance issues in mixed-use development as well as some less common approaches that have been devised to handle specific situations. It therefore develops some generalities and then provides illustrative examples as evidence of current and diverse practice. Because so many current and planned mixed-use properties operate under public/private and/or joint venture relationships, they have more complex and varied solutions to operations, management, and maintenance

Renovated and redeveloped in the 1980s, Tower City Center in Cleveland includes numerous buildings that have endured since the 1930s.

structures. The chapter also addresses special management issues, such as managing noise, odors, parking, traffic, and promotion, as well as asset management.

Operational Issues and Challenges

Mixed-use properties often require complex management structures, but the objective should always be to keep the structure as simple and straightforward as possible. This same objective drives the initial structure of a mixed-use development itself, but the very nature of projects with multiple uses makes them prone to complexity from the start that is then merely reflected in the operations, management, and maintenance structure needed. The added features of public/private joint ventures merely expand the number of operations, management, and maintenance issues that need resolution.

Two overriding questions should be addressed upfront in establishing a management plan: How will operating responsibilities and costs be allocated to the various entities? How can the detailed operating needs of each use be best served in the overall development and management plan?

Allocating Responsibilities and Costs
Centralized control, to the extent that it is possible, is still regarded as the most desirable (but not always achievable) strategy for successful operations, manage-

Yerba Buena Center has been under development for more than 20 years. One of the newest additions is the Four Seasons Hotel and Residences, at the center behind the park. The Yerba Buena Alliance, a membership organization of property and business owners and residents, provides publicity and public information, oversees and monitors the neighborhood, and facilitates outdoor events and programming.

ment, and maintenance of mixed-use projects. A typical mixed-use project has three or more separate and distinct income-producing entities, each needing distinct operations, management, and maintenance requirements. But unless these entities have an effective overriding operations and management structure responsible for oversight, management conflicts, operating difficulties, and varying maintenance standards, problems can adversely affect the whole project and the synergism of its components.

A central management entity can coordinate or provide security, ensure that the component uses do not metamorphose into incompatible uses, ensure that common areas and building exteriors are maintained, manage shared parking, and provide utilities and other commonly needed services. A central management structure does not, however, preclude allocation of operations, management, and maintenance to components. In some instances in fact, this strategy is the most desirable one for effective operations, management, and maintenance.

The two major challenges in managing mixed-use properties involve determining the best allocation of responsibilities and allocating the cost of common centrally provided services among the project's participants. These challenges are especially difficult when, as is often the case, participants have radically different operating needs and motivations. For example, a large retail component requires significantly different security arrangements, parking operations, waste removal, cleaning and delivery schedules, promotion, and events management from an office or residential component. Parking facilities require specialized operating skills not found in most development organizations. These differences have to be resolved in the design of the operations, management, and maintenance structure.

Too often in [mixed-use developments], common expenses are allocated among land uses on the basis of rote formulas such as square footage. The problem is that once these formulas are put in place, they usually cannot be changed without the consent of all property owners. For example, a community has 10,000 square feet [930 square meters] of commercial uses and 90,000 square feet [8,400 square meters] of residential uses, and common expenses are allocated on the basis of a 90-to-10 ratio. Rather than just assume that this ratio is correct, the property owners association should evaluate carefully the nature and extent of the expenses that each land use in the community might generate. As part of this process, each item in the budget of the property owners association should be evaluated to determine whether any one land use disproportionately generates shared expenses. Specific issues to be considered for each land use might include the following: the rate at which shared utilities are expected to be consumed; the traffic anticipated to be generated by each user on common roads; whether there will be limitations on the hours that each land user can operate; the expected costs of maintaining, insuring, and operating common property, facilities, and services; and the extent to which any land use will need to be monitored for security.[1]

Gloucester Green is a mixed-use development in Oxford, England, that includes retail shops and restaurants, private flats, offices, the refurbished Old Fire Station arts complex, a bus station, an underground parking garage, and public open space. A cinema, shops, and other town center uses are nearby. Most of the buildings as well as the bus station and the main "piazza" were built as a piece in the late 1980s. The development is situated approximately one-quarter mile (0.4 kilometer) from the main shopping center of Oxford. The main plaza space is entirely pedestrian, although one edge incorporates a taxi stand. The bus station forms a distinct and separate territory within the development as a whole. The main spaces are open 24 hours a day, and there is no control over pedestrian access.

Gloucester Green is an urban development whose shops, restaurants, and main open space are mainly given over to leisure consumption aimed at a mix of predominantly upscale visitors and local businesses. The majority of retail outlets are specialty shops, boutiques, relatively expensive gift shops, and cafés. The arts complex, the Old Fire Station, is at one corner of the main open space. The space is also given over to a food market one day a week, which caters to a much broader range of users than the shops and cafés. A clear attempt has been made to create a definite place—a stylish quarter—in the city through the use of building forms to enclose the main spaces.

Gloucester Green involves a mix of ownerships, making its management complex. The office and residential elements are under freehold ownership, whereas the retail outlets are currently owned by a large development company, Guardian Properties. Guardian built the main piazza space as part of its planning obligations. The city council owns the main piazza space, and Guardian manages it under a somewhat vague leasing arrangement, allowing Guardian considerable control over the use of the space but also implying that Guardian is responsible for providing security for the space. The arrangement between Guardian Properties and the retailers who lease outlets is somewhat similar to that in many shopping centers. The owners manage the space on behalf of the retailers and levy a service charge to pay for maintenance, promotions, and advertising. Although privately managed, the piazza remains under ownership of the city council, which, in Guardian's view, makes it difficult to control users and uses.

The intent of management's leasing policy has been to create an upscale retail environment. The model that the company had in mind was a continental square served by street cafés aimed at attracting middle-class consumers drawn for the most part from staff and students at the university. This plan has been very difficult to achieve because of legal requirements to allow access for emergency vehicles to the buildings themselves and a requirement to keep the central space clear for the weekly market. Moreover, management found the market itself detrimental to the tone it wished to convey. Another significant factor that has constrained the creation of an upscale ambience is the presence of fast-food outlets and a betting shop on one side of the square owned by a company whose leasing policy is somewhat different from Guardian's.

Source: Resource for Urban Design Information, www.rudi.net, accessed October 30, 2000.

■

When a public component and public participation or interests are involved, other issues may be raised. The public's ability, or inability, to provide services or share costs is often at odds with private requirements for a reliable management, maintenance, or operations model. For example, public officials are more concerned with initial capital cost than with future operating costs. They often find ongoing operations and maintenance costs a fiscal burden and thus tend to underestimate them. In contrast, to remain competitive, the private sector may urge public agencies to provide higher-than-average maintenance or operating standards that public agencies find difficult—if not impossible—to provide. Politics enters the picture, making it difficult to hold public agencies to any consistent, continuing financial support for operations and maintenance. Under these circumstances, projects with public participation, whether true codevelopment projects or merely the public sector's requirements for certain performance from the developer as a prerequisite for approval, present particular and difficult challenges. Solutions should always call for management arrangements that put a premium on strong central control, effective mechanisms for resolving conflicts, and flexibility.

Understanding Operational Details

All too often, developers do not give priority to the details of postdevelopment operations and management as the project is conceived and is evolving. Although this timing suffices for projects with one owner or one use, developers of more complex mixed-use developments have found that arrangements for operations, management, and maintenance must have equal priority with physical planning and design and financial planning, and must be reassessed at various stages of a project.

Thus, initial planning and deal making for complex mixed-use projects must also include planning for how the project will be operated, managed, and maintained not only after it is constructed but also during phases when the entire project infrastructure is still incomplete. This approach ensures that a logical and efficient operations, management, and maintenance strategy—one that supports the objectives of the various participants effectively and thus enhances the value of the project for tenants, owners, and the community—is available during design and phasing of the development.

The following management, maintenance, and operations issues must be addressed upfront:

- configuration, ownership, and sharing of spaces and systems;
- definition of rights of use for common areas;
- assignment of responsibilities and allocation of costs for maintenance and operation of common and public areas;
- allocation of costs and responsibilities for maintenance of external site components, including landscaping, parking areas, and building exteriors;
- parking management and sharing;
- controls on and approval of exterior signage, exterior changes, and maintenance responsibilities;
- assignment of costs for utility systems (which may overlap among areas);
- responsibilities for trash disposal, snow removal, and other public services;
- provision of security and safety, particularly at the boundaries of public and private areas;

- assignment of responsibilities for promotion and marketing;
- liability for accidents or damages occurring in common areas;
- event management, social programming, and liveliness of common areas and open spaces;
- hours of operation and possible conflicts between the right of access to public spaces (such as transit system entries and public throughways in a project) and security, especially after operating hours, for various uses.

Operating problems are much easier to address and solve in the planning and design stage of the development process than they are in the operating stage.

Negotiating Management and Maintenance Agreements

Management and maintenance agreements involve varying degrees of complexity, depending on the nature and number of parties involved, the configuration and design of the project, and the role of the public sector. Success requires cooperation among these parties to result in legal agreements that are equitable, agreeable to all, and carefully crafted to reflect current and future ownership and operational issues.

Photographer: C.J. Walker; courtesy of Elkus/Manfredi Architects Ltd.

CityPlace was developed by Related Urban Group (formerly Palladium), a diversified real estate company with expertise in a wide range of property types and in developing mixed-use projects. With more than 600,000 square feet (55,742 square meters) of retail space, the retail component of CityPlace enjoys the coordinated marketing and management of a regional shopping mall.

WestEnd City Center was developed through a joint venture between Hungarian and North American development firms, with the expertise of each important in establishing operational plans for the project.

The Participants

Although many mixed-use properties are created by a joint venture of one or more private entities, many include some degree of public or quasi-public participation. For example, one of the parties might be an institution such as the Massachusetts Institute of Technology, whose objectives are long term and may or may not be the same as the public partner's interests.

An overseas project such as WestEnd City Center in Budapest, Hungary, that is a joint venture partnership (TriGranit) of a North American developer, TrizecHahn Corporation, and a Hungarian development company, Granit Polus R.A., required the two companies with different business cultures to resolve their different management and operational behaviors. In addition, the North American company had to learn the operational practices of various levels of government and the expected concessions required to obtain approvals from the Hungarian Ministry of Transportation for transportation issues, the city of Budapest for some approvals, a district government in the city for others, the national Historical and Cultural Assets Commission, and a government architectural committee, to name a few. Having knowledgeable local partners was crucial to the success of the project. Although this example might be replicated in the United States, power sharing and the approval process differ. Thus, local expertise is always needed.

Many mixed-use properties have participants with overlapping and divergent interests, not all of which are profit motivated, particularly when public, quasi-public, or nonprofit entities are involved. Developers must fully understand their own objectives, some of which may be variations of profit motives, for example, the creation of value for the tax base and long-term appreciation for quasi-public participants to which project ownership eventually will revert.

Often, a public party's objectives involve creating jobs or open space, or providing public facilities. For example, nonprofit organizations such as museums or performing arts groups want to pour all the resources they can into their primary objective and thus are inclined to want relief from certain costs, such as common area maintenance (CAM) costs. Thus, it is necessary to identify all participants' objectives as the project is conceived and refined so that divergent objectives can be addressed in the operational, management, and maintenance structure.

Structuring the Agreement

When it comes to the creation of management and maintenance agreements, common objectives should be identified, particularly with respect to cost efficiency and operational effectiveness. It is also important to recognize that each party may be able to provide certain operations, management, or maintenance skills and that, conversely, some entities may be adverse to or unable to provide specific operations, management, or maintenance functions or even funding. For example, at Lindbergh City Center in Atlanta, MARTA, the local transit authority, was averse to paying CAM charges but could provide security for the project.

The maintenance and management agreement, sometimes referred to as a Construction, Operation, and Reciprocal Easement Agreement, should create a "three-dimensional subdivision that includes one or more street-level and air space or air rights parcels," according to Edward C. Hagerott. The agreement should include provisions dealing with easements; each owner's construction obligations; the use, operation, maintenance, and alteration of each component; insurance requirements; restrictions on transfer and preferential purchase rights; remedies; and mortgage rights and protections. "The [agreement] should describe all of the shared project components in a precise manner to help ensure that it creates all of the necessary easements and properly allocates the maintenance responsibility for each component."[2]

A developer will place restrictive covenants against a property to achieve one or more of the following:

- to restrict the use of the property and thereby preserve and enhance value and ensure orderly functioning and operation;
- to provide for maintenance, repair, and replacement of facilities that are shared by individually owned units;
- to grant easements and other rights of use in favor of the owners of units of the real estate in any common areas and facilities and in other units;
- to provide a means of describing, in a legally sufficient manner, units of real estate that are to be separately owned (for example, condominium units consisting of individually owned spaces in a single building); and
- to address what will be done in the event of damage or destruction.

Legal requirements are imposed by two basic bodies of law: common law, largely derived from Anglo-Saxon jurisprudence and established by decisions rendered by the appellate courts of the federal government and the states in controversies that are brought before them; and statutory law, enacted by the legislatures of the United States and the states and codified in the statutes of the United States and the states.

The threshold issue underpinning every effort to impose restrictive covenants upon real property is whether, under common law, they are enforceable in the first place. In general, common law has upheld restrictive covenants not contrary to law or public policy. However, a fundamental concept recognized in most jurisdictions is that such covenants are to be strictly and narrowly construed in favor of the free use of property. The basis of this doctrine is that the conveyance of fee simple title (that is, complete ownership) of property is inconsistent with the imposition of limits on its use. Thus, the courts of most states are under a mandate imposed by existing case law not to expand the effect of restrictions beyond the evident intent of the drafter. For example, a restriction against mobile homes or trailers might not prohibit a manufactured home that does not have axles and has been placed on property in the same manner as a stick-built house.

Covenants will have limited value if they do not bind and obligate every party thereafter owning the real estate covered by those covenants. As between the parties to the initial conveyance, the covenants should be enforceable in any event. But if they are not "real" covenants that "run with the land," they may not be enforceable against and among purchasers who acquire their lots from the original buyers. Courts have drawn elaborate and somewhat illogical rules for determining whether or not a developer can enforce covenants against second-generation buyers, and whether such buyers can enforce the covenants against each other. Courts also have shied away from enforcing covenants that do not "touch and concern" the land as "real" covenants. For example, a restrictive covenant establishing a minimum setback pretty clearly touches and concerns the land. But a requirement that a property owner maintain a membership in a club that owns recreational amenities adjoining the subdivision might not be a "real" covenant and thus might not bind a subsequent owner of the real estate.

Another principle recognized in many state courts is that affirmative obligations, especially monetary obligations (such as the payment of assessments), are to be carefully scrutinized and will not be enforced as covenants running with the land unless stated with enough specificity to withstand scrutiny as enforceable contracts. Therefore, an obligation of an owner to pay assessments to a property owners association for common area maintenance, where the common areas are defined in general rather than specific terms, may not be enforceable under common law. The standard imposed is a high one, and may be impossible to achieve in the phased development of a large tract over several years. In such developments, it is impossible at the outset to predict the extent of common areas that might ultimately be incorporated (for example, the number of miles of roads, the acres of common space open area, the number of entrance features and signs, and similar common features).

An additional principle derived from case law is that, to be enforceable, restrictions must promote a uniform scheme of development. The ability of a developer under restrictions to modify those restrictions unilaterally might destroy a uniform scheme of development and render the restrictions unenforceable. In a large, multiphase, multiyear development, it is impossible to know initially everything a declaration might need to cover. And yet no developer wants to be compelled to approach previous purchasers and ask for consent to a declaration modification for fear that the owners to whom the request is made will ask for something in return or will refuse outright—perhaps due to dissatisfaction with an unrelated matter.

The common law is rife with cases on the specificity with which real estate must be described. The preferred methods are by reference to a recorded plat, or by a metes-and-bounds description drafted from a current survey. This need for a specific description creates challenges with air parcels and air rights, although as this becomes a more common method of ownership, attorneys are developing ways to describe air parcels and air rights under common law principles. However, to describe a block of enclosed space within a building with the specificity required by these common law principles is prohibitively cumbersome, and thus statutory law providing for the creation of condominiums must be relied upon to enable lawyers to draft a legally sufficient description of a unit within a building.

Finally, many restrictive covenants, and especially those for commercial developments, include first refusal or first offer rights in favor of the developer with regard to the resale of undeveloped parcels, or rights of repurchase in favor of the developer relating to parcels upon which construction does not start within a specified time after the closing. These rights might be held unenforceable under the common law Rule Against Perpetuities, the bane of many a law student. The Rule Against Perpetuities invalidates interests in real estate that do not "vest" within a required period of time. Most states have adopted statutory modifications of the Rule Against Perpetuities that eliminate its strict application. Even if there is no problem with Rule Against Perpetuities, however, such rights might be stricken by a court under its equity powers if they are not reasonable in terms of duration and pricing.

Fortunately, most states have enacted legislation that mitigates the effect of these common law principles. Without this legislation, structuring enforceable restrictive covenants would be a haphazard endeavor. However, these common law principles cannot be ignored. They are not abolished by the enactment of legislation, and the positions reflected in the decisions of the appellate courts on these principles indicate how those courts will interpret the statutes.

Source: Brian P. Evans, "Restrictive Covenants for Mixed-Use," *Urban Land*, February 2003, pp. 25–26. Evans is a partner in the real estate department in the Charlotte office of Kennedy Covington Lobdell & Hickman, LLP.

Agreements must be carefully tailored to the project and the parties involved, and structuring them is a multidisciplinary effort involving operational, design, financial, legal, and perhaps other types of expertise. This effort should begin at project conception and, for the most part, should be worked out in general if not specific terms during predevelopment.

Negotiations for an operations, management, and maintenance agreement encompass several phases:

- recognizing that the appropriate operations, management, and maintenance responsibilities are necessary parts of a development agreement package among the participants;
- establishing the public or private nature of each major component;
- determining public and private objectives for the areas common to both;
- assessing the operation, management, and maintenance skills and propensities of each participant as well as each one's ability and willingness to fund the specific tasks identified;
- estimating the benefits and costs of operating, managing, or maintaining the project by alternative means;
- agreeing on a specific operations, management, or maintenance structure for meeting the objectives;
- defining costs for operations, management, or maintenance that should be allocated;
- agreeing on how such costs should be shared.

The negotiations must balance the interests of all parties involved. Because reaching a specific agreement may be a lengthy process, it may be necessary to fashion an interim, more general, memorandum of understanding that simply designates the management structure and duties but leaves room for further negotiations about the mix of participants and sharing of costs. Initial estimates of costs assist in determining expenses to be negotiated. Other factors shaping the agreement are each party's interest in participating in the operation of the project and the public entity's objectives and experience in similar projects. In every case, however, the key to a successful operations and management strategy is centralized control, even when subactivities are delegated to one or more of several participants in a mixed-use development.

Public/Private Negotiations

Cities with experience in public/private projects usually attempt to minimize the public role in operations or management, except when a specific public service can be performed on publicly owned space, for example, a public parking garage. Public agencies may prefer to avoid making decisions or signing agreements on operations and management issues upfront and would rather defer agreement until problems arise that necessitate negotiation. Because they are at greater risk if maintenance is inadequate or a management problem needs immediate action, developers should seek to

Kuala Lumpur City Centre in Malaysia, featuring the twin Petronas Towers, is one of the largest and most complex mixed-use properties in the world.

avoid this approach. Like the need for central control, the need for certainty in operations and management responsibilities should be settled as soon as possible in the development process.

Negotiations regarding public use areas present some special issues:

- Although development will be approved by appointed planning and elected bodies, some aspects of operations, management, or maintenance may involve government departments or quasi-independent agencies that may not have the same commitment to equitable resolution, which can lead to conflicting public objectives.
- Public disclosure of negotiating positions, which may be required under certain conditions, should be avoided to the extent possible. Reporting positions and objectives in the media may create expectations in the community that make it more difficult for all parties to achieve an agreement.
- Negotiations by the public sector are often burdened with the requirement to satisfy a negotiations policy committee. Such a body may have to approve the initial negotiating position, provide specific guidance for "agreements in principle," and approve final binding agreements. The process of keeping the committee on board throughout negotiations may be difficult for all involved.

Key Topics in a Management and Maintenance Agreement

The nature and operational requirements of mixed-use properties vary, and thus the features of operations, management, or maintenance agreements are often quite different, depending on the location, physical configuration, ownership, and other aspects of the project itself. Several basic concepts and issues are generally addressed in any agreement, however, including common area maintenance and use standards, utilities and HVAC systems, design approval, security, and financial administration.

Basic Issues and Concerns

A number of underlying concerns are common to nearly all agreements for professional management. Parties to such agreements should ensure that the following issues are addressed:

- Does the agreement provide for effective management of common areas and internal boundaries where two uses adjoin?
- Does it establish uniform standards for maintenance, operation, and use, regardless of ownership?
- Does it provide mutual protection for all owners against deterioration and adverse use of separately owned or leased portions of the project?

At Mizner Park in Boca Raton, Florida, the development process and thus its management, maintenance, and operations are almost the reverse of most public/private projects—being more a private/public project. City planners had identified the site as desirable for redevelopment and had a concept of what they wanted to happen. The city, through its redevelopment agency, was exploring acquisition through purchase or eminent domain. The developer, Crocker & Company, asked the city to determine whether it could avoid competitive selection if it controlled the land. Upon securing a positive determination, Crocker & Company purchased the land. The developer then sold the land to the redevelopment agency subject to a 99-year lease for a series of five building pads; those leases were subject to a whole range of reciprocal cross-easements to ensure access. The responsibility for CAM evolved. As owner of the site, the Community Redevelopment Agency (CRA) is legally responsible for maintaining everything but the five pads—the central plaza, Mizner Park, the streets and the outside sidewalks (those not under the arcades fronting the buildings lining the two streets on either side of the park), and various accessways. The developer built the parking structures within the boundaries of the five pads and therefore is responsible for their construction, maintenance, and operation. Although CRA did not participate in the parking structures, the master lease agreement provides that the developer make available a certain number of spaces at all times. To date, parking (except valet parking) is free; however, the lease reserves the developer's right to charge for parking.

The solution for the provision of maintenance is also complicated by some unanticipated circumstances. Development approval required covenants governing maintenance and operation of the common areas and a provision that allows the developer to provide operations and maintenance to a higher standard, with the increased costs of doing so expensed against lease charges. The lease requires a base rent and a participating rent based on net operating income.

The first complication was that, in the last minutes of negotiations, an error was found in terms of certain requirements for the bond coverage. To remedy this problem so as not to delay the closing, the developer agreed to assume responsibility for CAM for five years. This solution took an estimated annual budget obligation off the tax increment and land rents and brought the transaction into the bond coverage requirement. The developer had never intended to take on any responsibility for maintenance, and at the end of five years, the issue came to the fore. The developer would not accept the city staff as the maintenance agency, recognizing that they would not meet the desired standard. As a result, the city sought open bids on a maintenance contract, awarding it to the

Mizner Park involves a public/private management agreement whereby the city of Boca Raton and its redevelopment agency are responsible for maintaining the central plaza and park, the streets, and various accessways, while the owner is responsible for maintaining the parking structures and buildings.

low bidder (which was not the developer). An attempt to prevent award of the contract to the low bidder failed. Within less than two months, CRA received complaints about the quality of maintenance, resulting in termination of the contract. CRA then entered into a negotiated agreement with the developer to provide CAM; CRA makes an annual payment to the developer that is less than the actual cost of maintaining the common areas.

Another complication surfaced. The original plan reserved two sites for future cultural users, the International Museum of Cartoon Art and the Center for the Arts. Their leases make them responsible for maintenance and operations on their pads, but the developer has assumed responsibility for maintenance of all common areas of the nonprofits, reflecting a concern about the nonprofits' ability to provide the desired standard of maintenance.

Could this series of circumstances be anticipated? Unlikely. But the provision that allows the developer to apply a higher maintenance standard and charge such additional costs against the lease base and participating rent works to reduce the unrecoverable costs to the developer and still ensures the long-term quality of this mixed-use project.

The developer of Abacoa Town Center in Jupiter, Florida, created an umbrella association to provide for operations, management, and maintenance of common areas and facilities, including tracts for parking, parking structures, and the theater green and stage.

Courtesy of de Guardiola Development, Inc.

- Does it incorporate promotional mechanisms and responsibilities, with fair representation of diverse interests?
- Does it provide for equitable sharing of financing by the project's beneficiaries?
- Does it ensure continuity in public participation, where appropriate, despite policy or organizational changes in the public agency's participants?
- Does it ensure continuity of private responsibilities to the public should ownership or control of pieces of the project change?
- Does it provide a mechanism for change and flexibility where needed to deal with unforeseeable circumstances and events?

The alternatives are articulated in a prototype agreement in which a specially created corporation bears responsibility for the operations and management of a mixed-use development and the maintenance of common areas, which might include public areas. The corporation has the authority to use its own staff or other contractors to provide services to owners or operators of various components of the project. The structure of such a corporation is established by its bylaws. The corporation thus becomes the single operations and management entity with responsibilities established in the articles of incorporation and operational expectations, management practices, maintenance responsibilities, and funding as set forth in its bylaws or ancillary legal documents and agreements among the interested parties.

In this model, the corporation is a nonprofit organization and does not issue stock. Each participant entity in the mixed-use development is entitled to the number of votes proportionate to the value of money and/or service it contributes to the corporation. Nonvoting members might be appointed to maintain coordination with units of government or private groups.

Daily operations, management, and maintenance are the responsibility of a general manager, with oversight by an executive committee. The general manager could be one of the members of the corporation (for example, the principal developer) or a separate management firm; it carries out daily maintenance in accordance with the policies determined by the corporation and the approved budget. The manager recommends changes in the policies or budget, keeps accounts for the maintenance entity's income and expenses, hires and discharges personnel and contractors for the range of responsibilities required of the corporation, and keeps members of the corporation informed of general operations through periodic performance reports and notification of extraordinary events that might require resolution by corporate members. The corporation, through its general manager, is responsible for major operating functions.

Common Area Maintenance and Use Standards

With mixed-use properties varying from mixed-use towers to multibuilding complexes and multiblock town centers and districts, the type and extent of the common area varies widely as well. Whatever the configuration of common areas, the corporation is responsible for all maintenance services in those areas. Depending on the nature of the common area, it might include everything from building and systems maintenance to street cleaning, snow removal, landscape maintenance, trash removal, space renovation, and any other activities needed to keep the facility maintained to a defined standard. It might also be required under contract to provide similar or specialized services in noncommon areas of the project. The corporation should be free to fulfill these responsibilities by the most efficient means available: hiring employees directly, subcontracting services to an independent maintenance firm, or purchasing management services from the developer, for example.

At Tabor Center, a multibuilding complex in downtown Denver, the original management plan called for Williams Realty to manage common facilities, the project's exteriors, and the office building, while the Rouse

Company managed the retail space and Westin managed the hotel. Common facilities include the parking garage and loading dock and a central chilled-water plant. Williams also managed a life safety/security system, which includes four separate fire command centers and one 24-hour security command post. The development has since been sold and is now managed by Equity Office Properties and Urban Retail Properties.

At Abacoa Town Center in Jupiter, Florida, the developer has created an umbrella association to provide for operations, management, and maintenance of all common areas, including tracts for parking, parking structures, an outdoor theater green, and special events. The association's costs are built into rents for the residential units and into the CAM charge for the retail component. In Downtown Silver Spring, Maryland, Montgomery County plans to create, under a special provision of Maryland law, the Silver Spring Urban District Corporation to provide common area maintenance; at MetroTech Center, a mixed-use development in Brooklyn, a business improvement district (BID) provides public area maintenance in the common areas where superior maintenance standards are needed.

Whether common areas are enclosed or exterior open space, the corporation establishes standards for the use of the common area under its authority and maintains control over activities carried out there. It ensures that the general public, tenants, merchants, workers, and customers are afforded appropriate access to the areas during normal business hours and regulates access after hours. This function includes issuing permits to merchants, other tenants, the developer, the city, civic organizations, or anyone else who wants to use the area for sales, shows, special displays, other promotional activities, and special events deemed appropriate for the space. The corporation might collect fees to defray the costs of maintenance and utilities for such special events.

Utilities and HVAC

The corporation might furnish some or all utilities, including lighting, electrical power, natural gas, and water, by whatever method it deems most appropriate. A requirement to maintain separate accounting and billing for the common areas means that metered wiring, plumbing, and other utilities would have to be designed and constructed for each entity for which it is required. The design of the project determines the feasibility of accommodating these requirements. The feasibility of such an arrangement should be determined before the corporation is formed. An alternative to separate metering of utilities is the assessment of charges based on the square footage or some other fair method, which again should be determined in advance of finalizing various operations, management, and maintenance agreements.

The corporation maintains and operates HVAC systems for enclosed common areas, and it should be free to manage the systems in the optimum manner. The need for separate cost accounting and control over these systems probably requires that they also be physically independent from the privately controlled facilities in the complex. The feasibility of establishing separate systems should be determined by engineering studies. Again, if separate systems are not feasible, charges should be based on some method for prorating shares of benefits.

In San Diego's Ballpark Neighborhood, utility facilities are shared by reciprocal easements set forth in a declaration of covenants, conditions, and restrictions between the parcels and project elements and then maintained by the Park Owners Association, a nonprofit mutual benefit corporation. The utility facilities include:

> . . . all intake and exhaust fans, storm and sanitary sewer systems, drainage systems, common ducting systems for ventilation and utility services, domestic water systems, natural gas systems, electrical systems, fire protection water systems, telephone systems, cable television systems, telecommunication systems, fiber-optic systems, chilled water and heated water systems, central utility services, and all other utility systems and facilities reasonably necessary to service improvements situated in, on, over, and under the Parcel.

Each mixed-use development has a somewhat different set of utility services that might be best served by a central entity. It is important that these services be identified early in the conceptual stage of the mixed-use development and be thus accommodated by the legal structure and physical design.

Numerous entities are involved in development of the proposed San Diego Ballpark District, including the San Diego Padres organization; Hines, which is the development manager of the ballpark; JMI Realty, which is undertaking development of hotel and condominium properties in the district; and the city of San Diego, the Center City Development Corporation, and the port of San Diego, which are providing financing. The plan was developed by Roma Design Group.

Design Approval

Approving design changes that affect the physical appearance, safety, convenience, or efficient use of the common areas is a responsibility of the corporation after the project is completed. This requirement may also apply to various elements under private control such as signs, permanent advertisements, and decorations and to exterior design changes for various buildings in a multibuilding complex and for such things as rooftop appurtenances. Although such constraints might affect the marketability of the overall project, failure to establish such control may be detrimental to the long-term value of the mixed-use development.

At WestEnd City Center, both the national Historical and Cultural Assets Commission and a local government architectural committee had to approve the initial design and any subsequent changes. At University Park at MIT, the Declaration of Covenants and the Design Guidelines are used to tie the interests of the developer, the city of Cambridge, and MIT together to establish design standards that were used to control the initial design and to manage design changes over time.

Security

The corporation is responsible for protecting the physical security of persons and property in the common areas. It provides security personnel during and after normal hours of operation, coordinating measures with security personnel who operate in adjoining public and private spaces. It might operate a centralized surveillance system, or it might hire a private security service. The corporation might also negotiate operating agreements for extra patrols with the city police department. Thus, the corporation continuously coordinates and maintains security arrangements with both public and private security forces.

A major concern in eastern Europe is security. In some eastern European countries, organized crime syndicates prey on small retailers through extortion, and the local police are often ineffective at curbing the problem. Ensuring the safety of both customers and tenants at WestEnd City Center in Budapest was therefore a top priority. In the shopping mall, hotel, and office areas, uniformed security personnel form a highly visible presence, and all entrances to the project are protected by cameras. These measures, along with a generally proactive approach to safety and security, have been very successful. Not a single major security incident has occurred at the center since the project opened.

At Lindbergh City Center in Atlanta, plans call for MARTA to provide security under the cost-sharing agreement in exchange for relief from CAM charges. At University Park at MIT, private security is provided 24 hours a day in several ways. Each building has a security guard; a security van tours the interior streets, the perimeter of the park, and the parking garages; foot and bike patrols are active; and a guard will escort tenants to their vehicles in the garages upon request. At MetroTech Center in Brooklyn, 28 public safety officers with special status

MARTA will provide security at Lindbergh City Center in Atlanta under a cost-sharing agreement in exchange for relief from common area charges.

as peace officers provide 24-hour, seven-day-a-week patrols throughout the district.

Financial Administration

The corporation is authorized to collect and manage fees from the various parties of the management corporation for the services it provides. A formula for assessments and fees might be stipulated in land disposition or land leasing agreements between public and private participants in the development, but a mechanism should be provided to modify the formula when changed circumstances result in inequities. Because the public also uses common areas, the corporation retains the ability to receive and manage funds from the city or other public bodies. At Mizner Park, the developer provides all CAM. The master land lease with the city contains a base rent and a participating rent, and covenants set the standards for operations and maintenance but allow the developer to expense above-normal costs against his lease charges.

Approaches to Operations and Management

Operations and management in typical mixed-use developments have evolved through trial and error into major participants' striking a deal acceptable to all. For mixed-use projects in general, the early tendency to divide a project into separately managed components or spaces gradually yielded to a perceived need for more central management. Possibilities range from a single private management ownership entity to private associations, public/private management entities, and business improvement districts.

General Approaches and Issues

Developers have used several general approaches, each offering a variety of techniques and differing in various ways from the model corporation described in the previous section:

- developer's ownership and/or management of all uses, with subcontracts for specialized uses;
- creation of a distinct operations/management/ maintenance entity separate from the principal parties but representing their interests;
- division among the project's participants of responsibilities for specific components or geographic sectors;
- when numerous owners are involved, delegation of responsibilities for common areas or a specific management/operations function to an involved party, usually the developer but occasionally another participant in the project;
- creation of an areawide management system for a mixed-use district with a large number of separate ownerships.

Often one of the major issues is the division of responsibilities between public and private entities. Although the various private entities presumably can agree on sharing costs and responsibilities because they recognize the desirability of establishing the most cost-effective and profitable approach to such division, the public sector is often driven by public interests and political concerns that are different from those of the private participants and thus more difficult to resolve. The following examples of various operations, management, and mainte-

nance structures demonstrate the wide range of solutions that have been created for mixed-use developments.

Direct Management by the Developer

The most straightforward management approach involves strictly private projects where the master developer/ owner handles management largely in house, with subcontracts to other entities when specialized expertise is required. At Peabody Place in Memphis (see Chapter 8), Belz Enterprises, the owner and developer, markets and oversees the management of the Peabody Place properties, subcontracting for the day-to-day management of the residences and office space and directly managing the hotel and the retail, including a general manager for the entire retail portion of the project.

At Sony Center am Potsdamer Platz (see Chapter 8), Tishman Speyer Properties Deutschland, under a property management and leasing agreement, is fully responsible for leasing and property management, including lease administration, service and security contracts, budgeting and procurement, and tenant support and coordination. These functions are handled by a full-time staff of 16 people. Costs are allocated to tenants according to a complex formula that splits common area costs four ways: costs related to a specific tenant, costs related to a specific building, costs related to the use of a tenant, and costs related to the overall project. By using direct costs incurred by the tenant and by allocating a portion of the common area costs according to this formula, all

Courtesy of de Guardiola Development, Inc.

At Abacoa Town Center in Jupiter, Florida, apartment residents pay for common area maintenance strictly through rents while retail tenants are assessed common area maintenance charges.

Although the apartment and retail uses at Pentagon Row were developed separately by separate owners, the two owner/operators have created a management structure and a formula to manage the shared spaces.

tenants are ensured that they are paying a fair share of the project's common area costs.

At WestEnd City Center in Budapest, TriGranit Management Company, a subsidiary of the developer, is property manager for all the property's common areas, excluding the hotel interior. A separate company manages the parking facilities, and all costs and revenues incurred by this company are part of a separate third-party contract with TriGranit. Operational expenses for the common areas are shared by the different users. The office tenants and the hotel pay a defined contribution for the maintenance of the exterior common areas, while the retail tenants pay a prorated share of the remaining exterior common area costs. Tenants in the shopping center also pay for 100 percent of the enclosed retail common area costs, and office tenants and the hotel operators pay for 100 percent of the enclosed office and hotel building costs.

Separate Management Entities and Associations

Associations and other separate management entities are also often employed to manage the development.

> Although master associations can be set up in a variety of ways, . . . a basic framework might include two subassociations—one for residential and one for nonresidential owners. In addition to being members of their respective subassociation, all property owners also would be members of the overall master association. Master associations provide a vehicle through which owners of different types of property can communicate regularly with each other and resolve differences. Over time, such associations can foster a greater sense of community and enable each property owner to have a better understanding of where he or she fits in the larger scheme of the development.[3]

At Abacoa Town Center, a single developer and one entity maintain common areas and facilities. Rather than keep these functions within the development company, however, the developer created an umbrella association to provide for the management, operations, and maintenance of all common areas. Because individual tenants in the rental residential units could not be assessed a CAM charge, the cost of their participation in the umbrella association is built into the rent. For the retail component, the cost is built into CAM charges and transferred to the umbrella association. This model is relatively simple but still meets the needs of the mixed-use development for which it was devised.

Another example of an association is Phillips Place in Charlotte. The development strategy for this multi-building mixed-use development was to have each major component of the project separately owned and managed. The Harris Group owns and manages the retail portion; Post Properties owns and manages the apartments; and a partnership of the Harris Group and the Panos Hotel Group owns the hotel, with the latter managing the property. Ownership of the residential and retail portions of the buildings that include residential over retail space is divided between the residential and retail owners/developers. Maintenance of landscaping along the entrances is shared by Post Properties, the Harris Group, and the hotel partnership. The hotel pays a set monthly fee for its share of landscaping and lighting. Retail tenants pay for their share of common area maintenance based on the size of their space. The retail, residential, and hotel pay a share of the common area maintenance cost to a master association, similar to Abacoa, that is managed by the retail entity.

At Rowes Wharf in Boston, a master condominium association involving three voting units—hotel, office/retail, and residential—manages the project. Rowes Wharf Associates holds the votes for two of the units, and the residential condominium association holds the vote for the third. Each component has its own internal management. Formulation of the management plan began early in the development process, as Beacon Management Corporation participated in the design process. Because of the developer's long-term commitment to the project, long-term management efficiencies were a concern.

Another variation on this model can be found at Pentagon Row in Arlington, Virginia. This project is located on a 14-acre (5.6-hectare) site owned jointly by H Street Properties and the Cafritz Foundation and leased with separate 65-year ground leases to two developers—300,000 square feet (28,000 square meters) to Federal Realty and 540,000 square feet (50,000 square meters) to Post Properties. The two developers elected to jointly contract to build separately using the same general contractor so that liability is separated, but the project has many shared spaces so a single management structure has been created with a prorated formula for costs.

Public/Private Approach in Downtown Silver Spring

At Downtown Silver Spring in Montgomery County, Maryland, redevelopment is taking place under a general development agreement that was awarded to a joint venture partnership of the Peterson Companies, Foulger Pratt Companies, and Argo Investments. The development will include 500,000 to 600,000 square feet (46,500 to 55,800 square meters) of private development in a mixture of retail, restaurant, and entertainment uses, with a food market and a multiscreen movie complex, a 150- to 200-room hotel, 150,000 to 200,000 square feet (14,000 to 18,600 square meters) of Class A office space, and residential space. The project also includes a multitude of public facilities and improvements, including a civic building, a garage, a restored theater, an arts center, a town square with a skating rink, a pavilion, a fountain, and improvements to the streetscape. The site is bisected by two major streets.

Under an unusual feature of the development agreement, the developer is the sole contractor for all public improvements. This arrangement was devised to eliminate the conflicts and delays that would invariably arise in such a complex project where pubic improvements are tightly integrated into the fabric of the mixed-use development. It is intended to ensure coordinated development of the public and private features. The agreement sets forth the estimated cost of all public improvements, which will be funded by the county. Each public improvement will be designed by the developer and approved by the county, and the maximum total development cost is set under a development improvement contract. The developer receives a 4 percent development fee and is encouraged to seek cost savings, with 70 percent of such savings going to the county and 30 percent retained by the developer.

Ongoing maintenance of the public spaces is proposed under a somewhat unusual structure. Under Maryland law, Montgomery County can create the Silver Spring Urban District Corporation, which would be responsible for promotion, organization, and support of cultural, recreational, and business activities for Town Square, events on interior Ellsworth Drive (originally a public street that will be vacated and sold to the developer so it becomes a private street with rights of public access), maintenance of streetscaping for public rights-of-way and sidewalks, enhanced security, and other initiatives to advance the business and residential environment and sense of community. For all intents, this corporation would act like a BID.

In addition, the developer must create an association for the ownership and maintenance of interior Ellsworth Drive. This association could either contract with the urban district to provide enhanced security and/or maintenance. If the county chooses not to form the urban district, other provisions in the development agreement will achieve the same results. Funding for the district comes from assessments to property owners in the district. For the association, it would be done through the terms the developer chooses in its creation. Although some features of this development management agreement are specific to provisions of Maryland law, the various features could be duplicated in some way in most jurisdictions.

Institutional/Public/Private Approach in Cambridge

This example illustrates how a management and maintenance agreement can meet the concerns of both an institution that does not want to be a developer but wants to ensure a certain quality in a development that will ultimately revert to it and a city that wants to encourage economic revitalization while minimizing public burden.

The impetus for University Park at MIT was the desire of Massachusetts Institute of Technology through its endowment fund to develop a corporate office/R&D park adjacent to its campus that would help accelerate the transfer of technology to the commercial marketplace (see Chapter 8). The operations, management, and maintenance structure for University Park had to satisfy requirements of all three players: MIT, the developer (Forest City), and the city of Cambridge. It will ultimately revert to MIT.

Courtesy of the Peterson Companies

The Silver Spring Urban District Corporation provides a variety of management and maintenance functions at Downtown Silver Spring in Maryland.

A declaration of covenants at University Park at MIT sets forth management responsibilities, the basis for assessments, and the relationship between the common areas and tenant buildings.

Property management at University Park is provided for in two documents that tie Forest City, MIT, and the city of Cambridge together: the *declaration of covenants* and the *maintenance agreement.*

MIT's declaration of covenants brings all development contemplated for University Park under one management entity. The covenants run with the land. For example, if Forest City were to sell the property or if foreclosure were to occur, the terms of the declaration travel with the properties, and the obligations of the covenants become the obligations of MIT or a successor owner/land leaseholder. This provision is particularly important to ensure maintenance of the common, private, and public areas in University Park to the higher standards mutually expected by the city, MIT, and Forest City.

The covenants specify that the dominant owner (Forest City) is obligated to hire a professional management company. Forest City thus contracted with Forest City Commercial Management, Inc., a wholly owned subsidiary, for that function. Because this technique requires lenders to agree that the terms of the covenants are superior to their debt and the city expected the developer to take on what otherwise might be public maintenance responsibilities, it took two years to put this declaration in place.

The declaration sets forth management responsibilities, the basis for assessments, and the relationship between the common areas and tenant buildings. It provides for a single management entity for both and for certain open-space maintenance responsibilities for the Auburn Park residential area, regardless of the fact that the land is subleased and under a separate agreement.

In addition to maintenance of common open space, Forest City Commercial Management is responsible for maintenance of common areas and management of the traffic mitigation agreement, another requirement of zoning. The principal feature is participation in the Charles River Transportation Association, which operates a shuttle bus system serving its affiliate members. Property management inside the office/R&D buildings is a typical arrangement but also includes an exterior common area charge to cover grounds maintenance and exterior security.

Security is provided 24 hours a day through security guards in each building, a security van, and foot and bike patrols. Management uses its own security staff for all events except where alcohol is served, because such events require a city permit and a fee for the city to provide police oversight.

The maintenance agreement guarantees that Forest City Commercial Management or it successor will maintain various agreed-upon improvements in the public rights-of-way except where the developer has provided the city of Cambridge with spare parts for the city's maintenance of certain items. More important, it allows University Park's management to provide maintenance at a higher standard at its own expense. The agreement runs for 15 years, with provisions for extensions.

District Management in Brooklyn

District management is another area of development management that has evolved rapidly in recent years. Interested parties in a district with a large number of separate ownerships—such as a downtown or a designated arts or historic district—have incorporated elements of management used for complex projects into areawide management systems that endeavor to program development as well as manage existing spaces.

At MetroTech Center, Forest City Enterprises is a major participant in the 25-block MetroTech BID created to further the revitalization of downtown Brooklyn (see the accompanying feature box). This business improvement district provides a wide range of public safety and sanitation services as well as a variety of other activities intended to enhance the physical and social qualities of all the properties—public, private, and institutional—included in the district. The MetroTech BID includes large corporations as tenants in Forest City's MetroTech Center as well as other commercial properties; 150 stores,

The mission of the MetroTech BID is to provide top-quality, efficient, cost-effective service and support to its customers through program initiatives in neighborhood safety, sanitation, business development and services, real estate management, liaison with city agencies and elected officials, processing constituents' complaints, and development of new internal and external resources to support programs goals. Its mission is also to work closely with neighboring communities to support their efforts at improvement.

MetroTech BID Services
Public Safety
- 28 public safety officers with special patrol/peace officer status
- 24-hour, seven-day-a-week patrols throughout the district
- Three zero-emission electric scooters
- Bicycle patrol
- 23 cameras for a closed-circuit TV street monitoring system
- Sophisticated communications equipment linking the BID with the New York Police Department
- Officer training provided by the New York City Police Academy
- Area police–private security liaison hub

- Districtwide emergency notification system
- Special award for a recipient from the 84th Precinct of the New York Police Department

Sanitation
- Seven-day-a-week, year-round street cleaning
- 33 BID litter baskets mounted on streetlight poles and 27 Department of Sanitation baskets
- Ongoing removal of graffiti
- Seasonal tree maintenance for more than 200 trees
- Maintenance of area directory signage system

Economic Development
- Technical assistance and workshops for merchants
- Marketing of vacant retail space
- Merchant marketing initiatives
- Maps, banners, and promotional materials
- Streetscape improvements
- Special events
- Assistance for local schools and community service organizations
- Building facade improvement program, cash incentives for cleaning facades, store signage, store window displays, open-link security gates

The owners of MetroTech Center, a mixed-use project in Brooklyn, New York, are major participants in the MetroTech business improvement district, which provides a wide variety of public safety and sanitation services for a 25-block area.

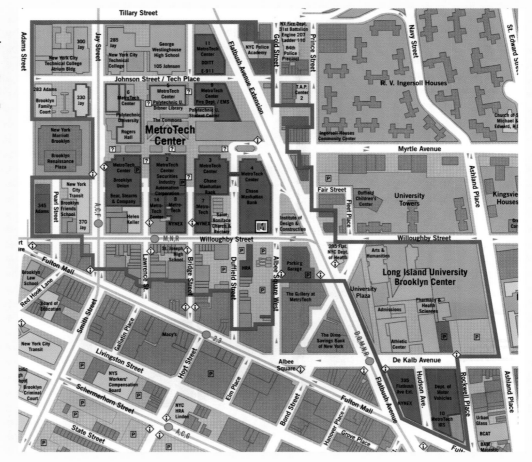

restaurants, and service establishments; city, state, and federal agencies; three universities, three high schools, and other academic institutions; and a small number of residents. With the BID's presence, the Forest City complex obtains the higher-level maintenance, management, and public safety required of a successful mixed-use development.

Managing Multiple Uses and Entities at Yerba Buena Center

When Yerba Buena Center was originally planned in the 1960s as an urban renewal project to provide sites for office development and convention facilities, it was primarily a clearance project without residential uses. As in most renewal programs, the focus was on physical revitalization with the presumption that once that objective was accomplished, the marketplace would sustain the revitalization.

A master developer was chosen, part of whose mandate was to maintain the open spaces. The master developer was unable to proceed, however, and the project has been developed following a master plan that evolved over time—following a series of lawsuits that halted the original plan—and included a great deal of community input. It is now a combination of public and cultural uses, private high-end commercial establishments, and residential uses with a significant amount of public open space built by a variety of developers rather than a single master developer.

The San Francisco Redevelopment Agency considered how to knit together the various public and private users so they could act cohesively to operate and maintain Yerba Buena Center. Achieving these ends was critical for maintaining this area in the heart of the city that is the focal point for the many visitors who come to the city and the Moscone Convention Center. The agency believed two elements were critical for maintenance of the area: funding to sustain the ten acres (four hectares) of open space and the cultural facility, and a group of stakeholders representing the neighborhood who would be invested in the area and oversee its ongoing inevitable changes.

The principal funding tool for maintenance of the project is the *separate account*, funded by contributions required in leases for the private developments, including the 1,500-room Marriott Hotel and Millennium Partners, developers of Sony Metreon and the Four Seasons Hotel. These uses front on the gardens. The fund is used to hire a maintenance/management firm to provide ongoing management and maintenance of the gardens, janitorial services, and 24-hour security, and to oversee all the activities in the gardens.

SFRA also provides management funding for 70 to 90 events per year by contracting with an events management firm. This effort enlivens the open space, which in turn contributes to its safety and attractiveness for residents and visitors alike. These events focus on the gardens, providing a citywide public amenity.

At Yerba Buena Center, a publicly initiated development, the principal maintenance funding tool is the separate account, which is funded by contributions required in leases to the private developments.

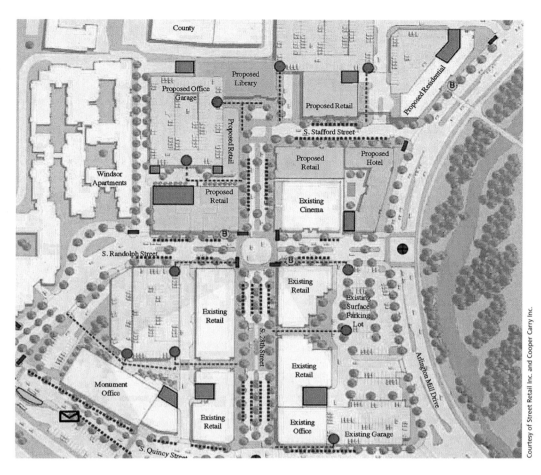

Building service and loading areas (highlighted in red) are away from the main streets and screened from view in the proposed expansion plan for the Village at Shirlington in Arlington, Virginia.

The funding source was carefully negotiated. To create a constituency of stakeholders, the Yerba Buena Alliance was created as a private membership organization that, as of 2001, had 153 members, including developer entities, businesses, cultural facilities, and residential complexes in the neighborhood. It is a nonpolitical group that addresses topics such as traffic management, transportation, and avoidance of undesirable uses. As such, it functions much like a traditional neighborhood civic association. In addition, a type of BID is being considered to address security and maintenance in the area to ensure that the surrounding areas not covered by the maintenance and management agreements are well cared for.

This approach may be applicable to what happens when projects begin to age. Cities now find that areas renewed years earlier have to be renewed again. The dual resources of a sufficiently funded and cohesive neighborhood group and a staff person or persons to ensure diligent maintenance of the public and private investments are critical.

Special Issues in Operations and Management

Several topics require special attention in an effective management plan and management agreement: controlling noise and odor, parking management, traffic and transportation management, and joint promotion

of the development. These generally thorny issues can create significant friction and problems for management if they are not properly addressed.

Controlling Noise and Odor

One of the most critical aspects of operating and managing a mixed-use property is the management of noise and unpleasant odors. Property management and operations must carefully control truck access, loading, dumpsters, restaurants, bars, nightclubs, entertainment facilities, and other sources of noise and odor that can offend tenants, residents, and visitors if not properly handled. Many management issues need to be carefully addressed during design, or they may become insoluble problems; in many cases, however, conflicts are unavoidable and thus must be addressed through careful management.

Managing noise and odor from a restaurant, especially when residential uses are nearby, is a particularly important issue for many mixed-use properties. Numerous questions should be addressed regarding the relationship between residential and restaurant uses:

- Should hours of operation or outdoor seating or outdoor music be limited somewhat to keep down noise that might disturb residents' sleep?
- Should decibels be restricted on the ambient noise generated by outdoor seating?
- If a restaurant might be added below or adjacent to residential units, has proper venting of food odors

been addressed in advance, and have easements been reserved to allow such venting?

- Should outdoor lighting (neon, flashing, or high-intensity lights) be limited?
- To what degree of architectural control should the restaurant be subject with regard to such matters as building design, redesign, signage, and outdoor seating?
- If commercial land uses generate significant amounts of garbage, should storage of garbage be controlled and times when garbage may be picked up limited?
- Should hours be limited during which deliveries can be made to restaurants?
- Should restaurant drive-through lanes or the types and overall number of restaurants be limited?
- Where will restaurant patrons park their cars? Is parking adequate? How will the mix of restaurants and other commercial uses affect the overall demand for parking and the timing of demand?
- Should restaurant patrons' access to parts of the community be limited?
- Should restaurant owners have access to recreational facilities located in other parts of the community?[4]

Noise and odors from loading docks and trash dumpsters present another potential problem. At Paseo Colorado, for example, loading is carefully controlled. Six loading docks, located on a side street, serve the development. Four docks are dedicated to the retail and restaurant portions of the project, and the remaining two are shared by the housing and the supermarket. Hours of use of these two bays are further controlled; the supermarket accepts deliveries in the early morning, and the apartments have access to the docks between 10:00 a.m. and 5:00 p.m. Noise levels are controlled in several other ways. Outdoor dining terraces must close by midnight on weekdays and 2:00 a.m. on weekends, and loud music is prohibited. Noise limitations are similarly written into the residential leases, and the pool deck has been located away from retail and public areas.

During the earlier phases of Addison Circle (see Chapter 8), trash produced by commercial and residential uses was deposited in the same collection area and hauled away by a private firm under contract to Post Properties. The common collection point was unpopular, however, because of the odors produced by the more organic wastes from the restaurants. Planning for the next phase of development at Addison Circle provides commercial trash to be segregated in a special utilities zone, separate from the residential trash.

Noise from temporary events and entertainment must also be carefully managed. In most cases, major entertainment shows and festivals should be held on weekends; holding them at those times appeals to residents, draws traffic to retail outlets, avoids conflicts with office tenants, and encourages weekend business for hotels.

Parking

The management of central parking has evolved in parallel with other aspects of management for mixed-use projects. Developers and operators point out the need to get professional advice early. Functional design, which addresses the general layout of spaces, locations of entrances and exits, and relationship to amenities in and around the project, is an essential ingredient in long-term operational success. Moreover, the effort can point out opportunities for enhancing the contribution of parking to the project as a whole.

Management of parking varies greatly, depending on the nature of the project. Several general concerns should be considered in determining the management approach suitable for a specific project:

- Traffic should be moved as quickly as possible to get maximum benefit from the parking provided. Traffic flow should be organized so that no particular group of users suffers delays beyond what would be experienced in a single-purpose parking structure. A central location for cashiers can help, and readily understandable rates make it easier for drivers to move through the system. Good design and signage are the bases of efficient movement.
- It is generally desirable to give parking levels adjacent to the project's amenities to short-term parkers, who are attracted by shade, shelter, and easier access to entrances and exits.
- A professional should help determine the price structure as a way of managing use of space.
- Price structure and design are important aspects of the project's management. Parking for retail tenants is a high priority in most projects; it is crucial to retail's success and the rents that can be charged. In general, reserved spaces should be avoided, but monthly spaces should be made available although not assigned.
- Parking lease rates should be separated from rents in most cases. The separation of these charges gives the parking manager flexibility to address changes in parking requirements as the project evolves and changes.

At Addison Circle, a series of gates in the lower decks of the residential parking structures are progressively unlocked during the business day to serve shoppers, and basement parking levels are reserved for valet parking at much higher densities. Restaurants and larger retail tenants thus are able to use a combination of on-street, valet, and designated off-street parking in adjacent parking structures.

At Valencia Town Center Drive, an agreement among owners provides for shared use of two parking structures for office tenants and retail customers. Behavior control gates were installed between the second and third levels of the two five-level parking structures to keep retail customers from going past the second level during the day; office tenants are required to park on the upper levels. At approximately 5:00 p.m., the control gates are opened; employees are required to start leaving at that time so their spaces are available during peak evening hours. If either owner group wants to modify the operating plan but a mutual resolution cannot be reached, the agreement provides for arbitration using a specified list of parking experts to determine how the situation might be corrected.

At Paseo Colorado in Pasadena, parking is segregated between residential and retail uses. Residents park in a separate section of the lower level of the two-story subterranean garage; they have card keys to access the express lanes of the garage entries. The 387 dwelling units are assigned 494 parking spaces, or 1.3 spaces per unit. For security, garage elevators serving the residential portion of the project do not stop on the retail levels, and retail access elevators do not stop on residential floors.

Traffic and Transportation Management

A mixed-use development of significant size is frequently the target of concerns about traffic generation. In most communities, these concerns result in the requirement for a traffic generation study as part of the submission to gain public approval. The results of the study are then used to establish conditions of approval that provide amelioration of whatever the community determines to be the negative impacts of the development.

Because each project is different, no recommendations exist for how this issue should be addressed. The hope is that the community's requirements are reasonable and are directly related to the legitimate excess impacts resulting from the mixed-use development. Thus, exactions that do not directly resolve the impacts of the development should be resisted and solutions that offset negative impacts offered.

At University Park at MIT, a traffic mitigation agreement was required by rezoning. The principal feature is participation in the Charles River Transportation Association, which operates the LINK shuttle bus system (see the accompanying feature box).

Joint Promotion

The management of promotions creating an appropriate image serves marketing objectives for retail and office space and is a key ingredient in the project's identity; it has become an increasingly important responsibility in management and maintenance agreements. In many cases, managers have assistance from specialized staffs that plan events throughout the year.

Promotional managers in mixed-use properties point out the need to coordinate activities on a regular basis, at least monthly, to discuss what management and individual tenants are doing. For example, booking a major performer or special event in a performing arts center will result in heavy restaurant traffic on that evening. Restaurant managers need to be aware of such bookings and plan for them. Similarly, major retail sales can be expected to increase traffic through other project spaces.

Central spaces like ice rinks provide an important amenity, although they may also present major drawbacks because they are costly to maintain and highly

Courtesy of Catellus

Mission Bay in San Francisco is a large project covering more than 300 acres (121 hectares) that will be phased over many years. The traffic management plan for the development includes a traffic construction management plan, with Web site postings on traffic restrictions for specific roads on specific dates.

University Park's comprehensive transportation demand management program promotes alternative modes of transportation and other services designed to reduce peak hour demands at the site:

- Shuttle Services—Forest City provides shuttle services for all tenants of University Park. The shuttle makes regular stops at various points at the site throughout the day and provides a direct connection to public transportation in Central Square. In addition to reducing peak-hour vehicle trips, the shuttle reduces off-peak trips by providing employees an alternative to driving their vehicles to run errands during the day.
- Public Transportation—Forest City promotes the use of public transportation by selling monthly passes on site, providing transit schedules to employees, posting transit schedules in public areas of University Park, and providing a toll-free phone number so that people can call for shuttle service during off-peak hours.
- Bicycle Amenities—University Park has enclosed and secured bicycle facilities throughout the site; many of the new buildings include showers and changing facilities. Free bicycle repair and maintenance is provided at the annual University Park Transportation Fair.
- Rideshare Program—Forest City provides rideshare programs to encourage commuters to ride with other commuters rather than drive alone. This program includes carpool/vanpool incentives and ride matching. The Guaranteed Ride Home Program ensures convenient travel options for vanpool/carpool/transit users if work-related activities require them to miss their regular ride home.
- On-Site Amenities—Restaurants, hotels, banks and ATMs, and a grocery store are provided on site.
- Electric Vehicles—Forest City encourages the use of electric vehicles by providing charging stations in the Pilgrim Street garage.

In addition to encouraging alternative forms of transportation, Forest City promotes programs designed to minimize the use of single-occupancy vehicles and to reduce peak-hour demands: improvements to pedestrian and bicycle transportation infrastructure, marketing the advantages of living nearby, parking supply and pricing policy, reduced truck traffic, and a potential airport shuttle. ■

A traffic mitigation agreement was a requirement of the rezoning for University Park at MIT.

Courtesy of Forest City Enterprises

agreed to it. Thus, both sides knew the estimated operating costs and the basis for splitting them.

Another issue that needed to be resolved in advance was an operating plan that would control retail and office parkers. The solution was to allow office workers to use the upper three levels of the parking structures during the day and retail parkers the ground and second floors.

Finally, if either owner group wants to modify the operating plan at some time in the future, the agreement provides that it can be done by mutual agreement if a set of standards are met. If an accord cannot be reached and there is thus no mutual resolution, the "major decision provisions" of the agreement allow for arbitration using a specified list of parking experts; the standards are used as a guideline to determine whether or not parking is inadequate and, if it is, how it might be corrected.

Maximizing an Asset's Value over Time

Asset management also involves strong ongoing strategic management that optimizes the value and performance of the property through ongoing market research, marketing, development, and leasing. In many cases, mixed-use projects become magnets for new tenants and new uses if they are properly managed, thus creating new opportunities for improving the asset. Mixed-use projects constantly evolve, grow, and improve, and financial performance can frequently change for the better as the project matures.

For example, at Redmond Town Center in Redmond, Washington, which was built by Winmar and first opened

in 1997, a number of changes in ownership and program have improved, or are expected to improve, the project's financial performance over time. Redmond Town Center serves a primary market of 198,000 residents with an average household income of $90,530. Including a secondary area, the property serves a total market of nearly 650,000 residents with an average household income of $86,056. Some 71 percent of adults have attended or graduated from college—well above the 44 percent rate for the entire United States.

The 120-acre (48.5-hectare), 1.15 million-square-foot (107,000-square-meter) mixed-use complex includes an outdoor lifestyle center that currently offers 100 stores, 15 restaurants and cafés, entertainment venues, office space, and lodging. The property is one of four Pacific Northwest regional properties acquired by Macerich Company and the Ontario Teachers Pension Board in February 1999. The property's retail and big-box space includes Borders Books & Music, Eddie Bauer, Z Gallerie, Bed, Bath & Beyond, and a Loews Cineplex. Nonretail uses currently include a 180-room Marriott Residence Inn and 692,000 square feet (64,000 square meters) of office space housing the world headquarters of AT&T Wireless and other major tenants. Upon final buildout, the property is expected to have upward of 1.8 million square feet (167,000 square meters) of gross leasable area, with additional retail space, an upscale residential component, and another hotel among the uses being considered.

Macerich, which acquired Redmond Town Center in Redmond, Washington, in 1999, has undertaken several strategies to enhance financial performance, including attracting the Bon Marché department store to the development.

Since Macerich's acquisition, sales at specialty stores (less than 20,000 square feet [1,860 square meters]) in Redmond Town Center's core retail area grew 41.4 percent, from $285 per square foot ($3,100 per square meter) in February 1999 to $403 per square foot ($4,300 per square meter) for the 12-month period ended July 2001. For the entire center, sales for stores less than 20,000 square feet (1,860 square meters) grew 27.2 percent, from $272 per square foot ($2,900 per square meter) to $346 per square foot ($3,700 per square meter). Nearly 100,000 square feet (9,300 square meters) of new retail and restaurant space has opened at the property since the acquisition, highlighted by a 49,850-square-foot (4,600-square-meter) gourmet superstore. Openings in late 2001 included two restaurants to complement the center's six full-service restaurants: Todai, a Japanese sushi and seafood buffet, and Golden Chopsticks, serving modern Chinese cuisine.

More recently, Macerich announced that the Bon Marché will become the first department store at Redmond Town Center. The new 110,000-square-foot (10,200-square-meter), two-level building is expected to open in fall 2003. The full-line store, being built just across from the property's core retail area, will offer moderate and better apparel, accessories, and home merchandise. A pedestrian bridge will link the store to the two-story buildings in the core area. Bruce Johnston, Macerich's regional vice president for leasing, expects Bon Marché's presence to result in a healthy increase in daily retail shop-ping traffic. It allows Macerich to reopen discussions with merchants who typically are not represented in unanchored centers, which may convince them that Redmond Town Center is an excellent alternative to typical enclosed malls.

The long-term success of complex mixed-use properties hinges on the developer's ability to negotiate good operating and management agreements and on active management and reinvestment in the property to ensure it is kept up to date, takes advantage of new market opportunities, and performs at an optimum level (see Chapter 5 for other examples of developers' reinvesting in, redesigning, and renovating mixed-use properties to enhance value).

Assessing Performance

Management and operations must ultimately be concerned with the development's financial performance, seeking full occupancy at maximum rents and reasonable operating expenses to achieve an attractive stabilized income stream. Mixed-use projects have a mixed record of performance, and several high-profile projects such as CityPlace in West Palm Beach and Hollywood & Highland in Los Angeles have encountered some problems with financial performance. But considerable anecdotal evidence also suggests that many mixed-use projects achieve higher rents and sales than new or established stand-alone suburban real estate products.

Nearly 100,000 square feet (9,300 square meters) of new retail and restaurant space has opened at Redmond Town Center since it was acquired by Macerich, and sales per square foot have increased substantially.

The following information is from a variety of mixed-use developments in the United States; it is current as of the end of 2002.

Reston Town Center. The 20-acre (8-hectare) Phase I of Reston Town Center, which opened in October 1990, was constructed by the original owner, Mobil Land Development Corp. It included 530,000 square feet (49,000 square meters) of office space, 240,000 square feet (22,000 square meters) of specialty retail and restaurants, a 13-screen movie theater, a 517-room Hyatt Regency hotel, a post office, a one-acre (0.4-hectare) central plaza, and a skating pavilion.

Dallas-based Terrabrook, which now owns Mobil Land's Reston Town Center properties, is continuing the development program. Phase II, which broke ground in 1998, is scheduled for completion in 2004. Phase III, which broke ground in 2001, is scheduled for completion in 2005. Together, the two additional phases comprise 30 acres (12 hectares) of new development with approximately 1.5 million square feet (139,400 square meters) of office and retail space, 700 townhouse-style four-story rental apartments and for-sale condominiums, new parks and plazas, and an amphitheater. An additional building will be constructed for office, residential, or retail use according to market demand, and another building will be developed as a 500-room hotel or high-density residential building depending on the economy and the market.

- Office—Office space at Reston Town Center leases faster and at higher rates than the surrounding Dulles Corridor market. In 2002, when that market had softened compared with the previous year and suffered from excess supply, three new Reston Town Center office buildings opened. Two were 90 percent leased by September 2002. The third, which opened in August, was already 65 percent leased by September.

  Whether the local office market is up or down, Reston Town Center commands a premium. In mid-2001, for example, annual office base lease rates at Reston Town Center ranged from $34.00 to $44.00 per square foot ($365 to $475 per square meter), 10 to 15 percent higher than comparable buildings in northern Virginia. In the slow market of 2002, comparable office buildings outside Reston Town Center rented in the low to middle $20s per square foot ($215 to $270 per square meter), while Reston Town Center buildings rented in the high $20s and low $30s per square foot (approximately $325 per square meter).
- Retail—In mid-2001, Reston Town Center's retail properties enjoyed a 10 to 15 percent (and sometimes higher) rental premium over comparable retail facilities in northern Virginia. In 2002, per-square-foot sales were substantially above national averages for restaurants, fashion merchandise, and service retailers like photo processing.
- Hotel—The Hyatt Regency Reston is one of the top two northern Virginia hotels in revenues and room rates.
- Adjacent Property Values—Office rents within walking distance of Reston Town Center are very close—

Both office and retail space at Reston Town Center have achieved rent premiums over comparable space in the area, and the hotel is one of the top two in terms of room rates in northern Virginia.

in some cases identical—to Town Center rates. Residential properties also enjoy a Reston Town Center halo effect. The 700 new townhouse-style rental apartments and for-sale condominiums, developed by Trammell Crow Residential of Atlanta, Georgia, are within walking distance of Reston Town Center. In October 2002, townhouse units sold for $200 per square foot ($2,150 per square meter), compared with $150 per square foot ($1,600 per square meter) in the metropolitan area.

CityCenter Englewood. In 1998, the city of Englewood, Colorado, a working-class suburb just south of Denver, demolished the failed Cinderella City mall—the largest enclosed mall west of the Mississippi River when it opened in 1968—and began constructing on its 55-acre (22-hectare) site CityCenter Englewood, a transit-oriented village with a city hall, library, courts, and administrative offices around a civic plaza, a cultural and performance center, residential units, and retail space.

The Civic Center, light-rail transit station, and Phase I retail space opened in 2000. Gart Sports Company, the second-largest sporting goods retailer in the United States, moved its headquarters from downtown Denver to a renovated 92,000-square-foot (8,550-square-meter) former warehouse across Hampden Avenue from CityCenter Englewood in 2002 because of its central location and access to light rail.

- Office—In June 2002, CityCenter's average annual office rents were $21.00 to $25.00 per gross square

At CityCenter Englewood in Englewood, Colorado, office space was 100 percent leased and retail space was 90 percent leased in 2002.

Courtesy of David Owen Tryba Architects

In 2002, Easton Town Center's retail rents averaged $35.00 per square foot, the highest in the greater Columbus area.

Courtesy of Development Design Group Inc.

foot ($225 to $270 per square meter), compared with $13.50 to $17.00 per square foot ($145 to $185 per square meter) in the city of Englewood, which has little Class A space. CityCenter's office occupancy rate was close to 100 percent, compared with 89.9 percent in the Denver metropolitan area.

- Retail—In June 2002, annual rents for CityCenter stores averaged $18.00 to $20.00 per square foot ($195 to $215 per square meter), triple net, while in the city of Englewood, gross retail rents averaged $8.00 to $14.00 per square foot ($85 to $150 per square meter). Approximately 90 percent of CityCenter's existing retail space was leased and occupied, compared with approximately 80 percent in Englewood.

Town centers like CityCenter Englewood also generate above-average sales tax revenues. In the mid-1970s, for example, Cinderella City accounted for 52 percent of Englewood's sales tax revenue; by 1994, however, it provided only 2.6 percent of the city's

sales tax revenues. In comparison, between January 1 and April 30, 2001, with just 25 percent of CityCenter Englewood completed, the city collected $301,189 in sales tax revenue from CityCenter, more sales tax than the mall generated in its last two years of operation combined ($180,240 in 1996 and $78,694 in 1997). The city had estimated that CityCenter's retail development would generate $2 million to $2.5 million in sales tax revenue annually. In 2001, CityCenter generated more than $2 million in sales tax revenue.

- Residential—In June 2002, CityCenter apartments averaged $1,005 to $1,735 per month for rent, compared with $500 to $700 per month for multifamily housing in Englewood and $550 to $750 per month in the metropolitan Denver area.

Easton Town Center. Scheduled for buildout in 2010, the new 1,200-acre (485-hectare) Easton Town Center in the new master-planned community of Easton in Columbus, Ohio, will include 3.3 million square feet (306,700 square meters) of retail space, 5 million square feet (465,000 square meters) of office space, 1,000 multi-family residential units, 1 million square feet (93,000 square meters) of hotel and conference facilities, restaurants, and entertainment venues for 43,000 workers.

Phase I, which opened in June 1999, includes 13 buildings for retail, restaurants, and entertainment on six city blocks around a landscaped town square; it drew close to 10 million people in Easton Town Center's first year. This commercial space, which has been almost fully leased since 1999, currently enjoys a 97 percent occupancy rate.

- Office—Annual full-service office rents averaged $23.00 per square foot ($250 per square meter) in October 2002, compared with $15.65 to $18.57 per square foot ($170 to $200 per square meter) in the rest of Columbus's suburban office markets. In the first quarter of 2002, Easton Town Center had a 78.8 percent occupancy rate, compared with 70.2 percent to 89 percent for Columbus's suburban office markets.
- Retail—In October 2002, Easton Town Center's annual retail rents averaged $35.00 per square foot ($375 per square meter), the highest rents in the greater Columbus market, and its retail space was 95 percent occupied. Retail sales were higher than $400 per square foot ($4,300 per square meter), and restaurant sales were higher than $600 per square foot ($6,455 per square meter). In contrast, regional shopping centers in the United States in 2002 averaged $220 to $230 per square foot ($2,365 to $2,475 per square meter) in sales. Some stores did exceptionally well: the Town Center's Virgin megastore reportedly averaged $1,000 per square foot ($10,760 per square meter) in sales in the first year after it opened in July 2000.
- Residential—Multifamily residential units in and near Easton Town Center have performed very well. In October 2002, rents for multifamily units within two miles (3.2 kilometers) of Easton were 12.5 percent

(for studios) to 60.8 percent (for three-bedroom units) higher than those in the Columbus metropolitan area. The overall occupancy rate for the Easton multifamily market was 95.2 percent, compared with 94 percent occupancy for greater Columbus.

- Hotel—In September 2002, room rates for the Hilton Hotel in Easton Town Center ranged from $134 to $219 per night, compared with an average daily rate of $57.96 to $103.38 for greater Columbus. The occupancy rate was 85 percent, compared with the average of 59.3 percent in greater Columbus.
- Adjacent Property Values—The presence of Easton Town Center has substantially increased adjacent property values. In early 2002, the last property within one block of Easton Town Center sold for $750,000 an acre ($1.8 million per hectare). In October 2002, property zoned for office development within one block of Easton Town Center was quoted at $1 million an acre ($2.5 million per hectare). Land zoned for office development approximately one mile (1.6 kilometers) from the Town Center was listed at $250,000 an acre ($617,500 per hectare).

Southlake Town Square. The 130-acre (53-hectare) Southlake Town Square broke ground in February 1998 in Southlake, Texas, northwest of Dallas. At buildout in 2020, it will have up to 1,000 housing units and 2.5 million square feet (232,300 square meters) of retail, restaurant, office, theater, and hotel space. The first phase was completed in 1999.

- Office—"The town square's office rates enjoy a 10 percent premium in the Southlake market," says Brian Stebbins, chief executive officer of Southlake-based Cooper & Stebbins, the developer. "Compared with the overall Dallas/Fort Worth metroplex, the town square commands a 25 to 30 percent premium. While the office rental rate in the metroplex dropped 4.8 percent between the first quarter of 2001 and the first quarter of 2002, Southlake Town Square's rate increased by approximately 5 percent."

Office and retail space at Southlake Town Square in Southlake, Texas, has achieved 10 percent rent premiums over comparable space in the Southlake market. The parks and squares in the center are popular spots for events.

Courtesy of Cooper & Stebbins

Both retail and residential uses at Winter Springs Town Center in Florida have outperformed the competition during the early phases of development.

Courtesy of Dover Kohl Partners

In the first quarter of 2002, while the metroplex was struggling with a 74.6 percent office occupancy rate, the office occupancy rate in Southlake Town Square was 95 percent. In October 2002, the town square's office occupancy rate was still at 95 percent, while that in surrounding Tarrant County ranged from 85 percent to 90 percent.

- Retail—In October 2002, retail rents in the town square enjoyed a 10 to 15 percent premium over the South-lake market and a 25 to 30 percent premium over the Dallas/Fort Worth metroplex. The town square's retail occupancy rate remained stable at 98 to 100 percent, compared with 90 percent in the Tarrant County market and 88.5 percent in the metroplex. "In October 2002, the town square's retail sales were $357.50 to $385.00 per square foot ($3,850 to $4,145 per square meter), significantly higher than the average of $220 to $230 per square foot ($2,370 to $2,475 per square meter) achieved in regional malls across America in 2002, and 30 to 40 percent higher than that achieved in a typical suburban retail strip center," says Stebbins.

The city of Southlake benefits from its new town square in many ways. The town square, for example, now generates more than $7 million in annual sales tax revenue. By the end of 2002, it had also provided employment for more than 1,500 people.

- On-Site Property Values—In October 2002, property values of undeveloped town square parcels generally commanded a 5 to 25 percent premium over compa-rable sites in the metroplex and a 10 to 20 percent premium over comparable lots in the town of South-lake. "The greater value is attributable to these parcels' being within the town square and to the efficiencies gained through the greater level of site coverage and density made possible by the zoning that was put in place," says Stebbins.

- Adjacent Property Values—By October 2002, South-lake Town Square's halo effect had improved the value of surrounding properties by 5 to 10 percent over comparable Southlake properties and 5 to 25 per-cent over similar metroplex properties.

Winter Springs Town Center. The 240-acre (97-hectare) Winter Springs Town Center in Winter Springs, Florida, broke ground in 2002. By the end of the year, the 30-acre (12-hectare) Phase I, planned for 17 buildings, included three completed buildings and six other buildings under construction. The town center will include office, retail, and residential space, a city hall complex, entertainment, a daycare center, a proposed hotel and convention center, a municipal park, and two public squares. The town cen-ter's main street will end at a pedestrian pier on a lake.

- Retail—The first completed buildings in Winter Springs Town Center are already demonstrating the power of new suburban town center development. In October 2002, annual retail rents at Winter Springs Town Center averaged $18.00 to $23.00 per square foot ($195 to $250 per square meter) plus $3.25 per square foot ($35.00 per square meter) CAM charges. The annual rate at the nearest shopping center, about one mile (1.6 kilometers) away, was $16.50 per square foot ($180 per square meter).

Retailers are more than willing to pay the above-average rents for Winter Springs Town Center. "In the first phase of the town center's development, we leased 90,000 square feet (8,365 square meters) of 135,000 square feet (12,500 square meters) of retail space before the first building had even been com-pleted," says Mayor Paul P. Partyka.

- Residential—From the start, the town center's resi-dential projects have outperformed nearby proper-ties. The first completed residential project, an 85-unit multifamily building, sold 45 units at $325,000 each (10 to 15 percent higher than comparable housing in the larger market area) in its first few months of sales.

Rents and Returns. Although many mixed-use proper-ties achieve higher-than-average rents and/or occupancy levels, they do not necessarily also outperform the competition in terms of return on investment. Their complexity may push development costs substantially higher than those of the competition, which affects their return on investment, higher rents and values notwithstanding. In addition, mixed-use properties are often targeted toward higher-end markets, resulting in higher-cost and higher-priced development products, which likely will be rewarded with higher rents but not necessarily with higher returns.

Return on investment data for mixed-use properties are not easily obtained because most developers and owners do not want to divulge this information and because their financial performance is not tracked nationally as it is for office, industrial, retail, and apartment property categories. Thus, it is difficult to know what returns these projects have provided to investors. Nonetheless, the data and results discussed above do suggest that mixed-use properties can achieve quite favorable market results. The challenge for developers is to achieve these enviable results within a reasonable development and operating cost budget.

Notes

1. Seth G. Weissman, "Lawyering the New Urbanism," *Urban Land,* October 2000, p. 116.
2. Edward C. Hagerott, Jr., "Drafting Construction, Operation, and Reciprocal Easement Agreements for Vertical Mixed-Use Projects," *The Practical Real Estate Lawyer,* November 2002, pp. 15–25.
3. Weissman, "Lawyering the New Urbanism," p. 89.
4. Ibid., p. 88.

8. Case Studies

Addison Circle, Addison, Texas
An urban village organized around a circle and streets, including apartments, office, and retail uses.

CityPlace, West Palm Beach, Florida
An urban town center featuring a main street with retail, entertainment, cultural, and residential uses and additional office and hotel uses planned.

Jin Mao Tower, Shanghai, China
An 88-story mixed-use tower with hotel over office space and a retail facility at the base of the structure.

Peabody Place, Memphis, Tennessee
A downtown redevelopment project that mixes new and historic buildings and includes hotel, office, residential, and retail space.

Phillips Place, Charlotte, North Carolina
A suburban town center featuring a main street with retail, entertainment, apartment, and hotel uses.

Sony Center am Potsdamer Platz, Berlin, Germany
A downtown redevelopment project organized around a central atrium with office, retail, entertainment, and residential uses.

University Park at MIT, Cambridge, Massachusetts
An urban village organized around a central square and including office/R&D, apartment, hotel, and retail space.

Valencia Town Center Drive, Valencia, California
A town center in a planned community featuring a main street with retail, entertainment, office, hotel, and apartment uses.

WestEnd City Center, Budapest, Hungary
A mixed-use center adjacent to a transit station that is organized around both a retail mall and adjacent streets, with office and hotel uses as well.

Yerba Buena Center, San Francisco, California
A publicly initiated downtown redevelopment project and district with convention, hotel, cultural, entertainment, retail, residential, and office uses.

Addison Circle
Addison, Texas

Addison Circle is a mixed-use urban village built around a circle and a grid street system, with apartments and office space as the primary uses. The development has brought density—and a sense of community—to a classic edge city. Located in Addison, Texas, a northern suburb of Dallas, the 80-acre (32.5-hectare) mixed-use project is the result of a public/private partnership between Post Properties, Inc., and the town of Addison. Designed by RTKL Associates in conjunction with Post Properties and a team of consultants, Addison Circle's master plan calls for some 2,700 to 3,000 dwelling units intermixed with neighborhood retail, parks, and civic space, as well as 3 million to 4 million square feet (278,800 to 371,700 square meters) of offices and commercial uses. At about 50 dwelling units per acre (125 per hectare), the mostly rental project is more than twice as dense as a typical North Dallas garden apartment project. Yet Addison Circle has a sense of place and community not often seen in new development.

The Site and the Development Process
Despite its small size, the town of Addison had always attracted more than its fair share of commercial development. Permitting liquor by the drink long before other North Dallas suburbs, it became the focus for restaurant and hotel development and has been at the epicenter of Dallas's northward growth corridor since the mid-1970s. But as sales tax revenues from the restaurants were beginning to decline in the early 1990s and competition was emerging from newer suburbs, Addison town officials focused on the need to create a physical focal point as well as a stronger population base for the town to support and anchor the town's commercial uses.

The idea for a higher-density, mixed-use, residential neighborhood was first suggested in Addison's 1991 comprehensive plan and more recently in a community-based visioning program (Vision 2020). Though land-locked and about 80 percent built out, one of the few remaining undeveloped sites in Addison proved to be ideally suited for a higher-density mixed-used development. The site, adjacent to Addison's old town, was within walking distance of employment, retail, and entertainment establishments; adjacent to a Dallas Area Rapid Transit station; close to Addison's conference and theater center; and, not incidentally, controlled by a single landowner. Encouraged by town officials, the landowner, Gaylord Properties, teamed with Columbus Realty Trust (later acquired by and now known as Post Properties), an

apartment real estate investment trust, to develop a program and plan for the site.

To develop a project like Addison Circle—radically different from and denser than typical suburban projects—the developer and the city worked closely to formulate the program and design, to educate the public about the benefits of the more urban design, and to establish the terms of the public/private partnership. In addition to the more usual public workshops, the development and education process went so far as to have city staff travel to Chicago and Boston to observe and measure streets and setbacks in several universally admired older urban neighborhoods.

Eventually, a set of design and development standards were hammered out with the town and codified in a Planned Development District approval, covering such items as density, lot coverage, exterior building materials, setbacks, and street landscape standards. Working with town staff, the developer also evaluated phasing and development options and their likely impacts on municipal operating and capital budgets. The developer also identified funding gaps that needed to be resolved to provide the infrastructure and quality desired by the town and the developer.

The final agreement with the town of Addison committed the town to spending a total of $9.5 million of its general funds over the life of the project: $5.5 million on upfront infrastructure, street, and public open space improvements and the remaining $4 million in the second phase of development. As Art Lomenick, formerly of Post Properties concluded, "It cost an awful lot of money to build Addison, but unlike some other developments, Addison Circle will be there 100 years from now."

Seven phases are planned at Addison Circle, with expected buildout in 2003 to 2005. Three phases have been completed. The first phase, including 460 dwelling units, 20,000 square feet (1,860 square meters) of retail space, and a half-acre (0.2-hectare) park, was completed in 1997. A second phase, with 610 dwelling units, 90,000 square feet (8,365 square meters) of retail space, 41,000 square feet (3,810 square meters) of office space, and a 1$^1/_2$-acre (0.6-hectare) park, was completed in 1999, as was Addison Circle One, a 303,000-square-foot (28,160-square-meter) office building developed separately by an office developer but within the overall master plan. Phase III, consisting of 264 rental residential units, was completed in December 2000.

Although most of the housing at Addison Circle consists of rental units, Post Properties constructed six units

Addison Circle includes a pedestrian-friendly grid of streets and narrow mews, with a circle as the focal point. True to urban form, entrances open to the street, with a separation created by elevating buildings several steps above the sidewalk.

of for-sale townhouses during Phase II, and Amicus Properties developed an 86-unit, eight-story condominium project that was completed in spring 2002.

Planning and Design

The master plan for Addison Circle establishes two subareas: a residential neighborhood of mid-rise housing with supporting retail uses, parks, and other amenities, and a higher-density office and commercial district adja-

cent to the North Dallas Tollway. Linking the two areas is a framework of open space: a traffic roundabout (Addison Circle) and an axial green called Esplanade Park.

Streets and Public Spaces. Attention to streets and open space (public space in general) is one of the elements that makes Addison Circle so appealing. The circle itself is the symbolic center of the project. But in addition to its symbolic role, the roundabout serves to calm traffic that flows along Quorum Drive, a preexist-

Addison Circle brings dense urban forms to a suburban edge city. Residential neighborhoods consist of four-story buildings, some with retail businesses on the first floor.

ing major thoroughfare that cuts through the middle of the site. Not without controversy, a special roundabout consultant was required to convince skeptical officials to permit construction of what was to be the first public traffic circle in the area in more than 50 years. A design competition was also held to create a sculpture for the center of the circle; the winner, "Blueprints at Addison," establishes the circle as the focal point of the project and of the larger community.

Craig Blackmon

Buildings exude a solid permanence. Built of red brick with a course of stone at the base, they are finely detailed with painted metal balconies and cast stone arches and lintels.

Substantial investment is also evident in the treatment of Addison Circle's residential streets and boulevards. Sidewalks and crosswalks in many cases are paved in brick, with mature shade trees planted at 25-foot (7.6-meter) intervals. Larger specimens were specified in many cases to provide an instantly mature streetscape. Decorative metal guards, similar to those found in English gardens, define the edges of the tree wells. Bike racks, benches, litter containers, and other street furniture are provided as well.

Reversing the typical suburban norm of deep building setbacks and narrow sidewalks, the residential building facades at Addison Circle are close to the street, and sidewalks are generous. Sidewalks are 12 feet (3.6 meters) deep on residential streets, and buildings are set just six feet (1.8 meters) back of the sidewalk (18 feet [5.5 meters] from the curb). The six-foot (1.8-meter) setback allows for a landscape buffer as well as entries and stoops between sidewalk and building. On boulevards, the sidewalk is 14 feet (4.3 meters) wide, and buildings are set back 24 feet (7.3 meters) from the curb, allowing a ten-foot (three-meter) zone for landscaping or outdoor dining.

The buildings at Addison Circle are typically doughnut-shaped courtyard buildings. All residences have direct access to a private, secured interior courtyard. Some buildings have a second courtyard that is shared between the residential and nonresidential (retail and office) uses. The latter courtyards are open to employees, visitors, and residents alike. In general, the courtyards are carefully designed and often engaging spaces with lush landscaping, benches, fountains, sculptures, and shaded arcades rather than simply leftover voids between buildings.

Similarly, apartments open directly onto the several small parks dotting the neighborhood. Low stone walls edge the parks in places, defining pedestrian walkways between park and building. Hiking and biking trails are also being developed, and a large open space has been dedicated to the town for town-sponsored special events.

Buildings fronting major streets include neighborhood-serving retail shops on the first level. Mature trees line the sidewalks, providing shade for pedestrians. They also give the impression of a stable, well-established town rather than a new development.

Residential Units. A wide range of dwelling unit types is provided at Addison Circle, ranging from 570-square-foot (53-square-meter) efficiencies that rent for as little as $645 per month to 3,200-square-foot (295-square-meter) lofts that rent for $4,000 a month and up. Although most units (45 percent) are one-bedroom models, the planned mix also includes two- and three-bedroom units, townhouses, and live/work units.

Residential buildings have double-loaded hallways, with major entries and windows looking out over the street as well as the interior pool and courtyard areas. The intent of the full-block-closure building is to avoid functionally ambiguous space: one is either in the public realm, policed by the many windows overlooking the street and public courtyards, or within the security zone of the building and private courtyards.

Both the architecture and site planning contribute to the urban texture of Addison Circle. The residential buildings are primarily four stories high; in some cases, three residential levels are located above ground-floor shops and small service businesses. Building designs are modern but domesticated by balconies, bays, gables, and brick. Typically, residential buildings are stone at the base topped by a red brick facade. Brick bands in contrasting colors introduce a variety of detail to the finish. Similarly, window elements help to create architectural diversity; for example, large bay window structures are painted to contrast with the brickwork. Facades are further articulated with cast stone sills and lintels, dark-green painted metal balconies, and awnings.

Commercial Uses. Retail and other commercial uses are located at the street level in most buildings, with approximately 50 small retail and service businesses occupying 110,000 square feet (10,225 square meters) of ground-floor space in Addison Circle. The businesses range from convenience retail and personal services to restaurants and art galleries. As with most mixed-use communities, the neighborhood-serving commercial uses were initially somewhat slower to lease, based as

they are on the demand generated by housing and other local uses. Construction of a significant amount of office space has greatly strengthened the patronage base of the restaurants and other neighborhood businesses, however.

In addition to housing and retail space, Addison Circle has a significant office component. To date, approximately 340,000 square feet (31,600 square meters) of office space has been constructed, principally in two buildings, one six stories and one ten stories. The mid-

Most residential buildings face on the street and on an inner landscaped courtyard with a pool. All outdoor space is in full public view—with informal eyes-on-the-street surveillance—or within the security of an enclosed courtyard.

rise structure is a mixed-use building with ground-floor retail space, three floors of office space, and a double-height (floor and mezzanine) level of loft residences on top. The building, which includes office space for Post Properties, contains approximately 40,000 square feet (3,720 square meters) of offices and four office tenants. The Post Properties building fronts on Esplanade Park and is located between two residential buildings.

The high-rise office structure, Addison Circle One, sits at the end of Esplanade Park, with frontage overlooking the North Dallas Tollway. The 303,000-square-foot (28,160-square-meter) structure was developed by Champion Partners, a Dallas-area real estate developer, on land purchased from Gaylord Properties, the original owner of the Addison Circle land. Thus, Addison Circle One, although not developed by Post Properties, was subject to the Addison Circle master plan, and Champion was party to reciprocal obligations with Post with regard to parking and other issues. Completed in

Each courtyard is carefully designed and distinctive, and provides amenities such as benches, fountains, and sculptures.

early 1999, Addison Circle One is a Class A structure with large (30,000-square-foot [2,790- square-meter]) floor plates, enhanced electrical load capacities, and state-of-the-art mechanical systems. Major tenants of the $55 million structure include the corporate headquarters of the Staubach Company and Cap Rock Communications. Addison Circle One shares a parking garage with the adjacent residential building and health club. The garage, constructed by Champion, is partially leased to Post Properties for the residential and retail spaces and health club. As in the other Addison Circle garages, each use follows code and is physically separated from other uses in the parking structure.

Parking and Service Areas. Parking is provided in above-grade structures typically located behind each residential block, thus allowing for residences and shops to open directly onto the street. Residential and nonresidential uses share the same parking garages but do not share space within the garages; the number of parking spaces required by code is met or exceeded for each individual land use. For residences, the structured parking provides for one parking space per bedroom, a ratio that amounts to approximately 1.4 spaces per dwelling unit.

All vehicles access the parking garages from the same entry points. Commercial tenants, patrons, and residential visitors park without charge on the ground floor in an unsecured area; residents proceed through a security gate to park on the upper floors. Pedestrian access to the garages from the retail areas is often through one of the public courtyards.

Secondary auto and pedestrian circulation is provided by mews—45-foot-wide (14-meter) fire and access lanes located between buildings. The 45-foot (14-meter) right-of-way, paved from building face to building face, consists of two 12-foot (2.6-meter) vehicular lanes flanked by 10.5-foot-wide (3.2-meter) "sidewalks," defined with street trees but no curbs. Residential building entries and apartments face the mews, which also serve as pick-up and drop-off points for building residents.

Loading for the commercial uses is handled from the street, as there are no designated loading zones at Addison Circle. For the most part, this design is not a problem, notes Cindy Harris, vice president of development for Post Properties. Loading is mostly accomplished using small trucks, as is typically done in urban areas; however, the Addison Circle policy regarding loading is being revised as a result of larger trucks' blocking traffic on some of the larger streets. The revised policy is expected to restrict loading to the smaller streets and restrict the hours of deliveries.

Trash removal is another area where proximity of residential and nonresidential uses requires special consideration. In the earlier phases of Addison Circle, trash produced by commercial and residential uses was deposited in the same collection area and hauled away by a private firm under contract with Post Properties. Common collection points have proved to be unpopular, however, because of the odors produced by waste from the restaurants. Planning for the next phase of development at Addison Circle provides for the segregation of commercial trash into a special utilities zone separate from the residential trash.

Marketing and Promotion

Overall marketing of the project has benefited from the public/private partnership with the town of Addison, resulting in substantial positive public relations for the development. For example, all Addison residents, businesses, and employees were invited to the grand unveiling in April 2000 of "Blueprints at Addison," a piece of public art located in the circle that celebrates Addison's history and future. The piece, intended to symbolize the town and its development concept, consists of 25 metal poles topped with five floating art panels depicting blueprints of some phase of Addison's past and future. Post Properties contributed $450,000 of the total cost of $2.1 million.

Post Properties markets the development as a sophisticated urban-lifestyle community that, according to its Web site, "offers an attractive blend of European charm and modern urban vitality. Post Addison Circle is located in a thriving new neighborhood. With its tree-lined, brick-paved streets and stunning landscaping, Post Addison Circle allows you to enjoy a lifestyle of quiet elegance—just minutes from the best that the city has to offer."

To a large extent, the market for Addison Circle is those who rent by choice, not from necessity. According to Paris Rutherford, vice president and director of urban design for RTKL/Dallas, they are often "double-income couples with no children, empty nesters, and young professionals, typically between 30 to 55 years old. They rent by choice, preferring the urban lifestyle Addison Circle affords."

For this market segment, quality of life is a key issue. Developers like Post Properties are finding that amenities such as pools and health clubs are a starting point but that for many renters, the idea of convenience and community—everything from having a dry cleaners

The community will ultimately include 2,700 to 3,000 residential units, neighborhood retail shops, and up to 1.3 million square feet (120,774 square meters) of office space.

downstairs to a coffee bar to a secure place to stroll or sit—is an increasingly sought-after amenity. "The success of Addison Circle," notes Art Lomenick, former senior executive vice president for development at Post Properties, "is directly tied to an informal sociability created by the mixed-use development pattern."

The development has been able to achieve some premiums in the market for both the apartments and office space. Apartment rents as of 2002 generally ranged from $1.40 to $1.60 per square foot ($17.20 per square meter), well above average rents for the area (around $1.00 per square foot [$10.75 per square meter]) and approximately 10 percent above comparable new developments in the area. Premiums for office space are also evident, even for the office parcels that were sold off. Though developed in a competitive market, Addison Circle One started out strong and has remained strong. The building was 86 percent leased at completion, 100 percent within a few months thereafter. Lease rates at Addison Circle One are about $2.00 to $3.00 per square foot ($21.50 to $32.25 per square meter) higher than in comparable Tollway properties. According to Paul McCrea, senior partner of Champion Partners, these indicators of market strength are attributable to the quality of the building and its physical association with Addison Circle. "We are able to achieve above-market lease deals," notes McCrea, "because of the Addison Circle environment." Keying in on one of these environmental attributes, Cindy Harris of Post Properties credits the attractiveness to all the restaurants within walking distance of Addison Circle: "In the Texas heat, office workers are happy not to have to get in their cars and drive to lunch."

Experience Gained

If cities want the development of quality town centers, they must play a proactive part in the development process. First, successful rezoning for public/private partnership developments of this type must use the joint efforts of city staff and the developer's team. In this case, the

To improve the streetscape, parking is located in above-grade structures behind each residential block.

strategic planning process incorporated the developer, the consultants, and a task force comprising town technical and managerial staff and policy makers, who worked together as a project team. The purpose of this close working relationship was to provide technical and political advice and to ensure agreement and understanding on the form and substance of planning concepts, traffic issues, and development standards. Ultimately, the team worked together to attain a final consensus for the adoption and implementation of these concepts.

To develop quality housing and sustainable communities, the development process must allow time to market the concept. Background data, slides, and videos from comparable U.S. or foreign developments should be presented to illustrate proposed standards of quality, tenant profiles, and design features. The characteristics and advantages of proposed building types and the mix of uses must then be communicated to city staff, policy makers, and community leaders completely and cohesively.

Cities must be proactive in the development process and must agree to a number of development commitments, including incentives to seed initial development, creation of a pedestrian-friendly environment that supports neighborhood services, and flexibility in zoning that encourages mixed-use and medium-density development. Density is important, because it ultimately funds both parties' obligations.

Under this new covenant, each party wins. The developer's investment hurdle rates are achievable, and the city reaps additions to its tax rolls, which generate revenues to cover the cost of upgraded public infrastructure and city services. The outcome is a sustainable, integrated mixed-use residential development that serves as a vibrant life force for the community and a blueprint for future projects.

One area where the project has struggled a bit is in the retail space. The project was not developed to be a major retail destination, and Post Properties is not a retail developer. As a result, retail space has been slow to take root. In many of its more recent projects, Post has sought to develop partnerships with retail developers to undertake the retail portions of their urban village developments.

Site plan.

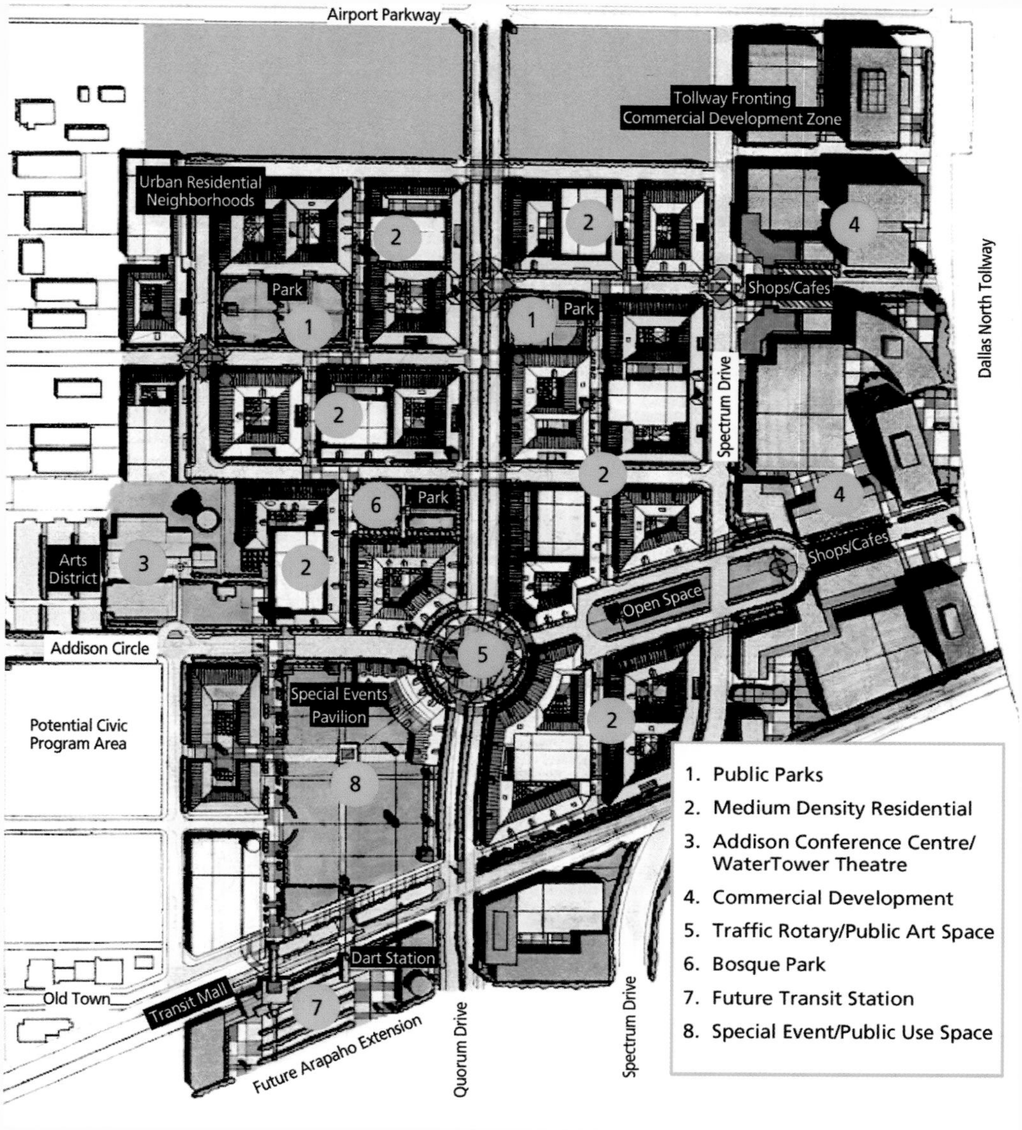

Airport Parkway

Tollway Fronting
Commercial Development Zone

Urban Residential
Neighborhoods

Park

Shops/Cafes

Spectrum Drive

Dallas North Tollway

Arts
District

Addison Circle

Open Space

Shops/Cafes

Potential Civic
Program Area

Special Events
Pavilion

1. Public Parks
2. Medium Density Residential
3. Addison Conference Centre/
   WaterTower Theatre
4. Commercial Development
5. Traffic Rotary/Public Art Space
6. Bosque Park
7. Future Transit Station
8. Special Event/Public Use Space

Dart Station

Old Town

Transit Mall

Future Arapaho Extension

Quorum Drive

Spectrum Drive

Craig Blackmon

Project Data: Addison Circle

Land Use and Building Information

Site Area	80 acres (32.5 hectares)

Gross Building Area (GBA)

Use	Existing Gross Square Feet (Square Meters)	Planned Gross Square Feet (Square Meters)
Office	340,000 (31,600)	1,000,000 (92,900)
Retail	110,000 (10,220)	250,000 (23,230)
Residential	1,276,800 (118,660)	2,592,000 (240,900)
Hotel	0	150,000 (13,940)
Restaurant	20,000 (1,860)	40,000 (3,720)
Public park	121,680 (11,300)	425,260 (39,500)
Parking	640,000 (59,500)	1,296,000 (120,400)
Total GBA	2,508,480 (233,130)	5,753,260 (534,690)

Land Use Plan

	Acres (Hectares)	Percent of Site
Buildings	39 (15.8)	48.8%
Streets/surface parking	16 (6.5)	20.0
Landscaping/open space	10 (4)	12.5
Public Parks	15 (6)	18.7
Total	80 (32.4)	100.0%

Residential Information

Unit Type	Unit Size (Square Feet/ Square Meters)	Number of Units	Rent Range
Phases I & II			
Efficiency	570–772 (53–71.7)	214	$645–786
1-Bedroom	681–1,079 (63.3–100)	482	$800–1,220
2-Bedroom	870–1,521 (80–141)	203	$1,013–2,015
3-Bedroom	1,501–1,507 (139–140)	11	$1,591
Lofts	807–3,219 (75–299)	160	$870–4,400
Phase III			
Efficiency	559 (52)	102	$681
1-Bedroom	777 (72.2)	106	$920
2-Bedroom	1,100 (102)	58	$1,300

Office Tenant Information

Occupied NRA	100%
Number of Tenants	14 (10 at Addison Circle One)
Average Tenant Size (Addison Circle One)	5,335–92,358 square feet (495.8–8,585 square meters)
Annual Rents	$22–25 per square foot ($237–269 per square meter)
Average Length of Lease	2–10 years (7–10 at Addison Circle One)
Typical Terms of Lease (Addison Circle One)	Rent is net of electricity and parking

Retail/Entertainment Tenant Information

	Number of Stores	Total GLA (Square Feet/ Square Meters)
General merchandise	6	10,605 (985)
Food service	11	30,561 (2,840)
Personal services	10	12,050 (1,120)
Health club	1	10,957 (1,020)
Other	21	36,097 (3,355)
Vacant	5	6,463 (600)
Total	54	106,733 (9,920)

Percent of GLA Occupied	94%
Annual Rents	$16–20 per square foot ($172–215 per square meter)
Average Length of Lease	3–5 years
Typical Lease Provisions	Triple net

Development Cost Information[1]

Phase I	$31,000,000
Phase II	$83,000,000
Phase III	$20,000,000
Total	$134,200,000

Financing Information[2]

Financing Source	Amount
Post Properties (65% debt/35% equity)	$134,000,000
Town of Addison	$10,200,000
Total	$144,200,000

Notes

[1] For Phases I to III, not including the $55 million Champion Building or $10.2 million from the town of Addison.

[2] The town of Addison contributed $10.2 million—$9 million for infrastructure plus an additional $1.2 million for the featured sculpture.

Development Schedule

1994	Planning started
1995	Site purchased (Phase I)
1995	Construction started
1997	Sales/leasing started
1997	Phase I completed
1998	Phase II completed
2001	Phase III completed

Developer

Post Properties, Inc.
4401 Northside Parkway
Suite 800
Atlanta, Georgia 30327
404-846-5000

Architect and Master Planner

RTKL Associates, Inc.
1717 Pacific Avenue
Suite 100
Dallas, Texas 75201
214-871-8877

Engineering and Landscape Architect

Huit-Zollars
3131 McKinney Avenue
Suite 600
Dallas, Texas 75204
214-871-3311

Other

Town of Addison
5300 Beltline Road
Addison, Texas 75001
972-450-7078

CityPlace

West Palm Beach, Florida

CityPlace is a mixed-use town center that currently brings together residences, cultural facilities, restaurants, and national and regional specialty retailers in a European-style village setting; office, hotel, and conference space is also planned for future phases. CityPlace offers open-air shopping plazas, handsome tree-lined esplanades and streets that invite strollers, and winding walkways that lead to sidewalk dining establishments, entertainment venues, and family-friendly activities such as free concerts and dancing fountains.

CityPlace currently has 600,000 square feet (55,760 square meters) of retail space and nearly 600 residential units, including condominiums, townhouses, live/work units, and rental apartments. Three office towers totaling 750,000 square feet (70,000 square meters) will eventually round out the mix along with a 400-room hotel and the Palm Beach Convention Center, which is scheduled to open in 2003. The cultural infrastructure adjacent to CityPlace, which currently includes the Kravis Center for the Performing Arts, is being expanded to include the new home of the Palm Beach Opera and the Norton Museum of Art.

The Site and Development Process

CityPlace is located on a 72-acre (29-hectare) site in the heart of West Palm Beach, near the intersection of I-95 and Okeechobee Boulevard, a major thoroughfare leading to the Palm Beaches and a ten-minute drive from Palm Beach International Airport. Affluent communities such as Palm Beach, Hobe Sound, Delray Beach, and Boca Raton are all nearby. More shopping areas can be found across the intracoastal waterway at Worth Avenue and at the Clematis Street district, West Palm Beach's earlier downtown development success story.

CityPlace was made possible by an innovative combination of public and private financing and development expertise. Although West Palm Beach enjoys proximity to the area's beaches and affluent tax base, it enjoyed none of the advantages, and by the 1980s the downtown held little appeal to city residents and outside visitors. Little downtown activity occurred beyond the nine-to-five office hours, and major pockets of vacant land and poorly maintained, underused buildings had become eyesores. In the mid-1980s, developer Henry Rolf began to quietly assemble 340 separate parcels of land equaling 73 acres (29.5 hectares) in the short span of nine months. His plans to create a "Downtown/Uptown" project as a gateway to Palm Beach collapsed with the real estate depression of the late 1980s and early 1990s.

Although that project failed, the successful land assembly created a tremendous opportunity for the city to undertake redevelopment of the site, allowing it to bypass the onerous land assembly process that often impedes downtown redevelopment projects.

When Nancy Graham became mayor in 1991, she was faced with a dying downtown and very few resources to bring it back to life. In 1993, Graham attended the Mayor's Institute on City Design sponsored by the National Endowment for the Arts. She learned of the importance of good urban design and the role design plays in revitalizing cities after hearing Mayor Joseph Riley discuss Charleston's revitalization. West Palm Beach's planning regulations and zoning, however, made it illegal to build attractive, exciting urban places like Charleston. To clear a path for redevelopment required the overhaul of the city's planning and regulatory codes and the appointment of new staff and commissions receptive to change. The urban design firm Duany Plater-Zyberk and retail expert Gibbs Planning created a new downtown master plan using principles of new urbanism.

The transformation began with the construction of a new fountain in Centennial Plaza near city hall and significant public investment on Clematis Street—the city's historic but then dormant retail spine. The fountain became a popular gathering spot and site for special community events and street entertainment, and Clematis Street evolved into a vibrant oasis of small local retailers, cottage businesses, restaurants, and nightlife spots. With community use and pride reestablished in West Palm Beach, Mayor Graham next set out to create value in the nearby 72-acre (29-hectare) no-man's-land.

Accordingly, the mayor issued a request for proposals for redevelopment of the 72-acre (29-hectare) site previously assembled by Rolf. The city ultimately awarded a contract to a development team led by the Palladium Company of New York and its CEO, Ken Himmel. Himmel brought his experience with numerous large mixed-use projects, including Reston Town Center in northern Virginia, Copley Place in Boston, Water Tower Place in Chicago, and Pacific Place in Seattle. Himmel's lead designer for the latter three projects was Howard Elkus of Elkus/Manfredi Architects, and the reunion of this team set the tone for the urbane design of CityPlace.

The city also acted as a financial partner in the transformation of West Palm Beach's business district. It borrowed the $20 million required to acquire the site for CityPlace and leased the parcel to Palladium for 75 years, with payments tied to the debt service on the loan. The

Palladium Plaza at CityPlace is the focus of the cultural, economic, and social life of West Palm Beach.

city also raised $55 million in tax increment financing to pay for 30 percent of the parking deck construction as well as for the landscaping, fountains and artwork, lighting, and public space improvements. The city also took on all permitting work for the project to ensure that the regulatory process did not impede development.

Of the $142 million financed by the developers, 77 percent was provided by commercial banks, led by Key Bank for first mortgage construction and miniperm financing, with the remaining 23 percent representing equity investment by the Palladium Company and an equity partner, a Midwest pension fund.

Planning and Design
Background research for the design of CityPlace took Elkus, Himmel, and Graham to Europe on an intense seven-day tour of southern Mediterranean architecture and urbanism in search of inspirational buildings, plazas, fountains, and urban landscapes. While traveling, Elkus and his team sought the right scale of spaces in arcades from Rome to Venice; the knowledge gathered on this trip was key to the success of the design and was influential in the shaping of the streets, public spaces, buildings, and arcades so that they are welcoming for both pedestrians and businesses.

The plaza in front of the restored church—now the Harriet Himmel Gilman Theater—is the center of gravity for the development, providing a grand public room that draws visitors from throughout West Palm Beach and Florida's Gold Coast. The church, the outdoor din-

ing areas that spill out onto the plaza, the fountain, and the urban landscaping create a sense of enclosure and a European atmosphere. A dramatic fountain in the church plaza stands as civic art during the day and provides water, light, and fog shows choreographed to music each night. Smaller plazas, courtyards, and fountains are located on the first and second levels of the project, and streets can be closed for festivals and events.

The former First United Methodist Church at the center of the plaza, built in 1926, was one of the largest Spanish colonial revival structures of its day. The building has been carefully restored and adapted at a cost of $5 million and provides an 11,000-square-foot (1,020-square-meter) hall for cultural performances, community events, and art exhibits. The building provides an important visual anchor that lends elements of history and authenticity to the project. The CityPlace development team was careful to preserve the dramatic views of the building by carefully designing the Italian-style plaza in front of the church and by curving the commercial streetwall to open up around the plaza.

The church and the plaza are located near the intersection of two principal pedestrian-friendly streets, and together the plaza and these two streets define the central core area and public spaces of the town center. South Rosemary Avenue, running perpendicular to Okeechobee Boulevard, is the main retail street in the project, while Hibiscus Street intersects with South Rosemary at the church. Retail parking is located in several garages, with the main parking garage on Hibiscus located on

The Harriet Himmel Gilman Theater for Cultural and Performing Arts is a historic Spanish colonial revival church located at the heart of CityPlace that has been restored as a new performance theater.

Shoppers pause in the large, Italian-style plaza to admire the dancing waters of the Palladium Plaza Fountains set to music and lights.

the eastern portion of the site. A hotel and convention center are planned for a parcel across Okeechobee Boulevard.

The plan also includes a diverse assortment of 586 housing units (with more planned) as well as plans for three office towers totaling 750,000 square feet (70,000 square meters). The CityPlace development team believed that the provision of various housing options was important to achieving 24-hour street life integral to the project's success. Housing options include 51 townhouses, 33 garden apartments, 128 luxury high-rise apartments, 264 mid-rise apartments, 38 flats, and 56 live/work units above the storefronts on Rosemary Avenue. Housing is concentrated in the western portions of the site closest to the major cultural institution, running along the entire length of Sapodilla Avenue and enveloping large interior-block parking garages.

To create an area encompassing five city blocks without introducing the sameness of a project, the designers worked hard to introduce individual design features in the buildings, walkways, and landscaping throughout CityPlace. Various column types and different combinations of stone, brick, and tile were used for walkways, crosswalks, and plazas. Individual plantings were selected to match the architecture rather than following a uniform pattern of identical trees and plants. Elkus expanded on the intent of CityPlace architecture in a 1998 interview with the *South Florida Business Journal:*

I think it's an architecture of freedom. You can be as informal or formal as you want within that context. You can be your most relaxed self or you can be eloquent. . . . There is a greater unity in the overall approach than, say, on Clematis Street, which can be southern Mediterranean and South Beach. You will not find the use of pink within CityPlace. We don't think it belongs within the palate that we've chosen. It has been so exaggerated in all-pink developments that by the elimination of pink we're making sure CityPlace doesn't run that way.[1]

Inspired by the grandeur and elegance of the Paris Opera House, the Muvico Theater on the second level features upscale concessions and valet parking.

©2001 C.J. Walker

The design creates highly textured streetscapes and a variety of building scales.

Courtesy of Elkus/Manfredi Architects Ltd.

Using a mix of styles, colors, elevations, and materials, the facades of the two- to three-story buildings along the main retail street—Rosemary Avenue—create the illusion of many smaller buildings. The architectural details play off the southern Mediterranean theme with exposed rafters, canvas awnings, and tile and metal rooftops. Wrought iron and wooden balconies on the upper floors allow residents to overlook the street life below. "It's an architecture of out-of-doors," explains Elkus, "of a very different climate. It embraces landscaping. It does not have hard edges between the inside and outside. It uses patios, arches, and trellises between the buildings and surrounding them."[2]

Tenants, Marketing, and Management

From the beginning, the CityPlace development team knew that a distinctive mix of shops, restaurants, entertainment, and housing options would be required to live up to the project's vision. For the retail compo-

nent, the developers assembled a core of experienced "main street" retailers, including Restoration Hardware, Barnes & Noble, FAO Schwarz, Ann Taylor, Williams Sonoma, Pottery Barn, and a variety of anchors, including Macy's, the Muvico Theaters, and a 23,000-square-foot (2,140-square-meter) gourmet grocery store. They then set out to recruit ten high-profile destination restaurants, including the Cheesecake Factory, Mark's, Angelo and Maxie's, and Boston's Legal Seafood. A few dozen smaller high-end fashion, home, and lifestyle shops are sprinkled throughout, ranging in size from a few hundred to a few thousand square feet.

Many of the retailers chose to design their buildings specifically to blend in with CityPlace's special urban environment. Macy's introduced a new store concept— a resort flavor in a two-story, 11,000-square-foot (1,020-square-meter) building that is smaller than its traditional department stores. Muvico Theaters, a Fort Lauderdale–based cinema operation, built a 20-screen theater designed to evoke the grandeur and elegance of the Paris Opera House; the theater features upscale concessions, a supervised children's playroom, and valet parking. FAO Schwarz created a two-story, custom-designed building as well. Even retailers that did not drastically alter their internal layouts were willing to experiment with external appearances. Pottery Barn negotiated a two-story facade on its one-story store, with the second floor serving as residential space.

CityPlace enjoys the coordinated marketing and management of a regional shopping mall. The city supports the programming of community festivals and events. The project has had a positive impact on adjacent properties, and cultural institutions such as the Kravis Center are initiating projects to improve the connections between their institutions and CityPlace.

CityPlace quickly gained momentum, and its retail, restaurant, and entertainment spaces were more than 60 percent leased one year before its opening in October 2000. Residential units sold briskly and often before construction began. The project's 51 townhouses sold out in ten days with sale prices of $252,000 to $418,000, and the 33 condominiums sold out in three weeks for $139,000 to $349,000. Apartment leasing has moved more slowly, however, which observers attribute to the lack of neighborhood retail shops, forcing residents to drive some distance to buy groceries and sundries.

Retail and restaurant sales have ranged from $350 to $1,200 per square foot ($3,765 to $12,900 per square meter), and the ten restaurants have been strong performers, with long waiting times on weekends, offering diners the opportunity to visit the shops or stroll through the plaza.

Retail itself has not been so successful, and overall the financial performance of CityPlace, according to Ken Himmel of the Related Companies, has been "well below initial expectations." He further notes that "people are not coming here to do comparable apparel shopping." As of 2003, Himmel was reviewing new strategies to improve the viability of retail: one strategy under consideration is to shift away from expensive clothing retailers and toward home furnishings, art galleries, and more restaurants and nightclubs. Roche Bobois, a high-end home furnishings store, recently opened in CityPlace.

Although the project is currently having problems, the addition of office, hotel, and convention uses in the coming years should bolster performance, and Himmel predicts that CityPlace will achieve an 8.5 to 9 percent return on cost by 2005 to 2006.[3]

Experience Gained

CityPlace is an example of how large-scale redevelopment projects can proceed when municipalities and the private sector work closely together toward the realization of a shared vision. Key factors helped to smooth a clear path for development:

- land assembly completed before the project's start;
- strong local leadership and support with a clear vision of how the property should be developed;
- West Palm Beach's regulatory reform process, which had removed major impediments to a compact, mixed-use development in the downtown before the start of construction;
- the city's willingness to jump-start the development project by taking on financial risk and providing public funds to obtain the property and make infrastructure improvements;
- conducting a competitive RFP process that allowed the city to select a development team with experience in town center development based on traditional urban design principles, making the best possible marriage between public and private sector partners;
- the city's being responsible for all the permitting and pushing the project through the approvals process, allowing the development team to focus on financing, leasing, and building the project.

Fountains located throughout CityPlace are richly detailed and designed to showcase the region's Mediterranean aesthetic heritage.

The Cheesecake Factory is one of the project's most successful restaurants, with weekend waiting times for a table exceeding an hour.

©2001 C.J. Walker

Residential lofts and apartments above retail shops feature a combination of mellow Tuscan colors and warm earth tones. Wrought iron and wooden balconies on the upper floors allow residents to overlook the street life below.

©2001 C.J. Walker

The preservation and adaptive use of the Spanish colonial revival church was an investment in CityPlace's distinctive identity and established a connection with the community's history that elevated the project's authenticity.

The grand, Italian-style plaza provides a powerful center of gravity for the project, attracting people to live, work, or visit CityPlace regardless of their motivation to shop.

The articulation of CityPlace's southern Mediterranean theme in terms of stylistic elements and the indoor/outdoor character of the buildings and spaces provide a strong sense of place connected with the vernacular tradition of Florida's early Gold Coast communities.

Retail in a mixed-use project should find a niche and not compete directly with major malls. In general, a retail facility of 400,000 to 700,000 square feet (37,000 to 65,000 square meters) in a mixed-use project will find it difficult to compete directly against malls of larger than

1 million square feet (93,000 square meters) with three or more department stores.

The experience at CityPlace suggests that retail in mixed-use developments must be carefully sized and positioned so as not to overreach. Most retail components in mixed-use developments are smaller than 300,000 square feet (28,000 square meters) and focus on restaurants, entertainment, lifestyle retail, and other specialty niches; trying to compete directly with malls for comparison apparel shopping is risky business.

Notes

1. Carole Clancy, "CityPlace Architect Draws Inspiration from Italy," *South Florida Business Journal*, May 15, 1998, p. 3A.

2. Ibid.

3. Paul Owers, "Can CityPlace Survive?" PalmBeachPost.com, accessed April 7, 2003.

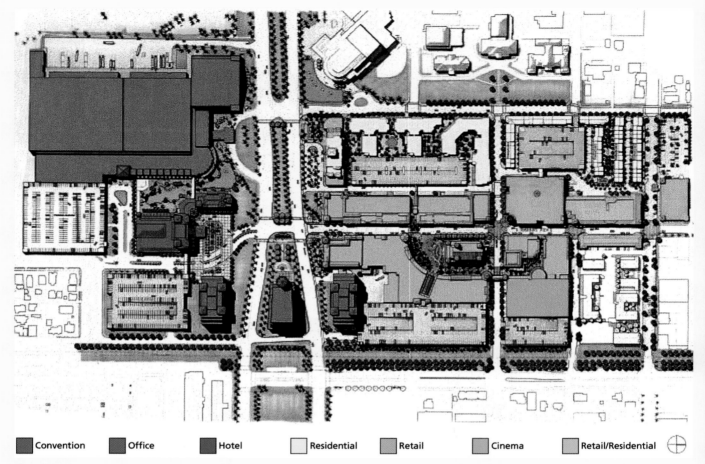

Convention   Office   Hotel   Residential   Retail   Cinema   Retail/Residential

Site plan.

Project Data: CityPlace

Land Use and Building Information

Site Area   72 acres (29 hectares)

Parking Spaces   3,300

Gross Building Area (GBA)

Use	Existing Gross Square Feet (Square Meters)		Planned Gross Square Feet (Square Meters)	
Office	0		750,000	(70,000)
Retail	689,836	(64,100)	–	
Residential	647,209	(60,150)	NA	
Hotel	–		280,000	(26,000)
Convention center	–		300,000	(27,900)
Total GBA	1,337,045	(124,260)	1,080,000	(100,370)

Leasable Area or Units/Rooms

	Existing	Planned
Office net rentable area (square feet/square meters)	0	450,000 (41,820)
Retail gross leasable area (square feet/square meters)	627,124 (58,280)	627,124 (58,280)
Residential (units)	586	935
Hotel (rooms)	0	350

Retail Information

Tenant Classification	Number of Stores	Total GLA (Square Feet/ Square Meters)	
Food service	3	5,521	(513)
Clothing and accessories	30	204,400	(19,000)
Shoes	2	5,501	(510)
Home appliances/music	2	4,726	(440)
Gift/specialty	7	10,410	(970)
Jewelry	5	8,646	(805)
Home accents	10	92,185	(8,570)
Personal care	2	4,535	(420)
Restaurants	8	81,570	(7,580)
Toys	2	19,870	(1,845)
Books and cards	2	43,810	(4,070)
Cinema	1	92,000	(8,550)
Supermarket	1	23,000	(2,140)
Vacant	–	31,102	(2,890)
Total	75	627,085	(58,280)

Percent of GLA Occupied   95%

Annual Rents $35–50 per square foot ($375–540/square meter)

Average Annual Sales $350–1,200 per square foot ($3,765–12,900/square meter)

Average Length of Lease   10–15 years

Residential Information

Unit Type	Unit Size (Square Feet/ Square Meters)	Number of Units	Number Sold/Leased[1]	Rent and Sale Price Range
A Tower	805–1,243 (75–115)	128	110 Leased	$1,226–2,130
B Courtyard	766–1,405 (71–130)	264	185 Leased	$950–1,945
B Flats	900–1,300 (84–120)	54	30 Leased	$1,195–2,900
C Lofts	936–2,459 (87–230)	56	13 Leased	$1,940–5,680
D Townhouses/ Condos	1,000–1,700 (93–158)	84	84 Sold	$150,000– 380,000

Development Cost Information

Retail development	$200,000,000
Residential development	50,000,000
Anchors	50,000,000
Tenant improvements	50,000,000
Planned future development	200,000,000
Total	$550,000,000

Development Schedule

1996–1997	Planning started
5/1998	Site purchased
12/1998	Construction started
Spring 1998	Sales/leasing started
10/2000	Phase I completed
2003	Project completed (estimated)

Developer

The Related Companies, LP (The Palladium Company)
625 Madison Avenue
Ninth Floor
New York, New York 10022
212-421-5333

Architects

Elkus/Manfredi Architects, LP
530 Atlantic Avenue
Boston, Massachusetts 02210
617-426-1300

REG Architects, Inc.
120 South Dixie Highway
Suite 201
West Palm Beach, Florida 33401
561-659-2383

Note
[1] As of early 2002.

Jin Mao Tower
Shanghai, China

Jin Mao Tower is an 88-story skyscraper containing office, hotel, and retail uses on a 5.9-acre (2.4-hectare) site in Shanghai, China. The tower, a triumph of engineering and technology and a symbol of China's economic and political resurgence, was the third tallest building in the world when it was built. One observer has described it as "China's locomotive ego in built form." Located in the rapidly developing Pudong area of Shanghai, China's largest city, the development lies directly across the river from downtown Shanghai. Jin Mao Tower features more than 1.3 million square feet (123,000 square meters) of office space, a 555-room luxury hotel, and 347,362 square feet (32,280 square meters) of retail uses. Jin Mao Tower is a prime example of how a vertical mix of uses on a large scale can result in a landmark building, in this case resulting in the creation of an international icon and symbol for a city and a country.

The Site and Development Process
The development is the centerpiece of the 10.8-square-mile (28-square-kilometer) Lujiazui Finance and Trade Zone, part of the Pudong New Area and across the river from Bund—a riverfront boulevard that is the traditional commercial heart of Shanghai. A century ago, Pudong was notorious as an area of gangsters, prostitutes, shabby warehouses, and run-down shacks. Redevelopment has taken place rapidly and on a large scale in recent years, with whole neighborhoods torn down in a matter of weeks to make way for new buildings and infrastructure. Jin Mao towers over neighboring high-rise office buildings and fronts onto a wide arterial road that bisects the Pudong district. New bridges and tunnels connect Pudong to downtown Shanghai.

The symbolism of developing this location should not be overlooked. In the 1840s, China was humiliated in the First Opium War. The British and other colonial powers occupied Shanghai and other cities along the Chinese coast as a foothold in the lucrative opium trade. The great trading houses of the day set up their elegant headquarters along the Bund, where executives could view the loading and unloading of their ships. Today, those buildings still stand but are dwarfed by Jin Mao Tower and its neighbors across the river.

The Pudong New Area represents one of the keystones of China's economic development strategy. The Lujiazui Finance and Trade Zone is designed as a financial center to rival Hong Kong, with the Jin Mao Tower as the physical and symbolic centerpiece. Office space in Shanghai has been built rapidly in recent years, and

the inventory is now equal to Hong Kong's, which took 50 years.

Jin Mao Tower was developed and is now owned by the China Shanghai Foreign Trade Center Company, known as the China Jin Mao Group. The Chinese Ministry of Foreign Trade and Economic Cooperation formed the Jin Mao Group from a consortium of 14 Chinese shareholding companies that focus on import/export activities, technology, development, and business management.

The development strategy and financing for Jin Mao Tower was quite different from that used in the West and other capitalist countries, and the role of the Chinese government was fundamental in the undertaking. Jin Mao Tower cost $540 million to develop. As in the West, financing for this type of project was a combination of equity investment and debt. In China, however, equity investors are often state-owned enterprises or parastatal companies that often face very soft budget constraints as a result of their direct government support. Moreover, debt financing is often provided by Chinese banks, which are controlled by the state and are notorious for their lack of rigorous underwriting standards and levels of bad debt. Compounding this situation, the central Chinese government gave the Shanghai municipal government permission to lease publicly owned land on a long-term basis for development and use the funds generated to finance local infrastructure projects—leading to a serious glut of available land for development. As a result of all these government investment strategies and the provision of incentives to develop buildings without market demand, office vacancy levels in Shanghai in the late 1990s reached almost 70 percent.

Any real estate development in China needs political support to succeed. As Shanghai is known as the golden goose of the Chinese economy, it rarely goes lacking in government support for its redevelopment projects. In the case of Jin Mao Towers, the full force of the central Chinese government was behind the project from start to finish, which greatly expedited the development process. Deng Xiaoping, China's leader until his death in 1997, called for the redevelopment of the Pudong New Area generally and the construction of Jin Mao Tower specifically.

Planning, Design, and Construction
Jin Mao Tower was intended to be an architectural landmark. The government master plan for the Lujiazui district specified Jin Mao Tower as one of the focal points of the area, surrounded by smaller buildings of 30 to

© Hedrich Blessing

40 stories and ample park space. The government sponsored an international architectural competition in 1993 to select the tower's design. The competition specified a design with a mix of uses, including a hotel and offices. The jury looked for a design that was modern yet distinctively Chinese.

The Chicago office of Skidmore, Owings & Merrill won the competition, submitting a design inspired by the architecture of traditional Chinese pagodas. Architect Adrian Smith wanted to create a building that successfully combined a feeling of modernity with explicit reference to traditional Chinese aesthetics and cultural principles. Chinese numerology figures prominently in the tower's design. The number eight is particularly auspicious in Chinese culture; thus, the tower is 88 stories and employs the number eight in various other ways. The tower is also tapered by a series of segmented setbacks, resulting in 13 separate segments, with the larger segments at the bottom gradually giving way to smaller segments near the top, evoking a Chinese pagoda. Jin Mao means *much gold* in Chinese.

Like that of the pagodas of the past, the design is strong yet light and serves as a reference point for development in the rest of the district. The result is neither a pastiche of Chinese design elements nor a strictly modernist building. This impressive building is undeniably Chinese and entirely appropriate to its location and purpose.

The Jin Mao Tower is the tallest building in China. Office space is found on the third through 50th floors above a two-story entrance lobby. The Grand Hyatt Shanghai Hotel occupies floors 53 to 87, with an observation deck on the 88th floor. Employing a curtain wall of steel, aluminum, and glass, the tower sparkles with the changing light of the Shanghai skyline. Attached to the tower is a six-story retail and entertainment venue known as the Podium. Visually, the Podium serves as a base for the neighboring tower and is designed with a lofty atrium

The design of the Jin Mao Tower successfully blends elements of modern architecture with traditional Chinese principles.

More than 1 million people have already visited the observation deck at Jin Mao Tower, the tallest building in China and third tallest in the world.

and a blend of modern elements. Landscaping and parking spaces surround the building on the 258,342-square-foot (24,000-square-meter) site.

The interior throughout Jin Mao Tower is modern, elegant, and inviting. Steel and glass blend with marble and wood to create a sophisticated atmosphere. High-quality materials and fixtures were installed with creative workmanship, something that is often lacking in other development projects in China. Office floor plates range from 25,000 to 30,000 square feet (2,325 to 2,790 square meters), with no columns; floor-to-ceiling height is 8.9 feet (2.7 meters).

A hexagonal concrete core surrounded by an array of eight composite mega columns supports the building's height. Two sets of outrigger trusses connect these columns to the core, allowing the building to efficiently resist wind and earthquake forces. The building contains 235,440 cubic yards (180,000 cubic meters) of concrete. To support this weight, more than a thousand structural steel piles were driven 272 feet (83 meters), the longest steel pipe piles ever used in a land-based building. The project has a completely self-contained infrastructure system, including electric generators, a sewage treatment plant, and a potable water plant. Copper and fiber-optic cables connect the building's systems and provide broadband communications connections.

The tower is easily accessible by several modes of transportation. It has 900 auto parking spaces, 800 of them in an underground garage, and 1,000 bicycle parking spots. The Number Two subway line runs directly from downtown Shanghai to Pudong, with a stop just outside Jin Mao Tower. Office tenants can take the free shuttle bus from Jin Mao Tower across the river to People's Square. The building contains 61 high-speed elevators.

A truly international team of contractors and consultants worked on the project, with more than 70 firms ultimately involved in the construction process. Coordination and dialogue were carefully considered among all parties working on the project. Despite the challenges of working in China and the potential for misunderstandings between local and foreign firms, a high level of cooperation was achieved. Still, it was exceptionally difficult to manage the construction process, even with full-time translators. Dozens of meetings were held with local and government agencies to determine how Chinese and international building and engineering codes should apply to this massive building. Meetings were required on a regular basis to review and approve every revision and refinement of the architectural plan.

Marketing and Performance

Jin Mao Tower offers the best office space in all of Shanghai, with rents ranging from $12.00 to $20.00 per square foot ($130 to $215 per square meter) per year, near the top of the market. A number of Chinese import/export firms and a number of prominent Western firms such as Dow Jones, Dresden Bank AG, Asahi Bank of Japan, and Compaq have their offices in the building. The first tenants moved into the building in February 1999,

and occupancy rates are near 70 percent, which is remarkable, given the oversupplied office market in Shanghai. In the surrounding Pudong/Lujiazui market area, the Chinese government has imparted a host of incentives to encourage companies to locate there. The office vacancy rate is estimated at 35 to 60 percent, however.

The Grand Hyatt Hotel, on floors 53 to 87, is the highest hotel in the world. A stunning 498-foot (152-meter) atrium in the core of the hotel has been described as *Guggenheim on steroids*. The hotel has won several awards and in 1999 was named the best business hotel in Asia by *Asia Business Week* and *Bloomberg*. The hotel offers guests a variety of deluxe services and amenities. Rooms offer marble baths, spectacular views, and art deco–inspired interiors. A dozen restaurants and lounges are located in the hotel, and the Oasis Club swimming pool and fitness center is found on the 57th floor.

All this luxury is not cheap, however, with room rates starting at $175 per night and going to $4,500 for the

© Hedrich Blessing

The six-story Podium building stands next to the tower and houses most of the project's retail and entertainment components.

chairman's suite. Occupancy at the hotel is more than 70 percent despite the high prices, as a result of a steady stream of foreign business travelers. The hotel hosts many VIP functions, and PU-Js, the hotel's nightclub, is one of the most fashionable places to party in the city.

Despite the large number of office workers in Jin Mao Tower and the surrounding Pudong area, the 344,456-square-foot (32,000-square-meter) retail component in the six-story Podium building has not been successful. The varied shopping districts in Shanghai offer better selections and value, making the retail component unnecessary at this time. Moreover, the design of the retail space makes it feel separated from the offices and hotel. The top four floors are now closed to the public. The second floor contains an exhibition of the construction of Jin Mao Tower; the first floor has a few small retailers such as a bookstore, gift shop, and airline ticket office. Only the food court in the basement is doing a brisk business serving lunch to nearby office workers.

Leasing efforts for the space continue, however, and managers hope that the market for retail services will improve once the remainder of the Pudong area is built out. Like office space in Shanghai, retail space is oversupplied, with vacancy rates for modern retail space at 30 percent.

The Podium building provides access to the observation deck on the 88th floor. The deck allows a view of the many high-rise buildings, all built within the last ten years, stretching over the horizon. There is no better place to appreciate Shanghai's beauty. The observation deck is a popular attraction, and more than 1 million people have visited it since it opened in March 1999. The tower has quickly become a landmark in China, with images of the building in advertisements for the city of Shanghai and its attractions. The building is popular with locals, and people line up along the Bund across the river to have their pictures taken with the tower in the background.

The interior of the Podium building is beautifully designed, but retailers there have not done well. Much of the space now houses nonretail uses.

© Hedrich Blessing

The Grand Hyatt Shanghai is arguably the finest hotel in the city. Guestrooms surround a 498-foot (152-meter) atrium that rises almost to the top of the building.

A highly articulated steel, aluminum, and glass facade allows the Jin Mao Tower to sparkle on the Shanghai skyline.

Strong property management is a hallmark of the development. Repairs are made quickly when needed, tenants' needs are met, and the overall service is outstanding. A quarterly newsletter keeps people up to date on building happenings, and ongoing training helps to improve the building staff's performance. Statements from the board of directors emphasize providing service with near-religious zeal. This high level of service is especially valued in China, where such service can be hard to find.

Experience Gained

One of the greatest risks in developing mixed-use projects is getting the mix wrong. When properly planned and guided by market research, a mix of uses creates a positive feedback system where each use supports the success of the others. This kind of synergy exists to a degree at Jin Mao Tower, where the hotel helps meet the needs of office tenants and the office space allows the hotel to offer spectacular views for guests. Synergy is not guaranteed, however, as exemplified by the retail space. Although market miscalculations played a role, the poor retail performance can be attributed in part to the design and configuration of the tower, whose office and hotel users must go out of their way to reach the Podium building's shops and services. It remains to be seen whether the retail space will improve once the tower is fully leased and the surrounding area is built out.

The design and construction of Jin Mao Tower was a complex undertaking that required a truly international effort and a lot of special coordination to overcome language and cultural obstacles and miscommunications. Managing a diverse group of professionals was difficult, as members of the development team had to understand each other on both personal and cultural levels. This learning process paid off, as the team was able to work together to complete the project.

Jin Mao developers learned that quality sells. In an office market with abysmal vacancy rates, the tower has achieved a 70 percent occupancy rate in less than two years, and the hotel has done even better. The tower offers the best offices, hotel rooms, and restaurants in the entire city. No other address in Shanghai is as synonymous with prestige and quality as Jin Mao Tower.

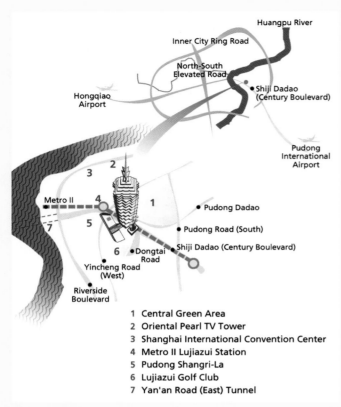

Huangpu River

Inner City Ring Road

North-South
Elevated Road

Shiji Dadao
(Century Boulevard)

Hongqiao
Airport

Pudong
International
Airport

Metro II

3

2

1

4

Pudong Dadao

5

Pudong Road (South)

7

Shiji Dadao (Century Boulevard)

6
Dongtai
Road

Yincheng Road
(West)

Riverside
Boulevard

1 Central Green Area
2 Oriental Pearl TV Tower
3 Shanghai International Convention Center
4 Metro II Lujiazui Station
5 Pudong Shangri-La
6 Lujiazui Golf Club
7 Yan'an Road (East) Tunnel

Location map.

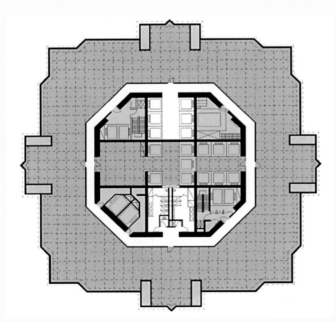

Typical office floor plan.

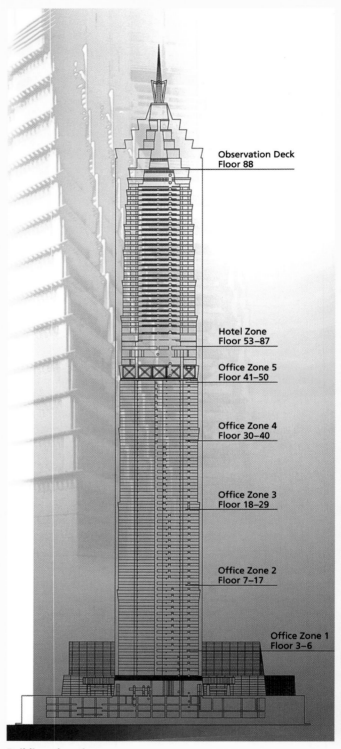

Observation Deck
Floor 88

Hotel Zone
Floor 53–87

Office Zone 5
Floor 41–50

Office Zone 4
Floor 30–40

Office Zone 3
Floor 18–29

Office Zone 2
Floor 7–17

Office Zone 1
Floor 3–6

Building elevation.

Project Data: Jin Mao Tower

Land Use and Building Information

Site Area	258,342 square feet (24,000 square meters)
Gross Building Area (GBA)	3,121,636 square feet (290,000 square meters)
Building Height	1,379.5 feet (420.5 meters)

Land Use Plan (Existing)

Office Net Rentable Area	1,330,721 square feet (123,675 square meters)
Retail Gross Leasable Area	347,362 square feet (32,280 square meters)
Hotel Rooms	555
Parking Spaces	900 (800 in garage)
Observation Deck	16,361 square feet (1,520 square meters)

Office Information

Percent of NRA Occupied	70%
Number of Tenants	55
Tenant Size	Up to 161,463 square feet (15,000 square meters)
Annual Rents	Approximately $12–20 per square foot ($130–215 per square meter)
Average Length of Lease	2-year minimum

Hotel Information

Number of rooms	555
Room rates	$175–4,500 per night
Occupancy rate	70–80%
Number of meeting/function rooms	12
Capacity of largest function room	900
Guest amenities and facilities	Swimming pool; fitness center; airport limousine; 24-hour business center; 24-hour concierge; 24-hour room service; 9 restaurants, lounges, and nightclubs
Guestroom features	Marble bathrooms, 2-line telephones, computer dataport with high-speed modem, interactive television

Development Cost Information

Total development cost to date	$540 million

Development Schedule

1993	Competition held/planning started
6/1994	Construction started
2/1999	First office tenants
3/1999	Observation deck opened
8/1999	Project completed

Developer

China Jin Mao Group Co.
8F Jin Mao Tower
88 Shiji Dadao
Pudong New Area
Shanghai, 200121 PRC
8621-5047-6688

Architect/Engineer

Skidmore, Owings & Merrill
224 South Michigan Avenue
Suite 1000
Chicago, Illinois 60604
312-554-9090

Shanghai Institute of Architectural Design & Research
1368 Xizang Road
Shendu Building
Shanghai, 200011, PRC
8621-6321-9500

East China Architectural & Design Institute
151 Hankou Road
Shanghai, 200002, PRC
8621-6321-7420

General Contractor

Shanghai Jin Mao Contractor
Jin Mao Tower
Pudong New Area
Shanghai, 200002 PRC
8621-5876-3063

Peabody Place

Memphis, Tennessee

Peabody Place, in the heart of downtown Memphis, is one of the largest mixed-use developments in the country. The total project area covers about 2 million square feet (185,900 square meters) in several buildings and includes space for retail, commercial, office, residential, and entertainment uses as well as four parking garages with 3,300 spaces. The redevelopment of the urban area to create Peabody Place has included the restoration of several historic buildings in the Gayoso-Peabody Historic District (listed on the National Register of Historic Places), and construction of a new 15-story, Class A office tower and a 320,000-square-foot (30,000-square-meter) retail/ entertainment center with a 22-screen movie theater. From the restoration and reopening of the historic Peabody Hotel in 1981 to the 2001 grand opening of the Peabody Place Entertainment and Retail Center, the project is widely recognized as a cornerstone for the revitalization of downtown Memphis.

The developer, Belz Enterprises, is a major family-owned real estate development company based in Memphis, with interests throughout the South and much of the country. Belz develops, owns, and manages more than 25 million square feet (2.3 million square meters) of industrial/warehouse/distribution centers, shopping centers, office buildings, mixed-use centers, and corporate campuses.

Belz is one of the nation's largest developers of factory outlet malls, a field that it pioneered. The company also owns and manages convention centers and hotels, including the Peabody hotels in Memphis and Orlando. Although urban infill projects have not been typical of Belz Enterprises's real estate developments, the family was especially interested in the revitalization of downtown in its home base of Memphis.

The Site and Development Process

Peabody Place occupies an eight-block area in downtown Memphis on the city's west side, a few blocks from the Mississippi River and Beale Street, an area renowned for its blues clubs. The site is anchored to the east by the historic Peabody Hotel, to the south by Beale Street, to the east by the Peabody Place Entertainment and Retail Center, and to the west by the corporate headquarters of AutoZone, an auto parts chain based in Memphis. In this city of 1.1 million residents, more than 220,000 people live within 10 minutes of downtown Memphis. Downtown is home to 10,000 residents and 80,000 workers, and hosts 6 million visitors each year. Annual retail spending by visitors totals $1.7 billion.

In addition to Peabody Place, other attractions and developments contributing to the revitalization of downtown Memphis include the Beale Street Entertainment District, the Orpheum Theatre, the Pyramid Arena, AutoZone Park (home to the Memphis Redbirds baseball team), the Gibson Guitar Factory and Museum, the Mud Island Mississippi River Park, the Main Street Pedestrian Mall and Trolley Line, and the National Civil Rights Museum. Planned for downtown Memphis are the Cannon Center for Performing Arts and the renovated and expanded Cook Convention Center.

Downtown Memphis had experienced significant deterioration and blight in the late 1960s and 1970s: neglect and vacant buildings permeated large swaths of downtown. In 1976, the city of Memphis sought to rebuild downtown with the construction of a pedestrian mall on Main Street linking downtown points of interest. (In 1993, this pedestrian mall was turned into a transit mall, home to the 2.5-mile (four-kilometer) Main Street Trolley line that interconnects the central business district, Main Street Mall, and several Memphis landmarks.) In 1977, the city of Memphis and Shelby County governments established the Center City Commission (CCC) to direct the comprehensive redevelopment of downtown Memphis and serve as the official partnership between private business and government in the revitalization.

The restoration and reopening 20 years ago of the historic Peabody Hotel, built in 1925, is widely credited with launching the renewal of downtown Memphis. Belz Enterprises purchased the hotel property in foreclosure for $410,000 in 1975 and has invested nearly $35 million in its restoration. At the same time, the company acquired the land immediately south of the hotel and three-fourths of a block parcel south of Gayoso Avenue. After much debate, the city agreed to close Gayoso Avenue, allowing adjacent parking for the Peabody Hotel.

In 1981, the Peabody opened its doors again as a premier hotel, complete with the famous Peabody ducks. (In the 1930s, general manager and hunter Frank Schutt began a practice of placing live ducks in the lobby's marble fountain. Today, the tradition continues as the Peabody ducks descend from their Duck Palace on the hotel's rooftop each morning at 11:00 a.m., march out of the elevator down a red carpet to inhabit the fountain by day, and ascend back to the rooftop each evening.) Since then, Belz has developed Peabody Place in several phases. After the refurbishment of the Peabody Hotel, Belz sought to persuade AutoZone to choose downtown Memphis for the relocation of its corporate

Peabody Place, located in the heart of downtown Memphis, is one of the largest mixed-use developments in the country. The project, which covers eight city blocks, features restored historic buildings, modern office towers, apartments, retail and entertainment, restaurants, and gathering places.

headquarters. After more than two years of negotiations, AutoZone agreed to the deal. The $30 million, eight-story, 270,000-square-foot (25,100-square-meter) office building on a bluff overlooking the Mississippi River opened in 1995, bringing nearly 1,000 employees downtown.

Across Front Street from the site of AutoZone, Belz had acquired six historic buildings in 1994 (in a real estate auction in which there were no other bidders) to develop the next phase of Peabody Place, the largest historic preservation project in the state of Tennessee. This block of buildings included the former Gayoso Hotel, the city's first luxury hotel, built in 1842, and later the site of Goldsmith's department store.

The original plan for the block had been to build a regional shopping mall with department store anchors. The closing of Goldsmith's department store as a result of the consolidation of Federated Department Stores in the early 1990s, however, derailed this effort. Belz de-

cided instead to pursue a mixed-use development with entertainment anchors. In 1995, Belz renovated the former Gayoso Hotel to become Gayoso House Apartments, the first residential component of Peabody Place. Other components in this historic block include 50 Peabody Place, which houses office space and street-level retail shops, and Pembroke Square, with apartments and office and retail space.

On the four square blocks just to the east of the historic block and south of the Peabody Hotel, Belz proceeded with the next phases of Peabody Place: the 185,000-square-foot (17,200-square-meter) Tower at Peabody Place (opened in 1997), the 320,000-square-foot (30,000-square-meter) Peabody Place Entertainment and Retail Center, a Hampton Inn (opened in 2001), and parking structures. A third hotel is also planned. The project included a special financial partnership among Belz Enterprises, the city of Memphis, Shelby County, and the federal government.

The 468-room Peabody Hotel is a 14-story Italian Renaissance Revival building, built in 1925 in the era of grand hotels. The masonry building has a terra-cotta and limestone base with terra-cotta cornices, pilasters, balustrades, and window surrounds on the upper levels.

The Center City Commission has been an important player throughout the progress of Peabody Place. The CCC is a combination of separate development interests providing funding, tax incentives, and other benefits to attract new development to downtown Memphis. These investments have paid off, and since the 1990s, downtown Memphis has seen a marked upswing, with more than $2 billion invested in current developments. This new construction and renovation is a blend of public and private development projects, but the great majority represent private investment. Strategically allocated public funds and the commission's awarding of tax abatements and development loans have encouraged private development and raised public confidence in the development in downtown Memphis.

Architecture and Design

Historic preservation and elegant new construction characterize the multiple components of Peabody Place, which ranges across some or all of seven contiguous downtown blocks. In 1935, historian David Cohn proclaimed, "The Mississippi Delta begins in the lobby of the Peabody Hotel." The 468-room hotel is a 14-story Italian Renaissance Revival building, built in 1925 in the era of the grand hotels. The masonry building has a terra-cotta and limestone base with terra-cotta cornices, pilasters, balustrades, and window surrounds on the upper levels. The two-story main lobby, which provides a dramatic entrance to the hotel, features marble columns and an ornate beamed ceiling. The renovation of the Peabody sought to restore, refurnish, and reequip the building as a first-class hotel. In 1994, the Peabody Hotel completed the final phases of the multimillion dollar renovation, which included the complete refurbishment of every guest room, the addition of an exclusive concierge-service level, new carpeting and paint in the mezzanine-level meeting rooms and ballrooms, and the demolition and renovation of the Grand Lobby Bar.

The other historic portion of Peabody Place is located one block from the hotel; it consists of a block of historic structures at the heart of Peabody Place containing more than 500,000 square feet (46,500 square meters) of space built from the late 1800s and the early 1900s, including what is now Pembroke Square, Gayoso House, and 50 Peabody Place. This portion of the project consisted of four major building renovations and the addition of a building, called the "Grand Lobby," that internally ties the existing buildings together. These buildings have been transformed to modern apartment residences, offices, restaurants, and retail establishments. Many of the historic architectural details have been carefully preserved, including high ceilings, oversized windows, elegant limestone columns, and original ceramic tile floors. The apartments range from 557 to 1,380 square feet (52 to 128 square meters), and some include loft-type bedrooms or bay windows that offer views of the city or the Mississippi River. The convenient downtown location offers residents shops and restaurants nearby and retail shopping on the ground floor; the Main Street Trolley stops right outside.

Local, state, and national historic preservation groups have applauded the restoration in the Gayoso-Peabody Historic District. The preservation of this historic block has earned 16 local, regional, and national design awards, including its selection as the Design of the Decade (the 1990s) by the Memphis Chapter of the American Institute of Architects, which recognizes the project as one of the most significant pieces of architecture in Memphis during the decade.

Across the street from this historic block and at the edge of the development is the AutoZone corporate headquarters, perched on a bluff overlooking the Mississippi River to take advantage of the site's attributes and views. The river side of the structure features a modern, curved glass facade, while the side facing the city is more in keeping with the historical buildings in the old Cotton Row. Because the project is located in an earthquake zone—30 miles (48 kilometers) from the New Madrid fault—the building is the first seismic base–isolated structure to be built in the central Mississippi Valley. This state-of-the-art engineering design is to reduce damage by cushioning buildings against earthquake shaking. The AutoZone building has won several awards for architecture, including the AIA Memphis Award of Honor in New Construction Architecture.

The Tower at Peabody Place, near the center of the site and considered the signature office address for downtown Memphis, features a polished granite base, glass towers with bay windows at all four corners, and marble, granite, and wood finishes in lobby areas. The 15 stories include eight levels of Class A office space, six levels of parking, and one level of retail shops and commercial space.

The heritage of Memphis music and the legacy of the grand movie palaces is the theme of Peabody Place Entertainment and Retail Center, located roughly between the Tower building and the Peabody Hotel. The center

The Peabody Place Entertainment and Retail Center covers more than 300,000 square feet (28,000 square meters) in a streetscape environment. The three-story retail/entertainment center's varied and smaller-scale streetscape is organized along a multilevel atrium courtyard. The first-floor retail space faces both the street and the courtyard, while the 22-screen cinema anchor occupies the top floor.

The heritage of Memphis music and the legacy of the grand movie palaces were used for the theme of the Peabody Place Entertainment and Retail Center.

The Entertainment Center from another perspective.

The Hampton Inn and Suites at Peabody Place.

The Tower at Peabody Place is considered the signature office address for downtown Memphis. Its 15 stories include eight levels of Class A office space, six levels of parking, and one level of retail shops and commercial space.

Courtesy of Belz Enterprises

covers more than 300,000 square feet (28,000 square meters) in a distinctive streetscape environment and is accessible from any one of three connected indoor parking garages. The three-story retail/entertainment center's varied and smaller-scale streetscape is organized along a multilevel atrium courtyard. First-floor retail space faces both the street and the courtyard, while the multiplex cinema occupies the top floor.

The 22-screen cinema anchor, Muvico Theaters, boasts a 110,000-square-foot (10,200-square-meter) turn-of-the-century train station motif for its themed movie theater, welcoming moviegoers into an expansive picturesque railway yard complete with model trains, stone walls, and train trestles.

Financing

A package of public incentives was incorporated into the financing program for Peabody Place to make it feasible. Approximately 23 percent of the nearly $285 million cost of Peabody Place was funded through a series of low-interest loans, grants, and direct public investment. Peabody Place was one of the later projects to receive an Urban Development Action Grant from HUD, with a total of $14.95 million allocated in two separate funding rounds. In addition, $6.45 million was made available through the Community Development Block Grant program. These funds were provided by no-interest 30-year loans made through the city, with the city participating in the net annual cash flow. Other HUD funds involved in the project included a Section 108 loan for $12 million and a CD float loan for $4 million.

The Economic Development Administration provided a loan guarantee to finance the improvements associated with the Peabody Hotel, involving approximately $2.7 million that was used for sidewalks, streets, and other public infrastructure improvements in the vicinity of Peabody Place. City general obligation bonds for $9.92 million were used to finance the Tower parking garage. Shelby County (where Memphis is located) issued general obligation bonds for $9.7 million to finance a portion of the parking garage for the Entertainment and Retail Center and Peabody Hotel, with the remaining $5.12 million for parking expenses provided by city of Memphis general obligation bonds.

In addition to these loans and grants, the city of Memphis and Shelby County froze property taxes on the various components of Peabody Place. These freezes ranged from ten to 25 years, depending on the component. In addition, incentives were provided through federal investment tax credits for historic properties, including the Peabody Hotel, the Pembroke Square building, Gayoso House, and 50 Peabody Place. Federal credits were also provided for low-income housing, which makes up a portion of Gayoso House.

The tax credits assisted the developer in raising equity for the development. A number of local and national lenders provided construction financing and long-term financing of the various components of Peabody Place, including a consortium of nine banks that assisted in financing the Peabody Hotel. Total private funding was in excess of $200 million.

Tenants and Management

Belz Enterprises markets and oversees the management of the Peabody Place properties, subcontracting for the day-to-day management of the residences and office space and directly managing the hotel and the retail space, including a general manager for the entire retail portion of the project. In its management of the retail space, Belz emphasizes cleanliness, security, and response to customers' requests. The Peabody Hotel is managed by the Peabody Hotel Group (PHG), a subsidiary of Belz Enterprises, which owns and operates another Peabody Hotel in Orlando, Florida, and nine other hotels throughout the country. Overall, performance for each use in Peabody Place is above average for downtown and in line with or slightly above the greater Memphis metropolitan area.

In the historic block, the Gayoso House, Pembroke Square, and 50 Peabody Place are home to mixed-income apartments, luxury townhouses, a food court and other dining facilities, a grocery store, a bakery, a card shop, luxury office space, and specialty retail stores. Although a grand lobby serves as the ground-level main entrance for the retail, office, and residential users of each building in the block, separate elevator banks go to the apartment residences and offices in the upper levels of the buildings. The alternate entrances to the block for apartments and offices are also separate.

Typical apartment residents include upper-income residents, young professional singles, tourism-/service-related employees, families, empty nesters, and college students. Exceeding expectations, the apartments have maintained a near-capacity occupancy rate, often at 99 percent. Rents in Peabody Place apartments range from $550 to $1,400 per month. At $.90 per square foot ($9.70 per square meter) or an average $804 per month,

The block of historic structures at the heart of Peabody Place, built during the late 1800s and early 1900s, has been restored to its original grandeur, housing modern apartment residences, offices, restaurants, and retail establishments. Pembroke Square is in the foreground.

Courtesy of Belz Enterprises

The AutoZone corporate headquarters, perched on a bluff overlooking the Mississippi River, takes advantage of the site's attributes and views. The river side of the structure features a modern, curved glass facade, while the side facing the city is more in keeping with nearby historical buildings.

Courtesy of Belz Enterprises

apartment rents are above the average downtown apartment rent of $.82 per square foot ($8.80 per square meter). Average apartment rents in the greater Memphis metropolitan area are $.58 per square foot ($6.25 per square meter).

Pembroke Square houses two cultural attractions as well: the Center for Southern Folklore and the Peabody Place Museum and Gallery. The Center for Southern Folklore is a private, nonprofit organization dedicated to preserving Southern culture, with an emphasis on music and art. The interior, decorated by local artists, is eclectic and includes a gift shop and coffee bar with books and albums featuring Memphis and Memphis artists. The center hosts live music at lunch each day and on Friday and Saturday evenings.

The Peabody Place Museum and Gallery offers a permanent display of Chinese art from the personal collection of Jack Belz, chair and CEO of Belz Enterprises, and his wife, Marilyn. In addition to Chinese art and sculpture extending back as far as 2,000 years, the collection includes Judaica, European contemporary art glass, a mineral collection that includes a 75 million-year-old bird fossil from the Liaonins province of China and a petrified dinosaur egg, and Italian mosaics, boxes, and obelisks.

The Tower at Peabody Place, in addition to serving as the headquarters for Belz Enterprises, is occupied by tenants such as an accounting firm, law firms, and an engineering firm. Office and retail occupancy rates for

Peabody Place buildings (50 Peabody Place, 85 percent; Pembroke Square, 90.5 percent; Tower at Peabody Place, 84.5 percent) have been at or above the average for downtown Memphis (82.8 percent for office space and 86 percent for retail space). Rental rates for the office and retail space in the historic block have been consistent with, or slightly above, the downtown average of $15.51 per square foot ($167 per square meter), while the Tower at Peabody Place commands the highest rents, $20.50 per square foot ($220 per square meter), compared with the downtown average for Class A office space of $17.00 per square foot ($183 per square meter).

The newly opened Peabody Place Entertainment and Retail Center beckons people to "come downtown and play," offering a range of lifestyle-oriented tenants, including music stores, specialty retailers, and restaurants. Entertainment anchors include the 100,000-square-foot (9,300-square-meter) Muvico Theaters 22-screen cinema with stadium seating and 55,000-square-foot (5,100-square-meter) Jillian's. The movie megaplex includes a theater with a six-story-high screen, concessions with offerings ranging from quesadillas and popcorn shrimp to traditional popcorn, and a child care center for parents who need a babysitter.

Jillian's is a three-story multidimensional food and entertainment retailer with a sports video café, dance club, bowling alley, tournament-quality pool tables, and more than 150 electronic simulation games under one roof.

The entrance and interior of the new Pembroke Square Grand Lobby, a new structure that ties together the buildings of the historic block—Pembroke Square, Gayoso House, and 50 Peabody Place—and serves as the ground-level main entrance for retail, office, and residential users.

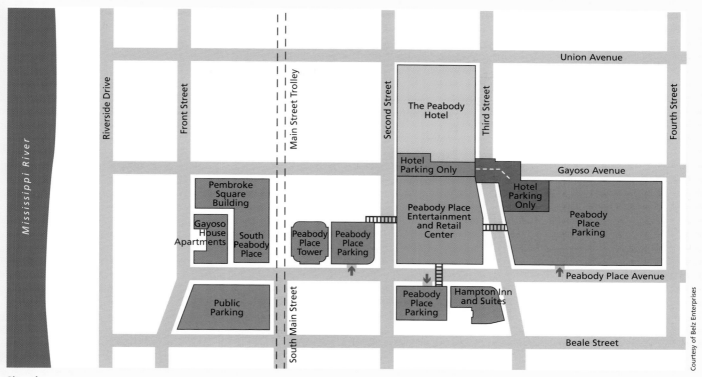

Site plan.

Other tenants include Tower Records and Video, Kidder Entertainment, Memphis Motor Sports, Ann Taylor Loft, Gap and Gap Kids, Victoria's Secret, Starbucks coffee, the Isaac Hayes restaurant "Music~Food~Passion," a Mrs. Fields Bakery Café, Texas de Brazil, A&W All American Food/Long John Silver's, and Rocky Mountain Chocolate Factory.

The mixed-use character of the development benefits multiple users of the parking garages. For example, in the 700-car parking garage attached to the Tower at Peabody Place, where office tenants rent parking spaces for $90.00 per month, apartment residents of the Gayoso House and Pembroke Square may also lease parking spaces for $35.00 per month.

Experience Gained

It is important to have a large contingency factored into a historic restoration project, as certain conditions in an older structure may be unknown or unpredictable until actual construction begins. In the Peabody Place historic block, the renovation cost 30 percent more to build than the original estimate calculated. Although it can be more expensive to reuse historic features, the results provide added value to the final product.

Infill construction on a tight downtown site is expensive to stage and build. The higher costs demand the construction of premium office and retail space. It is possible to command premium rents, based on the development's distinctiveness and the downtown market, but the market must see the value and be willing to pay more for that kind of environment.

Multiple levels of an entertainment/retail center can create challenges for putting retailers in a prime loca-

tion. The connected parking garages ease that difficulty, however, as they bring people into the building on various levels.

A variety of available local and federal government tax incentives, loans, grants, and subsidies were key to making the investment financially feasible.

Although mixed-use developments can be quite complicated and more expensive to build, urban mixed-use development is very rewarding, frequently resulting in distinctive properties and settings that can command higher rents and create higher property values.

Pembroke Square

Land Use and Building Information

Site Area   0.86 acre (0.35 hectare)

Building Area

	Gross Square Feet (Square Meters)	Leasable Square Feet (Square Meters)
Office	139,946 (13,000)	109,495 (10,175)
Retail	34,275 (3,185)	34,275 (3,185)
Residential	44,000 (4,090)	41,620 (3,870)
Concourse	27,169 (2,525)	27,169 (2,525)
Total	245,390 (22,800)	212,559 (19,755)

Land Use Plan

	Existing Square Feet (Square Meters)
Buildings	37,489 (3,485)

Residential Unit Information

Unit Type	Unit Size (Square Feet/ Square Meters)	Number of Units	Rent Range
1-Bedroom Platform	630–712/ 59–66	8	$660–700
1-Bedroom Platform	821–1,032/ 76–96	31	$800–1,000
1-Bedroom Loft	989–1,129/ 92–105	4	$950–975
2-Bedroom Loft	1,381/128	2	$1,400–1,425

Office Tenant Information

Occupied NRA	92%
Number of Tenants	14
Average Size	5,000 square feet (465 square meters)
Annual Rents	$16-20 per square foot ($172–215 per square meter)
Average Length of Lease	5–10 years
Typical Term of Lease	7 years

Retail Tenant Information

Tenant Classification	Number of Stores	Total GLA (Square Feet/ Square Meters)
General merchandise	3	10,283/956
Food service	3	17,872/1,661
Hobby/special interest	1	1,000/93
Gift/specialty	1	1,800/167
Personal services	1	1,500/139
Financial	1	18,000/1,673
Total	10	50,455/4,687

GLA Occupied	70%
Annual Rents	$15–19 per square foot ($161–204 per square meter)
Average Annual Sales	$300 per square foot ($3,228 per square meter)
Average Length of Lease	5–10 years
Typical Term of Lease	7 years

Development Schedule

1993	Site purchased
1993	Planning started
1995	Construction started
1994	Sales/leasing started
1996	Phase I completed
1997	Project completed

Gayoso House

Land Use and Building Information

Site Area   0.75 acre (0.3 hectare)

Residential Parking Spaces   45

Gross Building Area

	Gross Square Feet (Square Meters)	Leasable Square Feet (Square Meters)
Retail	10,543 (980)	10,543 (980)
Residential	152,821 (14,203)	109,089 (10,138)
Parking	12,000 (1,115)	–
Concourse, health club, leasing office, storage	20,914 (1,944)	15,101[1] (1,403)[1]
Total	196,278 (18,241)	134,733 (12,522)

Note
[1] Concourse only.

Land Use Plan

	Existing Square Feet (Square Meters)
Buildings	29,946 (2,783)
Streets/surface parking	2,604 (242)
Total	32,550 (3,025)

Residential Unit Information

Unit Type	Unit Size (Square Feet/ Square Meters)	Number of Units	Rent Range
1-Bedroom	557–765/52–71	127	$660–675
2-Bedroom	700–979/65–91	25	$670–925
1-Bedroom Loft	968–1,151/90–107	3	$900–1,100
2-Bedroom Loft	1,007/94	1	$1,050

Retail Tenant Information

Tenant Classification	Number of Stores	Total GLA (Square Feet/ Square Meters)
Food service	1	8,743/812
Gift/specialty	2	1,800/167
Total	3	10,543/980

GLA Occupied	91%
Annual Rents	$15–18 per square foot ($161–194 per square meter)
Average Annual Sales	$300 per square foot ($3,228 per square meter)
Average Length of Lease	5–10 years
Typical Term of Lease	10 years

Development Schedule

1993	Site purchased
1993	Planning started
1994	Construction started
1994	Sales/leasing started
1995	Project completed

50 Peabody Place

Land Use and Building Information

Site Area   0.26 acre (0.1 hectare)

Gross Building Area

	Gross Square Feet (Square Meters)	Leasable Square Feet (Square Meters)
Office	50,570 (4,700)	41,320 (3,840)
Retail	8,900 (827)	8,900 (827)
Concourse	8,400 (781)	8,400 (781)
Total	67,870 (6,308)	58,620 (5,448)

Land Use Plan

	Existing Square Feet (Square Meters)
Buildings	11,250 (1,045)

Office Tenant Information

Occupied NRA	90%
Number of Tenants	7
Average Size	2,500 square feet (232 square meters)
Annual Rents	$15–17 per square foot ($161–183 per square meter)
Average Length of Lease	5–10 years
Typical Term of Lease	7 years

Retail Tenant Information

Tenant Classification	Number of Stores	Total GLA (Square Feet/ Square Meters)
General merchandise	1	3,000/279
Personal services	2	5,900/548
Total	3	8,900/827

GLA Occupied	100%
Annual Rents	$16–20 per square foot ($172–215 per square meter)
Average Annual Sales	$300 per square foot ($3,228 per square meter)
Average Length of Lease	5–10 years
Typical Term of Lease	7 years

Development Schedule

1993	Site purchased
1993	Planning started
1994	Construction started
1994	Sales/leasing started
1996	Project completed

Grand Lobby

Land Use and Building Information

Site Area   0.126 acre (0.05 hectare)

Gross Building Area

	Gross Square Feet (Square Meters)	Leasable Square Feet (Square Meters)
Office	2,239 (208)	2,239 (208)
Retail	2,455 (228)	2,455 (228)
Lobby	2,409 (224)	–
Total	7,103 (660)	4,694 (436)

Land Use Plan

	Existing Square Feet (Square Meters)
Buildings	7,103 (660)

Office Tenant Information

Occupied NRA	100%
Number of Tenants	1
Average Size	2,400 square feet (223 square meters)
Annual Rents	$15–17 per square foot ($161–183 per square meter)
Average Length of Lease	5–10 years
Typical Term of Lease	7 years

Retail Tenant Information

Tenant Classification	Number of Stores	Total GLA (Square Feet/ Square Meters)
Food service	1	1,705/158
Gift/specialty	2	750/70
Total	3	2,455/228

GLA Occupied	70%
Annual Rents	$15–22 per square foot ($161–237 per square meter)
Average Annual Sales	$300 per square foot ($3,228 per square meter)
Average Length of Lease	5–10 years
Typical Term of Lease	7 years

Development Schedule

1993	Site purchased
1993	Planning started
1995	Construction started
1994	Sales/leasing started
1996	Project completed

Tower at Peabody Place

Land Use and Building Information

Site Area	0.706 acre (0.28 hectare)
Public Parking Spaces	700

Gross Building Area

	Gross Square Feet (Square Meters)	Leasable Square Feet (Square Meters)
Office	152,000 (14,126)	140,929 (13,097)
Retail	18,409 (1,711)	18,409 (1,171)
Parking	270,500 (25,139)	–
Concourse	16,600 (1,543)	8,500 (790)
Total	457,509 (42,519)	167,838 (15,598)

Land Use Plan

	Existing Square Feet (Square Meters)
Buildings	42,500 (3,950)
Landscaping/open space	3,500 (325)
Total	46,000 (4,275)

Office Tenant Information

Occupied NRA	84%
Number of Tenants	8
Average Size	5,000 square feet (465 square meters)
Average Length of Lease	5–15 years
Typical Term of Lease	10 years

Retail Tenant Information

Tenant Classification	Number of Stores	Total GLA (Square Feet/ Square Meters)
General merchandise	2	8,522/792
Food service	1	6,000/558
Financial	1	3,887/361
Total	4	18,409/1,711

GLA Occupied	54%
Annual Rents	$18–25 per square foot ($194–269 per square meter)
Average Annual Sales	$300 per square foot ($3,228 per square meter)
Average Length of Lease	5–15 years
Typical Term of Lease	10 years

Development Schedule

1980	Site purchased
1992	Planning started
1996	Construction started
1995	Sales/leasing started
1997	Project completed

Peabody Place Entertainment and Retail Center

Land Use and Building Information

Site Area	6.5 acres (2.6 hectares)
Parking Spaces	1,600

Gross Building Area

	Gross Square Feet (Square Meters)	Leasable Square Feet (Square Meters)
Retail	531,950 (49,438)	313,000 (29,089)
Parking	584,500 (54,322)	–
Total	1,116,450 (103,760)	313,000 (29,089)

Land Use Plan

	Existing Square Feet (Square Meters)
Buildings	268,000 (24,907)

Retail Tenant Information

Tenant Classification	Number of Stores	Total GLA (Square Feet/ Square Meters)
General merchandise	4	32,410/3,012
Food service	11	47,380/4,403
Clothing and accessories	8	31,430/2,921
Gift/specialty	6	6,780/630
Jewelry	1	1,000/93
Entertainment	5	194,000/18,030
Total	35	312,950/29,085

GLA Occupied	82%
Annual Rents	$30–50 per square foot
	($323–538 per square meter)
Average Annual Sales	$300 per square foot
	($3,228 per square meter)
Average Length of Lease	5–10 years
Typical Term of Lease	10 years

Development Schedule

1979	Site purchased
1990	Planning started
1998	Construction started
1997	Sales/leasing started
2001	Phase I completed
2001	Project completed

Owner/Developer

Belz Enterprises
The Tower at Peabody Place
Suite 1400
Memphis, Tennessee 38103
901-767-4780

Project Team for Pembroke Square, Gayoso House, 50 Peabody Place, and Grand Lobby

Architect

Hnedak Bobo Group, Inc.
104 Front Street South
Memphis, Tennessee 38103
901-526-8386

Landscape Architect

Jackson Person & Assoc.
66 Monroe Avenue
Suite 104
Memphis, Tennessee 38103
901-526-8386

Structural Engineer

Jamnu H. Tahiliani & Assoc.
474 Perkins Road Extension
Suite 21
Memphis, Tennessee 38117
901-767-5393

Mechanical Engineer

Gala Engineering
7975 Stage Hills Boulevard
Suite 5
Bartlett, Tennessee 38133
901-384-8400

Electrical Engineer

Metz/DePouw, Inc. (now DePouw Engineering, LLC)
5118 Park Avenue
Suite 500
Memphis, Tennessee 38117
901-685-2834

General Contractor

Metro Construction, LLC
1936 Vanderhorn Drive
Memphis, Tennessee 38134
901-386-0094

Project Team for Tower at Peabody Place and Peabody Place Entertainment and Retail Center

Architect

RTKL/JMGR
One South Street
Baltimore, Maryland 21202
901-528-8600

Landscape Architect (Tower at Peabody Place)

Jackson Person & Assoc.
66 Monroe Avenue
Memphis, Tennessee 38103
901-526-8386

Landscape Architect (Peabody Place Entertainment and Retail Center)

Mahan Rykiel Associates
1330 Smith Avenue
Baltimore, Maryland 21209
410-435-1700

Structural Engineer, Mechanical Engineer, Electrical Engineer

JMGR
100 Peabody Place
Suite 300
Memphis, Tennessee 38103
901-260-9600

General Contractor

Tri-Tech
50 Peabody Place
Suite 210
Memphis, Tennessee 38103
901-432-4300

Phillips Place
Charlotte, North Carolina

Phillips Place is a suburban mixed-use development that combines specialty retail, a multiplex cinema, apartments, and a hotel, all organized around a main street. The project is located on a 35-acre (14-hectare) parcel in the SouthPark area of Charlotte, known for its high-quality office and retail development, well-established neighborhoods, and strong demographics.

The objective and the challenge for the developer was to develop a thriving mixed-use town center for a traditional low-density suburban business district and residential neighborhood, something that had not been done before in the Charlotte area. The developer sought to achieve this goal by creating a retail main street environment anchored at one end by a 124-room hotel and at the other by a multiplex cinema, apartments built over retail stores on one side of the retail street, and several separate apartment buildings located in a residential area behind the main street. The result is an inviting new pedestrian-friendly retail, entertainment, and residential district—and an important new gathering place—for a typical low-density, auto-oriented suburban environment.

The Site
The site is located 15 to 20 minutes from downtown Charlotte, the airport, and the Outer Loop in the rapidly developing SouthPark area. SouthPark includes the Carolinas' second largest business district and also has a residential base with one of the highest income levels in the Southeast. Half the residents of SouthPark have annual household incomes of more than $60,000, more than 75 percent attended college, a full quarter spend an average of $100 or more per shopping trip, and nearly 25 percent are 25 to 35 years of age.

The site includes substantial frontage on Fairview Road, southeast Charlotte's major east/west thoroughfare, but it is not served by any other adjacent streets. Thus, all access to the project, including three separate entrances, is provided by Fairview Road, a site constraint that limited the ability of the developers and designers to connect the project to its surroundings. Residents to the south did not want any significant connection, especially additional traffic flowing through their neighborhood on the way to and from Phillips Place. Commercial properties lie to the north and west, residential properties to the south and east.

Other site features and constraints that affected the development and its design include high-tension power lines located at the front of the property along the arterial frontage, an electrical substation located adjacent to the property to the east, and terrain that slopes downward as one moves into the property from the arterial.

Development Process
From the outset, the developers pursued a mixed-use town center development for the property, believing that this concept for SouthPark and for the specific site was desirable and highly marketable. The site was in a prime location and of sufficient size to allow the concept to work.

The site originally was owned by the D.L. Phillips Trust, a family trust, and some of the family members live adjacent to the property to the south. Thus, while these family members had a strong economic interest in development of the land, they also were interested in a development that did not detract from the surrounding residential areas. As a result, they exercised considerable influence on the nature of the project and how it would affect their neighborhood.

To develop a mixed-use project on the property required rezoning. In the South District Plan, the site was recommended for multifamily housing at a density of 22 units per acre (54 per hectare), which would potentially have allowed 770 units and significant traffic during peak hours. The developers sought to amend the plan to incorporate nonresidential uses, which they successfully argued would reduce peak traffic, avoid placement of residential housing adjacent to high-tension power lines, and provide retail stores not presently in the Charlotte market and public spaces that would be an amenity for the surrounding area—while still providing for the multifamily housing originally targeted by the plan.

To complicate the rezoning approval process, the county had no mixed-use zoning classification. Thus, the developer had to apply for an amendment to the CC–General Commercial zoning category to allow residences above retail uses, further lengthening the approval process even though city staff and elected officials supported the project. The conditional rezoning plan required sensitivity to the surrounding land uses and residents, as it involved achieving residential densities higher than those previously approved for the area.

The master developer, the Harris Group, sought several partners to make the complicated concept work. Although the company had extensive experience in retail and hotel development, it had not pursued a substantial residential project, nor was it a hotel operator. It therefore sought a partner to develop the apartments, finally settling on

Rick Alexander

Post Properties, a major real estate investment trust that develops, owns, and operates apartments. It also sought a hotel partner and operator, settling on the Panos Hotel Group, a hotel operator. The group chose TBA^2, a local firm with which it had worked extensively, as architect.

The developers used essentially one contractor to handle the retail, hotel, and cinema development, eliminating numerous coordination issues that could have arisen if more than one contractor built the project. The general contractor's attention to detail and to coordination of the utilities that service the project—and the contractor's insistence on staying a phase ahead on site work—allowed the project to be delivered on time. Construction began in November 1995, the first phase was completed in June 1997, and the entire project was completed in March 1998.

The retail and entertainment component, which includes 130,000 square feet (12,080 square meters) of space configured as an open-air retail village along a main street, targets specialty retailers and upscale restaurants; the program currently includes 32 tenants, including six restaurants, ten clothing stores, five gift/specialty stores, four home furnishings stores, and a ten-screen theater cinema that incorporates stadium seating and an attractive marquee that is visible from most points along the main street.

The residential portion of the project comprises several components, all owned and developed by Post Properties. They include 32 apartments/townhouses that face the main street and are located over the retail uses in three-story buildings and 68 units that surround a garden area in three-story buildings just off the main street. The residential component also includes 302 apartments in 12 separate garden apartment buildings with attached and detached garages. Apartment residents also have access to a clubhouse, a residential business center, a fitness center, a swimming pool, and two tennis courts. The apartments facing the courtyard near the main street

Phillips Place is a mixed-use town center that is home to high-end retail stores and restaurants.

Steve Hinds

are designed to include urban lofts with 14-foot (4-meter) ceilings and two-story townhouse apartments.

The hotel is a 124-room Hampton Inn and Suites; it includes 86 rooms and 38 suites developed to higher standards than Hampton Inn's typical product. The hotel does not include a restaurant, but all the numerous restaurants in Phillips Place are within easy walking distance; the Palm Restaurant is adjacent to the hotel.

Planning and Design

The developers and designers were challenged to create a town center on a pedestrian scale along a heavily traveled six-lane arterial. The solution involved internalizing the main street, which provided a slower, more controlled environment than the fast-paced, auto-oriented environment on surrounding thoroughfares. Contrary to standard suburban retail design, storefronts along this internal street are not visible from the adjacent thoroughfare, although some of the larger stores have signage that is

Rick Alexander

The lighted fountains at both ends of the retail/residential street feature rampant lions derived from the project's logo, which is based on the Phillips family crest, the site's original owners.

visible and others also have back entrances that face the thoroughfare. The developers considered the layout essential to the success of the pedestrian environment they were seeking. To mitigate the lack of visibility from the thoroughfare, tenants without signage on Fairview Road are given prominent signage on two entrance features.

One premise on which the project is built is that the spaces between buildings are just as important as the buildings themselves. Two landscaped courts terminate the east/west axis of the main street and showcase the two anchors, the hotel and the cinema. These two buildings establish the visual endpoints of the main street, and they serve as primary destinations and activity generators, enhancing pedestrian movement along the street. Several octagonal pavilion buildings help to shape the courts at both ends of the street, which include traffic circles surrounding lighted water fountains that feature four heraldic-style standing lion sculptures holding the fountain bowl. Angled parking with landscape dividers also is provided along the street.

The streetscape and lighting were emphasized to ensure that pedestrians would be safe and have a pleasant experience, day or evening. Brick sidewalks and outdoor seating encourage people to relax and enjoy themselves. Decorative street signs can be found in all areas of the project. The general lighting level is less intense than that typically found in shopping centers, but it gives pedestrians a sense of safety and invites strolling. The glow of the subdued lighting also enhances the romantic nighttime mood of Phillips Place. Special attention was given to the lighting of the fountains, the theater marquee, and the hotel porte-cochere to give them the necessary presence along the main street.

The project's architectural influences range from the commercial streetscapes of Charleston and Savannah to the public gardens and residential townhouses of Bath, England. Colorful awnings over streetside windows accent the beige, taupe, and peach exterior walls inspired by historic Charleston's Rainbow Row. Building surfaces are made of synthetic stucco using an exterior insulation and finish system. Variegated Mexican sandstone forms exterior building bases, and classical columns are abundant. Gabled and mansard roofs are accented with twin domes at the center, further enhancing the European ambience.

All the stores front on main street, and they have numerous large windows. The retail buildings on the north side of the main street are two stories high to balance the three-story buildings to the south; however, zoning for the property does not allow for the second-level space to be developed as retail. As a result, with 24- to 26-foot (7.3- to 8-meter) ceiling heights, retailers on this side of the street have opportunities to make creative use of the space—as storage or as attractive high ceilings, for example—depending on the needs of the retailer. Retail buildings on the south side of the street have more conventional ceiling heights, as these spaces include second- and third-level residential apartments, some of which have balconies. The mixed-use buildings use post-tension concrete slabs on the roof of the retail stores and wood-frame construction for the residential units above.

The developers emphasized continuity of design along the main street. All the buildings and facades along the street—including the retail and residential spaces, hotel, and cinema—were designed by the same architect, TBA[2] Architects. They draw from the same palette of colors and architectural themes.

The project includes three two-level parking structures, two of which are divided between retail and residential uses. The retail component uses the upper level and the apartments the lower; there is no shared parking on the property. The sloping site benefited the parking structure design. Because of the slope, the top retail parking level is at grade with the main street and is not an obtrusive visual element when viewed from the main street. The lower residential parking level can be reached at grade from the south, but only by residents or guests, who must pass through the security gate to get to the lower-level parking entrance.

The apartment community on the southern half of the site is a gated, secure environment. The architecture of these units is more conventional than that used in the commercial portion of the project. The apartments can be accessed via two separate road entrances. All units are in walkup buildings, and many include balconies; there is a variety of floor plans, some of which include direct access to garages.

Limited land area was available to meet stormwater retention requirements for the site, so vaults were constructed under tennis courts and a large stormwater management pond—located along the southern border of the property—was created as an amenity for the residential area.

The large-lot residential uses to the south, including the residences of the former landowners, required considerable buffering and careful attention to tree preservation and landscaping along the southern property line.

Marketing/Management/Finance

Construction of the project was phased, starting with the 302 garden apartments and the cinema and 20,000 square feet (1,860 square meters) of adjacent retail stores. The second phase included the remainder of the retail space, 100 additional residential units, and the hotel. Parking was a challenge when the cinema first opened, as not enough spaces were available. The problem was remedied upon completion of the second phase by creating more parking behind the cinema, which required an administrative site plan amendment.

Each major component of the project is separately owned and managed: the Harris Group owns and manages the retail space; Post Properties owns and manages the apartments; and the hotel is owned by a partnership of the Harris Group and the Panos Hotel Group, with the latter managing the property. Ownership of the residential and retail portions of the buildings that include residential over retail space is divided between the residential and retail owners/developers.

The multiplex theater features state-of-the-art sound and stadium seating coupled with the nostalgic architecture of an old movie house.

Maintenance of landscaping along the entrances is shared by Post Properties, the Harris Group, and the hotel partnership. The hotel pays a set monthly fee for its share of landscaping and lighting. Retail tenants pay for their share of common area maintenance costs based on the size of their space. Most of the retail tenants finished their own space with a tenant allowance.

The town center concept—with its specialty retail and entertainment attractions—helped draw desirable nationally known retailers to the project. Careful attention was paid to attracting national tenants not presently in the Charlotte area, most of which would have only one store in the market, to provide Phillips Place with a unique collection of tenants. The project was marketed to prospective tenants as a regional destination.

One of the leasing advantages for Phillips Place was that the rents—$28 to $34 per square foot ($300 to $365 per square meter) net of common area charges—were roughly half those of the nearby mall. Many of the tenants originally were mall candidates who were attracted to Phillips Place in part because of its unusual outdoor pedestrian-oriented environment and specialty retailing. The project also benefited from a tight retail space market in the SouthPark area. Sales averaged around $400 per square foot ($4,300 per square meter) through the end of 2001.

The first tenant to sign on was the theater, followed by the Palm Restaurant, which set the tone for the leasing, and Dean & Deluca, which generated daytime traffic and continued the upscale tone of the center. Other key restaurants and retailers followed, including Bertolini's Italian Trattoria, Via Veneto Fashion Shoes, Restoration Hardware, and P.F. Chang's China Bistro.

An executive for one of the signature retailers in the project—Restoration Hardware—notes, "As a retailer, we love the outdoor, plaza environment. Our customers love going back to Main Street, where there is an outside presence and a meandering atmosphere. We wanted

Domed corner pavilions mark key intersections. Facades recalling historic Charleston or Savannah are clad with synthetic stucco above Mexican sandstone bases.

Residences adjacent to and over retail stores enjoy a landscaped private courtyard.

Post Park at Phillips Place has the ambience of a pedestrian-friendly small town, yet it is just steps away from fine restaurants, cafés, trendy boutiques, and a multiplex movie theater.

a place where there were a host of interesting tenants so our customers could walk from shop to shop and sample the fare. We liked the fact that Phillips Place has hints of a historic nature."

The retail portion of the project was 90 percent occupied by December 1997 and achieved 95 percent occupancy by May 1998. The retail center does not have a marketing fund, which has limited the center's ability to sponsor events and promote the center broadly. The developer, however, contributes annually to several events and advertising, and most large tenants do their own promotions. The developer also provides 24-hour security.

The hotel is an inn and all-suite hotel owned 50/50 by the Harris Group and the Panos Group. It offers its guests far more service than the typical limited-service hotel. The inn and suites attract both corporate clients and those visiting Charlotte for the weekend, which allows guests an easy walk to a variety of retail entertainment venues. Hotel occupancy averaged around 78 percent through the end of 2001.

Rents in the apartment buildings range from $840 per month for 650 square feet (60 square meters) to $3,040 per month for 2,200 square feet (205 square meters); rents generally range from $1.10 to $1.30 per square foot ($12.00 to $14.00 per square meter) per month. Rents are highest in the areas nearest the retail space, especially those directly over the retail stores on the street. The residential portions achieved 98 percent occupancy shortly after opening, and they are now 100 percent leased.

Construction financing for the retail portion of the project was provided by Southtrust Bank, while Compass provided construction financing for the hotel. First Union later provided two separate permanent loans for these elements. A ten-year nonrecourse permanent loan for $25,350,000 at 6.79 percent interest for the retail portion was closed on March 12, 1998. The developers found that the retail portion of the project required substantially more equity than a typical retail development, but

the project was well received by financing sources once completed and leased.

Experience Gained

Phillips Place is a prime example of how a mixed-use town center can be successfully developed in a rapidly growing suburban business district. The project provides an important urban gathering place for the low-density suburban community and illustrates how the relatively dense mix of a variety of uses can create synergy and a whole that is greater than the sum of its parts. The leasing of the retail space and apartments was quick, easily achieving pro forma rents. The hotel occupancy rate is higher than average for the area, and sales per square foot are above average for a retail center of this type.

Although Phillips Place is pedestrian oriented within, it remains very much a suburban development in that it is primarily reached by car. Although apartment residents and hotel guests can and do walk throughout the center, few of those living or working in the surrounding community are likely to come to the project on foot, because no attractive pedestrian pathways serve the project. The project cannot be integrated with an existing street system —it is served by only one roadway—and it is separated from adjacent residential neighborhoods by fences. Moreover, few major generators of pedestrian traffic lie within easy walking distance, even if attractive pathways existed.

Nonetheless, Phillips Place brings to the Charlotte suburbs a new urban element, giving its residents the opportunity to walk to many conveniences and providing visitors and nearby residents and workers with an exciting combination of dining, shopping, and entertainment in one location. Phillips Place is a major step in the right direction for suburban place making and pedestrian-oriented, mixed-use development.

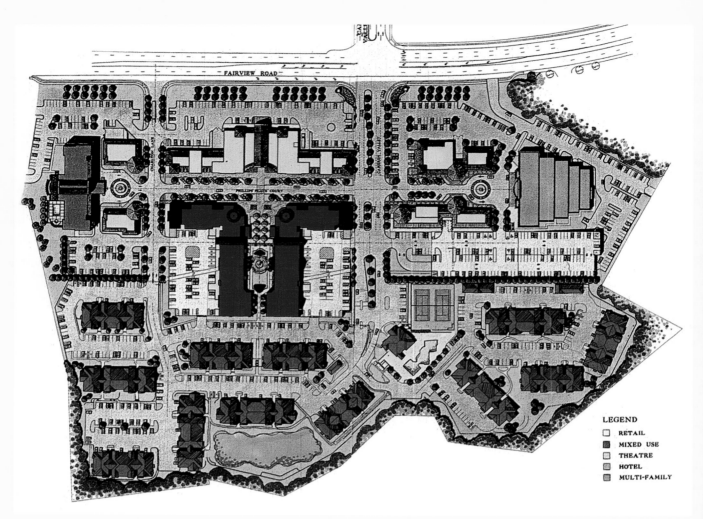

FAIRVIEW ROAD

LEGEND

☐ RETAIL
■ MIXED USE
☐ THEATRE
▨ HOTEL
▨ MULTI-FAMILY

Site plan.

Project Data: Phillips Place

Land Use and Building Information

Retail	129,394 square feet (12,025 square meters)
Residential	402 units
Hotel	124 rooms
Parking	790 spaces
Site Area	35 acres (14 hectares)

Residential Information

Unit Type	Unit Size (Square Feet/ Square Meters)		Rent Range
Freestanding Apartments			
1-Bedroom	650–1,050	(60–97.5)	$840–1,050
2-Bedroom	965–1,335	(90–124)	$1,300–1,825
3-Bedroom	1,980	(184)	$1,790–1,925
Apartments over Retail Space			
1-Bedroom	700–1,500	(65–140)	$870–1,545
2-Bedroom	1,055–1680	(98–156)	$1,440–2,075
3-Bedroom	1,980–2,200	(184–204)	$2,600–3,040

Retail Information

	Number of Stores	Total GLA (Square Feet/ Square Meters)	
Food service	6	31,770	(2,953)
Clothing and accessories	10	23,653	(2,200)
Shoes	1	3,100	(290)
Home furnishings	3	12,859	(1,195)
Home appliances/music	1	1,500	(140)
Hobby/special interest	2	6,877	(640)
Gift/specialty	5	9,705	(900)
Personal services	3	8,775	(815)
Recreation/community	1	30,000	(2,790)
Total	32	128,239	(11,914)

Gross Leasable Area (GLA) Occupied	95%
Annual Rents	$28 to $34 per square foot ($300 to $365 per square meter)
Average Annual Sales	$400 per square foot ($4,305 per square meter)
Average Length of Lease	5–10 years

Development Cost Information

Site Costs

Site acquisition	$11,950,000
Site improvement	3,907,842
Parking deck	1,700,000

Construction Costs

Retail	$14,254,000
Residential	38,000,000
Hotel	8,000,000
Total	$60,254,000

Soft Costs

Leasing	$1,600,000
Construction interest/fees	786,825
Startup costs	167,000
Legal and accounting costs	45,000
Total Development Cost	$80,410,667

Development Schedule

11/1995	Site purchased
11/1995	Construction started
6/1997	Phase I completed
3/1998	Project completed

Master Developer/Retail Developer

Lincoln Harris (formerly the Harris Group)
100 North Tyron Street
Charlotte, North Carolina 28202
704-714-7600

Apartment Developer

Post Properties
3350 Cumberland Circle
Suite 2200
Atlanta, Georgia 30339
404-846-5076

Hotel Developer

The Harris Group
The Panos Group
Charlotte, North Carolina

Architect

TBA^2 Architects
112 South Tryon Street
Suite 200
Charlotte, North Carolina 28284
704-333-6686

Site Planner

LandDesign
223 Graham Street
Charlotte, North Carolina 28202
704-376-7777

Sony Center am Potsdamer Platz

Berlin, Germany

Only rarely do cities have an opportunity to redevelop entire districts at their core. But in Berlin, a city that today is in a state of constant change as it reemerges as one of Europe's most important centers, that is exactly what is happening at Potsdamer Platz. One of the most significant contributions to this redevelopment is the Sony Center am Potsdamer Platz. This architecturally compelling and award-winning development features 732,760 square feet (68,100 square meters) of office space, 285,140 square feet (26,500 square meters) of residential space, and more than 451,920 square feet (42,000 square meters) of retail and entertainment uses.

The development represents one of the clearest expressions of the Berlin that is emerging today, and it sets a high standard for large-scale urban mixed-use projects around the world. The development is a prime example of a modernist downtown mixed-used development organized around enclosed public spaces, a style of development not frequently employed in the United States today but still used in other areas of the world, especially Europe and Asia. It has refined this model, however, by creating a space that is accessed through open-air passageways, ensuring that the space can be easily reached from surrounding buildings and streets and resulting in a space that is not mechanically climate-controlled, allowing it to feel more a part of the sights, sounds, smells, and climate of the surrounding city.

The Site and Development Background

In the 1920s, Berlin was one of Europe's cultural capitals, and Potsdamer Platz was at its heart. Characterized by outstanding architecture and a vibrant social and intellectual environment—not to mention throngs of traffic—Potsdamer Platz was the dynamic hub of the city. All that changed with World War II. By 1945, most of Potsdamer Platz had been reduced to rubble. In the years following the war, Potsdamer Platz was remarkable only for the fact that it served as the meeting point of the Soviet, British, and American sectors of occupied Berlin. But as the deep freeze of the Cold War swept in, the fate of Potsdamer Platz seemed to be sealed. When the Berlin Wall was built in 1961, it ran right through the middle of what had been Potsdamer Platz. On either side was a heavily fortified wasteland, and the glory days of the 1920s were a distant memory.

In November 1989, however, the world watched in amazement as the Berlin Wall fell. Berlin was on the cusp of another transformation, and after the fall of the wall the government in Berlin was eager to rebuild the city. In 1991, the Berlin Senate Department of Town Planning and Environmental Protection held a competition to develop an appropriate plan for the entire Potsdamer Platz district. The German architectural firm Hilmer und Sattler won the competition. Its plan provided the basis for the subsequent competitions that were used to select the architectural teams that would fill in the district plan with detailed designs for each building site. A central goal of the master plan was to re-create the preeminence of Potsdamer Platz as a location for shopping, entertainment, and culture and the sense of excitement that had once been characteristic of the square. Hilmer und Sattler's plan specified such items as the dimensions of sites at Potsdamer Platz, the layout of streets, and the height and massing of buildings, but it did not address the uses that would be permitted or the architectural form that the new buildings should take.

During this time, the Berlin Senate gave the Sony Corporation an opportunity to purchase a property, hoping that a firm with Sony's reputation and international standing would create a development of the highest quality. Sony officially signed the purchase contract in June 1991. Apart from the broad planning framework set out in Hilmer und Sattler's plan, the contract also specified certain other obligations for Sony, including the on-site preservation of the former Hotel Esplanade as a historic structure and Sony's having to build a permanent home for the Filmhaus, an important organization in the German film industry, and offering a long-term subsidy on its rent.

With its purchase contract in place, Sony then held a competition of its own and invited seven renowned architectural firms to take part. Helmut Jahn's bold design was unanimously selected as the winner in August 1992. Although some people in the local government were initially unenthusiastic about Jahn's decidedly modern design, eventually Sony was able to persuade the regulators that it was the best design for the site. In 1994, Sony formed a joint venture with New York–based Tishman Speyer Properties and the Kajima Corporation of Japan to make good on its plans for the Potsdamer Platz site. Within the joint venture, Tishman Speyer was given responsibility for developing, managing, and leasing the project, while Kajima served as an equity partner and technical adviser.

The site of the Sony Center is one of the largest inner-city development sites in all of Europe. Immediately to the north is the peaceful Tiergarten park, and just beyond

In the 1920s, Potsdamer Platz was the intellectual and social hub of Berlin.

Most of Potsdamer Platz was destroyed during World War II. After the construction of the Berlin Wall in 1961, the area became a no-man's-land.

Today, Potsdamer Platz is being radically transformed. In addition to the Sony Center, a variety of projects are bringing offices, hotels, residences, shops, and entertainment facilities to the area.

it stand the famous Brandenburg Gate and the German parliament building. To the west of the site is the Berlin Kulturforum, where the Berlin Philharmonic Orchestra, the Chamber Music Concert Hall, and the Neue National-galerie designed by Mies van der Rohe are located. The Potsdamer Platz district is well integrated into the city's transportation system.

A number of different building sites are located on all sides of Potsdamer Platz itself, all of which are being rede-veloped in spectacular fashion. As in other parts of Berlin, massive amounts of public money are being invested to build or upgrade infrastructure. In and around Potsdamer Platz, the city government, the federal government, and the German railway company collectively invested more than DM4 billion ($2.4 billion) in infrastructure improve-ments in recent years.

As part of the planning process, Tishman Speyer had to work with a host of different government agencies.

The Forum, a 43,040-square-foot (4,000-square-meter) public space, is the centerpiece of the Sony Center. Capped by its signature roof, the Forum is enclosed by the buildings of the Sony Center and is animated at all hours of the day with people coming and going.

For instance, the Berlin state government had the approval authority for the master plan, while the Tiergarten district government made the decisions on day-to-day matters and issued building permits. Plans for the Sony Center had to be submitted for public review and comments for a period of three months. A number of changes to the plan emerged from this review process. For instance, the configuration of open space on the site was changed, and the cinemas were moved below grade.

Planning, Design, and Construction

The Sony Center is truly a mixed-use project, with eight separate buildings providing space for office, retail, entertainment, and residential uses. The buildings range from eight to 26 stories, and together they offer approximately 1.4 million square feet (132,500 square meters) of space. These buildings are arranged around an elliptical public open space called the Forum, which is capped by a dramatic roof. Each building maintains a distinct identity, but the project also presents a coherent overall vision.

The overarching goal of the site plan was to make sure that each building and use component would function properly as individual entities but also give the project a coherent architectural design and provide a space where users could come together in a lively and engaging setting. The Forum is the glue that holds the project together. It provides a visual and functional axis around which the other uses are arranged. At the same time, the design team sought to ensure that the project was easily accessible visually and functionally from the areas around the site.

This goal has been achieved through the use of multiple open-air passageways that lead to and draw one's attention to the Forum space from the surrounding buildings and streets. The Forum is the place where everyone comes together and the synergies between the different uses are most evident. Around the Forum, individual uses generally have been grouped together so that each user group has a space to claim as its own without creating conflicts with the other components of the project. Given that the site is triangular in shape, the individual buildings in the project were designed to maximize the use of the land while still leaving enough room to create the Forum space at the center of the site and to present a clear edge to the surrounding streets.

At an area of 43,040 square feet (4,000 square meters), the Forum represents a type of public space that one rarely finds in new construction projects today. Many offices and residences at the Sony Center look out onto the Forum, creating a sense of enclosure and interaction. With a fountain at its center, skylights offering a view into the theaters below, and outdoor seating for the surrounding cafés, the Forum is a engaging public space used for a variety of events.

High above the Forum is one of the signature components of the Sony Center. Immediately recognizable on the Berlin skyline, the tent-like Forum roof is a marvel of engineering developed by Helmut Jahn and Ove Arup and Partners. Made of 56,500 square feet (5,250 square meters) of Teflon-coated fabric and 37,660 square feet (3,500 square meters) of laminated glass, the roof follows the shape of a hyperbolic cone and is more than 325 feet (100 meters) across at its widest spot. The roof peaks 246 feet (75 meters) above the Forum and creates the single largest covered outdoor area in all of Berlin. By alternating transparent and opaque materials in a folded-over design, the roof allows a never-ending variety of light and shadow on the spaces below, and it is lighted in vivid colors at night. Because the Forum roof does not completely seal off the space below and several open-air passageways are included, the Forum space is not mechanically heated or cooled; the design offers protection from the elements while still permitting air to circulate.

The construction of the Sony Center presented tremendous difficulties for the development team. First, the site had been heavily bombed during World War II, so initial excavations had to be done with extreme care because of the risk of finding unexploded shells. A major soil cleanup then followed. A second difficulty was that the water table at the site was only about 6.5 feet (2 meters) below the surface, requiring the use of deep slurry wall perimeter foundation construction and the injection of a gel blanket 72 feet (22 meters) below the surface.

Strict environmental and other regulations shaped the plan. Germany is known for the rigor of its environmental legislation, and regulators watched construction of the Sony Center closely. Regulations on historic preservation also meant a lot of work for the development team. For instance, building permits for the Sony Center stipulated that no columns could penetrate the historic rooms at the Esplanade Hotel. Therefore, the development team decided to literally hang seven floors of apartments from gigantic roof trusses right above the Esplanade. These trusses form a bridge structure that alone weighs more than 570 tons (520 metric tons), and all of the apartments are attached to the trusses by steel rods.

Likewise, the site plan and the need to widen one of the roads adjacent to the Sony Center meant that the historic Kaisersaal (Emperors Hall), a luxurious room where the German kaiser used to hold functions, had to be moved. Moreover, the room had to be moved in one piece. Even though the room weighed 1,430 tons (1,300 metric tons), it was successfully lifted on air cushions and delicately moved 246 feet (75 meters) to its new home beside the other historic rooms of the Esplanade Hotel. Despite all these challenges, Tishman Speyer was still able to use a variety of value engineering techniques to save almost DM300 million ($180 million) on construction costs. Coordinating all this activity was a management task of enormous proportions. And although the city government was very supportive of the Sony Center, innumerable special permits were required to bring the project to completion.

The concerns of the development team did not end at the edge of the site. Tishman Speyer worked closely with the city of Berlin to build an underground arterial road running north/south next to the Sony Center site, a road that offers the additional bonus of providing access to the loading docks at the Sony Center. The developers also worked with Deutsche Bahn to reconstruct the neighboring Potsdamer Platz subway and rail station. The reconstruction included the creation of a below-grade connection to the Sony Center site.

Architecturally, the Sony Center is stunning. Helmut Jahn's design makes extensive use of steel and glass to create a series of buildings that are highly transparent but still show a great deal of character and attention to detail. One of Jahn's goals was to combine traditional notions of urbanism and public space with a vision for the technologically oriented city of the future. The project achieves this goal. Further, the design of the Sony Center creates a coherent image and sense of enclosure, yet it is also porous enough that it provides good connections with the surrounding area and pedestrians can easily access the Forum through attractive passageways without passing through doors. Mixing different uses was also a central part of the vision and design for the Sony Center, reflecting a belief that diverse activities and an interaction between public and private spaces are essential components of great urban places. Although some local residents have complained that the architecture of the Sony Center is too modern for their taste and inappropriate for Berlin, the design has generally been very well received and clearly stakes out Berlin's position as one of Europe's leading centers of contemporary architecture.

The Sony Center is connected with the subway and regional rail transit station next door, and 980 parking spaces are provided for tenants and visitors in an underground garage. Because the different pieces of the Sony Center depend on each other, phasing the development was not considered an option, even though doing so reduced the margin for error during construction.

The Development Program and Tenants
Fundamental to the development program, especially the retail space, is the Forum, the place where all the

The architecture of the Sony Center is strikingly modern. Designed by Helmut Jahn, the buildings use steel and glass to achieve a high degree of transparency while setting out a futuristic vision for contemporary architecture.

Despite slack conditions in the Berlin market, all the office space at the Sony Center was leased before opening.

different users of the Sony Center can interact. Retail uses at the Sony Center, clustered around the Forum, comprise 87,200 square feet (8,100 square meters) of space. Apart from its exciting architecture, the vitality of the Forum is generated by all the people coming and going, heading to offices and entertainment functions or visiting one of the cafés or restaurants. Tishman Speyer has concentrated its leasing efforts on retailers and restaurants that would add to this atmosphere. A run-of-the-mill clothing store, for example, would not be particularly welcome at the Sony Center. Instead, one can find retailers like the Sony Style store, a high-tech environment spread over four stories that offers an innovative range of products and stands at the contemporary nexus of shopping, lifestyle, and entertainment venues. Other retailers at the Sony Center include WebFreeTV.com and Volkswagen AG, both of which have developed stimulating retail/entertainment environments.

Despite the leading-edge design of the Forum, the space also takes advantage of the old European tradition of outdoor cafés and restaurants. The Sony Center offers both tenants and visitors a number of places where they can relax, eat, and watch people go by. Although the Sony Center opened in June 2000, not all of the retail space had been leased, in part because Tishman Speyer was holding out for the sort of tenant that would fit in with the Sony Center concept. Given the attractiveness of this project, Tishman Speyer does not expect these retail vacancies to last very long.

Another key part of the Sony Center is the 371,220 square feet (34,500 square meters) of entertainment space, which has contributed greatly to the project's success. One building at the Sony Center is devoted to the 188,300-square-foot (17,500-square-meter) Filmhaus and the German Mediatheque. The Mediatheque is devoted to the study of radio and television, while the Filmhaus offers space to a variety of users, such as the German Film and Television Academy. The Filmhaus

also offers exhibitions open to the public, including the Marlene Dietrich Collection, a film museum celebrating the career of the famous actress from Berlin. Also at the Filmhaus is the Arsenal repertory cinema. As noted earlier, the development team was obliged to provide space for these uses, but they also fit well with the goals of the overall plan for the project.

Any good mixed-use project draws outside visitors to the site, and the Sony Center succeeds with a host of other entertainment options in addition to the Filmhaus. Another 182,920 square feet (17,000 square meters) of space is devoted to other entertainment uses. For example, an eight-screen CineStar multiplex underneath the Forum offers the latest in new releases, and a 550-seat CineStar offers IMAX 3-D cinema. These users have helped to make the Sony Center an attractive destination for residents and visitors and have raised the project's public profile.

Sony itself has contributed to the entertainment facilities in the form of the Music Box. This exciting new concept uses cutting-edge technology to offer patrons a variety of interactive and informative activities, including the Beatles Yellow Submarine Adventure, where visitors can ride in a simulated-motion submarine. Standing in front of a series of screens, visitors can try conducting the Berlin Philharmonic Orchestra. A harp makes music with jets of running water instead of strings, and a recording studio brings a virtual Beethoven back to life. The focus is on fun in a stimulating and educational environment that uses the latest in computer technologies.

Offices, however, actually take up the majority of the space at the Sony Center, offering tenants one of the most prestigious addresses in the city with state-of-the-art telecommunications infrastructure and security systems. Space is available in four buildings with a total floor area of 731,680 square feet (68,000 square meters). One building, a 26-story tower, features a semicircular glass facade and offers stunning views of the city. The entire building has been leased to Deutsche Bahn AG, the

Residential units at the Sony Center have been designed and built to the highest standards of luxury. They are selling well at the highest prices in the market.

Entertainment facilities such as a 3-D IMAX theater and innovative retail concepts draw customers to the Sony Center.

German railway company. The remaining space is spread around the other buildings on the site.

Not surprisingly, the headquarters of Sony Europe is to be found at the Sony Center. Other major tenants include Sanofi-Synthelabo and Sony Music.

In 1990, real estate market forecasts for Berlin were uniformly optimistic, forecasting that office absorption would top 10.8 million square feet (1 million square meters) per year at increasingly higher rents. Reality turned out quite differently. Even in the late 1990s, vacancy rates were touching 10 percent, with more than 16.1 million square feet (1.5 million square meters) of space on the market. It is therefore all the more remarkable that the office space at Sony Center was fully leased before opening day, well ahead of schedule and at a premium price.

Even with all the attention to technology and the future at the Sony Center, the past also finds a home in the development. The Grandhotel Esplanade was once a major meeting place in Berlin's social scene. Built around 1910, the hotel had beautiful sandstone facades and a luxurious neo-Baroque interior. Unfortunately, the building barely survived World War II with only a few of its public rooms remaining. In the development of the Sony Center, one of the conditions imposed by the city government was that these historic spaces be saved and restored.

One of the historic rooms, the Breakfast Hall, was broken down into 500 pieces, moved, and reconstructed elsewhere on the site. The Kaisersaal, on the other hand, had to be moved en masse. Having found their new homes on the site, the rooms have been painstakingly restored and now serve as restaurants that are also available for private functions. Two of the former interior walls of the Breakfast Hall were left behind in their original location when the rest of the room was moved. These walls now form part of the Sony Center's outer facade and are on view to the public through a specially designed series of protective glass panels, thus creating an intriguing blend of old and new.

The residential units at the Sony Center may not dominate the project, but they are an important part of its overall concept. The Forum Apartments, 67 rental units, are situated above the public urban piazza at the center. An open-plan architectural concept means that the living units, on average 970 square feet (90 square meters), offer flexibility in both horizontal and vertical layout. The five floors of apartments start at a height of 82 feet (25 meters), giving them the character of a penthouse. The urbane heart of the Sony Center and the Kulturforum, situated to the southwest, can be seen from the apartments.

The 134 spacious condominiums of the Esplanade Residence have been fitted into a futuristic bridge structure that spans the former Grand Hotel Esplanade. Luxury and tradition have been combined with ultramodern architecture and fittings. The part of the former Grand Hotel that is listed as a historic monument has been elaborately restored, giving the apartments, which

A marvel of engineering, the Forum roof is already a landmark on the Berlin skyline. The roof sits on a gigantic ring beam and offers protection from the elements while creating an endless play of light and shadow in the space below.

Thousands of people attended the gala opening of the Sony Center in June 2000.

range from 645 to 2,260 square feet (60 to 210 square meters), a special flair.

Residences have been built to the highest quality, and they rent and sell for some of the highest prices in the Berlin market. Rents for the apartment units range from DM28 to DM42 per square meter ($1.55 to $2.35 per square foot), sale prices for the condominiums from DM8,500 to DM12,500 per square meter ($475 to $695 per square foot). Solid wood and natural stone, custom fittings, separate climate controls for individual rooms, concierge service, and valet parking all help to create a special atmosphere for residents.

Financing, Marketing, and Management

Building the Sony Center was not cheap. Total development costs for the project were roughly DM1.5 billion ($900 million). Nineteen banks were involved in putting together the DM975 million ($585 million) nonrecourse debt package—the largest real estate project financing scheme in German history. Dresdner Bank and Westdeutsche ImmobilienBank were the lead financial sources, and Sony was the major equity investor.

Because of the problems that the Berlin real estate market had gone through in the years leading up to this development, it took much convincing, thorough due diligence work, and an agreement to meet strict reporting requirements to get the banks on board. Trusting the outstanding reputations of Sony and Tishman Speyer, however, the banks were eventually convinced

of the project's viability. The lenders required the project be 30 percent preleased before releasing the funds for development.

Managing all the different uses and users is a complex task. Under a property management and leasing agreement, Tishman Speyer Properties Deutschland is fully responsible for leasing and property management at the Sony Center. Specifically, Tishman Speyer is responsible for all lease administration, service and security contracts, budgeting and procurement, and tenant support and coordination. These functions are handled by a full-time staff of 16 people.

Costs are allocated to tenants according to a complex formula, which splits common area costs four ways: costs related to a specific tenant, costs related to a specific building, costs related to the use of a tenant, and costs related to the overall project. By using direct costs incurred by the tenant and allocating a portion of the common area costs according to this formula, all tenants are ensured that they are paying a fair share of the project's common area costs.

The Sony Center has been a tremendous financial success. Office space in the project was completely preleased, and all the uses have generated premium rents. Overall, the project is 98 percent leased. Achieving this level of success was by no means assured, however; despite its history, Potsdamer Platz was not obviously the best location in the market. In fact, the Sony Center and the other projects at Potsdamer Platz have faced fierce competition from other more established locations in Berlin, such as the Kurfuerstendamm area in the former West Berlin and Friedrichstrasse in the former East. Understanding the market situation, Tishman Speyer undertook a major marketing effort more than five years before the opening of the project. The InfoBox, for example, was an information center where visitors to Potsdamer Platz could learn about the area and the development projects. It attracted more than 2 million visitors a year. Good marketing, outstanding architecture, a high-caliber mix

The historic Emperors Hall and the Breakfast Hall have been painstakingly restored and are now used as restaurants.

of tenants and uses, and a high-profile location have made the Sony Center as successful as it is.

In 2000, the Sony Center received a ULI Award for Excellence. The jury's citation summarized why this project is so compelling:

> The Sony Center, at the symbolic ground zero of the no-man's-land that once separated East and West Berlin, leads the way in restoring Potsdamer Platz's preeminence as a cultural and retail center. Simultaneously, it points to a new approach to European urban life, using 21st-century technologies and techniques to fill in the core of a city hollowed out by the Cold War.

Experience Gained

Architecture is absolutely central to the identity and attractiveness of this project. The design of the Sony Center distinguishes it from the competition and helps to make it a compelling destination for businesses and consumers. Creating a special urban place through architecture is worth the investment; in this case it was worth going through an extensive competition to get a great design.

Developers and planners need to think carefully about how the pieces of a mixed-use project fit together. Not all uses are compatible, and some combinations of uses generate more interaction and activity than others. Achieving this kind of synergy between uses is the hallmark of a good mixed-use project. The cafés, retailers, and entertainment uses grouped around the Forum make the space come alive at all hours of the day, while residential and office users have greater privacy in their dedicated spaces.

Developers must carefully consider the positioning of their project in the market; understanding and finding the right combination of location, accessibility, and target market were essential to the success of this project. Understanding the nature and level of competition for different land uses in a market will shape the uses that are chosen for the project. It took some courage to develop office space at the Sony Center, given the conditions in the local market. On the other hand, Tishman Speyer decided not to build more retail space at the Sony Center than it did, because the surrounding area was becoming saturated with retail uses.

The time has come for mixed-use projects. Consumers and businesses are showing increased interest in interesting and attractive urban places. Well-designed mixed-use developments can be just the kind of destination such consumers are looking for, whether in Europe or in North America. Mixed-use projects like the Sony Center attract and engage people in a way that single-use projects can never achieve.

Good project management was absolutely key to the success of the project. Especially given the scale and the complexity of the Sony Center development, the developer had to have a strong handle on all aspects of the development process (particularly construction) to make sure that the project could be completed on time and on budget.

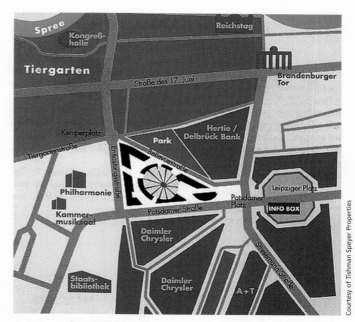

Area map showing the Sony Center and Potsdamer Platz. Cultural facilities, a large park, and the German parliament (Reichstag) are all nearby.

No urban site or development, no matter how large, should be isolated. It is therefore important to cooperate with both neighbors and local planning authorities to ensure that the project is properly and carefully integrated with the surrounding area.

Especially in the case of a joint venture, frequent and open communication between the parties is vital. From the beginning of the project, developers need to make sure that all members of the development team are on the same page and that any problems that arise are dealt with as soon as possible. When the people working on project teams are not accountable and when they do not understand or communicate with each other, problems can build up, often with disastrous results for the project.

Uses are interspersed among the eight buildings of the Sony Center. Retail and entertainment functions are concentrated at ground level to provide a high degree of activity.

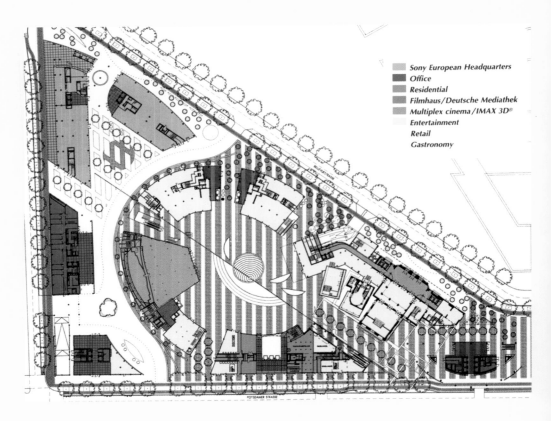

Sony European Headquarters
Office
Residential
Filmhaus/Deutsche Mediathek
Multiplex cinema/IMAX 3D®
Entertainment
Retail
Gastronomy

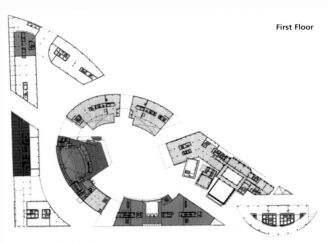

First Floor

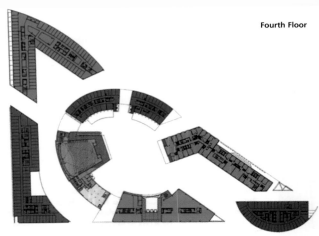

Fourth Floor

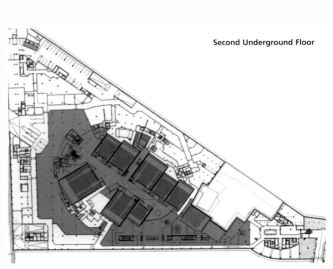

Second Underground Floor

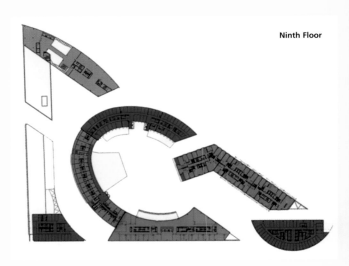

Ninth Floor

Project Data: Sony Center am Potsdamer Platz

Land Use and Building Information

Site Area — 284,540 square feet (26,444 square meters)

Gross Building Area (GBA) — 1,425,700 square feet (132,500 square meters)

Existing Land Uses

	Square Feet (Square Meters)
Office net rentable area	733,000 (68,100)
Retail gross leasable area	87,160 (8,100)
Residential units	285,140 (26,500)
Parking spaces	980
Entertainment	182,920 (17,000)
Filmhaus	188,300 (17,500)

Residential Information

Unit Type	Unit Size (Square Feet/ Square Meters)	Number of Units Sold/Leased	Rent/Price per Square Foot
Apartments	365–1,130 (34–105)	67	$1.55–2.35
Condominiums	645–2,260 (60–210)	134	$475–695

Office Tenant Information

Occupied NRA — 100%

Number of Tenants — 4 main tenants, 6 smaller tenants

Average Tenant Size

Main tenants average	172,160 square feet (16,000 square meters)
Smaller tenants average	3,230 square feet (300 square meters)

Average Length of Lease — 10 years

Main Tenants

Sony Europe
Sony Music
Deutsche Bahn AG
Sanofi-Synthelabo

Retail/Entertainment Information

Number of Tenants — 15, including movie theaters

Major Retail/Entertainment/Restaurant Tenants

Sony Style Store
Volkswagen AG
WebFreeTV.com
CineStar Multiplex (8 screens)
IMAX 3-D Cinema

GLA Occupied — 80%

Average Length of Lease — 10 years

Total Development Cost — $900 million (DM1.5 billion)

Development Schedule

1991	Sony Berlin founded
6/1991	Site purchased
1992	Architectural competition
1993	Murphy/Jahn plan developed
1995	Planning completed
9/1995	Ground breaking
3/1996	Moving of the Kaisersaal
1997	Leasing begins
1998	Construction completed
1/2000	First parts opened to the public
6/2000	Grand opening

Developer

Tishman Speyer Properties
Quartier 205 Friedrichstadtpassagen
Friedrichstrasse 67
10117 Berlin, Germany
49-30-2094-5400

Architect

Murphy/Jahn Inc. Architects
35 East Wacker Drive
Chicago, Illinois 60601
312-427-7300

University Park at MIT

Cambridge, Massachusetts

University Park at MIT is a mixed-use urban campus that features office, R&D, apartment, hotel, and retail uses organized around a common. Adjacent to the campus of the Massachusetts Institute of Technology, the development was initiated by MIT and undertaken through a joint venture with Forest City Enterprises.

Conceived as a technology-oriented business park providing state-of-the-art, high-tech, flexible, first-class facilities in a thriving campus environment, University Park has evolved into one of the premier centers for biotech and biomedical research in Cambridge. When fully developed in 2005, University Park will comprise 2.3 million square feet (213,755 square meters), including more than 1.6 million square feet (148,700 square meters) of office and research space, a 210-room hotel and executive conference center, 100,000 square feet (9,300 square meters) of retail space and restaurants, 460 rental housing units, three structured parking facilities for 2,800 cars, and four acres (1.6 hectares) of parkland.

The development is distinctive among mixed-use urban village development in that unlike many of these projects that are dominated by residential and retail uses, this development is an office-focused urban village and serves as an important model for effectively combining office and research space with other uses in an attractive urban campus setting.

The Site and Development Background

MIT had been acquiring land for 25 years for the development of a corporate office and research park adjacent to its campus. The strategy was to invest portions of the MIT endowment in ways that would generate economic returns while also helping to accelerate the transfer of technology into the commercial marketplace. In 1982, with a site assembled, MIT issued an RFP.

MIT's objectives were to:

- secure a good economic return for the endowment fund;
- protect long-term campus growth;
- foster technology transfer;
- create employment opportunities for students and graduates;
- provide collaborative or advisory opportunities for faculty.

The university did not want to use the site to develop academic research or incubator space or to direct the location of the patent assets and technology investments of the faculty. The RFP was issued to seek a for-profit developer with deep pockets and staying power, long-term investment objectives, and expertise across several product types—offices, R&D space, residences, and retail uses. The university also wanted the developer to obtain the necessary public approvals while performing its duties at arm's length from the university, thus protecting MIT's relationship with the Cambridge community.

The RFP received 38 responses. The finalists were Forest City Enterprises, Trammell Crow, and Beacon Properties. Forest City's proposal was the only mixed-use concept incorporating residential and retail components with the core office/R&D uses. In 1983, MIT selected Forest City, and the parties signed a 20-year development agreement that will expire in 2003. Under the terms of this agreement, Forest City will develop University Park using a series of 75-year ground leases, with each lease term to begin as each portion of the site is developed. Thus, the terms of each lease convey with its parcel, and the property gradually will revert to MIT, with all leases ending no later than 2078. No provisions exist for lease renewal; however, there is also no prohibition if MIT and Forest City choose to add one.

Forest City's objectives as expressed in its proposal to MIT were to:

- create a campus environment offering a mix of complementary uses;
- build flexible, quality buildings to support those uses over time;
- develop a concept that would allow the project to respond to evolving market parameters;
- have approvals ensured over the project's buildout;
- achieve an attractive return on investment.

The city of Cambridge also had objectives:

- taxable development;
- development at least cost to the city, effected through developer-funded provision of all infrastructure with long-term maintenance agreements for the infrastructure provided;
- the creation of jobs, particularly for entry-level personnel;
- limited neighborhood retail uses to augment but not compete with existing retail establishments;
- construction of affordable housing.

Aerial view of the common, with two office/R&D buildings on the left and the U-shaped Kennedy Biscuit Lofts apartment building just beyond. The yet-to-be-developed 23 Sidney Street parcel—planned for development in Phase V—is the green space adjacent to the Kennedy Biscuit Lofts and between the common and the Market Square Park and historic structures at the entrance.

University Park is built largely on what once was blighted, unused industrial land in Cambridge across the Charles River from Boston. The 27-acre (11-hectare) site, assembled by MIT through its acquisition of 25 individual parcels, fronts on Massachusetts Avenue, the major artery of the city of Cambridge that connects the MIT and Harvard campuses with Boston. Like the Back Bay section of Boston, this area used to be marshland that gradually was filled in and used for industrial purposes.

For most of the 20th century, the major user on the site was the 12-building Simplex Wire and Cable Company, manufacturers of everything from electric stoves to deep-sea telegraph cables. It left Cambridge in the 1970s, and by the 1980s, most of the site was vacant.

Although there were no apparent significant environmental hazards on the site, its urban industrial character suggested that some cleanup would be necessary. Forest City and MIT share the cost of environmental remediation 50/50, with MIT's reimbursement to Forest City eligible for inclusion in its cost basis of the land.

After careful evaluation, only two buildings on the site were deemed suitable for adaptive use: the Jackson Building, a five-story industrial loft building that was once a Sears shoe factory, for R&D use, and the F.A. Kennedy Steam Bakery, where the Fig Newton was created, for conversion to rental apartment units and the Bright Horizons Child Care Center. The remaining development is in new buildings designed to meet the needs of potential tenants.

Master Planning and Public Approvals
University Park can be likened to a private urban renewal project. MIT, Forest City, and Cambridge all intended the project to be a for-profit private real estate investment, not an expansion of the MIT campus, and thus university uses are not permitted. With the project having residential, retail, and office/R&D uses and featuring a

community-friendly design, the concept of urban design was seen as an advantage in the Cambridge market. Master planning and public approvals required four years, however, before MIT, Forest City, and the city of Cambridge reached a consensus.

One of the developer's key objectives was to plan for the flexibility needed in the 21st century. Thus, a primary concept was to build an infrastructure backbone in the streets and buildings that would prove adaptable over time. The project was to be an urban campus; thus, the existing streets would remain and, in some cases, be extended as public or private streets to maintain the neighborhood's existing grid. On one location only, a larger superblock was required to accommodate the combination of hotel, grocery, and parking garage uses.

The urban design plan uses a framework of street edges and axially related parks and open spaces to help integrate the development into the surrounding commu-

The landscape elements of the common include brick-edged walkways and plazas, low lighting standards, and a variety of sculptural pieces.

Star Market is located on the second level of the same building that houses the University Park Hotel. The main entrance to the hotel is just to the right of the entrance to Star Market. Many customers arriving by car do not use this entrance, which has both escalators and elevators to the market, but instead park on the third level of the adjacent parking structure and then enter directly from there.

nity. The centerpiece of the interconnecting open-space system—and the heart and soul of the master plan—is the University Park Common. Located along Sidney Street, the main north/south thoroughfare, the common not only attracts business tenants from University Park but also brings neighbors from the surrounding Cambridgeport community to the center of University Park, helping to foster a vibrant, lively atmosphere.

The strategy for University Park could not have been successful without the close cooperation of three entities —MIT, Forest City, and the city of Cambridge—and their collaborative and creative approach to land use planning and zoning. Existing zoning ordinances could not accommodate the desired objectives and mix of uses; the solution that was chosen was to develop a master plan and to zone the property in conformity with the plan. This planned district zone—the Cambridgeport Revitalization Development District—allowed all three parties to achieve their objectives.

The plan's first phase focused on mid-rise office and R&D buildings around the common that essentially fill separate blocks, while several office/R&D buildings in later phases surround the Landsdowne Quadrangle on Landsdowne Street. Residential uses are located primarily along the western edge of the development on Brookline Street, including low- and mid-rise wood-frame buildings surrounding small courtyards and the refurbished Kennedy Biscuit Lofts in a mid-rise historic structure. One additional 11-story apartment building—91 Sidney Street—is located on the southern portion of the site and overlooks the common. The hotel is located near the entrance in a prominent location along Sidney Street, and retail uses are located near the entrance and adjacent to the hotel, principally in 350 Massachusetts Avenue (where a restaurant is located) and in 20 Sidney Street (where a Star Market grocery is located).

In addition to the district plan and zoning requirements, additional agreements ensure the plan's implementation and guarantee long-term maintenance of the

quality of the project for the mutual benefit of the parties. Along with the new zoning, Forest City, MIT, and the city of Cambridge together executed several contractual agreements, including a land transfer agreement, a set of design guidelines, a traffic mitigation agreement, and a housing plan. Subsequently, Forest City and MIT instituted a declaration of covenants establishing responsibilities and commitments for common maintenance.

The Cambridgeport Revitalization Development District establishes the overall parameters for the project. It sets the maximum total gross building area at 2.3 million square feet (213,755 square meters), limits the amount of retail space to a maximum of 150,000 square feet (13,940 square meters) of GBA, and specifies that at least 400,000 square feet (37,175 square meters) of GBA be devoted to housing. It also specifies the construction of 100 low-income units, defined as 80 percent of the community median income, and 50 moderate-income units, defined as 110 percent of median income. These

The landscape elements of the common include a variety of sculptural pieces, including this cable reel, a reminder of the Simplex Wire and Cable Company that once occupied much of the site.

The University Park common and the main Sidney Street axis, with the 64 and 38 Sidney Street buildings in the foreground and the University Park Hotel at MIT in the background. The fog fountain and the various sculptural elements of the Traces program make the common a special place.

units would remain thus designated for 30 years. The zoning also establishes the minimum amount and general location of open space. It specifies floor/area ratios and height limits for various portions of the site. It also establishes some timing requirements for the completion of the housing units and open space in relation to other development. Finally, it sets a requirement for the submission of a master plan and design guidelines along with procedures for incremental approvals.

MIT's declaration of covenants is used to bring under one management entity all development contemplated for University Park. These covenants run with the land. For example, if Forest City were to sell or if there were a foreclosure, the terms of the declaration would convey with the properties and the obligations of the covenants would become the obligations of MIT or a successor owner/land leaseholder. This conveyance is particularly important to help ensure maintenance of the private and public common areas in University Park

to the higher standards mutually expected by the city, MIT, and Forest City.

The covenants specify that the dominant owner is obligated to hire a professional management company. As the dominant owner, Forest City chooses the management company; it contracted with Forest City Commercial Management, Inc., a wholly owned subsidiary, to manage the project. This arrangement required the lenders to agree that the terms of these covenants would be superior to their debt, and the city expected the developer to take on what otherwise might be public maintenance responsibilities. It took two years to put this declaration in place.

The design guidelines, comprising both text and graphics, is a 25-page agreement among Forest City, MIT, and the city of Cambridge. In the text, bold-face type identifies requirements that must be met, while the remainder of the text is only for explanatory purposes and to give general, nonbinding direction for design.

These guidelines embody the developer's master plan, in many cases either refine or modify the specifics of the zoning district, and establish the ground rules for specific approvals as development proceeds. Among other items, they set forth the primary use patterns and general plan, quality standards for open space and the streetscape, building design and heights, parking, and pedestrian and traffic circulation.

The maintenance agreement guarantees that Forest City Commercial Management or its successor will maintain various improvements in the public rights-of-way agreed to in the design guidelines, except where the developer has provided the city of Cambridge with non-standard spare parts, such as streetlight fixtures, for the city to use in its maintenance of the city-owned areas of University Park. More important, it allows University Park's management to provide a higher standard of maintenance at its own expense. This agreement runs 15 years and has a provision for extensions.

Design of Common and Public Spaces

University Park contains four landscaped parks. At the Massachusetts Avenue entrance is Market Square Park, an attractive entry feature that surrounds an adjacent historic building and tower. At the center of the development is the largest common area, University Park common, adjacent to Sidney Street. One short block away off both sides of the common are two smaller parks that are visually connected to the common. In the Auburn Court residential area along Brookline Street is Auburn Park, and on the other side along Landsdowne Street is the Landsdowne Quadrangle, both surrounded by buildings. These parks were strategically placed at the pedestrian cross axis of University Park to attract tenants and neighbors into and through the series of public open spaces.

As designated in the master plan, the University Park common was envisioned as a common area for Cambridge residents and University Park office and residential tenants rather than as a corporate enclave isolated from the neighborhood. With its walkways, seating areas, lawns, trees, and plantings, the common is the focal point of University Park.

Art is prevalent in the common. Traces, a series of plaques and sculptures, depicts the history of University Park. Once part of the Charles River, the site was filled to expand Cambridge's land area. Oyster shells and other marine sculptures in bronze are reminiscent of the park's natural history. Once fill operations were completed, a variety of industries opened shop, including Simplex Wire and Cable, a shoe factory, a book publisher, a bakery, a candy maker, an audio products manufacturer, and a telescope manufacturer. These industries are represented by various symbolic sculptures, including a shoe, a cable spool, and a copper candy vat, placed throughout the common.

The major new tenants at University Park produce pharmaceutical and biotech products and are represented as well. Also featured in the public art program and placed throughout the park are 18-inch-square (45-centimeter-square) granite blocks with sandblasted symbols of hydrogen, lithium, and other elements of the periodic table. They are intended to reflect the project's association with MIT. Some are freestanding on the lawn, others laid out in a row near the main entrances to the buildings.

A final design element worth mentioning is the fog fountain. Because Boston's frigid winters make it difficult to operate a fountain year round, the design team came up with the concept of a fog fountain, which would graphically convey the site's beginnings as a salt marsh yet not freeze. It is powered by a compressor pump that forces water through a high-pressure hydraulic line and out of nozzles to produce fog. All these sculptural elements serve as place makers that help distinguish the common and mark the history of the University Park site.

Office Buildings

Flexible and high-quality architecture and engineering drove much of the project's office building design, which had to appeal to MIT, the community, and the tech/biotech markets. Because they had to serve all users, all office/R&D buildings were designed with above-standard flexibility and capacities. Floor-to-floor heights are 15.5 feet (4.7 meters) on the first floor and 13 feet, 8 inches (0.2 meter) for upper floors of most buildings, compared with a standard of 12.5 feet (3.8 meters) slab to slab for office buildings. Later buildings will have heights of 15 feet (4.6 meters) on the upper floors and 18 feet

The entrance pylon in Market Square Park and the historic tower mark the entrance to University Park at MIT.

(5.5 meters) on the first floor. Floors are designed for loads of 125 pounds per square foot (610 kilograms per square meter), compared with a standard of 80 pounds per square foot (390 kilograms per square meter). Power capacity is 25 watts of power per square foot (270 per square meter), compared with the standard of eight to ten watts per square foot (86 to 108 per square meter) for modern office space. All buildings have freight elevators and interior loading docks concealed from the street.

The buildings are designed to allow for flexibility, and the developer does not provide any special features to meet tenants' specific requirements. Such features must be paid for using buildout funds in each lease. The general character of design is spelled out in the design guidelines, with each building having a clearly identifiable base, middle, and top; brick and stone are the major facade materials.

Private conduits in all the streets are stubbed up to all the building sites, providing the flexibility to meet almost any utility requirements in the future without having to tear up the streets. Because the developer owns these conduits, their use by a tenant can be negotiated in the lease, with future additional use requiring payment of an access fee.

Extra vertical mechanical chases in the buildings will accommodate future demand for utilities and telecommunications cables. All buildings have redundant power feed to two separate substations to minimize power interruptions.

Although the master plan limits the allowable amount of retail space to 150,000 square feet (14,000 square meters), the developer recognized that the city's attitude toward permissible retail use might change. Therefore, it designed the fronts of the buildings along Sidney Street so that they can be easily converted to retail use without remodeling street-level facades.

Housing

Although Cambridge was once a mainly blue-collar city, it has seen an influx of wealthy residents over the past decade, driving up housing costs. Cambridge already has many traditional public housing units. For this project, however, the city wanted a significant number of affordable housing units that would help fill the gap between true public housing and the increasingly expensive open market. Thus, of a minimum total of 400 units, the plan for University Park requires that at least 150 be affordable—100 units for low-income families and 50 for moderate-income residents. The remaining units may be leased at market rate.

The majority of this requirement for affordable housing was provided through the subleasing of a site in University Park, adjacent to the existing residential neighborhood, to a nonprofit housing developer, Homeowners Rehab, Inc. (HRI). At Auburn Court, HRI has developed 137 rental units in two phases, 91 of which are reserved as affordable units. In conjunction with Keen Development Company, a local residential developer, Forest City

also converted the F.A. Kennedy Steam Bakery into the 142-unit Kennedy Biscuit Lofts, which has 64 affordable units. Even though the zoning required 400 units, it did not preclude a greater number of units, provided there was an equivalent reduction in the amount of office/R&D space. As the project evolved and with the elimination of rent control in 1996, improving the financial feasibility of developing rental apartments, the total number of housing units to be built has increased. The current ratio of 24 percent affordable units is well above municipal goals for the city as a whole.

The most recent addition is 91 Sidney Street, completed in 2002, which features 135 market-rate apartment units in an 11-story, concrete-frame brick and glass building overlooking the common.

Financing

Forest City acquired each development parcel in the park through a 75-year ground lease, taken down at the start of construction, which marks the final acquisition date and triggers the lease period. Base rent is calculated as a percentage of MIT's average basis in land value, adjusted for certain cost factors and for inflation between the execution of the initial development agreement and the time each ground lease is consummated. For the initial parcels, the cost basis was about $13.00 per square foot ($140 per square meter); by 2000, it had risen to about $40.00 per square foot ($430 per square meter). MIT was responsible for the demolition of existing build-

Auburn Court is an affordable housing community along one edge of University Park that was developed by Homeowners Rehab, Inc., using a ground sublease ($2,000 per unit) from Forest City, the master developer.

ings (with the cost included in its basis), and both parties share equally in the cost of environmental remediation. Otherwise, the land is delivered as is; therefore, ground rent is net to MIT. This component of ground rent is senior to first-mortgage debt but is relatively small; hence, it has not impeded the securing of mortgage financing.

In addition, MIT participates in the growth of income derived from the project over time, receiving 15 percent of cash flow above a base established when each building is initially 90 percent leased, as well as a 15 percent participation in net refinancing and sales.

Forest City is a nonrecourse borrower. Each commercial building project was financed separately using conventional financing, and most financing was done on the basis of small incremental mortgages that are converted to a master mortgage when further financing is no longer needed. The residential projects, particularly those with affordable components, have been financed with Massachusetts bond funds or other financing sources dedicated to housing. During the downturn in the market in the early 1990s, financing generally was not readily available. Although space was in demand, biotech tenants were not generally financeable at the time.

Tenants and Marketing

One of Forest City's principal strategies for University Park—with its proximity to MIT and Harvard—was to develop office buildings flexible enough to address the evolving needs of high-tech companies while responding to fundamental shifts in the high-tech industry over time. The first buildings targeted high-tech industries such as defense, computer, and software firms. In the late 1980s, however, just as these first buildings were completed, demand from these previously hot sectors in Cambridge slowed and a new technology-based industry—biotechnology—emerged from university research laboratories. Startup biotech companies may require as long as a decade to achieve significant revenues, let alone a profit, so many developers and lenders were not inclined to risk their capital to build facilities for the fledgling biotech industry. Forest City, however, although recognizing the inherent risk also understood this opportunity to serve an emerging market niche during a time when other sectors of the economy were in decline.

The flexibility built into the structures at University Park—generous floor-to-ceiling heights, large ventilation shafts, and greater-than-average power capacity—was originally geared for high-tech users but also met the functional needs of the growing biotech sector. Biotech research facilities, however, have significant requirements for HVAC, plumbing, and electrical distribution, driving the cost of improvements to three to four times that of traditional office space. Working creatively with lenders, Forest City identified ways of financing tenant improvement allowances of $75.00 to $90.00 per square foot ($810 to $970 per square meter), achieving commensurately higher rental rates in return. Experience has proved that despite the high initial investment they require, biotech

The bridge between these buildings was added during construction to provide a connection, because the buildings were leased to one tenant. The vista under the bridge leads to the Auburn Court residential component and then to the adjacent community.

research facilities hold their value well and in fact are generally adaptable by second- and even third-generation occupants with very little modification. Although Forest City did not initially intend to develop a biotech park, biotech firms now occupy 90 percent of the 700,000 square feet (65,055 square meters) of R&D space offered at the park.

Although the quality of the project and the master plan always have been important components of University Park's marketing program, prospective tenants generally have not been willing to pay higher rents to acquire them. In fact, some discounts had to be offered until the common was finished and the master plan became obvious. Costs associated with the parks and streetscape and the significant private investment in infrastructure have been absorbed into the project's overall cost structure.

Marketing was accomplished by establishing a relationship with Meredith & Grew, a premier and well-

Millennium Pharmaceuticals
and Cereon Genomics occupy
two R&D high-tech buildings
at 45 and 75 Sidney Street.

Courtesy of Forest City Enterprises

known Boston brokerage firm. Because of Meredith & Grew's reputation, Forest City did not advertise locally or nationally. Moreover, the hotel has served as a marketing tool for the entire development.

All office buildings were preleased before the start of construction. For example, in Phase III, Millennium Pharmaceuticals and Cereon Genomics, which became the tenants of 45/75 Sidney Street, approached the developer looking for space with a time deadline. In Phase IV, two buildings provided expansion space for Millennium and one building for Alkermes, a biotech company that was a startup in the first phase. Millennium will occupy about 50 percent of the total R&D space in University Park and has become a campus within a campus. Thus, many tenants in later phases are the result of early tenants' internal growth.

On the residential side, Kennedy Biscuit Lofts and 91 Sidney are marketed by Forest City Residential Group from its headquarters in Cleveland, with on-site managers. Because rental units are in short supply in the Cambridge market, leasing has generally occurred as soon as units become available. With their location in University Park, market-rate rental units have been able to obtain a 15 to 20 percent premium over the going market rate.

Because Auburn Court was developed independently as units for moderate- and low-income residents, the marketing strategy targeted the pent-up demand for affordable housing.

University Park's Web page is used as a marketing and informational tool for both new and existing audiences.

Management

Property management at University Park is provided for under an unusual legal structure. A declaration of covenants and a maintenance agreement jointly commit Forest City, MIT, and the city of Cambridge to the management and maintenance of University Park. The declaration sets forth management responsibilities, the basis for assessments, and the relationship between the common areas and tenant buildings, providing for a single management entity for both. It also specifies certain responsibilities for the maintenance of Auburn Park's open areas, regardless of the fact that this land is subleased and under a separate agreement.

Maintenance responsibilities for the common area include those for the common open space, the outside walls of buildings and garages, and management of the traffic mitigation agreement, another requirement of zoning. Its principal feature is participation in the Charles River Transportation Association, which operates the EZLink shuttle bus system that provides its affiliate members with access to each other and to public transit facilities, including North Station in downtown Boston.

Property management inside the office/R&D buildings is typical for the area. Building common area maintenance charges in 2000 were $6.30 per square foot ($70 per square meter) net rentable space, not including taxes, and exterior CAM charges were $0.88 per square foot ($9.50 per square meter). The latter covers grounds maintenance and exterior security. For tenant improvements, the chief engineer oversees construction and manages contractors' access. All cable and power suppliers must use the University Park conduits in the streets and pay use fees. For the buildings, use of risers is defined in the lease agreement.

Security is provided 24 hours a day. Each building has a security guard; a security van tours the interior streets, the perimeter of the park, and the parking garages; and foot and bike patrols are present. A guard escorts tenants to their vehicles in the garages upon request. Management uses its own security personnel for all events except for those where alcohol is served, as serving alcohol requires a city permit and a fee for the city to provide police oversight.

Management also programs activities in the common areas. Current activities include festival events, tenants' use of open spaces (for a fee) for their own special events, tenant appreciation days, and seasonal decorations. Any revenues generated by these activities are used to offset assessments. Other tenant amenities include an arrangement with the hotel for shared concierge services.

Experience Gained
Many features of University Park at MIT increase its likelihood of success:

- It has an optimal ownership/financial structure for carrying the land at a low cost.
- It was undertaken in a high-value market where supply was tight, allowing it to achieve the higher rents necessary to support the higher costs of an urban campus.
- The master plan incorporates flexibility, allowing changes to be made over time to respond to the market.
- It was designated as a special zoning district.
- It has the right location and a high-quality urban campus environment, which allowed the project to weather the economic downturn of the early 1990s.

Several things could have been done differently:

- Underestimating the difficulty of working with a community and having a major institution as an arm's-length partner caused tension, and the community's expectations extended the time needed to obtain approvals.
- As the project has evolved, it has become clear that the developer should have sought a greater amount of retail space, both to help create a sense of place and to meet the needs of the market.

Site plan.

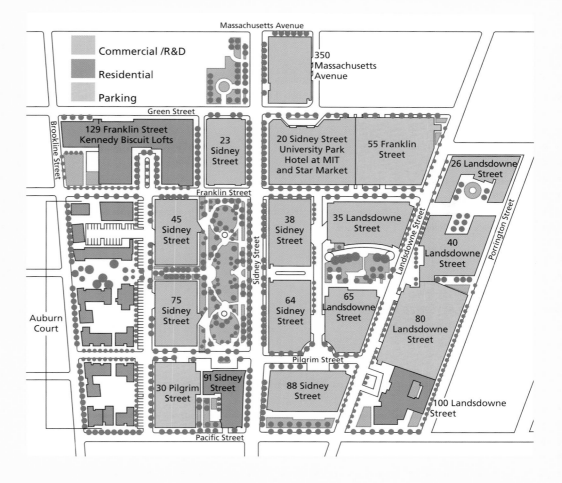

Project Data: University Park at MIT

Land Use and Building Information

Site Area — 27 acres (10.9 hectares)

Gross Building Area — 2.3 million square feet (213,755 square meters)

	Existing Square Feet (Square Meters)	Planned Square Feet (Square Meters)	Total Square Feet (Square Meters)
Office net rentable area	703,100 (65,345)	681,000 (63,290)	1,400,000 (130,110)
Retail gross leasable area	75,000 (6,970)	25,000 (2,325)	100,000 (9,295)
Hotel rooms	210	0	210
Residential units	414	46	460
Structured parking spaces	2,800	0	2,800

Floor/area ratio — 7.4

Building Phase	Use	Size Square Feet (Square Meters)	Cost (Million)
Phase I: 1987–1996			
26 Landsdowne Street	R&D	100,000 (9,295)	
38 Sidney Street	R&D	122,000 (11,340)	
64 Sidney Street	R&D	126,000 (11,710)	
Total R&D		348,000 (32,340)	$57.6
Kennedy Biscuit Lofts	Residential	142 units	$21.2
Auburn Court, Phase I[1]	Residential	77 units	
Total Phase I			$78.8
Phase II: 1996–1998			
350 Massachusetts Avenue	Office	100,000 (9,295)	
350 Massachusetts Avenue	Retail	18,000 (1,675)	
20 Sidney Street	Hotel	210 rooms	
20 Sidney Street	Grocery	50,200 (4,665)	
55 Franklin Street	Garage	950 spaces	
Total Phase II			$78.7
Phase III: 1997–1999			
45/75 Sidney Street	R&D	276,700 (25,715)	
30 Pilgrim Street	Garage	600 spaces	
University Park Common	Open Space	1.25 acre (0.5 hectare)	
Total Phase III			$70.0

Phase IV: 2000–2002			
35 Landsdowne Street	R&D	201,300 (18,710)	$59.4
40 Landsdowne Street	R&D	212,000 (19,705)	$66.0
65 Landsdowne Street	R&D	122,400 (11,375)	$37.5
80 Landsdowne Street	Garage	1,130 spaces	$20.8
88 Sidney Street	R&D	145,300 (13,505)	$48.3
91 Sidney Street	Residential	135 units	$36.2
Auburn Court, Phase II[1]	Residential	60 units	
Landsdowne Quadrangle	Open space	0.5 acre (0.2 hectare)	
Total Phase IV[2]			$332.5

Phase V: 2002–2004		
100 Landsdowne Street	R&D	241,130 (22,410)
23 Sidney Street[3]	Residential/retail	In planning

Development Cost Information

Total development cost — $600 million

Residential Information

Location	Unit Size (Square Feet/ Square Meters)	Number of Units	Rent[4] Range
Kennedy Biscuit Lofts	692–1,800/64–167	142	$1,800–3,800
Auburn Court	670–1,200/62–111	137	$1,850–2,950
91 Sidney Street	580–1,300/54–120	135	$2,000–4,000

Office Tenant Information[4]

Net rentable area occupied	100%
Number of tenants	16
Space occupied	2,000–200,000 square feet (185–18,600 square meters)
Annual rents	$12–60 per square foot ($129–645 per square meter)
Average length of lease	5–10 years
Typical terms of lease	Triple net

Retail/Entertainment Tenant Information

Star Market	50,200 square feet (4,665 square meters)
The Asgard Restaurant	5,800 square feet (540 square meters)
Cambridge Trust Bank	3,400 square feet (315 square meters)
Espresso Royale Café	1,400 square feet (130 square meters)
GLA occupied	100%
Annual rents	$25-30 per square foot ($270-325 per square meter)
Average annual sales at Star Market	$434 per square foot ($4,670 per square meter)
Average length of lease	10–15 years

Notes

[1] Developed by Homeowners Rehab, Inc., on land subleased from Forest City for $2,000 per unit.

[2] Estimated.

[3] 23 Sidney Street is the last University Park parcel to be developed. Its use and building size are not yet determined.

[4] As of July 2002.

Development Schedule

1982	Planning started
1983	Developer selected
1987	Zoning district approved
1988	Master plan approved
2004	Projected project completion

Developer/Manager

Forest City Enterprises, Inc., and its wholly owned subsidiaries:
Forest City Commercial Group, Inc.
Forest City Residential Group, Inc.
38 Sidney Street
Cambridge, Massachusetts 02139
617-225-0310

Landowner

Massachusetts Institute of Technology
Master Plan/Urban Design Guidelines
Koetter Kim & Associates
University Park Common Design
The Halvorson Company

Architects

Arrowstreet, Inc.
Burt Hill Kosar Rittelmann Associates
Elkus | Manfredi Architects, Ltd.
Koetter Kim & Associates
Tsoi/Kobus & Associates, Inc.
Walker Parking

Valencia Town Center Drive
Valencia, California

Valencia Town Center Drive is a suburban mixed-use town center developed in the heart of the new town of Valencia, California, 30 miles (48 kilometers) north of downtown Los Angeles on I-5. It is the centerpiece of this 36,000-acre (14,575-hectare) master-planned community that was started in the 1960s by the Newhall Land and Farming Company. The town center features a pedestrian-friendly main street with office space above ground-floor retail uses, restaurants, movie theaters, apartments, and a hotel and conference center.

Valencia Town Center Drive is a prime example of suburban place making. As it took shape in the late 1990s, Valencia Town Center Drive stood at the forefront of a national trend that is remaking the suburbs. A main street and town center provide the public realm that is absent from most master-planned communities and suburban areas of the last five decades, and it meets the growing consumer demand for greater community.

The Site and Development Process
The Newhall Land and Farming Company, a publicly traded company and developer of new towns and master-planned communities in California, is the developer of both Valencia and Valencia Town Center Drive. Founded in 1883, the company owns approximately 50,000 acres (20,245 hectares) of property throughout California. In addition to Valencia, the company is building Newhall Ranch, a 12,000-acre (4,860-hectare) community located across I-5 from Valencia. Partly located within the city of Santa Clarita, Valencia has more than 40,000 residents and 40,000 jobs and is part of the Santa Clarita Valley, whose population is 200,000.

Newhall Land has always taken a long-term perspective for its real estate activities. The company broke ground for Valencia in the late 1960s, but it will not complete this new town until early in the 21st century. The company used a similar long-term approach in planning and building Town Center Drive. Its objective was to create an easily recognizable and easily marketable community center and identity within a very suburban area, thereby strengthening the regional perception of Valencia as a distinctive, attractive, pedestrian-friendly destination, not just another shopping mall surrounded by highways and housing tracts.

The 80-acre (32.4-hectare) site was surrounded by Valencia's three main arterials, had easy access to the I-5 freeway, and was the focal point for Valencia's extensive paseo (pedestrian walkway) system. Valencia Town Center, a successful regional mall designed by RTKL,

opened in 1992 and anchors the eastern edge of Town Center Drive.

Population projections and market analysis for Valencia and the surrounding Santa Clarita Valley suggested that Town Center Drive could be supported in the market by the mid-1990s, but the real estate recession of the late 1980s and early 1990s made it difficult to proceed. Nevertheless, Newhall Land decided to proceed with the project, using a conservative and methodical phased approach, despite the difficult market. Newhall Land's gamble in the real estate market paid off, and in four short years it had created a thriving half-mile (0.8-kilometer) main street with a wide mix of uses. Town Center Drive celebrated its grand opening in 1999, making it one of the first new main street projects completed in the United States.

Planning and Design
Legendary planner Victor Gruen designated the town center in Valencia's 1965 master plan as a dense downtown for the Santa Clarita Valley featuring retail space and high-rise office buildings. As the town was developed in the 1970s and 1980s, Newhall Land realized that the community and market would not support a high-rise town center. Newhall Land wanted to build a traditional main street, and Tom Lee, Newhall Land's chair and CEO at the time, envisioned Town Center Drive as a genuine community hub and downtown for the entire Santa Clarita Valley. "We wanted a lively, small town main street," says Lee, "with a traditional mix of main street uses that really serve local needs and demographics." A true main street has a broad mix of uses—office, restaurant, entertainment, hotel, housing, and retail—that attract residents, workers, and visitors from early morning until late at night, seven days a week. Newhall Land particularly wanted to bring office users to Town Center Drive to create additional jobs in the community, enabling more residents to work close to home.

To begin the planning process, company executives toured and studied main streets from Santa Barbara, California, to Annapolis, Maryland, and talked to developers, city officials, storeowners, and planners to learn what worked and what did not work on a main street. Newhall Land also conducted a one-day design charrette in 1993 to gather input and ideas from real estate professionals, architects, and planners. Although each participant came with his or her own, usually differing, ideas for the necessary ingredients for a successful main street,

Valencia Town Center Drive is designed as a lively, small town main street with a traditional mix of main street uses that serve local needs and demographics.

the company used participants' advice to further refine goals and ideas for the project.

Town Center Drive was envisioned as a contemporary version of the pre–World War II small town main street, with the addition of contemporary amenities, including plentiful parking. The street would serve office users by day and community residents at night and on weekends while making financial sense for Newhall Land.

The company wanted the street to be less regimented and urbanized than Reston Town Center in Reston, Virginia, and less casual and focused on entertainment than Third Street Promenade in Santa Monica. Newhall Land insisted that the project evoke classical main street design with varying yet complementary architectural and building styles to create a street that seemed as though it had been developed over time. The company also wanted Town Center Drive buildings to follow a Mediterranean theme, like State Street in Santa Barbara. Designers wanted to capture a similar feel while fitting the individual buildings into a cohesive whole.

Part of creating that cohesive whole meant integrating the Valencia Town Center regional mall into Town Center Drive. Most regional malls are surrounded by a ring of surface parking lots, but when Newhall Land designed Valencia Town Center mall in the late 1980s, its land planning consultant, Skidmore, Owings & Merrill LLP, advised the firm to break that traditional ring of parking and set aside an area that would someday connect directly to Town Center Drive. Newhall Land did so, and

that area became the mall's main entrance, with movie theaters, a working carousel, and fountains all waiting to connect to the future Town Center Drive.

In designing the main street, Newhall Land paid particular attention to building heights and was careful not to give Town Center Drive an urbanized appearance. Architect Scott Johnson of Johnson Fain Partners designed the office buildings to be tall enough to create a focal point along the street and adjacent buildings with gradual steps down to complement the two-story regional mall. Most office buildings are three to five stories tall with "punched" or recessed windows rather than smooth banded glass. Punched windows are more human in scale and inviting than the smooth glass corporate image look of traditional main streets.

Despite their somewhat fanciful Mediterranean facades, Town Center Drive's office buildings were designed to fit the needs of contemporary users by providing 20,000-square-foot (1,860-square-meter) floor plates and Class A interiors. The building's rear facades also have a more conventional glass wall that creates a strong office image. Additional entrances in the rear of the building allow for direct access to surface lots and multistory parking garages for use by both office workers and shoppers.

To further strengthen the pedestrian-friendly environment, the office building's ground floors feature stores and restaurants that contribute to a pleasurable sequence of sights, sounds, and experiences that encourage people

A contemporary version of the pre–World War II main street, Town Center Drive boasts many amenities, including plentiful parking and a direct connection with the main entrance of the regional mall, its eastern anchor.

to walk up and down the street. Designers created occasional interruptions in the street wall and store windows with miniplazas set into the buildings, courtyard entrances into office lobbies, and water gardens or plazas at the corners for outdoor dining or street entertainment. Ten- to 14-foot-wide (3- to 4.3-meter) sidewalks with mature shade trees, arcades, plazas, open space, and benches encourage strolling and window-shopping.

In designing the street systems, Newhall Land wanted to avoid turning Town Center Drive into a busy traffic artery. Designers specified a roadway of just 53 feet (16 meters) with on-street parking, but traffic codes demanded a four-lane, 64-foot-wide (19.5-meter) street that prohibited on-street parking to facilitate traffic flow. Fortunately, the company owned the Town Center Drive site and chose to develop the street as a private 53-foot-wide (16-meter) roadway with one lane of traffic in each direction and angled curbside parking. The company also sold land to the city of Santa Clarita to develop a

transit hub at the Town Center, which will bring more people to Town Center Drive.

The alignment of McBean Parkway proved to be a challenge for the project's designers. This six-lane north/south arterial road divides Town Center Drive in half. To create visual and functional connections between two portions of the development, Newhall Land divided the street into quadrants that choreograph activities into defined clusters, luring pedestrians from one quadrant to the next. For example, the hotel and conference center in the western half of Town Center Drive are located diagonally across McBean Parkway from the 130,000-square-foot (12,080-square-meter) Valencia Entertainment Plaza on the eastern half of Town Center Drive. The entertainment retail center acts as a strong lure that pulls pedestrians across McBean Parkway; conversely, the hotel and conference center also attract people across this arterial. The beautiful town green, which is the terminus of the western end of Town Center Drive, also is a strong visual landmark that attracts pedestrians' attention to that part of the street. And Newhall Land used the same sidewalks, tree plantings, light fixtures, and signage along the entire length of Town Center Drive to create cohesion and unity.

Mix of Uses

Finding the right mix of tenants and uses was critical to the project's success. Newhall Land sought uses and tenants that would complement and support each other. Offices feed retail shops by supplying customers for the stores and restaurants. At the same time, retail uses support offices by providing important amenities—restaurants, bookstores, clothing stores, gift shops, and coffee bars—that make employees happier and the main street an attractive location for employers.

In terms of total space, Town Center Drive has more than 400,000 square feet (37,175 square meters) of office space in four separate three- to six-story buildings ranging in size from 57,000 square feet (5,300 square meters)

The Mediterranean-inspired buildings evoke a classical main street design, as if it had been developed over time.

Designers created occasional interruptions in the street wall and store windows, inserting miniplazas, courtyards, and water gardens and plazas at the corners for outdoor dining or street entertainment.

The six-story, 244-room Hyatt Valencia Hotel and the adjacent conference center have generated considerable pedestrian traffic for the shops, restaurants, and cinema.

to 132,000 square feet (12,270 square meters). An additional 483,000 square feet (44,890 square meters) is planned. The buildings are designed and programmed to attract corporate tenants in signature buildings.

Retail space makes up 114,000 square feet (10,595 square meters) of the project, with an additional 76,000 square feet (7,065 square meters) planned. Newhall Land programmed the retail to complement, not compete with, the middle-market orientation of the Valencia Town Center mall, which anchors the eastern edge of the street. Above all, the company wanted to avoid a row of chain stores that would resemble traditional malls. For Town Center Drive, the company focused on higher-end men's and women's apparel, home furnishings, gift shops, restaurants, and cafés. Thus far, Town Center Drive has attracted Ann Taylor, Talbots, Zany Brainy, Chicos, Borders Books & Music, and many others. In addition, everyday local services such as a florist, dry cleaner, beauty parlor, medical practices, lawyers, and

accountants leased space, attracted to the project's main street ambience.

Office and retail uses were just the first programming decisions. Although hotels are missing from many of the new main street projects sweeping the nation, Newhall Land knew that a hotel would be important to the project's success. A hotel is a destination unto itself, creating important spillover that puts people (particularly business travelers) onto a street, especially in the evening. The six-story, 244-room Hyatt Valencia Hotel and the adjacent 26,000-square-foot (2,415-square-meter) conference center have generated considerable pedestrian traffic for the town center. Guests eat at the restaurants on Town Center Drive, shop at the clothing stores and bookstores, and go to the movies at the Valencia Entertainment Plaza cinema complex.

In addition, Newhall Land recognized that an entertainment center with movie theaters would be a regional draw that would strengthen the street. The 130,000-square-

The Valencia Entertainment Center is a regional draw with an 11-screen multiplex, an IMAX 3-D theater, and several restaurants and retailers.

foot (12,080-square-meter) Valencia Entertainment Center offers an 11-screen multiplex, an IMAX 3-D theater, several restaurants, and local and national retailers. The 55,000-square-foot (5,110-square-meter) Spectrum Health Club provides another regional attraction in fitness-conscious southern California.

Finally, Newhall Land sought residential uses to create a town center where people lived, worked, and visited. The 210-unit Montecito luxury apartment development surrounding the town green serves as a terminus for the western end of Town Center Drive. The town green is modeled after an English garden and features flower beds, benches, shrubs, and a fountain that is illuminated at night. The apartments add a residential base and village quality to the town center, while also creating additional pedestrian traffic on evenings and weekends, adding movement to the street and customers for the retail and entertainment venues.

From studying other main streets around the country, Newhall Land knew that the placement of different uses along Town Center Drive was just as important as the mix of uses. For example, a cinema and bookstore work well together, but higher-end retail stores do not prosper next to sit-down restaurants, so these uses were mainly positioned at opposite ends of the street.

Phasing, Marketing, and Financing

On September 15, 1995, Newhall Land broke ground on 24300 Town Center Drive, the first speculative office building constructed in greater Los Angeles since 1990 and the subsequent real estate recession. The three-story, 57,000-square-foot (5,300-square-meter) building was completed in 1996. The company did not market the building as the founding property of Town Center Drive. Instead, Newhall Land used conventional marketing, which focused on the building as a stand-alone project with a 20,000-square-foot (1,860-square-meter) floor plate, stressing the advantages of locating in Valencia and casually mentioning the plans for a future main

street. With 24300 Town Center Drive leading the way, Newhall Land had the marketing tool it needed to generate sufficient interest for additional buildings.

In June 1997, Princess Cruises, one of the nation's three largest cruise companies, signed a 15-year lease for 100,000 square feet (9,300 square meters) on the top five floors of 24305 Town Center Drive. When the building was completed in 1998, the company relocated 600 employees from its Century City headquarters to Valencia. Peter Radcliff, president of Princess Cruises, said one reason his company chose to locate in Valencia was the city center environment. In early 2001, Princess Cruises moved the rest of its headquarters to two new Town Center Drive buildings, bringing a total of 1,500 employees to the street.

In August 1998, the Hyatt Valencia Hotel opened, and in mid-1999, Town Center Plaza, a two-story mixed-use building, opened just west of the hotel. This 26,000-square-foot (2,415-square-meter) retail and office building serves a variety of locally owned retail and professional tenants. Mid-1999 also saw the opening of the Valencia Entertainment Plaza; the two-story Entertainment South Building with restaurants and stores opened across from Valencia Entertainment Plaza in 2000.

Newhall Land celebrated the official opening of Town Center Drive in October 1999, but the company is still exploring additional development, including office, apartment, and retail opportunities on the west side of McBean Parkway. The company would also like to add

Princess Cruises moved its headquarters into three buildings along Town Center Drive because of the project's city center environment.

civic uses on or adjacent to Town Center Drive, such as a library or community theater.

In phasing and financing Town Center Drive, Newhall Land did not have the luxury of taking the everything-at-once approach used at other pioneering town centers, such as Reston Town Center and Celebration, Florida. The company developed Town Center Drive piece by piece to fit with market demand and its own budget requirements. Thus, Town Center Drive was built project by project over four years.

In phasing and financing the project, however, the company did enjoy the advantage of owning the land without debt. As the landowner and a publicly traded company, it was able to completely self-finance the new $100 million main street. The company, in partnership with Urban Properties for the retail properties, also manages much of Town Center Drive and its buildings. Newhall Land undertook the phasing and financing of the project with the understanding that it needed patience and financial staying power to let a new town center evolve, and it stuck with the long-term plan, despite the ups and downs of the economy and the real estate cycle.

Newhall Land sold the four office buildings in the fourth quarter of 2000 to Thomas Properties Group, LLC, which acquired the four properties on behalf of a public pension fund. Thomas Properties will lease and manage these buildings on behalf of its client.

Experience Gained

Newhall Land learned numerous lessons and had to overcome numerous obstacles in building the new main street. For example, Valencia's six-lane McBean Parkway, which intersects half-mile-long (0.8-kilometer) Town Center Drive at its middle point, could have been a serious impediment to pedestrian traffic. Careful design and planning of uses allowed Newhall Land to create a strong, functional connection between both ends of its new main street.

The ground-floor retail space in Town Center Drive's office buildings filled more slowly than Newhall Land had originally anticipated, because those shops were completed before the opening of destination restaurants and the 130,000-square-foot (12,080-square-meter) Valencia Entertainment Plaza. Those two uses are important local and regional draws to the entire street, bringing the customers that retailers need. If Newhall Land had it to do over again, the company might have phased the retail space to open when the Valencia Entertainment Plaza and other destination uses were in place.

To prove to residents and visitors that a Main Street exists, the developer must program events that lure people to the street. In particular, many of the post–World War II generations who did not grow up in a traditional town with a main street must be reeducated and shown how much fun it is to be in a mixed-use pedestrian-friendly environment compared with an enclosed mall. Newhall Land carefully encouraged events—a jazz festival, a concert series, family activities such as the Italian

The town green, a small urban park near the 210-unit Montecito luxury apartments, serves as a terminus for the western end of Town Center Drive.

Street Painting Festival—to lure people to Town Center Drive so they could see it for themselves.

When phasing a main street development, a special lease deal for the first tenants will compensate them for the marooned feeling of being first in an unfinished project. Retailers in particular will struggle getting the customers they need to succeed until a full retail street is in place and a critical mass of retailers has been achieved.

The private developer of a new main street must establish a strong working relationship with the local government for several reasons. Through this relationship, the municipality may provide the developer with money for costly infrastructure improvements like parking or street improvements. In return, the local government gets a new source of tax revenues, jobs, and residents. Working with the local jurisdictions can also help modify the traffic and zoning codes, which often hinder pedestrian-friendly mixed-use developments of this kind.

Most important, the developer of a new main street needs patience—lots of patience. Developers are often oriented toward short-term profits. A mixed-use main street must achieve a critical mass to succeed, which means planning for long-term profits. Staying power is critical to achieve the attractive returns that can accrue as the project is completed and matures.

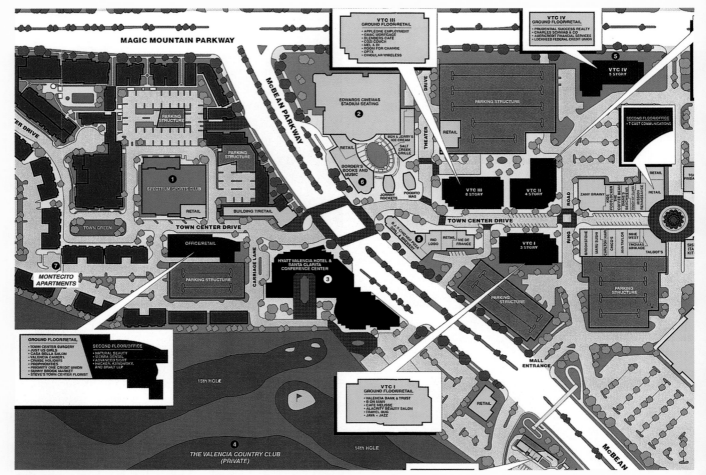

Site plan.

Newhall Land carefully encouraged events such as a jazz festival, a concert series, and the Italian Street Painting Festival (shown here) to lure people to Town Center Drive.

Project Data: Valencia Town Center Drive

Land Use and Building Information

Site Area	80 acres (32.4 hectares); one-half mile (0.8 kilometer) long
Gross Building Area (GBA)	800,000 square feet (74,350 square meters), excluding hotel, apartments, and regional mall

Land Use Plan

	Existing Square Feet (Square Meters)	Planned Square Feet (Square Meters)
Office net rentable area	400,000 (37,175)	483,000 (44,890)
Retail gross leasable area	114,234 (10,615)	76,000 (7,065)
Regional mall	790,000 (73,420)	–
Residential	210[1]	5,000[2]
Hotel rooms	244	0
Entertainment gross leasable area	108,000 (10,040)	0
Miscellaneous gross leasable area	86,000 (8,000)	0

Office Building Information

Building Name	Number of Stores	Square Feet (Square Meters)
24300 Town Center Drive	3	87,000 (8,085)
Princess Cruises I	6	132,000 (12,270)
Princess Cruises II	5	127,000 (11,800)
Princess Cruises III	4	84,000 (7,805)

Entertainment Information

Building Name	Number of Stores	Square Feet (Square Meters)
Edwards and IMAX Theaters	11 Screens + IMAX	108,000 (10,040)

Development Cost Information

Total development cost	$100,000,000

Development Schedule

1883	Site purchased
1965	Planning started
9/1991	Construction started
9/1995	Sales/leasing started
2002/2003	Project completed

Owner/Developer

Newhall Land and Farming Company
23823 Valencia Boulevard
Valencia, California 91355
615-225-4000

Principal Architects

Johnson Fain Partners
800 Wilshire Boulevard
Los Angeles, California 90017
213-622-3500

Altoon + Porter
444 South Flower Street
48th Floor
Los Angeles, California 90071
213-225-1900

Street Landscape/Hardscape Design

HRP LanDesign
3242 Halladay
Suite 203
Santa Ana, California 92705
714-557-5852

Planners

RTKL Associates Inc.
333 South Hope Street
Suite C200
Los Angeles, California 90071
213-627-7373

EDAW
350 South Grand Avenue
Suite 3920-A
Los Angeles, California 90071
213-229-0150

Skidmore, Owings & Merrill
725 South Figueroa Street
Suite 910
Los Angeles, CA 90017
213-488-9700

Notes

[1] At the west end of the street.

[2] Within one-half mile (0.8 kilometer).

WestEnd City Center
Budapest, Hungary

For more than a decade, Hungary has undertaken a remarkable transformation from its communist past toward a democratic, market-oriented future. WestEnd City Center in Budapest, the Hungarian capital, is symbolic of this dramatic change. Developed by TriGranit Development Corporation, this 2.1 million-square-foot (192,000-square-meter) project combines a hotel, offices, shopping, and leisure facilities in one of the city's best locations. With a distinctive architectural character, high-quality design and construction, and an attractive mix of uses, the project has already had a tremendous impact on the local market and has set a new standard for future development projects in the city.

TriGranit Development Corporation is a joint venture of Canada's TrizecHahn Corporation and Granit Polus R.A., a Hungarian company with extensive development experience in the Eastern European market. TriGranit was formed in 1996 with the goal of developing high-quality office and mixed-use projects in Hungary and Slovakia. WestEnd City Center is one of the company's first, and certainly its most ambitious, development efforts. Staff from TrizecHahn supervised a local project team in all aspects of the development process. WestEnd City Center formally opened in November 1999, just in time for the holiday shopping season. On opening day, thousands of people jammed into the center to see one of Budapest's most remarkable new real estate projects.

The centerpiece of the development is the shopping mall. It features nearly 400 stores in a space of 532,620 square feet (49,500 square meters), including 33 restaurants and cafés in a food court and other locations. Apart from the shops, the mall features a 14-screen multiplex cinema, a variety of active water features, and a 236,720-square-foot (22,000-square-meter) roof garden and park. WestEnd City Center also includes 204,440 square feet (19,000 square meters) of Class A office space, a new Hilton Hotel with 230 rooms, and parking facilities for 1,500 cars. The development scheme also involved the restoration of a historic building on the site and the reconstruction of a bridge over the railway tracks adjacent to the site. All these facilities are tied together by a distinctive modern design that still manages to relate well to the other buildings in the neighborhood.

The Site
WestEnd City Center is located at one of the most accessible points in Budapest. Next door to the project is the Nyugati railway station, one of the city's two main stations. Apart from being the city's major destination for com-muters, the station is itself a treasured landmark, having been designed and constructed by Gustav Eiffel, also famous for his tower in Paris. The site is served by a metro station as well as numerous bus and trolley lines. Also adjacent is Vaci Road, a major arterial street that connects downtown Budapest with the suburbs to the northeast. The result is that more than 400,000 people reach the site daily.

The traditional commercial center of Budapest is only a few minutes away from the site, and approximately 220,000 people live within a 1.2-mile (2-kilometer) radius. Moreover, Budapest as a whole has 2 million residents and receives 20 million tourist visits per year. But despite the apparent strength of the local market, there are no developments in the city that offer the scale or the quality of the shops and services found at WestEnd City Center.

The 624,080-square-foot (58,000-square-meter) site was a difficult one to develop. It was previously occupied by disused railway tracks and assorted railway buildings in various stages of collapse. Other development firms had shown some interest in the site, but none were able to move ahead into the development process. Granit Polus, the Hungarian partner in TriGranit, felt that it could do better; it acquired the site in 1997 and began to prepare plans.

Development Process
A number of obstacles stood in the way of development, the most important of which was the need for extensive negotiations with a variety of local authorities to come up with a plan acceptable to all parties. Before TriGranit even came into the picture, the city had been contemplating different uses for the site, including turning it into a municipal park. To receive approval for the project, TriGranit had to agree to a host of concessions to public authorities, including the restoration of a historic building on the site that had once been a customs house, the reconstruction of an adjacent bridge over the railway tracks (in cooperation with the city government), the improvement of a commuter railway facility, and the relocation of other buildings associated with the railway station.

TriGranit had to deal with a variety of public agencies during the development process. For example, the Hungarian Ministry of Transportation previously had control of the site and had to be consulted regarding changes to the railway facilities. The city of Budapest had authority for the zoning of the site, while a district

With its strikingly modern design, mix of uses, central location, and strong transit connections, WestEnd City Center has become one of the most important business and retail addresses in Budapest.

government in the city was responsible for issuing permits. The national Historical and Cultural Assets Commission had to be consulted throughout the development process, and a local government architectural committee had to approve the initial design and all subsequent changes. In all these cases, having knowledgeable local partners was crucial to the project's success.

Public consultation proved to be an important component in the development process for WestEnd City Center. Although the consultative mechanisms in the Hungarian planning process are perhaps not as thoroughly ingrained as in the United States, an effort was made during planning to gauge local reactions to the proposed design and to help generate the required level of political support. For instance, TriGranit sponsored a public concert at the site as a show of good faith and to give the local population a flavor of the amenities that they might be able to expect from the center. Apart from

Located next to the Nyugati train station designed by Gustav Eiffel, WestEnd City Center has one of the best locations in downtown Budapest.

these direct efforts at public relations, however, it was also essential to work within the political system of committees and approving agencies to get the project approved. In this regard, the local partners in the joint venture and the project's architect (a highly respected Hungarian firm) were indispensable. In fact, without their network of contacts and deep understanding of the nuances of the local planning and approval process, the project may never have proceeded.

Financing for WestEnd City Center was handled by local staff, who worked with four local banks to arrange a financing package worth approximately $127 million, including both construction and permanent financing. The developers had to contribute approximately $35 million in equity to the project. Of the total construction cost of $121.3 million, almost $12 million was devoted to site and building amenities such as the landscaping, water features, furniture, and signage and for utility connections for electricity, gas, water, and sewage. At $82.5 million, the retail component of the project absorbed the largest share of the construction costs.

Arranging the financing was easier said than done, however. No local banks had ever seen a project the size and scope of WestEnd City Center, so it took quite a bit to convince them that the project was not just viable but would be a success. Although this financing arrangement clearly was sufficient to get the project built, it did have its frustrations; in retrospect, the developers believe that it might have been better to arrange financing with western banks, many of whom are increasingly interested in the Eastern European market. To facilitate their future sale, the different components of the project are actually on separate parcels, a legal arrangement that does not detract from the functional integration of the center.

TriGranit used a variety of techniques to ensure that the development would be completed on time and within budget. Construction projects in Hungary sometimes suffer from poor information, poor-quality materials, and murky financial accounts. Therefore, TriGranit hired

a North American construction manager with extensive experience working in Eastern Europe to avoid these pitfalls. Materials were purchased locally if possible, but TriGranit did not hesitate to buy materials in other countries if they were more appropriate. Moreover, TriGranit insisted that construction be done with high-quality materials and methods to ensure the quality of the finished product.

All components of the project were built simultaneously, with no phasing of different components, although components with different uses were completed at slightly different times to accommodate the needs of different tenants. For instance, the retail component needed to be open in time for the Christmas rush, so the shopping mall opened in November 1999, requiring the project management team and construction crews to compress the schedule. This rush to completion was not considered as essential for the other components of the project, so they opened after all the interior fit-out work had been completed. Thus, offices were opened in July 2000, the hotel in September the same year.

An adjunct to WestEnd City Center is the historic building that formerly housed a customs office serving the nearby railway tracks. The building, considered a historic structure, had fallen into disuse. TriGranit agreed to restore the building as a condition for allowing new development on the remainder of the site and absorbed the cost of this renovation. Today the building, with a lofty atrium flooded with natural light, houses some of the offices of TriGranit staff; additional space is available to other users.

Similarly, the new commuter rail facility adjacent to the project site is functionally separate from WestEnd City Center, although it does enhance access to the development. Renovating the tracks and providing this facility was another condition imposed on the development team. Despite the fact that the Hungarian Rail Company clearly benefits from the facility, it did not contribute to it financially. Rather, it was simply a cost that

TriGranit had to absorb to proceed with plans for the remainder of the project. Although the main Nyugati railway station building was not changed in any way, upgraded platforms and a new side entrance allow commuters to exit onto the plaza in front of the main entrance to WestEnd City Center. Architecturally, this new entrance uses the same materials and style as the center next door.

Planning and Design

One of the most intriguing aspects of WestEnd City Center is its design. It is thoroughly modern in character, with the widespread use of steel and glass in the facades. A highly distinctive angled steel and glass canopy is a featured element of the main entrance to the center. An important consideration in designing the project was to ensure that it did not have a monolithic appearance. This concern was addressed by giving the center a highly differentiated facade punctuated by street entrances to the different components of the project and by varying materials and colors used. Despite the unique architectural character of WestEnd City Center, it also manages to blend successfully with the other buildings in the area, particularly with respect to height and massing. The linear arrangement of the project on its site reinforces the traditional character of the streetscape, with the architecture still respecting the forms and details of nearby buildings. Newer development projects being built in the surrounding area echo WestEnd City Center's design themes.

The layout of the project's different uses conforms to the site's distinctive shape and the need to restrict height and massing of the structures. Therefore, the uses are arranged essentially linearly. The shopping mall, which generates the most traffic and requires the highest accessibility, runs the entire length of the site, connecting the subway stop and bus/tram areas at the pointed end of the site with the parking garage at the wider far end of the site. In fact, a direct underground connection runs from the subway stop to the shopping mall.

Away from these transit connections, the hotel is nested on top of and within the envelope of the shopping center. It is separate enough from the shopping mall to achieve its own atmosphere and character, but it has a direct link from the lobby into the mall as well as a substantial street entrance and driveway.

Office space is located near the opposite end of the site from the subway connection in three buildings, and office tenants can choose to walk through the shopping mall, which runs under portions of the office buildings, or around it to get to their buildings. The offices do not have a particularly obvious interior connection to the shopping mall or the hotel but have an architecturally distinct entrance on the street. This arrangement helps to give the office component of the project its own character and helps to improve security by controlling access to the buildings.

Beyond the office space is the historic former customs house; it is separate, physically and functionally, from

The 230-room Hilton Hotel at WestEnd City Center. The lobby is decidedly modern yet comfortable and luxurious. Rooms at the Hilton have been built to the highest international standards.

the rest of WestEnd City Center. Located between this historic structure and the railway tracks at the far end of the site is a parking garage, which also includes retail space on the upper levels.

In terms of appearance, the 532,620-square-foot (49,500-square-meter) shopping mall at WestEnd City Center would be familiar to any North American consumer. Storefronts have high-quality signage; TriGranit insisted that tenants present an attractive image to shop-

Each component of WestEnd City Center has a distinctive entrance, but all are integrated into a coherent architectural whole.

pers. Public areas of the mall are spacious and bright, thanks to their generous proportions and the extensive use of skylights. Natural plants soften the environment, a 66-foot (20-meter) waterfall graces the main entrance, and other fountains are located inside and outside the center.

The shopping mall at WestEnd City Center opened fully leased in November 1999. This achievement is particularly remarkable, as the vacancy rate for retail space in Budapest shopping centers in 1999 was 18 percent. Rents for the retail space average $35.60 per square foot ($383 per square meter) per year. Since the opening, some turnover of tenants has occurred, and some flaws in the design have been revealed. For instance, because the floor plan of the mall looks something like a stretched out "B," foot traffic tends to flow into the straight part of the layout rather than the curved part, resulting in insufficient pedestrian flow for some of the smaller retailers located off the main axis. TriGranit is trying to enhance their exposure by creating stores with frontage on both walkways.

The interior design and facilities of the 230-room Hilton Hotel meet international standards. Three restaurants and cafés offer hotel guests a variety of options; the hotel also has ten conference rooms of varying sizes to offer. In addition to a state-of-the-art fitness center, the hotel features an executive floor with additional guest facilities such as access to a rooftop terrace with views of the Budapest skyline. The hotel is well inte-

grated with the rest of the project, with direct access from the lobby to the shopping mall and the nearby transit facilities.

Office space at WestEnd City Center is built to the highest international standards. The project offers more than 206,290 square feet (19,172 square meters) of space in three six-story buildings; architecturally, they blend with the rest of the center.

The primary public open space for the development is the 236,720-square-foot (22,000-square-meter) roof garden, which sits atop much of the retail space. It features abundant natural grass and an array of trees and flowers, futuristic light standards that make the garden usable at all hours, and many tables and benches where workers or shoppers can have lunch or relax. TriGranit carefully attends to the maintenance of the roof garden, and despite its location, no problems have occurred with the viability of the plantings or damage to the roof below.

Despite the center's being highly accessible by public transit, parking was a major concern in planning and design. The project currently provides 1,500 parking spaces in both underground garages and a multilevel parking structure built above a section of active railroad tracks leading to the nearby Nyugati station. As it turns out, parking is ample at WestEnd City Center. The facilities have never been full, and it is unclear when or whether they will be. Part of the issue is the cost of parking, as patrons of the shopping center have to pay to use the parking structure. This arrangement is somewhat unusual for the Budapest market, and finding the right pricing level for the parking facilities is ongoing.

The California-based Jerde Partnership International, a firm with experience in planning and architecture in countries all over the world, designed the retail concept for WestEnd City Center, with Finta Studios, a local Hungarian architect, serving as project architect responsible for most of the detailed design work. Having two architects for the same project had certain strengths and weaknesses. On the one hand, the design is cutting edge and in touch with international design trends for shopping centers while also considering local sensibilities. On the other hand, tensions between the two architects sometimes arose over the importance of certain components in the project or how some of the details of the design would be worked out. In the end, none of these tensions were destructive. The lesson that emerged from the design process was that developing a shared vision and mutual trust were essential to achieving a successful design.

Marketing, Operations, and Management

In terms of attracting attention and customers to the project, it has certainly helped WestEnd City Center that it sits on a landmark site with exceptionally high visibility in the local market. Moreover, because it was (and is) the largest development of its kind in Hungary, there was no lack of media attention about its development. More traditional methods of advertising the center have also been important. Walking around downtown Budapest, one frequently sees posters advertising

WestEnd City Center, particularly as a destination for fashion. Recognizing the importance of the tourist market, one can also find advertisements for the center in hotel rooms around the city and in the free guidebooks given out to tourists arriving in the city.

TriGranit did all the marketing and leasing in house. Expatriate staff from TrizecHahn worked on leasing with international tenants, while Hungarian staff worked with local tenants. Although a number of western retailers have set up shop at WestEnd City Center, Hungarian tenants predominate. Unlike some of the other centers in the Budapest market, all the retailers at WestEnd City Center are well established and have extensive experience in the market. When the shopping mall opened, it was fully leased.

Almost half the retailers are fashion oriented, making WestEnd City Center the largest concentration of such stores in Budapest. An interesting aspect of the Buda-

The shopping mall is the centerpiece of WestEnd City Center. It surpasses all its competitors in the local market in terms of store selection, amenities, and design.

The roof garden at WestEnd City Center provides a valued amenity and public open space for all the uses in the project, especially the hotel and office buildings, which overlook the space.

pest retail market is the relative absence of department stores, compared with similarly sized cities in Western Europe, and WestEnd City Center is no exception. The center is anchored by a 14-screen multiplex theater, a Media Markt electronics store, and a Julius Meinl supermarket. Nevertheless, these anchors, particularly the movie theaters, have been effective in drawing customers to the center. With top-quality seating and sound and a good selection of the latest films, the movie theaters have attracted more than 2 million visitors, making the WestEnd City Center cinemas the most successful ones in all of Hungary by a substantial margin.

One definite strength of the shopping mall is its opening hours. Unlike many of its competitors in Budapest, the WestEnd City Center is open weekdays from 10:00 a.m. until 9:00 p.m. It is also open late on weekends, and the entertainment facilities draw people throughout the evening. Giving consumers this added degree of choice and flexibility has helped WestEnd City Center to succeed.

A distinctive glass and metal canopy helps to define the architectural character of WestEnd City Center.

As per the management agreement, Hilton Hotels is the operator of the hotel at WestEnd City Center, although it did not participate as an equity investor in the project. Occupancy rates initially showed steady upward movement. By February 2001, the occupancy rate was still languishing at approximately 40 percent, a situation that can be attributed primarily to a substantial increase in hotel competition in the local market. Typical room rates at the Hilton are $125 to $300 per night.

To be competitive with the numerous other recently built office projects in Budapest, WestEnd City Center is targeting tenants who want to be close to a transit station and other concentrations of businesses in the city. Office tenants get the latest in communications equipment, climate control, and security features. Major tenants include Vodafone and Lucent Technologies. As of February 2001, 80 percent of the office space at WestEnd City Center had been leased, with the remainder under negotiation. Annual rents for the office space are $17.20 per square foot ($185 per square meter) per year.

Users share operational expenses for common areas at WestEnd City Center. For instance, tenants in the shopping center pay 100 percent of common area costs for the enclosed retail space; similarly, office tenants pay for 100 percent of the enclosed office building costs. Hilton provides for the maintenance of its own interior space. The office tenants and the hotel pay a defined contribution for the maintenance of exterior common areas, while retail tenants pay a prorated share of the remaining exterior common area charges.

TriGranit Management Company provides property management services for all the property's common areas, excluding the hotel interior. A separate company manages the parking facilities at WestEnd City Center, and all costs and revenues incurred by this company are part of a separate third-party contract with TriGranit. No parking contribution or reciprocal revenue credit is made to or by any of the other tenants or operators in the project.

Project rendering.

A major concern in operating in Eastern Europe is security. In some Eastern European countries, organized crime syndicates prey on small retailers through extortion rackets, and the local police are often ineffective at curbing the problem. Ensuring the safety of both customers and tenants at WestEnd City Center was therefore a top priority. In the shopping mall, the hotel, and the office areas, uniformed security personnel form a highly visible presence, and all entrances to the project are protected by cameras. These measures, along with a generally proactive approach to safety and security, have been very successful since the opening of the project.

Experience Gained

WestEnd City Center clearly demonstrates why mixed-use developments are garnering increased attention. At WestEnd, each use generates a level of activity that supports the other uses in the project. The proportions of various uses have been correctly gauged for the needs of the local market. Architecturally, WestEnd City Center shows that different uses can still have separate identities within a coherently designed and built whole. Perhaps most important, one can see from this project that mixed-use developments generate a level of interest and activity that single-use projects find hard to achieve. Whether they are tenants, shoppers, hotel guests, or simply visitors, people are drawn to WestEnd City Center, and once there, they have any number of reasons to stay.

A joint venture proved to be ideal for the development of WestEnd City Center. Each partner brought different yet complementary skills and knowledge to the development process, and both were therefore able to contribute substantially to successful completion of the project. The partners had to recognize each other's strengths and weaknesses and be able to trust the other to further the goals of the joint venture company.

Being able to compromise—with the joint venture partner, the designers, and the local authorities—was

vitally important to the project's success, especially in light of its complexity.

Substantial challenges were associated with developing a project in the Hungarian market, and some aspects of the development process, such as financing and construction, were particularly tricky. They required persistence as well as in-depth knowledge of the local partner to carry out successful negotiations.

The landmark location of the center, its exceptional access, and the high-quality mixed-use concept were compelling in the market. These factors made it worth the time and effort that it took to overcome all the obstacles.

Financing the project in euros rather than U.S. dollars would have been more appropriate, given the location of the project, the financing, and the source of materials. It also would have helped to arrange financing sooner in the development process.

Controlling the timing of the development was very important. Delays are always a possibility, but in the case of WestEnd City Center, it took an exceptional effort to ensure that the shopping mall would open in time for the Christmas season.

Given usual construction practices in Eastern Europe, it was vital to maintain strict control over construction. It was also necessary to introduce high standards to ensure the success of the final product.

An active and multifaceted approach to leasing and marketing the project was important in securing tenants for the project and in attracting customers.

Project Data: WestEnd City Center

Land Use and Building Information

Site Area   624,080 square feet (58,000 square meters), including 107,600 square feet (10,000 square meters) of air rights over the railroad tracks

Gross Building Area   2.1 million square feet (192,062 square meters)

	Square Feet (Square Meters)
Office net rentable area	206,290 (19,172)
Retail gross leasable area	532,620 (49,500)
Hotel rooms	230
Parking spaces	1,500
Roof garden/park	239,700 (22,276)

Land Use Plan

	Square Feet (Square Meters)	Percent of Site
Buildings	1,816,140 (168,786)	88%
Landscaping/open space	239,700 (22,276)	12
Total	2,055,840 (190,994)	100%

Office Information

NRA Occupied	80%
Number of Tenants	3
Major Tenants	Vodafone
	Lucent Technologies
Annual Rents	$17.20 per square foot ($185 per square meter) per year
Average Length of Lease	5 years
Typical Terms of Lease	Net lease with prorated share of building common area space

Hotel Information

Typical Room Rate	$125–300 per night
Occupancy Level	40%

Retail/Entertainment Information

Major Tenants	Square Feet (Square Meters)
Star Century Multiplex	91,400 (8,492)
Media Markt	46,270 (4,300)
Julius Meinl	39,900 (3,706)
Play Station West	25,000 (2,322)
Giacomelli	19,900 (1,846)
Marks & Spencer	9,740 (905)
Mango	7,330 (681)

GLA Occupied	98%
Annual Rents	$35.60 per square foot ($383 per square meter) per year
Average Length of Lease	10 years

Development Cost Information

Site Costs

Site acquisition	$14,200,000
Site improvement	500,000
Total	$14,700,000

Construction Costs

Office	$13,400,000
Retail	82,500,000
Hotel	13,600,000
Building owner expenses	11,800,000[1]
Total	$121,300,000

Soft Costs

Office, retail, and hotel	$27,900,000
Tenant allowance	17,000,000
Total	$44,900,000
Total Development Cost	$180,900,000

Note

[1] Includes common building and site amenities such as landscaping, water features, signage, and utility connections.

Development Schedule

3/1997	Planning started
12/1997	Site purchased
1/1998	Sales/leasing started
6/1998	Construction started
11/1999	Retail mall completed
7/2000	Offices completed
9/2000	Hotel completed

Developer

TriGranit Development Corporation
Vaci ut. 3
1062 Budapest, Hungary
36-1-238-7738

Retail Architect

The Jerde Partnership International
913 Ocean Front Walk
Venice, California 90291
310-399-1987

Project Architect and Planner

Finta Studios
Margit K`rut 39
1024 Budapest, Hungary
31-1-374-3374

Director of Construction

Otto Blau Associates Inc.
29 Arjay Crescent
Toronto, Ontario
M2L 1C6 Canada
416-445-3731

Yerba Buena Center

San Francisco, California

Yerba Buena Center is a large-scale urban mixed-use district in downtown San Francisco that has been under construction since the 1960s. The development was initiated and planned by the San Francisco Redevelopment Agency, with numerous private developers and other entities undertaking much of the development on the site. The development is anchored by the Moscone Convention Center, developed largely underground at the center of the site, and a variety of cultural institutions.

The statistics attest to the breadth and success of Yerba Buena Center: the 87-acre (35-hectare) mixed-use redevelopment project in San Francisco's South of Market Street (SOMA) district currently includes the 1.3 million-square-foot (121,000-square-meter) Moscone Convention Center, 2,600 hotel rooms, more than 20 museums and galleries, a 350,000-square-foot (32,530-square-meter) urban entertainment center (Metreon), some 2,500 newly constructed or renovated housing units, 1.5 million square feet (139,000 square meters) of office space, a block of children's facilities, and more than ten acres (4 hectares) of public gardens.

And building on the spiraling success of Yerba Buena Center, considerably more is on the way: recently opened or currently under construction are three museums/cultural centers, a 775,000-square-foot (72,030-square-meter) expansion of the Moscone Center, three hotels with approximately 800 rooms, several residential projects totaling approximately 1,000 dwelling units, and several other major retail and mixed-use projects. All told, in the next few years the project will represent more than $3 billion worth of investment in the San Francisco economy.

The magnitude of Yerba Buena Center's development is matched only by the length of its gestation. Though most of its construction has occurred in the last five to ten years, Yerba Buena Center—also known as Yerba Buena Gardens—has been nearly 50 years in the making. The project's history dates back as far as 1953, when redevelopment of some 1,100 acres (445 hectares) south of Market was first proposed. The first construction—the Moscone Center (south portion)—was completed in the early 1980s. Today, Yerba Buena Center is distinctive not only for its size but also for its focus and approach to city building. At its core is the notion that public amenities—gardens, museums, and cultural facilities—can act as a catalyst for reinvestment in a distressed urban district and serve as the nucleus for a new mixed-use neighborhood.

Development History and Process

Market Street has always been a line of demarcation in San Francisco; the wide avenue physically divides the street pattern to the north and south and psychologically separates SOMA from the more northerly precincts. As the North of Market area evolved into the city's business center and elite address, the once fashionable SOMA gradually drifted into industrial and secondary commercial uses interspersed with deteriorated hotels and other lower-rent uses. By the 1950s, considerable interest had arisen both in "reclaiming" the district and in providing for the city's growing hospitality industry.

In 1961, a 156-acre (65-hectare) area was designated as a redevelopment area but later reduced to 87 acres (35 hectares), with a core 25-acre (10-hectare), three-block area. Federally funded acquisition of properties began in the 1960s. In 1964, under the direction of Justin Herman, the city's redevelopment director, the noted Japanese architect Kenzo Tange was retained to develop a plan for the central three blocks of Yerba Buena. The Tange team's plan called for 9 million square feet (836,400 square meters) of development, including a convention center, sports arena, and 1 million square feet (93,000 square meters) of offices. Adopted five years later, in 1969, the plan envisioned futuristic-looking megastructures on each block, with prominent spiral-ramped parking garages. In the spirit of the times, the plan was self-contained, without reference to its neighborhood setting, and in fact consciously walled off its urban context.

Implementation of the plan was slow as a result of lawsuits filed on behalf of displaced residents of the area, which rendered development unfinanceable. In 1971, Schlesinger/Arcon Pacific was selected to develop the project. An apparel mart was proposed in lieu of a portion of the office uses, and ultimately the sports arena was scrapped as well. But with the project still stalled by budget issues and community opposition, in 1976 the new mayor, George Moscone, formed a "select committee" to reconsider the undertaking. The committee "included everyone from advocates of lawn planting to [adherents of] the original plan," recalls Helen Sause, deputy executive director of the San Francisco Redevelopment Agency and project manager for Yerba Buena since 1980.

In six months of intensive public hearings and meetings, the select committee along with the redevelopment agency forged a consensus plan: public amenities—open space, cultural facilities, and children's uses—would be central to the project's concept; the convention center could proceed but only if primarily below grade; and

Yerba Buena Center is a diverse district that relies on attractive public spaces and a variety of uses, especially cultural uses, to create a strong sense of place in the heart of San Francisco. In the background is the Four Seasons Hotel and Residences.

replacement housing would be integrated into the project's design. Based on these concepts, the Board of Supervisors approved the project in 1978, and the pending lawsuits were settled. The first phase of the convention center, named for Mayor Moscone (who was assassinated in 1978), soon began construction on Central Block 3 (the third block south of Market Street); it opened to the public in 1981, almost 20 years after it was first planned.

Initially, the agency sought a master developer to formulate and implement a plan for developing the central three blocks. The developer would build both the public and private portions of the project. Based on a 1980 Request for Qualifications, a team headed by Olympia & York and including the Marriott Corporation and Willis Associates, was selected to negotiate a development and disposition agreement (DDA) with the city. The 14-volume agreement was signed four

The San Francisco Museum of Modern Art (left) and the new W San Francisco Hotel (right), directly to the east of the Esplanade. The museum, completed in 1995, is one of the most distinctive buildings at Yerba Buena Center and one of the biggest draws.

years later in 1984, and the Olympia & York team completed the first project—a 1,500-room Marriott hotel—by 1989. Concurrently, other developers began to construct replacement housing and other residential and commercial projects on adjacent blocks in the larger project area.

At the end of the 1980s, the economy took a downturn, however, and it eventually became clear that the Olympia & York team would not be able to fulfill its obligations. It also became clear that to attract investment to the project, the agency would have to take a greater hand in sponsoring and directing the design of the central open space—the Esplanade Gardens—and the cultural facilities, in particular the Yerba Buena Center for the Arts. In 1993, the agency terminated its agreement with the Olympia & York team, and the developer forfeited some $26 million it had paid the agency for a series of time extensions.

Over the years of false starts, the plans for Yerba Buena moved steadily away from the monolithic early plans and the strategy of a single master developer to a more complex urban and architecturally richer matrix of individual but interrelated projects. Phase II of the convention center—Moscone North—a mostly underground facility below Central Block 2, opened in 1992, and the 6.5-acre (2.5-hectare) Esplanade Garden and East Garden on its roof was completed in 1993 along with the two Center for the Arts buildings. The Museum of Modern Art, SFMOMA, opened in January 1995. The

ten-acre (four-hectare) children's facility constructed on the roof of the first phase of Moscone Center (Central Block 3) opened in October 1998, followed by Metreon (built over the Marriott's subterranean ballroom) in June 1999.

Planning and Design

The central feature of the Yerba Buena plan is Esplanade Garden, located above Moscone Center North. Designed by Romaldo Giurgola with MGA Partners and Omi Lang, the garden is used by workers, residents, tourists, and convention visitors alike. Within the garden are several smaller theme gardens and areas as well as café structures and the offices of the nonprofit Yerba Buena Alliance and the garden's management. Esplanade Garden is the location of organized events programmed by Yerba Buena Alliance as well as informal activities. Adjacent to Esplanade Garden, between the two Center for the Arts buildings, is the more intimate East Garden.

Esplanade Garden on Central Block 2 is connected to the children's facilities on Central Block 3 by a pedestrian bridge over Howard Street; it will eventually be connected north to Market Street and the Bay Area Rapid Transit (BART) station by Yerba Buena Lane, a new mid-block pedestrian way through Central Block 1. A new public plaza is now open at the Market Street end of Yerba Buena Lane, and a second plaza—Jessie Square—will be constructed in front of the historic Jessie Street substation, tying the planned Jewish and Mexican museums and the 1872 St. Patrick's church into Yerba Buena Lane. The strategy of the Yerba Buena plan is to use this open space as the common link between the various uses and structures in Yerba Buena Center and as the common focus and amenity for the greater Yerba Buena neighborhood and SOMA district.

The corollary of the gardens-as-central-focus concept is a reliance on a multiplicity of developers and designers to build out the Yerba Buena Center plan around the gardens. To date, more than 15 developers and 20 architects have been active within the project area's boundaries. The intention of this strategy is to echo the more fine-grained nature of the surrounding city. The redevelopment agency is also consciously encouraging design excellence at Yerba Buena as a means of creating a special identity and attraction at Yerba Buena Center. The list of architects at Yerba Buena, from Japan's Fumihiko Maki to San Francisco's Stanley Saitowitz, represents some of the best architectural talent practicing today.

Yet while some of the buildings produced at Yerba Buena Center are acknowledged for their design, compromises have had to be made that affect the cohesiveness of Yerba Buena Center from the standpoint of design and function. Because of a high water table, the Moscone Center could not be completely built underground. As a result, Esplanade Garden is raised up to four feet (1.2 meters) above grade in places, making the pedestrian connection somewhat less clear and inviting. Complicating the issue further were the challenges of accom-

Yerba Buena Center for the Arts Theater, designed by James Stewart Polshek, is an example of the exceptionally high quality of design at Yerba Buena Center.

modating structures required for below-grade ventilation, exits, and service entrances, which have resulted in further visual and physical obstruction. The issue is most pronounced along Third Street, where blank walls and a full grade level separate SFMOMA from the Yerba Buena Center for the Arts and Esplanade Garden. Efforts have been made to mitigate this condition by the installation of the East Fountain and park along the street edge, intended to announce the gardens beyond.

An aerial view of Esplanade Garden, with the Center for the Arts and the San Francisco Museum of Modern Art in the background.

These issues aside, Yerba Buena has become a powerful economic and urban development engine. A rundown of the multiple components of Yerba Buena Center reveals a diverse district with an enviable momentum. The overall plan generally concentrates the convention center, gardens, and cultural and entertainment facilities at the center of the site, hotel uses on the northern edge, housing on the southern and western edges, and office and commercial uses on the eastern and southern edges, although there is a general mixture of uses throughout the site.

The Development Program

The development program is driven by convention facilities, cultural facilities, hotels, retail/entertainment/recreation facilities, and housing, which together with the public open spaces are the dominant land uses and main generators of activity in the district. Office uses are also important elements that have been drawn to the district because of the amenities and sense of place that have been created.

Convention Facilities. Convention facilities are the focus of Yerba Buena Center; they currently include 1.3 million square feet (120,800 square meters) of space located primarily underground at Central Blocks 2 and 3. Eight years after its first expansion, the center is being enlarged once again. The current expansion—Moscone West—with approximately 775,000 square feet (72,000 square meters), began construction in early 2000 and was expected to open by spring 2003.

Cultural Facilities. The primary cultural facilities are concentrated along Third Street at the edge of Central Block 2. The San Francisco Museum of Modern Art, completed in 1995, is perhaps the highest-profile cultural facility at Yerba Buena Center. In the year after its distinctive Mario Botta–designed structure opened, SFMOMA attendance quadrupled, from an average of 220,000 visitors in its old Civic Center facility to 820,000 in its first year at Yerba Buena Center.

The nonprofit Yerba Buena Center for the Arts, located adjacent to Esplanade Garden and directly across the street from the SFMOMA, is a second major contributor to Yerba Buena Center's reputation as an arts center. Consisting of two separate facilities and structures, the Galleries and Forum, and the Theater, the facility hosts the productions of local arts groups as well as national and international artists and performers.

Three new cultural facilities were expected to open in 2003: 1) a Jewish museum designed by Daniel Libeskind in the historic 1905 Jessie Street power substation, 2) a Mexican museum designed by Ricardo Legorreta adjacent to Jessie Square along Mission Street, and 3) the African American Cultural Institute.

Hotels. Hotels are generally concentrated on the north side of the Yerba Buena Center, including four major hotels in the district and others just beyond the boundary. Demand for hotel rooms has been strong and growing, based on the strength of the Moscone Center convention business, the general strength of San

Metreon, an urban entertainment center developed by Sony and Millennium Partners/WDG, opens onto the street and the Esplanade Gardens. It has surpassed expectations for attendance, with 8 million to 10 million visitors in the first year of operation.

Courtesy of Perretti & Park Pictures

Francisco tourism, the local strength of Yerba Buena Center as a tourist destination, and improvement of the Yerba Buena Center/SOMA district. The 1,500-room San Francisco Marriott, located just north of the Moscone Center and one of the oldest hotels in the district, is reportedly one of the chain's best-performing hotels. A more recently developed hotel—W San Francisco—which opened in 1999 next to the Museum of Modern Art, is a 30-story, 423-room convention hotel operated by Starwood Lodging. A 280-room Four Seasons Hotel, opened in 2001 next to the Marriott and behind the historic St. Patrick's church, is part of a mixed-use facility by Millennium Partners and WDG Ventures, Inc.

Other projects under construction or in planning include the St. Regis, another hotel/residential project with an expected completion date of 2004. Developed by Carpenter & Co., the building will contain 269 hotel rooms, 102 residences, commercial facilities, and an African American cultural center. A mixed-use project being developed by Forest City Development, 835 Market Street, is also expected to open in 2004. Plans for the project include a 250-room hotel as well as retail space, entertainment, and condominiums.

Retail/Entertainment Space. The principal retail/entertainment focus of Yerba Buena Center is Metreon, an urban entertainment center jointly developed by Sony and Millennium Partners/WDG. Located on Central Block 2 and fronting on Esplanade Garden at the heart of the project, Metreon has surpassed attendance expectations, with estimates of 8 million to 10 million visitors for its first year of operation. The 350,000-square-foot (32,500-square-meter) complex includes themed amusements based on the work of well-known authors such as Maurice Sendak, games, special retail tenants such as Sony Style and a Discovery Channel store, several restaurants, and a 16-theater cineplex including a Sony IMAX theater.

A second major commercial complex, 835 Market Street, was developed by Forest City Development and

The Children's Center can accommodate 90 children in its daycare center; it includes a vintage carousel, a 12-lane bowling alley, an ice skating rink, a rooftop garden, and Zeum, a 34,000-square-foot (3,160-square-meter) art and technology center aimed at youth aged 8 to 18.

Courtesy of Perretti & Park Pictures

Courtesy of Perretti & Park Pictures

is being constructed within the historic Emporium building—just to the west of the boundary of the original Yerba Buena Center district; it is expected to open late in 2004. Anchored by Bloomingdale's, the project is expected to include 900,000 square feet (84,000 square meters) of retail space, 250,000 square feet (23,000 square meters) of entertainment uses, offices, condominiums, and a hotel.

Children's Facilities/Recreation. Yerba Buena Center includes a considerable amount of recreational and other facilities oriented toward youth and families, all concentrated on Central Block 3 above Moscone South. The recently opened Children's Center includes a child care facility for 90 children as well as a 12-lane bowling alley, a vintage carousel, a National Hockey League regulation-size ice skating rink, and Zeum, a 34,000-square-foot (3,160-square-meter) art and technology center aimed at youth aged 8 to 18. Zeum's facilities include video production, stop-motion animation, digi-

tal photography, Web page design, and a variety of other digital and multimedia tools. A two-acre (0.8-hectare) rooftop garden with interactive play facilities provides an outdoor extension of the Children's Center.

Housing. Yerba Buena Center includes a notable mixture of housing types, from single-room occupancy and subsidized senior and family projects to high-end condominiums. Housing is concentrated principally to the south and west, although newer luxury housing has been developed more recently on the north. Several smaller existing buildings at the periphery of the project have been rehabilitated for subsidized housing, and several market-rate infill projects have been constructed. One development, the Mendelsohn House, has been developed for low-income seniors.

Many of the newest developments are luxury properties. The residential portion of the Four Seasons Hotel project developed by Millennium/WDG, located on Market Street, has been very successful and has achieved

384 **Mixed-Use Development Handbook**

very attractive prices. The development includes 142 residential units (nearly all presold at prices ranging from $1.5 million to $14 million), a 100,000-square-foot (9,300-square-meter) sports club, and 60,000 square feet (5,580 square meters) of retail space. The Paramount, a 486-unit residential tower located at the corner of Third and Mission streets, offers attractive views of the city and Yerba Buena Center. Developed by the Related Companies and opened in 2002, 900-square-foot (85-square-meter) units rent for $2,000 per month or more, although 20 percent of the units in the Paramount are reserved for low-income tenants. Another 92-unit condominium building was recently completed, and two loft-style condominiums are being added to the mix. Yerba Buena Lofts also recently opened.

Offices. More than 1 million square feet (93,000 square meters) of office projects has been completed in the Yerba Buena Center project area, including buildings for AT&T and Pacific Telephone. Office buildings are located primarily on the western and southern edges of the district. Newer projects include the SOMA Square project adjacent to Yerba Buena Center.

Parking and Transit. Nearly 3,900 parking spaces are provided in several parking facilities around the district; the principal structure is the 2,515-space Yerba Buena Garage off Fourth Street on the western edge of the project across from the Metreon. A second major facility is the Moscone Center garage on the eastern edge of the development along Third Street across from Moscone South. The project is also well served by transit, with its own Yerba Buena BART station adjacent to the new Four Seasons Hotel along Market Street, and two other BART stations are located nearby along Market Street.

Financing and Management

The strategy adopted by the redevelopment agency for developing Yerba Buena Center was for the city to build or subsidize project amenities, thereby creating an environment conducive to private sector investment. The value of this investment would then be tapped to provide a source of revenue to maintain the public facilities. Thus, the city acted as developer for Esplanade Garden, Center for the Arts, and the Children's Center, and subsidized the museums through land sale writedowns. Sources of financing for the city have been multiple: tax increment revenue bonds, hotel sales tax revenue bonds, sale and lease of land and air rights, and contributions from developers.

The city retained ownership of the land under Metreon and the Marriott, and rental income from both projects is dedicated to the maintenance, operations, security, and management of the gardens, the Center for the Arts, and the Children's Center. Specifically, the city's lease for Metreon includes a base rent and a percentage rent required of the project's owners, and an obligation for garden maintenance and security assessed on Metreon tenants based on their square footage. A private firm retained by the redevelopment agency provides property management services, including maintenance and security.

In 1991, the redevelopment agency and a private developer founded a not-for-profit membership organization, Yerba Buena Alliance. The intent was to create an organization of stakeholders for the new neighborhood. Headed by executive director Anita Hill, the alliance plays a variety of roles on behalf of some 150 members, including property and business owners and residents of Yerba Buena Center and in the larger neighborhood. The Yerba Buena Alliance provides publicity and public information services on behalf of Yerba Buena Center, oversight and monitoring of the neighborhood, a forum for members and stakeholders through its monthly meetings, and generally acts as an advocate for the neighborhood. In addition, the alliance works with the staff of the Center for the Arts in facilitating outdoor events and performances in the gardens. Ranging from poetry readings to performance art, dance, and music, a schedule of events is programmed from May to October. The

Mendelsohn House, an AIA award–winning apartment complex for low-income seniors, is located on Folsom Street just south of Moscone South.

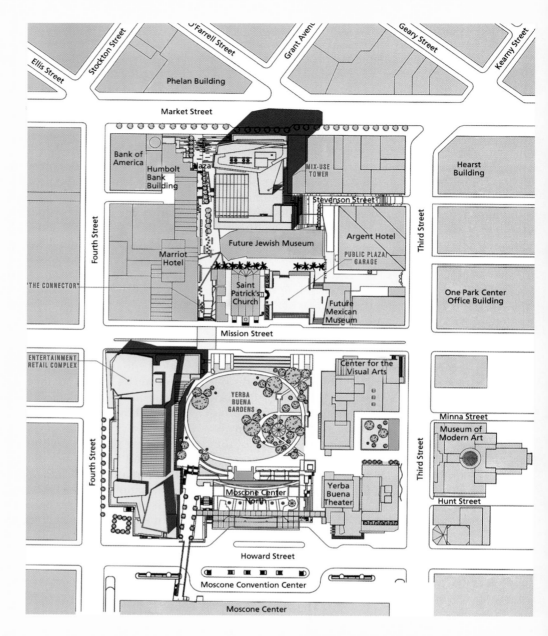

Site plan for Four Seasons Hotel and Residences and surrounding spaces at Yerba Buena Center.

operational budget of Yerba Buena Alliance is funded primarily by its members and special events income, though the redevelopment agency also contributes to the organization's operations.

Experience Gained

Development strategies at Yerba Buena Center have included developing public amenities to encourage private investment, using cultural facilities as anchor tenants, and mixing arts and entertainment to provide a richer and more varied attraction. Although many cities will not be able to bring the same level of cultural infrastructure to a redevelopment area, the concept remains valid. Cultural amenities and attractive public spaces are strong anchors for redevelopment areas and should be encouraged and nurtured.

Design strategies have included the orchestration of multiple developers to build in diversity rather than relying on a single master developer, tying land uses together using a public open-space network, and maintaining an intensity and diversity of use by mixing land uses vertically as well as horizontally. A diverse mixed-use strategy implemented over time has resulted in a district that looks like it developed over time, not all at once. This desirable outcome has greatly enhanced the diversity and appeal of this urban district.

Financing strategies have included the provision of a land lease mechanism by which the private sector provides a reliable revenue stream for the ongoing maintenance and protection of the public gardens and amenities. Mechanisms need to be in place to make certain that private properties and businesses can participate in and contribute to the ongoing management and development of the district.

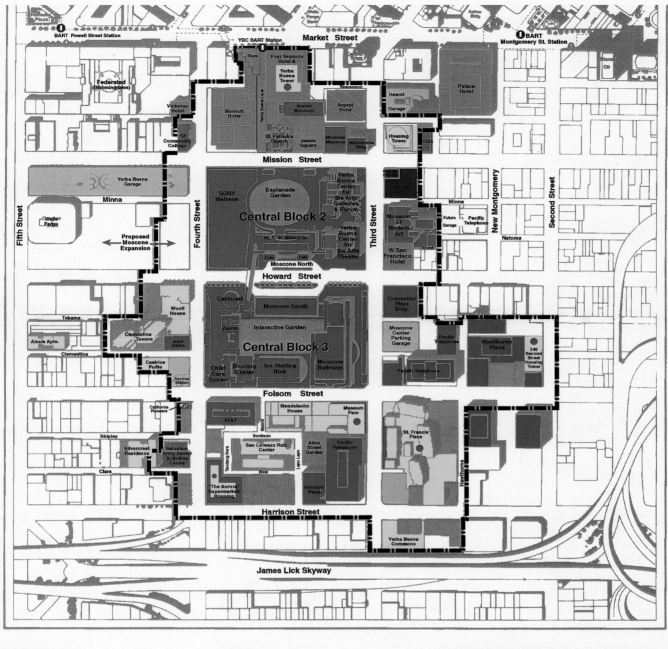

CENTRAL BLOCKS

HOUSING

MARKET RATE HOUSING

MAJOR OFFICE/COMMERCIAL/ RETAIL

HOTEL

INSTITUTIONS, PUBLIC SERVICE

AUTO-RELATED USAGE (Gas Station, Parking)

OPEN SPACE/GREENERY

RETAINED USAGE-REHABILITATION (Commercial, Office, Light Industry)

PARCELS UNDER NEGOTIATIONS

Site plan for Yerba Buena Center.

Project Data: Yerba Buena Center

Land Use Information

Site Area	87 acres (35 hectares)
Parking Spaces	3,877

Master Planner/Developer

San Francisco Redevelopment Agency
770 Golden Gate Avenue
San Francisco, California 94102
415-749-2506

District Property Manager

Yerba Buena Alliance
760 Howard Street
San Francisco, California 94103
415-541-0312

Development Schedule

1950s	Planning started
	Site purchased
1968	Construction started

Project	Architect	Uses	Construction Costs	Completion Date
Hotels and Convention Facilities				
The Moscone Center 747 Howard Street 415-974-4027	• Phase I: HOK • Phases II and III: Gensler/DMJM	1.3 million-square-foot (120,800-square-meter) convention center	$550 million	• Moscone South: 1982 • Moscone North:1992
Marriott Hotel 55 Fourth Street 415-442-6000	DMJM	1.9 million-square-foot (176,600-square-meter) convention hotel with 1,500 rooms and 135,000 square feet (12,500 square meters) of convention space	$300 million	October 1989
W San Francisco Hotel 181 Third Street 415-817-7878	Hornberger Worstell Associates	30-story, 423-room convention hotel with full-service restaurant and bar	$73 million	June 1999
Moscone West	Gensler/Kwan Hemmi/ Michael Willis Associates	775,000-square-foot (72,000-square-meter) convention center expansion	$170 million	Spring 2003
Public Spaces				
Yerba Buena Center KTB Realty Partners 750 Howard Street 415-247-6500	MGA Partners with Romaldo Giurgola	• 0.5-acre (0.2-hectare) East Garden • 5.5-acre (2.2-hectare) Esplanade • MLK Jr. memorial and waterfall • 2 cafés • Sister Cities Garden	$40 million	October 1993
Jessie Square	CTLK	30,000-square-foot (2,800-square-meter) plaza	$3 million	Mid-2003
Cultural Facilities				
Yerba Buena Center for the Arts 701 Mission Street 415-978-2710	• Galleries and forum: Fumihiko Maki • Theater: James Stewart Polshek	• 100,000 square feet (9,300 square meters) • Three galleries • Video screening room • Multipurpose forum • 775-seat theater	$43 million	October 1993

Project	Architect	Uses	Construction Costs	Completion Date
San Francisco Museum of Modern Art 151 Third Street 415-357-4172	Mario Botta	200,000-square-foot (18,600-square-meter) museum	$85 million	January 1995
Jewish Museum of San Francisco 166 Geary Street, Suite 1500 415-788-9990	• Original structure: Willis Polk • Expansion: Daniel Libeskind	70,000-square-foot (6,505-square-meter) museum	$53 million	Late 2003
Mexican Museum Fort Mason Building D 415-202-9711	Ricardo Legorretta	65,000-square-foot (6,040-square-meter) museum	$28 million	Late 2003

Entertainment/ Recreation Facilities

Project	Architect	Uses	Construction Costs	Completion Date
The Children's Center KTB Realty 750 Howard Street 415-247-6500	• Adele Naudé Santos • Landscape architect: M. Paul Friedberg & Partners	• 261,360-square-foot (24,300-square-meter) children's center • Ice rink/bowling center/café • Zeum • Carousel • Child care facility • Play circle	$56 million	October 1998
Metreon 101 Fourth Street 415-369-6005	SMWM	• 350,000-square-foot (32,500-square-meter) urban entertainment center • 15 movie theaters • IMAX • Retail • High-tech entertainment • Restaurants	$125 million	June 1999

Parking Facilities

Project	Architect	Uses	Construction Costs	Completion Date
5th & Mission Yerba Buena Garage	• 1969 phase: Bushness, Jessup, Murphy & VandeWeghe • 1993 expansion: Whisler Patri	2,515 parking spaces and service retail	$15.8 million expansion	Expansion opened 1993

continued

Project	Architect	Uses	Construction Costs	Completion Date
Residential Projects				
Woolf House I, II, III 801 Howard TODCO 230 Fourth Street 415-896-1882	Robert Herman & Assoc.	212 units for low- and moderate-income elderly	$14 million	• I: 1970 • II: 1982 • III: 1995
Ceatrice Polite 321 Clementina TODCO	Robert Herman & Assoc.	90 units of housing for lower-income elderly	$8 million	1984
St. Francis Place Third & Folsom 415-284-3014	Kaplan McLaughlin Diaz	• 410 market-rate rental units • 81 low- and moderate-income units • 30,000 square feet (2,800 square meters) of retail and office space	$50 million	1985
Mendelsohn House TODCO 230 Fourth Street 415-896-1882	Robert Herman & Assoc.	• 190 units of housing for low- and moderate-income elderly • Ground-floor commercial	$15 million	1989
Museum Parc 300 Third Street 415-495-8547	J. Stavi	• 233 market-rate residential units • Ground-floor commercial retail space	$40 million	1990
Yerba Buena Commons 88 Perry Street AMB Properties 415-975-5890	Kwan Hemmi	• 246 units of low- and moderate-income housing • Tax credit financing	$16 million	March 1997
The Aurora Apartments 788 Harrison Street 415-956-7100	VBN Architects	• 160 market-rate apartments • 17,000-square-foot (1,580-square-meter) supermarket with 73 parking spaces • 112 residential parking spaces	$31 million	January 2000
246 Second Street Monahan Pacific 1101 Fifth Street Suite 150 San Rafael, California 415-456-0600	Rony Rolnizky	• 92 condominium units (9 affordable) • Parking garage with 82 spaces	$23 million	August 2000

Project	Architect	Uses	Construction Costs	Completion Date
The Paramount The Related Companies 18201 Von Karman Avenue Suite 400 Irvine, California 92612 949-660-7272	Howard Elkus	• 492,000-square-foot (45,725-square-meter), 43-story residential tower • 500 housing units (100 affordable) • Parking structure with 292 spaces • 35,000 square-foot (3,255-square-meter) retail space	$90 million	Summer 2001

Mixed-Use Projects

Project	Architect	Uses	Construction Costs	Completion Date
Four Seasons Hotel and Residences Millennium Partners and WDG Ventures, Inc. 720 Market Ninth Floor 415-274-9150	Gary Edward Handel & Assoc.	• 750,000-square-foot (69,700-square-meter) building • 5-star 280-room hotel • 142-unit residential complex • 100,000-square-foot (9,300-square-meter) sports club • 60,000-square-foot (5,575-square-meter) retail • Landscaped pedestrian way with 35,000 square feet (3,250 square meters) of shops, public art, and waterway • 803 underground parking spaces	$215 million	2001
St. Regis Carpenter & Co. 90 New Montgomery Suite 1320 415-243-9080	SOM	• 555,000-square-foot (51,580-square-meter), 40-story mixed-use tower • 269-room hotel • 102 residential units • Commercial facilities • 20,000-square-foot (1,860-square-meter) African American cultural center	$125 million	2003
835 Market Street (Bloomingdale's) Forest City Development 785 Market Street 14th Floor 415-863-5980	KPF, RTKL, Carey & Company	• 900,000 square feet (83,600 square meters) of retail space, including a Bloomingdale's department store • 250,000 square feet (23,200 square meters) of entertainment space, including 8 movie theaters • 55,000 square feet (5,100 square meters) of office space • 250-room hotel • 65 condominiums	$400 million	Late 2003

9. Trends and Outlook

Unfavorable conditions in commercial property markets will slow mixed-use development over the near term, but long-term prospects are quite good. Even with exceptional development concepts in strong markets, starting major new mixed-use developments will be difficult until markets recover.

Over the longer term, however, the dominant trends of growing urbanization, increasing traffic congestion, rising land values, and new smart growth initiatives will lead to more mixed-use development in prime locations in both central cities and suburbs. These new projects will be shaped by a variety of trends, including growing public involvement, main street designs, new intown housing products, transit, infill development, and a variety of other issues.

Main Streets, Blocks, and Squares

Perhaps the most important trend shaping mixed-use development in recent years—and one that will continue for the foreseeable future—is the continuing shift toward traditional urban forms and urban design concepts. Whereas most mixed-use developments before 1990 were organized around pedestrian plazas, atriums, or malls, the mixed-use projects of tomorrow will be

Zlote Tarasy is a mixed-use project in Warsaw that includes retail, entertainment, office, and hotel uses.

organized around pedestrian-friendly streets, blocks, and squares. Whether it is called urbanism, traditional urbanism, or new urbanism, urbanist design approaches will dominate the mixed-use developments of the future—especially in the United States and Europe, although Asian mixed-use projects are starting to move in this direction as well. Urbanist and new urbanist design ideas permeate most of the development plans now on the drawing board, and this approach to mixed-use development will only grow over the coming years. Crocker Park in Westlake, Ohio—featuring residential, retail, and office space—uses such an urbanist approach, with the marketing theme "Inspired by Tradition—Designed for the Future."

Many mixed-use schemes will not strictly adhere to new urbanist design principles, however, and for practical and economic reasons will frequently combine mixed-use and new urbanist design approaches with single-use development approaches, each on distinct parcels but all in one plan. These plans will generally provide strong pedestrian connections between the mixed-use and single-use parcels, and developers will use these hybrid models to cast broader nets and to serve a broad range of tenants' needs and preferences.

As a result, we will increasingly see town center plans that include significant outparcels for major office tenants, big-box retail stores, or other users that are economically necessary to make the project work but do not wish to be directly in the town center. The Ayrsley develop-

Crocker Park, a proposed town center in Westlake, Ohio, features ample public open space.

ment in Charlotte, North Carolina, is an example of this approach; plans include a town center, an office district, and a multifamily neighborhood. King Farm in Montgomery County, Maryland, uses a similar approach. Birkdale Village in Charlotte includes both main street retail and big-box retail in separate sections. Many of these hybrid developments will also include large surface parking lots, at least in the short run, until future phases make development of these lots feasible.

Growing Public Sector Support and Involvement

The public sector will be a dominant force behind mixed-use development over the next five years as local jurisdictions become more proactive in planning specific areas, implementing mixed-use zoning, and building new civic uses to create places in the suburbs. Public sector planners generally are much in favor of smart growth, new

Miramar Town Center, a publicly initiated town center planned for Miramar, Florida.

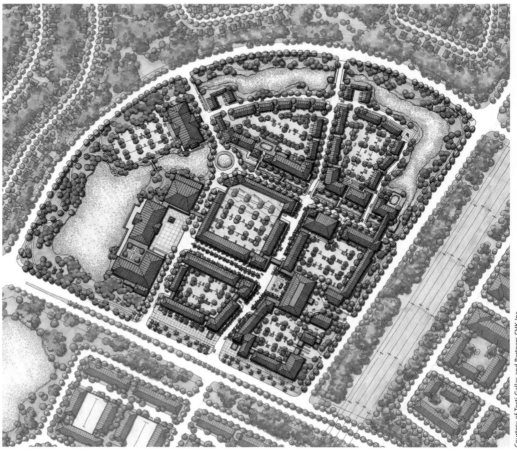

The Pleasant Hill BART Station in California, a planned transit village in the East Bay region of San Francisco.

urbanism, and mixed-use development strategies, and for significant and strategic development parcels—whether downtown, on suburban infill sites, or greenfield locations —public planners will favor or even seek to foster mixed-use development. Notably, the growing scope of public involvement in *suburban* mixed-use development is a new trend that will play a significant role in shaping the suburbs of the future.

One prevailing model for future mixed-use development is likely to be a suburban town center initiated by a local government seeking to create a sense of place for its community. Miramar Town Center, for example, is a proposed mixed-use town center being initiated by the city of Miramar, Florida. The plan involves major civic elements, including a city hall, cultural arts center, library, and education center. Initial plans also call for 437 apartments, 89 townhouses, 101,000 square feet (9,400 square meters) of retail space, and 78,000 square feet (7,250 square meters) of office space, all set among streets and boulevards with plazas and parks among them. The impetus for the project has come from growth pressures, the need for new public buildings, and the desire to create a civic identity for the community.

Lenexa, Kansas, plans a similar town center, Lenexa City Center. The idea for the town center resulted in part from a strategic planning process in which Lenexa citizens identified a desire to create a city center that would serve as a central gathering place. Because millions of square feet in the area is expected to be developed in coming years, Lenexa chose to take proactive steps to shape development in this area into a community asset, creating a special place that all citizens and visitors can enjoy.

Transit-Oriented Mixed-Use Projects

Mixed-use transit villages will emerge as an important new type of mixed-use development with their own peculiar

designs and mix of uses. The many new transit systems being developed or expanded are frequently underused, especially in the United States. The public sector increasingly recognizes that investing in transit is unproductive unless transit stations are surrounded by dense, pedestrian-friendly zones. Thus, local jurisdictions are increasingly seeking to channel higher-density development into such locations. Transit-oriented development is ripe for growth, and mixed-use projects are well suited to these locations.

Most of the many examples of transit-oriented development already in place are loosely organized districts that have not been carefully planned, and few of them can be characterized as mixed-use transit villages. Over the next five years, this situation will change as new and carefully planned transit villages are developed. These transit villages will be built principally in suburban locations, often following station area development plans and frequently involving public/private partnerships. Numerous new mixed-use transit villages are being planned around suburban transit stations in the United States, including Peterkort Station and Cascade Station near Portland, Oregon, Pleasant Hill BART Station and Richmond Transit Village in San Francisco, and North Bethesda Town Center and Twinbrook Commons in Montgomery County, Maryland.

North Bethesda Town Center, near Washington, D.C., is planned for a 32-acre (13-hectare) site at the White Flint Metrorail station in Montgomery County, Maryland. The development was initiated by the Washington Metropolitan Area Transit Authority (WMATA), which owned the land and selected the developer. The plan includes approximately 1.4 million square feet (130,000 square meters) of office space, 1,400 multifamily residential units, and 200,000 square feet (18,600 square meters) of retail space. The development is one of the largest joint development projects ever approved by WMATA and is expected to generate almost 6,500 additional daily trips at the station.

The massing plan for the proposed town center in RiverPark, a planned community near Oxnard, California.

Town Centers in Planned Communities

Mixed-use town centers in planned communities are a relatively new form of mixed-use development that will become increasingly more important in coming years. A significant percentage of suburban residential development is in planned communities of all types and sizes, and suburban housing development within planned communities is expected to remain strong over the next five years. But the single-use, low-density approach to these developments is now evolving into more varied concepts that include higher densities and mixed-use development in town or village centers. Most of the larger planned communities going forward today have been planned to include some form of town center or village with a mix of uses, and many of the larger communities include multiple mixed-use villages. Although these village and town centers are most likely to appear in newer planned communities, many older planned communities, such as the Woodlands near Houston, also are proceeding with town center developments.

A mixed-use town center on the boards for a planned community is the town center for the 700-acre (285-hectare) RiverPark near Oxnard, California, which is being billed as a "planned live-work community." At the heart of the community will be a town square surrounded by a commercial district that will include a mix of local and national retailers, the Food & Wine Expo, a convention hotel, and an adjoining office campus. The town center is planned to serve a broad surrounding market, including regional shoppers, office workers, and tourists. It is located adjacent to a freeway to increase its visibility and accessibility. Retail uses are focused around the town square and along pedestrian streets linked to nearby residential neighborhoods.[1]

Other examples include town centers for Southwood in Tallahassee, Florida, Coffee Creek in Indiana, and Verrado in Buckeye, Arizona.

More Intown Housing, More Housing Variety

Housing is the use that will drive mixed-use development over the next five years, partly because of the strong housing market and weak demand in most other sectors. Housing in mixed-use developments will be fueled by the growing diversity of housing markets and available housing products, and by growing demand for intown and urban housing products. One result will be a growing number of urban villages, a type of mixed-use project that will have a distinctly residential feel.

Housing is increasingly a market of demographic niches, each with its own housing preferences. Specifically, the number of childless households—young and old—will increase. The various segments of this group are likely candidates to choose urban lifestyles and housing products, including a growing array of intown and urban housing products such as apartments over retail, loft apartments, luxury high-rise condominiums, mid-rise apartments with structured parking, garage townhouses, and live-work units. These products fit well with mixed-use programs.

The greatest variety of housing will be most notable in suburban mixed-use settings, in both urban villages and town centers that will offer an array of housing products, with the densest urban products at the center and the least urban near the edges. One example of how this variety of housing types will be developed is the plan for Baldwin Park in Orlando, a large redevelopment proj-

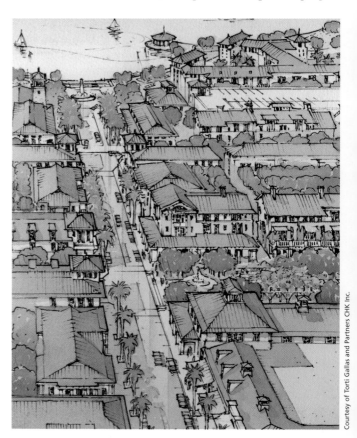

The town center planned for Baldwin Park near Orlando will include a variety of housing types and densities.

ect on the site of the former Orlando Naval Training Center. The overall plan adapts housing types traditional to the American South into a variety of new prototypes, including rowhouses, a variety of "plexes," and garden apartments. The Town Center will include 1,200 housing units in a mix of for-sale, loft, rental, townhouse, and manor house units.

Other developments that will offer a wide variety of urban housing in town centers and urban villages include Stapleton near Denver, Mission Bay in San Francisco, and Potomac Yard in Alexandria, Virginia.

Mixed-Use Retail Niches

Retail in mixed-use developments will increasingly take on the form of main street lifestyle centers, relying on a mixture of restaurants, bookstores, entertainment, and lifestyle retailers such as Banana Republic and Pottery Barn. They will most often be configured somewhere in the range of 100,000 to 300,000 square feet (9,300 to 27,900 square meters), will frequently include a combination of indoor and outdoor spaces, and will increasingly incorporate big-box retail stores in some fashion. In a few cases, mixed-use projects will include very large retail components with more than 1 million square feet (93,000 square meters), such as the project planned for Belmar in Lakewood, Colorado. For the most part, however, they will stick to smaller and more manageable retail niches.

Retail trends will continue to favor big-box stores such as Wal-Mart, Target, and Best Buy, and they will start to appear more frequently in mixed-use properties. Specialty retailers, traditionally located in malls, will increasingly be attracted to lifestyle centers and main street settings that offer lower common area costs and greater identity. Many retailers increasingly are interested in creating their own special identity and in controlling storefront design—difficult to do in many traditional mall and strip center locations.

Finding and exploiting defensible niches will be a dominant theme for mixed-use retail development. Main street retail has its limits and still faces stiff competition from the dominant malls and the plethora of big-box retailers that dominate the retail landscape. Several major mixed-use projects with sizable retail components—including CityPlace in West Palm Beach, Hollywood & Highland in Pasadena, and Santana Row in San Jose—have had difficulty, in part because they are trying to compete as regional shopping destinations without having the full range of stores offered at major malls. In the future, most mixed-use retail will likely avoid direct competition with dominant malls and will instead carve out a small but viable niche that relies in part on creating a compelling and memorable atmosphere.

Kent Station in Kent, Washington, for example, is a relatively small project of 540,000 square feet (50,000 square meters) that proposes to mix retail, office, and residential uses in a main street configuration on a 19.9-acre (8-hectare) site. The retail/entertainment component will be modestly sized and will include a cinema, supermarket, restaurants, and other retail. Even though it is relatively small, the project will be phased.

Offices and Hotels Gravitating toward Mixed-Use

Office and hotel uses will increasingly favor mixed-use environments, but in some cases they will prefer to be in adjacent rather than central locations in a mixed-use development. Because of high office vacancy rates in most areas of the United States, Europe, and even Asia, office uses will not be major drivers of mixed-use projects over the next five years. In fact, the trend in mixed-use projects in recent years has been away from office and hotel uses and toward residential and retail uses. This trend will continue over the next three to four years. Once office and hotel development markets begin to pick

Kent Station in Kent, Washington, will include a modestly sized retail main street featuring a cinema, supermarket, restaurants, and lifestyle retail.

Courtesy of LMN Architects

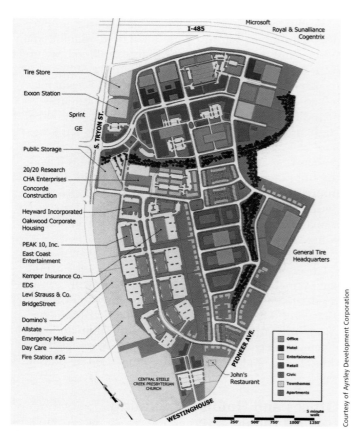

The plan for Ayrsley in Charlotte, North Carolina, includes a mixed-use town center, an office district, and an apartment district.

Courtesy of Ayrsley Development Corporation

up in four to five years, however, new office development will likely gravitate toward new and existing mixed-use districts that offer a better office environment than free-standing sites. This trend will certainly not represent a majority of the total office market, but the shift will be significant for mixed-use developments.

Mixed-use developments must remain flexible, however, to take advantage of this trend, and mixed-use design will increasingly involve low-cost low-rise office buildings, some of which will be in office campuses adjacent to mixed-use centers. At Belmar in Lakewood, Colorado, office uses in the project are being marketed as space that represents "a whole new generation of technology and office design, a low-profile, modern suburban floor plate in a high-density, urban environment."[2] The development plan for Ayrsley—a 140-acre (56-hectare) development in Charlotte, North Carolina—is being marketed as a "diverse urban tapestry of homes, shops, offices, and parks" in southwest Charlotte's growing business community. The plan accommodates offices in the town center portion of the project as well as on separate freestanding parcels.

Asian Mixed-Use Development: High Rises with Growing New Urbanist Trends

Mixed-use developments in Asia will reflect many of the trends discussed earlier, but several trends will be distinc-

tive for Asia. One is the continued preference for high-rise and high-density mixed-use projects in megastructures. Developers' and governments' preferences for major icon buildings will remain a strong force in many of these cities, and the market demand for malls and high-rise office, hotel, and residential towers will support these preferences, especially in rapidly growing areas such as Shanghai and Pudong in China. The Shanghai World Financial Center, planned to be the world's tallest building, is a prime example of this continuing trend; other examples include Kowloon Station in Hong Kong and Plaza Rakyat in Kuala Lumpur, Malaysia.

More district-based models are likely, however, to become more prevalent as new urbanist and street-oriented approaches to planning and development begin to take hold in these countries. Many western firms that are well versed in these approaches are now working in Asia. The Yangpu district master plan along the Huangpu River in Shanghai, for example, uses such an approach. These more urbanist approaches will likely be quite dense, incorporating a variety of mid- and high-rise buildings. They will also incorporate strong regional flavors, both in their mix of uses and in their designs. This combination should result in many diverse new urban districts that will represent distinctly different new models for mixed-use development.

European Mixed-Use Development: Urban Redevelopment

European mixed-use development will be driven largely by urban redevelopment; it will also reflect many of the trends discussed earlier, especially public involvement, transit-oriented development, intown housing, and the use of main streets and squares. In fact, these trends will be even more pronounced in Europe than in the United States, given Europe's strong urban traditions and preference for using more urban patterns for directing growth.

Because priorities for planning and development in many European cities generally favor redevelopment over greenfield development, mixed-use development will generally be focused in existing districts and will involve urban redevelopment sites, either in central cities or in underused industrial zones. The Gasometer project in Vienna, which involved the redevelopment and adaptive use of a historic gas plant, is a good example. Other projects in various stages of planning and development include Spinningfields in Manchester, England, River City in Prague, Zlote Tarasy in Warsaw, and Millennium City in Budapest.

Europe will also see some new urbanist mixed-use developments in outlying suburban locations that will incorporate mixed-use town centers. The Wilanow project, located adjacent to a historic palace five miles (8 kilometers) from downtown Warsaw; Genitoy, part of the new planned community of Bussy St. George in France; and Poundbury in England are examples of this trend.

The Chinese government is planning several large urban mixed-use districts along the Huangpu River in Shanghai that feature large waterfront parks, including the Yangpu district, pictured here.

A countervailing trend that will continue in Europe is the use of retail malls in some mixed-use projects. The relative lack of malls in Europe makes them a novelty that can serve untapped demand. Continued demand for more malls in both Eastern and Western Europe will lead to a higher percentage of mall-based mixed-use projects than is expected in the United States. This trend will be especially pronounced in Eastern Europe, as exemplified by WestEnd City Center, but Western European cities have also seen this trend, as exemplified by the mall planned for Diagonal Mar in Barcelona.

North American Mixed-Use Development: Infill and Greyfield Development

Peculiar to North America will be the opportunity for infill mixed-use development on surface parking lots and other underused land—often referred to as *greyfields*—in both downtown and suburban commercial areas. The downtowns in many of the newer cities throughout the South and West—including Dallas, Houston, Phoenix, Albuquerque, Salt Lake City, Tucson, Denver, Charlotte, and Atlanta—have large areas of surface parking lots and a general lack of pedestrian-friendly environments. These cities already have strong grid systems in place, and with creative planning and infill development, including residential- and retail-driven mixed-use projects, new pedestrian-friendly mixed-use districts can be profitably developed there. Denver has already made visible strides in this direction, and most of the other cities are pursuing redevelopment programs as well that will foster new mixed-use projects. Many older cities in the Northeast—Detroit, Cleveland, Buffalo, and Cincinnati, for example—have some of the same problems and opportunities.

The U.S. suburbs are also full of surface parking lots in low-rise suburban office parks and districts; these areas can also benefit from diversification through new uses on these underused parcels. These office parks are in-creasingly viewed as bland, sterile, lacking in amenities, and unnecessarily inconvenient. They have much underused land, and those that are well located will increasingly undergo redevelopment and densification programs that will lead them toward mixed-use development.

Finally, many retail malls and other shopping center sites dominated by large surface parking lots are underdeveloped or need redevelopment. These sites offer a variety of opportunities for infill development. At Brookfield Village in Brookfield, Wisconsin, proposed plans call for using underused parking lots and other adjacent parcels to diversify uses around an existing mall. Belmar in Lakewood, Colorado, is being built on the 103-acre (42-hectare) site of the former Villa Italia shopping center; it will include 1.2 million square feet (111,500 square meters) of retail space, 1,300 homes, 900,000 square feet (83,600 square meters) of office space, a 250-room hotel, and four acres (1.6 hectares) of parks, plazas, and greens.

Other examples of greyfield redevelopment projects in various stages of planning include Cherry Hill Town Center on the site of a horse racing track in Cherry Hill, New Jersey, and Brookwood Village in Birmingham, Alabama, on the site of a mall.

Creating Manageable Development Projects

A fundamental issue facing developers of mixed-use projects over the next decade is managing the considerable risk involved and controlling development costs. Well-designed mixed-use projects can generate rent premiums, but if these premiums come with higher development costs, returns will be no different from more ordinary products. Higher risk should generate higher returns. Over the next several years in a generally less than favorable development market, developers of mixed-use projects will focus like a laser on managing risk and controlling development and construction costs.

Downtown Main Street is a proposed new mixed-use retail core for downtown Dallas, Texas.

The shortcomings and financial difficulties of many large and/or ambitious mixed-use projects can be attributed to many things, including poor design, mismanagement of construction, and overly ambitious schemes that were too large, cost too much, and took too long to build. Many have suffered from sharp market shifts as the economy turned south in 2001. High-profile projects such as Hollywood & Highland, CityPlace, and Santana Row have all suffered from one or more of these problems. Mixed-use projects going forward over the next five years will tend to be less ambitious, at least in their early phases, and will be more conservative in their approach.

Developers of mixed-use projects over the next five years will increasingly employ one or more of several techniques to reduce their risk:

- developing smaller projects;
- developing projects with low-rise buildings, which are less costly to construct;

- minimizing the layering of uses where possible to reduce complexity and development costs;
- carefully phasing the project so as to not overshoot the market;
- creating innovative development partnerships that spread the risk and improve the expertise involved without adding conflict;
- working closely with the public sector in public/private partnerships.

Smaller mixed-use projects are likely to be more prevalent over the coming years, partly because commercial property markets are slower but also because smaller projects are more doable and less risky. Many smaller developers, attracted to mixed-use projects, are unwilling or unable to take on the risk of large, ambitious developments. Many smaller cities and towns are interested in mixed-use development but can support only small projects. Smaller mixed-use projects with modest amounts of residential, office, and retail space are much simpler to develop and can serve niche markets very well in the right location.

For larger projects, developers will manage development costs by minimizing the layering of uses, by designing simpler low-cost buildings that will still fit into mixed-use plans, and by creating strategic partnerships and careful phasing plans. Mixed-use projects will likely be developed increasingly through partnerships between smaller developers who know their local market well but do not have the resources to develop a large mixed-use project by themselves. Notes Paris Rutherford of RTKL in Dallas, "We are seeing more well-established local developers pursuing the larger local opportunities in teams. This may be attributed to their political connections and special knowledge or site issues."

The public sector has and will continue to play a critical role in managing risk for mixed-use projects through the many public initiatives and subsidies discussed earlier. Mixed-use development is in the public interest, and the public sector will be very active in fostering mixed-use projects through planning, investment, subsidies, financing, and facilitation of the approval process. Although it will come with a price for private developers, in most situations the benefits will outweigh the costs. In fact, public involvement will be the reason that many mixed-use projects happen over the next five years; the role that the public sector can play in providing leadership, shaping development concepts, and enhancing feasibility will be an integral part of the mixed-use landscape. Developers interested in mixed-use projects will increasingly seek out the public sector as strategic partners.

Notes

1. Richard W. Thompson and Nathan B. Cherry, "A Broad Mix," *Urban Land*, May 2002, pp. 44–49.

2. www.villa-lakewood.com, accessed May 16, 2003.

Bibliography
and Index

Bibliography

Books

Ames, Steven C., ed. *Guide to Community Visioning*. Chicago: APA Planners Press, 1998.

Barton-Ashman Associates, Inc. *Shared Parking*. Washington, D.C.: ULI–the Urban Land Institute, 1983.

Beyard, Michael D., et al. *Developing Retail Entertainment Destinations*. Washington, D.C.: ULI–the Urban Land Institute, 2001.

Beyard, Michael D., W. Paul O'Mara, et al. *Shopping Center Development Handbook*. Third Edition. Washington, D.C.: ULI–the Urban Land Institute, 1999.

Bohl, Charles. *Placemaking: Developing Town Centers, Main Streets, and Urban Villages*. Washington, D.C.: ULI–the Urban Land Institute, 2002.

Booth, Geoffrey, et al. *Transforming Suburban Business Districts*. Washington, D.C.: ULI–the Urban Land Institute, 2001.

Calthorpe, Peter. *The Next American Metropolis*. Princeton, N.J.: Princeton Architectural Press, 1993.

Calthorpe, Peter, and William B. Fulton. *The Regional City: Planning for the End of Sprawl*. Washington, D.C.: Island Press, 2001.

Congress for the New Urbanism, with the Great American Station Foundation. *The New Transit Town: Best Practices in Transit-Oriented Development*. San Francisco: Congress for the New Urbanism, 2003.

Council on Development Choices for the '80s. *The Affordable Community: Adapting Today's Communities to Tomorrow's Needs*. Washington, D.C.: ULI–the Urban Land Institute, 1981.

Coupland, Andy. *Reclaiming the City: Mixed-Use Development*. London: E&FN Spon, 1997.

Davidson, Michael, and Fay Dolnick, eds. *Parking Standards*. APA Planning Advisory Report No. 510–511. Chicago: American Planning Association, 2002.

Dinsmore, Clement. *The Impact of Public Capital Markets on Urban Real Estate*. Washington, D.C.: Brookings Institution, 1998.

Duany, Andres, Elizabeth Plater-Zyberk, and Jeff Speck. *Suburban Nation: The Rise of Sprawl and the Decline of the American Dream*. New York: North Point Press, 2000.

Fadar, Steven. *Density by Design: New Directions in Residential Development*. Washington, D.C.: ULI–the Urban Land Institute, 2000.

Funders' Network for Smart Growth and Livable Communities. *Real Estate Finance and Smart Growth Project Report, 2002*. www.fundersnetwork.org.

Garreau, Joel. *Edge City: Life on the New Frontier*. New York: Anchor Books/Doubleday, 1991.

Gause, Jo Allen, et al. *Office Development Handbook*. Second Edition. Washington, D.C.: ULI–the Urban Land Institute, 1998.

Great Britain Department for Transport, Local Government and the Regions. *Mixed-Use Development: Practice and Potential*. London: Stationery Office, 2002.

Gruen, Victor, and Larry Smith. *Centers for the Urban Environment: Survival of the Cities*. New York: Van Nostrand Reinhold, 1973.

Hall, Kenneth B., and Gerald A. Porterfield. *Community by Design: New Urbanism for Suburbs and Small Communities*. New York: McGraw-Hill, 2001.

Hirschhorn, Joel S., and Paul Souza. *New Community Design to the Rescue: Fulfilling Another American Dream*. Washington, D.C.: National Governors Association, 2001.

Jacobs, Jane. *The Death and Life of Great American Cities*. New York: Random House, 1961.

Katz, Peter. *The New Urbanism: Toward an Architecture of Community*. New York: McGraw-Hill, 1994.

Kelbaugh, Douglas. *Common Place: Toward Neighborhood and Regional Design*. Seattle: University of Washington Press, 1997.

Langdon, Philip. *A Better Place to Live: Reshaping the American Suburb*. Amherst: University of Massachusetts Press, 1994.

Minnesota Institute of Legal Education. *New Urbanism, Smart Growth*. Minneapolis: Author, 2001.

Mumford, Lewis. *The City in History: Its Origins, Its Transformations, and Its Prospects*. New York: Harcourt, Brace & World, 1961.

National Capital Planning Authority–Australia and Better Cities Program–Australia. *Facilitating Mixed Use Development*. Canberra, Australia: A.G.P.S., 1995.

New Urban News. *New Urbanism: Comprehensive Report and Best Practices Guide*. Ithaca, N.Y.: Author, 2003.

Oldenburg, Ray. *The Great Good Place*. New York: Paragon House, 1989.

O'Neil, David. *The Smart Growth Tool Kit*. Washington, D.C.: ULI–the Urban Land Institute, 2000.

Oregon Transportation and Growth Management Program. *Commercial and Mixed-Use Development Code Handbook*. Salem, Ore.: Author, 2001.

Peiser, Richard, and Anne Frej. *Professional Real Estate Development: The ULI Guide to the Business*. Second Edition. Washington, D.C.: ULI–the Urban Land Institute, 2003.

Petersen, David C. *Developing Sports, Convention, and Performing Arts Centers*. Washington, D.C.: ULI–the Urban Land Institute, 2001.

PKF Consulting. *Hotel Development*. Washington, D.C.: ULI–the Urban Land Institute, 1996.

Porter, Douglas. *Making Smart Growth Work*. Washington, D.C.: ULI–the Urban Land Institute, 2002.

PricewaterhouseCoopers. *Greyfield Regional Mall Study*. San Francisco: Congress for the New Urbanism, 2001.

Procos, Dimitri. *Mixed Land Use: From Revival to Innovation*. Stroudsburg, Pa.: Dowden, Hutchinson & Ross, 1976.

Rovig, Steven R., and Timothy R Osborn. *Drafting Real Estate Documents That Work. Part I. Condominiums, Master-Planned Communities, and Mixed Use*. Seattle: Washington State Bar Association, 2001.

———. *Drafting Real Estate Documents That Work. Part II. Commercial Projects*. Seattle: Washington State Bar Association, 2001.

Royal Institution of Chartered Surveyors. *Mixed-Use Development: Concept and Realities*. London: Author, 1996.

———. *Planning Mixed-Use Development: Issues and Practices*. London: Author, 1998.

Schmitz, Adrienne, et al. *Multifamily Housing Development Handbook*. Washington, D.C.: ULI–the Urban Land Institute, 2000.

———. *The New Shape of Suburbia: Trends in Residential Development*. Washington, D.C.: ULI–the Urban Land Institute, 2003.

Schneekloth, Lynda H., and Robert G. Shibley. *Placemaking: The Art and Practice of Building Communities*. New York: Wiley, 1995.

Schwanke, Dean, et al. *Resort Development Handbook*. Washington, D.C.: ULI–the Urban Land Institute, 1997.

Sitte, Camillo. *City Planning According to Artistic Principles*. New York: Random House, 1889, reprinted 1965.

Snedcof, Harold R. *Cultural Facilities in Mixed-Use Development*. Washington, D.C.: ULI–the Urban Land Institute, 1985.

Unwin, Raymond. *Town Planning in Practice: An Introduction to the Art of Designing Cities and Suburbs*. New York: Princeton Architectural Press, 1909, reprinted 1994.

ULI–the Urban Land Institute. *Property Development Europe: Case Studies in Innovation*. Washington, D.C.: Author, 2003.

Wener, Richard, et al. *Placemaking for Change: 2001 Rudy Bruner Award for Urban Excellence*. Cambridge, Mass,: Bruner Foundation, Inc., 2001.

Whyte, William H. *City: Rediscovering the Center*. New York: Doubleday, 1988.

Journal Articles

Beakley, Paul. "Financing Mixed-Use." *Urban Land*, October 2002: 120–121+.

Bucher, David C. "Case Study: Greyfields as an Emerging Smart Growth Opportunity with the Potential for Added Synergies through a Unique Mix of Uses." *Real Estate Issues*, Summer 2002: 46–54.

Cohen, Andrew P., and Marty Borko. "The Community Mall." *Urban Land*, November/December 2002: 100–105.

Corso, Stacey. "Creating the Perfect Blend." *Real Estate Forum*, June 2001: 38–44+.

Cupkovic, Noel L. "The Secrets to Success of Today's Mixed-Use Developments." *Shopping Center Business*, March 2002: 58+.

Dawe, Patric. "Mixed-Use Transportation Projects: Catalysts for Urban Revitalization." *Urban Land*, October 2002: 96–97.

Eade, Christine. "Mixed Messages." *Property Week*, October 27, 2000: 42–44.

Egan, Nancy. "Mixing It Up." *Urban Land*, April 1999: 66–71.

Evans, Brian P. "Restrictive Covenants for Mixed Use." *Urban Land*, February 2003: 25+.

"Focus on Mixed-Use Development Projects: Mixed-Use Projets a Mixed Bag." *Economic Development Now*, January 31, 2003: 5–8.

Grant, Jill. "Mixed Use in Theory and Practice." *Journal of the American Planning Association*, Winter 2002: 71–83.

Grogan, Bradley C. "From Majesty to Mixed Use." *Urban Land*, April 1999: 80–83.

Hagerott, Edward C., Jr. "Drafting Construction, Operation, and Reciprocal Easement Agreements for Vertical Mixed-Use Projects." *Practical Real Estate Lawyer*, November 2002: 15–25.

Handel, Gary E., Blake Middleton, and Glenn Resclavo. "Vertical Urbanism: Mixed-Use Residential Projects Are Experiencing Success in America's Downtowns." *Urban Land*, May 2002: 65–70.

Hibbard, Forrest N. "Parking Structures for Mixed-Use Developments." *Parking*, March 2003: 24–26.

Hightower, David. "Healthy Mixed-Use Environments: The Macro, the Micro, and the Nano." *Development*, Summer 2002: 40–43.

Hudnut, William H. "Mayor's Forum: Mixing Uses." *Urban Land*, 2002: 51–56.

Lewis, Steve. "Zoning Trends: The Mixed-Use Puzzle." *Shopping Center World*, May 1, 2002: 86, 88.

Lynne, Natalie. "Mix 'n Match." *Journal of Property Management*, May/June 2002: 28–30+.

Macht, William P. "Mixed Media." *Urban Land*, March 2002: 32–33.

Miara, Jim. "The Manchester Mix." *Urban Land*, February 2003: 78–81.

Miller, Robert L. "Suburbia Mixed." *Urban Land*, November/December 2000: 48–51, 128–129.

Murray, Michael. "Suburbs Look to Public Funds for Mixed-Use Project." *Real Estate Finance Today*, January 21, 2002: 8.

Rutherford, Paris, AICP, and Ray Peloquin AIA. "Making Mixed-Use Work." *Shopping Center Business*, August 2001: 62+.

Scavo, James J. "How to Draft Mixed-Use Community Restrictive Covenants." *Practical Real Estate Lawyer*, November 2002: 27–45.

Stephens, Paula. "Together Wherever We Go." *Shopping Center World*, November 2001: 76–78.

Trischler, Thomas J. "In the Mix: Determining What Uses Work Together Most Successfully." *Development Magazine*, Fall 2001: 40–46.

Weissman, Seth G. "Lawyering the New Urbanism." *Urban Land*, October 2000: 84–85, 88–89, 116–117.

Periodicals

Architecture
www.architecturemag.com

Architectural Record
www.archrecord.construction.com

Building, Design & Construction
www.bdcmag.com

Buildings
www.buildings.com

Commercial Investment Real Estate Journal
www.ccim.com

Development
www.naiop.org

Development Case Studies—ULI
www.casestudies.uli.org

Downtown Idea Exchange
www.downtowndevelopment.com

Economic Development Now
www.iedconline.org

Estates Gazette
www.estatesgazette.com

Europroperty
www.europroperty.com

Hotels
www.hotelsmag.com

Hotel Business
www.hotelbusiness.com

ICSC Research Bulletin
www.icsc.org

Information Packet: Mixed-Use Development—Selected References
www.uli.org

Information Packet: Place Making and Town Center Development—Selected References
www.uli.org

Journal of the American Planning Association
www.planning.org

Journal of Property Management
www.iem.org

Lodging Hospitality
www.lhonline.com

Metropolis
www.metropolismag.com

Multifamily Trends
www.urbanland.uli.org

Multi-Housing News
www.multi-housingnews.com

National Real Estate Investor
www.nreionline.com

New Urban News
www.newurbannews.com

Parking
www.npapark.org

PAS Memo
www.planning.org

Planning
www.planning.org

Practical Real Estate Lawyer
www.ali-aba.org

Professional Parking
www.parking.org

Property Week
www.propertyweek.com

Real Estate Forum
www.reforum.com

Real Estate Issues
www.cre.org

Retail Traffic
www.retailtrafficmag.com

Shopping Center Business
www.shoppingcenterbusiness.com

Shopping Centers Today
www.shoppingcenterstoday.com

Urban Land
www.urbanland.uli.org

Zoning News
www.planning.org

Organizations

American Hotel and Lodging Association
Washington, DC
(202) 289-3100
www.ahla.com

American Institute of Architects
Washington, DC
(202) 624-7300
www.aia.org

American Planning Association
Chicago, IL
(312) 431-9100
www.planning.org

American Resort Development Association
Washington, DC
(202) 371-6700
www.arda.org

Congress for the New Urbanism
San Francisco, CA
(415) 495-2255
www.cnu.org

European Academy of the Urban Environment
Berlin, Germany
49-30-89.59.99.0
www.eaue.de

European Institute for Comparative Urban Research
Rotterdam, the Netherlands
31.10.4081186
www.euricur.nl

Funders' Network for Smart Growth and Livable Communities
www.fundersnetwork.org

Great Buildings Collection
www.greatbuildings.com

International Council of Shopping Centers
New York, NY
(646) 728-3800
www.icsc.org

International Downtown Association
Washington, DC
(202) 393-6801
www.ida-downtown.org

International Network for Traditional Building,
    Architecture & Urbanism
London, UK
44 20 7613 8520
www.intbau.org

International Network for Urban Development
The Hague, the Netherlands
31 (0)70 324 45 26
www.inta-aivn.org

Livable Places
Los Angeles, CA
(213) 622-5980
www.livableplaces.org

Local Government Commission
Center for Livable Communities
Sacramento, CA
(916) 448-1198
www.lgc.org

National Association of Industrial and Office Properties
Herndon, VA
(703) 904-7100
www.naiop.org

National Charrette Institute
Portland, OR
(503) 233-8486
www.charretteinstitute.org

National Multi Housing Council
Washington, DC
(202) 974-2300
www.nmhc.org

National Restaurant Association
Washington, DC
(202) 331-5900
www.restaurant.org

National Retail Federation
Washington, DC
(202) 783-7971
www.nrf.com

National Town Builders Association
Washington, DC
(202) 333-1902
www.ntba.net

National Trust for Historic Preservation's National Main Street Center
Washington, DC
(202) 588-6219
www.mainst.org

New Urbanism: Creating Livable Sustainable Communities
Alexandria, VA
(703) 549-6296
www.newurbanism.org

Placematters.com
Denver, CO
(303) 964-0903
www.placematters.org

Project for Public Spaces
New York, NY
(212) 620-5660
www.pps.org

Resource for Urban Design Information
Headington, Oxford
44 (0) 1865 483602
www.rudi.net

Royal Institution of Chartered Surveyors
Coventry, UK
44 (0)870 333 1600
www.rics.org

Royal Town Planning Institute
44 20 7929 9494,
London, UK
www.rtpi.org.uk

Smart Growth Network
www.smartgrowth.org

ULI Development Case Studies
www.casestudies.uli.org

ULI Smart Growth Case Studies
ULI Smart Growth News
SmartGrowth.net
www.smartgrowth.net

Index